W9-BIQ-486

MIDLOTHIAN
PUBLIC LIBRARY

HISTORY OF THE AMERICAN CINEMA

Volume 6

1940-1949

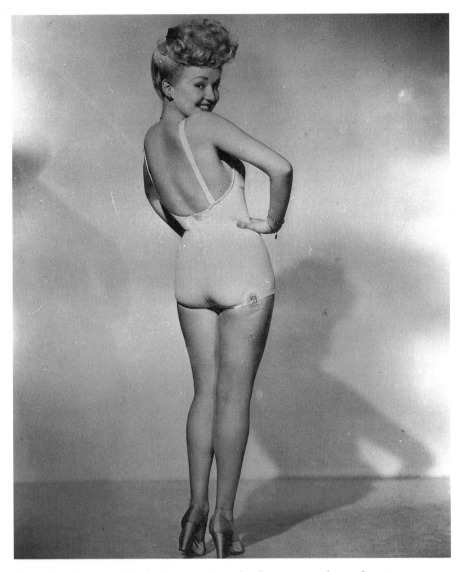

Betty Grable, one of 20th Century–Fox's leading stars, whose ubiquitous pinup served the World War II cause offscreen as well as on.

HISTORY OF THE AMERICAN CINEMA

CHARLES HARPOLE, GENERAL EDITOR

6
BOOM AND BUST: THE AMERICAN CINEMA IN THE 1940s

Thomas Schatz

Charles Scribner's Sons
Macmillan Library Reference USA
Simon & Schuster Macmillan
NEW YORK

Simon & Schuster and Prentice Hall International
LONDON   MEXICO CITY   NEW DELHI   SINGAPORE   SYDNEY   TORONTO

Charles Scribner's Sons
Macmillan Library Reference USA
Simon & Schuster Macmillan
1633 Broadway
New York, NY 10019

Library of Congress Catalog Card Number: 97-16335

Printed in the United States of America

Printing Number
1 2 3 4 5 6 7 8 9 10

Library of Congress Cataloging-in-Publication Data

Schatz, Thomas, 1948-
    Boom and bust : the American cinema in the 1940s / Thomas Schatz.
        p.   cm.—(History of the American cinema ; v. 6)
    Includes bibliographical references and index.
    ISBN 0-684-19151-2
    1. Motion pictures—United States—History.   2. Motion picture
industry—United States—History. I. Title. II. Series.
PN1993.5.U6H55   1990 vol. 6
791.43'0973'09044—dc21   97-16335
                                                                              CIP

This paper meets the requirements of ANSI/NISO Z.39.48-1992
(Permanence of Paper).

Advisory Board

Coordinator
IAN JARVIE
York University

JOSEPH L. ANDERSON
WGBH, Boston

TINO BALIO
University of Wisconsin—Madison

EILEEN BOWSER
Museum of Modern Art

HENRY S. BREITROSE
Stanford University

PETER J. BUKALSKI
Southern Illinois University at Edwardsville

JACK C. ELLIS
Northwestern University

RAYMOND FIELDING
Florida State University

DONALD FREDERICKSEN
Cornell University

RONALD GOTTESMAN
University of Southern California

JOHN G. HANHARDT
Whitney Museum of American Art

LEWIS JACOBS

GARTH JOWETT
University of Houston

RICHARD KOSZARSKI
American Museum of the Moving Image

JOHN B. KUIPER
University of North Texas

DANIEL J. LEAB
Seton Hall University

JAY LEYDA†
New York University

JOHN MERCER
Southern Illinois University at Carbondale

JEAN MITRY†

PETER MORRIS
York University

CHARLES MUSSER
Yale University

JOHN E. O'CONNOR
New Jersey Institute of Technology

EDWARD S. PERRY
Middlebury College

VLADA PETRIC
Harvard University

ROBERT ROSEN
University of California, Los Angeles

DONALD E. STAPLES
University of North Texas

ALAN WILLIAMS
Rutgers University

The Cinema History Project and the
History of the American Cinema
have been supported by grants from the
National Endowment for the Humanities and the
John and Mary R. Markle Foundation.

Contents

Acknowledgments

This volume is indebted to the Efforts of Charles Harpole, General Editor of the History of American Cinema series. At Scribner's, John Fitzpatrick and his assistant, Leroy Gonzalez, provided invaluable editorial support as well.

While researching and writing this book, I received crucial support from the University Research Institute at the University of Texas at Austin and also from the National Endowment for the Humanities. The Humanities Research Institute at the University of California—Irvine also provided valuable assistance in the form of a research fellowship (and a place to work with a number of top film scholars from various UC system schools). I am especially grateful to Nick Browne of UCLA, who organized the UC—Irvine research project.

I also wish to acknowledge the numerous archives, libraries, and special collections used in conducting the primary research for this book, and to thank the many individuals who assisted in that research. Chief among these sites in terms of my own research were the Department of Special Collections at USC; the Harry Ransom Humanities Research Center at the University of Texas at Austin; the Margaret Herrick Library at tge Acaemy of Motion Pictures Arts and Sciences; the Wisconsin Center for Film and Theatre Research at the University if Wisconsin—Madison; and the Theatre Arts Library at UCLA.

Locating the many images and illustrations for this book was a challenging task and would not have been possible without the help and expertise of Mary Corliss of the Museum of Modern Art, Marc Wanamaker of Bison Archives, Ron and Howard Mandelbaum of Photofest, Mike Mashon of the Broadcast Pioneers Museum at the University of Maryland, and George Barringer at the Georgetown University Library.

I also want to thank my contributors—Chris Anderson, Tom Doherty, Mary Beth Haralovich, Hap Kindem, Clayton Koppes, Lauren Rabinovitz, and Janet Staiger— whose efforts and support as colleagues and collaborators are most appreciated.

Many other individuals contributed to the project in various ways, ranging from casual but highly valuable conversations about my research to close readings of the manuscript as it developed. I am especially grateful to Ed Buscombe, Carol Clover, Garth Jowett, George Lipsitz, Michael Rogin, Vivian Sobchack, and Linda Williams. I'd also like to thank several of my colleagues at Texas, particularly John Downing and Horace Newcomb, for making my life easier during the course of this long-term project. And a final note of thanks and gratitude goes out to my recent and current students at UT, who probably have heard quite enough by now about war films and *film noir*, tax codes and defense plants, HUAC and the *Paramount* decree. They are, finally, what this project is all about.

Contributors

THOMAS SCHATZ is Philip G. Warner Regents Professor in the Department of Radio-Television-Film at the University of Texas at Austin. His books include *Hollywood Genres: Formulas, Filmmaking, and the Studio System* and *The Genius of the System: Hollywood Filmmaking in the Studio Era.*

CHRISTOPHER ANDERSON is Associate Professor of Telecommunications and Film Studies at Indiana University. He is the author of *Hollywood TV: The Studio System in the Fifties.*

THOMAS DOHERTY is Associate Professor of American Studies and Chair of the Film Studies Program at Brandeis University. He is the author of *Teenagers and Teenpics: The Juvenalization of American Movies in the 1950s* and *Projections of War: Hollywood, American Culture, and World War I.*

MARY BETH HARALOVICH is Associate Professor and Chair of the Media Arts Department at the University of Arizona. She has published widely on both film and television, including studies of the Hollywood star system and Warner Bros. poster publicity of the 1930s and 1940s.

GORHAM KINDEM is Professor of Communication Studies at the University of North Carolina at Chapel Hill. His books include *The American Movie Industry* and *The Live Television Generation of Hollywood Film Directors.* He is producer-director of several documentary films.

CLAYTON KOPPES is Professor of History and Dean of the College of Arts and Sciences at Oberlin College. He is the author (with Gregory Black) of *Hollywood Goes to War: How Politics, Profits, and Propaganda Shaped World War II Movies.*

LAUREN RABINOVITZ is Associate Professor of American Studies and Film at the University of Iowa. She is the author of *Points of Resistance: Women, Power and Politics in the New York Avant-Garde Cinema* and coauthor of *The* Rebecca *Project,* a CD-ROM.

JANET STAIGER is Professor of Radio-Television-Film at the University of Texas at Austin. She is coauthor (with David Bordwell and Kristin Thompson) of *The Classical Hollywood Cinema: Film Style and Mode of Production to 1960* and author of *Interpreting Films: Studies in the Historical Reception of American Cinema* and *Bad Women: Regulating Sexuality in Early American Cinema*.

HISTORY OF THE AMERICAN CINEMA

Volume 6
1940-1949

1

Introduction

The American cinema in the 1940s was an industry at war, fighting monumental battles at home and overseas, both on-screen and off. Chief among those battles, of course, was World War II, the defining event of the decade for the movie industry and for the nation at large. Never before had the interests of the nation and the industry been so closely aligned, and never had its status as a national cinema been so vital. The industry's "conversion to war production" from 1942 to 1945 was eminently successful, as Hollywood enjoyed what may have been its finest hour as a social institution and a cultural force. The war also ignited a five-year economic boom, pushing box-office revenues and film studio profits to record levels.

While World War II was the signal event of the decade, however, Hollywood's fiercest and most significant battles were waged on the domestic front—battles with the Justice Department over antitrust violations, battles with Congress over "un-American activities" in Hollywood, battles with labor unions for control of the Hollywood workforce, battles with the growing ranks of freelance talent and independent producers for control of the filmmaking process, battles with theater owners for control of the movie marketplace, battles with censors over subject matter. These and other crises reached their flashpoints in the late forties as the war boom was followed by a disastrous postwar bust.

Although the bust was very much a postwar phenomenon, the industry's decline actually began in the early 1940s during the odd, intense interval between the Great Depression and World War II. The sociologist (and sometime screenwriter) Leo Rosten provided a prophetic assessment of that decline in his acclaimed study, *Hollywood: The Movie Colony*, published in November 1941. Rosten had begun the book in the late 1930s, at the height of Hollywood's golden age, but he soon found himself charting what he termed the "end of Hollywood's lush and profligate period." By 1941, observed Rosten, the movie industry was in serious straits:

> Other businesses have experienced onslaughts against their profits and hegemony; but the drive against Hollywood is just beginning. No moving picture leader can be sanguine before the steady challenge of unionism, collective bargaining, the consent decree (which brought the Justice Department suit to a temporary armistice), the revolt of the independent theater owners, the trend toward increased taxation, the strangulation of the foreign market, and a score of frontal attacks on the citadels of the screen. (Leo Rosten, *Hollywood: The Movie Colony* [New York: Harcourt, Brace, 1941], p. 78)

Rosten's assessment is notable for two principal reasons: first, its accurate inventory of the crises facing the industry in the early 1940s; and second, how completely those crises would dissolve within weeks of the book's publication, following Pearl Harbor and the entry of the United States into the war. That wartime reversal did not invalidate Rosten's appraisal, however; in fact, the crises he described would return with a vengeance immediately after the war. And thus the governing paradox of the era: the closer one looks at the film industry during the 1940s, the more evident it becomes that World War II marked an extended, dramatic, and most welcome interval in a decade-long period of industry decline.

The Prewar, Wartime, and Postwar Motion Picture Industry

The 1940s, then, was a decade of momentous reversals for the American cinema. The most significant and striking reversals came immediately after Pearl Harbor, particularly in terms of the industry's relationship with the U.S. government. In 1940–1941, Hollywood had been mired in federal lawsuits and congressional hearings over various issues, from antitrust violations and racketeering to allegations of Communist ties and on-screen warmongering. But with the nation suddenly plunged into a global war, Washington saw the movie industry in a very different light. Hollywood's control over every phase of the industry was now deemed a key asset, and the movies an ideal source of diversion, information, and propaganda for citizens and soldiers alike. President Franklin D. Roosevelt, a longtime supporter and canny manipulator of the movie industry, allowed Hollywood to continue commercial operations so long as it cooperated with Washington in actively supporting the war effort.

The industry readily complied, although wartime filmmaking and exhibition were scarcely business as usual. The studios and the nation's theater owners cooperated with the government and the military in selling war bonds, providing live entertainment for the troops all over the globe, promoting charity and relief efforts, and cranking out hundreds of war-related features, documentaries, newsreels, and even military training films. Meanwhile, the surging war economy and myriad war-related restrictions created a public with the war on its mind and money in its pockets—and with little to spend it on other than the movies. Moviegoing became an essential wartime ritual for Americans, as weekly attendance and industry revenues soared. It was an essential ritual for the military as well, a "two-hour furlough" in makeshift theaters and "beachhead bijous" around the globe, with films supplied through a worldwide distribution system created by Hollywood and the War Department.

Another significant wartime reversal involved Hollywood's aggressive on-screen support of the war effort. In 1940–1941, as war raged overseas and as Roosevelt actively supplied England with arms and initiated a "defense buildup" at home, Hollywood's treatment of the war had been remarkably tentative, especially in feature films. That changed dramatically after Pearl Harbor, and by late 1942 nearly one-third of the features produced dealt directly with the war effort. The war claimed a number of top stars—primarily leading men like Clark Gable, Tyrone Power, and James Stewart, who joined the service, but also a few top female stars like Carole Lombard, who died in a plane crash during a war-bond drive, and Myrna Loy, who went to work for the Red Cross. Meanwhile a new generation of wartime stars like Betty Grable, Greer Garson, and Abbott and Costello emerged, and a number of established stars like Bob Hope, Bing Crosby, and Humphrey Bogart saw their careers surge during the war.

Familiar film genres, from musicals and crime films to women's pictures and historical epics, were reworked to invoke "war themes." Hollywood also developed a cycle of combat films like WAKE ISLAND (1942), BATAAN (1943), THIRTY SECONDS OVER TOKYO (1944), and THE STORY OF GI JOE (1945), providing fictional accounts of actual Allied battles. These combat films, along with the massive output of war-related documentaries and newsreels, effectively serialized the Allied war effort while bringing a new level of realism to American movie screens. Indeed, wartime Hollywood was more focused than ever before on real-world events as the lines between factual and fictional films steadily blurred.

A significant counter to Hollywood's war-related output emerged in *film noir,* a cinematic style which first took shape before the war in dark, expressive dramas like REBECCA (1940), CITIZEN KANE (1941), and THE MALTESE FALCON (1941). During the war, *film noir* coalesced into a distinctive period style in two distinctive cycles: "hard-boiled" crime thrillers like MURDER, MY SWEET and DOUBLE INDEMNITY (both 1944), and "female Gothics" like SUSPICION (1941), SHADOW OF A DOUBT (1943), and GASLIGHT (1944). Far afield from the heroic posturing and documentary realism of the combat films and home-front dramas, these *noir* films evinced the "dark side" of the wartime experience, coexisting in dynamic tension with Hollywood's onslaught of war-related films.

As the emergence of *film noir* suggests, the movie industry's wartime worldview was neither unified nor one-dimensional, and this applied to off-screen industry conditions as well. Despite the war-induced prosperity and the overall effort to present a united front, the film industry underwent its share of internal conflicts and contradictory developments during the war. There was intense debate about the "entertainment value" of war films, with the nation's theater owners continually lobbying for more escapist fare or at least for more upbeat war-related efforts—military musicals like THIS IS THE ARMY (1943) or home-front romances like SINCE YOU WENT AWAY (1944). Meanwhile, advisers from the Office of War Information (OWI) bickered constantly with Hollywood's own Production Code Administration (PCA) about the on-screen depiction of various war-related issues and events.

Conflicts arose in the filmmaking ranks as well, as studio control was challenged and steadily undermined by the shift of top talent to freelance status, and also by the surge in independent production. These trends had been evident earlier but accelerated dramatically during the war due to various factors—war-related income tax hikes which induced Hollywood's high-paid talent to "go freelance," for instance, and the growing demand for A-class pictures in the overheated wartime marketplace that forced the studios to rely on independent producers for additional high-end product.

As the war came to a close, any semblance of a united industry front quickly faded, and the postwar era soon proved to be the most turbulent and crisis-ridden period in industry history. Indeed, the "drive against Hollywood" described by Rosten in 1941 resumed with even greater force after the war. The studios were hit by a major strike in early 1945 even before the fighting stopped overseas, and in October, within weeks of the Japanese surrender, the Justice Department renewed its antitrust case against the studios in federal court. Hollywood's economic boom continued into 1946, but by 1947 the film industry had begun a steady, seemingly inexorable slide.

The industry's box-office decline in the late 1940s was spurred by various developments both at home and overseas. On the home front, the millions of returning servicemen who had fueled record box-office revenues in 1946 soon began marrying and starting families in the suburbs, far from the industry's vital downtown theaters. With "suburban migration" and the "baby boom" came commercial television and other shifts in patterns of media consumption, as moviegoing ceased to be a ritual necessity for most Americans. And while the nation at large enjoyed a huge economic surge in the postwar era, this only meant rising costs for the film industry. Hollywood faced serious problems overseas with the outbreak of the cold war in 1946, which disrupted trade behind the "Iron Curtain." Equally troublesome was the growing protectionist trend in key European markets like England, Italy, and France, which were trying to promote their own film industries and limit Hollywood's domination.

As economic conditions rapidly deteriorated in 1947–1948, the film industry suffered three crucial setbacks: a motion picture trade war with Britain severely undercut Hollywood's most important overseas market; a congressional investigation of Communist infiltration of the movie industry led to the infamous Hollywood blacklist; and the Supreme Court handed down the momentous *Paramount* decree, an antitrust ruling which forced the major studios to divorce their all-important theater chains.

Despite these deepening crises, however, filmmaking in the late forties held up remarkably well. Indeed, Hollywood seemed to be energized by the internal discord and external threats of that turbulent era, and also by a remarkable influx of talent during and just after the war. The atmosphere in Hollywood and the tenor of its films changed in the late 1940s, as critics noted a new maturity and heightened realism in the American cinema. The war film was a tremendous influence here, of course, although interestingly enough, Hollywood's output of war-related features and documentaries simply stopped soon after the war. By 1946, the war itself and its social impact—including the plight of returning veterans and the postwar "return to normalcy"—were deemed box-office poison by filmmakers and exhibitors alike. But equally remarkable is the fact that, after a three-year moratorium, the war film staged an unexpected comeback in late 1949, fueled by the critical and commercial success of BATTLEGROUND, SANDS OF IWO JIMA, and TWELVE O'CLOCK HIGH.

With the war film on hiatus in the late 1940s, the realism and propaganda function of that recent cycle emerged in the "social problem dramas" and so-called message pictures—perhaps the single most significant on-screen development during the postwar era. The trend began immediately after the war with the December 1945 release of THE LOST WEEKEND, a powerful drama of an alcoholic binge that was a solid box-office hit and won the Academy Award for best picture. Despite the rising tide of cold war conservatism, Hollywood's output of message pictures intensified, most notably perhaps in a succession of prestige-level dramas from 20th Century–Fox that were huge commercial and critical hits: GENTLEMAN'S AGREEMENT, a 1947 drama involving anti-Semitism that won the Oscar for best picture; THE SNAKE PIT, a 1948 study of mental illness; and PINKY (1949), a "race film" set in the Deep South that confronted a social problem that the industry had systematically avoided for decades.

Hollywood's newfound maturity also was evident even in more traditional genres—in Westerns like DUEL IN THE SUN (1946) and RED RIVER (1948), which addressed more "adult" themes, for instance, and in musicals like THE PIRATE (1948) and ON THE TOWN (1949), which integrated modern dance and ballet. The postwar penchant for realism and social critique had a significant impact on the crime drama and *film noir* as well. *Noir* thrillers like THE POSTMAN ALWAYS RINGS TWICE (1946), OUT OF THE PAST (1947), THE LADY FROM SHANGHAI (1948), and KEY LARGO (1948) featured maladjusted males whose alienation and anxiety clearly invoked the general postwar climate. And in crime films like CROSSFIRE and BOOMERANG (both 1947), two "police procedurals" centering on ex-servicemen accused of murder, the dark expressionism of *film noir* effectively merged with the realism and social impulse of the message picture.

Hollywood's progressive postwar impulse reached a peak of sorts in 1949 with PINKY and several other race-related dramas, notably INTRUDER IN THE DUST, LOST BOUND-ARIES, and THE HOME OF THE BRAVE, and also a fictionalized biography of Huey Long, ALL THE KING'S MEN, which was perhaps the best of the postwar message pictures. Shot entirely on location in the Deep South, ALL THE KING'S MEN took on a range of social issues, from alcoholism and adultery to political corruption and the role of media in modern politics; it also was the third postwar social drama to win the Academy Award for best picture. But remarkably enough, these films marked not only the culmination but the abrupt end of Hollywood's postwar progressivism. Message pictures, political dramas, and even the antiheroic and vaguely antisocial *noir* thrillers all but disappeared after 1949, as the industry took a decidedly conservative turn both on-screen and off.

Hollywood's conservative turn reflected the rapid escalation of the cold war in 1949—the year of the Alger Hiss trial, the Soviet A-bomb, and the fall of China to the Communists—as America drifted into what W. H. Auden had so aptly termed "the age of anxiety."[1] While that anxiety was soothed somewhat by the tremendous economic boom, the movie industry found no such solace. As television swept across the newly suburbanized American landscape in 1949, the movie industry's slide worsened. Box-office revenues and theater admissions plunged, movie budgets and studio payrolls were slashed, and thousands of personnel were laid off. As the anthropologist Hortense Powdermaker noted at the time, the operative term was not "anxiety" but "panic":

> In Hollywood there is far more confusion and anxiety than in the society which surrounds it. Even in its most prosperous periods when net profits were enormous, far surpassing those of other businesses, everyone was scared. Now, when diminishing foreign markets, increasing costs of production, competitions with European pictures, and changing box-office tastes threaten the swollen profits of past prosperity, fear rises to panic. (Hortense Powdermaker, *Hollywood: The Dream Factory* [New York: Grossett & Dunlap, 1950], pp. 308–9)

The decade ended on an appropriately climactic note with the "dis-integration" of Paramount, Hollywood's most powerful studio. As the company with the largest theater chain, Paramount had been the main target of the government's decade-long antitrust suit, and in the wake of the Supreme Court's 1948 *Paramount* decree, the studio also became the first of the Hollywood powers to divorce its theater chain. At the stroke of midnight on 31 December 1949, Paramount formally split into two separate entities: Paramount Pictures and United Paramount Theaters.

The American Cinema in the 1940s

The Paramount divorce capped the government's ten-year antitrust campaign and the drive against Hollywood as well. The war boom had suspended that drive—had seemed, in fact, to stifle it altogether—but it had only postponed the inevitable. The resumption of the drive against Hollywood and Hollywood's rapid decline in the late 1940s well indicate the potency of the prewar threats to the industry, which took on a new intensity after the war. Those postwar developments also underscore the paradoxical status of the 1940s as a distinct period in American film history.

The war era represents far more than simply an interlude in Hollywood's decline, of course, particularly in light of the industry's social status and extraordinary economic prosperity during World War II. But like the war itself, the wartime movie industry can be understood only in terms of the conditions and events which both preceded and precipitated it. And the postwar era, in turn, can be understood only in relation to the tremendous impact of the war, not merely on the film industry but on the nation and the world at large.

This study therefore treats the 1940s as a distinct, coherent period in American film history, but one which necessarily must be examined in three phases: the prewar (1940–1941), wartime (1942–1945), and postwar (1946–1949) eras. The first three parts of the book are organized around these three subsequent phases, examining the "larger" social and industrial forces as well as the films and filmmaking during the prewar, wartime, and postwar eras. The opening chapter in each of the three sections surveys the general industry context—the prevailing social and economic conditions, the movie marketplace at home and abroad, incursions by powerful outside forces like organized labor, the federal government, and so on. The second chapter of each section examines Hollywood's studio-based production system, which changed dramatically in the course of the decade as the factory-oriented filmmaking procedures steadily gave way to a more "independent" and unit-based approach. The third chapter in each section examines the stars, genres, and production trends of the period, which are covered via general surveys and detailed case studies. The wartime section also includes a specialized chapter by Clayton R. Koppes on the Office of War Information, which played a crucial role in regulating movie content. Additionally, chapter sections on specialized topics have been contributed by Janet Staiger (on B movies and their audiences), Mary Beth Haralovich (on studio marketing practices), and Gorham Kindem (on the Screen Actors Guild and the blacklist).

A fourth section examines various decade-long developments which were of "ancillary" concern to Hollywood and mainstream commercial cinema and yet were of crucial importance to the general history of American film. This section includes chapters on documentary and newsreel production (by Thomas Doherty), on the emergence of experimental and avant-garde cinema (by Lauren Rabinovitz), and on the development of the television industry during the 1940s (by Christopher Anderson).

The research for this book emphasizes primary sources and materials, particularly industry trade paper accounts and studio archives. Of particular interest among the archival materials are production records, interoffice memoranda, contracts and legal documents, financial reports, and correspondence between the studio and the home office in New York. The principal news sources are *Variety* and the *Motion Picture Herald,* along with the *Wall Street Journal* and the *New York Times.* Two film critics also figure heavily in this study: Bosley Crowther, the dean of American newspaper critics in the 1940s and the lead reviewer for the *New York Times* (and the only critic there to receive a byline during the entire decade); and James Agee, an astute magazine critic who wrote during much of the decade for both *Time* (1941–1948) and *The Nation* (1942–1948). Industry biographies, insider accounts, interviews, and oral histories also are utilized, principally to supplement the more reliable archival material and news accounts. Previous historical accounts are considered as well—although, incredibly, no in-depth, comprehensive history of Hollywood in the forties has yet been attempted.

A final word about the case studies: while it is crucial to examine the American cinema as a commercial industry and a social institution, it is equally important to maintain focus on actual films and filmmaking. Close study of specific cases reveals the complex interplay of historical forces which affect the making of movies and which ultimately shape individual films. And it is at this level of analysis, finally, that one is most keenly aware of the stakes involved in the practice of film history—that is, an understanding and appreciation of the social impact, cultural value, and lasting appeal of the movies themselves.

PART 1

☆

The Prewar Era

THE GREAT DICTATOR (1940).

2

The Motion Picture Industry in 1940–1941

Prologue: January 1940

The American cinema in early 1940 was a study in paradox, with Hollywood in the full flowering of its "golden age" while the industry foundered economically and was beset by crises both at home and abroad. In terms of filmmaking achievements, Hollywood was just coming off what many considered its best year ever—a view underscored in January 1940 when several top holiday pictures went into widespread release. Those late-1939 releases included Mr. SMITH GOES TO WASHINGTON, THE HUNCHBACK OF NOTRE DAME, DRUMS ALONG THE MOHAWK, DESTRY RIDES AGAIN, and GONE WITH THE WIND. The most significant of these, without question, was GONE WITH THE WIND, an industry phenomenon of the first order and striking evidence of the movie industry's paradoxical state.

Released in late December 1939, GONE WITH THE WIND was an immediate hit of such magnitude that it redefined what one trade paper termed "how big and how important a motion picture can be."[1] David O. Selznick's massive Civil War epic was certainly the "biggest" production in Hollywood annals: a $4.25 million, 220-minute, star-laden Technicolor spectacle far beyond the scale of even the "prestige pictures" of the era. GONE WITH THE WIND proved to be the biggest of commercial hits as well. In that era, a $5 million box-office gross was considered exceptional; over the previous decade, only Disney's SNOW WHITE AND THE SEVEN DWARFS (1937) had surpassed that mark. In January 1940, GONE WITH THE WIND averaged roughly $1 million *per week* while playing in fewer than 500 of the nation's 17,500 theaters.[2]

Despite the runaway success of GONE WITH THE WIND, the overall economic state of the industry in early 1940 was shaky at best. Box-office receipts for January were down about 5 percent compared with January 1939, and in fact the studios' combined profits during that halcyon 1939–1940 period were well below their net income in 1936 and 1937, when Hollywood's Depression-era recovery first took hold. The studios had responded to that earlier economic upturn by increasing both the quality and quantity of their productions in the late 1930s, a strategy which now seemed somewhat ill advised. As *Variety*'s Roy Chartier noted in January 1940, many leading exhibitors felt that Hollywood's high-end pictures, "regardless of how fine they are, have gone entire-

Hollywood, 1940.

ly out of proportion to the potentialities of the market as it stands today."[3] Interestingly enough, GONE WITH THE WIND was the exception that proved the rule; that single picture accounted for over one-half of Hollywood's net profits in 1940.[4]

The glut of "quality" pictures indicated not only a misfired market strategy but the gradual erosion of studio control over the filmmaking process as well. While the studios still ruled the industry at large, they were forced to contend with the growing power and leverage of independent filmmakers and top freelance talent, who tended to specialize in prestige-level production. The status of major independent producers like Selznick, Walt Disney, and Sam Goldwyn signaled this trend, as did the steadily increasing clout of top stars and filmmakers. The producer-director Frank Capra in January 1940, for example, had recently ended a decade-long relationship with Columbia Pictures after completing MR. SMITH GOES TO WASHINGTON and was negotiating a one-picture deal with Warner Bros. for MEET JOHN DOE (1941). RKO, meanwhile, was trying to rein in its recently signed multitalented prodigy, twenty-five-year-old Orson Welles. In January 1940, the studio announced that it was shelving the boy wonder's first project, a film adaptation of Conrad's *Heart of Darkness,* owing to projected cost overruns, and that Welles would begin work (as producer-director-writer-actor) on another project, "John Citizen, U.S.A."—released in 1941 and retitled CITIZEN KANE. And Hollywood's consummate independent filmmaker, the producer-director-writer-star Charlie Chaplin, was shooting "Chaplin #6" in January 1940 at his personal production facility on La Brea

Avenue under the usual shroud of secrecy—although it was widely known to be a comic biography of Adolf Hitler.[5]

Another clear display of individual clout among Hollywood's creative community in January 1940 involved Katharine Hepburn. The actress had fled Hollywood for the Broadway stage in 1938, having been dubbed "box-office poison" by leading exhibitors, and had starred in a stage hit, *The Philadelphia Story*. Hepburn had the foresight to purchase the screen rights to Philip Barry's hit play, and now she was back in Hollywood, auctioning both the presold story property and her own renewed star status to the highest bidder. As of January 1940, both Warners and MGM were still in the running; Hepburn would decide on MGM.[6]

While the increasing authority of top talent was a matter of some concern for the Hollywood studio powers in early 1940, the industry faced even greater threats from various outside forces and from external industry developments. The most serious, of course, involved the outbreak of war in Europe in late 1939, which threatened Hollywood's crucial overseas trade. In January, the war's impact on foreign markets, particularly in Europe, was still uncertain. After the Nazi invasion of Poland in September 1939 and ensuing declarations of war on Germany by both England and France, there had been very little active warfare. Thus, an eerie calm pervaded the Continent, and the Hollywood studios had no real conception of how the war in Europe would affect their foreign trade. Nor was there any clear indication of whether the war-related U.S. defense buildup, just under way in early 1940, would affect the film industry. As Chartier described the situation in January 1940: "The war, and any boom resulting from that industrially in this country, might mean generally renewed vitality in theater receipts. It also might mean nothing and, so far, it hasn't except in a very isolated way through stepped up grosses where production has spurted, notably steel centers."[7]

While war conditions intensified both at home and abroad in early 1940, so did the growing discord between Hollywood and the U.S. government. When Congress reconvened in January, Hollywood suffered a series of verbal assaults on Capitol Hill. Senator Burton K. Wheeler of Montana, an avowed isolationist, publicly chastised Hollywood for pro-war and pro-military propaganda and promised to propose legislation restricting any overtly interventionist films. Hollywood was accused of a different brand of propaganda by Congressman Martin Dies of Texas, who in his opening address to the House requested additional funding for his investigation of "un-American activities" in the United States. Dies singled out Hollywood in his January 1940 address, suggesting that the movie industry, and particularly its labor unions and talent guilds, was rife with subversives and Communists. And organized labor suffered a setback in January when a federal grand jury indicted Willie Bioff, the Hollywood-based chief of the industry's dominant labor organization, the International Alliance of Theatrical and Stage Employees (IATSE), in a major racketeering and bribery scandal.

Yet another congressional assault came from Senator Matthew Neely of West Virginia, an outspoken critic of motion picture trade practices. In past years, Neely had sponsored bills against the block booking of pictures, a practice by which the studios forced exhibitors to take a studio's entire annual output, sight unseen, in order to get the more desirable A-class pictures. Neely's anti-block-booking bills had passed the Senate in 1938 and again in 1939, only to fail in the House.[8] Neely vowed in January 1940 to reintroduce that legislation and to sponsor additional bills outlawing double features and, on a more serious note, prohibiting studios from owning theater chains.

This threat of theater "divorcement" already had been posed by another and considerably more potent governmental force: the antitrust division of the Department of Justice. In 1938, the Justice Department filed an antitrust suit against the major Hollywood studios—the so-called Paramount case, named for the first defendant cited—which challenged the studios' ownership of theaters and various other trade practices as well. The studios had managed to keep the Justice Department at bay until January 1940, when the senior federal judge John C. Knox set a trial date of 1 May.

The announcement of a trial date in the Paramount case sent shock waves through the industry, initiating a decade-long succession of legal proceedings—hearings and trials, appeals and reversals, and eventually a series of Supreme Court rulings late in the decade. The government's antitrust campaign was in many ways the single defining industry event of the 1940s, striking at the very essence of the Hollywood studio system and bringing about the wholesale transformation of the American movie industry.

The Studio System and the Antitrust Campaign

The major combatants in the movie industry's antitrust battles during the 1940s were the Department of Justice and Hollywood's major studio powers: MGM, Paramount, Warners, 20th Century–Fox, RKO, Universal, Columbia, and United Artists (UA). Through the 1920s and 1930s, these studios steadily refined a "vertically integrated" system of film production, distribution, and exhibition, creating what economists term a "mature oligopoly"—that is, a cartel of companies cooperating to control an industry.[9] In the Justice Department's view, the net effect of that control was a veritable monopoly of the movie business, a view that led the attorney general to file the 1938 antitrust suit against the studios.

Actually, the Justice Department's antitrust suit was simply one facet of a widespread government initiative against the studios. Scarcely coherent or unified, the antitrust campaign against the movie industry was waged on numerous fronts, from local courts and state legislatures to Congress and the Justice Department; it also involved a range of legal and regulatory efforts, from civil and class-action suits to state laws and federal regulations. Because of the structure of the movie industry, however, only the federal government had the authority to regulate the complex nationwide system of marketing and exhibiting movies. Moreover, the antitrust battles eventually involved not only the Hollywood studios with their affiliated theater chains but also several large unaffiliated theater circuits.

The Roosevelt administration, the Justice Department, Congress, and the federal courts were in many ways at odds with one another about whether any antitrust action against the movie industry was necessary, and if so, exactly what action to take. And this disagreement applied to many other industries besides motion pictures. Since the mid-1930s, in fact, the antitrust division of the Justice Department had been involved in a fierce, ongoing battle with the White House over the New Deal and, more specifically, over the National Recovery Act (NRA), which FDR pushed through Congress shortly after his inauguration in 1933. The NRA, in essence, provided government sanction for monopolistic trade practices in certain industries, including motion pictures, as a means of combating the Depression. Significantly enough, the Supreme Court had declared the NRA unconstitutional in 1935, but by then trade practices were in place which clearly were benefiting leading U.S. industries, and which the dominant powers in those industries were altogether unwilling to give up.

*Justice Department "trustbuster"
Thurman Arnold.*

Thus, the Justice Department became heavily involved in "trust-busting" in the late 1930s—seeking, in effect, to undo what had been done under NRA sanction during the first few years of FDR's administration. The head of the department's antitrust division was Assistant Attorney General Thurman Arnold, who by 1938 already had won antitrust cases in the medical, oil, dairy, fertilizer, and construction industries, among others. Arnold fielded countless complaints about unfair trade practices from the movie industry's so-called independent exhibitors—the theater owners with three or fewer movie houses whose business dealings were virtually dictated by the studios. Arnold grew increasingly sympathetic to their plight, and on 20 July 1938, he filed *U.S. v. Paramount Pictures et al.* in New York Federal District Court, citing the so-called Big Eight Hollywood studios for violating the Sherman Antitrust Act.[10]

Interestingly enough, the suit against the studios did not center on film production but rather on two other factors: first, the integration of production and distribution through various trade practices, which were facilitated by the Big Eight's trade association, the Motion Picture Producers and Distributors of America (MPPDA); and second, the further control of distribution and exhibition by the five studios which also owned theater chains. Although their control of actual film production was not central to the suit, there was no question but that the Big Eight studio-distributors dominated that end of the business as well. By the late 1930s, they produced about 75 percent of all U.S. feature films, which generated 90 percent of all box-office revenues. Hollywood features also accounted for some 65 percent of all films exhibited worldwide; one-third of the studios' revenues came from abroad.[11] The studios' foreign and domestic revenues enabled them to keep their production factories running at full capacity; in the late 1930s, that meant turning out about one feature film per week, along with assorted serials, newsreels, shorts, and cartoons. The lone exception was UA, which was not a studio per se but rather a distributor for Hollywood's major independent producers; UA released only fifteen to twenty pictures per year.

As important as film production was to the major studios—and to the studio system—the real key to studio control of the industry lay in the distribution and exhibition sectors. In fact, the single most complex question raised by the antitrust suit, and a question which would plague the Justice Department and the courts for a full decade, was whether film distribution or exhibition was the key to studio hegemony. The Big Eight had a virtual lock on all feature film distribution, completely controlling the movie marketplace and taking in around 95 percent of all domestic (U.S. and Canada) rental receipts.[12]

Studio control had steadily consolidated during the 1920s and 1930s, when the major Hollywood powers refined an array of sales policies and trade practices which dictated the flow of movie product through the nation's movie theaters, minimizing their own risks while maximizing the earning potential of their top features, and effectively stifling any form of competition in the mainstream movie marketplace. Chief among these tactics were blind selling (also known as blind bidding) and block booking. Equally important was the elaborate "run-zone-clearance" system, which favored A-class studio pictures and the all-important first-run movie market. Indeed, studio control of the first-run market was in many ways the essential feature of the Hollywood studio system.[13]

According to the *1941 Film Daily Year Book*, there were some 17,500 movie theaters in operation in 1940—one for every 8,000 persons in the United States. The total first-run market in 1940 included 1,360 theaters in the 400 largest cities in the United States and Canada (i.e., those with a population of at least 12,500). All told, first-run houses generated well over one-half of the industry's total domestic revenues. The most important of these were the first-run metropolitan houses, which in 1940 comprised about 450 downtown deluxe palaces in the 95 U.S. cities with over 100,000 population.[14] These theaters seated thousands of spectators, ran only top features, which played day and night, and generated the lion's share of movie revenues.

The run-zone-clearance system sent a picture, after playing in the lucrative first-run arena, through the 16,000 "subsequent-run" movie houses; "clearance" refers to the amount of time between runs, and "zone" refers to the specific areas in which a film played. Typically, a top feature would play its second run in smaller downtown theaters and then move steadily outward from the urban centers to the suburbs, then to smaller cities and towns, and finally to rural communities, playing in ever smaller (and less profitable) venues and taking upwards of six months to complete its run.[15] The average daily attendance per theater was 500, and average attendance per show was 250.[16] But because of the enormous differences in moviegoing patterns and in theater size, ranging from rural houses with only a few hundred seats to the metropolitan movie palaces which seated thousands, these average figures were virtually meaningless. In REBECCA's record-setting run in early 1940 at New York's Radio City Music Hall, for instance, a reported 750,000 saw the picture in its first five weeks—an average of 20,000 per day.[17]

Thus, the logic of the studios' effort to own and/or control (through joint-ownership ventures) the nation's first-run theaters. As Mae Huettig stated in her landmark 1939 study, *The Economic Control of the Motion Picture Industry,* "Despite the glamour of Hollywood, the crux of the motion picture industry is the theater." Huettig acknowledged the importance of the studios' movies as the means of attracting audiences to those theaters, aptly describing the movie industry as "a large inverted pyramid, top-heavy with real estate and theaters, resting on a narrow base of the intangibles which constitute films."[18] Figures from the *1941 Film Daily Year Book* indicate just how top-heavy the industry actually was at that time. In 1940, the U.S. movie industry was a $2 billion enterprise; of that total, some $135 million was invested in the Hollywood studios and about $25 million in distribution operations, while the exhibition sector was valued at a staggering $1.9 billion.[19]

The overall importance of the exhibition sector was further reinforced by the vastly superior power of the studios which also owned theaters. Those vertically integrated companies—MGM, Paramount, Warner Bros., 20th Century–Fox, and RKO—were without question the governing powers in the movie industry. In fact, there was no real comparison between these so-called Big Five companies and the Little Three noninte-grated studios (Universal, Columbia, and UA) in terms of power, size, and economic value. The net worth of the Big Five in 1940–1941, including their theater holdings, ranged from MGM and Warners at about $165 million each to Fox at $130 million, Paramount at $110 million, and RKO at $70 million. Universal and Columbia were each valued at about $16 million, most of which was tied up in their production-related facil-ities. UA had little book value or assets to speak of, since it was essentially a distribution company.[20]

Taken together, the Big Five studios either wholly owned or held controlling interest in a total of about 2,600 "affiliated" theaters in 1940, most of which were first- and sec-ond-run theaters in major urban markets. While their collective theater holdings amounted to only about 15 percent of the nation's total, they included over 80 percent of all metropolitan first-run theaters.[21] The integrated majors also completely controlled exhibition in 73 of the 95 U.S. cities with over 100,000 in population.[22] And significant-ly enough, the studios' affiliated and first-run theaters were not subject to compulsory block booking. In these lucrative venues, the companies cut exclusive deals with one another and played only the best of each others' pictures.[23] Not surprisingly, this prac-tice reinforced the general perception of collusion among the Big Five.

Another crucial aspect of studio collusion, in the Justice Department's view, was the geographical dimension of their theater holdings. While each of the Big Five's chains included several dozen first-run theaters in major cities nationwide, the bulk of each company's holdings was concentrated in particular regions. Thus, the Big Five cooper-ated with one another in order to control the first-run market and to gain the full bene-fit of a nationwide first-run release.

Paramount's chain was by far the largest, totaling some 1,250 theaters in 43 states, but it was especially strong in the upper Midwest (chiefly the Chicago area), the Deep South, and New England. Fox owned around 600 houses in 1940 through its National Theaters subsidiary, most of them west of the Rockies, along with limited holdings in various areas in the Midwest. Warners' chain of about 475 theaters dominated the mid-Atlantic states and the Northeast. MGM (via Loew's, Inc.) and RKO both had relative-ly small theater chains—barely one-tenth the size of Paramount's—but they had two dis-tinct advantages: a relatively high proportion of first-run theaters, and shared dominion over the New York City area, the nation's leading movie market. Loew's New York the-aters made up one-half of its chain of 150 houses; most of its other holdings were first-run houses in the eastern half of the United States. RKO, meanwhile, was the least regionally oriented of the Big Five; its slightly more than 100 theaters, most of them for-mer vaudeville houses, were located in major cities across the United States.[24]

These theater chains provided the Big Five with profitable exhibition venues and also valuable real estate holdings, giving them increased leverage with the financial institu-tions that underwrote production costs. Being in this position enabled them to produce a generally higher grade of pictures than their competitors could, pictures ideally suited for display in their deluxe theaters. Their affiliated chains also enabled the Big Five to control the point of entry for top features into the movie marketplace. "As a control device, the development of strategic first-run theaters as the showcase of the industry proved remarkably effective," stated Huettig. "Ownership of these relatively few theaters gave [the integrated majors] control over access to the market."[25] For the Justice Department, this "barrier to entry" was yet another factor in its case against the studios.

The affiliated chains were clearly the privileged class of movie theater by the late 1930s; they included the majority of first-run houses, relied almost exclusively on top features, and were not subject to block booking.[26] Another privileged class—and another eventual target of the Justice Department's antitrust division—was the large unaffiliated theater circuits. Because some of the larger circuits included several hundred theaters, they were able to do volume business and had considerable buying power with the studios. Also, some circuits dominated particular regions of the country—the Schine circuit in the Southeast, for instance, or the Griffith circuit in the Southwest—thus complementing the majors' regional strengths (as exhibitors) and further enhancing the circuits' status and preferential treatment by the studio-distributors.[27]

Meanwhile, the independent theaters—about 60 percent of all theaters in the United States—had been systematically relegated to the weakest and least profitable position in the movie marketplace. As Garth Jowett has noted, by the late 1930s the "independent theater was in a rapid decline." Although "by far the largest group numerically," these theaters were "the least important source of film rentals. More and more, these tended to consist of the smallest houses in the less lucrative locations."[28] Independent theater owners had been battling the studios and the large circuits since the 1920s. In 1929, they formed their own trade organization, Allied States Association (ASA), to counter the powerful Motion Picture Theater Owners of America (MPTOA), which was dominated by the affiliated chains and large circuits.[29] The independents saw little success, and their situation worsened dramatically with the Depression and with FDR's National Recovery Act, which enabled the studios to codify, quite literally, such practices as block booking, blind bidding, and run-zone-clearance as standard industry policy. Indeed, the NRA provided what Tino Balio has termed "government sanction for the trade practices that [the majors] had spent years developing through informal collusion."[30]

As mentioned earlier, the plight of the independent theater owners—whose overall numbers and sheer persistence earned them political clout—was the prime motivation for the Justice Department's antitrust suit against the Big Eight. In *U.S. v. Paramount*, the studios were held in violation of the Sherman Antitrust Act for a range of trade practices—principally block booking, blind bidding, arbitrary designation of play dates, forcing shorts and newsreels (along with features) on exhibitors, discriminatory film rental rates, prohibition of double features (of A-class product), admission-price fixing, pooling of filmmaking talent, and assorted lesser charges. Also at the behest of independent theater owners, Attorney General Arnold filed antitrust suits against several powerful theater circuits, charging them with restraint of trade within specific geographical locales.[31]

In the initial Paramount suit, the Justice Department named all of the Big Eight producer-distributors as defendants, since their collective trade practices had rendered the entire industry a vertically integrated system. But the Little Three protested that, without their own theaters, they exercised nowhere near the same control as their theater-owning counterparts—and, in fact, UA did not even practice block booking. The Little Three's protest raised the crucial question of whether distribution or theater ownership was the key to studio control; at this point the Justice Department opted simply to deal separately with the Big Five and the Little Three. In 1939, the Paramount suit was emended, effectively splitting the defendants into two groups according to theater ownership. While still suing Columbia, Universal, and UA for unfair trade practices, the government increasingly shifted the focus of its case to the five integrated major studios.

The 1940 Consent Decree

The studios' initial response to the Paramount suit was rather cavalier, just as it had been to other challenges to their hegemony. As the *Motion Picture Herald* described the situation, "Time was, back in the summer of 1938, and for many months following, when many a motion picture corporate executive, and many a motion picture corporate counsel, held the opinion—never expressed publicly—that the United States Government's 'key' antitrust case to divorce production-distribution from exhibition, break up the 'talent pool' in Hollywood, and otherwise refabricate most of the industry's pattern, never would reach trial."[32] But the government pressed on; the *Wall Street Journal* predicted in January 1939 that the studios' "high, wide and handsome days are coming to a close," and that "henceforth there will be increasing control and regulation" of the industry.[33]

Ensuing events in early 1939 certainly bore out that prediction. In January, the studios submitted (via the MPPDA) a sixteen-point proposal outlining a new trade agreement, which within days was rejected by the theater owners. In February, Thurman Arnold told the Economic Society of New York that the Justice Department's primary goal was "absolute divorcement of production and distribution from exhibition" and he even broached the possibility of cinema as a "government regulated monopoly."[34] That same month, the Supreme Court handed down its first post–New Deal decision related to the movie industry, citing the Big Eight and two large unaffiliated circuits for attempting to fix prices and to prohibit double billing of top product in subsequent-run theaters.[35] This decision was a severe setback and a worrisome signal for the Hollywood powers. In the words of a *Variety* editorial, the decision "unwinds much of the complicated industry texture which had developed in the past decade," and seriously threatened both the "large affiliated and independently owned theater circuits, now in control of first-run exhibition."[36]

By March 1939, over thirty antitrust lawsuits had been filed against the majors in federal, state, and local courts, and the Senate's Interstate Commerce Committee had resumed hearings on the Neely anti-block-booking bill in the Senate.[37] The majors responded by offering to stop forcing shorts on exhibitors (which *Variety* termed "a sop to the Government monopoly suit"), and by proposing yet another draft of revised trade practices to theater owners—which again was rejected.[38] The government, meanwhile, increased the pressure in May by bringing another antitrust suit against several large unaffiliated circuits as well as attaching a partial "bill of particulars" to the New York suit, citing Paramount for forty-three specific offenses.[39] In June, another MPPDA proposal was rejected by Allied, and *Variety* signaled a Justice Department ultimatum under a front-page banner headline: "Divorcement or Else, Says D.C."[40] In late summer, the Senate again passed the Neely bill, sending it on to the House; that it was not expected to pass did little to assuage the growing concerns among Hollywood's major studio powers.

This general pattern of lobbying, negotiating, and political maneuvering continued, both in the press and behind the scenes. In January 1940, the *Film Daily Year Book* listed the war in Europe as the number-one news story of the past year, followed by the trade reforms, the Neely bill, and antitrust litigation; *Variety* named the federal antitrust suit as "No. 1 on the list of current nightmares" for the industry.[41] Once the trial date was set (eventually it was moved from May to June), the majors began negotiating directly with the Justice Department. Meanwhile, the MPPDA president, Will Hays, working behind the scenes, even made overtures to Roosevelt himself.[42] Neely, despite the continued reluctance in the House to pass his anti-block-booking bill, submitted a bill to the Senate in April demanding complete theater divorcement; Thurman Arnold supported the bill in Senate testimony.[43]

Clearly the government's antitrust campaign was gaining steam, and the Hollywood powers—and their armies of attorneys—worked furiously to reach a satisfactory compromise. The case did finally go to trial on 6 June, only to be immediately adjourned by Judge Henry W. Goddard, with the attorney general's approval, to allow further settlement explorations.[44] That adjournment was the first of thirteen trial postponements over the next four and a half months as the Justice Department and the Big Five hammered out a consent decree. Signing such a decree was, for the studios, a submission of a no-contest plea and an implicit admission of guilt, as well as an effort to rectify the situation. The key points of the 1940 consent decree, signed on 29 October 1940, were: block booking would continue, but in blocks no larger than five films; trade shows would be held regularly to provide exhibitors with advance screenings; forcing of shorts and newsreels was banned; and the majors could not expand their holdings without federal approval. An arbitration board was set up to settle disputes involving clearance and the like. And the issue of divorcement was tabled for three years, left by the Justice Department and the court to hang like the sword of Damocles over the majors' heads.[45]

Two points should be underscored here. One was that the independent exhibitors, on whose behalf the antitrust suit had been filed, had begun protesting the consent decree as soon as drafts of the document began circulating in the summer. The independents' main concern was the blocks-of-five compromise, which they argued would do little to stop the blocking of weak pictures together with more desirable ones and thus would allow the present abuses to continue. Moreover, the trade shows would cause additional expense and hassle for the independent exhibitors. A more favorable plan, Allied suggested, was to continue the policy of buying a full season's program, sight unseen, but with more liberal cancellation allowances—letting exhibitors cancel up to 20 percent of a seasonal block.[46] In fact, Allied's Northwest office sponsored just such a bill in Minnesota immediately after the decree was signed. The bill passed both houses in early 1941, causing severe problems for all involved, including Minnesota exhibitors who grew desperate for product when the Big Five refused to deal with them on the terms dictated by the legislation.[47]

The second point relates to the Little Three and the so-called escape clause in the 1940 consent decree. Because UA, Universal, and Columbia did not own theaters, they considered themselves exempt from the government's antitrust charges. (UA sold its pictures individually, while Universal and Columbia relied heavily on block booking.) Still, Justice pressed its suit against the Little Three; the consent decree included a clause stipulating that if the government's case against the Little Three had not been resolved as of 1 June 1942, then the entire consent decree was void and the Big Eight could resume their earlier trade practices.

All in all, the majors emerged from the antitrust suit in remarkably good shape. As D. W. Churchill of the *New York Times* suggested in early October 1940, "From tentative drafts of the consent decree already produced, it appears that the government has taken a generous attitude toward the peculiar marketing system under which the industry operates, and that the studios will get off a lot easier than they had at first anticipated." Churchill also criticized the exhibitors for their "desire to share in all of the profits without wanting to assume any of the risks." But there was no doubt that independent theater owners had been systematically denied a fair share of those profits—as the majors acknowledged when they entered into the decree.[48]

Because the decree was signed after the 1940–1941 season commenced on 1 September 1940, the new selling setup with its blocks-of-five provision did not take effect until the 1941–1942 season. The majors did start holding trade screenings for exhibitors in early 1941, however, and arbitration tribunals also were set up in each of the thirty-one key distribution exchanges to hear complaints. By mid-July, nearly one hundred arbitration cases had been filed, the vast majority of them involving clearance; about half had been resolved, with only eight favoring the complaining exhibitor.[49] Not surprisingly, both the circuits and the independent exhibitors were as unhappy with the arbitration system as they were with the blocks-of-five provision. In December 1941, the MPTOA president, Ed Keykendall, stated that "the consent decree is a mess," and that "the benefits promised to exhibitors have completely failed to materialize."[50] A short time later, he wrote a piece for the *Film Daily Year Book,* suggesting that, for the theater owner, "the problem now is how to get out of the costly blunder without becoming even further involved in litigation and statutory regulation."[51] In that same volume, Allied's board chairman and general counsel termed the decree a "lamentable failure," insisting that theater owners in 1941 suffered "the blackest year in their history."[52]

The Justice Department shared the exhibitors' concerns about the effectiveness of the consent decree, and in fact the Justice Department clarified its concerns in a statement issued in January 1942 reviewing the first year of operation under the decree. While "the net result of the decree" was still uncertain, Justice questioned whether continued "discrimination" against the independents "may be remedied by measures short of divorcement."[53] But any claims regarding the exhibitors' undue suffering in late 1941 were dubious at best considering the recent box-office surge due to the improving economy and the U.S. government's massive defense buildup. Indeed, as discussed later in this chapter, the domestic movie marketplace by late 1941 was booming while Hollywood's overseas markets were imperiled. It was the major studio-distributors who were feeling the squeeze.

The War and Hollywood's Overseas Markets

Besides the government's antitrust campaign, Hollywood's chief concern in the early 1940s was the war overseas, which affected its foreign trade as well as the domestic market as the United States shifted into an extended and increasingly intense prewar mode. The prewar period began with the outbreak of full-scale war in Europe and steadily intensified from the fall of France and the Battle of Britain in mid-1940 until the United States entered the war in December 1941. During that time, the country underwent a complete social, political, industrial, and economic transformation, keyed by a massive military and defense buildup, which stimulated the national economy, and by an ideological shift from isolationism to uneasy neutrality to open support of Britain and the Allies.

In the early months of the war in Europe, Hollywood's primary concern was the prospective decline of its foreign trade. Ironically, the situation at the outset of World

War II contrasted sharply with the impact of the First World War, which came as a tremendous windfall for the nascent American movie industry. As the film critic Frank Nugent of the *New York Times* recollected in September 1939: "Prior to 1915, the American picture industry was a puny brat living on a diet of one and two reels. Germany, Italy and Sweden were the flourishing film makers; France was not far behind. The war changed all that. Hollywood was a war baby." Nugent noted that the elimination of foreign competition during World War I enabled the Hollywood studios to corner the U.S. market and to establish a foothold internationally. That foothold became a stranglehold in the 1920s with the steady consolidation of the studio system and Hollywood's successful introduction of sound—to a point where, in Nugent's words, "Hollywood's standards generally have become the world's standards."[54]

With the deepening military crises overseas in the mid to late 1930s, Hollywood again was benefiting from weak foreign competition. Moreover, the studios' ongoing efforts to pursue overseas markets despite the war put the movie industry in a rather unique position among U.S. industries. As the *Wall Street Journal* noted, "The moving picture industry was one of the very few American businesses that had a vital stake in foreign trade when the war broke out."[55] Maintaining that trade had not been easy, of course, particularly with the loss of major foreign markets in the late 1930s. Germany in 1937 severely cut its import of Hollywood films and also reduced the revenues remitted to the studios. Japan followed suit in 1938, reducing the number of U.S. imports to about sixty films (down from an average of about four hundred before the war) and freezing virtually all U.S. motion picture revenues in Japan.[56] Nazi expansion into central Europe in 1938 further undercut Hollywood's overseas business, contributing to a fall of 6 percent in the studios' overseas revenues compared to 1937.[57] In January 1939, Italy nationalized the film import business, at which point the MPPDA announced that all studio trade with that country was suspended. In July, *Variety* reported that Hollywood's foreign revenues were off nearly 10 percent compared with the first six months of 1938, owing mainly to the losses in central Europe and Italy.[58]

In mid-1939 there were 62,000 movie theaters wired for sound worldwide. This number included 17,500 in the U.S. domestic market and about 1,225 in Canada; 33,000 in Europe; 5,250 in Latin America; and some 6,200 in the Far East. Despite the lost Axis markets, which included 6,500 theaters in Germany and 4,000 in Italy, Europe remained the key region in Hollywood's overseas trade, with England's 5,300 theaters and France's 4,600 accounting for the vast majority of Hollywood's overseas revenues.[59] According to a *Variety* survey of the global movie marketplace in September 1939, the market shares (percentage of total foreign revenue) of Hollywood's chief overseas clients at the time were: Great Britain, 45 percent; France/Belgium, 13 percent; Australia, 11.2 percent; Central and South America, 9 percent; Scandinavia, 4.2 percent; Holland, 1.5 percent; Bulgaria/Greece/Turkey, 1.2 percent; neutral central Europe, 1 percent.[60]

Variety routinely estimated Hollywood's overseas income as 40–50 percent of its total movie revenues in the late 1930s; other more conservative (and perhaps more reliable) estimates were somewhat lower. In October 1939, the *Wall Street Journal* reported: "The situation may be summed up as follows: American film producers obtain about 30 percent to 35 percent of their total film rentals from abroad. This varies somewhat from year to year. Around half of the foreign income . . . comes from Great Britain. South America supplies 10 percent to 15 percent and the rest is scattered. The Continent of Europe, due to government regulation and exchange difficulties, has provided little profit in recent years."[61] In the ensuing months, Hollywood's trade on the Continent would be reduced to virtually nil as the Nazi blitzkrieg eliminated one European market after another, culminating in the fall of France in June 1940. By late 1940, all of Europe except Sweden, Switzerland, and Portugal was lost, owing either to Nazi-imposed trade embargo or to political alliance with the Axis. That left England standing virtually alone in the face of Nazi aggression in the West—and alone, too, as Hollywood's last significant European market.[62]

Britain traditionally had generated the lion's share of Hollywood's overseas income, providing the majors with $35 million per year throughout the 1930s.[63] Hollywood product accounted for well over 80 percent of the films screened in England, and by the late 1930s Britain had become, in effect, a direct extension of the American market; it was, as *Variety* suggested in January 1939, "a country that is closer to America in language, thought and ideals than any other in the world."[64] But as war conditions in Europe and England worsened, Hollywood seemed ever on the verge of writing off its British income. After its declaration of war on Germany in September 1939, Britain closed all its theaters—a move termed by George Bernard Shaw, in an open letter to the *London Times,* "a master stroke of unimaginative stupidity" considering the cinema's importance to morale and social cohesion, as well as its role as simple diversion from the events at hand.[65] Within two weeks, 65–70 percent of British theaters had reopened, primarily those outside London, and by early 1940 business was nearing prewar levels.[66]

Conditions worsened in late 1940 with the Battle of Britain, a sustained German air attack designed to soften England for an all-out invasion later that year. In September, the German *Luftwaffe* began its nightly air raids over London—the so-called London Blitz—and within two weeks the total number of war-related theater closings surpassed one hundred. The nightly bombing raids on London and other key industrial targets continued, and by December the number of London theaters closed due to bombings reached two hundred. The courageous British resistance stalled Hitler's plans for an invasion in 1940, and by 1941 those plans were abandoned altogether and the Battle of Britain finally ended. In June 1941, as England entered a summer free of blitzes, some 650 theaters were closed, at least 500 owing directly to the war, and attendance was down 25 percent. But remarkably enough, British cinemas during the first two years of the war had generated nearly $50 million in rentals for Hollywood's major producer-distributors.[67]

Getting that money out of England was quite another matter, however. As of September 1941, British trade restrictions had frozen an estimated $35 million of Hollywood revenues in British banks. The freeze caused considerable concern among the majors, whose foreign income had fallen more than 50 percent in the previous year.[68] The freezing of British funds dated back long before the war, to the so-called Films Act of 1927, also known as the "quota law," which was renewed by Parliament in 1938. The act set limits on remittance of revenues and also set quotas on the proportion of domestically produced and imported films that British theaters could screen, thus encouraging American companies to invest in British production (or to coproduce). Once the war broke out, filmmaking in Britain fell to under one hundred films per year, and its facilities were converted to factories, offices, warehouses, and so on. These changes reduced American investment opportunities; Britain desperately needed cash for its war effort, however, and so it increased the remittance restrictions. In October 1940, U.S. distributors were allowed to remit only $17.5 million; in January, a new agreement lowered the ceiling for that year to $12.5 million.[69] Finally, in October 1941, after a full year's negotiation and cajoling by Ambassador Joseph P. Kennedy, Britain agreed to allow withdrawal of $37.5 million and lowered the quota of British films to only 2.5 percent.[70]

The Luftwaffe *bombed Britain's production facilities as well as its theaters. Actress Deborah Kerr stands amid the ruins of the Denham Studio outside London in 1941.*

England yielded on the issue of remittances in response to the U.S. government's active support of the British war effort, notably the Lend-Lease Act (which became law in March 1941), whereby the United States supplied England with weapons, ships, planes, and other war-related materiel. By mid-1941, Hollywood also became more aggressive in its on-screen support of the British war effort, producing a number of features and documentaries designed to solidify American support of England and also to boost British morale.

Outside the United Kingdom, Hollywood's prewar overseas interests focused increasingly on Central and South America. In January 1939, the *Motion Picture Herald* announced that "plans are under way [in Hollywood] for the intense cultivation of the Latin American countries," in hopes of offsetting the expected losses in Europe and the Far East. Many of these plans involved production outside Hollywood. UA already had been producing and releasing Spanish-language pictures for several years through facilities in Spain and Mexico, and of the thirty or so pictures planned for release in 1939 in Central America, fewer than half were to be produced in the United States. The widespread conviction was that, even with imported Latin talent, the Hollywood studios were fundamentally ill equipped to produce "a genuinely Spanish film." Thus, these coproductions were coordinated through the State Department's Division of Cultural Relations, whose "good neighbor policy" with Latin America well indicated the larger political and economic stake of the United States in that region.[71]

Hollywood was particularly sensitive to the cultural and language barriers between the United States and Latin America, although there were several other drawbacks to developing those markets as well. First, the dominant Latin American nations, unlike those in war-torn Europe, were in relatively good economic shape and were producing their own films. In fact, Hollywood in 1939 was supplying talent and equipment as well as financing to various Latin American countries.[72] By early 1940, Brazil, Argentina, and Mexico all had surpassed Britain as top consumers of film stock from the United States.[73] A second concern was that other foreign nations besides the United States, notably Nazi Germany, also were cultivating the Latin American market—and like the United States, primarily for political rather than economic reasons.[74]

By 1941, various Hollywood studios were designing major productions for the Latin American market—and for domestic audiences as well, in hopes of improving America's interest in its neighbors to the south. These included Fox's THAT NIGHT IN RIO (1941), DOWN ARGENTINE WAY (1940), and BLOOD AND SAND (1941), and RKO's THEY MET IN ARGENTINA (1941), and MGM's THE LIFE OF SIMON BOLIVAR. The improving Latin American market was often referred to as a "bright spot" in Hollywood's otherwise dismal or uncertain overseas trade, showing a 10 percent improvement between 1940 and 1941. But in fact, Hollywood's cultivation of the Latin American market was an economic disappointment and something of a cultural and political debacle.[75] In May 1941, ARGENTINE NIGHTS (1940), a Ritz Brothers–Andrews Sisters musical comedy from Universal, was banned in Buenos Aires after opening-night demonstrations against the picture. The chairman of the U.S. Cultural Relations Committee, Jock Whitney, blamed the problem on "anti-American and anti-free forces," but actually such protests were not uncommon, nor were they confined to films designed specifically for the Latin American market. That same month, Mexico banned a seemingly innocuous Western, KIT CARSON (1940), for its offensive portrayal of Mexicans.[76]

In late 1941, the State Department began suggesting topics for films designed for export to Latin America, and it supported a fact-finding and goodwill tour of South

Among Hollywood's A-class star vehicles geared for the Latin American market was BLOOD AND SAND *(20th Century–Fox, 1941), with Tyrone Power and Rita Hayworth in conspicuously Latin roles.*

America by a Hollywood contingent that included Jock Whitney, Bing Crosby, and Walt Disney.[77] The *1942 Film Daily Year Book* lauded that effort and again cited the improving Latin American market, though the improvement was attributed as much to the general economic and social development of the region as to any of Hollywood's efforts.[78] And *Variety's* year-end survey reported that efforts by cinema, radio, and other U.S. media industries to promote the good neighbor policy was "pretty much a flop." As a State Department study at the time suggested, despite their good intentions, "Americans still do not appreciate the tastes, interests and conditions of countries below the Rio Grande."[79] But U.S. government and industry could ill afford to ignore the Latin American market, given the immediate political stakes and the long-term economic prospects, and so Hollywood's good neighbor initiative continued throughout the prewar era and into the war years.

The U.S. Defense Buildup and the Domestic Movie Market

The war-induced decline in foreign revenues and the problems over British remittances forced the studios to focus more heavily than ever on the domestic market. In 1940, the movie industry gauged its "potential" audience (comprising "frequent" and "occasional" moviegoers) at 90–100 million out of a total population of just over 130 million. According to the *Film Daily Year Book*, weekly ticket sales in the United States totaled 80 million in 1940, and 55–60 million Americans went to the movies every week.[80] Movie tickets made up one-fifth of all U.S. amusement expenditures and fully four-fifths of all spending on spectator amusements, including theater and sports.[81] Although moviegoing was integral to the everyday lives of most Americans in 1940, the industry still was struggling to shake the lingering effects of the Depression and harbored grave concerns about the effects of war on the domestic market.

As the U.S. defense buildup gained steam in 1940, however, it became clear that the motion picture industry would be a major beneficiary, particularly because the buildup was centered in the urban-industrial areas where Hollywood did most of its business. Thus, the film industry's guarded optimism about a possible war boom tended to grow right along with the defense buildup. A June 1940 report from Poor's on Wall Street suggested that the improving domestic movie market should more than compensate for losses overseas.[82] Industry performance in 1940 actually bore out that prediction: domestic revenues climbed from $659 million in 1939 to $735 million in 1940, up nearly 12 percent.[83] In January 1941, the *Wall Street Journal* reported that "Hollywood is on the road to becoming more domestically self-contained, even though the road may be a rough one," and went on to note that the movie industry "has by now pretty well adjusted to the loss of a large part of its foreign revenues."[84]

While the movie industry was enjoying the benefits of the defense buildup by late 1940, it actually lagged behind other major industries as the buildup went into high gear in the early months of 1941. In fact, many feared that the full force of the defense boom might not reach the movie industry. "All Other Biz Up But Pix," ran a banner *Variety* headline in May 1941, and in June Bosley Crowther of the *New York Times* devoted several columns to what he termed Hollywood's "Boxoffice Blues."[85] By late June, according to the Office of Government Reports, defense contracts and expenditures totaled $17 billion, but still the movie business was in the doldrums.[86]

All that changed overnight—or over a single weekend, actually. During the Fourth of July holiday weekend, theaters reported a surge in attendance—and in fact, virtually all amusement and recreational spending in the United States surged.[87] The *Wall Street Journal* reported in September 1941 that the boom was still going strong. "The amusement world says the Fourth of July touched off a spending explosion," said the page-one story. "So sharp and so sudden was the spurt that those affected dismissed it as a flash in the pan. But succeeding summer weeks . . . continued to pile up cash in the box offices, book and liquor stores, railroad, bus, and airline ticket offices."[88]

By the autumn of 1941, the sustained boom had become an accepted way of life in the movie industry, with even better business expected as new factories, urban labor migration, the draft, new army camps, and rearrangement of work schedules (night shifts, swing shifts, and the like) all pushed movie attendance and ticket sales ever upward. The box office was up a reported 20–25 percent in Washington, D.C., and about 15 percent in the Twin Cities. Business in Indianapolis was even better, with city payrolls having increased 50 percent over the preceding year. The boom also hit heavily in Detroit and Los Angeles owing to the concentration of airplane factories in those areas. One city that lagged behind, ironically enough, was New York, the nation's movie exhibition leader, since there were relatively few defense plants in the metropolitan area.[89]

Perhaps the number-one beneficiary of the defense buildup was Pittsburgh, the nation's steel center and capital of heavy industry, and thus a crucial city in the U.S. defense arsenal. New munitions factories, shipyards, airplane plants, and military bases added millions of dollars to payrolls and pushed movie theater revenues up well over 20 percent—and even higher in department store sales, auto purchases, home building, and some luxury expenditures. Factories were still being built as of 1 November 1941, with 22,000 new jobs expected within the next fifteen months. Virtually all of the city's 150 theaters were feeling the effects of the boom, with the biggest rise occurring in the neighborhood and suburban houses.[90]

This latter point touches on one of the more interesting aspects of prewar exhibition, namely, the trend in American life toward suburbanization as the population shifted away from urban centers to outlying suburbs and small communities. Prior to the defense buildup, in fact, the population shift away from the downtown theaters where the industry did most of its business had been a growing concern among exhibitors. In August 1940, the *Motion Picture Herald* reported that Census Bureau figures indicated that "a substantial part of the future of motion picture exhibition lies in the suburbs." This change reversed the trend of the 1910s and 1920s when urban centers grew rapidly. According to the Census Bureau, the total population of nine of the thirty U.S. cities with over 300,000 in population had actually declined since 1930.[91]

One obvious factor in this shift, stated the *Herald*, was the "commuter mode of life," which was also contributing to the slow but steady rise of the drive-in movie theater—a trend that accelerated in 1941 with the development of in-car speakers.[92] There were some sixty-five drive-ins operating in 1941, with another fifty or so under construction, most of them in the South and in California, spurred by population growth and favorable weather. Another phenomenon related to suburban and commuter lifestyles, said the *Herald*, was "the construction of well planned 'shopping centers' . . . creating situations in which motion picture theaters can and do thrive." Los Angeles provided a prime example. Downtown retail sales in L.A. had been declining since 1929, while department stores like Bullock's and the Broadway had opened successful suburban branches. Sears, Roebuck, and Company had five stores in the L.A. area, none of which was located downtown.[93]

Along with the antitrust suit, noted the *Herald,* the move to the suburbs and shopping centers could render the industry's movie palaces "unprofitable" and could even "break the first-run monopoly which the 'downtown' theatres have enjoyed." But as yet, these trends were deemed to be "of too recent origin for any conclusive results."[94] Those "results" would not be forthcoming for quite some time, since the defense buildup and the ensuing war conditions would keep the population concentrated in urban centers. In fact, in 1941 the suburban trend was effectively quashed by government mandate: new home construction was suspended so that both labor and material could be utilized for war-related production. For the time being, however, the limited suburban boom provided a strong complement to soaring downtown movie attendance and helped push revenues to record levels.

Another factor in the improving market situation in 1941—and another distinct manifestation of the nation's deepening prewar mentality—was the public's growing appetite for news about the war overseas as well as about U.S. "preparedness." By late 1940, Hollywood newsreels, documentary shorts, and features were increasingly devoted to war-related subjects. The public was buying, and, in fact, news-hungry audiences were changing the very nature of moviegoing. By spring 1941, theaters routinely interrupted their programs to provide news bulletins, and some houses actually began scheduling radio broadcasts of FDR's Tuesday evening "Fireside Chats"—broadcasts which were drawing total radio audiences of up to 70 million, fully one-half the U.S. population.[95] Another barometer of public interest in the war was the prewar rise of the newsreel theater. These theaters enjoyed their heyday before and during World War II, with approximately twenty-five in operation in the largest U.S. cities by late 1941. Nearly all of these were converted second-run downtown houses, and many had news tickers in the lobby and radio piped into the auditorium between newsreel programs.[96]

Newsreel houses were one of several forms of specialty theaters operating in the United States in 1940, virtually all of which were affected by the defense buildup and the war. The effects were most pronounced in those theaters that catered to foreign films, including both ethnic theaters and art-cinema houses. The former were located in ethnic neighborhoods in large cities, primarily in the Northeast, although Spanish-language theaters in the Southwest were not uncommon. Art cinemas catered to the growing ranks of cinephiles and connoisseurs interested in critically acclaimed foreign films, primarily from France, Germany, and England. Just before the war in Europe, the *Motion Picture Herald* reported that foreign-language films played regularly at about 175 theaters in 85 different localities, about 100 of which screened only foreign films. That total actually had declined during the 1930s, with the assimilation of immigrant audiences into the American (and Hollywood) mainstream and also the increased control over the movie marketplace by the Big Eight. By 1940, in fact, the ethnic theater was being eclipsed by the art cinema as a site for viewing foreign-language films. With the war in Europe, however, the market for foreign-language films quickly dried up altogether.[97]

By far the most significant form of specialty theater in the United States at the time was the so-called Negro theater. The number of these theaters, designed to serve the nation's 12 million African Americans, had increased steadily in the 1930s and would explode during the 1940s as African-American participation in the war effort made that population an increasingly viable market segment. Not surprisingly, given the marginal social and economic status of blacks before the war, statistics on these theaters and

This marquee on Hollywood Boulevard illustrates the war-related focus of the news-reel theater in the early 1940s.

their audiences are even less accurate and reliable than those on mainstream moviego-ing. According to an in-depth *Motion Picture Herald* story in July 1939, the Motion Picture Division of the Department of Commerce estimated that there were some 400 Negro theaters in 175 cities in 28 states at the time—an increase of 65 percent in the previous two years.[98] *Variety* in January 1940 reported that there were some 500 the-aters in the United States devoted to "all-Negro" films. Most of these were located in the Deep South, although New York City's Harlem district alone boasted seventeen Negro theaters.[99]

Variety also noted that an increasing number of mainstream theaters in more openly segregated areas, especially in the Deep South, were adopting policies to accommodate blacks, such as reserving a portion of the theater for blacks (usually the balcony, entered through a separate entrance) or devoting the final screening of the day (usually a late-night program) to black-only audiences. These changes enabled blacks to see Hollywood films at the same time as white audiences in these areas, which was scarcely the case in Negro theaters.[100] The latter generally received Hollywood films in their final runs—sometimes one to two years after their initial release in large cities in the North, and about six months later in the South.[101] But the Negro theaters also had the advantage of being able to run all-Negro films created specifically for African-American audiences.

By late 1941, the U.S. movie marketplace was booming and Hollywood's late-Depression economic woes clearly were over. The industry had become "domestically self-contained" to an unprecedented degree, no longer relying on overseas revenues to turn a profit. Domestic revenues reached a record $809 million in 1941, up from $735 million in 1940. And the British remittances in late 1941 came as a tremendous windfall, pushing studio profits to their highest levels in over a decade. The combined profits of the Big Eight totaled $35 million, nearly double the $19 million profits of 1940.[102]

Labor Pains

Adding to the chaos and uncertainty of the prewar era was a deepening labor crisis, which involved powerful forces both inside and outside the motion picture industry. In fact, a number of long-simmering labor conflicts reached a boiling point in 1940–1941, signaling not only the severity but also the increasingly political nature of Hollywood's labor crisis. The conjunction of these conflicts also indicated the inability of the studios—and their trade association and public relations branch, the MPPDA—to manage these crises. Hollywood's labor conflicts centered on three distinct areas: first, jurisdictional battles for control of the unions and guilds by national labor organizations; second, government prosecution of film industry labor leaders for racketeering; and third, investigations by local and federal authorities into alleged Communist infiltration of Hollywood labor unions.

A catalyst of sorts in each of these conflicts during the prewar era was the official formation of Hollywood's top talent guilds. The directors' and writers' guilds were founded in the mid-1930s, but as of 1939 they still had not signed contracts with the studios (which, in this context, were routinely referred to as the "producers").[103] The Screen Actors Guild (SAG) won recognition from the producers in 1937, signing a contract that made SAG the sole bargaining agent for all of Hollywood's actors, from top stars to bit players.[104] The leverage of top stars over the studios proved crucial in winning SAG approval, and in turn the Actors Guild helped win approval for both the Screen Directors Guild (SDG) and the Screen Writers Guild (SWG). Both SDG and SWG sorely needed this support, since both were deemed a greater threat to studio control over filmmaking than SAG and thus both faced much heavier producer resistance to their respective guild agreements.

The first of these two guilds to win recognition was SDG. A key figure in the effort was the Columbia producer-director Frank Capra, arguably Hollywood's top filmmaker at the time and a savvy political infighter. Capra was the first president of SDG and also happened to be president of the Motion Picture Academy in 1939 (having won three best-director and three best-picture Oscars in the preceding five years), and he deftly played SDG and the Academy against each other. Capra also won the support of SAG and played the industry's top stars and directors against the studios.[105] In early 1939, the directors, after threatening to strike and desert the Academy en masse, signed a three-year pact with the producers.

The writers had much more difficulty reaching an agreement, owing to chronic internal conflicts and a lack of leadership, as well as a history of battling the studio brass. SWG had won certification in August 1938 from the National Labor Relations Board (NLRB) to act as bargaining agent for screenwriters, then spent two years haggling with the producers over an agreement. By 1940, writers were the only Hollywood workers

The smiles of writer Sheridan Gibney, Paramount executive Frank Y. Freeman, MGM executive Eddie Mannix, and writer Sidney Buchman (newly elected president of the Screen Writers Guild) belie the bitter, seven-year struggle which preceded the signing of the SWG pact.

with no protection or bargaining rights with the studios. The NLRB was highly critical of the producers' intractable stance, and also of studio efforts to set up a competing union dominated by highly paid contract writers. SWG eventually prevailed, however, signing a six-month pact in 1940 and then a seven-year deal in June 1941. While *Variety* termed this agreement "a major victory for the scribes," it was a bitter, hard-won victory.[106] As Leo Rosten observed, "The obstinacy and indiscretion with which the producers opposed Hollywood writers in their fight for recognition, basic working conditions, and a code of fair practice, is one of the less flattering commentaries on the men who control movie production."[107]

With the unionization of top filmmaking talent, the stakes in Hollywood's ongoing jurisdictional battles rose considerably. In general, these battles over jurisdiction resulted from two factors: the enormous size and complexity of the movie industry, and the fact that Hollywood labor had not organized extensively until the Depression. During the 1930s, in fact, Hollywood had rapidly evolved from essentially an "open shop" to a "union town," leading *Variety* to posit in January 1939 that "the major studios are now 100 percent organized."[108] As David Prindle has noted, "When several unions are attempting to move into an unorganized city, or when technological change creates new and different jobs, jurisdictional strife is inevitable. Because Los Angeles was the least organized large city in America [in the early 1930s], and because the motion picture was using a rapidly evolving technology, Hollywood was a union battleground during those decades [the 1930s and 1940s]."[109]

The chief antagonist in these battles was the International Alliance of Theatrical and Stage Employees (IATSE), a labor organization under the American Federation of Labor (AFL). Created in the 1890s on the East Coast as a stage union, IATSE came to dominate the ranks of movie theater employees, particularly through its control of the nation's projectionists. This control gave IATSE the power to shut down the entire movie industry and provided tremendous leverage for its successful assault on Hollywood in the 1930s. By decade's end, IATSE's ranks totaled some 40,000 members in 849 studio and exhibitor unions in the United States and Canada, including about 12,000 of Hollywood's 30,000 workers. In 1939, IATSE began vying for complete control of Hollywood's labor force, hoping to create "one big union" of motion picture employees.[110]

IATSE faced opposition from three parties. First and foremost were the studios, which had formed an uneasy alliance with IATSE; they recognized its obvious power but were adamantly opposed to the organization of all filmmaking talent into a single labor organization. IATSE also faced opposition from the AFL's chief national (and international) adversary, the Council of Industrial Organizations (CIO). In the late 1930s, the CIO began an incursion into Hollywood, until then an impregnable AFL stronghold, through the United Studio Technicians Guild (USTG), a group of Hollywood unions which bolted IATSE for CIO affiliation.[111] The third party opposing IATSE's "one big union" effort was SAG, which, despite its AFL affiliation, had been fiercely independent since its founding in 1933. During its formative years, SAG resisted horizontal affiliation with actors unions in other industries or other parts of the country and maintained a tenuous rapport with the AFL. Since winning official recognition in 1938, SAG was fast becoming Hollywood's most powerful union, and it openly refused to submit to IATSE jurisdiction.[112]

SAG demonstrated its growing power and influence in the battle between IATSE and the USTG, which escalated rapidly in 1939. By early summer, the USTG had won the support of the major studios, which were always looking for ways to undercut both IATSE's power and the further consolidation of organized labor. In July, the NLRB set a September date for a certification election to determine whether USTG had sufficient support to be awarded NLRB recognition. In August, SAG announced that it was on the verge of bolting the AFL and joining the CIO. That same month, the government announced that a federal grand jury would be looking into a $100,000 "loan" made two years earlier by the chairman of the board of 20th Century–Fox, Joe Schenck, to IATSE's Hollywood labor boss, Willie Bioff—a loan which was discovered by detectives hired by SAG. Now on the defensive, IATSE moved to shore up its votes against the USTG in the coming election. In September, the IATSE president, George Browne, signed a "peace treaty" with SAG assuring the guild its autonomy in exchange for AFL allegiance and an endorsement of IATSE. Bioff also began fomenting strike threats at the studios, resulting in a 10 percent pay hike on 25 September for IATSE's Hollywood members. Not surprisingly, the USTG lost its bid for NLRB certification.[113]

While IATSE prevailed in its battle with the USTG, its problems in Hollywood steadily worsened in 1940–1941. In January 1940, Bioff was indicted for failing to report the $100,000 loan to the IRS.[114] In June, Joe Schenck was indicted on thirty-nine counts ranging from tax fraud and conspiracy to perjury. Schenck was tried in a New

York federal court in March 1941, found guilty on two counts, and sentenced to one year in prison. What became evident at his trial was that Schenck, in his capacity as representative of the producers and head of the studios' labor negotiations committee, had acted as a "bag man" on behalf of his fellow producers, delivering payoffs to IATSE's Bioff and Browne. Moreover, the $100,000 was simply one installment in a total of over $1 million paid by the studios to avert strikes by IATSE-member unions.[115] In May 1941, Browne and Bioff were indicted by a New York grand jury for extortion. The two were ousted from IATSE in August and were tried and found guilty later that fall. Browne was sentenced to eight years in prison, Bioff to ten.[116]

Thus, after a decade of tremendous success, IATSE's power quickly eroded while its reputation and credibility, already suspect due to mob ties and strong-arm tactics, were in absolute shreds. Moreover, IATSE faced yet another formidable challenge in 1941 when several renegade IATSE unions formed the Conference of Studio Unions (CSU). Although affiliated with the AFL (as was IATSE), the CSU was a very different organization in two primary ways. First, it comprised mainly preproduction craft unions, versus IATSE's strength among technical and production-related unions; and second, it was an openly leftist organization, while IATSE was avowedly right-wing. The CSU was led by Herbert Sorrell of the Painters Union, a canny politician and experienced labor militant, who had organized the Cartoonists Guild under his own Painters Union and in 1941 waged a bitter, protracted, and successful strike against Disney.[117]

The Screen Actors Guild, meanwhile, emerged from the USTG fray and the IATSE debacle as, in Prindle's words, "the strongest and most prestigious labor union in Hollywood."[118] But SAG ran into trouble of its own in 1940–1941 when it became the focus of allegations of Communist infiltration. Most of these came from Congressman Martin Dies of Texas and his House Committee on Un-American Activities. Since its creation in 1938, the Dies Committee had been taking broad swipes at Hollywood's labor unions for leftist sympathies.[119] In February 1940, the Dies Committee targeted forty-three stars as having ties to the Communist Party.[120] In August, Dies interviewed a number of stars and other key industry figures in a San Francisco hotel, and afterward he publicly exonerated James Cagney, Humphrey Bogart, Fredric March, and the writer Philip Dunne. But Dies also reasserted that "numerous actors and screen people" were either Communists or red sympathizers.[121] In that same month of August 1940, a Los Angeles County grand jury began investigations of SAG along similar lines. While that inquiry found nothing, the allegations of Communist infiltration continued and steadily spread to other labor organizations.

In 1941 the Los Angeles County grand jury, the California General Assembly, the Dies Committee, and various other political groups conducted probes for "subversives" and Communists in various studio unions.[122] These efforts also came to naught, resulting in a *Variety* banner headline in August, "Can't Make Red Slur Stick."[123] By then the anti-Communist fever was subsiding, owing mainly to Nazi Germany's June 1941 invasion of the Soviet Union. Thus, a U.S. alliance with the Soviets seemed likely—and did occur with the U.S. entry into the war, at which point the anti-Communist probes ceased altogether. In fact, Hollywood's labor conflicts all but disappeared in December 1941. Both Sorrell and the newly elected IATSE president, Richard Walsh, made no-strike pledges on behalf of their member unions, promising labor unity and full support of the industry's war effort. Thus, the *Film Daily Year Book* noted the "stabilization of labor relations throughout the motion picture industry" in late 1941.[124]

Actor James Cagney with Congressman Martin Dies in August 1940, after the Warners star was cleared of having Communist ties by Dies's Un-American Activities Committee.

Propaganda, Politics, and the Production Code Administration

Interestingly enough, the anti-Communist political probes during the prewar era focused on the infiltration of leftist ideologues into Hollywood labor unions rather than on the infiltration of leftist ideology into movies themselves. Other groups were sounding this alarm, however, notably conservative political and religious organizations like the American Legion and the Catholic Knights of Columbus. At the same time, isolationist politicians and political groups were increasingly vocal in their criticism of the movies' pro-war, pro-military, and pro-Allies themes and subjects. As with the labor discord, these conflicts indicated the heightened political stakes for Hollywood before the war, as well as the general inability of the industry's internal mechanisms, especially the MPPDA and its subagency, the Production Code Administration (PCA), to manage these crises.

The PCA was scarcely designed or equipped to handle overtly political matters, of course. Its primary function was to uphold the Production Code, a doctrine of movie ethics written in 1930 at the request of the MPPDA president Will Hays and designed, in the words of its preamble, to uphold "the larger moral responsibility of the motion pictures."[125] This responsibility was defined almost entirely in terms of sexual and criminal deviance, which were very much at issue in the early 1930s. Since its creation in 1934 under the leadership of Joseph Breen, the PCA (also known as the Breen Office) had interacted with producers and studio executives to regulate movie content, while the MPPDA fended off outside efforts to censor or otherwise control movie content.

Code enforcement had become standard operating procedure in the industry by 1940, with the vast majority of pictures made in complete compliance with the Code. But there were a number of serious internal Code challenges, particularly from leading independent producers on high-stakes, first-run productions. Most of these involved familiar PCA territory—sex, violence, profanity, criminal behavior—as with the well-known 1939 controversy over Rhett Butler's parting epithet to Scarlett at the end of GONE WITH THE WIND. The latter was little more than a Selznick-inspired publicity stunt, however, and scarcely indicated what the PCA was up against at the time. A much better indication was another Selznick production, REBECCA, based on Daphne du Maurier's best-selling novel whose male hero gets away with murder. The PCA found that plot line unacceptable, leading to a bitter, yearlong struggle with Selznick over the adaptation. The PCA prevailed: in the film version the death is accidental. This change incensed Selznick, who appealed to his partners to mount a "fight against so insane and inane and outmoded a Code as that under which the industry is now struggling."[126]

That campaign was conducted behind the scenes, but other producers were willing to go public about the Code. The most notable of these was the independent producer Howard Hughes, who conducted a much-publicized battle over THE OUTLAW (1943), an "adult Western" featuring Hughes's most recent female protégée, Jane Russell. The PCA approved the script, a bit of revisionist Western history featuring Russell as a libidinous dance-hall girl who comes between Pat Garrett and Billy the Kid. But then in early 1941, the PCA rejected the finished film, which had been directed by Hughes himself after Howard Hawks left the project. PCA concerns about THE OUTLAW centered on several dozen "breast shots"—scenes in which camera position or costuming, in the PCA's view, overemphasized Russell's figure. Breen instructed Hughes to reshoot the scenes with Russell "recostumed," or the PCA would not grant THE OUTLAW a Code seal. Without a Code seal, a film could not be released through any of the eight MPPDA distributors.[127] Hughes refused to comply and publicly chastised Breen, the Code, and the MPPDA's "monopoly" not only over movie distribution but also over the nation's social and sexual mores. While THE OUTLAW was shelved for the time being, Hughes's well-orchestrated anti-Code publicity campaign kept the picture (and Jane Russell's image) very much in the public eye.

Breen's battles with Selznick and Hughes indicated two important factors in prewar Hollywood: first, that there was growing resistance within Hollywood to the strictures of the Code; and second, that Code resistance was more likely to come from major independent producers and in pictures geared to more sophisticated urban audiences. These challenges involved areas that the PCA was designed to regulate, and the PCA generally did handle such challenges, although often with obvious difficulty. There were other challenges of a more topical and political nature, however, which the PCA—and the MPPDA as well—proved woefully ill equipped to handle. Most of these involved political and war-related issues, and here too the challenges tended to involve independent prestige-level pictures.

Among the chief critics of the Code's political constraints was Walter Wanger, a leading independent producer whose battles with Breen over political content dated back to

This pose by Howard Hughes's discovery Jane Russell keyed the publicity campaign for THE OUTLAW *(1943) and generated a firestorm of controversy.*

BLOCKADE, a 1938 picture set against the Spanish Civil War. In 1939, Wanger again was battling the PCA, this time while making FOREIGN CORRESPONDENT (1940), an espionage thriller set in Europe with Nazi antagonists and based on a recent nonfiction best-seller, *Personal History* by Vincent Sheean. PCA restrictions infuriated Wanger, resulting in a very public debate with the MPPDA president Will Hays conducted in speeches, in the pages of trade journals, and in the *New York Times* and various national news magazines. In a February 1939 letter to the *New York Times,* Wanger argued that the PCA was wedded to a "formulated theory of pure entertainment," which was "making impossible the honest handling of important truths and ideas."[128] Days later, Will Hays issued his annual MPPDA report, which reasserted precisely that theory: "The screen has handled successfully themes of contemporary thought in dramatic and vivid form and presented the subject matter as splendid entertainment, rather than propaganda."[129] A few weeks later, in response to the suggestion that there was a movie trend, as *Variety* put it, toward more "realistic and contemporary themes," the PCA flatly denied that there would be "any tampering with the production code or lightening of PCA regulations."[130]

By 1940–1941, however, as the war in Europe intensified and as the likelihood of U.S. intervention increased, Hays and Breen could scarcely discourage filmmakers from taking on geopolitical and war-related subjects. Indeed, Roosevelt personally appealed to the movie industry in 1940 to support both the defense buildup at home and the Allied effort overseas. The industry complied, initially with documentary and newsreel coverage, and by 1941 with a steady increase of war-related features. The studios also began producing training and informational films for both the government and the military. Roosevelt responded to these efforts with a letter of appreciation to be read at the Academy Awards banquet in early 1941. Meanwhile, the nation's isolationist contingent chastised Hollywood's interventionist turn and frequently invoked the term "propaganda"—a loaded term at the time, of course, given the nationalization of the film industries in Germany and Italy and their conversion into state propaganda agencies.[131]

In the midst of the growing turmoil, Hays and the PCA were hit with a severe shock in May 1941 when Joe Breen announced his resignation. After running the PCA with single-handed, single-minded authority since its creation in 1934, Breen unexpectedly decided to take a position at RKO as general manager of the studio.[132] Breen was replaced as PCA president by his former assistant, Geoffrey Shurlock, then the senior member of the nine-man Hollywood-based censorship board. The British-born Shurlock was a devout Anglican with cultivated tastes and considerable PCA experience, having been with the MPPDA since 1932, but it soon became evident that he was less adept than Breen at handling the problems that now faced the agency.

Perhaps the best indication of Shurlock's deficiencies—in judgment as well as political savvy—occurred a few months later in a confrontation with the PCA's familiar nemesis, the Catholic Legion of Decency. In October 1941, Shurlock awarded a Code seal of approval to MGM's new Greta Garbo picture, TWO-FACED WOMAN. The picture was a follow-up to Metro's 1939 comedy hit NINOTCHKA, again teaming Garbo and Melvyn Douglas in a screwball romance—this time in a tale of mistaken identity wherein Garbo masquerades as her own twin sister, seduces her wayward husband, and finally reveals her true identity in a climactic comic comeuppance. *Variety*'s review of the film termed it "a wild and occasionally risqué, slapstick farce" but questioned "just how some of the lines of dialogue escaped the [PCA] scissors." The Legion of Decency wondered the same thing and gave TWO-FACED WOMAN a "C" (condemned) rating—which rendered the film off-limits to the millions of American Catholics.[133]

Both MGM and the PCA initially tried to weather the storm, and *Variety* noted in early December that the outcry actually may have boosted the picture's box office.[134] But the opposition steadily grew. TWO-FACED WOMAN was banned by censor boards in Providence, Boston, and elsewhere, while scenes were ordered cut by boards in Omaha, Chicago, Milwaukee, and other cities.[135] The Catholic Church continued to pressure MGM, with Archbishop Francis Spellman of New York reiterating the Legion's condemnation. In December, MGM finally relented and, in an unprecedented and costly move, withdrew the movie from release. Garbo and Douglas were called back to Metro to film a new scene in which the husband learns of his wife's masquerade early in the story and thus simply pretends to be yielding to his sister-in-law's charms.[136] The picture was then re-released, but the damage apparently was done: TWO-FACED WOMAN died at the box office.

The TWO-FACED WOMAN flap coincided with another regulatory crisis in late 1941, and one which underscored the increasingly complex political stakes for Hollywood, as well as the industry's vulnerability to outside attack. This crisis involved the so-called propaganda hearings convened in Washington, D.C., in September 1941 by a cadre of isolationist senators who decided to take on the movie industry in a grandiose (if somewhat desperate) stand against the tide of interventionism. Gauging Hollywood as an ideal target due to the antitrust and anti-Communist assaults it had sustained, Senators Burton K. Wheeler of Montana and Gerald P. Nye of North Dakota demanded that the

Interstate Commerce Committee investigate what Nye termed the Hollywood "propaganda machine," which was run by the studios "almost as if they were being operated by a central agency." The committee hearings focused on seventeen "war-mongering" feature films, a dozen of which were produced in Hollywood—including Wanger's FOREIGN CORRESPONDENT and Charlie Chaplin's THE GREAT DICTATOR (1940)—along with four British imports and one other studio-released foreign picture.[137]

The Senate hearings convened on 9 September 1941, with the former Republican presidential nominee and renowned jurist Wendell Willkie serving as Hollywood's counsel (for a fee of $100,000). Will Hays was called to testify along with several top studio executives, but the MPPDA and its president were scarcely a factor in the hearings. Indeed, it was Willkie who mounted Hollywood's defense and quite literally stole the show. Senator Nye set the tone of the investigation by describing the movies in question as "the most vicious propaganda ever unloosed on a civilized people" and suggesting they were the result of a veritable conspiracy by a cabal of foreign-born Jews. Willkie deftly reframed the terms of the isolationists' argument, putting the senators on the defensive from the outset. Nye repeatedly played into Willkie's hands—denying, for instance, that prejudice or xenophobia motivated his allegations, then adding: "If anti-Semitism exists in America, the Jews have themselves to blame."[138] Willkie mounted a spirited, high-minded defense, charging that Nye and Wheeler hoped "to foster and

Wendell Willkie, pictured here during his failed 1940 presidential bid, successfully defended Hollywood in the Senate propaganda hearings of 1941.

create public prejudice against the industry," to discourage "accurate and factual pictures on Nazism," to influence industry portrayal of "the national defense program," and "to divide the American people in discordant racial and religious groups in order to disunite them over foreign policy."[139]

Public and press support immediately swung to Willkie and the movie industry. Soon there was open support from Washington as well, with FDR praising Hollywood's war effort and Senator Ernest McFarland of Arizona threatening to ask the Dies Committee to investigate the isolationists.[140] By October, Nye and Wheeler had completely lost the initiative, and the hearings lapsed into a series of adjournments and postponements. In mid-November, the proceedings were suspended for Thanksgiving; on 26 November, they were postponed indefinitely with no plans for resumption.[141]

The Japanese attack of Pearl Harbor and U.S. entry into World War II only a few weeks later not only rendered the charges of propaganda moot but resulted in the government effectively ordering Hollywood to become precisely the kind of national propaganda agency the isolationists feared. There were no further outside attacks once Hollywood assumed that role, of course. After Pearl Harbor, the movie industry's rapport with the government changed completely, as did its role in setting the nation's social and political agenda. In fact, U.S. entry into the war stemmed the tide of industry criticism and interference from virtually all outside forces—Congress, the Justice Department, the Legion of Decency, anti-Communist crusaders, national labor organizations, and so on. The drive against Hollywood was, in the parlance of the day, suspended "for the duration."

3

The Hollywood Studio System in 1940–1941

By 1940, the major motion picture companies had refined a production system acutely attuned to market conditions and to the industry's vertically integrated structure. This system was the essential feature of Hollywood's "classical" era, the basis for what Tino Balio has called the "grand design" of 1930s American cinema. But as we have seen, the American cinema faced myriad challenges both inside and outside the industry in 1940–1941. These would have enormous impact on the studio production system during the 1940s, forcing Hollywood's major powers to adjust the way they rationalized and organized production, and the way they produced and marketed individual films as well. In the course of the decade, the studio system that had been refined over the previous quarter-century would be steadily, inexorably, and permanently transformed.

That transformation scarcely occurred overnight, and, in fact, Hollywood's studio-based production system was still essentially intact in 1940, despite the challenges that threatened the industry. That system was essentially a factory-oriented mass-production operation wherein revenues from distribution and exhibition enabled the studios to keep their production plants running at full capacity. This system enabled the major producer-distributors to turn out roughly one feature film per week along with assorted serials, shorts, newsreels, and so on. Hollywood's principal product, of course, was the feature film, which in 1940 accounted for over 90 percent of the $150 million invested in studio-based production.[1] Feature production at all of the major studios included both A-class and B-class movies, with the proportion of the former to the latter dependent on the company's resources, theater holdings (or lack thereof), and overall market strategy. The majors also turned out occasional "prestige" pictures—bigger and more expensive features that were heavily promoted and usually released on a special "road-show" basis. Prestige films of 1940 included Paramount's NORTHWEST MOUNTED POLICE, Selznick/UA's REBECCA, Chaplin/UA's THE GREAT DICTATOR, and MGM's THE PHILADELPHIA STORY.

While prestige pictures played an increasingly important role in the prewar movie marketplace, Hollywood's key commodity was the A-class picture, particularly the routine, studio-produced "star vehicle." These films dominated the first-run market, generated the brunt of studio revenues, and provided veritable insurance policies at the box office—not only with the public but with unaffiliated theater owners as well, since a

The Paramount "front gate" in 1939—perhaps the most famous and familiar studio entrance in Hollywood.

company's A-class features effectively carried its entire block of pictures. Thus, each studio's stable of contract stars and its repertoire of presold genre variations were its most visible and viable resources. There was a direct correlation, in fact, between a studio's assets and revenues, the number of star-genre formulas in its repertoire, and the size and quality of its star stable—ranging from the talent-laden MGM, with over a dozen top stars on its roster, to lesser companies like RKO, Columbia, and Universal, each of which had only one or two top stars under exclusive contract and produced only a half-dozen or so A-class features per year.

Each studio's A-class star-genre formulations also were the prime factors in its distinctive "house style." Warner Bros. by 1940, for instance, had fashioned its corporate identity and signature style around a steady output of crime films with James Cagney and Edward G. Robinson, crusading biopics with Paul Muni, Bette Davis melodramas, and romantic swashbucklers with Errol Flynn and Olivia de Havilland. These star-genre formulas were the key markers of Warners' house style, the organizing principles for its entire operation, from the New York office to the studio-factory a continent away. They were a means of stabilizing marketing and sales, of bringing efficiency and economy to high-end feature production, and of distinguishing the company's collective output from that of its competitors.

To supplement their A-class product and to render overall production and marketing operations more efficient, the studios relied heavily on B pictures. This distinctive class of low-grade feature film developed early in the Depression with the emergence of double billing and the general need to economize production. B movies were made quickly and cheaply, with second-rate stars and running times of about sixty minutes. They were ruthlessly formulaic, designed to play double bills in the subsequent-run market. Often referred to as "programmers," B's were packaged with another feature—either another B or a top feature working its way through the subsequent-run market—along with various shorts, newsreels, and cartoons in a full afternoon or evening "program" of films. All of the studios except UA produced B's, which, in fact, comprised up to one-half the output of Warners, RKO, and Fox by 1939–1940. While most of the studios' revenues were earned from first-run features, B-movie production enabled them to keep operations running smoothly and contract personnel working regularly, to develop new talent, and to ensure a regular supply of product. And given their established block-booking and blind-bidding policies, the major studios were assured of an outlet for their B-grade products.

Executive management—that is, the coordination of production and marketing operations by corporate and studio executives—was a crucial facet of the vertically integrated studio system, and one which changed considerably in the late 1930s and 1940s. The Depression-era collapse of five of the Big Eight studios had put several Wall Street firms in direct control of four motion picture companies (Paramount, Fox, RKO, and Universal), and the results were complex and somewhat paradoxical. While these studios became more efficient and market-driven, they never quite conformed to Wall Street's rigid notions of production efficiency and sound business practice. Moreover, efforts to force the studios to conform to these notions simply failed. Thus, by the late 1930s, as Robert Sklar has pointed out, "all of the studios were back under the management, if not the ownership, of men experienced in the world of entertainment." And in terms of actual studio operations, notes Sklar, "the ultimate issue is not who owns the movie companies but who manages them."[2]

Significantly enough, however, the newly appointed chief executives at Paramount, Fox, RKO, and Universal all came from the business side of the industry—a clear indication of Wall Street's influence and the general development of the cinema into a modern business enterprise. Tino Balio considers the ownership-management split which developed during the 1930s a necessary result of industrial and economic growth. "As they grew in size," writes Balio, the studios "became managerial, which is to say, they rationalized and organized operations into autonomous departments headed by a professional manager." The studio founders themselves either became "full-time career managers"—the Cohns at Columbia, for example, and the Warners—or, as was more often the case, relinquished direct control to salaried executives. Balio also notes that although most of the chief executives appointed during the 1930s came from either distribution or exhibition, the management of actual filmmaking operations invariably was left to a salaried executive with a production background.[3]

Thus, the ownership-management split in the late 1930s was accompanied by a split between the management of the corporation and the management of studio and production operations—a split that would grow even more acute during the 1940s. In the early studio era, management of the corporation, of the studio-factory, and of actual production was a top-down process with a clear chain of command. The New York office, the site of ultimate authority, dictated the direction of capital, controlled marketing and sales, and, for the Big Five, oversaw theater operations. The New York office also set the annual budget and general production requirements of the studio. The Hollywood plant, in turn, was managed by one or two corporate vice presidents—usually a "studio boss" and a "production chief"—who were responsible for day-to-day studio operations and for the overall output of pictures. The chain of command extended from the studio front office into the production arena via supervisors or "associate producers" who monitored production on behalf of the higher corporate executives.

This type of central-producer system, wherein one or two executives supervised production, had all but disappeared by 1940. The studios still were managed by a studio boss and a production chief, but these individuals rarely had the kind of direct influence and authority over actual filmmaking as the studio executives of the past. Instead, the studios gradually shifted to a so-called unit-producer system during the 1930s. This system, as Janet Staiger has noted, involved "a management organization in which a group of men supervised six to eight films per year, usually each producer concentrating on a particular type of film." While actual production remained centralized in the studio-factory and fell under the ultimate control of the executive hierarchy, the unit system clearly entailed a dispersal of administrative authority and creative control into the producer ranks.[4]

Until the late 1930s, unit production was generally a studio-based process involving top talent and A-class pictures. The studios learned during the 1930s that unit production provided a means of ensuring quality and consistency in high-end production while controlling not only costs but temperamental high-end talent. These units invariably formed around top stars and the other high-salaried "creative" personnel—notably directors, writers, cinematographers, and composers—and were keyed to specific star-genre formulas. Some of these units were informal and fluid, changing somewhat from one star-genre formulation to the next except for a few key personnel, as with the writer Casey Robinson and the composer Max Steiner on the Bette Davis melodramas at Warners. Other units were remarkably consistent, like the so-called Seitz unit at MGM, which cranked out Hardy Family pictures every four to six months, each of which depended on the collaborative efforts of the regular cast (Mickey Rooney, Lewis Stone, et al.), the director George B. Seitz, the associate producer Lou Ostrow, the writer Kay

*Warner Bros. studio boss Jack
Warner and company president
(and Jack's elder sibling) Harry
Warner in early 1940.*

Van Riper, the script supervisor Carey Wilson, the cinematographer Lew White, the editor Ben Lewis, and dozens of others.

The producer was in many ways the key figure in these units, and the unit's relative autonomy in terms of studio management was a function of both the producer's track record and the leverage (contractual or otherwise) of the top talent involved. At the A-class feature level, where product differentiation was essential, the "creativity" of the collaborators was a veritable requirement; indeed, unit production at that level was a means of managing (and limiting) innovation. At the low-budget feature level, conversely, where the "regulated difference" of products was the prime concern, the studios maintained a mass-production, assembly-line mentality. In fact, by 1940 the most obvious remnant of Hollywood's central-producer system was in the B-picture arena: each studio assigned a foreman of sorts—J. J. Cohn at MGM, Bryan Foy at Warners, Sol Wurtzel at Fox, Harold Hurley at Paramount, and Lee Marcus at RKO—to oversee production operations.

In 1940–1941, unit production began shifting to a more genuinely independent status, owing to several related factors, and three in particular: first, the increasing leverage of top filmmaking talent; second, the growing demand for A-class product which accompanied the improving market; and third, the 1940 consent decree with its blocks-of-five and trade-show provisions, which forced the studios to have A-class product on hand well in advance of release. This shift was widely anticipated in the industry, and in fact the *New York Times* ran an in-depth story on the coming trend in February 1940, noting: "The long-predicted bloodless revolution in picture-making appears imminent.

Unit production—that system by which independent producers operating under the protective wings of major lots are encouraged to use initiative and imagination while obtaining the benefits of factory costs and methods—has become an accepted practice at four studios: Warners, RKO, Universal, and Columbia."[5] In April, *Variety* ran a lead story under the banner headline "Film Unit Production Grows," reporting that the trend to studio-based independent filmmaking was accelerating, spurred by rising production and studio overhead costs and by the fact that some independents had their own outside funding.[6]

As discussed earlier, top talent began deserting the studios for freelance status in 1939–1940, many of them actually creating their own companies—a tactic which would accelerate rapidly in 1941–1942 as the war-related income tax codes took effect (see chapter 6). While UA was an obvious option for independents and freelance talent, other studios began modifying the "UA model" and were beating the company at its own game. While UA offered greater autonomy perhaps, a studio could provide an in-house independent with financing, distribution, superior resources (production facilities, talent pool, etc.), and, in the case of the integrated majors, direct access to the first-run market.

Given the market and regulatory conditions, the studios were willing to consider deals with outside producers and other top talent, often on unprecedented terms, simply to secure proven filmmakers who could reliably deliver A-class features. This new leverage for independents affected studio-based contract talent as well in that the studios were forced to grant more creative and administrative authority to above-the-line personnel—stars, top directors and writers, as well as staff producers—in order to keep them under contract. The most important filmmakers in this regard, without question, were producer-directors like Frank Capra, John Ford, Leo McCarey, and Cecil B. DeMille. In fact, the number of these so-called hyphenates increased substantially in 1940–1941, and their number would continue to grow throughout the decade.

As top filmmaking talent began to enjoy more creative freedom and authority in the early 1940s than they had known in two decades of studio rule, the studios' once-absolute control of the filmmaking process steadily diminished, particularly in the realm of A-class feature production, where the economic stakes were highest. The studios still dominated and effectively controlled the production system, of course, owing to their overall command of filmmaking resources as well as their command of distribution and exhibition. Significantly, each studio responded somewhat differently to these changing industry conditions in 1940–1941. The studio system may have been an integrated industrial and economic system, but each company actually manifested the system in a different and distinctive way.

The following survey of the Hollywood studios in 1940–1941 well indicates both the similarities and differences in studio operations and output in the prewar era. It provides, in brief, a sense of each studio's house style and corporate identity at this remarkable moment in American film history—that is, at the culmination of the studio era and the height of Hollywood's golden age, as the industry entered a period of dramatic and lasting change. This survey tracks the management and production operations, key resources, and market strategies of the five integrated majors (MGM, Paramount, 20th Century–Fox, Warner Bros., and RKO), the three major-minors (United Artists, Columbia, and Universal), and the struggling "Poverty Row" companies (Republic, Monogram), indicating both the continuity and the complexity of the studio system in prewar Hollywood and the range of studio strategies which were deployed during the volatile prewar era.

The Major Studios

The principal Hollywood powers in 1940–1941 were, of course, the so-called Big Eight studios, with the five theater-owning integrated majors by far the dominant companies. As discussed earlier, a clear rift existed between the five integrated majors and the three major-minors in terms of assets, resources, and overall industry power. That rift is readily evident in table 3.1, which charts the revenues, profits, and number of releases for each of the Big Eight companies in 1940 and 1941:

Table 3.1
STUDIO OUTPUT/INCOME, 1940–1941

Studio	1940			1941		
	No. of Releases	Revenues ($ millions)	Profits	No. of Releases	Revenues ($ millions)	Profits
MGM	48	121.9	8.7	47	113.9	11.0
Paramount	48	96.0	6.4	45	101.3	9.2
20th Century–Fox	49	47.8*	(0.5)	50	49.6*	4.9
Warners	45	100.3	2.7	48	98.1	5.5
RKO	53	54.2	(1.0)	49	53.3	1.0
Universal	49	27.6	2.4	58	30.2	2.7
Columbia	51	22.2	0.5	61	21.6	0.6
UA	20	22.5	0.2	26	23.9	0.1

Source: Joel Finler, *The Hollywood Story* (New York: Crown, 1988), pp. 280, 286–287.
*Revenues for Fox do not include theater earnings.

Besides indicating the clear superiority of the Big Five in terms of revenues and profits, these figures also show that all of the studios were beginning to capitalize on the pre-war market surge by 1941. That was, in fact, the first year since 1929 that all of the Big Eight companies turned a profit. That trend would continue through the coming war boom, with the integrated majors enjoying the benefits of that boom to a far greater degree than the other studios. As discussed in chapter 2, the Big Five were ideally positioned to capitalize on the movie industry's post–Depression, war-induced recovery, thanks largely to the courts' allowing them to retain their theater chains and thus ensuring their continued domination of the industry. In fact, with the improving economic and market conditions, the Big Five's collective domination could only increase.

These conditions brought a significant shift in the power structure within the Big Five, however. During the Depression, the theater-heavy companies—Paramount (with some 1,250 theaters), Fox (650), and Warners (500)—had taken a beating due to heavy mortgage commitments and overhead costs. Now these companies stood to realize a far greater share of the war-fueled market than MGM and RKO, which had relatively meager chains of only around 150 theaters. While this was business as usual for RKO, traditionally the weakest of the Big Five, it marked a serious reversal for MGM.

METRO-GOLDWYN-MAYER

MGM, the only company to turn a profit in each year of the 1930s, had closed that decade still very much in command of the industry. In 1939, MGM produced five of the ten

Aerial view of MGM, Hollywood's leading studio in 1940.

biggest hits and four of the ten Academy Award nominees for best picture. Moreover, its 1939 profits of $9.5 million were roughly equivalent to the net profits of all the other major studios combined. But in 1940–1941, MGM's decade-long dominance began to erode, with Paramount nearly pulling even in both gross revenues and net earnings in 1941.

MGM would not be overtaken easily, however, because its relatively limited theater holdings were offset by the tremendous resources it developed during the 1930s. Chief among these assets was the company's vastly superior star stable. MGM still could boast "all the stars in the heavens" in 1940, with a roster that included the three top box-office stars—Mickey Rooney, Clark Gable, and Spencer Tracy—and some two dozen other marquee names as well. Loew's/MGM also had the industry's foremost sales and distribution setup, which further enhanced the market value of its pictures. In fact, Selznick released GONE WITH THE WIND through MGM largely because of its unparalleled sales and exhibition operations.

MGM's superior resources enabled the company to emphasize top feature production—more so, in fact, than any of the majors. Metro's high-end output in 1940 featured lavish costume dramas, literary adaptations, historical epics, biopics, and musicals. While these enhanced Metro's critical stature and reputation for being the Tiffany's of the industry, the high costs on these pictures often reduced (or precluded) their profitability. Much more profitable among its top features were the contemporary romantic comedies and dramas starring Clark Gable, invariably teamed with one of Metro's many female stars.

The most profitable and cost-efficient MGM releases were its series pictures, most of which were produced by Joe Cohn's low-budget unit. These included the hugely successful Hardy Family pictures starring Mickey Rooney, the Thin Man series with William Powell and Myrna Loy, the Dr. Kildare series with Lew Ayres and Lionel Barrymore, the Maisie series with Ann Sothern, and the Tarzan series with Johnny Weissmuller and Maureen O'Sullivan. Because of MGM's superior resources, however, its series pictures qualified for first-run release. Budgeted in the $300,000 range (the industry average for all features in 1940), MGM's series pictures carried production values well beyond their B-grade counterparts from the other studios. One indication of the superior production values of Metro's series pictures, besides the casting of top stars as regulars, was their A-class running time of about ninety minutes, versus the sixty- to seventy-minute range of most series pictures. (The average running time for MGM's six Hardy Family pictures of 1939–1941, for instance, was ninety-one minutes.)

Like most of the studios, the Loew's/MGM management setup featured a chief executive in the New York office and a vice president who ran the studio and oversaw production—Nicholas Schenck and Louis B. Mayer, respectively. While Mayer acted as studio boss over MGM's 187-acre facility in Culver City, California, actual filmmaking at MGM was supervised by a staff of executive producers. In fact, a distinctive feature at MGM—and an increasingly severe problem at the studio—was its bureaucratic management-by-committee setup in the production realm and the sheer number of contract producers. When Irving Thalberg was production chief at MGM in the 1920s and 1930s, he relied on a half-dozen supervisors to oversee forty-five to fifty pictures a year. Once Mayer went to a management-by-committee setup after Thalberg's death in 1937, the number of producers and executives expanded enormously. By 1941, there were forty highly paid producers and studio executives at MGM. While this number included a few top producers like Mervyn LeRoy, Hunt Stromberg, Robert Z. Leonard, and Joe Mankiewicz, the majority of Metro's producers were middle-management types with little production experience, rendering MGM more conservative and less efficient than any of the other majors. And while MGM's staff of directors included such top filmmakers as George Cukor, Victor Fleming, King Vidor, and W. S. Van Dyke, they enjoyed less creative and supervisory authority over their pictures than their counterparts at the other major studios.

WARNER BROS.

Warner Bros., the only company besides MGM among the Big Five to avoid financial collapse during the Depression, was actually antithetical to MGM in many ways. While MGM had remained flush throughout the Depression, Warners had survived by siphoning off roughly one-quarter of its assets in the early 1930s and by developing a ruthlessly cost-efficient, factory-oriented mass-production mentality.[7] That meant tighter budgets on all features, a more streamlined studio operation, cutbacks in contract personnel, and a highly formulaic and routinized approach to its films and filmmaking. Warners split its output about evenly between the A-class star vehicles mentioned earlier and a steady output of B pictures. And unlike MGM's low-end products, there was no mistaking a Warners B picture for anything else. Moreover, Warners often assigned its mid-range stars like Ann Sheridan and Humphrey Bogart to low-budget jobs and promptly suspended them if they balked.

Warners was the only family-run studio among the Big Five. The company president (and elder sibling), Harry M. Warner, was widely considered the most cost-conscious of the Big Five chief executives. The younger brother, Jack Warner, ran the studio-factory; filmmaking operations were supervised by two longtime studio executives: Hal B. Wallis oversaw the production of all A-class pictures, while Bryan Foy handled Warners' B-picture production. Wallis was an able administrator and certainly qualified as a "creative" executive—although he was not perhaps on a par with Darryl Zanuck, his predecessor as production chief at Warners, who rose through the screenwriting ranks to executive status. Wallis relied on a staff of associate producers, who would not receive screen credit until 1942 but wielded considerable authority over A-class production at Warners. Many of them—notably Henry Blanke, Robert Lord, Jerry Wald, and Mark Hellinger—were former directors or writers and were closely involved in all phases of production. Warners also had a staff of capable, efficient directors, notably Michael Curtiz, William Dieterle, Lloyd Bacon, William Keighley, and Raoul Walsh. A few of them had considerable authority over specific star-genre formulations—Curtiz on the Flynn vehicles, for instance, and Lloyd Bacon on Cagney's action pictures.

Warners' strategy of relying on a half-dozen star-genre formulas for its A-class pictures began to change in the prewar era, for a number of reasons. In late 1939, Paul Muni left to seek freelance status, leaving Edward G. Robinson to fill in as resident biopic star while the studio brass reconsidered their commitment to the genre. Meanwhile, musical production was phased out when Busby Berkeley defected to MGM. Warners also responded to the increasingly competitive market by varying its formulas and by teaming and "off-casting" its top stars—recasting Flynn's swashbuckling Brit as a westerner, for instance, or teaming Davis and Cagney in a screwball comedy.

Equally uncharacteristic was Warners' pursuit of outside deals and presold story properties. In 1940, Harry Warner signed one-picture deals with the freelance producer-director Frank Capra for MEET JOHN DOE (1941), and also with the independent producer Jesse Lasky for SERGEANT YORK (1941). Both pictures were produced on the Warners lot using contract personnel, but both involved a number of outsiders as well—most notably the freelance star Gary Cooper, who played the title role in both pictures. Meanwhile, the traditionally tightfisted Warners turned spendthrift in the pursuit of presold story material. In 1940, Warners led the industry in expenditures for stage properties, spending a total of $536,000, including the top price paid by any company that year, $275,000 for *The Man Who Came to Dinner.*[8]

Warners actually increased the pace in 1941, a year in which a record number of stage plays (fifty-seven) were filmed.[9] In a three-week span in early 1941, Warners paid $125,000 for George M. Cohan's *Yankee Doodle Dandy,* $135,000 for Emlyn Williams's *The Corn Is Green,* and $175,000 for Joseph Kesselring, Russell Crouse, and Howard Lindsay's *Arsenic and Old Lace.*[10] This last purchase, made at the behest of Frank Capra for his second outside deal with Warners, involved an elaborate profit-sharing deal for Capra and the playwrights—yet another radical departure from Warners' usual way of doing business.[11] Moreover, the picture starred Cary Grant, an even more unlikely "Warners type" than Gary Cooper, and yet another indication of how much the studio was changing in the early 1940s.

While the off-casting, outside deals, and presold story buys indicated a significant shift in Warners' A-class operations in 1940–1941, the studio still maintained an efficient, assembly-line approach to B-picture production. Interestingly enough, Warners did not develop series pictures or serials at the B-grade level. The studio did excel in series-oriented short subjects, however, especially in animation production—an area which, for Warners, was enjoying a golden age of its own at the time. Leon Schlesinger's

Actor Donald Crisp, producer Henry Blanke, producer-director Frank Capra, production chief Hal Wallis, and staff director Michael Curtiz at the 1941 opening of Meet John Doe.

animation unit came into its own in the late 1930s, dominated by the cartoon directors Friz Freleng, Tex Avery, and Bob Clampett. Its first real cartoon "star," Porky Pig, emerged in the late 1930s, and that stuttering, porcine player provided an ideal foil for future animated stars—notably Daffy Duck and Bugs Bunny. The latter's first star vehicle, "A Wild Hare," was released in July 1940, unleashing a wisecracking, anarchic screen personality who not only could compete with Disney's beloved Mickey Mouse but in the next few years would become the industry's top cartoon star.[12]

20TH CENTURY–FOX

Twentieth Century–Fox was in a resurgent position in 1940 after barely surviving the Depression. The turn in studio fortunes came in 1935 when Fox, still struggling after financial collapse in the early 1930s, merged with 20th Century Pictures. Twentieth, a successful independent company founded in 1933 by Joseph Schenck and Darryl F. Zanuck, had released through UA and supplied most of its product in 1934–1935. But Schenck and Zanuck's efforts to form a partnership with UA were repeatedly thwarted by Charlie Chaplin and Mary Pickford, who still controlled UA. So in 1935 Twentieth merged with Fox, which had been casting about for a new studio management team.

The Fox brass in 1940: vice president William Goetz, production chief Darryl Zanuck, president Sidney Kent, board chairman Joe Schenck, and distribution chief John Clark.

The merger was engineered by Fox's president, Sidney Kent, who continued to preside over sales and theater operations out of New York. Meanwhile, Schenck became board chairman (and studio boss) and Zanuck became vice president in charge of production.[13]

Zanuck had climbed through the writers' ranks at Warners in the 1920s to become the studio's top production executive and was the last real holdover from that era of central producers and "creative" executives. Schenck was an experienced producer. Thus, their move to Fox bucked the Depression-era trend toward sales-oriented studio executives—although Schenck and Zanuck were quite sensitive to economic imperatives. Indeed, at Fox they developed an efficient and unabashedly commercial strategy that emphasized formulaic A-class star vehicles and a heavy output of B pictures. That approach proved enormously successful in the late 1930s, with the company averaging $7 million in profits from 1936 through 1939. Losses of $500,000 in 1940, marking a momentary setback, resulted primarily from a few expensive flops—notably the ponderous historical biography BRIGHAM YOUNG—and a lavish costume Shirley Temple musical-fantasy, THE BLUE BIRD, which was Fox's answer, in effect, to Disney's SNOW WHITE AND THE SEVEN DWARFS and MGM's THE WIZARD OF OZ (1939).

Aside from those overblown misfires, Fox fared quite well with its high-end output in 1940–1941, notably with its energetic modest musicals, light comedy-drama, sentimental Americana, and what Zanuck himself termed "hokum"—adventure yarns and quasi-historical biopics. Fox's star stable was undergoing a transition in the prewar era as Shirley Temple, Alice Faye, and the skater Sonja Henie, all top stars in the late 1930s, began to fade. These declines were offset by the fast rise of Tyrone Power to top stardom and the appeal of the second-rank male lead Don Ameche. Zanuck also signed a number of promising new players in 1939–1940, including Dana Andrews, Betty Grable, Gene Tierney, Carmen Miranda, and Henry Fonda.

Fox signed several directors as well in 1939–1940, including John Ford, Fritz Lang, Henry King, and Henry Hathaway, which tended to reinforce what Joel Finler has termed the "split personality" that Fox was developing at the time.[14] Ford and Lang turned out "serious" films (usually literary adaptations or biopics done in black and white), while Hathaway and King produced commercially successful if critically suspect pictures—period musicals, quasi-historical action-adventure films, and the like, often done in Technicolor. Fox, in fact, led the industry in Technicolor production, releasing five of the eleven color pictures produced in Hollywood in 1940 and continuing to dominate color production throughout the decade.

While Zanuck oversaw production of Fox's A-class features in its main Westwood facility, Sol Wurtzel turned out a steady supply of B's in the company's smaller plant on Western Avenue. Like Warners, Fox relied on its B unit for roughly one-third to one-half its output by 1940. Unlike Warners, though, Fox sustained its B-picture output into the 1940s, and it relied heavily on series pictures as well. From 1939 through 1941, while Zanuck was upgrading Fox's high-end output, Wurtzel cranked out Charlie Chans, Mr. Motos, Jones Family comedies, Cisco Kid Westerns, and detective series featuring Michael Shayne, the Falcon, and Sherlock Holmes. The Holmes series, starring Basil Rathbone and Nigel Bruce as Holmes and Watson, was clearly the cream of Fox's B-movie crop, and, in fact, Fox initiated it in 1939 in an effort to upgrade its B product.

One important change in Fox's prewar production and management operations involved Schenck's trial and conviction in 1940 on income tax charges in the Browne-Bioff labor scandal (see chapter 2), resulting in his extended hiatus from the studio in 1941–1942. His absence gave Zanuck increased responsibility over day-to-day studio operations, although much of it was handled by the studio executive William Goetz, whose role would be upgraded further in 1941 when Zanuck committed both his own time and Fox's resources to producing films for the military. In the area of production supervision, Zanuck relied increasingly on a few top contract writers—principally Nunnally Johnson, Lamar Trotti, and Philip Dunne—who were approaching writer-producer status by 1940–1941, although Zanuck jealously guarded his command of A-class filmmaking operations.

PARAMOUNT

Paramount's fortunes were improving dramatically in 1940 as the company's long-term recovery strategy began to pay off. The key factor in that recovery was Paramount's massive theater chain of 1,250 houses, which gave the company a huge advantage over its competitors as the economy improved. Another was the management team of Barney Balaban and Y. Frank Freeman, two theater men who brought efficiency and a fiercely market-oriented approach to studio operations. Balaban, cofounder and long-time head of the Chicago-based Balaban and Katz theaters (the prime subsidiary in Paramount's affiliated chain), was appointed company president in 1936 in the wake of Paramount's early-Depression collapse and fiscal reorganization. In 1938, Balaban

Paramount Pictures' chief executive Barney Balaban (left) in 1941, with a Paramount News team.

hired Freeman away from a successful Paramount theater subsidiary in the South, installing him as vice president in charge of the studio.

Freeman had little direct involvement with filmmaking operations, concentrating instead on the day-to-day management of Paramount's twenty-one-acre studio and its three thousand employees. Supervision of top features was handled by Henry Ginsberg and Buddy De Sylva, while Harold Hurley oversaw the extensive B-picture operation. Paramount's B output included several successful series, notably the Henry Aldrich films, which were adapted from a successful NBC radio program in an obvious effort to capitalize on the popularity of MGM's Hardy Family saga.

Paramount's resurgence in the prewar era involved not only a new management setup but a reformulated house style as well. In the late 1930s, Balaban and Freeman embarked on what *Fortune* magazine termed a "deadwood clearance program," shuffling off the high-paid talent and high-cost genres which had pushed the studio overhead and star salaries to an exorbitant level during the Depression. Among the stars departing Paramount after Balaban's arrival were Marlene Dietrich, Gary Cooper, Claudette Colbert, Fredric March, Carole Lombard, and Mae West. They were replaced by a new generation of younger, lower-paid contract players and rising stars such as Bob Hope, Ray Milland, Fred MacMurray, Dorothy Lamour, Paulette Goddard, and Veronica

Lake. Balaban did maintain a nonexclusive deal with Barbara Stanwyck, as well as an exclusive contract with Bing Crosby, who had been with the studio for a decade.

Actually, Crosby's career was sagging somewhat when, in 1940, he was teamed with Hope and Lamour in a lightweight musical comedy, ROAD TO SINGAPORE. That unexpected hit hastened Paramount's recovery and initiated the hugely successful Hope-Crosby-Lamour Road series. It also typified the studio's shift to moderately priced contemporary comedies and dramas—an obvious departure from the stylish exotica and high-cost spectacles turned out in the 1930s by Ernst Lubitsch, Josef Von Sternberg, and Rouben Mamoulian. Those filmmakers also left upon Balaban's arrival, and by 1940 the only remnant of those heady, exorbitant years was Cecil B. DeMille. A Paramount cofounder back in the 1910s, DeMille built his career on historical spectacles and continued to turn them out under Balaban—including NORTHWEST MOUNTED POLICE in 1940, his first Technicolor production. The studio's other top filmmaker was Mitchell Leisen, who specialized in romantic comedy and also served as a mentor of sorts to Preston Sturges and Billy Wilder, who would emerge in the early 1940s as the studio's top writer-directors.

Paramount had a tradition of allowing its top directors considerable authority and creative freedom. In fact, Lubitsch not only had produced his own pictures but for a brief period in the mid-1930s had been the executive in charge of all production at Paramount. This trend continued with Leisen, Sturges, and Wilder, while DeMille worked out a contractual arrangement giving him quasi-independent producer status and a percentage of the profits on his pictures. DeMille also capitalized on Paramount's ties with radio and enhanced his own celebrity status as host of the popular *Lux Radio Theatre,* a weekly program which dramatized (and thus publicized) not only DeMille's own pictures but a wide array of Paramount stars and products.

RKO

RKO was unique among the Big Five in 1940–1941 in terms of studio operations and market strategy, owing largely to its limited resources and its brief but troubled history. RKO had been created virtually overnight in 1928 at the dawn of the sound era and flourished in the ensuing "talkie" boom. But the company quickly faded once the Depression hit and in 1934 suffered financial collapse. In 1940, RKO was just coming out of receivership under its recently appointed president—and the company's fourth chief executive in its brief life span—George Schaefer, who before coming to RKO in 1938 had been the top domestic distribution executive with UA. Its assets at the time were $68 million, barely half those of MGM and Warner Bros.

Schaefer's regime was quite distinctive among top studio executives in that he maintained direct control over both the home office in New York and the Hollywood studio. Thus, he shuttled continually from coast to coast and tried to supervise all production during his visits to Los Angeles. Schaefer's sporadic involvement in production infuriated Pandro S. "Pan" Berman, a top producer and capable production chief who left RKO for MGM in 1939 to escape Schaefer's interference. Berman was replaced by former agent Harry Edington, who had little authority over studio operations. As the RKO historian Richard B. Jewell states, Edington "was nominal head of production, but Schaefer continued to run things like a potentate, insisting on final say with regard to all important studio decisions."[15]

The RKO production plant in 1940.

Schaefer had come to RKO in 1938 with the idea of adapting UA's independent strategy to the resources and operations of a major studio. Interestingly enough, Walt Disney had deserted UA and gone to RKO the year before, and in 1938 Disney was enjoying terrific success with his company's first animated feature, SNOW WHITE AND THE SEVEN DWARFS (1937), which was released via RKO. Once at RKO, Schaefer strongly supported Disney's shift into feature production, and in 1940–1941 Disney delivered three more feature-length cartoons: PINOCCHIO, FANTASIA (both 1940), and DUMBO (1941). By then Schaefer was urging other leading UA independents to follow him to RKO—most notably Sam Goldwyn, who did in fact move to RKO in 1941.

Both Disney and Goldwyn were exceptional among RKO's unit producers in that both had their own production facilities and established lines of credit and thus were almost completely autonomous from RKO in terms of production operations and studio control. Schaefer also signed a number of so-called in-house independents—filmmakers who maintained their own production units but operated within the physical and administrative purview of the studio. This arrangement included several important producer-directors, including established talent like Leo McCarey and promising newcomers like Orson Welles and Alfred Hitchcock. Overall, these independent (and quasi-independent) filmmakers produced almost all of RKO's first-run product in the prewar era, supplying fifteen of the company's fifty-three releases in 1940 and thirteen of forty-six in 1941.[16]

Another of Schaefer's distinctive tactics, at least among the integrated majors, was his penchant for signing one- and two-picture deals with freelance stars like Irene Dunne, Cary Grant, Carole Lombard, and Charles Laughton. In 1940, RKO had only one major star, Ginger Rogers, under exclusive studio contract, and in 1941, after an Oscar-winning performance in KITTY FOYLE (1940), she too demanded—and received—a limited, nonexclusive deal.

While outside producers supplied a dozen or so A-class pictures per annum during the prewar era, RKO itself turned out another twenty-five to thirty features, most of them B-grade series pictures. RKO also released newsreels, shorts, and cartoons, with Disney's animated output by far the most reliable commercial products on its schedule. Roughly three-quarters of the RKO-produced features were budgeted at $200,000 or less; its cut-rate Westerns starring Tim Holt and George O'Brien cost under $100,000. Among its top series offerings were the Mexican Spitfire films with Lupe Velez and a crime series featuring George Sanders as the Saint. Besides complementing RKO's high-end independent productions, these series films also served as a training ground for contract talent specializing in low-budget production, including such emerging talents as the editors-turned-directors Edward Dmytryk and Robert Wise, the editor (and later director) Mark Robson, and the director Jacques Tourneur.

Another RKO tactic worth mentioning here, and one which anticipated major postwar developments, involved so-called package deals: a leading talent agency, the Music Corporation of America (MCA), packaged the script, director, stars, and producer for several RKO pictures in late 1939 and early 1940. *Variety* termed this "a scheme utterly new to the picture industry, a variation of the increasingly popular independent production unit idea."[17] MCA had no control over the actual production, nor did it have any financial stake in the finished pictures; still, the agency clearly was facilitating the shift in filmmaking authority—especially in terms of the initiation and development of movie projects—away from the studios and into the hands of individual filmmakers.

Significantly enough, George Schaefer's bold experiment was a decided failure commercially, and thus the Schaefer regime at RKO was essentially a prewar phenomenon. RKO's most costly and ambitious films invariably lost money—notably the critically acclaimed ABE LINCOLN IN ILLINOIS, with losses of $740,000 in 1940, and THE MAGNIFICENT AMBERSONS, an early-1942 release produced and directed by Orson Welles, which lost $620,000. Moreover, the Goldwyn deal involved such favorable terms for the independent producer that even major hits like BALL OF FIRE and THE LITTLE FOXES (both 1941) showed up as losses on the RKO ledger. Schaefer's failure in 1941 to re-sign Ginger Rogers, whose films were money in the bank for RKO, further undermined his position. Thus, Schaefer was ousted by the RKO board in June 1942 as the studio opted for a more conservative strategy during the war era.[18]

The Major-Minors and the Minor Studios

Outside the privileged cartel of integrated majors, the three most important studios were United Artists, Universal, and Columbia. These were Hollywood's Little Three major-minors—"major" because they produced first-run features and had their own distribution setups; "minor" because they did not own theater chains. Like the Big Five, the Little Three benefited from the improving market conditions in 1940–1941, although their lack of theater chains limited those benefits in two significant ways. First, it meant that the major-minors had to rely on the integrated majors for access to the first-run market, which the Big Five controlled. And second, it meant that the Little Three lacked the revenue flow and financial leverage—and thus the resources—to generate the same volume of high-end product as the Big Five studios.

UNITED ARTISTS

One of the Little Three, United Artists, focused even more heavily than the Big Five studios on high-end product, although it scarcely operated at the same volume. As mentioned earlier, UA was not a studio per se but a distribution company for Hollywood's major independent producers, serving as the industry's chief supplier of supplemental high-end product for some two decades. Founded in 1919 by Charlie Chaplin, Mary Pickford, Douglas Fairbanks, and D. W. Griffith, UA was designed to distribute its founders' prestige pictures and to ensure their independence from the emerging studio-factory system. UA changed radically, however, as the studio system took hold and as the founders' careers waned; by 1940, it relied for product almost exclusively on major independents like Goldwyn, David Selznick, Walter Wanger, and the British producer Alexander Korda. Of the founders, only Chaplin was still active in production—which in his case meant a new picture every four or five years.

Whatever their claims to independent status, UA's producers relied on the integrated majors in certain crucial areas. While a few of them had their own modest production facilities, they generally leased studio space from one of the majors for their more ambitious productions. And although all of the UA producers had top talent under contract, they also borrowed top personnel from the majors. Perhaps most important, UA's producers relied on the majors' first-run theaters for their productions. Thus, UA competed directly with the majors in the first-run market, while relying on the majors' theater chains for access to that market. The majors, in turn, relied on UA to provide supplemental high-grade product for their theaters. And with the accelerating first-run market and the flight of top talent to freelance status, in 1940–1941 UA saw its production operations and release schedule increase accordingly. UA released twenty pictures in 1940, slightly above its average for the previous five years; in 1941, UA released twenty-six films, its highest total ever. All were A-class pictures geared for the first-run market.

While industry conditions in the prewar era seemed to favor UA, the company actually was in a rather paradoxical state: its critical prestige and the demand for its product were at an all-time high, while its finances and management were shaky at best. UA reached a peak of sorts in 1940, scoring five of the ten Oscar nominations for best picture with REBECCA, FOREIGN CORRESPONDENT, THE GREAT DICTATOR, THE LONG VOYAGE HOME, and OUR TOWN. But UA turned a profit of only $200,000 on twenty releases in 1940, down from $400,000 on sixteen pictures in 1939. UA was the only company among the Big Eight to see its profits actually decline in 1941, netting only $100,000 on twenty-six releases. Clearly UA was not benefiting from the improving market conditions to anywhere near the extent of the other majors. The difference was due in part to weaker product, although UA's producers complained about the poor distribution terms secured for their pictures, especially theaters affiliated with the Big Five—as indicated by Selznick's decision to release GONE WITH THE WIND through MGM rather than UA.

Another significant problem for UA involved the management of the company. While Pickford was inactive and Chaplin had produced only two pictures in the last decade (MODERN TIMES in 1936 and THE GREAT DICTATOR in 1940), the cofounders still

The Selznick Studio in 1940.

controlled UA's board of directors and effectively undercut partnership deals with several top producers and production executives, including Schenck and Zanuck in 1935 and Walt Disney in 1937. Similar difficulties hampered a possible deal with Frank Capra, the industry's leading producer-director, who left Columbia in 1939 and began courting UA. Even more important was the highly publicized lawsuit from the falling-out in 1940 with Sam Goldwyn, who had produced some fifty top features for UA since the 1920s, many of them sizable hits. Goldwyn and UA settled the lawsuit in early 1941, with the producer following Disney to RKO. That left Selznick, who had been with UA since creating Selznick International Pictures (SIP) in 1935, as the company's top producer. Selznick took over the top management role at UA after Goldwyn's formal resignation in 1941, although he retreated from active production following his back-to-back blockbuster hits, GONE WITH THE WIND and REBECCA.

COLUMBIA AND UNIVERSAL

The two other major-minor studios had a great deal in common with each other but very little in common with United Artists—other than a similar reliance on the Big Five for access to the first-run market. Like UA, Columbia and Universal both increased their output by about 20 percent—from roughly fifty films in 1940 to sixty in 1941.[19] While both companies hoped to upgrade their A-class output, these increases were mainly in the realm of B-picture production, which was Columbia's and Universal's forte. Both companies were full-fledged movie factories with ample production facilities and nationwide distribution setups, but without theater chains they lacked the financial leverage and the resources to compete with the major studios at the A-class level. (The assets of both Universal and Columbia were roughly $16 million—barely one-tenth those of MGM and Warners.)

During the 1930s, Universal and Columbia had developed low-cost, high-volume production operations geared to the subsequent-run market. They sustained this strategy during the prewar era, releasing a plethora of B's, series pictures, and serials. One clear measure of their overall market strategy and the status of their product was the running time of their features. Well over half of Universal's releases in 1940 and 1941, for instance, ran sixty-five minutes or less, while only three each year exceeded ninety minutes. The average running time for all of Universal's features in each year was under seventy minutes.[20]

Universal and Columbia also turned out A-class pictures, which in fact were crucial to their established production and market strategies, for three basic reasons. First, an occasional first-run hit earned far more than even a dozen routine, reliable programmers. Second, top features brought credibility and prestige not only with critics and the public but with first-run exhibitors as well. And third, since both companies relied heavily on block booking, top features played a vital role in moving their annual output of primarily second-rate features. With the booming first-run market and the demand for high-end product in 1940–1941, both companies increased their A-class efforts. Doing so occasionally involved long-term deals with outside producers and independent units, but for the most part the two studios simply signed one- and two-picture deals with free-lance stars and filmmakers, who came in and worked with contract personnel under the usual factory conditions.

By 1940, both Universal and Columbia had devised similar strategies regarding A-class production, focusing in-house on a single star-genre formula built around the studio's one bona-fide contract star, while outside talent supplied a few additional first-run features. Universal's top contract star was Deanna Durbin, whose musicals were produced by the "Pasternak unit"—which included the producer Joe Pasternak, the director Henry Koster, the musical director Charles Previn, and the cameraman Joe Valentine—at the rate of two per annum. Universal also banked on a few B-plus formulas in 1940–1941, principally horror films with Lon Chaney Jr. and comedy musicals with second-rank stars (including W. C. Fields, Mae West, and Edgar Bergen on limited contracts). And in an interesting parallel to Paramount's Hope-Crosby pictures, Universal parlayed the unexpected success of the comedy duo Abbott and Costello into a succession of low-budget comedy hits.

Columbia's top product during the prewar era came primarily from a single genre, the romantic or "screwball" comedy. Frank Capra had refined the screwball comedy into Columbia's house genre during the Depression, and after Capra went freelance in 1939, Columbia signed one- and two-picture deals with top outside producer-directors like Howard Hawks, George Stevens, and Wesley Ruggles for its A-class product—invariably romantic comedies in the Capra mode. About half of these top features teamed Jean Arthur, the studio's lone contract star, with an outside male star, and the others featured freelance stars on limited studio contracts. Harry Cohn also signed several young contract players in 1939–1940, including William Holden, Rita Hayworth, and Glenn Ford, all of whom seemed well suited to Columbia's brand of light comedy.

Columbia's Harry Cohn (seated), the only chief executive to reside in Hollywood and double as studio boss, with his New York executives in September 1941.

Universal and Columbia also pursued similar strategies for their low-end series and serials. Universal's B-grade output included Johnny Mack Brown series Westerns and its ever-popular sci-fi serials (such as THE GREEN HORNET), many of which were produced and directed by the serial specialist Ford Beebe. Columbia's low-grade output included the Lone Wolf, Blondie, and Boston Blackie series and several serials adapted from comic strips, such as "The Shadow" and "Terry and the Pirates." Columbia also built a successful series of comedy shorts around the Three Stooges, as well as the silent-era comedy stars Buster Keaton, Charlie Chase, and Harry Langdon.

Despite their similar production and marketing strategies, Columbia and Universal were altogether different in other key areas, particularly their facilities and management operations. Universal City had been Hollywood's preeminent filmmaking facility when Carl Laemmle opened it in 1915, and in 1940–1941 it was still a first-rate movie factory. Columbia, conversely, began in the early 1920s in a ramshackle facility on the corner of Sunset and Gower on Poverty Row. Although Columbia steadily swallowed up the surrounding facilities and by 1940 occupied an entire city block, it still carried a Poverty Row stigma—which studio boss Harry Cohn seemed to regard as a badge of honor.

Both studios began as family-run businesses but underwent significant changes during the 1930s; by 1940, they evinced radically different management setups. Universal was run until 1936 by Carl Laemmle out of New York, with his son, Carl Laemmle Jr., overseeing production at the studio. Economic collapse led to the Laemmles' ouster, and in 1938 Universal replaced its company president and studio boss with two theater men, Nate Blumberg and Cliff Work—following Paramount's lead by installing exhibition executives in top management positions, even though Universal did not have a theater chain. Blumberg and Work quickly reversed Universal's fortunes: the company's net revenues in 1940–1941 exceeded those of not only Columbia and UA but RKO as well.

Columbia was founded in 1920 by Harry Brandt and the brothers Harry and Jack Cohn. Brandt and Jack Cohn ran the company out of New York while Harry, the younger Cohn brother, managed the studio, until Brandt's retirement in 1931 led to a fraternal power struggle for control of the company. Harry Cohn prevailed, thanks largely to support from A. H. Giannini of the California-based Bank of America. Consequently Columbia was the only major producer-distributor in Hollywood whose chief executive also ran the studio and oversaw production and whose second-in-command ran the New York office.

MONOGRAM AND REPUBLIC

The huge demand for low-grade product that accompanied double billing and frequent program changes during the 1930s created another class of Hollywood production company: the B-picture studio. Throughout the Depression, as Todd McCarthy and Charles Flynn point out, "there were literally dozens of tiny studios, usually with impressive corporate names, that lasted two or three years and then disappeared."[21] The most successful of these minor studios were Monogram and Republic, which set up their own distribution exchanges in major cities and thereby survived the Depression. The two companies' histories were closely intertwined, dating back to Monogram's founding in 1929 by W. Ray Johnston and its ongoing indebtedness to Consolidated Film Laboratories. Monogram was Hollywood's leading B studio by 1934, turning out thirty-six films per year and specializing in series Westerns. Monogram also accumulated a sizable debt to Consolidated, whose owner, Herbert J. Yates, became interested in production. In 1935, Yates foreclosed on Monogram and another small independent, Mascot Pictures, merging them into Republic Pictures.[22]

Republic quickly took off, thanks largely to its serials and the growing popularity of the singing cowboy Gene Autry. By 1939–1940, Republic was working in a wide range of genres, including a family series (the "Higgins"), a lawyer series ("Mr. District Attorney"), and even an occasional musical. Meanwhile, Johnston and his longtime associate Trem Carr left Republic in 1936 and resurrected Monogram, which soon was turning out about twenty B's of its own per year. Leaving serials to Republic (and the major-minors), the revived Monogram continued to specialize in series production, generally Westerns and action pictures. Other companies also challenged Republic in the late 1930s, although less successfully than Monogram. The most prominent of these was Grand National, which was created in 1936 and did well enough to take over another low-budget studio, Educational, in 1938. At that point, the Grand National president, James R. Grainger, tried to move into A-class production, an ill-fated effort that bankrupted the studio in 1939.[23]

That left the B-picture field more securely in the hands of Monogram and Republic as Hollywood entered the prewar era, and the two low-budget outfits made the most of their limited means and market niche. Republic, the stronger of the two, turned out some two dozen features per annum on a production budget of about $2 million (less than MGM spent on a single top feature), notably its trademark John Wayne and Gene

Monogram and Republic, Hollywood's leading B-movie factories in the early 1940s.

Autry Westerns and several popular serials.[24] By 1940–1941, Republic was doing
remarkably well, returning gross rentals of $6–7 million with profits of just over
$500,000. While its profits were roughly on a par with Columbia's, Republic assets of
about $3.5 million hardly compared. (Columbia's assets in 1940 were $16 million.) But
as a subsidiary of Consolidated Labs, Republic did enjoy greater financial stability than
any other minor independent.[25] Republic also enjoyed the benefits of having two stars
on its roster, and in fact Yates by 1940 was exploiting Autry and Wayne in quite different ways. He sustained Republic's signature Western series with three or four Autry pictures per year, while alternating Wayne between Republic Westerns and A-class loan-
outs—to UA in 1940 for THE LONG VOYAGE HOME, for instance, and to Universal for
SEVEN SINNERS (1940) opposite Marlene Dietrich.

Monogram had a more modest operation, with assets of just under $1 million and a
stable of second-class stars, notably Westerners Buck Jones and Tim McCoy. By 1940,
Monogram was concentrating almost exclusively on Westerns and "actioners," with gross
rentals that year of $1.9 million, which translated into a small net loss. Monogram's for-
tunes improved somewhat in 1941, when rentals of just over $2 million yielded a profit
of $11,000.[26] Johnston and Carr remained optimistic as the economy improved,
although the prewar industry shift away from B-grade product toward big first-run pictures did not bode well for the likes of Republic and Monogram.

Production Strategies for the Changing Marketplace

Among the challenges facing the Hollywood studios in 1940–1941, clearly the most significant were the war and the antitrust campaign. These challenges were especially
intense for the Big Five integrated majors, which stood to realize enormous gains if they
could both overcome their declining overseas income and respond to the trade restrictions mandated by the 1940 consent decree. Two points about the Big Five's response
to these challenges should be underscored here. First, the 1940 consent decree was
signed in October 1940 but was not scheduled to take effect until September 1941. This
period gave the studios ample time to adjust production operations to the new sales policies, and it also happened to coincide nicely with the defense buildup, which began
gathering steam in early 1941 and hit the movie industry in full force during the summer. The second point is that the Big Five responded to both the consent decree and
the surging domestic market with roughly the same strategy: scaling back low-budget
production and concentrating on high-end pictures geared for the first-run market.

As will be seen in more detail later in this chapter, the majors did reduce B-picture
production but did not eliminate it altogether. The market demand for low-grade product and the uncertainties of the prewar marketplace virtually demanded that the major
studios continue to produce B's—and that they cultivate various other defensive market
strategies as well. The most significant of these was an increased reliance on presold
movies and story properties; in the B-picture realm, such properties generally were
series pictures—films with recurring characters, settings, and plots whose market value
was firmly established. In 1940–1941, over 10 percent of Hollywood features were
series pictures, with all the studios except Warners and UA heavily invested in the practice.[27] The vast majority were B's, most of them Westerns; the presold status of some
series was doubly reinforced by their having been adapted from popular radio series—
for example, Paramount's Aldrich Family, RKO's Dr. Christian, Columbia's Blondie,

RKO's Fibber McGee and Molly, and Republic's Melody Ranch.[28] There were a few important A-class series as well—MGM's Thin Man and Hardy Family series, for instance—although the demand for product differentiation at the A-class level tended to discourage this strategy.

The Big Five developed defensive strategies for the first-run market as well. Here too the key was preselling, which at this level generally involved the reissue of A-class features and the adaptation of best-selling novels and hit stage plays. While reissues were scarcely an innovation, the trend saw a sharp increase in the prewar era. In April 1941 alone, for example, nineteen "new" reissues joined the dozens already in release. This number included several military and combat films, such as HELL'S ANGELS (1930), HERE COMES THE NAVY (1934), and DEVIL DOGS OF THE AIR (1935), along with more routine fare like RAIN (1932), SCARFACE (1932), and BRINGING UP BABY (1938).[29]

Meanwhile, the market for presold literary and stage properties was booming. In 1939, the number (and cost) of such purchases had increased substantially, and by 1940–1941 the studios and major independents were breaking one record after another in the amount paid for the screen rights to top novels and plays.[30] Back in 1936, Selznick had considered the $50,000 he paid Margaret Mitchell for *Gone with the Wind* (1936) to be exorbitant; in 1940, Paramount paid three times that amount for Hemingway's *For Whom the Bell Tolls* (1940).[31] That record was broken in early 1941 when Warners paid $175,000 for Edna Ferber's *Saratoga Trunk* (1941). Also in early 1941, Paramount paid $275,000 for the rights to Moss Hart's hit play *Lady in the Dark* (1941), and in fact higher prices for top plays had become the rule, since these were more easily adapted to the screen.[32] (Plays were in dialogue form, and the length of a stage play and a feature film was roughly equivalent.) To keep such expenditures down, Paramount, Warners, and MGM all provided financing for Broadway plays, literally banking on possible hits with minimal screen-rights costs.[33] Ultimately, however, this type of speculation proved less efficient than simply paying top dollar for proven hits.

The consummate presold picture in 1940–1941, of course, was Selznick's adaptation of *Gone with the Wind.* In fact, the phenomenal performance of that single picture taught the major studio-distributors a great deal about the full potential of the motion picture market in 1940–1941, and how to exploit it.

Beyond the presold value of the novel itself, Selznick enhanced audience interest with the much-publicized "Search for Scarlett" and the signing of Clark Gable to portray Rhett Butler. The promotion went into high gear in December 1939 with a press screening for 750 in Los Angeles' Four Star Theatre to launch a nationwide newspaper, magazine, and radio campaign. The world premiere of GONE WITH THE WIND—or simply WIND, in then-current industry parlance—was held on 15 December at the Loew's Grand Theatre in Atlanta, culminating a weeklong, citywide gala which was widely reported in the national press.[34] One week later, a double premiere was held in New York City at the Astor and Capitol Theaters, with the latter covered live by NBC-TV— the first movie premiere ever to be televised.[35]

When it finally opened in L.A.'s Cathay Theatre in late December, WIND already was breaking attendance records in New York; at the Capitol, for instance, the picture was averaging over 11,000 admissions per day.[36] The record attendance continued throughout its half-year road-show run, with the unprecedented admission prices (75¢ in the afternoons and $1.10 in the evenings, versus 25–50¢ for most first-run films) pushing its record box-office take ever upward. WIND produced record rentals for distributor MGM as well, which was collecting an unprecedented 70 percent of the box-office take

The lavish location premiere of GONE WITH THE WIND *(MGM, 1939) in Atlanta.*

as a distribution fee (versus the usual 30–35 percent) during the film's road-show run. And in the process, the blockbuster was steadily revising the definition of a long-running hit as it played for weeks and months on end in major metropolitan houses, in an era when even top features played only one to two weeks.

By July 1940, WIND reached saturation as a road show, and MGM revised its terms: the picture was sold on a 50–50 basis (i.e., 50 percent of the exhibitor's receipts would be returned to MGM) at prices of 40¢ in the afternoon and 50¢ in the evening; reserved seating was recommended but not contractually required.[37] By April 1941, with its road-show and first-run engagements finally played out, WIND had grossed $31 million and played to an estimated audience of 45 million in 8,500 theaters, with another 3,000 bookings still to be played as the film finally went into general release at "popular prices."[38]

While GONE WITH THE WIND clearly was an exceptional case, its release pattern and sales strategy had considerable influence on the marketing of top features in 1940–1941. Its most obvious impact was on asking prices for top features and the length of time those features played in metropolitan first-run theaters. In February 1940, RKO released Disney's PINOCCHIO on rental terms of 70 percent and an admission scale averaging 75¢ in New York City's 3,200-seat Center Theatre.[39] In March, UA released the Selznick-produced REBECCA, which surpassed SNOW WHITE AND THE SEVEN DWARFS to become the first picture to play six weeks at Radio City.[40] In late 1940, MGM's THE PHILADELPHIA STORY also ran six weeks at Radio City, while Chaplin's THE GREAT DICTATOR (sold by UA on a 70 percent rental basis) played twen-

Hollywood luminaries aboard the S.S. America for the world premiere of THE SEA
WOLF *(Warners, 1941), including star Edward G. Robinson (seated third from right)
and emerging star Ronald Reagan (far right).*

ty-three weeks at the Astor, one of New York's more modest (1,100-seat) first-run theaters.[41] By 1941, long-running hits were becoming routine, especially in New York; in
July, eleven of the fourteen first-run theaters on Broadway were playing "holdovers."
Among these was Warners' SERGEANT YORK, a surprise hit of such magnitude that after
doing six weeks of sold-out business at the Astor, it moved to the larger Hollywood
Theater on Broadway for an indefinite run (at 75¢ for matinees and $1.10 for evening
shows) on a 50–50 basis.[42]

WIND's heavily publicized location premiere in Atlanta was also crucial to its promotional campaign, and it represented Selznick's effort to take a recent marketing innovation to another level altogether. Until the late 1930s, virtually all prestige-level pictures
were launched with a Broadway premiere. Several major releases in early 1939 departed from this strategy—notably Paramount's UNION PACIFIC, which premiered with
much fanfare in Omaha, and Warners' DODGE CITY, which premiered in its namesake
Kansas town.[43] Similarly well-publicized openings were held in 1939 for YOUNG MR.
LINCOLN in Springfield, for ALLEGHENY UPRISING in Pittsburgh, and for MR. SMITH
GOES TO WASHINGTON in the nation's capital. *Variety's* year-end survey of "Film
Showmanship" termed the location premiere a "revolutionary method of exploitation"
in 1939, and a "breakdown of the long-established precedent of a Broadway premiere as
the accepted official first showing."[44]

The impact of WIND's weeklong Atlanta premiere underscored the promotional value of the location premiere, and the trend intensified throughout 1940. By then, in fact, even the minor studios were getting into the act. Monogram, for instance, held a gala premiere in Phoenix for the opening of THE GENTLEMAN FROM ARIZONA, a Technicolor picture shot entirely on location in Arizona (Hollywood's first).[45] Location premieres had become fairly commonplace by 1941, and in fact the more predictable ventures— BIRTH OF THE BLUES premiering in New Orleans, SUN VALLEY SERENADE in Salt Lake City, and KEEP 'EM FLYING in Detroit—were complemented by a few truly offbeat efforts like the premiere of UNDERGROUND in New Mexico's Carlsbad Caverns and of THE SEA WOLF on the SS *America* off the California coast.[46]

The location premiere phenomenon was cut short in late 1941 with the U.S. entry into the war, but it was a significant prewar marketing trend on several counts. It clearly signaled the rise of the big picture and a nascent blockbuster mentality in Hollywood as the studios began to recalibrate the profit potential, market impact, and promotional requirements of their top releases. These campaigns also provided nationwide multimedia exploitation, which sales offices were convinced had a much greater impact than national radio or magazine campaigns. The locale also invoked the epic stature and spectacle quality of the pictures, not only in terms of their production values (lavish sets and costumes, location shooting, Technicolor, and so on) but also in terms of the subject matter in that an increasing number of these were distinctly *American* pictures. As these pictures well indicated, the troubled overseas markets and the growing need to promote Americanism as the nation faced the prospect of global war provoked an on-screen emphasis on domestic settings, domestic issues, and the domestic marketplace.

The Emergence of Market Research

Owing to the growing uncertainties and instability of the prewar marketplace and the increased emphasis on high-stakes, high-end product in 1940–1941, the Hollywood studios substantially upgraded their market research efforts. This involved not only improving the studios' own internal research operations but turning to outside research firms as well, and in fact the 1940s would see motion picture research emerge as an important ancillary industry.

Before 1940, most movie research had been conducted either by the Big Eight's trade association, the MPPDA, or else on an ad-hoc basis by individual studio-distributors or independent producers. The MPPDA's figures were geared to the industry as a whole, providing data on weekly attendance, annual box-office returns, the number and size of the nation's movie theaters, and so on. This information rarely was gathered by the MPPDA itself but was culled from various federal agencies—for instance, the Commerce and Justice Departments, the Internal Revenue Service, and the Census Bureau. Although comprehensive, these data were notoriously vague and inaccurate and were frequently challenged by the fledgling independent research firms in the early 1940s.

While the MPPDA traditionally provided general information on the industry and its audience, individual studios developed their own methods of gauging audience interest in—and thus the marketability of—particular pictures or performers. Besides routine analysis of box-office returns, these methods included the occasional use of sneak previews and test screenings, analysis of fan mail, and various efforts to elicit and evaluate the opinions and preferences of exhibitors. Such studio-based research efforts were haphazard and quasi-scientific at best, but through the 1920s and 1930s they had been adequate to the industry's needs. In that era of block booking and virtually complete market control by the Big Eight, more reliable or systematic research simply was not necessary.[47]

Moreover, top motion picture executives, particularly those in New York with their fingers on the financial pulse of the industry, preferred to base their market strategies and sales policies on their own intuition and business acumen. Many of these executives had backgrounds in either distribution or exhibition and were reluctant to yield their decision-making authority to research experts or outside firms. Market research may have been making strides in other U.S. industries, but movie executives prided themselves on their knack for showmanship and taste-making and their perceptions of audience interest.

By 1940, however, the studio powers recognized the need to develop more sophisticated and accurate means of market research in order to respond to the massive challenges and changes facing the industry. This realization coincided, interestingly enough, with the rapid emergence of public opinion polling as a viable form of social research, primarily as an offshoot of consumer research by advertising firms. The pioneer of public opinion polling in the United States was George H. Gallup, whose research efforts would have tremendous impact on motion picture audience research throughout the 1940s. Trained in scientific sampling, Gallup had joined the New York ad agency Young and Rubicam in 1932 as vice president in charge of research, concentrating primarily on consumer and radio audience research. In 1935, while still with Young and Rubicam, Gallup founded the American Institute of Public Opinion, which gained considerable notoriety for its accurate prediction of the 1936 presidential election. Also in 1936, and again with Young and Rubicam's support, Gallup began the informal (and unsolicited) study of movie audiences, an effort he continued throughout the late 1930s.[48]

In 1940, with the Gallup poll now a fixture in the American press and Gallup himself the acknowledged leader in the growing field of market research, Gallup created the Audience Research Institute (ARI) (later Audience Research, Inc.), devoted exclusively to the study of the movie industry and its audience. ARI's first major client was RKO, which signed an exclusive one-year deal with the research firm in March 1940. In 1941, ARI expanded its commercial operations and began providing its services to a number of studios and to independent producers. That year also saw the emergence of ARI's chief competitor, Leo Handel's Motion Picture Research Bureau (MPRB), along with various other (and less significant) firms.[49]

One immediate effect of the research efforts by Gallup, Handel, and others was to indicate how difficult it was to generalize about audiences and moviegoing. As Handel himself would note in 1950 after a full decade of audience research, there was still "no agreement as to what constitutes a 'moviegoer,'" let alone the moviegoing audience at large.[50] In 1940, Gallup put ARI on the industry map by leaking information (while under an exclusive contract with RKO) that industry figures on weekly attendance were grossly overinflated, and that the percentage of non-moviegoers was increasing. MGM responded with outright disdain for any and all efforts to gauge weekly attendance or the size of certain audience segments. Where and how, asked MGM, did ARI or the MPPDA come up with attendance figures when ticket sales for MGM films varied up to 300 percent from week to week on different pictures?[51]

Pioneer public opinion pollster George Gallup.

The debate about audience figures persisted, and indeed it heated up in March 1941 after ARI completed its one-year deal with RKO and Gallup went public with his claims about the MPPDA's inflated figures on weekly attendance and the like. At that point, Gallup was selling ARI's services industrywide, and without question his selective disclosure of valuable—and controversial—research data was one way of promoting his firm. In his first trade press interview in July 1941, Gallup openly challenged the industry's research figures, touting the detail and precision of ARI's more "scientific" methods. His boldest assertion in the interview was that weekly attendance was only 54 million, versus the habitually cited industry figure of 80 million. He also noted that 65 percent of moviegoers were under 30 years of age, and he recommended that the studios increase their output of big-budget films targeted at the 19–25 age bracket. Just over half (51 percent) of the audience was female, said Gallup, although the proportion could vary up to 75 percent for both sexes depending on the specific film. He also noted that women tended to prefer romance and serious drama, while men preferred action and comedy.[52]

Efforts to gauge and subdivide the moviegoing audience continued, as did the debates about the nature and size of that audience. In fact, virtually all motion picture research tended to center on the audience, in an ongoing effort to assess the size, behavior, and general attitudes of "the moviegoing public." This research was done with increasing precision, parsing the audience demographically in terms of age, gender, income, education, and so on; in the process, a number of long-standing industry assumptions about audiences steadily eroded. Chief among these was the assumption that the majority of moviegoers were women; that idea was challenged by a 1941 study conducted by MPRB indicating the following attendance frequency for New York City, the nation's largest and most important movie market:

Table 3.2
AVERAGE MOVIE ATTENDANCE IN NEW YORK CITY, 1941

Times per Month	Percent
0	22.6
1–2	19.3
3–5	30.7
6–9	17.7
10+	9.7

Leo Handel, *Hollywood Looks at Its Audience: A Report of Film Audience Research* (1950; New York: Arno, 1976), p. 100.

In the same study, Handel found that men were more likely to be non-moviegoers than women (24.7 versus 20.6 percent), but that overall men and women attended movies at about the same rate: men averaged 3.7 movies per month, and women 3.75.[53]

Both ARI and MPRB advocated research conducted on a film-by-film basis. As Handel himself described it in a book-length study, *Hollywood Looks at Its Audience* (1950), this type of motion picture research developed throughout the 1940s along the lines of what he termed "the structure of motion picture concerns"—that is, the production, sales, promotion, and exhibition of individual films. Production research involved preliminary (preproduction) tests of audience interest in story ideas, titles, casting, and so on. During production, research involved test screenings of films or individual scenes in rough-cut and included an array of methods (and mechanisms) for gauging the response of spectators. Postproduction research used the same methods in test screenings and added sneak previews. At this stage, research was designed not only to gauge the audience appeal of a film but also to facilitate its promotional campaign. Advertising and publicity research assessed the potential audience for a film (geared to a "want-to-see" index), measured the "publicity penetration" of ad campaigns, and even conducted test screenings of movie trailers (previews).[54]

Not surprisingly, this kind of research was geared to prestige and A-class pictures and thus was utilized almost exclusively by the integrated majors and by major independent producers. Among the more vocal supporters of ARI, in fact, were Sam Goldwyn and David Selznick; producers of their stature clearly had the most to gain from the market research strategies being developed in the early 1940s. Goldwyn, in fact, used ARI not only for market research on his own productions but also as a means to publicize his outspoken condemnation of double billing. Double billing his A-class pictures with lesser product cost Goldwyn revenues and critical prestige, and in a larger sense, in Goldwyn's view, it demeaned the industry.[55] This view was scarcely shared by others in the industry—nor by a good many outside it. Indeed, the debate about B pictures and double billing, which had been brewing throughout the 1930s, reached the boiling point during the turbulent, uncertain prewar era.

Duals, B's, and the Industry
Discourse About Its Audience

Janet Staiger

As the majors shifted their emphasis to A-class pictures and eased out of low-budget production in 1940–1941, and as the government railed against the foisting of substandard product on both exhibitors and audiences, the industry discourse was increasingly devoted to the "problem" of B movies and double features. As has been seen, duals and B's did persist, owing to the prevailing market conditions and also to long-standing industry attitudes and practices. In fact, the industry discourse, especially that conducted in the trade journals, focused on the rationale behind B-movie production and double billing, and also on the industry's conception of its market and its customers. Thus, the answer to the rather obvious question, why program "B's" anyway? is most revealing in terms of the industry's governing theories about its audience, about moviegoing, and about the preferences of certain audience segments.

In terms of actual production, it should be noted that B pictures and double billing represented more of a problem for the integrated major studios than for any other area of the industry, and that this problem was both practical and political. It was a practical problem in that the 1940 consent decree and the improving first-run market both compelled the majors to concentrate more heavily on A-class pictures, which did their best business when exhibited on a first-run, singles-only basis. It was a political problem in that the major studio powers had in fact been forcing second-rate product onto unaffiliated theaters via block booking and blind selling for years, and by 1940 the negative fallout from that practice could scarcely be ignored.

Thus, the studios began planning cutbacks in B-picture production in early 1940—even before the defense buildup began to gather steam, in fact, an indication of the importance of the political pressures involved. In January 1940, *Variety* reported that, given the economic and regulatory situation, "there is no place left in the [majors'] setup for the large number of quickies they've been turning out in the past."[56] Consequently, Harold Hurley's B unit at Paramount reportedly was cutting its output from seventeen pictures in 1939 to about ten in 1940; Sol Wurtzel at Fox was cutting back from twenty-seven B's in 1939 to about thirteen; Bryan Foy at Warners was cutting back from twenty to ten. And while all three companies were cutting B production in half, they were planning to increase spending to obtain "better writing and more important players" and thus to enhance the production values on B movies. Moreover, Jack Warner claimed that the cutbacks at his studio were "in accordance with the policy of complete 'B' picture elimination."[57]

While the majors actually did scale back B production in 1940–1941, that effort was something of a public relations gambit as well. Whatever the practical and political imperatives involved, the majors could scarcely eliminate B-picture production altogether. Studio production operations and marketing strategies relied on B's and double bills, and the blocks-of-five clause in the consent decree allowed them to continue tying second-rate product to their A-class films. Thus, in late 1941, *Variety's* Arthur Ungar noted "the so-called abandonment—for publicity purposes, but not actually—of the 'B' class of product." Ungar reported that the majors had upgraded B production via better scripts, directors, and casts. "But as long as Hollywood has to meet the requirements of theatres playing double bills," he observed, "one finds films known as 'second features,' or 'bottom of the bill,' or 'going into slough houses,' never hitting the screens of the top first runs." Ungar also noted that Columbia and Universal, which had not signed the consent decree, still relied heavily on B's; forty-one of Columbia's 1941 releases and thirty-seven of Universal's fell into that category.[58]

There is no question about the persistence—indeed, the prevalence—of double billing in 1940–1941, despite the supposedly negative view of theater owners and audiences and the routine attacks by the Justice Department, Congress, and state and local legislatures. *Variety* reported that as of July 1940, about 8,700 theaters in America were "dualing," with over 50 percent of all bookings industrywide involving double bills.[59] The *1941 Film Daily Year Book* indicated that 10,350 of the nation's 17,500 theaters regularly double billed, and that half of all theaters relied exclusively on double features.[60] The single-feature policy tended to be strongest in the major first-run markets throughout the country, and also regionally in the South and Southwest. In general, however, double features were very common, and in fact, an ongoing battle in the Chicago area in 1940 centered on a move by the powerful Balaban and Katz chain to *triple* bill on a citywide basis after successful experiments with tripling in 1939.[61]

Without question, there were strong sentiments against B's and double features in some industry quarters, particularly among subsequent-run exhibitors. The reasons for exhibitor concern were evident enough. Double features meant dealing with more product and more logistical headaches, not only in terms of programming but also in handling shipping, promotion, and so on. Duals also were considered a drain on possible revenues, particularly if the second movie was a weak B film. Like various other competitive practices developed by subsequent-run theaters during the 1930s—notably giveaways connected with games such as "banko, bingo, and other [box-office] bait"— duals and B's were deemed undesirable but difficult to eliminate.[62] Who would be the first to pull back? How would audiences respond?

The attitude among producers and the major studios was somewhat more complex. Major independent producers tended to oppose B's and duals, predictably enough, since coupling one of their prestige-level features with a lesser product—especially a B-grade film—diminished both its stature and its income. The major studio-distributors also were voicing a more negative view as they steadily shifted their production and market strategy away from B's and concentrated more heavily on the first-run market; however, they continued to rely on double features in their own theaters. The major-minor and minor studios, meanwhile, continued to rely on B's for most of their output and to focus primarily on double features in the subsequent-run market.

As industry debate over B's and double billing intensified, various market researchers and social scientists addressed the problem in a range of studies; some were commissioned by the MPPDA or by specific producers like Goldwyn, and some were done independently. The first of these studies to be publicized were conducted by Gallup's ARI, and these were widely reported in the trade papers—not only to address the problem but also, thanks to Gallup's knack for self-promotion, to promote interest in ARI's services.

First of all, in 1940 ARI was separating Americans into distinct categories in terms of national region, urban versus rural locale, age, income bracket, and gender. In the case of double features, according to Gallup, the programming practice was most popular in New England and among urban, younger, and lower-income individuals. Specifically, in terms of age, those 6–12 favored double features by 77 percent; the ages of 13–17, by 58 percent; 18–24, by 40 percent; and over age 25, by 32 percent. In other words, the younger the audience, the more inclined it was to prefer double features. In terms of income, 58 percent of those on relief preferred double features; of lower-income people, 53 percent;

The attitudes of both exhibitors and audiences toward double-bill programs are evident in this subsequent-run theater marquee.

middle-income, 37 percent; and upper-income, 25 percent. Thus, the lower the audience's income, the greater the appeal of duals. ARI did note that if both pictures were equally good, then the figures would improve for the older and higher-income audiences.[63]

This statistical data about the preferences for double features could then be compared with other information that Gallup supplied. Gallup's statistics for 1940 also included who was most inclined to attend the movies. Gallup reported that moviegoing dropped after age 19, and that 57 percent of the U.S. population under 30 went to the movies at least once a week. Additionally, the poor and the lower and middle classes went more often than the upper class. In fact, in terms of total admissions, those segments of the audience accounted for 83 percent of ticket sales, although they had much less impact on the total box office since they were more likely to attend lower-cost showings and subsequent-run theaters. Further research indicated that afternoon audiences, "composed largely of housewives and children, want quantity for their money while the evening crowds want 'something good and not too much of it.'" Analyzing these findings, Sam Goldwyn remarked that programming ought to be designed for those who can afford to go, not "by what the children up to seventeen years of age and people on relief like." Gallup's research, however, indicated that those people most inclined to go to the movies were the people who preferred double features. Not surprisingly, exhibitors were prepared to accept such conclusions as confirmation of both their intuition and established trade practices.[64]

Additional research was conducted by Leo Handel's MPRB, and those findings were summarized in *Hollywood Looks at Its Audience*. Handel summarized the pros and cons of double features:

> The reasons most frequently given by those opposing double bills, in order of importance, were: (1) that one or both of the features are likely to be a "poor" picture; (2) that sitting through a double feature is fatiguing and takes too much time; (3) that seeing two full-length pictures is confusing because, as one woman puts it, "you generally think about a picture when you get home and a double feature gets you mixed up." Those who preferred double features gave as their chief reasons: (1) that a double bill gives moviegoers more for their money; (2) if one picture is inferior, the other is likely to be good and in any event adds variety; and (3) a double feature gives those who attend a chance to "kill more time." (Handel, *Hollywood Looks at Its Audience: A Report of Film Audience Research* [1950; reprint, New York: Arno, 1976], pp. 132–33)

In 1940–1941, the research findings by ARI, MPRB, and other social scientists reported in the industry trade papers tended to endorse the practice of double billing not only as more popular (relative to single features) but also as more profitable. Thus, any serious reservations about the wisdom of "balanced" and more-for-your-money programming were allayed for the time being.[65] Indeed, B's were promoted by the minor studios as a means of providing a variation in the genre from the main feature and thus an appearance of more for the customers' money. As Steve Broidy, president of Monogram/Allied Artists, suggested, "Not everybody likes to eat cake. Some people like bread, and even a certain number of people like stale bread rather than fresh bread."[66]

Clearly key factors here were the range of viewing options offered to moviegoers in different kinds of communities and the variety of films available. The Hollywood studio-distributors in 1940 were likely to have only about 250 prints of an A-class movie in simultaneous circulation. So although the industry judged 450 theaters to be metropolitan first-run theaters (large houses in cities with populations of over 100,000 people), one could not count on many choices about where to see the latest Bette Davis or Mickey Rooney film. This problem was alleviated, however, by the number of first-run movies circulating at any one time in major urban markets, since the studios sent anywhere from eight to ten features into national distribution every week and the major markets contained a number of first- and second-run theaters. Thus, while one might not see a new release at a favorite theater, he or she would not have to travel too far or wait too long to see it in another favorable venue.

Those in small-town or rural areas, where perhaps only one or two subsequent-run houses existed within reasonable driving distance, enjoyed fewer options in terms of available movie product. But the double-billing policies and frequent program changes in most subsequent-run theaters offered variety of a different sort—variety in terms of the sheer volume of films being booked in the local theater and the different types of films included in the programs. Although the programming strategy for the exhibitors who booked B films and ran double features was variety, it was important for the industry to acknowledge that while some types of films were of interest to certain subgroups of the audience, others were not.

In fact, the research studies of the early 1940s were an obvious extension of the informal "research" and speculation about audience tastes and preferences conducted by exhibitors since the earliest years of the industry. Exhibitors were well aware of audience resistance to certain types of films, and they provided various means to enable moviegoers to act on their tastes and preferences. By the early 1930s, for example, some theaters had begun to insert screening times in their newspaper ads. In an interesting variation on this effort, a New York theater in 1941 began routinely starting the feature at 9:00 P.M. so that patrons could time their arrival and avoid the B picture if they wished. Another industry analyst noted that sometimes one of the features would be considered inappropriate for children and knowing when it would be on might be useful to families.[67]

Subsequent research throughout the 1940s also tended to confirm the governing industry assumptions about various preconceived audience segments preferring specific types of stories. Much of this research focused on genre preferences. From the beginning of the industry, exhibitors assumed that while different people were attracted to different stars, another significant taste distinction involved genres and story types. Additionally, advertising advice consistently stressed selling to subsets of the mass audience. Those subsets were to be added together through the "balanced" program—based on story type—which would then attract the largest possible number of people. Among the most important constructed audience subsets were children and women.

Since the 1910s and 1920s, it had been common to program for children and women on the assumption that they had specific tastes in story types to which the theaters could appeal.[68] Furthermore, children and women were considered valuable in two special ways: (1) advertising consultants believed that women led purchase decision-making for a household; and (2) the presence of women and children in the theater gave the establishment an aura of propriety. Other subaudiences supposedly existed: the rural or small-town audiences, for instance, which exhibitors believed favored B-grade Westerns and action pictures.[69] Differences in terms of gender, income, ethnicity, and race were deemed important as well. By programming for various subgroups, exhibitors were able to hedge their bets. Programs with sufficient variety would appeal to multiple subaudi-

The most reliable B-picture fare in 1940, particularly with small-town and rural audiences, was the Western, and the most popular B-Western star was Gene Autry.

ences; two movies in two different genres would attract more than one audience subgroup. And generally one of the films, for cost purposes alone, fell into the category of the B picture.

While research firms provided the industry with a general view of audiences and of moviegoing, and one which reinforced the industry's own preconceptions, the actual situation was more complex and also more variable than the industry discourse at the time conveyed. Consider, for example, a brief case study of the sales and promotional practices conducted in the fall of 1940 by the Interstate Theater Circuit, a major chain of movie houses affiliated with Paramount and whose market area was Texas.[70] At the time, the Interstate embarked on a significant deviation from its usual trade practices. Traditionally, the Interstate prided itself on not having succumbed to the double-feature standards of exhibition prevalent elsewhere in the United States. It was one of the few circuits to continue the older pattern, dating back to the 1920s, of playing a single feature along with a large variety of shorts. Thus, it assiduously avoided the B picture, calling the double feature a "virus" in the film business.

However, the Interstate was always alert for new ways to make a profit. Hence, when the manager of the "New Ideal" in Corsicana, Texas, said that movie houses there had the "best week-end business in five months," the Interstate was willing to amend slightly its attitude about B's. The New Ideal was designed as a tactic for remedying the problem of selling B pictures "devoid of box office names." For promoting, as a company memorandum put it, "the little pictures about which we too often say, 'Sure, it's swell! But there's nobody in the cast. How we gonna sell it?'" The New Ideal's solution was to sell the 1940 Universal film LA CONGA NIGHTS as "the corniest pic ever." This release probably did not mark the beginning of the cult movie, but it has similarities, for the New Ideal did not ask the audience to laugh with the film but to take an ironic stance, appreciating the film's ineptitude.[71]

The standard array of tactics used by the New Ideal to promote LA CONGA NIGHTS, and copied by other enterprising circuit houses, was suggested in Interstate's management newsletter. Popcorn sacks were imprinted with the phrases: "Corn on film!" "Corniest-Funniest Picture Ever Made!" A mock candidate for election to "Assessor & Collector of Laughs—Mr. I. M. Corn," was put on crutches—supposedly he hurt himself laughing—and "called on every home in Corsicana." Ads for the film included drawings of Hugh Herbert, the main actor who played seven roles, with corn coming out of his ear. Other ads continued the theme. The theater was decorated with cornstalks. A series of teaser ads in the local paper's personals column told the story of the dangers of watching this film. A contest was held in which the person who could sit through the film without laughing would be given a month's pass. Consolation prizes included a case of corn, a case of cornstarch, a pan of cornbread, and a bottle of corn remover—all of which were tie-ins with local stores.

As successful as this promotion for one B picture might have been, the Interstate chain continued through the 1940s to advocate a high-value A picture combined with a series of shorts as its exhibition strategy rather than the double-feature plan so common elsewhere. The Interstate took the standard line about the disadvantages of double bills that economists had noted early in the 1930s.[72] For one thing, a typical minimum double-feature program with a short, trailers, and the news would run at least three hours; a single feature film with more shorts could be presented in much less time. Thus, a single-feature program could have four shows a day while the double-feature format could get in only three. The difference was one entire audience. In 1941, one programmer for the Interstate claimed that business at theaters that double-billed was off 10–30 percent compared with the Interstate.

A second disadvantage of the double bill was the recognized lower quality of the second feature, the B picture. In the industry's terms of the 1930s and 1940s, the B picture was defined by its *lacks*. In terms of content (no performers considered to have star status), length (sixty to seventy minutes running time), in production value (minimal), a B picture, as one Interstate manager politely put it, was "a small picture."[73] For the purposes of understanding the functions of the double feature and the B movie within Hollywood, this difference in quality helps explain the continuation of these exhibition strategies during the 1940s in spite of the evident "lacks" of B pictures. A second movie supplied quantity and variety to the program even if the variety came through unintentional "badness." If LA CONGA NIGHTS was one of the corniest films to be distributed, it was not the only film exhibitors booked for the mere sake of providing an assortment for a spectrum of movie audience tastes. At the end of the 1940s, double features were still regular policy at some 25 percent of theaters and a part-time policy at another 36 percent. Only 39 percent of the houses (down by 2 percent from the reports in 1939) indicated they did single-feature programming only. What had changed were the sources for the second feature, since some of the major firms had moved toward primarily supplying A product.[74]

4

Prewar Stars, Genres, and Production Trends

Authorship, Film Style, and the Rise of the Producer-Director

T he rapidly changing social, economic, and industrial conditions in 1940–1941 created a curious paradox in terms of the actual films and filmmaking of the period. On the one hand, the Hollywood studios enjoyed the benefits of the improving economy, especially in the surging first-run market, and they continued to rely on established star-genre formulas to exploit that market. Indeed, familiar stars and standardized story forms remained the chief organizing principles in virtually all phases of the industry. But on the other hand, the acute demand for A-class product and the increasing clout of top filmmaking talent created unique opportunities for innovation and individual creativity in the production process—opportunities which a good many filmmakers actively pursued. This had a significant effect on the films of the period, and in fact the early 1940s saw changes in both film style and the filmmaking process, particularly with regard to directorial "authorship," that would have enormous impact throughout the decade.

Tino Balio, in his study of 1930s Hollywood, *Grand Design*, aptly notes that filmmaking during that era of near-absolute studio control was characterized by three related factors: the "growing domination of producers" over studio filmmaking; the "diminished status" of top creative talent, especially directors and writers; and "the 'authorship' of studio house styles."[1] The established house styles would persist into the 1940s, keyed as always to each studio's star-genre repertoire. But the demand for first-run product in the early 1940s and the emergence of the producer-director as a major industry force marked a significant reversal of the trends Balio describes.

The steadily increasing demand for first-run product in 1940–1941 put greater emphasis on presold films and product differentiation, and in the process filmmakers themselves became a viable means of preselling and differentiating top pictures. Increasingly, the names of individual directors—Frank Capra, Cecil B. DeMille, Alfred Hitchcock, William Wyler, John Ford, and others—were invoked to assure audiences of the distinctive artistry and overall quality of high-end movie product. Employing name recognition was more than simply a marketing ploy. Top filmmakers did enjoy greater

79

creative freedom and administrative control in the early 1940s than they had known in over two decades of studio rule. This power led to increased innovation in feature production styles and a higher premium on directorial style as well, particularly in films geared for more sophisticated metropolitan audiences.

This trend also signaled a broadening conception of critical prestige. With the surge in high-end production and in the overall quality of top features in 1940–1941, the distinction between A-class and prestige pictures steadily diminished. Indeed, the distinction became almost meaningless with the shift to longer runs at higher prices for first-run releases, as well as the reliance on presold product. The deluge of top product did include the more predictable and commercial prestige fare—costume musicals, biopics, historical epics, and so on. But these high-end releases included riskier and more innovative ventures as well, such as the adaptations of John Steinbeck's *The Grapes of Wrath* and *Of Mice and Men,* the amalgam of Eugene O'Neill one-act plays into THE LONG VOYAGE HOME in 1940, and Orson Welles's monumental CITIZEN KANE in 1941.

Projects like these indicated not only the willingness of studio executives and independent producers alike to test the interests and tastes of first-run audiences but also the increasing clout and innovative impulses of top filmmakers. Indeed, the rampant critical debates and industry discourse about the Hollywood cinema as a "director's medium" indicated that the notions of film authorship and film style that Balio ascribed to 1930s filmmaking no longer quite pertained—or at least not in quite the same manner. Balio's observations about the dominant role of producers still applied, but what he saw as the "diminished status" of the director simply did not.

Indeed, the single most significant aspect of the shift to independent and unit production in prewar Hollywood was the rise of the producer-director. Invariably, this person was a director who had ascended to producer status, a career path that occurred with increasing frequency in 1940–1941 owing to industry and market conditions. The primary factors were the market demand for first-run product and the war economy; there were other factors as well, from the formation of the Screen Directors Guild and the 1940 consent decree to the desire for autonomy by top directors and the critical discourse about cinema as a director's medium.

Frank Capra and John Ford were prime examples of this shift in Hollywood's division of filmmaking labor, and in fact both became embroiled in controversies during the struggle in 1939 for approval of the Screen Directors Guild (SDG), approval which centered on the very issues of directorial independence and individual artistry. As mentioned in chapter 2, Capra was president of both the Motion Picture Academy and SDG in 1939, and he played a key role in winning Guild approval. Ford, meanwhile, had remained characteristically aloof from the fray but was drawn in after the release of STAGECOACH in February 1939, when the industry debate was at its height. The picture was independently produced (for UA) by Walter Wanger and became a *cause célèbre* for those advocating not only SDG but a view of the cinema as a director's medium. Much of the struggle went on behind the scenes, as when Wanger informed a UA executive: "While I am proud to be the producer of 'Stagecoach,' will you please do everything in your power to see that the picture is known as John Ford's achievement."[2] At about the same time, the screenwriter Dudley Nichols wrote a personal note to Ford about the STAGECOACH premiere in New York: "If there was ever a picture that was a director's picture it was that one, and I tried to make that clear to everyone who complimented me in New York."[3]

The debate also went public via the press. The *New York Times* film critics Bosley Crowther and Frank Nugent both wrote on the issue, and Nugent was particularly out-

Hollywood's leading producer-director "hyphenate" in 1940: Frank Capra (left), with writer (and partner) Robert Riskin.

spoken. There are those, he wrote in March 1939, who argue that "the motion picture is a director's medium rather than the player's or the writer's. And this, beyond question, is true." The best evidence, Nugent opined, was "John Ford's" STAGECOACH.[4] Two weeks later, Capra wrote an open letter to the *Times,* suggesting that the real problem resided with the studios' executive producers. "About six producers today pass upon 90 percent of the scripts and edit 90 percent of the pictures," lamented Capra, while "there are only a half a dozen or so directors who are allowed to shoot as they please and who have any supervision over their editing."[5]

The official recognition of SDG in March 1939 provided significant impetus for the growing producer-director trend in 1940–1941. The Guild agreement gave all directors the right to participate in casting, script development, and editing (ensuring them the first rough-cut or "director's cut" of a picture) and increased directorial authority over principal photography as well. Two objectives of SDG, as *Variety* noted, were, first, "the gradual elimination of associate producers" (i.e., middle-management functionaries who supervised production) and second, the right of top directors, "signing contracts as producer-director, [to be] responsible only to the production department and top studio executives."[6] The producer-director trend received additional—and perhaps far greater—impetus from the 1940 consent decree, which put a premium on proven ("bankable") directors who could dependably deliver their own films. As *Variety* noted in late 1940, "the decree, apparently, is bringing [directors] all they had hoped to win through their [SDG] pact, and more."[7]

Once the Writers Guild signed its agreements with the producers in 1940 and 1941, screenwriters also began enjoying increased status and authority. Indeed, the term "hyphenate" was becoming common in industry parlance by then, referring not only to producer-directors but to other combination roles as well, notably writers who had ascended to either director or producer status—the writer-director Preston Sturges at Paramount, for instance, or the writer-producer Dore Schary at MGM.[8] It should be noted, however, that although market conditions placed greater importance than ever on stars to sell pictures, stars rarely attained (or even pursued) producer status; the actor-producer was not a common figure in the burgeoning ranks of Hollywood hyphenates in 1940–1941.

The film historian and theorist David Bordwell, in his telling analysis of classical Hollywood cinema, has argued for the centrality of the director in any consideration of film authorship in prewar Hollywood. In his examination of the complex interplay of innovation and standardization in Hollywood filmmaking, of product differentiation and classical film style, Bordwell posits the director as the primary agent of both the articulation and innovation of that style: "The most influential argument for differentiation within Hollywood cinema has been advanced by *auteur* critics. To choose a body of works attached to a director's signature and to claim it as individual, personal, even subversive . . . does locate important differences within the classical style." Significantly enough, Bordwell takes most of his examples from precisely this period in American film history—Hollywood in the early 1940s—when film style was shifting from an institutional to a more identifiably personal and individualized phenomenon.[9]

Bordwell offers four basic notions of directorial authorship in classical Hollywood. The first treats the director as an "individual human agent" and sole creator of a film, with virtually absolute control over every aspect of its creation. The second regards the director as a "veritable trademark" attached to a product as an assurance of its distinctive quality—as implied in the argument that a film is worth seeing because it is "a

Hitchcock film" or "a Ford film." The third associates the director with distinctive "narrational" and stylistic operations within a particular film; the director, in other words, is treated as a storyteller with characteristic techniques that become evident in the "telling" of a particular film story. And fourth, the director is associated with a set of "common stylistic or thematic strategies" that gradually become evident throughout an entire filmmaking career in a cumulative "body of work." In Bordwell's view, the most valid arguments for directorial authorship rely on the fourth approach, identifying a director's "personal style" in terms of the formal, narrative, and thematic qualities which emerge in the course of an entire career. Bordwell downplays the third category because narrational and stylistic operations rarely are evident within a single film—particularly for veteran studio directors like John Ford, Howard Hawks, William Wyler, and others schooled in the high classicism of the 1920s and 1930s, with its premium on thematic subtlety and "self-effacing" narrative technique. And Bordwell virtually dismisses the first two notions of directorial authorship altogether, since only "rare exceptions" among Hollywood filmmakers enjoyed any real individual autonomy, creative control, or trademark status.[10]

What is ultimately so remarkable about the 1940–1941 period, however, is how many of those "rare exceptions" did emerge. Industry conditions rendered the prewar era a moment of remarkable opportunity for filmmakers willing and able to seize it, and quite a few did so. Significantly enough, many of these filmmakers came from outside the studio system, bringing a strong sense of personal style and individual creative authority to their work in Hollywood. Indeed, the early 1940s saw the sudden, explosive emergence of a new generation of Hollywood directors who would have tremendous impact on American film history. Some, like Alfred Hitchcock, Anatole Litvak, Robert and Curt Siodmak, and Jean Negulesco, came from abroad, mainly from Europe after the war broke out; others, like Orson Welles, Vincente Minnelli, and Jules Dassin, came from radio or stage backgrounds in New York.

Most of the leading filmmakers (and eventually canonized *auteurs*) of the prewar era, however, were established Hollywood contract directors who had attained producer-director status and operated either freelance or under a (variously controlling) studio contract, like Frank Capra, John Ford, Leo McCarey, and Howard Hawks. Equally important were contract writers, like Preston Sturges, John Huston, and Billy Wilder, who climbed to hyphenate status as writer-directors in 1940–1941. The ranks of producer-directors and writer-directors would grow steadily during the decade, and these clearly were the filmmaking elite, individuals whose commercial success and ability to work within the system, even as freelance producer-directors, translated into unprecedented creative and administrative authority.

Ford, Capra, and Hitchcock in Prewar Hollywood

While the majority of Hollywood hyphenates in 1940–1941 were former contract directors who parlayed past success and current conditions into producer-director positions, they did so in different ways and under very different circumstances. The careers of Frank Capra, John Ford, and Alfred Hitchcock during the prewar era provide excellent examples of both the producer-director trend and the differences involved. Their filmmaking experiences included both studio-based and independent productions, and their roles ranged from straight contract director to independent producer-director to in-house independent. Moreover, all three filmmakers specialized in A-class and prestige-level productions, all achieved considerable critical and commercial success, and all three were singled out in 1940–1941 as exemplary individual artists in Hollywood's factory-oriented production system.

JOHN FORD

Ford, as mentioned earlier, was held up as a veritable test case for the Hollywood cinema as a director's medium during the 1939 struggle for DGA recognition. Ironically, however, in that same year Ford signed on with 20th Century–Fox and submitted to the authority of Darryl Zanuck, one of the half-dozen production executives castigated by Capra in his letter to the *New York Times*. Actually, Ford had already achieved independent producer-director status by 1939 but compromised his hard-won autonomy by signing on with Fox, where the filmmaking resources were far beyond those available to an independent releasing through UA. So was Ford's salary at Fox, which at $235,000 in 1939 was just short of Zanuck's ($250,000), although there was no question about their respective positions in the studio power structure.[11] And while his rapport with Zanuck was somewhat strained, Ford's term with Fox was eminently successful—more so, perhaps, than any other period in his career. Ford's prewar stint with Fox thus provides an illuminating example of a top director's role in the studio-based filmmaking process, and particularly of the kind of creative collaboration possible in a studio production unit.

Zanuck established the Ford unit at Fox to handle relatively modest A-class productions designed to build up Henry Fonda's star stature as well as the studio's prestige. Zanuck himself personally supervised the unit's first three pictures: YOUNG MR. LINCOLN, DRUMS ALONG THE MOHAWK (both 1939), and THE GRAPES OF WRATH (released in early 1940). All three Fonda vehicles were solid critical and commercial hits, with THE GRAPES OF WRATH earning five major Oscar nominations, including best picture of 1940, best actor for Fonda, and best director for Ford.

Interestingly enough, Ford's only producer-director effort during the prewar period was on the sole outside picture which his Fox contract allowed. THE LONG VOYAGE HOME, a 1940 "John Ford Production" for UA, was adapted from Eugene O'Neill's one-act plays by Dudley Nichols, who had scripted STAGECOACH. The picture impressed critics and scored several Oscar nominations (including best picture), but it was Ford's lone box-office failure of the period. Ford returned to Fox for two 1941 pictures: TOBACCO ROAD and HOW GREEN WAS MY VALLEY. The latter was Ford's consummate achievement during the prewar years at Fox, earning five Academy Awards, including best picture (beating out CITIZEN KANE) and a second consecutive best-director Oscar for Ford.

While his work at Fox solidified Ford's position among Hollywood's leading filmmakers, one would be hard-pressed to term any of them a "John Ford film" in the same way his colleagues and critics had singled out STAGECOACH. During his stint at Fox, which was cut short by a wartime hitch with the Army Signal Corps, Ford was very much a studio contract director operating under the very constraints described by Capra in the *Times,* and indeed Ford's "creative" achievement was to provide a distinctive inflection on Fox's established studio style.

The chief arbiter of that style, without question, was Darryl Zanuck, who closely supervised every phase of the Ford unit's operations. Zanuck participated most during pre- and postproduction. He personally approved the stories and developed the screenplays for all of Ford's projects, working closely with the contract writers Lamar Trotti (on DRUMS ALONG THE MOHAWK and YOUNG MR. LINCOLN), Nunnally Johnson (on THE GRAPES OF WRATH and TOBACCO ROAD), and Philip Dunne (on HOW GREEN WAS MY VALLEY).[12] In each case, Zanuck hammered away at the importance of story and character, and the entertainment value of the story in particular. In fact, he took the writer Ernest Pascal off HOW GREEN WAS MY VALLEY because, as Zanuck put it in an interoffice memo, "it has turned into a labor story and a sociological problem story, instead of being a great human, warm story about real, living people."[13] Zanuck was much happier with Dunne, who already had scripted THE LAST OF THE MOHICANS (1936), SUEZ (1938), STANLEY & LIVINGSTONE (1939), and THE RAINS CAME (1939) for Fox. The script for HOW GREEN WAS MY VALLEY underwent six additional drafts once Dunne was assigned—including a "revised final draft" by Zanuck himself. And Zanuck continued to stress the story and character values even while Ford was shooting.[14] "This is going to be a masterpiece," he assured Ford in one such memo, "not only a classical masterpiece, but a masterpiece of surefire commercial entertainment."[15]

Fox star Henry Fonda and director John Ford on the set of THE GRAPES OF WRATH *(1940).*

This is not to suggest that Zanuck interfered with Ford once a picture was in actual production. Zanuck invariably brought Ford in during the latter stages of scripting to consult on the final draft(s) and also on casting, art direction, and so on. Once shooting began, Zanuck kept his distance, monitoring production through dailies and a regular stream of memos to the set. Zanuck clearly appreciated the quality of Ford's direction and his ability to work with actors, and he allowed the director virtual autonomy during production. But Zanuck did resume authority once shooting was completed, even on Ford's projects. Indeed, Ford himself considered Zanuck "a great cutter, a great film editor," and acknowledged that while at Fox, "I had this tacit agreement that he [Zanuck] would cut the picture."[16] Production records bear this out, indicating not only that Zanuck supervised the editing of both THE GRAPES OF WRATH and HOW GREEN WAS MY VALLEY, but that once Ford finished shooting, he did not even see either picture until it was ready for release.[17]

FRANK CAPRA

While John Ford's prewar career carried him from a position of relative independence to a restrictive but highly successful period as a studio-based unit filmmaker, Frank Capra's career during the same period traced roughly the opposite trajectory. Capra had been Columbia's top director since the late 1920s and by 1936 was producing his own pictures. In 1938, according to *Variety*, Capra had the most lucrative contract of any Hollywood director: it paid him $100,000 per film plus bonuses and 25 percent of the profits.[18] Capra maintained a first-class production unit at Columbia built around screenwriter Robert Riskin, cinematographer Joe Walker, and unit manager Sam Briskin; he also was assured the services of one of Columbia's contract stars (notably Jean Arthur or Barbara Stanwyck) teamed with a major star on loan, such as James Stewart or Gary Cooper. Cohn also provided Capra with top presold properties—Kaufman and Hart's Broadway hit *You Can't Take It with You,* for instance, which Cohn secured for $200,000.[19]

The Capra unit parlayed that investment into another huge hit. Released in late 1938, YOU CAN'T TAKE IT WITH YOU dominated the box office in 1939 and won Oscars for best picture and best director—Capra's third in five years. Capra followed that with MR. SMITH GOES TO WASHINGTON, a late-1939 release which was perhaps his most successful film for Columbia. But despite his continued success at the studio, Capra left Columbia in 1939 for three principal reasons: his bitter and well-founded antagonism toward Harry Cohn; the company's lingering Poverty Row stigma; and his fierce desire to create an independent production company. The time was right for such a move, and Capra entertained a number of attractive offers after he left Columbia. The most ardent suitor had been David Selznick, who offered Capra $200,000 per picture plus a cut of the profits to sign with Selznick International Pictures and release through UA. Selznick also offered Riskin a separate writing contract, with the option to produce and/or direct on his own.[20]

Capra failed to work out a satisfactory long-term deal with UA, however, so he aligned Frank Capra Productions (essentially a partnership with Riskin) with Warner Bros. in a one-picture deal signed February 1940 to produce and direct MEET JOHN DOE.[21] That late-Depression fable starring Gary Cooper recalled such earlier Capra comedy hits as MR. DEEDS GOES TO TOWN and MR. SMITH GOES TO WASHINGTON, but it also evinced a dark, brooding quality more typical of Warners at the time. Released by Warners in March 1941, MEET JOHN DOE was not up to Capra's previous standards but did well at the box office, earning $2 million and keeping Capra's market value relatively high.[22] Again Capra tried to work out a long-term deal with UA, where Selznick was now the chief executive following Sam Goldwyn's recent departure. But again negotiations stalled, and in August 1941 Capra signed another one-picture deal with Warners, this time to do a screen adaptation of a current stage hit, *Arsenic and Old Lace.*

Unlike MEET JOHN DOE, a downbeat story whose only presold appeal was the marquee value of its star and director, ARSENIC AND OLD LACE (1944) was an established commercial property. In fact, Capra deemed the project a money-in-the-bank venture to tide him over financially during a wartime stint with the Signal Corps. As with the previous deal, Warners paid Capra $5,000 a week for a minimum of twenty weeks plus 10 percent of the gross receipts in excess of $1.25 million—a far better deal than the percentage-of-net offers from Columbia and Selznick, since Capra's high-cost productions had to gross at least $2–3 million before they turned a profit. The cost of ARSENIC AND OLD LACE, for example, included $150,000 for the star Cary Grant and $175,000 for the screen rights to the play, which along with Capra's $100,000 minimum pushed the total to $400,000 before even a foot of film had been shot.[23]

A competent piece of "canned theater" and a surefire box-office prospect, ARSENIC AND OLD LACE evinced even less of the famed "Capra touch" than MEET JOHN DOE— although it was scarcely a typical Warners-style picture either. Capra shot the picture quickly, mainly because of his pending war-related commitments. ARSENIC AND OLD LACE was completed in early 1942 but remained on the shelf at Warners owing to agreements with the play's producers. Finally released in 1944, ARSENIC AND OLD LACE was a solid hit, further enhancing Capra's market value and bargaining position, while scarcely refining his personal style.

ALFRED HITCHCOCK

Alfred Hitchcock's career in 1940–1941 followed a path dramatically different from either Ford's or Capra's. By the late 1930s, Hitchcock was among Britain's leading filmmakers and was well known in the United States thanks to transatlantic hits like THE MAN WHO KNEW TOO MUCH (1934), THE THIRTY-NINE STEPS (1935), and THE LADY VANISHES (1938). Selznick began courting Hitchcock in 1937 and in 1938 convinced him to leave the deteriorating conditions in England. Hitchcock signed an exclusive seven-year contract (starting at $2,500 per week) after Selznick agreed to put up $50,000 for the rights to Daphne du Maurier's forthcoming novel, *Rebecca.*[24] Hitchcock had brought the book to Selznick just before its publication, and like *Gone with the Wind*— purchased for the same price in 1936—*Rebecca* was an immediate publishing sensation and an international best-seller.

Hitchcock began work on the adaptation in early 1939, while Selznick was preoccupied with the yearlong shooting and editing of WIND. Thus, there was little of the producer's characteristic interference during the scripting and production of REBECCA. Selznick did bring in another writer, Robert E. Sherwood, to collaborate with Hitchcock and his coscenarist, Joan Harrison, on the adaptation. Selznick also cast the picture, deciding on the freelancer Laurence Olivier and Joan Fontaine, who signed a long-term contract with Selznick to secure the role. There were considerable difficulties with Breen and the PCA about the story line, most of which were handled by Selznick's story editor, Val Lewton. Hitchcock shot REBECCA in the fall of 1939, meticulously planning

Alfred Hitchcock (left), Joan Fontaine (far right), et al. on the set of REBECCA *(1940).*

each camera setup and working at a pace that Selznick found maddeningly slow. The producer kept his distance, however, concentrating on WIND and knowing that he would take full control of REBECCA during postproduction. Indeed, Selznick made certain of that, while REBECCA was still in production, by agreeing to loan Hitchcock to Walter Wanger to direct FOREIGN CORRESPONDENT after shooting REBECCA. Hitchcock reported to Wanger in October 1939, at which point Selznick and his editor, Hal Kern, began editing REBECCA as they completed their work on GONE WITH THE WIND.[25]

Released in March 1940, REBECCA was a huge critical and commercial hit, establishing Hitchcock's "trademark" status in Hollywood and bringing Selznick back-to-back Academy Awards for best picture—an achievement still unmatched in industry history. Sold as both a "Selznick production" and a "Hitchcock picture," it did represent a melding of their respective styles and interests. Like GONE WITH THE WIND, REBECCA manifested Selznick's fascination with lavish adaptations of ill-fated love stories favoring the heroine's viewpoint, with the star-crossed lovers victimized by events beyond their control—and events which enhanced the film's capacity for visual spectacle. Hitchcock, conversely, was more interested in the psychological and "atmospheric" dimension, thus bringing to the romantic melodrama the qualities of a suspense thriller. Indeed, the melding of styles in REBECCA helped generate what came to be termed the "female Gothic" cycle in wartime Hollywood, with Hitchcock as its prime purveyor.

Significantly enough, Hitchcock did not pursue that effort in collaboration with Selznick, who was thoroughly drained after WIND and REBECCA. In fact, Selznick quickly adjusted his filmmaking role from producer to agent and "packager" in 1940–1941, a change that had considerable impact on the careers of Hitchcock and other contract personnel of Selznick's, including Joan Fontaine, Ingrid Bergman, and the director Robert Stevenson. Because he had signed them to exclusive service contracts, Selznick was committed to pay his talent only their stipulated salaries, regardless of their actual market value. So on the Hitchcock loan-out to Wanger, for example, Selznick collected $5,000 per week for Hitchcock's services but paid the director only $2,500. He then "pocketed the overage," which on FOREIGN CORRESPONDENT came to $40,000 in clear profit. Selznick did raise Hitchcock's weekly compensation to $2,750 in June 1940; then in August he cut a two-picture deal with RKO, loaning Hitchcock for a minimum of thir-ty-two weeks at $5,000 per week. Hitchcock found this maddening, but he clearly rel-ished the degree of independence it afforded.[26]

Thus, Hitchcock began an extended period of his career as a filmmaker-on-loan, dur-ing which he continued to refine his personal style and also to consolidate both his cre-ative autonomy and trademark status. FOREIGN CORRESPONDENT, released in the fall of 1940, was an espionage thriller in the tradition of THE THIRTY-NINE STEPS and THE LADY VANISHES and thus was something of a reversion to form. The first of the RKO pictures, MR. AND MRS. SMITH (1941), was a romantic comedy and thus a radical departure for Hitchcock, and its critical and commercial failure reinforced his commitment to the sus-pense thriller. He was back in his element on the next RKO project, SUSPICION (1941), another female Gothic à la REBECCA with Fontaine (on loan from Selznick) reprising her role as the naive bride who comes to suspect her husband (Cary Grant) of being a mur-derer.[27] As in REBECCA, she is mistaken, although in this case the happy ending did not play well with preview audiences. Hitchcock considered a revised ending for the film wherein Grant does indeed murder his wife, but RKO balked at the idea. The studio's reluctance was borne out when SUSPICION emerged as a solid commercial hit and scored several Oscar nominations, including best picture and best actress (which Fontaine won).

In November 1941, Selznick arranged another loan-out of his star director, this time as part of a package deal with Frank Lloyd, an independent unit producer at Universal who agreed to purchase the story, script, and direction for SABOTEUR, a war-related spy thriller. After raising Hitchcock's salary to $3,000 per week, Selznick sold Hitchcock's original story and the script (cowritten by Harrison, Dorothy Parker, and Peter Viertel) to Lloyd for $70,000 and loaned Hitchcock's directorial services for $9,000 per week with a fourteen-week minimum.[28] Thus, as Ford and Capra both were setting off to do armed services training films and war documentaries, Hitchcock settled in to do fic-tionalized war films, gaining a greater degree of authority and creative control with each subsequent "Hitchcock picture."

Hitchcock's increasing autonomy and success in 1940–1941 is instructive on several counts, particularly in contrast to Ford and Capra. Whereas those two longtime Hollywood filmmakers had difficulty operating outside the familiar factory system of film production, Hitchcock actively pursued independent status and clearly flourished as a freelance producer-director. And from all indications, that success came not despite but because of his lack of experience in Hollywood. As indicated earlier, Hitchcock came from outside the studio production system and brought with him a set of assump-tions about filmmaking, film style, and the filmmaker's role that were distinctly at odds with Hollywood's. The success of his films ensured his ongoing leverage within the sys-tem—and with Selznick—and thus ensured his continued independence as well.

Other newcomers to prewar Hollywood were even more aggressive in their efforts to redefine the filmmaker's role within the studio system and to redefine the bounds of cinematic and narrative expression in the process. The most aggressive of these filmmakers, without question, was Orson Welles, who arrived in Hollywood in 1939 from a brief but spectacular early career in theater and radio in New York, signed on with RKO as a quasi-independent producer-director-writer-actor, and proceeded in his very first picture, CITIZEN KANE (1941), to radically redefine not only the process of Hollywood filmmaking but the nature and range of cinematic expression as well.

Orson Welles and CITIZEN KANE

Orson Welles's emergence as a Hollywood filmmaker and the production and release of CITIZEN KANE provide an illuminating example of the rapid ascent of the producer-director as an industrial and artistic force in prewar Hollywood, as well as of the remarkable range of product differentiation and the license for stylistic innovation. Although still in his twenties and with no real filmmaking experience, Welles had the artistic credentials and celebrity status to secure a contract with RKO in 1939 giving him unprecedented creative and administrative authority. And he made the most of it on CITIZEN KANE, easily the most innovative and controversial picture in prewar Hollywood—and in the view of many critics and film historians, also the most important.

While the creation of this cinematic masterpiece invariably is ascribed to Welles's genius, CITIZEN KANE was scarcely the product of a single filmmaker. But Welles's multifaceted creative role (including his on-screen portrayal of the title character), his well-publicized RKO contract, and the controversy surrounding the release of the film all reinforced the conception of KANE as an "Orson Welles film." And recalling Bordwell's criteria for film authorship, KANE clearly represents not only the "rare exception" wherein the individual creative control and trademark status of the director should be taken into account but also that rare occasion when a director's distinctive style is evident within an individual picture—moreover, within his initial filmmaking effort.

Actually, Bordwell's criteria for directorial authorship may apply to Welles and CITIZEN KANE to a degree that is altogether unique in Hollywood annals. The film critic and historian David Thomson has noted "the fact that, before or since, no one in Hollywood has carved out such freedom for himself" as did Welles on KANE.[29] Welles's biographer Barbara Leaming, discussing the deal that Welles cut with RKO's George Schaefer, has said: "It was Orson's image, and his uncanny ability to attract attention to it, that impressed Schaefer. And, as he saw it, the generous contract was actually a publicity gimmick—a shrewd investment that began paying off the moment it became public."[30] And KANE was heralded (then as now) as vitally innovative in formal and narrative technique, introducing, in the words of *Time*'s reviewer, "new ways of picture-making and story-telling."[31]

Born in 1915 to a wealthy midwestern family and clearly a gifted and precocious child, Welles developed an early talent for theater and the arts. After completing prep school at age 16, and having traveled abroad extensively with his father, Welles set out for Europe on his own to pursue his acting and artistic interests. He had some success on the stage and in 1934 made his acting debut on Broadway and on radio. He also teamed up with another emerging theatrical talent, John Houseman, and in 1937 the two formed the Mercury Theatre, a stage company which quickly became known for its daring, innovative productions. In 1938, Welles landed his own drama program on CBS radio, aptly titled *First Person Singular*, which featured adaptations of familiar stories that Welles narrated in the first person and in his distinctive baritone. Welles frequently involved Houseman and other Mercury players—such as Agnes Moorehead, Joseph Cotten, and Ray Collins—in the CBS broadcasts, most notably on Halloween in 1938, when "Orson Welles and the Mercury Theatre on the Air" presented an adaptation of H. G. Wells's *The War of the Worlds* (1898). The program caused a national sensation (and a state of temporary panic) and firmly established Welles in the national consciousness as a prodigious talent and significant media personality.[32]

Welles parlayed his (and Mercury's) stage and radio success into the July 1939 contract with RKO—entered into primarily to raise funds for Mercury's stage productions. The deal called for Welles to produce, direct, write, and act in two pictures over the next two years; Welles and the company would receive $100,000 plus 25 percent of the net profits on the first picture, and $125,000 plus 25 percent of the profits on the second. RKO reserved story and budget approval if projected costs exceeded $500,000, but Welles had total control over story and script development, casting and crew assignments, and production supervision. Moreover, Welles was given "final cut" of the pictures so long as he stayed within the prescribed schedule and budget.[33] Welles actually had a preapproved project under way when he signed: an adaptation of Joseph Conrad's *Heart of Darkness*, which he planned to shoot entirely from the "first-person singular" viewpoint of Marlow, the novel's protagonist-narrator. The picture was in pre-production by November 1939, but a budget estimate of more than $1 million effectively sank the project. Welles briefly considered adapting a lightweight spy thriller, *The Smiler with the Knife*, as a Carole Lombard vehicle, but that also fell through.

In January 1940, Welles began casting about for another project, and he soon connected with Herman J. Mankiewicz on an idea for an epic-scale, quasi-fictional biopic. A veteran screenwriter and industry iconoclast, Mankiewicz had wanted for years to do a screen biography of William Randolph Hearst. Mankiewicz himself was a longtime friend of the newspaper magnate and his actress-protégée Marion Davies, as well as a frequent guest at San Simeon, Hearst's Xanadu-style estate. In his conversations with Welles, it soon became evident that Mankiewicz's ideas for the Hearst biopic jibed quite nicely with Welles's ideas about a suitable film project. While it is impossible to designate either Welles or Mankiewicz as the originator of the story for CITIZEN KANE, this much is certain: The first draft of the screenplay was written by Mankiewicz in the spring of 1940 under the editorial supervision and watchful eye of John Houseman, and it clearly was based on the life and career of Hearst. It is also clear that Welles heavily revised the script in May and June as he prepared the actual production. Welles's rewrites were so extensive, in fact, that he later claimed sole writing credit—resulting in a dispute with Mankiewicz that was settled by the two sharing credit for both story and script.[34]

Welles's revisions resulted not only from his own creative impulses but also from RKO's qualms about producing an obvious Hearst biopic. Welles was encouraged to further fictionalize the story, and he complied, maintaining Mankiewicz's multiple flashbacks to reconstruct Kane's life but introducing several crucial framing devices: the highly expressionistic prologue depicting the moment of Kane's death and his utterance of the enigmatic "Rosebud"; the "News on the March" newsreel which rehearses Kane's life story; and the ensuing projection-room scene wherein the newsreel's creators discuss its lack of a satisfactory "hook"—thus initiating the search for the meaning of "Rosebud" and setting the story in motion. Welles designed the numerous montages to both condense and speed up the story, thus providing yet another distinctive narrative

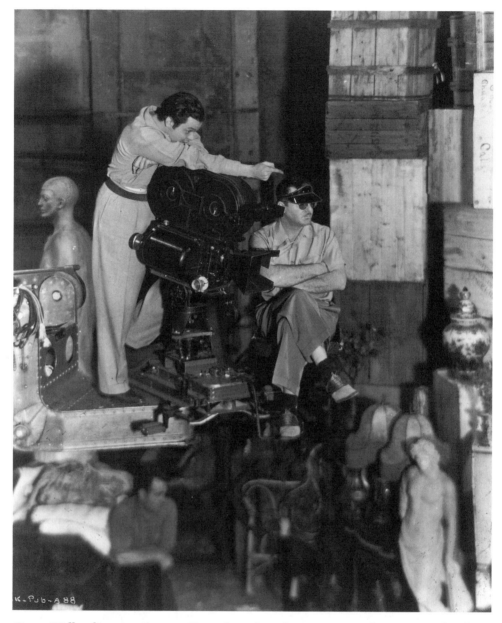

Orson Welles directing CITIZEN KANE *(1941), with cinematographer Gregg Toland (seated at right).*

device. And while he dismissed Mankiewicz's Rosebud-as-sled angle as "dollar-book Freud," he made eminently effective use of it in tying up the detective story.[35]

Welles took KANE into production in late June, at which point RKO set the budget at $740,000—actually quite reasonable for so ambitious a production. The final cost reached $840,000, some 15 percent over budget but scarcely enough to warrant the widespread rumors of Welles's extravagance. In fact, KANE was a relatively cost-efficient picture by current industry standards, owing in large part to Welles's effective collaboration with key creative and technical personnel. Percy Ferguson, for instance, designed the massive, imaginative sets so well suited to the film's visual technique. Remarkably, considering the number (110 in all) and size of the sets for KANE, Ferguson held the set costs to only $60,000, far below the usual for a top feature. Another key collaborator was Vernon Walker, who handled the special effects and optical printing (layering and assembling of images, etc.), which were more extensive on KANE than on any RKO picture since KING KONG in 1933.[36]

Perhaps Welles's most important collaborator on KANE was Gregg Toland, the cinematographer and in many ways the covisionary on the picture. Something of a prodigy in his own right, Toland had established himself as a leading cameraman while still in his twenties and by 1940 (at age 36) was among Hollywood's leading black-and-white cinematographers and visual innovators. Toland, then under contract to the independent producer Sam Goldwyn, had his own photographic unit (including camera equipment and two camera assistants) and was just reaching the peak of his creative and technical powers.[37] On recent pictures such as WUTHERING HEIGHTS (1939) and THE WESTERNER (1940), with the director William Wyler, and THE GRAPES OF WRATH and THE LONG VOYAGE HOME with Ford, Toland had been experimenting with high-speed film, wide-angle lenses, deep-focus cinematography (infinite depth of field), and what he termed "ceiled" (roofed-in) sets. Thus, Toland already had begun to refine the highly stylized "realism"—a term he frequently used in his own writing—and the visual style so often associated with KANE.[38]

Toland had yet to combine these elements satisfactorily in a single picture, and he saw KANE as "the opportunity for such a large-scale experiment."[39] In a June 1941 article in *Popular Photography* entitled "How I Broke the Rules on CITIZEN KANE," Toland related that "the photographic approach . . . was planned and considered long before the first camera turned," a procedure that was itself "most unconventional in Hollywood," where cinematographers generally had only a few days to prepare to shoot a film.[40] Robert L. Carringer, in his in-depth study of the production, writes that Welles and Toland "approached the film together in a spirit of revolutionary fervor," and that "Welles not only encouraged Toland to experiment and tinker, he positively insisted on it."[41] To accomplish the particular effects Welles was after on KANE—particularly the long takes from a fixed camera position, with the drama played out on multiple planes of action and in separately lit areas of the massive sets—Toland continued to innovate. He used arc lights rather than incandescents to achieve the chiaroscuro lighting effects (i.e., pools of light illuminating portions of an otherwise dark set) and used newly introduced coated lenses to eliminate glare and increase light transmission under low-level light conditions.[42]

While Welles and Toland were very much in sync in their conception of the look and the storytelling approach to KANE, they realized how unorthodox that approach was by Hollywood's standards. Thus, Welles decided to pass off the first days of shooting—which included the projection-room scene and a few other highly unconventional sequences—as photographic "tests." "What was shot on these first few days departed radically from the conventions of Hollywood filmmaking at the time," Carringer notes. "Much of it was openly, blatantly experimental."[43]

Equally unorthodox was the construction of Kane's story, not only the flashback structure and aggressive use of montages and temporal ellipses but also the optical effects used to give the film its distinctive narrative and visual flow. These were achieved primarily in post-production, with Welles working closely with the effects specialist Vernon Walker and the editor Robert Wise. Welles also experimented during post-production with sound as a means of both advancing and condensing the narrative (through sound montages), and he encouraged Bernard Herrmann to compose a score which conveyed more than simply the usual emotional cues for the audience. Thus, KANE's dialogue and sound-effects tracks and its musical score were laden with abrupt changes in tonality and sound level and contained as many distinctive "touches" and innovations as the visuals.

When post-production on KANE was completed in December 1940, the Hearst connection was still under wraps. A press screening in early January changed all that; the gossip columnist (and Hearst employee) Louella Parsons stalked out during the screening to inform Hearst that KANE was a thinly veiled biography and a veritable character assassination. Hearst immediately began a personal campaign against both the picture and the studio, refusing to review or to promote any RKO picture in his newspaper chain—beginning with RKO's KITTY FOYLE, then just going into release—until the studio agreed to withdraw KANE from release.[44] That set off a pitched battle over the picture, with top industry figures lining up both for and against KANE's release.

RKO postponed KANE's February release, choosing to build support for the film rather than openly defy Hearst. In a key strategic move, Schaefer held a special press screening of KANE in early March, with the magazine publisher Henry Luce (*Time, Life,* and *Fortune*) in conspicuous attendance. The screening was a success, owing mainly to the quality of the film itself. John O'Hara in *Newsweek,* for instance, called KANE "the best picture" he had ever seen. And the *Hollywood Reporter,* under the headline "Mr. Genius Comes Through; 'Kane' Astonishing Picture," began its review with a simple declaration: "'Citizen Kane' is a great motion picture."[45] The *Motion Picture Herald* ran a major story on the screening and related issues—Welles's threat to sue RKO, for instance, and Luce's offer to buy the film for a reported $1 million—and quoted *Time* magazine's assessment: "The objection of Mr. Hearst, who founded a publishing empire on sensationalism, is ironic. For to most of the several hundred people who have seen the film at private screenings, 'Citizen Kane' is the most sensational product of the U.S. movie industry."[46] Another successful press preview was held in early April, and by then the tide clearly was swinging to RKO.

Finally, on 1 May 1941, five days before Welles's twenty-sixth birthday, CITIZEN KANE premiered at the Palace in New York. The accolades continued, culminating in the New York Film Critics naming it the best film of 1941 and the Academy nominating KANE for nine Oscars, including best picture, director, and actor (Welles), and also for its cinematography, editing, and score. The public was less enthusiastic, however. KANE opened fairly strong—aided, no doubt, by the controversy generated by Hearst—but lost roughly $150,000 on its initial release.

Schaefer welcomed the critical prestige and was scarcely surprised by the box-office response. He continued to support Welles and his Mercury unit, which by late 1941 had two more RKO pictures in production: THE MAGNIFICENT AMBERSONS, an adaptation of Booth Tarkington's novel starring Joseph Cotten and the RKO contract player Tim Holt and scripted, produced, and directed by Welles; and JOURNEY INTO FEAR (1942), an

RKO studio head George Schaefer, Dolores Del Rio, Orson Welles, and Elsa Maxwell at the opening of CITIZEN KANE (*1941*).

adaptation of Eric Ambler's spy novel which Welles coscripted with Joseph Cotten, who also starred (Welles played a minor role). While AMBERSONS was another prestige-level "Orson Welles picture," JOURNEY INTO FEAR was a modest B-plus project directed by Norman Foster, a low-budget specialist who handled the Mr. Moto series for Fox. Although Welles had assured Schaefer he would codirect simply to get the project going, he served only as producer and creative consultant on JOURNEY INTO FEAR, which was in production in late 1941 while he and Robert Wise were cutting AMBERSONS.[47]

At that point, Welles's life and film career took a curious turn. After Pearl Harbor, at the behest of Nelson Rockefeller and in support of the good neighbor policy, Welles began serious work on "It's All True," a blend of fiction and documentary set in South America. Welles left for Brazil in early February 1942 to begin shooting, and thus he was not in attendance at the Academy Awards ceremony later that month when HOW GREEN WAS MY VALLEY took the major awards and when any mention of Welles and CITIZEN KANE reportedly was met with a smattering of boos and derisive laughter.[48] Of KANE's nine nominations, its only Oscar came for the Mankiewicz-Welles screenplay—which many saw as another slight of the boy genius.

The lingering resentment of Welles and KANE is perhaps not all that surprising, considering the young filmmaker's supreme self-confidence, his exceptional creative talents and contractual freedom, and his open disregard—if not outright disdain—for the conventions of Hollywood cinema and the commercial realities of the movie marketplace. Indeed, among the lessons learned on CITIZEN KANE were the limited market value of a filmmaker's trademark status and the limits of product differentiation as well. Welles was perhaps too "creative" for moviegoers, and KANE simply too different to attain popular or commercial success. These lessons were undoubtedly on the minds of Schaefer and his colleagues at RKO in early 1942 when they screened the completed versions of both THE MAGNIFICENT AMBERSONS and JOURNEY INTO FEAR and promptly demanded retakes and reediting to render the pictures more suitable for popular consumption.

So as Welles pursued an even more radical film experiment a continent away, RKO had begun to rein in its resident *auteur*. This scarcely signaled an erosion of directorial authority in the industry at large, however. While Welles charted the outer limits of individual autonomy and creative control in the prewar studio system, other filmmakers like Capra, Hawks, and Hitchcock managed to operate within those limits and to enjoy unprecedented creative and administrative authority over their work.

Stars and the Star System

While industry conditions in 1940–1941 clearly enhanced the status and power of Hollywood's leading filmmakers, the impact on its top stars—and on the star system in general—was less immediate and certainly less pronounced. For the most part, the crucial interdependence of the studio system and the star system remained intact during the prewar era. Stars continued to be closely associated with specific studios; the studios continued to rely on established star-genre formulations and to build "product lines" around new stars; and the overall box-office performance of top studio stars remained quite consistent.

The consent decree and the surging first-run market did, however, put more pressure than ever on stars to sell pictures, thus intensifying the interest in the marquee value of top stars. One clear indication of that intensified interest was the heavy focus of market research on film stars. Spearheading this effort was Gallup's Audience Research Institute, which advised its clients in the "selection of stories, titles and casts," providing a continuous reading of the "box-office temperature" and "personality values" of literally hundreds of top stars (see chapter 3).[49]

When Gallup began offering ARI's services on an industrywide basis in 1941, he openly acknowledged that "the best insurance against guess-work and the varying intangibles of successful entertainment" was a top star's name above the movie title. For the 1941–1942 season, a total of 342 starring roles already were set; of those, ARI placed 139 in the "name value" category but estimated that only about sixty stars had the capacity to "swing attendance" toward a particular picture.[50]

While ARI signaled the growing emphasis of market research on marquee value in the 1940s, the industry continued to rely on more traditional (and less scientific) measures of star appeal, principally the *Motion Picture Herald*'s annual "Exhibitors' Poll." This was a regular survey of the nation's theater owners, who ranked stars according to their total box-office performance over the past year. The results, published in the *Herald* in late December, included the twenty-five top-ranked stars according to both circuit theater owners and independents, as well as a combined listing. The combined Exhibitors' Poll rankings for the top twenty-five stars in 1940 and 1941 were as follows:[51]

Table 4.1
TOP TWENTY-FIVE FILM STARS, 1940–1941

1940	1941
1. Mickey Rooney	1. Mickey Rooney
2. Spencer Tracy	2. Clark Gable
3. Clark Gable	3. Abbott and Costello
4. Gene Autry	4. Bob Hope
5. Tyrone Power	5. Spencer Tracy
6. James Cagney	6. Gene Autry
7. Bing Crosby	7. Gary Cooper
8. Wallace Beery	8. Bette Davis
9. Bette Davis	9. James Cagney
10. Judy Garland	10. Judy Garland
11. James Stewart	11. Tyrone Power
12. Deanna Durbin	12. Alice Faye
13. Alice Faye	13. James Stewart
14. Errol Flynn	14. Errol Flynn
15. Myrna Loy	15. Dorothy Lamour
16. Dorothy Lamour	16. Betty Grable
17. Cary Grant	17. Bing Crosby
18. Bob Hope	18. Ginger Rogers
19. Henry Fonda	19. Wallace Beery
20. Gary Cooper	20. Jack Benny
21. Don Ameche	21. Robert Taylor
22. Jack Benny	22. Don Ameche
23. Ginger Rogers	23. Cary Grant
24. Ann Sheridan	24. Deanna Durbin
25. William Powell	25. William Powell

SOURCE: *Motion Picture Herald,* 28 December 1940, p. 13; *Motion Picture Herald,* 27 December 1941, p. 13.

Several key points are readily evident from these rankings. First, twenty-three of the top twenty-five stars (all but Gary Cooper and Cary Grant in both years) were contract stars with long-term studio ties. Second, the two lists display remarkable continuity with one another and also with the earlier "classical" era; twenty-two of the twenty-five stars appear on both lists, and all but Abbott and Costello and Betty Grable (both 1941) were established stars by the late 1930s. A third point is that the newcomers to the list, like virtually all of the established players, reached stardom via studio-based star-genre formulas. A fourth point is the obvious domination of MGM, which placed eight stars among the top twenty-five in both years, with Rooney, Tracy, and Gable ruling the roost.

Seven of those eight MGM stars were male, bringing us to the final point—the decided shift in the gender composition of the Exhibitors' Poll in the early 1940s. From 1932 (the first year of the poll) to 1939, over half of the top ten Hollywood stars were female, with the top spot occupied by a female every year but one. This changed dramatically in 1940, when males filled the top eight positions, thus beginning a general trend that would continue into the war years. Whether this shift represents a cultural transformation, a period of collective "gender crisis," or simply a momentary aberration is an interesting question. At the very least, the trend suggests that Hollywood was steeling itself and its audience for the impending social upheaval and military conflict by rehearsing various forms of male heroism (and in the case of Bob Hope and Lou Costello, of male cowardice) and also by investigating the prospect of male bonding and camaraderie, which was rapidly becoming a fact of life for millions of Americans.

Among the more remarkable aspects of the prewar star system was the phenomenal rise of Mickey Rooney, who succeeded Shirley Temple as the number-one star in 1939 and remained atop the Exhibitors' Poll in 1940 and 1941. As discussed in more detail later in this chapter, the key to Rooney's rapid rise was his recurring role as Andy Hardy, the model American adolescent, along with his appearances in a cycle of MGM musicals opposite Judy Garland. Rooney also established an odd rapport with Spencer Tracy, by costarring with him not only in MEN OF BOYS TOWN (a 1941 sequel to their 1938 costarring hit) but also in a 1940 biopic tandem playing the same Great American, Thomas Edison: Rooney starred in the adolescent version, YOUNG TOM EDISON, while Tracy did EDISON THE MAN. All three Tracy-Rooney films were successful, owing in large part to Tracy. Highly touted as an actor among movie stars, Tracy's talent and versatility took him from romantic comedies and biopics to epics (NORTHWEST PASSAGE in 1940) and horror films (DR. JEKYLL AND MR. HYDE in 1941). Tracy's portrayal of Father Flanagan in the Boys Town pictures is especially instructive, in that his sincerity and honest idealism somehow overcome both the mawkish sentimentality of the material and Rooney's usual histrionics.

While Tracy was prewar Hollywood's consummate actor-star and Rooney its crown prince, the acknowledged king was Clark Gable—the only star to appear in the Exhibitors' Poll every year from its inception in 1932. Gable's regal status was confirmed unconditionally by his portrayal of Rhett Butler in GONE WITH THE WIND, keeping him very much in view in 1940–1941 even though his other films were of little note. Gable remained Hollywood's top international star, and virtually everything he did for MGM turned a profit—notably BOOM TOWN with Tracy and Claudette Colbert in 1940, and HONKY TONK, an offbeat comedy-Western with Lana Turner in 1941.

MGM's other top-rate male stars were James Stewart, Wallace Beery, William Powell, and Robert Taylor, although only Stewart did any notable work in the prewar period. Indeed, the continued star status of Beery as a crusty character actor, Powell as a suave leading man, and Taylor as a square-jawed matinee idol was a tribute to MGM's canny reformulation of their familiar screen types. James Stewart, despite being dubbed *Variety*'s "cinematic man-of-the-year" in 1939, represented a very different challenge for MGM.[52] Until 1940, the studio seemed unable to develop suitable vehicles for Stewart's tongue-tied, awkward innocent, and thus most of Stewart's success came on loan—most recently to Columbia for MR. SMITH GOES TO WASHINGTON and to Universal for DESTRY RIDES AGAIN (both 1939). Stewart finally enjoyed an MGM hit in 1940 with THE PHILADELPHIA STORY, winning the Oscar for best actor and adding an edge to his screen persona as a savvy and vaguely cynical newsman. But then after three routine MGM features in 1941, Stewart left for the air force, joining Taylor in the first contingent of stars to enter military service.

While Fox, Warners, and Paramount could not match Metro's stable of male stars, each boasted a combination of talents who could fill the genre bill, from male action films and heavy drama to light comedy and musicals. Fox relied on Tyrone Power, Henry Fonda, and Don Ameche, with Power clearly the most vital company asset. His

Clark Gable and wife Carole Lombard at the Atlanta premiere of GONE WITH
THE WIND *(MGM, 1939), the film which confirmed Gable's status as the "king"
of Hollywood stars.*

virile self-confidence, rakish athleticism, blatant male beauty, and perpetual smile
served him well in JOHNNY APOLLO (1939), JESSE JAMES (1939), THE MARK OF ZORRO
(1940), and A YANK IN THE RAF (1941), all top hits that did little to vary his screen persona or tax his limited acting skills. Fonda was less popular but far more versatile, handling occasional action roles (THE RETURN OF FRANK JAMES, 1940), romantic comedies
(opposite Barbara Stanwyck in THE LADY EVE and YOU BELONG TO ME, both 1941), and
the Ford-directed social dramas and biopics mentioned earlier. Don Ameche, meanwhile, proved ideal for light comedy and drama, and particularly for Fox's trademark
musical biopics like SWANEE RIVER (1939) and LILLIAN RUSSELL in 1940.

Warners' top male stars in 1940–1941 were James Cagney, Errol Flynn, and Edward
G. Robinson, three heavily typecast stars whose prewar screen roles alternately reinforced and redefined their established personas. Cagney and Robinson continued to
portray gangsters and urban toughs—Cagney in CITY FOR CONQUEST and THE FIGHTING
69TH in 1940; and Robinson in BROTHER ORCHID (1940) and MANPOWER (1941). But
they also were "off-cast" in more ambitious Warners projects: Cagney in a period musical comedy, THE STRAWBERRY BLONDE (1941), and in a screwball comedy opposite Bette
Davis, THE BRIDE CAME COD (1941); Robinson in two biopics, DR. EHRLICH'S MAGIC
BULLET and A DISPATCH FROM REUTERS (both 1940), and an adaptation of THE SEA

WOLF (1941). Flynn's reformulation was less pronounced but no less significant, as his romantic, agile, and ever-smiling persona underwent a nationality shift. After establishing the Flynn persona via British outlaw-heroes like Robin Hood and Captain Peter Blood, Warners cast him as American hero in several Westerns: DODGE CITY (1939), SANTA FE TRAIL (1940), and VIRGINIA CITY (1940). Flynn reprised his swashbuckling Brit in THE SEA HAWK in 1940, but by then his American persona had caught on, and from 1941 onward he concentrated on American roles.

Paramount's top male stars in 1940–1941 were Bing Crosby, Bob Hope, and Jack Benny, all of whom were established stars in other media (radio, recording, vaudeville, and burlesque) and enjoyed increased popularity in the early 1940s. Their success came primarily in comedies, with Hope and Benny countering Hollywood's more heroic and romanticized male depictions. Benny's success as a film star came via three successive comedy-musicals produced and directed by Mark Sandrich: MAN ABOUT TOWN (1939), BUCK BENNY RIDES AGAIN (1940), and LOVE THY NEIGHBOR (1940). Benny then went freelance and enjoyed the biggest hit of his career, CHARLEY'S AUNT (1941), at Fox. The path to top stardom for Hope and Crosby, meanwhile, came via ROAD TO SINGAPORE (1940). Although the *New York Times* dismissed the film as "altogether too uneven for regular use," that film initiated Paramount's phenomenally successful Road series— ROAD TO ZANZIBAR (1941), ROAD TO MOROCCO (1942), ROAD TO UTOPIA (1945), ROAD TO RIO (1947), et al.[53] The increasingly outrageous Road pictures centered on Hope and Crosby, with Dorothy Lamour providing additional scenery and a requisite love interest.

The Hope-Crosby hits were yet another clear indication of Hollywood's male bias in the early 1940s, as was the rapid (and even more unlikely) ascent of Abbott and Costello at Universal in a succession of "service" comedies in 1941: BUCK PRIVATES, IN THE NAVY, and KEEP 'EM FLYING. Gene Autry was another extraordinary prewar star. The prototype "singing cowboy," Autry literally played himself in a half-dozen Republic B-grade Westerns per year and since 1937 had topped the list of Western stars—a separate (and exclusively male) Exhibitors' Poll category. In 1940–1941, Autry broke through to the list of A-class stars, demonstrating not only that B-grade Westerns were enormously popular but also that a B-picture series star, through sheer quantity of output and despite playing only in the subsequent-run market, could generate box-office revenues on a par with A-class stars.

Another important male star in 1940–1941—and in some ways perhaps the most important of the lot—was Gary Cooper, who year for year was the biggest movie star of the 1940s. Cooper had been an important contract star with Paramount in the 1930s but reached top stardom in the 1940s only after going freelance and signing on with the producer Sam Goldwyn. The "strong, silent type," Cooper had been typecast at Paramount in epic adventures and heroic biopics, culminating in BEAU GESTE (1939) and NORTHWEST MOUNTED POLICE (1940). Cooper's screen persona evinced a new sensitivity in his subsequent films, THE WESTERNER (1940), MEET JOHN DOE (1941), and SERGEANT YORK (1941)—now a man of action and integrity struggling to maintain his moral balance in an uncertain, corrupt, and chaotic world. Significantly enough, none of the three films was a love story per se, and in fact Cooper's principal cohort in each was Walter Brennan, another Goldwyn contract player and leading character actor, whose role in each film was crucial in defining and inflecting Cooper's. Both actors were critically acclaimed for these performances, with Brennan winning an Oscar for best supporting actor in THE WESTERNER (his third in five years), while Cooper won the best-actor Oscar for SERGEANT YORK.

Bing Crosby and Bob Hope in ROAD TO SINGAPORE *(Paramount, 1940), the first of their hugely successful series of Road pictures.*

The complexity of the Goldwyn-Warners deal for SERGEANT YORK also indicated the increased penchant for loan-outs, star swaps, and the like in the prewar era, as well as the increased power of independent producers. While YORK was produced for Warners by the independent Jesse Lasky, Goldwyn actually arranged the elaborate long-range deal with Warners, Paramount, and Selznick, which stretched out over several years and involved the lead roles in five films: SERGEANT YORK, THE LITTLE FOXES (1941), FOR WHOM THE BELL TOLLS (1943), CASABLANCA (1942), and SARATOGA TRUNK (1945).[54] Interlocking deals like these evinced the increasing mobility of stars and also the effort to find the right fit between top stars and high-stakes, presold vehicles.

As mentioned earlier, Katharine Hepburn herself engineered the deal on THE PHILADELPHIA STORY that paved the way for her triumphant return to Hollywood after a three-year hiatus on Broadway. Hepburn sold the screen rights to Barry's hit play along with her services as star to MGM for the Cukor-directed screen version in January 1940; she helped swing the deal for costars James Stewart and Cary Grant as well. When that movie became a hit in 1940, Hepburn went back to MGM with another project, WOMAN OF THE YEAR (1942), which she pitched as a costarring vehicle for herself and Spencer Tracy (whom she admired but had never met). She also wanted a long-term contract with story, script, and director approval. MGM complied, making Hepburn one of the highest paid and most powerful stars in Hollywood. WOMAN OF THE YEAR also initiated a series of Tracy-Hepburn pictures that would extend over the next three decades, including six during the 1940s.

WOMAN OF THE YEAR (*MGM, 1942*) *initiated a three-decade run of Tracy-Hepburn pairings.*

Hepburn was one of several top female stars who reached maturity in the early 1940s and exercised considerable leverage over their careers. Most of these were freelance artists such as Irene Dunne, Marlene Dietrich, Rosalind Russell, Claudette Colbert, Barbara Stanwyck, and Carole Lombard, all of whom preferred one- and two-picture deals or nonexclusive contracts to long-term studio ties. And although these were among the few female stars in prewar Hollywood who could individually carry a picture, none of them appeared among the top twenty-five box-office stars. Their absence from that ranking was due in part to their choosing to do fewer films per year than their studio-based counterparts, although the emergent male ethos in Hollywood was a factor as well.

The prewar period clearly was not a strong one for female stars and actresses, particularly at the box office. None of the female stars who did rank among the top twenty-five—Alice Faye, Judy Garland, Myrna Loy, Dorothy Lamour, Ann Sheridan, and the fast-rising Betty Grable—was deemed capable of carrying a picture without a prominent male costar. Indeed, most were known primarily as costars to a more celebrated male stars, with Lamour and Grable typecast and promoted as overt projections of male sexual fantasy. (This would change for Grable during the ensuing war years, when her ability to carry both a picture and a second-rate male lead was altogether evident.)

The period also saw the decline of several top female stars, notably Shirley Temple, Hollywood's top star from 1935 to 1938. Temple faded badly in 1939, buying out her Fox contract in 1940 (at age 12), only to struggle as a freelance star.[55] Universal's

Deanna Durbin survived adolescence—she turned 19 in 1940—but her distinctive musicals clearly were losing their appeal, and by late 1941 Universal began casting its highest-paid star in dramatic roles.

MGM, long known for its roster of female stars and its emphasis on women's pictures, saw a pronounced turnover in its female ranks in 1940–1941. The most significant decline was that of Greta Garbo, who had seemed primed for a shift from drama to comedy after her surprising 1939 hit NINOTCHKA, but who then retired in 1941 after TWO-FACED WOMAN. Garbo's sudden and unexpected retirement is often attributed to that film's disastrous reception, but the international market was also a crucial factor. Although Garbo was not ranked among even the top twenty-five stars by U.S. exhibitors in 1941, overseas exhibitors rated her second only to Gable.[56] But with the European market rapidly disappearing and her stock in the United States at an all-time low, Garbo opted for retirement. Other Metro stars on the wane were Norma Shearer, Joan Crawford, and Jeanette MacDonald, each of whom retired or was eased out in the early 1940s as MGM cultivated a new generation of female players—Hepburn, Lana Turner, Hedy Lamarr, and, from the MGM-British unit, Greer Garson.

Two female stars in 1940–1941 who definitely could carry a picture were Bette Davis and Ginger Rogers. Davis, Hollywood's consummate dramatic actress and the doyenne of women's pictures, had won her second Oscar in 1938 for JEZEBEL, which fleshed out the two distinctive dimensions to her screen persona—the ruthless bitch and the long-suffering victim—defining a dual trajectory over the next few years as Davis alternated between sympathetic and antipathetic roles in the best work of her career: DARK VICTORY and THE OLD MAID in 1939, ALL THIS AND HEAVEN TOO and THE LETTER in 1940, THE GREAT LIE and THE LITTLE FOXES in 1941. And interestingly enough, while other actresses working in the genre, like Irene Dunne, Claudette Colbert, and Margaret Sullavan, tended to alternate between women's pictures and comedies, Davis alternated between victim and ruthless victimizer, continually testing the emotional limits and polarities of the form. Her one significant departure came opposite Cagney in the 1941 screwball comedy THE BRIDE CAME COD, which did excellent box office but did not mark a new direction for her screen persona.

Ginger Rogers, just coming off a six-year, nine-picture stint as Fred Astaire's song-and-dance partner, had yet to establish her own individual screen persona by 1940. Rogers relished the opportunity to prove herself, however, after Astaire left RKO for freelance status in 1939, and she encouraged the studio to cast her in nonmusical roles. RKO complied, and Rogers quickly proved that she too could handle both comedy and drama. While Astaire's career temporarily flagged, Rogers scored in romantic dramas like KITTY FOYLE (1940), winning an Oscar for best actress, and in light romantic comedies like TOM, DICK AND HARRY (1941).

While the interdependence of the Hollywood studio system and the star system remained essentially intact in the early 1940s, there were clear danger signs for the studio powers. As Janet Staiger suggests, post-decree product differentiation put more emphasis on top talent, especially stars, "while selling by brand name decreased in value since the entire output of a firm was no longer a marketing point."[57] The trade discourse certainly bears that out, particularly in 1941 as the studios began adjusting to both the decree-related trade restraints and the improving market conditions. The *Motion Picture Herald* ran a story in March 1941, for instance, noting that the value of stars had increased, due to the decree, and also that "studios are in the main ceasing to be identified with a star or group of stars" to the same degree that they had been in the past. Equally significant were the growing ranks of freelance stars and "the intense amount of borrowing of name players in the last six months" as important first-run pictures were produced and promoted on their own merits rather than as factory-produced units to be blocked and sold with forty or fifty others.[58] In August, with the decree about to take effect, a *Motion Picture Herald* story on marquee names suggested that the major distributors were becoming "'personality conscious' to a degree not quite achieved before."[59]

CASE STUDY: MICKEY ROONEY AND JUDY GARLAND

Of Hollywood's leading stars in 1939–1941, Mickey Rooney and Judy Garland warrant close attention for several reasons. Both rose rapidly to top stardom during this period, and both became signature stars at MGM in an era when its star stable and house style underwent significant changes. Whether working separately or as costars, Rooney and Garland brought a new inflection and youthful energy to Metro, which had been showing signs of age and staid propriety. They also keyed two crucial star-genre formulas at MGM: the Hardy Family series, whose popularity was peaking in 1939–1940, and a cycle of juvenile show musicals in the early 1940s that solidified their costarring team. That cycle also marked the rise of the producer Arthur Freed and the so-called MGM Freed unit, which would revitalize the musical during the 1940s and generate the postwar golden age of the MGM musical.[60]

Not surprisingly, given their early polish and success, both Rooney and Garland were born to vaudevillian parents (in 1920 and 1922, respectively), and both began performing before school age. Rooney was a seasoned veteran of stage and screen by age 7, starring in comedy two-reelers as Mickey McGuire—a name he took legally during his five-year stint with the series. (His given name was Joe Yule Jr.) In 1932, he signed with Universal and became Mickey Rooney, and then signed with MGM in 1934. He caused a minor sensation as Puck in Warners' 1935 adaptation of A MIDSUMMER NIGHT'S DREAM, but he remained MGM's third-ranked juvenile behind Freddie Bartholomew and Jackie Cooper.

Rooney's breakthrough came in 1937, when he was cast as the son of a middle-class, middle-American couple (Lionel Barrymore and Spring Byington) in a domestic comedy-drama at Metro, A FAMILY AFFAIR. Audiences responded and exhibitors clamored for more, so MGM replaced Barrymore and Byington with two lesser stars, Lewis Stone and Fay Holden, and assigned J. J. Cohn's low-budget unit to develop a series. Cohn assembled the Seitz unit (see chapter 3), which turned out Hardy installments every three or four months in the late 1930s and early 1940s. Rooney's character took on greater importance with each installment to a point where, from 1939 on, every picture carried the name "Andy Hardy" in the title.[61] The Hardy pictures provided an ideal vehicle for Rooney's remarkable and still-developing skills and an ideal context for trying out new talent—particularly contract ingenues who could serve as friend or love interest for Andy. Besides Ann Rutherford, who became a series regular in 1938, the Hardy films enjoyed guest appearances from the emerging Metro stars Lana Turner, Ruth Hussey, Donna Reed, Kathryn Grayson, and most significantly (and most frequently), Judy Garland. It was Garland, in fact, who first introduced a musical dimension to the series, thus bringing out quite another facet of Rooney's character and talent. The first real Hardy *musical* was LOVE FINDS ANDY HARDY in 1938, which was in many ways Judy Garland's breakthrough film at MGM.

Unlike Rooney, who had extensive film experience early on, Garland grew up in vaudeville as one of the singing Gumm Sisters. (Born Frances Gumm, she and her sisters changed their stage name to Garland in 1931, and Frances became Judy a year later.) Garland had a rather discouraging early period with MGM, winning a long-term contract in 1936 over Deanna Durbin but then struggling while Durbin's career promptly took off at Universal. (In fact, Durbin and Mickey Rooney were awarded special Oscars in 1938 for "bringing to the screen the spirit and personification of American youth.") But then LOVE FINDS ANDY HARDY emerged as an exceptionally strong box-office hit, bringing a new dimension to the series and a new musical team to the MGM roster.

Garland's success in the Hardy film also confirmed MGM's decision to star her in THE WIZARD OF OZ (in a role initially conceived for Shirley Temple). The 1939 picture was MGM's riskiest and most expensive picture of the decade, and even with its ensemble, all-star cast, Garland's role clearly was crucial to its success. Garland was up to the task, striking an ideal balance of wide-eyed wonder, endearing vulnerability, and hesitant bravura, and she held her own musically alongside the veterans Ray Bolger and Bert Lahr.[62]

Garland closed out 1939 as a bona-fide MGM star and as a protégée of Arthur Freed. A longtime studio lyricist with aspirations to produce, Freed worked uncredited on Oz as an assistant to the producer Mervyn LeRoy, with MGM's assurance that he could produce a musical of his own after completing Oz. Freed convinced MGM to purchase the rights to a 1937 Rogers and Hart stage musical, *Babes in Arms,* and to bring Busby Berkeley over from Warner Bros. to choreograph and direct the film. He also convinced MGM to let him team Rooney and Garland as costars.[63] Freed's strategy was to combine the energy and appeal of the Hardy pictures with the backstage musical formula that Berkeley had refined in the early 1930s at Warners.

The Rogers and Hart musical was one of those "Hey kids, let's put on a show!" types, with the musical numbers passed off as rehearsals and building to a climactic amateur show. The kids were supposedly offspring of vaudevillians, a premise that added a degree of credibility—especially to Rooney's and Garland's characters—although realism was scarcely an issue in this upbeat adolescent fantasy. Freed and Berkeley designed the entire picture as a showcase for Rooney and Garland, bringing in Kay Van Riper for a script overhaul to add some of the Hardy series flavor but focusing most of their attention on the musical numbers. BABES IN ARMS was shot in only ten weeks for just under $750,000, a remarkably low figure for a major musical, although contributing to the low costs were the low salaries still being earned by its stars: Rooney made $900 per week on the film, and Garland only $500.[64]

Released in late 1939, BABES IN ARMS did excellent business through the holidays and into 1940, and it actually outperformed THE WIZARD OF OZ at the box office, grossing $3.3 million.[65] And while Oz and GONE WITH THE WIND had Hollywood rethinking its established production and marketing strategies, BABES IN ARMS underscored what the studios did best. It was an economical, efficiently produced star vehicle, an A-class genre amalgam with just enough novelty to satisfy audiences and ensure its success in the first-run market. It was also a prime candidate for reformulation, and in fact Freed, Berkeley, musical director Roger Edens, and their colleagues immediately went to work with Rooney and Garland on a follow-up picture, STRIKE UP THE BAND (1940). When that picture hit, Freed and company did BABES ON BROADWAY (released in January 1941), a sequel to Freed's initial Rooney-Garland musical and another solid hit.

*Judy Garland and Mickey Rooney
in their first costarring venture,
BABES IN ARMS (MGM, 1939),
and in one of the hit follow-ups,
BABES ON BROADWAY (MGM, 1941).*

Besides the cycle of show musicals, MGM reteamed Rooney and Garland in two additional prewar Hardy installments, ANDY HARDY MEETS THE DEBUTANTE (1940) and LIFE BEGINS FOR ANDY HARDY (1941), both of which sustained the series' musical dimension. In 1940, both also appeared in star vehicles of their own: Garland in another Freed unit musical, LITTLE NELLIE KELLY (1940), and Rooney in YOUNG TOM EDISON (1940). And in 1941, both were teamed with other top studio stars in prestige-level pictures: Garland and James Stewart were top-billed in an all-star musical, ZIEGFELD GIRL, while Rooney and Tracy teamed up in MEN OF BOYS TOWN. Clearly the youngsters had arrived, and unlike so many other adolescent stars who faded quickly, both Rooney and Garland seemed to be gaining in popularity as they matured.

Genres and Production Trends

As we have seen, star-genre formulation was still very much the rule in prewar film-making, with the genres of Hollywood's classical era maintaining their currency. Those genres were scarcely static or monolithic forms, of course, and in fact the changing social and industrial conditions in 1940–1941 clearly influenced the development of various genres. This influence was most evident perhaps in the realm of prestige production—those pictures featuring lavish production values, multiple stars, pre-sold stories, and a road-show release strategy. Tino Balio has pointed out that by the late 1930s virtually any genre was amenable to prestige-level treatment, but the majority of prestige pictures fell into three categories: biopics, epics, and adaptations.[66] These productions invariably employed top stars, of course, with their market appeal further enhanced by the pre-sold value of an established best-seller or stage hit or by the presumed interest in the historical figure or event.

As mentioned earlier regarding GONE WITH THE WIND, many of the period's prestige pictures were distinctly "bigger" in terms of narrative scope and spectacle, were more likely to be shot in Technicolor and to incorporate location shooting, and were focused on distinctly American subjects. Hollywood still adapted European classics and popular fiction, of course, like PRIDE AND PREJUDICE and REBECCA in 1940. And there were historical dramas about European events and figures—for example, Warners' two 1940 biopics, A DISPATCH FROM REUTERS (about the development of the first European news service) and DR. EHRLICH'S MAGIC BULLET (about the discovery of a cure for venereal disease). But the far greater tendency in 1940 was to adapt American literature (OF MICE AND MEN, THE GRAPES OF WRATH) and stage plays (OUR TOWN, THE LONG VOYAGE HOME, THE PHILADELPHIA STORY), and to dramatize events and lives from American history (NORTHWEST PASSAGE, ABE LINCOLN IN ILLINOIS, NORTHWEST MOUNTED POLICE.

The animated feature also emerged as a new type of prestige picture in 1940–1941. Disney began systematically producing feature-length cartoons in the wake of SNOW WHITE's success in 1937–1938, releasing PINOCCHIO and FANTASIA in 1940, and DUMBO and THE RELUCTANT DRAGON in 1941. While none was as successful as SNOW WHITE, these pictures did solidify the animated feature as an industry staple and the musical fantasy as its basic narrative form. They also established Disney as virtually the sole purveyor of the genre. Besides MGM's THE WIZARD OF OZ, a live-action variation of the animated musical fantasy inspired by SNOW WHITE's success, Disney's only real challenge came from Paramount via Max Fleischer's animation unit (the producer of the Popeye cartoon shorts), which produced two animated features: GULLIVER'S TRAVELS in

1939 and MR. BUG GOES TO TOWN in 1941. Both failed commercially, putting Fleischer out of commission and leaving Disney virtually alone in the animated feature market.

The animated features also indicated that the musical itself was undergoing a transition, and in fact many industry observers considered the genre to be in a period of serious decline in the late 1930s. Several important studio-based musical cycles either were fading badly or were phased out altogether at the time, notably RKO's Astaire-Rogers dance musicals, MGM's Jeanette MacDonald–Nelson Eddy operettas, Fox's Shirley Temple vehicles, and Warners' Busby Berkeley musicals. Astaire was scarcely going into retirement, however, and Berkeley was en route to MGM to rejuvenate the backstage formula with Rooney and Garland. And while the genre did undergo a crisis of sorts in 1939, sending musical talent back to Broadway or into other genres, by 1940 the trades were touting another musical cycle—the fourth since talkies, according to *Variety*.[67] By 1941, the genre was back in fashion, thanks primarily to the Disney features, the Rooney–Garland cycle at MGM, the Fred Astaire–Rita Hayworth musicals from Columbia, and Fox's Betty Grable vehicles.

The A-class Western also enjoyed a regeneration during the prewar era. In March 1939, just after the release of STAGECOACH, *Variety* noted that more "major budget westerns" were in release than at any time in the past decade and pointed to DeMille's UNION PACIFIC and Fox's JESSE JAMES (both 1939) as the films which "revived the cycle."[68] A few weeks later, Frank Nugent of the *New York Times* (who a decade later would be scripting Westerns for John Ford) noted that audiences had "formed the habit of taking our horse operas in a Class B stride. . . . But all that is changed now."[69] Like most critics, Nugent singled out STAGECOACH as key to this change. It is worth noting, however, that STAGECOACH, set in the mythic expanse of Monument Valley and starring the B-Western hero John Wayne as the Ringo Kid, and with its cavalry-to-the-rescue and shootout-on-Main-Street climaxes, was an unabashed genre film and thus was distinctly out of step with the other A-class Westerns of the time.

Indeed, most of the other A-class Westerns of the prewar era staked claims to respectability on the grounds of being more historically "authentic." Many of these were biopics, usually portraying outlaws—as in JESSE JAMES (1939), THE RETURN OF FRANK JAMES and WHEN THE DALTONS RODE (both 1940), BAD MEN OF MISSOURI (1941—about the Younger gang), and BELLE STARR and BILLY THE KID (both 1941). A number of historical epics also were set in the Old West, such as UNION PACIFIC (1939), NORTHWEST MOUNTED POLICE (1940), and VIRGINIA CITY (1940). Thus, the return of the A-class Western was, in one sense, another facet of the recent turn toward subjects taken from American history.[70]

While the A-class Western's resurgence was an important industry development, it actually involved a rather limited number of films. According to Ed Buscombe, the Big Eight released only nine A-class Westerns in 1939, thirteen in 1940, and nine in 1941. Meanwhile, Hollywood's output of B-grade Westerns, an industry staple throughout the 1930s, was simply astonishing. In fact, B-class Western output accounted for roughly 15 percent of all releases in the prewar era.[71] These films, shot in five to ten days and budgeted under $100,000, did steady if unspectacular business, reliably taking in $150,000 to $175,000.[72] The most successful B-class Westerns were the "singing cowboy" series featuring stars like Gene Autry, Roy Rogers, and Tex Ritter, whose popularity resulted from three factors: the commercial tie-ins with both radio and the record industry; their appeal to women as well as to men and boys, the predominant Western clientele; and the upgraded production values of their films, particularly Republic's Autry vehicles.

Screen comedy also underwent significant changes in 1940–1941, owing largely to prevailing industrial and social conditions. In 1941, with enlistment on the rise and the draft reinstated, service comedies reached a peak with CAUGHT IN THE DRAFT, a huge Bob Hope hit, as well as Abbott and Costello's BUCK PRIVATES, IN THE NAVY, and KEEP 'EM FLYING. The Hope-Crosby Road pictures took them overseas—to Singapore in 1940, Zanzibar in 1941, and Morocco in 1942—and a similar brand of bizarre burlesque was equally evident in the prewar comedies of Jack Benny and W. C. Fields. Many critics saw the accelerated turn toward comedy as a form of escapism in the face of world war, and indeed much of the male-dominant comedy was not only lightweight but utterly incongruous.[73] Each of the Hope-Crosby Road comedies, for instance, was increasingly zany and self-reflexive, with the artificial locations and throwaway plots serving simply as a pretext for stringing together topical gags and vaudeville routines.

Another significant prewar development was the evolution of the screwball comedy, which had so utterly dominated the 1930s. Crucial to that Depression-era comedy trend was the "unruly" woman, best characterized by Katharine Hepburn, Carole Lombard, Jean Arthur, and Barbara Stanwyck. But disappointing revenues on several 1938 comedies, especially HOLIDAY and BRINGING UP BABY, signaled a decline in the genre's popularity—leading *Variety* in 1939 to note the trend toward more staid romantic comedy, "with the screwball concoctions going out after a long cycle."[74] Subsequent hits like HIS GIRL FRIDAY and THE PHILADELPHIA STORY in 1940 and THE BRIDE CAME COD and THE LADY EVE in 1941, however, indicated that there was still life in that comic variation, although the couples involved—especially the woman—were indeed on noticeably better behavior than their screwball predecessors. Many prewar romantic comedies, in fact, have been aptly termed "comedies of remarriage," and their comic endorsement of the sanctity of matrimony was certainly more conservative than the Depression-era comedies, which tended to situate the marital embrace as an implicit outcome somewhere beyond the final fadeout.

Distinctly at odds with the general prewar taming of the screwball comedy was the offbeat comic vision of Preston Sturges, the longtime Paramount writer who graduated to writer-director in 1940 and quickly turned out four remarkable screen farces: THE GREAT MCGINTY, CHRISTMAS IN JULY (both 1940), THE LADY EVE, and SULLIVAN'S TRAVELS (1941). Deftly blending slapstick lunacy, social satire, sexual innuendo, and offbeat romance, Sturges established himself as a leading comic talent. Interestingly enough, Charlie Chaplin and Frank Capra also turned out prewar comedies that were darker and more politically astute than their previous work. Chaplin's THE GREAT DICTATOR and Capra's MEET JOHN DOE both begin as offbeat comedies but grow increasingly bleak, poised finally between social commentary and black comedy. Like Sturges's comedies, these addressed vital social and political issues—the rise of fascism, the confusion of hero-worship and celebrity status, the manipulative power of the media, the nature of political propaganda. And like Sturges's SULLIVAN'S TRAVELS, both THE GREAT DICTATOR and MEET JOHN DOE end not with a comic outburst but with a deadly earnest sermon delivered directly to the audience, underscoring the desperate social and political climate of a world on the brink of global war.

Despite the dominant male ethos in prewar Hollywood, the "woman's picture" maintained its currency. Focused on female protagonists and targeted primarily at female audiences, these films traced the seemingly inevitable loss or self-sacrifice that was woman's fate in a man's world—thus the term "weepies" to describe not only the films but the viewer's presumed emotional response to the heroine's plight. Women's pictures

Writer-director Preston Sturges (left) with Joel McCrea and Claudette Colbert on the set of SULLIVAN'S TRAVELS *(Paramount, 1941).*

in 1940–1941 generally fell into one of three categories: ill-fated love stories (ALL THIS AND HEAVEN TOO, 1940; WATERLOO BRIDGE, 1940; HOLD BACK THE DAWN, 1941; BACK STREET, 1941), sagas of marital or maternal sacrifice (PENNY SERENADE, 1941; THE GREAT LIE, 1941; BLOSSOMS IN THE DUST, 1941), or lighter working-girl romantic dramas (KITTY FOYLE, 1940; THE SHOP AROUND THE CORNER, 1940; TOM, DICK AND HARRY, 1941). Remarkably well tuned to the moral calculus of the Production Code as well as the popular tastes and sentiments of the era, these films were aggressively melodramatic, emotionally engaging, and often socially astute. They were not only commercially successful but critically acclaimed as well; in fact, four of the ten Oscar nominees for best picture in both 1940 and 1941 were woman's pictures.

As mentioned earlier, the genre's dominant figure at the time, Bette Davis, represented a fundamental ambivalence in the woman's film in her capacity to personify victimization and to willfully destroy those who might victimize her. And in films like THE LETTER and THE LITTLE FOXES, Davis also anticipated the *femme noire* of war and postwar thrillers. Equally important was the distinctive dimension that Joan Fontaine brought to the woman's picture with REBECCA (1940) and SUSPICION (1941), initiating the female Gothic cycle which would become increasingly prevalent during the war and postwar years, with its obvious ties to both the horror genre and the burgeoning *film noir.*

The horror genre itself had fallen into serious decline by the late 1930s but was resuscitated by Universal's successful reissue of DRACULA (1931) and FRANKENSTEIN (1931) as a double bill in 1938. That revived the studio's interests, and after some success with SON OF FRANKENSTEIN in 1939, the studio fully reactivated its horror cycle by teaming Lon Chaney Jr. (whose father had played the Hunchback of Notre Dame and the Phantom of the Opera for Universal in the 1920s) with the director George Waggner for two low-budget hits: MAN MADE MONSTER (1941) and THE WOLF MAN (1941). MGM made an unexpected venture into the horrific with its remake of DR. JEKYLL AND MR. HYDE (1941), costarring Spencer Tracy and Ingrid Bergman, which did reasonably well at the box office but did little to return the horror genre to respectability or A-class status.

CASE STUDY: THE WARNERS CRIME FILM

Among the more significant prewar genre developments was the reformulation of Warners' signature Depression-era genre, the gangster film. Key factors here were the unexpected rise to top stardom of the longtime contract player Humphrey Bogart and the concurrent emergence of a new crop of top filmmaking talent at Warners—notably Raoul Walsh, John Huston, Mark Hellinger, and Jerry Wald. And as with the regeneration of the MGM musical, the reformulation of the Warners crime film underscored both the viability of the studio's established house style and genre traditions and also the flexibility of that style when it came into contact with new elements.

Oddly enough, Warners in the late 1930s was trying not to redirect but to reassert its gangster formula, the cornerstone in its house style. Dating back to LITTLE CAESAR (1930) and THE PUBLIC ENEMY (1931), two films which established the genre in Warners' repertoire and made stars of Edward G. Robinson and James Cagney, respectively, the gangster film enjoyed tremendous popularity in the early Depression era. Despite efforts by the Legion of Decency, the PCA, and their ilk to subdue it, the gangster formula not only survived but flourished as the decade wore on in various subgenres—prison films, *policiers* (police dramas), juvenile delinquency films, and so on. Warners dominated the genre throughout the 1930s and closed out the decade with two successful Cagney vehicles, ANGELS WITH DIRTY FACES (1938) and THE ROARING TWENTIES (1939), both obvious throwbacks to the gangster sagas of the early 1930s. And among Warners 1940 hits was BROTHER ORCHID, with Robinson as a mob boss "on the lam" who finds religion in a monastery. The undercurrent of nostalgia and self-parody in these later gangster films indicated that perhaps the genre's classical period was on the wane. Moreover, both Cagney and Robinson wanted Warners to off-cast them in other types of roles, and both signed lucrative new contracts which guaranteed them that opportunity through story and role approval.[75] The stars' increased authority and studio clout was immediately evident, with Robinson portraying Dr. Paul Ehrlich and Paul Reuter in two 1940 prestige biopics, and Cagney playing light comedy in THE BRIDE CAME COD and THE STRAWBERRY BLONDE in 1941.

With Cagney and Robinson recasting their screen personas, Warners cultivated other actors as other gangster types, notably John Garfield and George Raft. Garfield signed a long-term deal in early 1939 (starting at $1,500 a week) and displayed the manic intensity and amoral charm of Cagney's early films in THEY MADE ME A CRIMINAL (1939), CASTLE ON THE HUDSON (1940), and OUT OF THE FOG (1941).[76] George Raft, who had established his gangster credentials as Paul Muni's sidekick in the 1932 gangster classic SCARFACE, signed a one-year, three-picture deal for $55,000 per picture in June 1939; that year Raft costarred with Cagney in EACH DAWN I DIE and then was top-billed in INVISIBLE STRIPES.[77] Second-billed in the latter was Humphrey Bogart, who also played key supporting roles in ANGELS WITH DIRTY FACES, THE ROARING TWENTIES, BROTHER ORCHID, and numerous other gangster pictures. Remarkably enough, Warners apparently did not deem Bogart a likely successor to Cagney and Robinson—at least in A-class crime films. Bogart, who appeared in twenty pictures from 1937 to 1939 and was making $1,250 per week at Warners, alternated between supporting roles in A-class crime films and lead roles in B-grade gangster sagas like YOU CAN'T GET AWAY WITH MURDER and KING OF THE UNDERWORLD (both 1939).[78]

Besides signing Garfield and Raft, Warners made a number of other moves in 1939 to sustain its gangster formula. The most significant of these were related to THE ROARING TWENTIES, which despite being cast in the gangster mold was also a catalyst in the reformulation of the Warners crime film. Mark Hellinger, a well-known New York journalist who had signed on as a writer at Warners in 1938, wrote the original story for the film, which was scripted by the team of Jerry Wald and Richard Macauley, then just making their way out of Bryan Foy's B-picture unit. Most significantly, Warners signed Raoul Walsh in May 1939 (at $2,000 per week) in a one-picture deal to direct THE ROARING TWENTIES.[79] Then in his early fifties and with a quarter-century of directing experience, Walsh proved to be ideally suited to the project and to the Warners style—and in fact would make a long-term commitment to the studio, sharing with Michael Curtiz the status of ranking house director during the 1940s.

The opening reel of THE ROARING TWENTIES is pure Warners, a montage of elliptical back story and intense action à la gangster classics like Public Enemy and I AM A FUGITIVE FROM A CHAIN GANG (1932). But once Cagney's ill-fated gangster-hero is set in motion, especially in terms of his hopeless love for the virtuous Priscilla Lane, THE ROARING TWENTIES changes gears, taking on an oddly self-conscious, near-tragic dimension. Realizing both the error of his ways and his own inevitable doom, Cagney undergoes a redemption of sorts. In the film's climax, he executes a cowering Bogart (who has

The demise of Cagney's reformed gangster at the end of THE ROARING TWENTIES (1940),
a key film in the reformulation of Warner's urban crime cycle.

taken over Cagney's mob and threatened Lane and her family) before being gunned
down by rival gangsters—thus fulfilling the genre's requisite death-in-the-gutter finale.

The success of THE ROARING TWENTIES won Hellinger hyphenate status as a writer-
producer and Walsh a five-year contract, and the two collaborated on three successive
crime pictures—THEY DRIVE BY NIGHT (1940), HIGH SIERRA (1941), and MANPOWER
(1941)—which further redirected the Warners crime film.[80] THEY DRIVE BY NIGHT was
scripted by Wald and Macauley and centered on two truck-driving brothers (Raft and
Bogart, with Ida Lupino costarring as Raft's wife) who become caught up in hijacking
and murder. THEY DRIVE BY NIGHT took the gangster from the confining urban milieu
to the open highway, effectively opening up the formula to new narrative and visual possibilities. The picture was a moderate hit, enhancing the Walsh-Hellinger unit's stature
and moving Bogart one step closer to a starring role.

Bogart soon secured that role when Raft turned down the part of the star-crossed gangster-hero, Roy "Mad Dog" Earl, in HIGH SIERRA. Although he was second-billed to Ida
Lupino, HIGH SIERRA was Bogart's first opportunity to play the male lead in an A-class picture—or a near-A anyway. That opportunity was bolstered considerably when the script
assignment went to John Huston, then a top Warners screenwriter who specialized in prestige-level biopics. Based on W. R. Burnett's novel of the same title, which Warners purchased immediately after its March 1940 publication, HIGH SIERRA had the earmarks of
the classic gangster saga, but it pushed even more aggressively beyond the confines of the
genre's conventional settings and characters.[81] The story centers on the career criminal

and "two-time loser" Roy Earl, who in the opening of the film leaves prison on a parole arranged by mobsters who want Earl to orchestrate a major heist.

Huston, who collaborated with Burnett on the adaptation, told the studio executive Hal Wallis that he wanted to retain the spirit of Burnett's story, which he considered "the strange sense of inevitability that comes with our deepening understanding of the characters and the forces that motivate them."[82] Huston and Burnett depicted "Mad Dog" Earl from the outset as an oddly sympathetic figure—a middle-aged, world-weary, and vaguely idealistic man whose only interest in the crime at hand is a function of his professionalism and his relief at being out of prison. Sympathy grows as Earl finds love and redemption en route to self-awareness and his inevitable demise, pushing the tragic qualities of the gangster-hero from latent subtext directly into the story itself. Huston stayed on the picture after shooting commenced in August 1940, and he soon realized that Bogart was ideal for the role. "Something happened when [Bogart] was playing the right part," Huston later recalled. "Those lights and shadows composed themselves into another, nobler personality: heroic, as in HIGH SIERRA."[83]

Bogart's low-key approach to the role jibed well with Walsh's direction, which was noticeably more subdued and deliberate than in THE ROARING TWENTIES. Crucial to the film was not only Bogart's masterminding of the crime but his inadvertent assembling of a "family" of losers and renegades—including Lupino and a mongrel dog, with whom Bogart flees into the mountains when the heist goes awry. Once in the Sierra Nevadas, both the love story and the flight take the gangster film into another realm altogether. David Thomson has noted that "visually, Walsh loves the long shot," and he also observes that "many of [Walsh's] films move inexorably towards remote, barren locales." This assessment includes HIGH SIERRA, which Thomson considers Walsh's "first clear statement of the inevitable destruction of the self-sufficient outsider."[84] This fate is most evident, of course, in the film's finale as Bogart's doomed hero, realizing his pursuers are about to close in, leaves his "family" and flees alone into the mountains, where he is gunned down by state troopers with high-powered rifles.

HIGH SIERRA marked a major breakthrough for Bogart and a major advance in Warners' treatment of the genre. Bosley Crowther in the *New York Times* termed Bogart's performance "a perfection of hard-boiled vitality," and the film itself "a perfect epilogue to the gangster film"—which Crowther clearly considered the studio's sole domain. "We wouldn't know for certain whether the twilight of the American gangster is here," wrote Crowther in his January 1941 review of the film. "But the Warner Brothers, who should know if anybody does, have apparently taken it for granted and, in a solemn Wagnerian mood, are giving that figure a titanic send-off befitting a first-string god."[85]

Walsh displayed his versatility on his next assignment, THE STRAWBERRY BLONDE, then reteamed with Hellinger, Wald, and Macauley on another male action picture, MANPOWER, starring Robinson, Raft, and Marlene Dietrich. While the picture itself did little to advance the Warners crime film—it was, in fact, a thinly veiled remake of a 1932 Hawks-directed Robinson vehicle, TIGER SHARK—the production of MANPOWER had considerable indirect impact on the form. Hellinger and Hal Wallis feuded throughout the shoot, and the conflict became so intense that Hellinger resigned during production.[86] Wald was then elevated to writer-producer status to complete the picture—the first of many he would produce for Warners during the 1940s.[87] There were conflicts on the set as well between Robinson and Raft, which Walsh handled well enough—and which did little to improve Raft's status at the studio. Because of his successful handling of that dispute, Walsh was asked to step in when Errol Flynn and his longtime director,

Michael Curtiz, had a severe falling-out during the shooting of THEY DIED WITH THEIR BOOTS ON (1941). Walsh got on well with Flynn, and the picture was a solid hit. As a result, Walsh's responsibilities at Warners changed radically. His next seven assignments, spanning the entire war era, were Flynn pictures, and thus Walsh necessarily shifted his focus to more upbeat and overtly heroic Westerns and war pictures.

With Walsh and Hellinger suddenly out of the picture, the revitalization of the Warners crime film—and the development of Bogart's screen persona—fell to John Huston. In May 1941, Huston signed a new pact with the studio, boosting his weekly salary to $1,500 and giving him the option of directing at least one picture during the sixty-eight-week term of the contract.[88] Huston already had a project in mind: THE MALTESE FALCON, based on Dashiell Hammett's pulp novel featuring the hard-boiled detective Sam Spade. Warners had adapted the novel twice before, in 1931 and 1936, but neither effort had been successful. The studio was willing to try the property again as a low-risk near-A, budgeted at a modest $380,000.[89] Raft was offered the role of Spade, which he turned down because, as Raft explained to Jack Warner in a 6 June 1941 letter, this was "not an important picture."[90] Warner was amenable, knowing that Huston preferred Bogart for the role and that Bogart was very interested in the part.

Despite the relatively meager budget for THE MALTESE FALCON (1941), Huston and the associate producer, Henry Blanke, mounted a first-rate production. Bogart was teamed with Mary Astor (as the *femme noire* Brigid O'Shaughnessy), and Blanke also signed freelancers Peter Lorre and Sidney Greenstreet (in his first screen role) for supporting roles. Huston brought the picture in some $50,000 under budget, and preview screenings indicated that Warners had an unexpected hit on its hands—and a new star in Bogart. Just before its October 1941 release, Warners revised the billing for THE MALTESE FALCON, moving Bogart from second-billed (after Astor) below the title to top billing above the title, with his name to appear in the same size type.[91] The picture was a modest commercial success but a tremendous critical hit, drawing rave reviews and Oscar nominations for best picture, best director, and best supporting actor (for Greenstreet). Typical of the critical response was Bosley Crowther's review in the *Times*, which termed THE MALTESE FALCON "the best mystery thriller of the year" and praised first-time director Huston's "brisk and supremely hardboiled" style.[92]

Thus, THE MALTESE FALCON marked an important development in the Warners crime film and an obvious departure from the gangster sagas of the previous decade, including HIGH SIERRA. The criminal element was well represented in THE MALTESE FALCON, of course, primarily by Greenstreet's well-bred, articulate, and utterly amoral heavy, Kasper Gutman, and by Astor's lethal seductress, whom Spade falls for but then turns over to the police at film's end for the murder of his partner. The story was only one episode in the ongoing pursuit of the "black bird" of the title, a jewel-encrusted statuette that actually is never found in the course of the film. Solving the crime, however, is scarcely the point of this particular strain of detective story, which is thoroughly focused on the style and worldview of the hero.

As a private eye, the hard-boiled hero was by nature an isolated loner, a rugged individualist, and a man with his own personal code of honor and justice. Indeed, in his murky past the detective invariably has resigned or been fired from an official law-and-order capacity, and he shares with the criminal element a deep resentment of the legitimate authorities. In that sense, he has more in common with the Western hero than either the gangster, the cop, or the more traditional Sherlock Holmes–style detective. Like the westerner, the detective's capacity for violence and streetwise savvy ally him

Humphrey Bogart (as Sam Spade), Sidney Greenstreet, Peter Lorre, and Mary Astor in THE MALTESE FALCON (*1941*).

with the outlaw element, while his personal code and idealism commit him to the promise of social order. And as portrayed by Bogart, the hard-boiled detective proved to be an ideal screen type for the prewar era—an irreverent, reluctant hero and rumpled idealist whose tough, cynical exterior conceals a sensitive, vulnerable, and fundamentally moral man. And significantly enough, this screen type also proved readily adaptable to a war-related context, as Bogart would demonstrate after Pearl Harbor.

The Emerging War Film

Perhaps the most significant and complex development in prewar Hollywood was the on-screen treatment of the war. While what might be termed the "war film" began to take shape during this period, this development was by no means a uniform or coherent process. Rather, the war film developed in different ways and at a very different pace in newsreels, documentary shorts, and features, with nonfiction films taking the lead in covering both the war overseas and war-related events at home. And when feature films did begin treating war-related stories and themes in 1940–1941, they were likely to do so in any number of genres and forms—from slapstick farce and romantic comedy to female Gothic and family melodrama, and most prominently in spy films and suspense thrillers. Noticeably lacking, in fact, were the combat films and home-front melodramas that would typify Hollywood's war-film production during and after the war.

Despite this rather uneven and haphazard treatment of the war in 1940–1941, most of the industry's war-related output shared a common thematic emphasis. With the outbreak of war in Europe, Hollywood's fiction and nonfiction films tended to be firmly pro-interventionist, pro-military, and anti-totalitarian. The newsreels, documentaries (both studio-produced shorts and imported features), and dramatic features released in the United States from 1939 through 1941 consistently portrayed the Axis powers, especially Nazi Germany, as a threat to the interests of America and its allies and to the American way of life. These films also depicted U.S. preparedness as absolutely necessary owing to what came to be perceived as America's inevitable entry into the war.[93] There were a few pro-Nazi films in circulation, most of them German-produced documentaries released by independent distributors on a very limited basis. By 1941, these had virtually disappeared from the U.S. market, which by then was dominated by pro-Allied and interventionist pictures produced either in the United States or Britain.

Actually, Hollywood's interventionist and pro-military—if not to say pro-war—stance was rarely evident in its feature films before 1940. As late as 1938–1939, with the European markets still open and isolationist sentiments at home still relatively strong, films criticizing fascism or promoting the U.S. military buildup were simply not considered good business. Before 1940, in fact, only Warner Bros. seemed willing to treat political conditions in Europe directly in feature films, owing largely to Harry Warner's virulent anti-Nazism. Bucking current industry wisdom, Warners released CONFESSIONS OF A NAZI SPY in April 1939. The documentary-style feature starred Edward G. Robinson as an FBI agent battling German espionage in the United States, and the film actually mentioned Hitler and Nazi Germany despite PCA objections. The critics raved, with the National Board of Review naming CONFESSIONS OF A NAZI SPY "the best film of the year from any country."[94] But the public was less enthusiastic; after doing moderate business in the United States, the picture was either banned or heavily censored overseas (including Great Britain).[95] Warners released a similar film in September 1939, ESPIONAGE AGENT, starring Joel McCrea; it too fared better critically than commercially, despite the outbreak of war in Europe that same month.

Conditions in Europe and the escalating U.S. defense buildup in late 1939 induced the other studios to deal with the war in dramatic features, although it would be well into 1940 before the results reached the screen. Warners remained the trendsetter, releasing THE FIGHTING 69TH in January 1940. The World War I drama starring James Cagney was important because it depicted Americans in combat against a German enemy (albeit a quarter-century earlier), and also because it involved the successful adaptation of both a Warners star and an established formula into a war story. THE FIGHTING 69TH depicts the conversion of Cagney's swaggering, self-centered tough guy, so familiar from crime and action films, into a team player on behalf of the war effort. Significantly enough, the conversion is sparked by a priest, played by Pat O'Brien— something O'Brien's clergyman had been unable to accomplish with Cagney's gangster a year before in ANGELS WITH DIRTY FACES. Cagney did "see the light" before going to the chair in the earlier film, but in THE FIGHTING 69TH his conversion results in a more heroic demise: Cagney gives up his life for his fellow soldiers by throwing himself on a German grenade.

THE FIGHTING 69TH was among Warners' biggest hits in 1940, and its popular and commercial success enhanced Hollywood's general shift to war-related features that year. By the spring and summer, as the Nazi blitzkrieg overran Europe and pushed to the English Channel, Hollywood had begun a blitz of its own—although with very few

In THE FIGHTING 69TH *(Warners, 1940), a World War I drama, Cagney's surly individualist is converted to the war effort by chaplain Pat O'Brien and drill sergeant Alan Hale.*

movies dealing directly with World War II. Indeed, one of the more interesting aspects of Hollywood's own "conversion" to war-film production in 1940 was its continued avoidance of the current war and its tendency, à la Warners in THE FIGHTING 69TH, to treat the war indirectly. According to one industry survey, Hollywood from September 1939 through August 1940 released 129 features (including 27 from Britain and France) and 60 shorts "dealing with the war and the troubles in Europe, national defense and preparedness, patriotism and Americanism, dictators and democracies."[96] This number included a remarkably wide range of genres, from Civil War epics and foreign legion films to westerns. In terms of features directly related to World War II, however, Hollywood's output was still quite limited. According to an in-depth study by James Earl Shain, Hollywood produced only six World War II–related films in 1939 (1.2 percent of its 483 releases), and twelve in 1940 (2.5 percent of 477 releases).[97]

Most of those appeared later in the year as the industry shifted noticeably to more militaristic, nationalistic, and political themes and to a heavier emphasis on U.S. preparedness. "By 1940 Hollywood had crossed an important threshold," note Clayton Koppes and Gregory Black in *Hollywood Goes to War.* "Some studios had begun to make explicitly interventionist films."[98] In September, Thomas Brady of the *New York Times* observed that "only in recent months" had the movies begun "proposing active American counteraction" to Nazi aggression.[99] Later that month, Bosley Crowther, noting the coming "wave of propaganda pictures" in his *Times* survey of the schedule of

1940–1941 films, commented that "films are fast assuming the role predestined for them in time of crisis."[100]

While Hollywood turned increasingly to war-related subjects in 1940, the studios relied on established genres and story formulas to dramatize those subjects. FOREIGN CORRESPONDENT, for instance, rehashed ESPIONAGE AGENT as well as Alfred Hitchcock's quasi-political "chase" films, THE LADY VANISHES and THE THIRTY-NINE STEPS (1935), and gave the espionage thriller a twist by adding a familiar 1930s screen figure, the crusading, wisecracking reporter (Joel McCrea). MGM's THE MORTAL STORM (1940), directed by Frank Borzage, was a domestic melodrama about a family torn apart by the Nazis when the family patriarch, a university biology professor, refuses to preach Aryan dogma to his pupils. Even the reviews tended to read the film in terms of family melodrama. Bosley Crowther, for instance, while recognizing the breakthrough status of the picture, opened his review with this assertion: "At last and at a time when the world is more gravely aware than ever of the relentless mass brutality embodied in the Nazi system, Hollywood has turned its camera-eye upon the most tragic human drama of our age."[101] Other films also tapped the family melodrama in anti-Nazi pictures—Fox's FOUR SONS (1940), for instance—though none as successfully as THE MORTAL STORM, due to Borzage's sensitive direction, the all-star cast (including James Stewart, Margaret Sullavan, and Robert Young), and the clear invocation of the "Jewish question."

Another interesting 1940 genre variation was Warners' THE MAN I MARRIED, which cast Joan Bennett in a female Gothic about a woman whose German-American husband gradually is won over by Nazi propaganda during a trip to Europe. The film is also notable for being one of the first mainstream features to actually use the word *Jew* in dealing with the Jewish question.[102] A more sanguine variation was ARISE MY LOVE (1940), an offbeat romantic comedy scripted by Charles Brackett and Billy Wilder about two reporters (Claudette Colbert and Ray Milland) who fall in love while covering the war in Europe.

Perhaps the most significant genre variation was THE GREAT DICTATOR, with Chaplin's Little Tramp transposed into a meek Jewish barber who is mistaken for the dictator Adenoid Hynkel. Released in late 1940, THE GREAT DICTATOR was a huge critical and commercial success, emerging as the number-two box-office hit of 1941. The number-one hit in 1941 was SERGEANT YORK, Warners' biopic of a reluctant World War I hero, and among the other top ten hits that year were A YANK IN THE RAF, DIVE BOMBER, and CAUGHT IN THE DRAFT. These clearly signaled an increased audience interest in war-related features in 1941, as Hollywood intensified its direct treatment of the current war. According to Shain, 32 of the studios' 492 releases (6.5 percent) in 1941 dealt with World War II. The majority were espionage thrillers, as the spy genre proved increasingly amenable to war-related adjustment. In fact, over one-third of the 50 Hollywood features from 1939 to 1941 related to World War II (18 in all) were spy films.[103]

Chief among the war-related spy films in 1941 was MAN HUNT, a Fritz Lang–directed thriller about an effete big-game hunter (Walter Pidgeon) who decides to take a shot at Hitler, simply for the sport of it. Like so many of the war films of 1940–1941, MAN HUNT featured a conversion narrative, with the hero eventually being caught and tortured by the Gestapo, escaping to England, then joining the military to get a legitimate shot at Hitler. The majority of conversion narratives were decidedly less offbeat than MAN HUNT, tracing instead the fate of the self-assured individualist who, in the course of military training, learns to subordinate his own interests to those of the group. This theme surfaced in a number of military training films—invariably complemented by a celebration of the arma-

Frank Morgan as the ethical professor and Robert Young as the Nazi zealot in MGM's
THE MORTAL STORM (1940).

Howard Hawks directs Gary Cooper in SERGEANT YORK *(Warners, 1941), another World War I drama with clear connections to the current European conflict.*

ment and technology involved, from tanks to dive bombers to submarines. Of the fifty war-related films of 1939–1941, thirteen involved soldiers at home, and virtually all of these focused on military training. The most popular and prevalent of these films were the service comedies mentioned earlier and aviation pictures like INTERNATIONAL SQUADRON (1941), FLIGHT COMMAND (1940), and I WANTED WINGS (1941).

Interestingly enough, only three of the fifty World War II films released in 1939–1941 dealt with soldiers in combat. This proportion would change dramatically in the next few years as the combat film came to dominate the standard conception of the war film and as the service comedies, military training, and espionage films declined. But given the conditions both at home and abroad before the war, it is scarcely surprising that political intrigue and military preparedness were the dominant themes in Hollywood's war-related output in 1940–1941.

While Hollywood features turned gradually and somewhat belatedly to the subject of World War II, there was extensive prewar treatment of war-related subjects in documentaries and newsreels. The most notable of these were the "March of Time" newsreels, produced by Louis de Rochemont, a young documentary filmmaker educated at MIT and Harvard. De Rochemont created the March of Time in 1934 with the backing of Time-Life, Inc., and by the late 1930s the international news service and its newsreels were a worldwide success. Issued monthly, usually about fifteen minutes in length but occasionally longer, the newsreels covered an array of issues and events. Virtually the only direct mention of Hitler and Nazi Germany on American movie screens before 1939 came via the March of Time, notably in a sixteen-minute May 1938 issue, "Inside Nazi Germany." From September 1939 to December 1941, over twenty newsreels covered the war and related events in Europe and the Far East.[104]

In 1940, de Rochemont produced the March of Time's first feature-length documentary, THE RAMPARTS WE WATCH. Released in September, one year after the outbreak of the war in Europe, the film combined a celebration of small-town American life with a biting critique of fascism. In 1941, the March of Time turned increasingly to U.S. preparedness, the defense buildup, and other domestic concerns (espionage, the disruption of shipping, etc.). De Rochemont resumed the anti-Nazi, anti-isolationist push in September 1941 with one of his most powerful films, "Peace—By Adolf Hitler," which traced the German leader's record of broken promises and devastation of Europe.

A very different form of war-related nonfiction filmmaking in Hollywood in 1940–1941 were the military training and informational films. The studios began to regularly produce these one- and two-reel films in late 1940, primarily through a Hollywood-based reserve unit of the Army Signal Corps comprising some two dozen officers and 300 GIs trained in film production. The unit was headed by Lieutenant Colonel Nathan Levinson, who also acted as vice-chair (under the chairman Darryl Zanuck) of the Motion Picture Academy Research Council, an organization which coordinated industry support for the Signal Corps' production efforts.[105] By 1941, these efforts were well under way and Zanuck was increasingly involved. In fact, Zanuck himself made a trip to Washington in August to meet with army brass about Hollywood's military-related filmmaking operations. Zanuck brought with him six of the one hundred or so training films already completed, including a Ford-directed one-reeler, "Sex Hygiene." (Another forty were in production, including Capra's "Combat Counter-intelligence.") The military leaders were favorably impressed, and Zanuck was forthright about the industry's pro-military, anti-isolationist stance—a position he and his fellow studio heads would publicly defend in the Senate propaganda hearings only a few weeks later.[106]

CASE STUDY: IN THE NAVY AND EAGLE SQUADRON

IN THE NAVY (1941) and EAGLE SQUADRON (1942) provide illuminating examples of Hollywood's prewar incursion into war-film production. Both were produced and released by Universal and directed by the staffer Arthur Lubin, and both signaled Hollywood's newfound resolve to cultivate a market for war films. But beyond that, the two films were radically different. IN THE NAVY was an Abbott and Costello service comedy (cum musical) and the second of eight Abbott and Costello vehicles that Universal cranked out in 1941–1942. EAGLE SQUADRON, conversely, was in production longer than all eight of the Abbott and Costello films combined and was an attempt by the independent producer Walter Wanger to integrate drama and documentary in an innovative portrayal of an RAF squadron during the Battle of Britain.

Thus, IN THE NAVY was by far the more routine production, demonstrating the studio's capacity to respond quickly and effectively to changing social and industrial conditions and to exploit the sudden emergence of new talent as well. Universal's Abbott and Costello films did exceptional business, averaging about $2 million in revenues and carrying the duo from obscurity in late 1940 to the number-three slot on the Exhibitors' Poll in 1941 and then, incredibly, to the top spot in 1942, displacing Mickey Rooney.

The lanky long-suffering straight man and his dumpy, bumbling sidekick had started in burlesque in the early 1930s, then moved to radio and Broadway late in the decade. They signed with Universal for a second-rate (even by Universal's standards) 1940 comedy, ONE NIGHT IN THE TROPICS, and then were featured in an early-1941 military farce, BUCK PRIVATES, as a pair of inept army draftees who comically survive basic training and become unlikely heroes. The plot was a pastiche of army jokes and vaudeville routines, interspersed with tunes performed by the Andrews Sisters—including the Oscar-nominated "Boogie Woogie Bugle Boy of Company B," which became a wartime standard.

By the time BUCK PRIVATES was released in February 1941, Universal already had finished shooting another Abbott and Costello vehicle, HOLD THAT GHOST (1941), a genre parody that melded gangster and horror formulas with the duo's verbal-physical comic style.[107] But when BUCK PRIVATES took off at the box office, Universal shelved HOLD THAT GHOST, planning to bring it in line with BUCK PRIVATES by adding a romantic subplot and a few Andrews Sisters musical numbers. Meanwhile, the staff producer Alex Gottlieb and the director Arthur Lubin, two B-movie specialists, set to work on a seafaring follow-up to the army comedy. Ten weeks later, IN THE NAVY was "in the can" and ready for release, an incredible feat even by B-movie standards, let alone for a picture destined for holdover first-run release.

Actually, the picture would have been ready even sooner except for problems with the Navy Department—problems suggesting that the regulation of movie content would

Costars Dick Powell, Lou Costello, and Bud Abbott in IN THE NAVY *(Universal, 1941).*

take on a new dimension during wartime. The plot had Abbott and Costello spatting, pratfalling, and ad-libbing their way through naval recruitment and training. After passing muster with Breen and the PCA, Universal requested official navy approval. The navy's reply that approval would "not be forthcoming on material of this sort" precluded Universal's use of navy facilities and file footage, both crucial to the rapid and efficient production of the film.[108] The script was rewritten to accommodate the navy's concerns, and Breen personally appealed directly to the secretary of the navy on Universal's behalf.[109] Breen secured navy approval, enabling Lubin to shoot much of the film at a naval training station near Los Angeles.

IN THE NAVY was shot in only twenty-three days at a cost of $479,207, most of which went to Abbott and Costello ($35,000), their costar Dick Powell ($30,000), and the Andrews Sisters ($15,000). Gottlieb earned $6,350 and Lubin $5,166 on the picture, based on their respective salaries of $300 and $350 per week. There were eight musical numbers in the picture (taking up thirty-five of its eighty-five minutes), including another 1940s standard, "Gimme Some Skin." Just before its release, Universal previewed the film for the navy—and again there were problems. In the film's chaotic climax, ship maneuvers are botched by Abbott and Costello's inept signaling, thus implicitly demeaning naval training. At the navy's behest, Universal sent the picture back into production. In yet another display of efficiency, additional scenes were written, shot, and edited into the picture in only three days, transforming the disastrous maneuvers into a Lou Costello dream sequence.[110]

IN THE NAVY was released in June 1941, and Universal's newly assembled Abbott and Costello unit—including Gottlieb, Lubin, writer John Grant, cinematographer Joe Valentine, and the Andrews Sisters—then went to work on HOLD THAT GHOST. The overhaul on that picture was completed by August, and the unit then cranked out an air force service comedy, KEEP 'EM FLYING, for a November 1941 release. Universal launched the film with a location premiere in Detroit, where retooled automobile plants were producing military aircraft at an incredible pace—although the factory system in Detroit had nothing on Universal's assembly-line production of Abbott and Costello comedies.

That same month, November 1941, Universal signed a one-picture deal with the independent producer Walter Wanger for EAGLE SQUADRON.[111] Interestingly enough, the Universal-Wanger deal was not to initiate but to complete the project, which already had been in the works for over a year. Difficult projects were not new to Wanger, a Dartmouth-educated Hollywood sophisticate who by 1941 had a reputation for taking risks and challenging industry convention. Wanger had worked his way up through the ranks as an executive and producer at several studios in the 1920s and early 1930s before signing a ten-year deal with UA in 1936, with UA to arrange both financing and distribution. The Wanger-UA union went very well for a few years, but after STAGECOACH in 1939 Wanger produced seven straight box-office flops, with Hitchcock's FOREIGN CORRESPONDENT and Ford's THE LONG VOYAGE HOME (both 1940) among the biggest losers at $370,000 and $225,000, respectively.[112]

That put considerable pressure on Wanger's EAGLE SQUADRON project, by far his most challenging to date and among the first Hollywood features designed to integrate documentary and fiction material. Wanger developed the project with Merian C. Cooper, a World War I flying ace who made documentaries during the 1920s before getting into movies as a producer. Cooper's partner in his documentary and early feature filmmaking efforts was Ernest B. Schoedsack; the two codirected such classic documentaries as GRASS (1925) and CHANG (1927) before coming to Hollywood, where their most successful collaboration was on KING KONG in 1933. Schoedsack was to collaborate on EAGLE SQUADRON as well, shooting and codirecting with the British filmmaker Harry Watt, who had recently completed an acclaimed documentary about the London blitz, TARGET FOR TONIGHT, which had been a success in the United States as well as England, winning a special Oscar in 1941.

The plan for EAGLE SQUADRON was to document the training, exploits, and day-to-day lives of a group of American pilots who joined the RAF during the Battle of Britain and the London blitz. Wanger and Cooper wanted to use actual combat footage and to have the pilots portray themselves. Some of the picture would be dramatized and in fact would incorporate a rather typical conversion narrative—not unlike the yarn that Zanuck conjured up for Tyrone Power at Fox in 1941, A YANK IN THE RAF, which depicts a Yank mercenary coming around to the British cause. But for the most part, EAGLE SQUADRON would be a factual account of Squadron 71 of the RAF and thus was quite innovative by Hollywood standards, although the number of feature documentaries on the market at the time did create a favorable climate for such an effort.

By the time UA announced EAGLE SQUADRON in July 1941, Watt and Schoedsack already had shot several thousand feet of film. But the Battle of Britain had ended two months earlier, and so Wanger spent much of that "blitzless" summer trying to figure how to reorient the narrative to accommodate the relative lull in the action. There were also problems with the British Air Ministry, which impeded correspondence between the filmmakers and balked at approving the aerial combat footage.[113] In mid-August, Watt and Schoedsack informed Wanger that they still felt that there was a "fine film" to be made on the subject, but that "getting a picture of feature length on the screen, using the boys of 71 Squadron in their actual parts, presents us [with] almost insurmountable problems." By September, Watt was convinced that "the only way this film now can be made is as a fictional one, using actors as the key members of the squadron, but always against a very factual and realistic background." The dramatic interplay of the fliers on the ground, now a virtual necessity because of the lack of action in the air, probably could not be "put across by amateurs," reasoned Watt. "In any case, their feelings would not allow them to reenact the most poignant episodes," especially those involving the deaths of their fellow fliers.[114]

Wanger agreed and assigned the screenwriter Norman Reilly Raine to do a dramatization of Squadron 71's story. Raine was ideal for the job, with a background in biopics and action pictures and more recently in war dramas—including THE FIGHTING 69TH and another Cagney film, CAPTAINS OF THE CLOUDS (1942), about an American flier in the Canadian Air Force. Wanger put Raine to work on the project and informed the UA board of directors of his decision to go with a dramatic approach. He figured that UA, which was responsible for funding his pictures, would be relieved at the decision, but this was hardly the case. UA already had sunk a considerable sum into the project, with little to show for it, and had been through a similar fiasco with FOREIGN CORRESPONDENT, on which Wanger had used over twenty writers and spent $213,000 in script costs alone. UA informed Wanger that there would be no additional funds for EAGLE SQUADRON, and so Wanger decided to leave UA and look for another producer-distributor. Wanger's split with UA gave the company his profit share on his most recent film, SUNDOWN (1941), and he in turn was able to keep the 14,000 feet already shot for EAGLE SQUADRON.[115]

Wanger shopped the project around Hollywood—but without Cooper, who had taken a commission in the Army Air Corps. The footage from the Battle of Britain and the

In EAGLE SQUADRON *(Universal, 1942), authentic battle footage was complemented by a documentary look for the dramatized lives of the men in Squadron 71.*

London blitz proved to be Wanger's ace in the hole, and several studios expressed interest. The best offer came from Universal, which agreed to put up $60,000 for Raine's script and another $50,000 for the documentary footage; the studio also agreed to hire Wanger at $2,500 a week as producer and to finance the completion of the picture. Wanger's contract gave him "complete supervision and control of this production," although the studio retained approval rights over the director, cast, and final cut. Wanger had full use of Universal's personnel and facilities and was allowed a budget "contemplated" in the $700,000 range. All net proceeds were to be split evenly between Universal and Walter Wanger Productions, Inc.[116]

Thus, Wanger became an in-house independent at Universal, with access to the studio's resources—including the director Arthur Lubin, who was between Abbott and Costello pictures at the time and was quite capable of completing EAGLE SQUADRON quickly and economically. Wanger and Lubin started shooting in January 1942, and the picture was completed and released by summer. By then, its costs were just over $900,000 and the market was glutted with war movies, but the Watt-Schoedsack footage gave the otherwise routine picture a distinctive edge. While the finished product was scarcely what Wanger initially had envisioned, EAGLE SQUADRON was a solid success. The picture grossed $2.4 million, and after Universal's production and distribution fees were extracted, it turned a profit of nearly $750,000.[117]

By the time EAGLE SQUADRON was released, the United States had gone to war and so had Hollywood. Any hint of caution or hesitation in the movie industry's support of the war effort was long forgotten by mid-1942—if anything, according to the bureaucrats in the Office of War Information in Washington, Hollywood's penchant for warmongering had grown too pronounced in the early months of the war. The industry would soon strike a more balanced treatment, however, and would be contributing to the Allied war effort as effectively as any major U.S. industry.

PART 2

☆

The War Era

CASABLANCA *(Warners, 1942)*.

5

The Motion Picture Industry During World War II

World War II was the best of times and the worst of times for the American film industry. It was a period of challenge and change, of anxiety and accomplishment, of intense focus on the task at hand and growing uncertainty about Hollywood's own long-term prospects once that task was completed. Within days of Pearl Harbor, President Franklin Roosevelt commissioned Hollywood to "emotionalize" the conflict and to mobilize public awareness and support by continuing to do what it did best—making and selling motion pictures, primarily feature films. But producing movies during the war was scarcely business as usual; on the contrary, it required a massive transformation of virtually every phase of industry operations.

Hollywood managed that transformation remarkably well, and its support of the war effort was successful by any number of criteria—by the overall quality of its films, by the well-regulated delivery of diversion, information, and propaganda to receptive civilian and military audiences, by the enormous revenues and profits for all concerned. This last point was of considerable consequence: World War II was indeed the best of times financially for the movie industry, and especially for the Hollywood studio powers. The prewar defense buildup initiated the economic upturn, with the Big Eight's combined profits surging from about $20 million in 1940 to $35 million in 1941. Those figures were far surpassed during the war: the Big Eight's combined profits neared $50 million in 1942 and then exceeded even pre-Depression totals, holding a sustained peak of some $60 million in each of the next three years.

While business was booming, however, the war also brought confusion and dislocation to the movie industry. In 1942, there were deep concerns about the war overseas, which was going badly for the United States and the Allies. Those concerns were compounded by severe problems at home due to wartime restrictions and shortages affecting every sector of the film industry, and due also to Hollywood's increasingly complex dealings with the government and the military. By 1943, as the tide of war began turning in both Europe and the Pacific, Hollywood was coming to terms with its role in the war effort and was stabilizing wartime operations. And as the Allies pressed toward victory in 1944–1945, Hollywood's concerns began to shift to the postwar era, which it faced with a mixture of unbridled optimism and genuine dread. Industry discourse at the time was rife with questions and doubts about the international marketplace, about the end of the war economy and the subsequent "reconversion," about urban relocation and population shifts away from the all-important first-run theaters, about the threats from commercial radio and television. At the same time, two serious prewar threats which had been subdued but continued to fester during the war—the government's antitrust campaign and Hollywood's internal labor discord—resurfaced in the late war years and reached crisis proportions in 1945, even before the war ended.

Whatever the immediate and impending problems facing the industry during the war, however, Hollywood never lost sight of its primary commitment to the national war effort, or of its unique and crucial role in that effort. In many ways, World War II was the best of times for the movie industry not because of its unprecedented economic prosperity, but because of its social and cinematic achievements. Hollywood made significant on-screen advances during the war in both features and nonfiction films. Established genres and stars were "converted to war production," while Hollywood steadily refined two distinctive narrative formulas, the combat film and the home-front melodrama, to dramatize the war effort. Many top filmmakers turned to the documentary form, which took on new significance during the war—and encouraged a new realism in fiction filmmaking as well. By 1944–1945, fictional and documentary treatments of the war had reached a remarkable symbiosis, creating an on-screen dynamic utterly unique to the war era. Meanwhile, a stylistic countercurrent developed in what came to be termed *film noir,* which explored the darker side of America's wartime psyche.

As long as the war lasted, the moviegoing experience remained the central, unifying wartime ritual for millions of Americans, from the war-plant worker in Pittsburgh to the foot soldier in the Pacific. Through it all, the movies effectively conveyed wartime conditions and gave shape to the sentiments of the vast Allied populace. "There was a day when it was considered smart to be cynical about Hollywood," wrote the war correspondent Robert St. John for *Look* magazine in 1944. "That was before the war."[1] Like many observers of the U.S. motion picture industry, St. John felt that Hollywood came of age during World War II, and indeed that period may have been Hollywood's finest hour as a cultural force and a social institution.

America and the War Effort

Hollywood's wartime role can only be examined and understood in terms of the larger social, economic, and material conditions at home during that era, as well as the military developments overseas. The retooling of the motion picture industry that accompanied the nation's entry into the war was simply one facet of a massive conversion of American industry and labor—indeed, of the American way of life—that began within days of Pearl Harbor and would extend not only through the war years but for years and even decades afterward.

From the moment the Japanese surprise attack was reported in Washington, D.C., on the afternoon of Sunday, 7 December (the attack actually began in Hawaii at 7:55 A.M. local time), the government kicked the defense buildup into high gear. The buildup was orchestrated through a network of agencies, principally the War Production Board (WPB), the civilian agency that coordinated the wartime economy and the production of war goods; the War Manpower Commission, which coordinated and allocated the overall human resources required for military, industrial, agricultural, and other civilian needs; the War Labor Board (WLB), which handled all labor-management disputes in

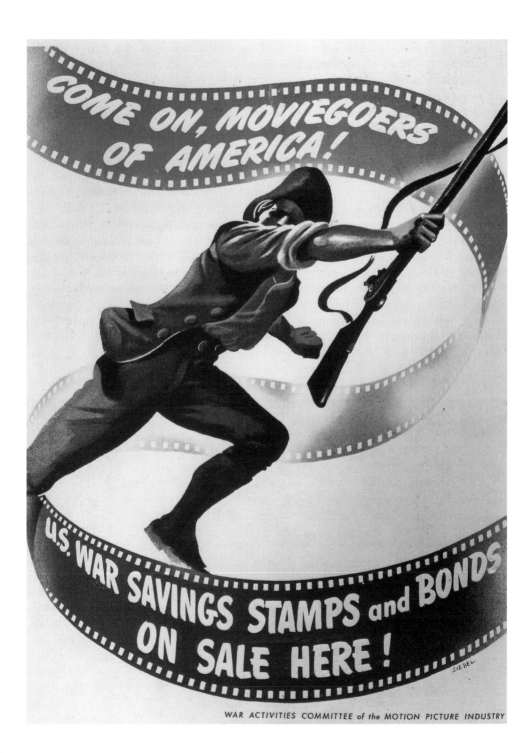

defense-related industries; the Office of Price Administration (OPA), which controlled prices and regulated the production and availability of civilian goods, including the rationing of virtually all the necessities of day-to-day life; and the Office of War Information (OWI), which handled all government news releases to the press, served as liaison between press and government, and supervised the dissemination of information and propaganda through the media, notably motion pictures and radio. Scores of other agencies and subagencies were created during the war, in addition to the myriad government and military organizations set up during the Depression and the prewar defense buildup.

Roosevelt and his colleagues in Washington well realized that Allied victory was essentially a matter of effective utilization of their military and industrial resources. As the historian R. A. C. Parker has noted in his study of World War II, "Superior resources won the war; the victors had greater numbers of men and women and made more weapons."[2] Initially, the government's prime objective was to assemble a national war machine by creating new industries and, to a far greater extent, by converting existing industries to war production. This effort required additional workers and increased productivity, and both of these areas saw enormous growth during the war. In 1939–1940, 8 million people—nearly 15 percent of the workforce—were unemployed in the United States, and the average factory was in operation for forty hours per week. The defense buildup sharply increased employment rates. By early 1942, as the government began awarding war contracts (which eventually would total $240 billion) and pumping $2.3 billion per month into the economy, unemployment had fallen to 3.6 million. By 1944,

"Rosie the Riveter": OWI photo of women working in war plants.

the U.S. workforce had increased by 18.7 million and unemployment bottomed out at 800,000. A total of 64 million Americans were at work, including some 10 million in the armed services. By then, the average factory was in operation for ninety hours weekly, and the United States was producing 40 percent of the world's armaments. The productivity of American workers was unmatched throughout the world—roughly twice that of Germany in 1944, and fully five times that of Japan.[3]

Millions of those factory workers were women, and in fact the war had a greater impact on the employment and economic status of American women than any other event in this century. More than 6 million women took jobs during the war, increasing the female workforce by more than 50 percent. Much of the work was in traditionally male roles, particularly factory work. Female employment in the aircraft industry increased from only 1 percent in 1941 to 39 percent in 1943, for example, while women came to comprise 15 percent of the workers in the previously all-male shipbuilding industry. Another one million women went to work as civil servants for the government, where they were hired at a rate four times greater than men.[4]

The most rapid and significant conversion to war production involved the automotive industry, which retooled by government mandate to produce aircraft, artillery, tanks, heavy trucks, and jeeps. On 10 February 1942, the last new civilian car (a Ford) rolled off the assembly line in accordance with a government order to halt all civilian automobile production. Within weeks, all of the major automotive companies had converted operations and were producing war-related materiel. Ford's new Willow Run plant, 50 miles from Detroit, for instance, was redesigned to mass-produce B-24 Liberator bombers. The plant covered 67 acres, employed 42,000 workers, and by the end of the war would produce 8,654 bombers, eventually turning them out at the rate of one per hour.[5] The Saginaw division of General Motors was retooled to produce Browning machine guns; by March 1942, it was cranking out over 7,000 per week. Pontiac, meanwhile, was producing anti-aircraft guns at the rate of 1,250 per month. The auto industry continued to produce trucks as well, turning out more than one million light and heavy trucks in 1943–1944—more than all of the other Allied and Axis powers combined.[6]

Parker has argued that "production of aircraft is the best single measure of industrial achievement in the war," and here the U.S. conversion and output were particularly impressive. In 1939, Roosevelt set a production target of 5,000 planes, and that total was surpassed by some 800 aircraft. In 1941, the defense buildup took off and over 26,000 planes were produced. That output was nearly doubled in 1942 and then doubled again in 1943, with production leveling off in 1944 at 96,000 planes—over twice the output of the two next-largest producers, Russia with 40,246 and Germany with 39,275. Between Pearl Harbor and D day in June 1944, U.S. aircraft production averaged 5,700 planes per month, a rate roughly equivalent to the nation's entire output during all of 1939.[7]

Conversion to a war economy boosted salaries, of course, with total wages and salaries increasing from $52 billion in 1939 to $113 billion in 1944. Under government-imposed salary limits on raises, average weekly earnings in manufacturing rose 65 percent during the war, from $32.18 in 1942 to $47.12 in 1945. Meanwhile, the production of civilian goods fell by about one third as U.S. workers found themselves with greater purchasing power but increasingly less available for purchase. Shortages and restrictions became a way of life, and as the war progressed virtually everything that Americans wore, ate, drank, drove, or otherwise used was rationed by the OPA.[8]

The war effort also required massive relocation of the civilian population. During the war, over 15 million persons, some 10 percent of the population, relocated in different counties, with about half that number moving to another state. Industrial centers in all parts of the country saw sizable population increases, particularly on the West Coast; San Diego, San Francisco, Los Angeles, Seattle, and Portland were all among the top ten cities in terms of population gains between 1940 and 1944. (The Los Angeles population increased 15 percent during that period, with an influx of about 440,000.)[9] Some of the population relocation, however, was neither voluntary nor related to war production. Soon after Pearl Harbor, Japanese and Japanese Americans were systematically removed from their homes and confined in internment camps. The total number of persons interned reached 110,000, roughly two-thirds of whom were U.S. citizens; 80 percent of those were from California.[10]

Not only were Americans moving in record numbers, but they were marrying and reproducing at a higher rate as well, despite the millions of men going into the service. Indeed, the early 1940s saw something of a "marriage boom" and a mild "baby boom" as well owing to various war-related factors: the prosperity of the period in the wake of the Depression, the prospect of separation due to military service, and no doubt the prospect of draft deferments as well. From 1940 to 1943, one million more families were formed than would have occurred under normal conditions, while the birthrate rose about 15 percent.[11] The number of family households increased by about two million during the war, despite a sizable countertrend toward "merging households" due to shortages of housing and consumer goods. The number of households with married women at the head and husbands absent increased from 770,000 in 1940 to 2,770,000 in 1945.[12]

While war production brought millions into the labor force and created real prosperity for the first time since the 1920s, the mobilization of millions of Americans into urban-industrial centers also brought labor conflicts, racial and ethnic discord, battles for women's rights, a surge in juvenile delinquency, and various other problems. Union membership grew along with the war plants, although both the unions and the factories experienced an erosion of authority and leadership. Despite the unions' no-strike pledges, labor strikes became a fact of life during the war, especially after 1942. The period saw record numbers of wildcat strikes—short-term, sporadic, unauthorized work stoppages within a limited labor arena. As Nelson Lichtenstein points out in *Labor's War at Home*, "The proportion of all American workers who participated in wartime strikes quadrupled after 1942, reaching an eighth of the workforce by the time of the surrender of Japan in September 1945." And in industries that suffered major strikes, such as mining and aircraft, the proportion of the workforce participating in strikes was 50 percent or higher per year.[13]

The surge in war-related employment of women and blacks in industry also was a source of conflict. Women suffered routine discrimination in terms of salary scales, work assignments, and limited advancement (especially into the growing supervisory and management ranks), but women rarely mounted any organized action to protest this treatment. Male coworkers tended to tolerate their invasion of the factories so long as women produced and remained within the newly defined arenas of "women's work"— aircraft riveting, welding, and wiring, for example.[14] Indeed, Rosie the Riveter became not only an accepted but an idealized figure during the war, best evidenced perhaps by Norman Rockwell's May 1943 *Saturday Evening Post* cover.

Black workers were given no such romanticized treatment, however; in fact, black workers were decidedly more militant and met with much greater resistance in their pursuit of equal opportunities in the workplace. Among the bleaker of these episodes were the Detroit "hate strikes" involving white workers who walked off the job to protest black integration of traditionally white shops. These strikes reached a climax of sorts in June 1943, when 25,000 workers at Packard staged a weeklong strike after two blacks were promoted to long-segregated machinist positions.[15] The conflicts spilled out into the streets of Detroit, which soon became inflamed in weeks of violent race riots, culminating on 21 June, when 25 blacks and 9 whites were killed and another 800 were injured.[16]

June 1943 also saw racial violence erupt in Los Angeles as white servicemen battled Latino youths in the "zoot-suit riots"—referring to the oversized, brightly colored jackets and trousers sported by Latino youths (and by blacks and whites as well). This kind of disturbance was not confined to Los Angeles, although the problem was particularly severe there because of the sizable Mexican-American population and the large numbers of servicemen passing through that city. Actually, the zoot-suit riots were also related to another wartime social problem: juvenile delinquency. During the war, teenage violence and vandalism were a problem in virtually every major city, particularly the war centers with their urban crowding, unchecked prosperity, late-night revelry, and general lack of parental supervision due to work schedules. Movie theater owners were among the more vocal critics of the situation, complaining about raucous disruptions of screenings, slashed

Teenage smoking and drinking in "Youth in Crisis," a 1944 "March of Time" newsreel on the wartime surge in juvenile delinquency.

theater seats, and the like. Nighttime curfews were imposed on teenagers in many cities, while the media constantly challenged parents to assume greater responsibility for their children's behavior.

Although the war industries disrupted urban life, they also energized American cities in more positive ways. Perhaps no city in the United States was as lively during the war as Los Angeles, owing to three factors: the booming aircraft industry; L.A.'s status as a point of embarkation for the Pacific war theater; and the movie industry's efforts, especially through the USO and the legendary Hollywood Canteen, to entertain troops en route to the Pacific. Los Angeles, like most other large cities, also saw a tremendous wartime boom in nightclubs and restaurants, in live music and dancing, and in various other forms of entertainment. While entertaining the troops had its place, entertaining the workers who stoked the war machine was crucial as well.

Complementing the assembly of America's industrial war machine was the buildup of its armed forces. By December 1941, the peacetime draft had increased the military to about 1.5 million men, and the total surpassed 2 million immediately after Pearl Harbor. This number, however, represented only a fraction of the required force, which eventually would peak at 11.7 million American servicemen.[17]

The first year of U.S. involvement in the war was devoted primarily to recruiting and training troops and to building the domestic war machine. But 1942 did not go well for the Allies: Japan won decisive victories in the Pacific, while the Nazis scored victories in the Atlantic and in North Africa. By late 1942 and early 1943, the tide began to turn, thanks in large part to the steady supply of American aircraft and warships. In the summer of 1943, the Allies had taken the offensive on all fronts, and by late 1943 there was little question of whether the Allies would prevail; it was simply a matter of how long it would take and at what cost.

At that time, U.S. troop strength overseas was only about 1.6 million, but that number increased dramatically as the Allies dug in for the long haul both in the Pacific and in Europe. American military forces were deployed to two major theaters of action: the Pacific, where primarily navy and marine forces battled the Japanese; and Europe (and North Africa), where army and air force contingents fought the Nazis. The Russian-German theater to the east represented a veritable war unto itself, waged from June 1941 (when the Nazis invaded Russia) to May 1945. In the span of only a few months in early 1944, the number of U.S. troops in the two theaters reached about 3.6 million; this period also saw the American war machine reach peak productivity.[18]

In the summer of 1944, Allied victory was assured with D day and the invasion of Europe and with a series of major victories over the Japanese in the Pacific. But Germany and Japan still fought fiercely, and casualties mounted as Roosevelt challenged the war-weary populace in early 1945 to upgrade the effort, issuing a "work or fight" mandate to increase both troop and war-plant strength.[19] Roosevelt's death in April preceded Hitler's suicide by only a few weeks as the war in Europe finally ended. Germany surrendered on 7 May; the following day was declared V-E Day (for "victory in Europe"). By then, the Allies had secured the Pacific (at an enormous cost in lives lost) and the United States was conducting regular bombing raids over the Japanese mainland in preparation for a November invasion. That invasion was precluded by Japan's unconditional surrender following the American atomic bombing of Hiroshima (6 August) and Nagasaki (9 August). The official Japanese surrender took place on 2 September, which President Harry S Truman proclaimed V-J Day.

Hollywood and Washington

On 17 December 1941, ten days after Pearl Harbor, Roosevelt appointed Lowell Mellett—an ardent New Dealer and Roosevelt aide who was a former editor of Scripps-Howard's *Washington Daily News*—to serve as coordinator of government films, acting as a liaison between the government and the motion picture industry and advising Hollywood in its support of the war effort. In his letter of appointment, FDR told Mellett: "The American motion picture is one of the most effective mediums in informing and entertaining our citizens. The motion picture must remain free in so far as national security will permit. I want no censorship of the motion picture."[20]

Roosevelt's message was of tremendous importance to the movie industry, indicating as it did that Hollywood would be allowed to continue commercial operations during the war, and without heavy interference from Washington. The motion picture industry, in other words, was not subject to the wholesale "war conversion" that was transforming other major U.S. industries such as steel, auto manufacturing, and construction. Many in Washington argued for conversion of the movie industry, similar to such conversions in Germany and Italy. Civilian production could be suspended, they argued, leaving distributors to rely on existing inventories (i.e., reissues), while the studios produced training, informational, and propaganda films. There was some merit to this argument, in that training films already were proving crucial to rapid deployment of recruits, while the movie-starved civilian population seemed generally satisfied with the growing number of reissues already in release.[21]

Roosevelt opposed conversion of the movie industry, however, realizing the importance of motion pictures as a form of diversion for civilians and soldiers alike. FDR realized, too, that the most effective propaganda often took the form of "mere" entertainment. The British government's ill-advised and much criticized closing of theaters and curtailing of production in England after the war broke out in Europe, along with the Britons' voracious appetite for Hollywood films in the interim, provided ample support for this view. Moreover, Hollywood already had demonstrated its willingness to produce training films, war-related shorts, and newsreels, while its feature films had begun to support FDR's unofficial interventionist policies—as the Senate's recent propaganda hearings had indicated. Considering the industry's proven ability to inform and entertain, along with its avowed commitment to assume a more aggressive propaganda role now that the war was at hand, FDR was confident that the government's political and military agenda and Hollywood's deep-seated commercial interests could be brought into workable alignment.

Thus, the costs and difficulties of full-scale conversion were averted, and indeed Hollywood was quite ready to embark on its own distinct form of war production. As the *Wall Street Journal* noted in a page-one story in January 1942: "The movie industry is fortunate in that its production facilities were ready for immediate utilization in the war effort. There was no problem in enlarging its 'plant capacity.' The industry is lucky, too, in that its chief 'raw material' is talent."[22]

Mellett informed all studio heads that there were six war-related subject areas which the government hoped to see treated in feature films, newsreels, shorts, and documentaries: the issues ("why we fight"), the enemy, the allies, the home front, the production front, and the U.S. armed forces. To facilitate Hollywood's treatment, Mellett set up an office on the West Coast under Nelson Poynter. Like Mellett, Poynter was a journalist-turned-bureaucrat and liberal New Dealer with no experience in the business or the

Elmer Davis, head of the Office of War Information.

production of motion pictures. It appeared that such experience would be unnecessary, since Poynter's role was to be purely advisory—which indeed it was, at the outset at least. Throughout the spring of 1942, Poynter and his staff devoted most of their efforts to meeting with studio executives, producers, and writers to outline and reinforce the government's strategy.

Hollywood's relationship with Washington assumed a more formal and bureaucratic dimension in June 1942 with the official creation of the Office of War Information (OWI), which amalgamated several related government agencies. Headed by Elmer Davis, a print journalist and broadcast news analyst, the OWI's function was to enhance public understanding of the war at home and abroad, to coordinate government information activities, and to serve as a liaison with press, radio, and motion pictures. With both a domestic and an overseas branch, the OWI handled virtually all domestic information and propaganda while sharing its overseas responsibilities with the Office of the Coordinator of Inter-American Affairs (CIAA), under Nelson Rockefeller, as well as the Office of Strategic Services (OSS), under William "Wild Bill" Donovan. Mellett's outfit, now the Bureau of Motion Pictures (BMP), was situated within the OWI's domestic branch.[23]

The BMP had three objectives: to produce war-related informational and propaganda films, primarily shorts; to review and coordinate the filmmaking activities of various other government agencies, which were substantial; and to act as liaison with the motion picture industry. This last objective involved securing optimal distribution for government films and assisting the studios in their war-related efforts.[24] Distribution of government shorts soon became routine, thanks largely to the Hollywood-based War Activities Committee (WAC), run by the former RKO executive George Schaefer. Formerly the Motion Picture Committee Cooperating for National Defense, the WAC worked with the BMP in lining up commitments from over 10,000 theaters to show government films—a total which would grow to over 16,000 by war's end.[25]

While the OWI-WAC handling of government film distribution ran quite smoothly, the BMP's efforts to work with Hollywood filmmakers on war-related pictures proved to be a far more complex and difficult task. Clayton Koppes traces these efforts in detail in chapter 8, but several points should be underscored here. First, while Mellett and Poynter generally abided by FDR's assurances that there would be no government censorship of motion pictures, the BMP did take an increasingly active role in analyzing and evaluating movie projects, promoting story subjects and plot lines, and applying various pressures on studio personnel to cooperate. During 1942, the BMP became highly critical of Hollywood's war-related filmmaking efforts and fashioned something of a second production code and a PCA-style review process to rectify the situation. Not surprisingly, this was not a welcome development in the movie industry.[26]

A second point is that the BMP and the PCA (and their respective codes) were politically and ideologically at odds, not only on the treatment of the war but on various other issues as well, from their respective conceptions of a "good" society to their notions of what constituted a good movie. The PCA's extreme conservatism and obsessive concern over moral and sexual issues was fundamentally at odds, as Clayton Koppes and Gregory Black point out in *Hollywood Goes to War*, with the OWI's ethos of "mild social democracy and liberal internationalist foreign policy."[27] Moreover, the PCA had considerably more experience than the BMP in dealing with studio executives and filmmakers, and it also had a much clearer understanding of how to work social and political themes into motion pictures. Thus, the OWI and the PCA often gave the studios conflicting and even contradictory input on the making of war-related films.

The OWI's ideological bent also created problems in 1942 with the newly elected, conservative-leaning Congress, which viewed the agency in general and the BMP in particular as blatantly pro-Roosevelt and dangerously liberal. Thus, in 1943 Congress cut off almost all funding for the OWI's domestic operations, resulting in Mellett's and Poynter's resignations and leaving the BMP with little to do on the home front except cooperate with WAC in the routine distribution of government shorts. That did not mark the end of the BMP in Hollywood, however. On the contrary, the agency actually gained a stronger hand by shifting its liaison activities to the still-active overseas branch under Ulric Bell, a former Washington correspondent for the respected *Louisville Courier-Journal* and head of the prewar interventionist group Fight for Freedom; he had developed a strong accord with the Office of Censorship. This shift raises a third important point: with its control over film exports, the Office of Censorship effectively put teeth into the BMP's advisory role, providing a post hoc threat to deny export to those films made without adequate regard for the BMP's input before and during production.[28] By 1945, the BMP's input was related not only to the war but to the anticipated postwar era as well, as the OWI steadily expanded its concerns to include the selling of democracy and free enterprise overseas.

Thus, the OWI, in cooperation with the Office of Censorship, exercised considerable influence over the wartime movie industry. As Koppes describes in chapter 8, the OWI significantly affected Hollywood's depiction of America's social and political issues, its allies and enemies, and its role in the envisioned postwar world. And as Richard Lingeman suggests, "FDR's promise of no censorship was not given cynically, but never in our history was the government to assume, albeit temporarily, such tacit power over a medium of mass communication."[29]

Beyond Washington's direct influence on the movie industry via the OWI, the government also had considerable indirect impact through the myriad war-induced regulations, restrictions, and shortages. Among the more severe of these was the drain on filmmaking talent, as the so-called manpower shortage seriously impaired every phase of the industry, particularly production. By late 1942, roughly 4,000 individuals, an estimated 22 percent of studio employees, had joined the armed forces.[30] The Screen Actors Guild reported in January 1943 that 900 actors had withdrawn to join the service; the Screen Writers Guild reported 168 withdrawals, and the Directors Guild 104. Another 40 or so had left the studio executive and producer ranks.[31] The most significant losses in terms of top feature filmmaking were male stars and directors. Clark Gable, James Stewart, Henry Fonda, Alan Ladd, Robert Taylor, and many other stars left for the military, as did such top directors as John Ford, Frank Capra, William Wyler, George Stevens, and John Huston. A tally in late 1944, when the number of studio employees in the service peaked, indicated that over 6,000 had entered the armed forces, including 1,500 actors, 230 writers, and 143 directors. Metro lost 1,090 to the service, Fox 755, Warners 720, Paramount 525, Universal 418, Columbia 289, RKO 224, Republic 134, and Monogram 129.[32]

The distribution and exhibition sectors lost more employees to the military (and the factories) than the production sector, although these were somewhat easier to replace. During the first year of the war, distribution lost 4,500 employees to the service, and exhibition some 18,000. The latter figure amounted to about 12 percent of all theater employees, and 29 percent of male workers in the motion picture industry.[33] These vacancies often were filled by women, and in fact the exhibition end of the business saw

*Hollywood writer-director Garson Kanin (seated at Moviola editing machine),
actor Granville Scofield, and Disney animator Ambrozi Paliwoda, in training with
the Signal Corps.*

pronounced changes as women moved out of ticket windows and usherette outfits and
into projection booths and management offices. In March 1943, Warners reported having the first theater in the United States staffed entirely by women, and in June 1943
Loew's reported that sixty-two of its theaters, roughly half, were being run by women.[34]

Other wartime shortages and restrictions affected the availability of raw film stock,
construction materials (especially steel and lumber), and transportation. The film stock
restrictions were imposed by the War Production Board, primarily to help meet government requirements of raw stock for training films. These restrictions initially set
allotments, per studio, at about 25 percent below 1941 usage; they gradually eased as
government and military requirements diminished. Despite ongoing complaints about
needing film stock both for production and for release prints, the industry quickly
adjusted by cutting down on the amount of stock allotted for each picture, and also on
the number of prints in circulation. The production cutbacks led to more careful pre-
production planning and to fewer takes of individual scenes being shot and printed.
And as seen in more detail later, the restrictions also gave companies a rationale for producing fewer features, increasing the length of runs, and stockpiling finished films—all
of which helped boost the studios' enormous wartime profits. Thus, the film stock

restrictions, as *Variety* put it in early 1944, "turned out to be more of a bookkeeping nightmare than an actual drawback to production and distribution" and in fact brought increased efficiency to production.[35]

Restrictions on construction also were mandated, by the WPB for the most part, and applied primarily to set construction and to theater building and remodeling. In 1942, the WPB imposed a limit of $5,000 on material expenditures for sets, and $200 on materials for theater construction.[36] The studios devised methods of recycling and constructing new sets within these guidelines and also increased location shooting in 1942 (Hitchcock, for example, shot SHADOW OF A DOUBT entirely on location). Exhibition, however, saw theater construction come to a virtual halt, and remodeling limited to the bare necessities. Theater owners also were hurt by curtailments of projection equipment (and parts) and were forced to rely on systems sorely in need of repair or replacement.

Transportation restrictions had an enormous impact on the movie industry in many ways, from the Office of Price Administration's pervasive gasoline rationing and its 1943 ban on pleasure driving to tire shortages, lowered speed limits, and the general dearth of civilian vehicles. After the brief surge in location shooting in 1942, travel restrictions late in the year made it almost impossible to leave the back lot. Distribution and the circulation of prints were hampered by the Office of Defense Transportation's cuts in truck delivery schedules—giving a literal meaning to the "bicycling" of prints from theater to theater. Most significantly, moviegoing underwent wholesale changes during the war owing to the combined effects of population relocation and travel restrictions: outlying theaters, especially small-town and rural movie houses, generally lost business, while major urban theaters thrived.[37]

Another government restriction which created a tremendous furor for a short period was a $25,000 salary ceiling decreed by the director of economic stabilization in October 1942, scheduled to take effect on 1 January 1943.[38] The announcement sent shock waves through the movie industry, whose top talent earned well over that maximum on individual pictures, and whose term contracts carried built-in pay hikes. (According to the Internal Revenue Service, eighty individuals at MGM alone earned over $75,000 in 1942.)[39] The studios dispatched a contingent of lawyers and executives to Washington to lobby various officials and agencies, including the Treasury Department, as cries of "Why work?" circulated among the Hollywood elite. The government backed off, and eventually Congress overruled the plan altogether, relying on the personal income tax codes to divert "excessive" earnings to the government. Thus, the high salaries in Hollywood continued, with an estimated 250 employees earning over $100,000 in 1944.[40]

Entertaining the Troops

Films, stage shows, and other diversions it provided for the men and women in uniform, both at home and abroad, were also a significant aspect of Hollywood's support of the war effort. This was yet another area where the government, the military, and the movie industry developed an efficient and successful working relationship. The crux of Hollywood's effort came via WAC cooperation with the War Department and the army to create the largest distribution and exhibition circuit in the world—and one that eventually encompassed the entire globe. In February 1942, the WAC delivered its first shipment of 16mm films (versus the usual theatrical film gauge of 35mm), free of charge, to soldiers in combat areas. Typical of the hundreds of regular shipments of gift films that followed, this first shipment comprised eighty prints of twenty different programs, each of which included one feature and one or two shorts and ran between ninety minutes and two hours.[41]

In the coming years, the OWI overseas branch and the WAC routed these packages to troops at every U.S. military base, command post, battlefront, and outpost. Films were delivered by jeep, parachute, PT boat, and any other conveyance available and soon became part of the everyday military routine.[42] Often referred to as a "two-hour furlough," these screenings were one way of keeping in touch with conditions back home; they also were considered crucial to morale and one counter to the critical problem of battle fatigue. It is worth noting, though, that the soldiers' tastes did not run simply toward escapist fare, particularly in the early war years. According to the *Motion Picture Herald*, the five most popular films in army theaters in 1943 were GUADALCANAL DIARY, CRASH DIVE, DESTINATION TOKYO, AIR FORCE, and SAHARA.[43]

In 1943, the system was well in place; that year the studios shipped 218 features to the War Department, delivering a total of over 6,100 16mm prints.[44] Many of these films were released to the military one to two months (and occasionally much earlier) before their general theatrical release. Warners' Capra-directed comedy ARSENIC AND OLD LACE, for example, enjoyed its world premiere in military theaters overseas in January 1943, more than a year before its U.S. release.[45]

This time lag was due in part to the majors' heavy backlog of unreleased features—the

Troops in the South Pacific enjoy a "two-hour furlough."

Military screening of ARSENIC AND OLD LACE (*Warners, 1944*)
for troops in the China-Burma theater of action.

Hollywood version of "hoarding" in the face of anticipated war shortages. Another very different reason had to do with the publicity advantages of these releases. Early in the war, Hollywood publicized the deliveries, hoping to get some mileage out of stunts like holding the May 1942 world premiere of TARZAN'S NEW YORK ADVENTURE on a base in Iceland, where the film was delivered by parachute.[46] As the system developed, however, the studios came to realize that servicemen writing home about films they liked provided even better publicity. *Variety* in April 1943 indicated that this unique form of word-of-mouth promotion generated "considerable pre-selling value," and the advance release setup with the army was "developing into an important merchandising channel."[47]

The sheer number of theaters, screenings, and servicemen involved underscores this point. In mid-1944, operations in North America (including Alaska and parts of Canada) stabilized at over 1,100 theaters and an attendance of 17 million per month.[48] By January 1945, the overseas service was estimating its weekly attendance at 7.7 million, with pictures shipped and screened daily "wherever men are fighting or are stationed."[49] In October 1945, the army set up five improvised 16mm theaters aboard the *Queen Mary* and the *Queen Elizabeth* for returning servicemen. By that time, Hollywood had delivered 43,189 prints of 1,941 features to the War Department, plus 33,189 prints of 1,050 shorts. The estimated number of showings per day, worldwide, was 3,500, with daily attendance of about 1.5 million.[50]

While the WAC coordinated 16mm film shipments to the service, the Hollywood Victory Committee coordinated live performances by film, radio, stage, and vaudeville personalities for the armed forces and related services. Formed three days after Pearl Harbor, the Victory Committee included representatives of the various talent guilds and unions who arranged everything from one-night stands (single performances) in the States to extended overseas tours. On the civilian front, the Victory Committee organized shows for various government agencies, notably the Treasury Department for its war-bond drives. But most of the committee's efforts involved entertaining the troops on several USO circuits: the Victory Circuit with 600 venues, most of them theaterlike facilities on army posts or naval stations which could accommodate full-scale revues, plays, and concerts; the Blue Circuit, where smaller troupes played, comprising some 1,150 limited base facilities; the Hospital Circuit, mainly wards and auditoriums in military hospitals; and best known perhaps, the Fox Hole Circuit with its impromptu performances in makeshift facilities at or near battlefronts.[51]

The Victory Committee's overseas operations did not pick up steam until late 1943, when the number of U.S. troops heading for the European and Pacific theaters increased sharply. By April 1944, there were 80 units touring overseas, with 38 of those in the British Isles. Between Pearl Harbor and V-J Day, the Hollywood Victory Committee booked 119 overseas tours, 2,700 hospital tour events, 3,050 camp tour events, and 2,500 bond tour events. All told, over 53,000 appearances were made during and just after the war by over 4,100 individuals.[52]

Two other methods of entertaining the troops on the home front also are worth mentioning. One was giving free passes to men and women in uniform, a practice that began before Pearl Harbor and became fairly routine during the war, owing in part to WAC

USO-CAMP SHOWS
★ ★ ★

The indefatigable Bob Hope and Frances Langford work the USO's "Fox Hole Circuit," providing live entertainment for troops at the front.

Bette Davis serves dinner to the troops inside the Hollywood Canteen.

Soldiers from all branches of the military outside the Hollywood Canteen.

lobbying of exhibitors. Accurate records were not kept, but one estimate put the number of free admissions to New York City theaters as of September 1943 at 2.4 million, with another 2 million passes given to servicemen in Chicago during the same period.[53] The second notable form of wartime entertainment on the home front was the legendary Hollywood Canteen, a refurbished livery stable just off Sunset on Cahuenga Boulevard. Inspired by the Stage Door Canteen in New York City, the Hollywood Canteen was created and run by a group of movie industry volunteers, many of them top stars—including its hard-driving president, Bette Davis. The Canteen opened in October 1942 and soon became a requisite stop for the hundreds of thousands of servicemen passing through Los Angeles en route to the Pacific. Every night at the Canteen, "the boys" enjoyed free refreshments, the company of stars, and the music of top bands.[54] Within a year of its opening, some 350 industry personnel had volunteered to dance, sing, serve Cokes, or simply wash dishes, and the Canteen had entertained its one millionth serviceman—who was honored with kisses from Marlene Dietrich, Deanna Durbin, and Lana Turner.[55]

America's Wartime Movie Marketplace

While Hollywood and the government cooperated to create the world's largest distribution-exhibition circuit during the war, the domestic motion picture market underwent a massive war-induced transformation of its own. With each successive year during the war, as American theaters set new box-office records, the very nature of movie exhibition changed rather dramatically—albeit temporarily. During the war, theaters took on a community role and import altogether different from any they held in any period before or since, and a role that was scarcely anticipated in the chaotic early months of the war.

In the first few months of 1942, despite Roosevelt's edict that the movie industry continue commercial operations, theaters were plagued by war-related problems and disruptions. Blackouts and "dimouts" were ordered for theaters on the coasts and in major war production centers. Air-raid orders from the Office of Civilian Defense required theaters to train personnel and install special equipment in the event of air attack.[56] The rationing of gasoline and other fuel affected theater operations, delivery of prints, and patronage. All theater construction and remodeling was suspended, with the burgeoning drive-in movie industry abruptly halted.[57] The drafting of young men into military service limited available theater employees, bringing not only women but more teenagers and older workers into the exhibition field. A momentary shock went through the industry when, in April 1942, government officials suggested that one-third of American movie houses be shut down.[58] That never occurred, but the WPB continually warned exhibitors that theaters might be closed owing to severe shortages.[59] Movie exhibition flourished despite these problems, even in that trying first war year. As a January 1943 *Variety* story concluded after presenting a litany of exhibitors' woes: "Offsetting the troubles is the turnaway business enjoyed by thousands of theaters from coast to coast."[60]

That first war year also saw movie theaters become war-oriented community centers, owing to the cooperative efforts of the WAC and the nation's exhibitors. The WAC's Theatre Division had two main tasks: to facilitate the distribution and exhibition of government films, and to facilitate the sale (in theaters) of war bonds and victory

Sign of the times: a poster for a German film is removed from a theater in "Little Germany" in Yorkville, New York, on 11 December 1941, after war was declared.

bonds. As mentioned earlier, the WAC managed by war's end to get nearly all the movie houses in the United States to pledge to screen government films—totaling over 77,000 prints of 171 films in the course of the war. Meanwhile, bond drives became a regular feature in movie houses, particularly in first-run theaters near defense plants. Perhaps the best indication of the importance of movie theaters to the government's bond-selling efforts was the role played by Ted R. Gamble. An exhibitor from Portland, Oregon, Gamble had been recruited before the war to advise the Treasury secretary on the role of movie theaters in government fund-raising. With the government's subsequent decision to keep bond-buying voluntary, Gamble was appointed head of Treasury's war finance division.[61]

During the various war bond sales campaigns, U.S. theaters held some 30,000 "bond premieres" and over 40,000 free movie days on which admission was free with the purchase of a war bond. Over one-third of the theaters participating in bond drives became official issuing agents for the U.S. Treasury, and they sold literally billions of dollars in war bonds in the course of the war. In fact, government estimates credit motion picture exhibitors with selling 20 percent of all "E" bonds (those issued to individual investors) during the war. Besides the Treasury Department, other agencies used movie theaters for various drives and initiatives, including the Red Cross, the March of Dimes, United Nations Relief, and Army-Navy Emergency Relief. Theaters also became collection centers for various "critical materials"—blood plasma, rags and paper, copper, rubber, and other needed items in short supply. A nationwide "Get in the Scrap" campaign also filled theater parking lots with tons of scrap metal.[62]

The war economy had a tremendous impact on theater trade, of course, and particularly in the downtown first-run houses that traditionally had been the chief source of box-office revenues. A typical trade press story appeared in April 1942 under the headline "Downtown Areas Boom"; the article noted that "business at the boxoffice has shifted markedly to the extent that the downtown theaters are cleaning up and the neighborhood or suburban houses are standing still or not doing as well as they did."[63] Losses of male patrons due to the draft were easily offset by increased business from defense plant workers; indeed, many downtown theaters were soon forced to expand their schedules. In Detroit, for instance, a United Auto Workers request induced the 5,000-seat Fox Theater to offer pictures from 1:00 A.M. to 5:30 A.M. for swing-shift workers—a contingent of at least 100,000, by UAW estimates.[64] By late 1942, midnight shows were becoming commonplace in theaters in defense plant areas, where exhibitors tried, as *Variety* put it, "to catch the trade piling into downtown zones at the late hour."[65]

By 1943, the development of another war-related trend not only added to the downtown exhibition surge but indicated a significant shift in production and distribution strategies. In July, the *Motion Picture Herald* reported that "customers are leaving the neighborhood second and subsequent run theaters for first run houses downtown," and

West Coast opening of Warners' AIR FORCE *in 1943. Note sign for "swing shift show" beginning at 1:30* A.M.

it suggested two principal reasons. First, patrons had more spending money and were willing to pay the increased admission price at downtown theaters. And second, first-run pictures were taking longer to move out of the downtown houses and into the "nabes" (neighborhood theaters). The latter point was crucial, as films were enjoying increasingly longer runs and thus generating more money for all concerned—even the subsequent-run exhibitors, who also ran top features longer than ever when they finally were able to get them.[66]

The penchant for holdovers and longer runs began before the war, of course, but it escalated sharply in 1942 and continued at record levels throughout the war. One well-publicized example was the run of MGM's MRS. MINIVER at Radio City Music Hall. That June 1942 release ran for a record ten weeks at Radio City, surpassing the six-week record held by three other recent upscale woman's pictures: REBECCA, THE PHILADELPHIA STORY, and WOMAN OF THE YEAR. In its ten-week run at Radio City, MRS. MINIVER played to a record 1.5 million persons and grossed $1.03 million, returning roughly half of the picture's production costs in that single venue. The picture continued at a record pace after ten weeks but was pulled owing to a contractual commitment to Disney for BAMBI (1942).[67] While few pictures did as well as MRS. MINIVER, the number of holdovers continued to increase. During 1943, a record low of 163 films played in New York City's first-run houses. Again Radio City provides an illuminating example of changing wartime distribution patterns. From 1936 to 1938, Radio City played thirty to thirty-two features per year; in 1939, the total fell slightly to twenty-eight and then held at twenty-six in 1940 and 1941. Then came the war years: Radio City played only sixteen pictures in 1942 and then played just ten or eleven in each of the next three years.[68]

Holdovers and long runs created serious booking problems for subsequent-run exhibitors, who turned increasingly to reissues to satisfy demand. By late 1943, exhibitors were actually requesting that the studio re-release old hits, and the companies readily complied. MGM announced plans to reissue pictures for the first time ever; Columbia planned to bring back its Capra hits, while RKO planned an elaborate re-release for SNOW WHITE.[69] Many of the reissues did excellent business; SNOW WHITE, for example, returned another $1.3 million in reissue.[70] The governing wisdom was that star vehicles released from two to ten years previously were the best candidates for reissue; the *Motion Picture Herald* reported that these pictures routinely returned $400,000–600,000 at the box office—a tremendous unexpected windfall for the studios and exhibitors alike.[71] Thus, Warners, Fox, and Paramount began re-release campaigns as well. By 1944, business for reissues was so strong that the studio-distributors began selling them at higher rates—even sometimes in percentage deals, a practice traditionally restricted to first-run features. MGM, responding to criticism by theater owners, announced that its reissues for 1944–1945 would be priced in a lower bracket, but only "in those areas where [exhibition] operations are suffering due to the big bottleneck in key situations."[72] By the summer of 1945, the trend was set, with dozens of reissues in circulation and another twenty announced for the beginning of the upcoming season.[73]

Because of the overheated first-run market, the success of reissues, and decree-related selling policies, the majors all but eliminated low-budget production during the war. But B pictures remained in demand, with the number of theaters playing B's and double bills actually increasing during the war.[74] Columbia and Universal continued to turn out B's at roughly the same rate as before the war, as did Republic, Monogram, and PRC

(Producers Releasing Corporation), although all these companies produced occasional top features as well.

Thus, the entire movie market was surging during the war era, with an increase in gross box-office receipts in each successive year. After previous highs of around $730 million during the pre-Depression talkie boom of 1929–1930, the total U.S. box-office take finally surpassed that record level in 1940, reaching $740 million. That total would double by the end of the war, as these figures indicate:

Table 5.1
U.S. BOX-OFFICE RECEIPTS, 1940–1945 ($ BILLIONS)

1940	0.74
1941	0.81
1942	1.02
1943	1.28
1944	1.34
1945	1.45

SOURCE: Joel Finler, *The Hollywood Story* (New York: Crown, 1988), p. 32; Christopher H. Sterling and Timothy R. Haight, *The Mass Media* (New York: Praeger, 1978), p. 188.

There were several key reasons for this wartime surge. One was a steady climb in admission prices, which rose from an average of 25¢ in 1942 to 30¢ in 1945.[75] (These figures do not include the federal admissions tax of 10 percent, which increased to 20 percent in 1944.) Another key reason was an increase in overall admissions, which, according to MPPDA figures, rose from around 85 million in 1941 to around 95 million by 1944–1945.[76] These figures were the subject of interminable debate, and they were challenged by an April 1944 Gallup/ARI study, which gauged weekly attendance at 62 million, plus another 10 million servicemen per week in military theaters.[77] More conservative estimates put admissions at 80 million before the war and 85 million by 1944–1945.[78]

The real key to the wartime box-office surge was the first-run market, which enjoyed a higher proportion of paying customers during the war than ever before, and also a higher proportion of moneymaking pictures. In 1942, 101 pictures (representing about three-fourths of all A-class releases) returned rentals of at least $1 million to their producer-distributors and took in a total of $182 million.[79] In 1943, 95 pictures did at least $1 million in rentals, returning a total of $211 million; 55 of those hits returned over $2 million.[80] By 1944, million-dollar rentals were altogether commonplace. It was becoming difficult by then to produce a top feature for less than $1 million, owing to inflation and other factors, but the first-run market was so hot that these releases were routinely recouping production costs within the first twelve weeks of general release.[81]

Despite higher first-run admission prices, as well as the numerous road shows and special engagements which pushed prices even higher, moviegoers flocked to downtown theaters as never before during the war. They enjoyed other entertainment forms as well, with radio, music, and theater also doing record business in the later war years.[82] Historians have argued that the American public grew war-weary in 1944–1945 as the Allies struggled toward victory and the U.S. war machine cranked away at maximum output. This may have been the case, but it scarcely diminished the public's appetite for diversion, relaxation, and the collective ritual of mass-mediated entertainment.

Premiere of GOING MY WAY
*(Paramount, 1944) in New
York's Times Square, and
playing at the Plaza Theater
on Regent Street in London.*

Foreign Markets

Hollywood's foreign trade during World War II focused primarily on the United Kingdom and Latin America, just as it had in 1940–1941. This orientation did not prove to be a serious liability, however, owing to the tremendous wartime moviegoing boom in England once the tide was turned against the Nazis in 1941–1942. In fact, Hollywood's wartime revenues from England far surpassed prewar totals, to a point where, by 1944–1945, the distributors again saw foreign markets providing about one-third of their income—a remarkable fact considering the record revenues at home. While the lion's share came from Great Britain, Hollywood continued to cultivate markets in Central and South America, with assistance from Rockefeller's Office of Inter-American Affairs, the State Department, and other government agencies. Persistent political and economic conflicts undercut this Latin American effort, but the studios and the government persevered, anticipating a more positive postwar situation. The State Department and the OWI intervened in other overseas markets as well, particularly in neutral Europe and in the Axis nations toward the end of the war. And as the government became more sensitive to America's image abroad, it became more concerned about Hollywood's role in projecting that image.

Canada, deemed simply an extension of the U.S. market by the studios (which included Canadian revenues in the "domestic" U.S. market figures), was, of course, a foreign market and thus warrants mention here. Undergoing an economic surge of its own during the war and, like the United States, untroubled by fighting on its own soil (or in its skies), Canada also enjoyed a motion picture boom. In 1939, according to government figures, paid admissions in Canada's 1,350 theaters totaled 138 million (versus about 4 billion in the United States), generating gross box-office revenues of $34 million.[83] By 1943, attendance had topped 200 million and receipts surpassed $50 million; those figures increased slightly in 1944 and 1945.[84] During that time, 95 percent of features screened in Canada were Hollywood product—including pictures dubbed into French for release in Quebec that the studios hoped to release later in France.[85]

Britain, too, was something of an extension of the U.S. movie market, although it was both more profitable and more complex. Early in the war, frozen assets continued to plague the U.S. companies, as they had in the prewar period. But late in 1942, Britain remitted nearly $50 million to the studio-distributors and effectively thawed the bulk of U.S. movie revenues for the duration, largely in response to the American lend-lease program and to heavy lobbying from the U.S. government.[86] Britain also eased its quota restrictions in late 1942, thus allowing U.S. product to occupy more screen time and cutting the requirement of U.S. production in England. The main reason for easing the quota restrictions was the general scarcity of British film product due to material and manpower shortages.[87] After turning out two hundred or more features per year before the war, British production fell drastically in the 1940s. The Board of Trade registered only forty-eight features in 1942, and between sixty and seventy in each of the next three years, when British-made product occupied only 15–20 percent of screen time in British theaters. Still, attendance climbed in England, surpassing 30 million in 1944 and 1945—25 percent above prewar figures.[88]

Wartime rentals for U.S. product in England in late 1944 were reportedly running over $90 million annually, with three-fourths of that total remitted to the distributors and the balance remaining in England as motion picture investments. As the war wound down, virtually all of the major U.S. companies began setting up production units or coproduction deals in England. (A few, like MGM and Warners, had had similar setups before the war. GOODBYE MR. CHIPS, for instance, was produced by the "MGM-British unit" in 1939.) These arrangements in the later war years were intended to provide, as *Variety* noted, "a hedge against possible postwar currency restrictions and not merely for quota-production purposes."[89]

While production in England was down, a number of British pictures did exceptional business in the United States during the war and held their own against Hollywood product in other foreign markets, especially in Europe and the Middle East. War films were particularly successful, notably Noël Coward and David Lean's IN WHICH WE SERVE (1942), Carol Reed's THE WAY AHEAD (1944; U.S. title THE IMMORTAL BATTALION), Anthony Asquith's THE WAY TO THE STARS (1945; U.S. title JOHNNY IN THE CLOUDS), and several by the London Films team of Emeric Pressburger and Michael Powell, including 49TH PARALLEL (1941; U.S. title THE INVADERS), ONE OF OUR AIRCRAFT IS MISSING (1942), and THE LIFE AND DEATH OF COLONEL BLIMP (1943; U.S. title COLONEL BLIMP). Most of these films featured a deft blending of wartime propaganda (with much speechifying), comedy, and action, and many incorporated war-related documentary footage as well.[90] Coward, Lean, and Reed were among a new generation of British talent that emerged during the war, along with the actors Trevor Howard, James Mason, and Rex Harrison—all of whom eventually would work in Hollywood.

The producer Alexander Korda remained an important figure in both England and the United States, as he had been in the 1930s, but J. Arthur Rank was without question the key individual in British cinema during the war. Heir to a flour and milling fortune, Rank had been in the industry since the mid-1930s as a producer, and by the war era he was building a massive film empire—and one that certainly was turning (and worrying) heads in Hollywood. By 1943, Rank owned or controlled both the Odeon and Gaumont theater circuits in England (totaling 650 theaters); he owned Eagle-Lion, a distribution company; he was chairman of the Gaumont British organization, which included Gainsborough Pictures and Gaumont British News, as well as the Denham and Pinewood studios, two fairly modest operations. In 1944, Rank had about $20 million tied up in nineteen of his own productions, resulting in such 1945 hits (in the United States as well as England) as BLITHE SPIRIT, A WALK IN THE SUN, THE SEVENTH VEIL, BRIEF ENCOUNTER, and Olivier's HENRY V.[91]

In 1944–1945, Rank made a number of cooperative deals with U.S. individuals and companies, including a five-year coproduction and global distribution deal with 20th Century–Fox; a two-picture production and distribution deal with RKO; a two-year, seven-picture distribution deal with UA; and a coproduction deal with David Selznick.[92] Rank's ultimate coup came in late 1945 with the creation of United World Pictures, a coproduction and global distribution setup with a major U.S. independent, International Pictures, as well as Universal Pictures. By then, his holdings had spread to Canada, Australia, and India as well as the United States, and he directly or indirectly controlled 80 percent of the film industry in Great Britain.[93]

Besides England, Hollywood's most significant wartime foreign markets were Mexico and Argentina. But unlike the booming British market, the two Latin American countries were notable more for Hollywood's efforts and their enormous potential than for producing revenues. While Britain was returning $70–80 million annually to U.S. distributors in the later war years, all of Central and South America combined generated only about $15 million per year. This level of revenue was deemed worthwhile in

*Britain's dominant film moguls
of the 1940s, J. Arthur Rank
and Alexander Korda.*

Hollywood for two reasons, both of which had to do with the political economy of the hemisphere. First and foremost, Latin America was a huge market within the U.S. "sphere of influence" and had only recently begun to develop a modern urban-industrial system. Much of the population was illiterate, only an estimated 10–15 percent were moviegoers (versus 80–90 percent in the United States and England), and there were only about 7,000 movie theaters in all of Central and South America. Nevertheless, these areas represented excellent postwar prospects for Hollywood.[94] Second, enormous pressure was applied by the U.S. government, and particularly by Nelson Rockefeller, the coordinator of inter-American affairs and architect of the good neighbor policy, who deemed movies an important means of advancing U.S. ideology in Latin America.

Although Mexico officially entered the war against the Axis in May 1942, it was not a principal participant and did not undergo a massive defense buildup or war economy as such. Still, its economic and industrial development during the war was substantial, including the rapid expansion of its own movie industry. Mexico produced eighty features in 1942, its highest since the coming of sound. Production fell below sixty in 1943, owing mainly to film stock shortages, then increased again in 1944–1945 despite recurring strikes and labor disputes in the production sector.[95] But by 1944, as Charles Ramirez Berg has pointed out, Mexico was becoming a film production and distribution power in Central America and something of a paradox vis-à-vis Hollywood. While relying heavily on Hollywood for imports, especially for its first-run theaters in Mexico City, Mexico exported its own productions to other Latin nations.[96] In 1944, Mexican films were occupying up to 60 percent of screen time in the major cities of Panama, Costa Rica, and Nicaragua, and even higher percentages in outlying towns and rural areas.[97]

Hollywood developed various strategies to enhance its fortunes in Mexico. Several studios entered into cooperative deals with Mexican producers to make Spanish-language films for the Latin American market, and some studios brought Mexican stars to

FOR WHOM THE BELL TOLLS *(Paramount, 1943) playing at Pathé's Capitolio Theater in Rio de Janeiro, October 1944.*

Hollywood. Most significant, perhaps, was the decision to begin dubbing rather than subtitling Spanish-language versions of Hollywood films (shorts and newsreels as well as features). This practice suited Mexican audiences, who apparently preferred dubbed versions, and it also overcame the illiteracy problem. Metro was the most aggressive company in this regard, creating a special dubbing facility in New York City with about one hundred actors, directors, and technicians, forty of whom were of Latin origin. MGM opened the facility to all the other studio-distributors and itself prepared eighteen features in the first year of operation for release in Latin America.[98]

Argentina presented Hollywood with a very different set of problems and possibilities during the war. Although officially neutral until March 1945, when it finally declared war against the Axis, the Argentine government was fairly sympathetic toward both Germany and Japan. Meanwhile, American and British pictures were routinely banned, newsreels were seized by the government on court orders for including captured German or Japanese footage, rentals were frozen and taxed at exorbitant levels (up to 50 percent), excessive quotas were set, and so on. Problems reached a peak in 1944, when Argentina began to censor Hollywood films as a means of pressuring the U.S. government to provide more raw film stock. The United States responded in August by banning all film and raw stock shipments to Argentina, effectively breaking diplomatic relations with that nation. That same month, strikes and film shortages closed down all production in Argentina.[99] Trade resumed a few months later, although relations remained strained at best. In fact in March 1945, the same month that Argentina declared war on Germany and Japan, it also banned all Spanish-language imports in an effort to stem the growing tide of U.S. and Mexican product. Two months later the ban was lifted by the Argentine courts, as were various other restrictions on U.S. products and revenues. So as the war wound down, prospects for Hollywood in that massive Latin nation began looking up.[100]

The postwar prospects in Nazi-dominated Europe were even better. By 1945, the estimated number of movie theaters worldwide was 60,000; one-third were closed to Hollywood product, and most of those were on the Continent.[101] (According to prewar figures, there were 15,000 theaters in Germany, Italy, and France alone.)[102] Hollywood began planning its postwar recovery in Europe in early 1943 and actually began implementing those plans later that year after Allied victories in North Africa, Sicily, and Italy.[103] Robert Riskin of the OWI did much of this planning, in cooperation with the military occupational forces and the psychological warfare branch of the Allied armies. Riskin even helped select the 40 features and 120 shorts for release in Italy—the first since December 1938—while the U.S. Army purchased and shipped 35mm projection equipment to facilitate exhibition.[104]

The U.S. government's support of Hollywood's postwar plans in Europe was motivated by both political and economic interests. Indeed, the two went hand in hand as the United States tried to sell democracy and free-market capitalism to those dominated by fascist and authoritarian regimes. Communism would be a crucial concern when the postwar era finally arrived, but in the later war years a much greater emphasis was placed on recapturing the French, German, and Italian markets. These countries not only had been closed to American products but had undergone extensive anti-American and pro-fascist propaganda campaigns. The U.S. government saw Hollywood movies as one means of effectively deprogramming the Axis-dominated populace—thus giving the term "postwar reconversion" a rather interesting connotation. The government encouraged Hollywood to consider the postwar political stakes as well. One good example occurred in January 1945, when the OWI and the Office of Censorship denied an export license to UA's TOMORROW THE WORLD (1944), a picture (based on a hit Broadway play) about an American college professor (Fredric March) who adopts his 12-year-old nephew, a German war orphan, and whose family then struggles to deprogram the dedicated young Nazi. In the OWI's view, the picture's portrayal of the Nazis was simply "too sympathetic."[105]

Hollywood executives not only tolerated but welcomed government assistance. They realized that without Washington's help, recovering the foreign markets lost during the war would be difficult if not impossible. The importance of Washington to Hollywood's postwar foreign trade is well illustrated in the industry's dealings with France after its liberation in 1944. The French government threw up one roadblock after another to prevent U.S. distributors from reclaiming the dominant position they had enjoyed before the war. Unlike Germany and Italy, whose production of escapist and entertainment-oriented pictures had all but ceased during the war, France had continued to turn out commercial features under German occupation. After liberation, Charles de Gaulle's government wanted assurances that French theaters would play domestic product in reasonable numbers, and also that French films would receive first-run release in the United States. Such assurances were not forthcoming, so the 108 features which the

Hollywood distributors had dubbed and readied for release were held up by the French government. Moreover, a proposed French ordinance would prohibit the release in France of any picture over two years old, which put 800 or so major Hollywood features released from 1940 to 1942 in jeopardy.[106]

One reason for Hollywood's concern about the French market was the relative health of its exhibition industry. Of the 4,600 theaters in France before the war, only an estimated 300 had been seriously damaged by the fighting, and only half of those were completely destroyed.[107] England, too, had weathered heavy fighting with relatively little damage to exhibition; nearly 5,000 of its prewar total of 5,300 theaters were running at the end of the war.[108] But fighting and air raids had severely depleted exhibition in other principal combatant nations, especially Germany and Japan. Heavy air raids over Germany in 1944–1945 devastated its movie theaters, with the total in Berlin, according to the Department of Commerce, falling from about 400 before the war to only 31 by early 1945. One U.S. official who visited Germany in April said that both the production and exhibition facilities would have to be completely rebuilt after the war.[109] In Japan, meanwhile, where the information dissemination section of General Douglas MacArthur's occupational army coordinated the release of 45 subtitled Hollywood features immediately after the war, the nation's total number of theaters had fallen from nearly 2,000 in the late 1930s to about 900.[110]

Despite devastation, political tangles, and burgeoning foreign competition from England, France, Mexico, and even Russia, the postwar prospects for Hollywood, overall, were extremely positive. In late 1945, reports of foreign revenues from Europe and the Far East indicated that in the three-month period following V-J Day, Hollywood distributors' overseas revenues exceeded those of the entire year of 1941.[111]

The Antitrust Campaign

As mentioned earlier, Hollywood's response to the 1940 consent decree ideally positioned the Big Five for the ensuing war boom. Selling in blocks of five and holding regular trade shows encouraged the major studios to scale back B-movie production and to concentrate on high-end product, and thus they were well prepared for the war-induced market surge of the early 1940s. Meanwhile, the independent exhibitors, whose complaints had initiated the Justice Department suit in 1938, continued to complain about block booking, the run-zone-clearance system, and other unfair trade practices that favored the studio powers. Thus, as the decree's new selling policies finally took effect in September 1941, Attorney General Thurman Arnold already had misgivings about the settlement. And as exhibitor complaints intensified and the market began its record surge in late 1941 and early 1942, Arnold began to seriously consider not settling with Columbia, Universal, and UA before the 1 June 1942 deadline. Not settling would activate the escape clause in the 1940 agreement, effectively voiding the consent decree after only nine months of actual operation, and would send the Justice Department and the majors back to the negotiating table.

The studios were well aware of the independent exhibitors' dissatisfaction with the decree, of course, and of Arnold's misgivings as well. The studios hoped the decree would stand, and those hopes were bolstered in early 1942 when unofficial word came from Washington that there would be a truce on antitrust suits for the duration in those industries involved in war production. But then in April, Arnold announced that the truce did not include the movie industry.[112] The majors, fearing that Arnold might let the escape clause deadline pass, had begun actively working with representatives of both Allied States and the Motion Picture Theater Owners of America on an alternative fair-trade policy. Spearheading this effort was the United Motion Picture Industry (UMPI), an industry organization formed immediately after Pearl Harbor.

The result was the so-called UMPI (or Unity) Plan, a selling formula designed to satisfy not only distributors and exhibitors but the Justice Department as well.[113] The key elements of the UMPI Plan were: features would be offered in blocks of twelve (approximately one-quarter of a company's annual output) and sold quarterly; five of the twelve pictures would be trade-shown, with the other seven identified by synopsis, star, and story (except for Westerns, which could be sold in blocks of six, unscreened, and identified by star only); cancellation would be allowed on none of the five trade-shown pictures but on two of the seven others; prices would be set at the time of booking or notice of availability.[114]

The UMPI Plan was delivered to Arnold in Washington in late May 1942, only days before the escape clause deadline. As expected, Arnold let the deadline pass in June, thus voiding the 1940 consent decree, but he made no immediate ruling on the new plan. Then in August, after two months of deliberation and consultation, Arnold rejected the UMPI Plan owing to concerns about the return to partial blind bidding and the ongoing inequities favoring the distributors' affiliated chains. "More and more competition must be shown," said Arnold in his statement rejecting the plan, "before the Federal Government will agree that the integrated companies are not suppressing competition between independent exhibitors and affiliated houses."[115] Arnold insisted that trade shows continue for all releases, but he left sales policies up to the individual distributors. Acknowledging that the consent decree had not accomplished its original objectives, Arnold warned the studio-distributors that he would continue to evaluate the situation until November 1943, when the three-year decree expired.[116]

In January 1943, Arnold issued another statement seemingly directed at Hollywood. While reaffirming that "our anti-trust laws have had to yield to the emergency," Arnold also asserted that the Justice Department's trust-busting efforts had not been "suspended for the duration."[117] But while those efforts did indeed continue, Arnold himself was no longer in charge. In February, Roosevelt named Thurman Arnold to the circuit court in Washington. Arnold's replacement was Francis Biddle, but the campaign against Hollywood was sustained primarily by Tom C. Clark, the assistant attorney general in charge of the antitrust division, who was as eager as his predecessor to undo the majors' control of the motion picture industry.[118]

The majors, meanwhile, continued to sell in blocks of five or fewer, with the exception of MGM, which went with the UMPI Plan's twelve-picture blocks and modest cancellation options. These sales policies continued through the 1943–1944 season, the only notable change being Warners' decision to adopt a single-picture sales policy.[119] And as negotiations with Clark and with the exhibitors continued, it became increasingly clear that a sales plan which satisfied all parties, including the Justice Department, was all but impossible. While the majors favored the status quo, predictably enough, the independents leaned toward full divorcement, as they had from the outset. The MPTOA favored a freeze on theater-chain expansion by the majors, a return to full-season blocks but with unrestricted 20 percent cancellation rights, and more effective arbitration machinery.

*Newly appointed "trustbuster"
Tom C. Clark.*

These policies, however, were clearly unacceptable to the government, which would not countenance any form of blind selling.[120]

Throughout 1943 and 1944, the majors and the government continued to submit proposals and counterproposals, with the MPTOA and Allied commenting on each round of negotiations. Divorcement was always a consideration, although the Big Five increasingly pinned their hopes on the Justice Department simply declaring a freeze in further chain expansion. Dissatisfaction with the arbitration system became an increasingly important factor, as the system proved so costly, unwieldy, and ineffective that exhibitors stopped filing complaints. Through 1941–1942, the arbitration machinery handled 276 complaints from exhibitors.[121] This was a rather low figure considering the endless complaints about clearance, and in fact about three-fourths of these cases did involve clearance.[122] But in 1943, only 74 cases were filed; in 1944, there were 29.[123]

Clearly the arbitration system was not working, although the declining filings also indicated the rather ambivalent situation for independent exhibitors in 1944. On the one hand, they were boycotting what they considered an inadequate and unfair system; on the other, business was so good that they really had very little to complain about. Indeed, by late 1944 many of the independents seemed to be falling in line with the MPTOA position favoring a freeze over divorcement. As the MPTOA president Ed Kuykendall said in September 1944, "No one in the industry will tell you seriously that theater divorcement will do anything but damage the industry, or will solve the problems of the independent exhibitor."[124]

Any hopes in the industry that Justice would go along with the freeze rather than divorcement were dashed in December 1944 by a Supreme Court decision against the Crescent theater circuit for antitrust violations. Crescent had been convicted in a lower court in Nashville in March 1943 of monopolizing a five-state area in the Southeast and of colluding with the majors for favorable distribution terms—a case quite similar to those pending against the Griffith and Schine circuits in other districts.[125] Crescent appealed to the Supreme Court, basing its defense on what the *Motion Picture Herald* described as "the broad question of the extent of Government power to regulate film trade practices by means of anti-trust actions."[126] But the Supreme Court upheld the lower court, breaking up the Crescent circuit and outlawing preferential treatment by distributors in exchange for favorable runs and clearance. Under the banner headline "Crescent Cues Vast Changes," *Variety* termed this a "smashing victory" for the government and one that "greatly strengthened" Justice's position in future antitrust battles with the other circuits and the Big Five.[127] The majors may have won acquittal in a few relatively minor antitrust suits during the war years, and the Minnesota antitrust laws may have been shot down in the courts, but the Crescent case clearly signaled that the majors were vulnerable on the antitrust issue.[128]

When Tom Clark was promoted to attorney general in early 1945, Robert Wright took over the antitrust division. Wright immediately made it clear that he considered vertical integration an illegal restraint of trade, and that he intended to press the matter in the courts.[129] Outgoing Attorney General Francis Biddle, with successor Clark at his side, stated in his parting address that "it is absolutely essential to divorce theaters from producers," and that doing so was the only way to keep independent exhibitors from "being pretty well squeezed out."[130]

As the war reached an end and the war boom continued, Clark and Wright showed little interest in any agreement with the majors that did not include divorcement. Thus, negotiations reached an impasse and the Paramount suit resumed. On Monday, 8 October 1945, Hollywood's eight major producer-distributors and the Justice Department were back in U.S. district court in New York. That same week, significantly enough, another federal court ruled that the Schine circuit was guilty of restraint of trade and ordered it dissolved. Meanwhile, the Griffith trial had concluded a month earlier and still awaited a decision.[131] With the Justice Department's antitrust campaign against the motion picture powers back in full swing, Wright made short work of the Paramount suit. The trial was concluded in mid-November after only twenty days in court, with oral arguments scheduled for January 1946 and a final decision expected by summer.[132]

While the Paramount suit hung in the balance, the Justice Department hit the industry—and Paramount in particular—with yet another blow on the antitrust front. As Christopher Anderson outlines in chapter 14, Paramount since the late 1930s had been investing in television research and development, had entered partnerships with several firms involved in the manufacture of television sets and video projection systems for movie theaters, and had been buying television stations. In December 1945, the Justice Department charged Paramount and its television partners (Scophony Ltd. of England, DuMont, General Precision Equipment, et al.) with creating a "world cartel and domestic monopoly" in the manufacture and sales of theater projection video technology, mainly through Paramount's control of Scophony's patents in the United States. A page-one *Variety* story on the government suit described Paramount's video holdings as the nation's largest, and also noted that the "FCC has the authority to yank [TV station] licenses and cancel applications" of any company found in violation of antitrust laws.[133] This observation referred, of course, to the other Paramount case being tried in New York federal court.

The new antitrust suit was a cruel coincidence for Paramount and a bitter irony for the studios. The government's laissez-faire attitude in the halcyon 1920s had allowed the studio system to develop, and in the 1930s Roosevelt's national recovery policies provided a government sanction to the studio cartel. By the 1940s, the Hollywood studios ruled the world's largest entertainment industry, but at the very height of their power they were plagued by the government's growing ambivalence about that power. While some in Washington, particularly in the executive branch, relied on Hollywood's support of the nation's wartime and postwar efforts—support that was of value precisely because of the studios' collective power—others sought to undercut that power. The Department of Justice was scarcely alone in this effort, but it had the means and the authority to bring down the Hollywood studios. And in going after the studios' television plans as well as their theater chains and sales practices, the government threatened to cut the studios off from their future as well as their past.

Labor

The motion picture industry, like most major industries in the United States, entered the war era with a firm commitment to increase efficiency and productivity. The unions and guilds made no-strike pledges, and for the most part these were honored from late 1941 until 1945. In Hollywood, which was almost completely unionized by 1941, organized labor's wartime performance was particularly impressive—certainly far better than in other major industries such as steel and mining, which were plagued by wildcat strikes from 1943 onward and in 1944–1945 suffered major strikes requiring government intervention.

The upstart Conference of Studio Unions (CSU), formed in 1941, made real strides during the war in its challenge of IATSE, which was still smarting after a series of prewar setbacks. As the Hollywood labor historian David Prindle aptly describes IATSE's plight: "Its president in prison, its connections to organized crime publicized to the world, its name a synonym for corruption and tyranny, the International Alliance of Theatrical and Stage Employees was, by the beginning of World War II, reeling and vulnerable."[134] Under Herb Sorrell, the CSU's membership grew to about 10,000 studio workers by 1945, while IATSE's fell to around 16,000.[135] IATSE's reach still extended well beyond Hollywood; its real power base was in exhibition (via the projectionists' union), and it also had a solid grip on distribution through the white-collar exchange workers. The only area of the industry outside Hollywood where IATSE's dominance was seriously challenged was New York City, where CIO unions controlled white-collar workers, both in the home offices of the major companies and in the regional exchanges.[136] During the war, in fact, the home offices and overall distribution sector reached the same stage of organization that Hollywood had before the war, with all but the top company executives becoming unionized. The exhibition sector lagged behind, with some work roles and some regions of the country still not organized by the end of the war.

After relative quiet through the early war years, several incidents in 1944 indicated Hollywood's increasingly volatile and politicized labor scene. The first involved the creation of two quasi-political organizations, the Motion Picture Alliance for the Preservation of American Ideals (MPAAI, usually MPA) and the Council of Hollywood Guilds and Unions (CHGU). The Motion Picture Alliance was formed in February 1944 by a group of notable Hollywood conservatives, including Gary Cooper, Walt Disney, King Vidor, the writer Casey Robinson, and the art director Cedric Gibbons; the producer-director Sam Wood was elected as its first president. According to *Variety*, the Alliance was formed in response to a Writers Congress meeting at UCLA that the Alliance founders felt was Communist-inspired; the organization's goal was to combat communism, fascism, and other alien "isms" in Hollywood.[137] In a brochure published in 1944, the Alliance defined its mission as follows:

> Our purpose is to uphold the American way of life, on the screen and among screen workers; to educate, not to smear.
>
> We seek to make a rallying place for the vast, silent majority of our fellow workers; to give voice to their unwavering loyalty to democratic forms and so to drown out the highly vocal, lunatic fringe of dissidents; to present to our fellow countrymen the vision of a great American industry united in upholding the American faith. (Reprinted in Eric Smoodin, *Animating Culture* [New Brunswick, N.J.: Rutgers University Press, 1993], p. 161)

Within weeks of the Alliance's founding, the House Committee on Un-American Activities, the so-called Dies Committee, began checking into the backgrounds of various studio employees; union leaders attributed this activity to the Alliance's efforts.[138] In late June, a counteralliance of sorts was formed by the constituents of 17 Hollywood labor organizations claiming to represent about half of Hollywood's 30,000 workers. In a mass meeting at the Hollywood Women's Club, the group denounced the Alliance as antilabor, anti-unity, racist, and reactionary and voted to create the Council of Hollywood Guilds and Unions. The Council's goal was to counter the Alliance's influence on all fronts, although its title well indicated that organized labor was its primary unifying force.[139]

Two other labor-related flaps in late 1944 indicated the growing tension between IATSE and the CSU, and its potential to generate a major strike. One involved a group of disgruntled extras and bit players who bolted SAG and created the Screen Players Union (SPU). Sorrell and the CSU backed the new union, and support was sufficient to warrant an NLRB certification election in December 1944. Predictably enough, given the ratio of extras and bit players to full-fledged screen actors—a distinction related to the issue of speaking parts, which was in fact key to this dispute—the SPU prevailed.[140] At that point, SAG and IATSE went into action (with heavy AFL support), forming the Screen Extras Guild (SEG) in direct opposition to SPU. Within a matter of months, virtually all screen extras had joined the SEG fold (and thus were under indirect SAG and IATSE control) and the SPU was finished.[141]

While the screen extras skirmish remained just that, another seemingly minor labor flap in late 1944 developed into a much more serious, long-term crisis. In October, a group of set decorators and painters, along with sympathetic machinists, walked out of

MGM when the studio refused to recognize the CSU-backed Studio Set Designers, Illustrators, and Decorators as an official bargaining agent. The studio refused because the seventy-eight-member union was not certified by the War Labor Board, and also because jurisdiction over the decorators was claimed by IATSE. The *Motion Picture Herald* termed the walkout the first major labor problem since 1937, and one of sufficient magnitude, potentially, to completely shut down production.[142] That was precisely what the CSU wanted to convey. There was no doubt of IATSE's ability to shut down production, due largely to its reach into the distribution and exhibition sectors; as the decorators' dispute developed, the central issue became the question of whether the CSU had that kind of clout.[143]

Sorrell tried to resolve the dispute through the WLB as well as the studios; when that effort failed, he officially led the local 1421 of the decorators union out on strike in March 1945. By then, the battle lines were clearly drawn, with the CSU facing off against IATSE not only in a battle for jurisdiction over the decorators but also in a struggle over whether the Hollywood filmmaking machinery would continue running. The studios' alliance with IATSE in the strike gave it an odd labor-management dimension by securing IATSE's commitment to keep the factories operating. (Actually Monogram and PRC, the two weakest studios, recognized CSU jurisdiction and were not subject to the strike.)[144] Thus began the so-called decorators strike of 1945, which dragged on month after month, steadily drawing in other craft unions until some 7,000 workers were

CSU boss Herb Sorrell, whose car window shows signs of a failed assassination attempt in October 1945.

on strike. Sorrell and the CSU were resolute, defying not only the studios and IATSE but the courts as well, which ruled that Walsh acted within his rights when he executed an emergency takeover of the decorators union.[145] By summer, the studios were operating near capacity despite picket lines, mounting tensions, sporadic violence, and rising studio overhead costs, which, according to Sorrell, had doubled since March. The strikers, meanwhile, were losing an estimated $2 million per month in wages.[146]

Hollywood became increasingly divided over the strike. The conservative Screen Actors Guild sided with IATSE, while the left-leaning Screen Writers Guild voted to support the CSU and to honor the picket lines. The AFL president, William Green, failing to resolve the dispute between the two AFL-affiliated groups, publicly criticized both parties and washed his hands of the entire affair. The AFL's archrival, the CIO, voted to support the strike, while the powerful Teamsters opposed it.[147] The war's end in August brought a sudden increase in the manpower supply in Hollywood, but V-J Day was tempered by what the *Motion Picture Herald* termed the "continuing state of strike-siege." The studios now had a huge supply of carpenters, painters, machinists, electricians, and others from the nearby aircraft plants to replace the CSU strikers. Still, noted the *Herald*, "the only way producers can avail themselves of a labor supply dumped at their door by the warplants is to route workers in via IATSE membership and across CSU picket lines. It can be done, but it isn't simple."[148]

That proved to be an understatement. The strike became steadily more militant after V-J Day, with sympathetic workers from Lockheed joining the CSU pickets, who battled IATSE strikebreakers outside various studios. In October, the isolated fistfights and rock throwings erupted into violent riots as the strike became front-page news nationwide.[149] The NLRB in mid-October announced the results of another election favoring the CSU-backed local (55 to 45), but that scarcely stemmed the tide of violence or moved the strike any closer to resolution. The heaviest violence occurred outside Warners, where production closed down completely for several days. While Jack Warner and his fellow executives looked on from studio rooftops inside the walled compound, studio guards and Burbank police waged a pitched battle with picketers. Sorrell then shifted the attack to Paramount, where about fifty were injured when IATSE workers crashed the CSU picket lines.[150]

Under pressure from Congress and the Labor Department, not to mention the California state authorities and an outraged public, the Hollywood powers finally resolved the dispute in late October during the thirty-second week of the strike. The key figure in that effort was a relative newcomer to Hollywood, Eric Johnston. A conservative businessman and recent president of the U.S. Chamber of Commerce, Johnston succeeded the venerable Will Hays as president of the MPPDA in September 1945. To his credit, Johnston quickly took charge of the strike situation. In a daylong session behind closed (and locked) doors at the Netherland Plaza Hotel in Washington, D.C., Johnston, Walsh, and various representatives of the industry and the AFL worked out an agreement whereby local 1421 was officially recognized and the 7,000 CSU workers returned to work, with their replacements kept on stand-by status for a 60-day arbitration period—at an added studio expense of an estimated $325,000 per week.[151]

In dollar figures, the strike wound up costing the strikers $15–16 million in lost wages, and it cost the studios around $10 million in additional overhead. But there were other costs as well. While Sorrell and the CSU won recognition for the decorators union, they failed to close down Hollywood production. The rift between competing labor factions, especially the CSU and IATSE, was now wider than ever, and the studios

The strike at Warners turns violent. Studio executives were on roof of building (upper right).

also had grown increasingly hostile toward and suspicious of the CSU and its supporters. That did not bode well for the postwar era: workers were demanding a larger share
of the industry's record profits, but the war-induced economic prosperity was bound to
level off. *Variety,* in its year-end story on the labor situation in Hollywood, termed the
decorators strike "the most disastrous strike in the film industry's history," but *Variety*
expected more of the same as new contracts were being negotiated for 20,000 studio
workers.[152]

Thus, 1945 ended with the prospect of labor strife and the antitrust trial casting a
dark cloud over what should have been Hollywood's brightest year ever. Indeed, these
events marked the rather ignominious end to the war era generally—an era that had
seen the Hollywood studios accomplish more than in any other four-year period in their
history.

6

The Hollywood Studio System, 1942–1945

At 11:26 A.M. on 7 December 1941, news of the Japanese attack at Pearl Harbor disrupted what was, by all accounts, a clear and quiet Sunday morning in Los Angeles. The news itself hit like an explosion, throwing the entire area into panic and confusion. The Hollywood movie colony, enjoying its weekly respite from an otherwise nonstop production schedule, was soon bustling with activity. In the first hours and days of the war, that activity had little to do with filmmaking. Makeshift air-raid shelters were constructed on movie lots, while dimout and blackout plans were quickly formulated. Studio employees fretted about Japanese attacks and the resemblance of the sound stages to aircraft plants.

Meanwhile, studio executives worried about the wartime status of Hollywood films and filmmaking. The U.S. entry into the war actually put the studios in a curious bind. On the one hand, there was the possibility of nationalization by the government and the suspension of all commercial operations "for the duration." On the other hand, the studios faced the prospect of playing a marginal role (or less) in Washington's overall war plans. After Pearl Harbor, as Richard Lingeman has noted, "the movie business was just another war industry eager to cooperate [with the government] out of fear that it would be considered 'non-essential' and strangled by lack of priorities."[1]

As seen in chapter 5, within two weeks President Roosevelt gave Hollywood the green light to continue commercial filmmaking, but with express instructions regarding the studios' active support of the U.S. war effort. Hollywood and Washington quickly adapted a workable wartime rapport, and the studios cooperated with both the government and the military in the production of war films. Several lesser Hollywood plants— Fox's old B-picture studio on Western Avenue, for example, and both the Disney and Hal Roach studios—were completely retooled for war-film production.

Hollywood swarmed with military personnel, including a number of filmmakers who joined up to do documentary work. Several top studio executives took military commissions, began wearing uniforms, and insisted on being addressed by rank. Jack Warner, for instance, signed up with the Army Air Corps and thereafter became "Colonel Warner," even in interoffice memos. Of the 2,700 workers who left Hollywood for active military duty in 1942, however, few were top studio executives. One notable exception was Fox's production chief, Darryl Zanuck, whose 1942–1943 stint as a commander in the Army Signal Corps included considerable action in North Africa.[2]

169

Moguls in uniform: Darryl Zanuck, Jack Warner, British General Bernard "Monty" Montgomery, and Harry Cohn.

Income, Output, and the Balance of Studio Power

The most significant developments in the Hollywood studio system during World War II were increased studio revenues (and profits) and decreased output. While the lower output of films was related to various wartime factors—the manpower shortage, for example, and restricted supplies of film stock—these cutbacks resulted more than anything else from surging wartime revenues. Simply stated, the first-run movie market was so bullish after Pearl Harbor that the major studios quickly saw the logic of increasing their emphasis on top product while cutting back on their overall output of films.

Indeed, the wartime reduction in motion picture production and overall releases was most acute, by far, among the Big Five integrated majors. During the five years before Pearl Harbor, the Big Eight producer-distributors together released 1,833 pictures. In the five years after Pearl Harbor (1942–1946), they released 1,395—a decline of 438 pictures, or nearly 25 percent. The three major-minors accounted for virtually none of that decline: Universal and Columbia averaged 50 pictures per year during both periods, and UA just over 20. The Big Five, meanwhile, declined from an average of 50 releases annually per company in the five prewar years to only 30 per year from 1942 through 1946.[3]

The Big Five had begun to scale back output in 1941, but clearly the real cuts came with the war itself. In a one-year span from 1942 to 1943, Warners cut its output from

34 to 21 pictures, MGM from 49 to 33, Fox from 51 to 33, and Paramount from 44 to 30. RKO's big drop came a year later, falling from 44 to 31 releases. Once instituted, these reductions held throughout the war, thus creating a very different release pattern for the early and later war years:

Table 6.1
MAJOR STUDIO OUTPUT, 1940–1942 AND 1943–1945

Company	Number of Releases		% Decline
	1940–1942	*1943–1945*	
20th Century–Fox	150	86	42.6
MGM	144	94	34.7
Paramount	137	85	37.9
RKO	136	108	20.5
Warner Bros.	127	59	53.5
Total	694	432	37.7

SOURCE: Motion Picture Year Book.

In terms of studio profits, all of the Big Eight fared well during the war, with the integrated majors enjoying the benefits of the war boom to a far greater degree than their

A Warner Bros. soundstage in 1942—shown here filming THIS IS THE ARMY *(Warners, 1943), a huge wartime hit, in between two other major studio productions.*

competitors. As in the 1930s and early 1940s, the Big Eight took about 95 percent of the total market, with the Big Five consistently accounting for 90 percent of industry profits. Revenues and profits for the integrated majors were far beyond Depression and prewar totals: combined industry profits climbed from just under $20 million in 1939 and 1940 to $34 million in 1941, $50 million in 1942, and then right around $60 million for the next three years.[4] A key factor here, of course, was the relative size of each major company's theater holdings. Its theater holdings gave Paramount a huge advantage over the other majors and left both MGM and RKO at an obvious disadvantage.[5] Thus, the balance of power among the Big Five that had begun to shift in 1940–1941 changed even more during the war; MGM was steadily overtaken by Paramount and Fox, with Warners close behind.

Looking at the total revenues, net profits, and profit shares of all the Big Eight during the war era, the collective domination of the Big Five and the relative balance of power among the majors—and especially Paramount, Fox, Metro, and Warners—is readily apparent.

Table 6.2

STUDIO FINANCES, 1942–1945

	Total Revenues ($ millions)	Net Profits ($ millions)	% Profit Share
Paramount	$575.6	$57.8	24.8
MGM	557.6	52.6	22.6
Fox	572.4°	46.5	20.0
Warners	519.8	33.7	14.5
RKO	321.2	18.8	8.1
Universal	188.2	14.1	6.0
Columbia	132.7	7.3	3.1
UA	109.5	1.4	0.6

SOURCE: Figures from Joel Finler, *The Hollywood Story* (New York: Crown, 1988), pp. 31, 286–87; and Christopher H. Sterling and Timothy R. Haight, *The Mass Media: The Aspen Institute Guide to Communications Industry Trends* (New York: Praeger, 1978), p. 184. See also Douglas Gomery, *The Hollywood Studio System* (New York: St. Martin's, 1986).

°Note that the Fox revenue total for 1942 does not include its theater income. Factoring this in would increase Fox's revenue total to about $625 million—the highest revenue total for the war era.

It is important to note that the majors did not enter the war with plans to reduce output but did so rather haphazardly in 1942–1943 in response to changing industry conditions. Consider the case of 20th Century–Fox during this period. In May 1942, Fox announced plans to spend $28 million on fifty-two features for the 1942–1943 season.[6] Three months later, as the marketplace continued to heat up, Fox decided to cut ten B's out of its schedule (following the lead of Paramount and Warners).[7] Then in September 1942, Fox announced that its profits for the previous six months were up 300 percent compared with the same period in 1941; Fox planned further reductions, with an even heavier concentration on first-run features.[8]

The wartime decrease in output among the Big Five was accompanied by steadily increasing production costs. Between 1942 and 1945, the average cost per feature rose from $336,600 to $554,386, and the average number of shooting days per picture climbed from twenty-two to thirty-three. The total cost for all film production in Hollywood more than doubled in that period, from $198.5 million to $402 million.[9] This increase was due in part to war-induced inflation, of course, but the primary factor was the steady shift to high-end production. By 1945, the Big Five were concentrating almost exclusively on A-class product for the first-run market, the major-minors dominated the middle ground (though they put out a few modest A pictures and a few low-grade B's), and the minors concentrated on the low end. A clear indication of this general range is provided by these figures charting the estimated costs on 300 studio productions in 1944:

Table 6.3
BUDGET RANGE OF STUDIO FEATURES, 1944

Company	Over $500,000	$200,000– 500,000	$100,000– 200,000	Under $100,000
MGM	21	5	0	0
20th Century–Fox	20	2	3	1
Paramount	17	2	4	4
Warner Bros.	12	2	2	0
RKO	9	12	9	1
UA	3	10	0	0
Universal	10	17	17	5
Columbia	5	10	24	3
Republic	1	3	12	7
Monogram	0	2	3	21
PRC	0	0	2	19

SOURCE: "All Features Released in 1945," *Box Office Digest*, 6 January 1945, p. 18.

Another factor in the majors' decreased wartime output was the stockpiling of product. Initially the impulse to stockpile pictures resulted from the sales policies under the 1940 consent decree. Since blind bidding was prohibited and all pictures had to be trade-shown, the studios were compelled to have their pictures ready well in advance of release. Once the war broke out, large trade shows and national sales conventions became impractical and were phased out in lieu of advance screenings of individual films at key exchanges prior to release. Thus, the studios could have reverted to a tighter schedule from completion to release, but by then war conditions encouraged stockpiling.

Early in the war, interestingly enough, stockpiling was the result of the studios stepping up production in response to war-related restrictions, anticipated shortages, and general uncertainties. As *Variety* noted in late 1942: "In a race against the time when wartime exigencies are expected to circumscribe activities via further inroads on talent, technicians, material and equipment, Hollywood studios are steaming ahead at the speediest production clip in history in order to build up their picture stocks."[10] As those stockpiles grew, along with inflated costs and first-run revenues, the studios found that they could continue stockpiling while actually cutting back production.[11]

In other words, as the war went on, stockpiling was essentially a function of the over-heated first-run marketplace. As revenues and market conditions outran even the most optimistic projections year after year from 1942 to 1946, long runs and holdovers became the rule as the studios milked their top features for every possible dollar. Thus the urge to stockpile product—studios shelved pictures which were ready for release for two years or more. Indeed, much of the falloff between 1942 and 1943 was less a matter of the Big Five *producing* fewer pictures than of *releasing* fewer pictures.

The backlogs grew rapidly in 1942 and early 1943, ranging between 100 and 200 features completed and awaiting release.[12] At the end of the war, the *Motion Picture Herald* pegged the backlog at 203 pictures, while *Variety* estimated an industrywide inventory of $250,000,000.[13] By then, the backlogs were part of overall postwar strategy; the studios anticipated changes in the tax codes as well as a box-office surge when servicemen returned and wartime restrictions were eased.[14] That strategy paid off: 1946 saw the Big Five's revenues and profits burst to even higher levels in the last shuddering concussion of the war boom.

Studio Operations and Market Strategies

THE MAJOR-MINORS AND THE MINOR STUDIOS

The war era saw a growing rift between the Big Five and the other studios in terms of production and management operations as well as overall market strategies. The major studios, with their superior resources, were able to respond to the wartime market more aggressively than the lesser studio powers. While the Little Three and the Poverty Row studios certainly benefited from the war boom, their overall production and sales strategies, for the most part, remained quite consistent during the war.

The one exception was United Artists. Its wartime success is scarcely surprising, given its established focus on high-end releases and the wartime premium on A-class pictures. While Universal and Columbia were content to simply sustain their prewar policies and enjoy the financial benefits of the war boom, UA under David Selznick lined up an impressive array of talent and film projects. Selznick signed the MGM producer Hunt Stromberg to a lucrative five-picture deal in 1942, for instance, and in early 1943 he closed a five-picture deal with James Cagney, just off his Oscar-winning performance in YANKEE DOODLE DANDY (1942).[15] Both contracts involved financing as well as distribution, a significant innovation for UA in the 1940s, and one that attracted a number of independents. In late 1943, the *Motion Picture Herald* reported that UA had a record sixteen units "currently active."[16]

While those units were active, however, they were not all that productive, and in fact UA was in desperate need of product. Thus, in a stunning reversal of form, the UA board decided in mid-1942 and again in mid-1943 to purchase packages of stockpiled second-rate pictures from Paramount. UA paid $4.8 million for a total of twenty-one pictures in the two deals—less than $250,000 per film. The studio acquired a few A pictures, but most were B's and series Westerns, including a number of Hopalong Cassidy programmers—hardly in the UA tradition. And in a further break with tradition, UA abandoned its long-standing singles-only policy and sold these pictures in blocks.[17]

The Paramount packages covered UA's shortfall, although they did not keep UA in the black. Incredibly, UA actually showed a net loss in 1944—the only company to accomplish such a feat during the war. But as Tino Balio suggests, the most severe loss was UA's prestige, since by 1944 it was "supplying second features for double bills almost exclusively."[18] Moreover, Selznick's relationship with the UA board, and particularly with Chaplin and Pickford, deteriorated steadily during the war, thus aggravating the company's long-standing instability.

Wartime production and market strategies on Poverty Row, meanwhile, were still geared to the subsequent-run markets—especially at Monogram and PRC, which continued to struggle simply to break even, despite the war boom. But Republic, always the strongest of the minors, enjoyed annual profits in the half-million-dollar range and thus was able to venture cautiously into A-class production.[19] President Herbert J. Yates replaced Gene Autry with Roy Rogers as Republic's resident singing cowboy star, and Rogers likewise played himself in an uninterrupted series of near-A formula Westerns.[20] Equally important to Yates's A-class aspirations was John Wayne, who continued to alternate between loan-outs to the majors and starring roles in high-end Republic productions.[21] His value to the studio was underscored in 1945, when Republic signed Wayne to a star-producer deal which included 10 percent of the gross on his pictures. Yates made other important moves to crack the first-run market in 1945, including deals with the producer-director Frank Borzage and the writer-producer-director Ben Hecht.[22]

The most significant wartime development at Monogram was the production of what were being termed "exploitation pictures," which *Variety* defined as "films with some timely or currently controversial subject which can be exploited, capitalized on in publicity and advertising." These ranged from offbeat actioners like WOMEN IN BONDAGE (1943), about a women's prison, to topical melodramas like WHERE ARE YOUR CHILDREN? (1943), an exposé of juvenile delinquency. The most successful of these was DILLINGER (1945), Monogram's first release to earn over $1 million, and a picture whose graphic violence and glorification of the legendary gangster incurred the wrath of critics and parents' groups.[23]

PRC made some efforts to upgrade its product line during the war, but it continued to specialize in exceptionally low-budget Westerns (some shot in only two to three days), along with its signature B-grade crime dramas and actioners. While none of these broke through commercially on the scale of DILLINGER, several PRC pictures directed by Edgar G. Ulmer were modest hits and have become minor classics, including offbeat musicals like JIVE JUNCTION (1943) and CLUB HAVANA (1945) and provocative thrillers like STRANGE ILLUSION and DETOUR (both 1945).[24]

THE MAJOR STUDIOS

The integrated majors saw radical changes during the war, owing primarily to the volatile market conditions and the increased importance and clout of producers and top talent. Perhaps the single most important development was the sharp acceleration of unit production and hyphenate status for above-the-line contract talent. While these changes had considerable impact on production management, studio management—executive control of the company at large—changed very little. In fact, the war boom reinforced the Big Five's established hierarchy of executive power, with ultimate studio authority still residing in the New York office.

Both Fox and RKO underwent changes in top management early in the war that underscored the market-driven mentality of the period. In March 1942, Fox's president, Sidney Kent, died suddenly of a heart attack at age 56.[25] Coming in the wake of the Fox board chairman Joe Schenck being sentenced to federal prison, Kent's death left a void

Republic's Herb Yates signs Ben Hecht to a producer-director-writer deal in 1945.

atop the executive ranks. The Fox board responded in April by appointing Spyros Skouras, then head of Fox theater operations, as company president. The board also named as its chairman Wendell Willkie, just off his successful industry defense at the Senate propaganda hearings in late 1941. Willkie served essentially as a figurehead, assuming various public relations duties, but that role was cut short by his own untimely death (at age 55) in 1944. At that point, Spyros Skouras became the sole chief executive, while his brother Charlie, another theater man, took over Fox's exhibition operations.[26]

RKO, meanwhile, underwent a management shake-up which accompanied the ascent of the Wall Street financier Floyd Odlum to board chairman of the company. Odlum's Atlas Corporation had begun investing in RKO in the 1930s, and by 1942 Odlum had acquired controlling interest.[27] Odlum promptly fired RKO's president, George Schaefer, who had overseen both the New York office and studio operations, and replaced him with two executives: Peter Rathvon, a Wall Street colleague of Odlum (and longtime RKO financial adviser), who took over the New York office as president of the RKO parent company; and the sales chief Ned Depinet, who became president of RKO-Radio Pictures. Meanwhile, Odlum replaced Joe Breen as studio production chief with the head of RKO theater operations, Charles Koerner. The new team quickly turned things around: RKO's profits rose from $600,000 in 1942 to $6.9 million one year later.[28]

Thus, Fox and RKO followed the prewar strategy of Paramount and Universal, installing men with theater and sales backgrounds as top corporate executives. *Variety* speculated in March 1942 about the role of these former theater executives "in shaping

Old power/new power: Paramount's Barney Balaban, new UA independent James Cagney, Loew's Nicholas Schenck, and new Fox president Spyros Skouras in August 1942.

studio production policies," but in fact the chief executives at all of the integrated majors had even less control over actual filmmaking operations than ever.[29] A governing paradox of the period was that market conditions, and particularly the increased emphasis on A-class product, brought a general shift in production management away from corporate and studio executives and into the hands of top talent. This shift was more pronounced at some companies than others, of course, as the studios responded in quite different ways both to market conditions and to the prospect of yielding more creative control to their top producers, directors, and writers.

MGM and Warner Bros. provide an illuminating contrast in this regard. Warners, without question the most factory-oriented of the Big Five in the 1930s, overhauled both its market strategy and production operations during the war. In cutting its output in half during the war, Warners completely abandoned both B-picture production and block booking, producing only A-class products which were sold on a unit basis. The last vestiges of the old Warners vanished with two telling events at the dawn of the war era. In September 1941, Warners' veteran B-unit head Bryan Foy was released from his contract. (Fox, less eager to eliminate B production, immediately picked him up.)[30] Then in February 1942, Warners made an even more dramatic change: the longtime studio production chief Hal Wallis stepped down, signing a new contract as a unit producer.[31] Jack Warner continued to oversee plant operations and to negotiate contracts and such, but for the first time since the 1920s—dating back to Darryl Zanuck's regime as production boss at Warners—no individual executive oversaw production. Thus, Warner Bros. underwent a belated shift during the war from a central-producer system to a unit-producer system and actually began assigning on-screen producer credit for the first time in 1942.

MGM, meanwhile, did reduce its output by some 30 percent during the war but proved altogether unwilling to adjust its basic production and management policies. MGM continued to turn out high-gloss, high-cost product, with Louis B. Mayer actually expanding the studio's bloated and inefficient supervisory system despite the decreased output. All production decisions were made by Mayer and his executive committee, comprising four MGM vice presidents and an elite group of eight producers, with another thirty or so producers supervising actual filmmaking. Metro also maintained the factory-system model, with multiple writers and directors working on individual pictures—a practice by then deemed wasteful and counterproductive by the other majors. An MGM study done in 1942 indicated that fourteen to sixteen writers worked on the average studio project, far more than was common elsewhere.[32] And in 1945, a trade journal reported that MGM had 116 writers under contract—three to four times the number of contract writers at the other studios.[33]

Despite MGM's efforts to maintain a central-producer (by committee) system, however, studio authority over actual filmmaking continued to erode during the war, because of the unprecedented demand for A-class product and the consequent increase in independent and unit production.

The Wartime Surge in Independent Production

In February 1942, *Variety* ran a prescient analysis of the unit phenomenon as it had developed over the preceding months. In 1941, noted *Variety,* "company after company has swung away from the system of front-office assignment of producers, which they have used for years, toward the unit idea." Now the war economy "is expected to still further spur the rush toward unit production which has marked the Hollywood scene for the past few months." Thus, predicted *Variety*, "virtually all of Hollywood's important pictures will be coming from these more-or-less independent producers."[34] The qualifier "more-or-less" was necessary because of the studios' ultimate control of distribution and first-run exhibition, and because the studios provided financing and production resources for most independents.

This latter point meant, in effect, that some filmmakers were more independent than others. *Variety* posited a "first class" of independents which included producers like Goldwyn and Selznick, who relied on particular studio-distributors but had their own production facilities and contract personnel, and who could handle their own financing. In the "second class" were contract producers and hyphenates like MGM's Hunt Stromberg and RKO's Orson Welles, who could "walk out at any time" and sign with a rival studio. Industry conditions were such that top producers were becoming increasingly mobile: "Hollywood has become such a checkerboard of jumping producers that it's almost impossible to keep up with the moves."

Variety concluded with the results of a "quick industry survey" naming the top ten unit heads in Hollywood: Sam Goldwyn, David Selznick, Jesse Lasky, Cecil B. DeMille, Walt Disney, Charlie Chaplin, Orson Welles, Preston Sturges, Jules Levey, and Alexander Korda. This group included filmmaking hyphenates, straight producers, and even a few production executives, suggesting that the term "independent" still was being applied rather haphazardly, even in the trade press. And interestingly enough, only a few of those among *Variety*'s top ten were very productive during the war in terms of a steady output of "important" pictures. But their varied efforts illustrate the range of independent activity during the war, and so a brief survey of *Variety*'s 1942 inventory of top independents proves rather illuminating.

Charlie Chaplin and Orson Welles, Hollywood's two most celebrated independents at the time, were essentially inactive during the war. This was no surprise in Chaplin's case, because he typically spent four or five years between finished films. Since the release of THE GREAT DICTATOR in late 1940, Chaplin still had not decided on his next project. Welles's situation was quite another matter. His 1942 excursion to South America for the experimental amalgam of documentary and fiction IT'S ALL TRUE went badly owing to cost overruns, inclement weather, and other complications. RKO eventually stopped funding the project, and Schaefer's departure left Welles without support at the studio. RKO's new chief executive, Peter Rathvon, refused to renew Welles's contract, so Welles went freelance and spent the rest of the war era trying in vain to buy the IT'S ALL TRUE footage from RKO so he could complete the project. He also tried to initiate other independent projects, including an experimental documentary-drama about the infamous French "Bluebeard," Henri Landru. Welles eventually sold the idea to Chaplin and it provided the basis for Chaplin's controversial postwar satire MONSIEUR VERDOUX (1947).[35]

The two other hyphenates on *Variety*'s list, the producer-director Cecil B. DeMille and the writer-producer-director Preston Sturges, had units at Paramount and enjoyed considerable success during the war. DeMille produced two prestige pictures, REAP THE WILD WIND (1942) and THE STORY OF DR. WASSELL (1944); both were commercially successful but failed to impress the critics. Sturges, on the other hand, enjoyed tremendous critical success but only modest box-office returns in a succession of outrageous comedies, including THE PALM BEACH STORY (1942), THE MIRACLE OF MORGAN'S CREEK, HAIL THE CONQUERING HERO, and THE GREAT MOMENT (all 1944). After a bril-

Orson Welles in Brazil, 1942, working on his ill-fated RKO production IT'S ALL TRUE
(shot 1942; released 1993).

liant creative run of eight pictures for Paramount from 1940 to 1944, and at the peak of
his success, Sturges decided to leave for an independent alliance with Howard
Hughes—an ill-fated decision that effectively stalled his career.[36]

Three other independents on *Variety*'s list simply were not all that productive during
the war. Jules Levey and Jesse Lasky produced just three pictures between them, none
of which was successful. The British producer Alexander Korda began the war with a
hit UA release, TO BE OR NOT TO BE (1942), but his London Films company was
plagued by financial problems which eventually caused a split with UA. In early 1943,
the *New York Times* announced that Korda was taking over the MGM-British unit, but
that union resulted in only one picture, PERFECT STRANGERS (U.S. release 1945; British
title VACATION FROM MARRIAGE [1944]). Korda also coproduced several wartime pictures, including SAHARA (1943), directed by his brother Zoltan Korda for Columbia.[37]

The other three on *Variety*'s list, Sam Goldwyn, David Selznick, and Walt Disney,
formed an elite trio as Hollywood's dominant major independent producers, although
they too underwent very different wartime experiences. Of the three, only Goldwyn
maintained business as usual during the war, turning out BALL OF FIRE in 1941, THE
PRIDE OF THE YANKEES in 1942 and THE NORTH STAR in 1943, THE PRINCESS AND THE
PIRATE in 1944, and UP IN ARMS in 1944. All were released by RKO, and all but THE
NORTH STAR were major hits.

Disney continued to release through RKO, but virtually all of Disney's wartime output
directly supported the war effort. A financially crippling studio strike (and settlement) in

1941 and the disappointing box-office returns of the prewar features (PINOCCHIO and FANTASIA in 1940; DUMBO and THE RELUCTANT DRAGON in 1941) encouraged Disney to abandon commercial operations after the release of BAMBI in June 1942 and to concentrate almost exclusively on war-related films. The Disney studio with its 1,200 employees was the only one designated as an official war production plant by the government, and it turned out scores of animated military training films and informational shorts. Disney's cartoons were geared to the war effort as well, although they remained extremely popular with wartime moviegoers. Disney's only feature during the war was an animated documentary on strategic bombing, VICTORY THROUGH AIR POWER (1943).[38]

Selznick, meanwhile, remained inactive as a producer during the early war years, but he quickly expanded his efforts as a talent agent to include the packaging of movie projects. He made enormous profits loaning out such contract talent as Ingrid Bergman, Joan Fontaine, Gregory Peck, Jennifer Jones, Joseph Cotten, Shirley Temple, Dorothy McGuire, and the directors Alfred Hitchcock and Robert Stevenson. Selznick also packaged star, story property and/or script, and other top talent for such films as CLAUDIA (1943) and JANE EYRE (1944), both purchased by Fox. In 1944, Selznick returned to active production with three projects, SINCE YOU WENT AWAY, I'LL BE SEEING YOU, and SPELLBOUND (1945).

The wartime careers of *Variety*'s top ten indicate both the vagaries and the variations of Hollywood independence during that turbulent era, which saw the ranks of so-called independents swell enormously. Indeed, the term was applied to virtually any above-the-line talent not under conventional long-term studio contract—a roster which included James Cagney, Gary Cooper, Lester Cowan, Buddy De Sylva, Arthur Freed, William Goetz, Howard Hawks, Ben Hecht, Mark Hellinger, Alfred Hitchcock, Fritz Lang, Leo McCarey, Dore Schary, Jack Skirball, Edward Small, Leo Spitz, Hunt Stromberg, Jerry Wald, Hal Wallis, and Walter Wanger. Many of these would have been considered simply freelance talent a few years earlier, but the economic and regulatory conditions during the war encouraged noncontract talent to set up independent production companies.

The wartime income tax was a crucial factor in the rise of independent companies. Its effect was described in detail by the industry executive Ernest Borneman in a *Harper's* piece, "Rebellion in Hollywood: A Study in Motion Picture Finance." The "rebellion," said Borneman, involved Hollywood's "inner circle of top producers, high-priced writers and directors, and the cherished stars," who were "clutching the banner of artistic freedom in one hand and an income tax blank in the other." The rebellion was "touched off inadvertently by the Treasury Department" in that Hollywood filmmakers and artists, "dismayed by wartime tax rates, went into business for themselves as independent producers in order to pay capital gains tax rather than income tax." This invariably entailed setting up a so-called single picture corporation—that is, a film production company created to produce a single feature. After the film's release, the company would be dissolved, its stocks sold, and the profits taxed at the capital gains rate of 25 percent.[39]

This arrangement proved most attractive to those who, by 1942, found themselves in the 80–90 percent income tax bracket. James Cagney, for example, readily acknowledged that his move to independent status with UA in 1942 was motivated largely by the fact that, in 1941, his earnings of over $350,000 with Warners yielded an after-tax income of only $70,000.[40] Established independents took to this strategy as well. Sam Goldwyn, for instance, was advised in November 1942 by his New York accounting firm

Walt Disney (right) confers with Alexander P. de Seversky, author of VICTORY
THROUGH AIR POWER.

to liquidate Samuel Goldwyn, Inc., and create a succession of "collapsible corporations" for each of his RKO productions, so that he could "convert ordinary income into capital gains." Goldwyn readily complied, and thus his wartime productions were put out by a series of new companies, including Avalon, Regent, Beverly, and Trinity Productions.[41]

As the independent trend accelerated and the market continued to heat up, the movie industry also underwent dramatic changes in production financing. As Borneman noted in his 1946 article: "In the unprecedented boom market of the past five years, it has no longer been necessary [for independents] to make pre-production deals with a major distributor in order to get production capital." Not only were independents less dependent on studios for financing, notes Borneman, but they also found a viable alternative to banks in the form of companies designed to finance movies. "Motion picture finance corporations have arisen in Hollywood, New York, and Chicago, which will put up all the necessary production capital, put up all the salaries, including that of the producer-promoter himself, and take one half of the net proceeds for their pains." Lester Cowan, for instance, used Domestic Industries, Inc., of Chicago to finance Tomorrow the World (1944) and The Story of GI Joe (1945), both of which were produced by single-picture corporations and released through UA.[42]

Studio-based Units and In-house Independents

The studios had little choice but to accommodate filmmakers who expressed independent inclinations, given the wartime demand for top talent and for a steady flow of high-end product. Thus, by early 1944, according to *Variety,* "Hollywood's most important independent producers [were] setting virtually their own terms with distributors."[43] At that time, 71 units were scheduled to deliver 196 features over the coming year at a total projected cost of $180 million—a figure equal to the combined production budgets of several major studios.[44] UA, a company designed solely to release major independent pictures, accounted for half of these. But UA's declining wartime fortunes due to management and marketing difficulties encouraged other studios to compete with it— invariably adapting the "UA model" to their own production needs. Thus, by 1944–1945, many independents were finding better terms elsewhere, particularly at Universal and RKO.

Universal signed deals with many in-house independents during the war, including Charles K. Feldman, Gregory La Cava, Frank Lloyd, Jack Skirball, and Walter Wanger. The most significant of these was Wanger, who entered a quasi-permanent relationship with Universal after producing Eagle Squadron in 1942. Wanger then signed to produce Arabian Nights (1942), a costume romance with Jon Hall and Maria Montez, and Universal's first Technicolor feature. The picture was a success, and it set the pattern for a series of limited contracts between Wanger and the studio. The deals called for Wanger to supply the story idea for each picture; once it was approved, he received $50,000 for script development. Wanger and the studio boss Cliff Work worked out the cast, crew, and budget, and Wanger then had complete control until the preview stage. He was paid a weekly salary during production and then split any net profits with Universal after release. Most of Wanger's films were scripted by Norman Reilly Raine and directed by Jack Rawlins, both freelancers; otherwise, he relied on Universal's contract talent.[45]

Thus, Wanger, even without the production facilities and contract personnel of film-makers like Goldwyn and Selznick, became a major independent producer through his connection with Universal. He maintained creative and supervisory control of his pictures, while providing Universal with a prestige-level unit and a steady string of commercial hits, including GUNG HO! (1943), LADIES COURAGEOUS (1944), and SALOME, WHERE SHE DANCED (1945). Wanger's commercial success at Universal enabled him to pursue a more ambitious venture with the studio in 1945. After signing another five-picture deal with the studio to deliver more standard A-class fare, Wanger entered a very different kind of arrangement in the form of Diana Productions. Wanger set up the company as a partnership with his wife, the actress Joan Bennett, and the director Fritz Lang, with Universal to supply one-half the finances and to distribute Diana's output of one or two pictures per year—beginning with SCARLET STREET in 1945.[46]

Universal entered several other new independent arrangements in 1945, signing Mark Hellinger Productions as well as Leo Spitz and William Goetz's International Pictures. Those deals, along with already established ones, gave Universal as strong a lineup of independent unit producers as any of the Hollywood majors except RKO.[47] At that point, RKO's outside-producer ranks included Walt Disney, Sam Goldwyn, Arthur Rank, Liberty Pictures (Frank Capra, George Stevens, and William Wyler), Jesse Lasky, Alfred Hitchcock, and Dore Schary. Several of these producers, however, were signed

Walter Wanger signing one of his many quasi-independent deals with Universal's Nate Blumberg.

in 1945 as the boom reached its peak, although Goldwyn, Disney, and Hitchcock (via Selznick) had played a crucial role in RKO's wartime success.

While RKO and Universal successfully exploited the in-house independent trend during the war, both studios also were shifting to a unit-production system for top contract talent. In fact, both developed a clear three-tier system during the war, with in-house independents supplying most of the A-class product, contract talent in studio-based units turning out a few A's but mainly near-A's, and the factory assembly line cranking out routine B's. The most significant of Universal's studio-based units was overseen by the writer John Grant, who graduated to writer-producer status in 1944 and produced the Abbott and Costello vehicles. Another important studio-based setup was the Sherlock Holmes unit under the producer-director Roy William Neill. Just before the war, Universal bought the rights to Arthur Conan Doyle's detective stories along with the contracts of Basil Rathbone and Nigel Bruce from Fox. Neill put Holmes and Watson through their paces in a dozen pictures during the war, developing a unit that was as consistent and dependable—if not quite as profitable—as Grant's Abbott and Costello unit.

RKO, meanwhile, enjoyed considerable success with a series of near-A horror films produced by Val Lewton, who left Selznick in early 1942 and signed with RKO as writer-producer. The first of these was CAT PEOPLE, a late-1942 release which was a modest commercial and critical hit and established what Lewton described (in a letter to Selznick) as "our little horror unit."[48] The Lewton unit continued to turn out modest horror films—notably I WALKED WITH A ZOMBIE and THE LEOPARD MAN in 1943, THE CURSE OF THE CAT PEOPLE in 1944, and THE BODY SNATCHER and ISLE OF THE DEAD in 1945—which were consistent moneymakers for RKO. These were scarcely on a par with RKO's A-class projects, however, nor was Lewton, because of his contractual status with RKO, in the same league with the in-house independents.

This distinction is crucial, particularly with regard to the other integrated major studios. Simply stated, the rest of the Big Five had both the production resources and the economic leverage to resist the in-house independent trend, and they went on record publicly—and often quite vocally—as being utterly at odds with the trend. *Variety* in July 1943, for instance, in one of the many trade press stories about the majors' resistance to "indie units," noted that "Paramount, Warners and 20th Century–Fox have no outside producers."[49] But in actuality, the majors were, in various ways, modifying the trend toward independent units to accommodate their top talent, usually through the relative autonomy of unit status and, in rare cases, profit-participation deals.

MGM and Fox remained most resistant to the in-house independent trend during the war, with MGM granting unit status to contract producers like Arthur Freed and Dore Schary, while Zanuck eschewed unit designation even for his top producers and directors. Interestingly enough, Fox had begun to develop unit production under Bill Goetz in the early war years while Zanuck was away with the Signal Corps, and Goetz actually signed a few outside deals—including a two-picture deal with Selznick for Hitchcock's services. Zanuck's return in 1943 effectively stifled that effort, however, and it ended Goetz's tenure with Fox as well. Goetz left in late 1943 to form International Pictures in partnership with Leo Spitz. The longtime Fox writer-producer Nunnally Johnson also left upon Zanuck's return, because Zanuck refused to let him have his own unit and a profit participation deal.[50] Johnson went on to form a successful independent company with Gary Cooper.

The situation was more varied and complex at Warners, which developed a range of strategies to accommodate the independent urge of top talent. Ample evidence of these varied strategies is provided by three early-1942 deals between Warners and Hal Wallis, Howard Hawks, and Mark Hellinger. The Wallis contract of January 1942, as mentioned earlier, signaled the end of Warners' central-producer setup. Because neither Wallis nor Warners wished to produce "as large a number" of pictures as in previous years, Wallis became responsible for only four pictures per annum. The contract was to run four years, starting at $4,000 per week, with Wallis to receive an additional 10 percent of the gross receipts once his pictures returned 125 percent of their costs. The participation angle marked a radical departure for Warners, as did the degree of Wallis's authority over his pictures: he had first choice of story properties, directors, performers, and other contract talent. He was to supervise the scripting and editing, although Jack Warner had the last word in any disputes. Each of Wallis's pictures was to be billed as "A Hal B. Wallis Production," in type at least 50 percent the size of the title.[51]

The Hawks and Hellinger deals of February 1942 differed considerably from the Wallis deal in that neither was granted the same degree of authority or a cut of the profits. But the two deals did further indicate Warners' shift to an in-house unit setup. Warners signed Hawks to a five-year, five-picture deal at a salary of $100,000 per picture, with his duties described as those of "Director and/or Supervisor." This designation gave Hawks authority over both scripting and editing, and his pictures were to be billed as "A Howard Hawks Production" in a type size 25 percent that of the title. Hawks was sufficiently comfortable with Warners to sign an exclusive deal, which meant he could work for no other company while the contract was in effect.[52] The writer-producer Mark Hellinger had left Warners in 1941 rather than submit to Wallis's authority. But with Wallis's shift to unit producer, Hellinger now was willing to return. On 26 February, he signed a five-year deal at $3,000 per week "as producer and/or executive and/or director and/or writer," and his contract stipulated a separate producer credit on all his pictures with his name at 25 percent the size of the title.[53]

Also of note in this context is an arrangement made with Bette Davis. In June 1943, Warners created B.D. Inc., an in-house independent setup for Bette Davis giving her 35 percent of the net profits on her pictures. That company folded, however, after a single picture; Davis ultimately had little interest in becoming her own producer.[54]

As mentioned earlier, Paramount had maintained a special arrangement with Cecil B. DeMille since the late 1930s but otherwise avoided in-house independent deals. This policy began to change during the war. In 1944, Hal Wallis left Warners and signed a deal with Paramount giving him an independent unit on basically the same terms that DeMille had been operating under for years. Shortly thereafter, the longtime Paramount production executive Buddy De Sylva demanded, and received, a similar deal from the studio.[55]

The easing of Paramount's resistance to the independent unit trend was further underscored by a 1944 deal with Leo McCarey. During the war, McCarey was virtually the only established freelance producer-director to maintain that status, relying on one-picture deals with various studios. After a modest 1942 hit for RKO, ONCE UPON A HONEYMOON, McCarey approached Paramount with an original story (his own) about two priests struggling to make ends meet in a New York City parish. McCarey convinced Paramount that it might make an ideal Bing Crosby vehicle, and the studio agreed to finance and distribute the picture. But Paramount also was sufficiently leery of the project to oblige McCarey's request to waive his salary in lieu of a share of the profits. The result, of course, was GOING MY WAY, the single biggest hit of 1944; McCarey's share was reportedly in excess of $1 million.[56]

Hollywood's leading independent producer-director during the war era, Leo McCarey, on the set of THE BELLS OF ST. MARY'S *(1945).*

McCarey then reasserted his independence and market value by spurning Paramount and striking a deal with RKO for THE BELLS OF ST. MARY'S, the sequel to GOING MY WAY. This, too, would star Crosby, whom Paramount had granted quasi-independent status, opposite Ingrid Bergman (on loan from Selznick). That 1945 production gave McCarey another huge hit, confirming his stature as Hollywood's leading freelance producer-director.

It confirmed, too, the validity of RKO's wartime courtship—which by 1945 had become remarkably aggressive—of outside independents. One of the more significant deals was with Dore Schary, a producer loaned to RKO in 1945 by another leading independent, David Selznick, as part of a multifilm package. The deal marked another stage in Schary's remarkable wartime ascent from contract writer at MGM to prestige-level independent—an ascent worth tracing in some detail.

CASE STUDY: DORE SCHARY AT MGM, VANGUARD, AND RKO

The career of Dore Schary during World War II demonstrates the range of independent and unit production strategies at the time, and several other wartime trends as well—particularly the emergence of the writer-producer as a significant industry force and the hyperactivity of A-class (and near-A) feature production. Schary's career in 1944–1945 also was directly related to two other significant developments in Hollywood's independent filmmaking arena: the return of David O. Selznick to active production, and Selznick's increasingly elaborate packaging of movie projects.

In late 1941, Dore Schary was a 36-year-old contract writer at MGM earning $1,000 per week; his more significant screen credits included BOYS TOWN (1938) and YOUNG TOM EDISON (1940). Schary wanted to produce, and he impressed Louis Mayer with his ideas about improving Metro's low-budget output. So in November 1941, Mayer signed Schary to a new one-year contract, at $1,750 per week, as executive producer and put him to work with Harry Rapf on MGM's mid-range product—its near-A pictures.[57]

Harry Rapf was a Metro executive (and corporate vice president) who not only lacked experience as a "creative" producer but did not even read the story properties or scripts that his unit developed.[58] MGM's near-A operations quickly changed under Schary's supervision, and in fact the Rapf-Schary unit (as it was termed in interoffice memoranda) soon became known on the lot—and well beyond it—as the Schary unit. Schary chaired weekly meetings with the unit's producers, going over story material, making cast and crew assignments, and monitoring production. He also played an active role in story and script development, serving as story editor and closely supervising postproduction. The Rapf-Schary unit included about a dozen producers; the total varied as some producers graduated to the A ranks while others were let go. Schary also joined Rapf on MGM's elite executive committee, not only to tap into the available studio talent and personnel but also to pass along promising projects deemed too ambitious for the B unit. Schary used top talent in some of his near-A productions—Robert Taylor in BATAAN, for instance—and also developed new talent that could work in both A and B pictures, such as Margaret O'Brien and Elizabeth Taylor.

The Schary unit started strong with JOE SMITH, AMERICAN, a home-front drama released in early 1942 and starring Robert Young as a munitions plant worker who faces problems at home and on the job. He eventually is kidnapped by enemy agents trying to discover the workings of a new bomb sight, and he is able to endure by fixing his mind on the values of home and family. The film avoided the jingoism and spy-thriller mechanics of so many early war films, however, and in fact critics were impressed by both its unassuming story and its modest production values. "In its own simple and unassuming way," stated the *New York Times*, "'Joe Smith, American' does more to underscore the deep and indelible reasons why this country is at war than most of the million-dollar epics with all their bravura and patriotism." It was "not a 'big' film as Hollywood productions go," noted the *Times*, "but it pulls a good deal more than its own weight."[59]

JOE SMITH, AMERICAN was budgeted at $280,000 and came in $44,000 under budget; it turned a profit of $240,000.[60] Although the film was invariably held up as a working model for the Schary unit, few others were produced as efficiently or did as well. The unit turned out thirteen films in 1942 at an average cost of $275,000. Most of these were crime thrillers, home-front dramas, Westerns, and combat films—all standard B-grade wartime fare—with the war-related pictures by far the more successful.

In 1943, the Schary unit's average cost per film rose to nearly $400,000, owing both to inflation and to Schary's growing ambition. Its two biggest pictures at that time were JOURNEY FOR MARGARET (1942), a rehash of MRS. MINIVER (1942) that cost $463,000, and LASSIE COME HOME (1943), which cost $564,000. Both were hits, although the real payoff was the introduction of 5-year-old Margaret O'Brien in the former and 11-year-old Elizabeth Taylor in the latter. (Their weekly salaries in 1943 were $150 and $75, respectively).[61] The unit's biggest project was BATAAN in late 1943, which cost $789,000 and costarred Robert Taylor, Thomas Mitchell, and Robert Walker; it was directed by Tay Garnett while he waited to start a big-budget Greer Garson vehicle. Clearly Schary's near-A productions were edging closer to A-class status, although the unit was operating only at about a break-even level. Still, Mayer was satisfied. He raised Schary's salary to $2,000 per week in November 1942 and then offered him another raise in late 1943.

By then, Schary had other plans. He wanted to personally produce A-class pictures, and despite Mayer's assurances, he was not optimistic about that possibility at MGM. There were other offers in late 1943, including one from Selznick, who finally was returning to active production. Selznick had two prestige-level projects in the works, SINCE YOU WENT AWAY and SPELLBOUND, and he wanted Schary to produce more modest A-class pictures through his Vanguard Films to complement Selznick's own prestige productions. Schary agreed, signing on in November 1943 at $2,500 per week plus 15 percent of the net profits on all his Vanguard releases.[62] A few weeks later, he purchased the screen rights to an original radio drama, *Double Furlough* by Charles Martin, for $2,500.[63] The story centered on a shell-shock victim who, while home for Christmas, falls in love with a woman on holiday furlough from prison. Schary convinced Selznick to bring in the freelancer Ginger Rogers for the lead, while costarring roles went to two Selznick contract players, Joseph Cotten and Shirley Temple, who also were appearing in SINCE YOU WENT AWAY.

Schary managed to keep his initial Selznick project on target at $1.3 million, proving that he was ready to handle A-class productions. He also displayed a canny feel for the marketplace by convincing Selznick to change the title to "I'll Be Seeing You," which Schary suggested in early 1944 after first hearing the Tommy Dorsey–Bing Crosby song.[64] Although Selznick was wary of the war-related title "Double Furlough," he balked at the suggestion. But when "I'll Be Seeing You" became the number-one coin-machine hit in the United States in July 1944, Selznick assigned Gallup's ARI to market-test the title.[65] ARI's research supported the change, and so the film was released just before the Christmas holidays under the title I'LL BE SEEING YOU. By then, the song had fallen from its extended run atop the charts but had become a wartime standard,

Dore Schary with Ginger Rogers and Joseph Cotten during production of Vanguard's I'LL BE SEEING YOU *(1944).*

and its use as both a title and a musical theme undoubtedly enhanced the film's popularity. Total earnings on I'LL BE SEEING YOU reached $3.8 million—giving Schary a profit share of $97,000 (beyond his salary of $105,000 on the picture) and securing his role with Vanguard.[66]

By early 1945, Selznick was preparing another Hitchcock picture, NOTORIOUS (1946), and a big-budget Western, DUEL IN THE SUN (1946). Schary had two comedies in the works: THE BACHELOR AND THE BOBBY-SOXER (1947), with Cary Grant and Shirley Temple, and THE FARMER'S DAUGHTER (1947), with Joseph Cotten and Loretta Young. Selznick's operations were plagued by various problems in 1945, however, principally cost overruns on DUEL and the decorators' strike, which completely closed down production in April while Selznick continued to run up huge overhead costs.[67] Selznick decided to unload all of his current projects except DUEL, making a series of immensely profitable deals in the summer of 1945 with RKO. These involved the outright sale of the NOTORIOUS, BACHELOR AND THE BOBBY-SOXER, and FARMER'S DAUGHTER packages (with profit participation to Selznick), and also the loan of the Selznick contract talent attached to each project—including Dore Schary.[68]

Thus, Schary joined Sam Goldwyn, Walt Disney, Leo McCarey, and others as an outside producer at RKO. His efforts there were eminently successful—so successful, in fact, that within a year he would be installed as RKO's production chief after the death of Charles Koerner. That promotion marked the culmination of Schary's remarkable climb through the filmmaking and executive ranks in wartime Hollywood, and it also indicated that the industry's "independent" ranks were still intimately tied to the major studio powers. Those ties would continue, of course, as long as the studios controlled the means of production and distribution, and as long as it remained necessary to rely on outside talent to satisfy the market demand for A-class product.

The studios also had the resources to exploit these A-class pictures, and in fact their sales, promotion, and marketing operations were geared up to another level during the war years. Indeed, not only the war-related market surge but also the post-decree sales policies, which took effect in late 1941, virtually demanded that the studios adopt more aggressive strategies in promoting and selling their high-end pictures. Some companies were more aggressive than others, but all recognized that both the war and the antitrust campaign meant that the marketing as well as the making of motion pictures was changing dramatically.

Working the First-Run Market

With the financial stakes and profit potential going up with each wartime release, and with the 1940 consent decree spurring a move to unit sales, the studios steadily adjusted both their market strategies and their marketing operations. *Variety* reported in September 1942 that the majors were increasing their "exploitation" budgets by 25 percent that year, and in April 1943 *Advertising Age* noted that overall motion picture advertising in all media—radio, newspapers, magazines—was up 10 percent.[69] Newspapers continued to be the primary means of movie advertising and promotion, although radio became increasingly popular during the war. Spot radio ad campaigns pushed individual pictures in specific first-run markets, and radio adaptations of top releases became a viable promotional strategy as well.

With its reduced output, increased emphasis on top product, and single-unit sales policy, it is scarcely surprising that Warners was the most aggressive in its promotion and advertising.[70] The other majors followed suit in 1943 as they, too, shifted to unit sales. The last to come around was MGM, which in 1943 still was selling groups of eight to twelve pictures. (MRS. MINIVER was the only picture Loew's sold singly in the early war years.) Metro had little choice but to adjust, however, since the trend toward longer runs and holdovers virtually demanded that pictures be marketed individually.

Most of Warners' efforts to promote its top features involved product tie-ins, which effectively sold the film while creating (or enhancing) the story property's currency in other media venues. During a single month in 1943, for instance, Warners featured condensed radio versions of seven releases, including YANKEE DOODLE DANDY (1942), NOW, VOYAGER (1942), and CASABLANCA (1942).[71] For an early 1944 biopic, THE ADVENTURES OF MARK TWAIN, Warners came up with five 15-minute programs to promote the picture on 200 network radio stations.[72]

The war boom also brought an increased emphasis on presold story properties, especially best-selling novels and hit plays. Relying on presold properties had a long history in the movie industry, of course, but the trend took a slightly different turn during the war, when presold stories were generally perceived as one means (like the use of Technicolor) of offsetting the loss of top male stars.[73] Here again, Warner Bros. led the

way, and its success in securing presold properties was due largely to its willingness to
make participation deals with authors and playwrights. This practice generally was
avoided by the other studios, particularly MGM and Paramount, and for good reason.[74]
Warners' deal with George M. Cohan for YANKEE DOODLE DANDY, for instance, paid
Cohan $125,000 up front plus 10 percent of the gross revenues over $1.5 million, which
turned out to be another $320,000.[75] But Warners was satisfied with such arrangements
and continued to cut participation deals throughout the war.

The significant increase in book sales early in the war skewed the presold story market toward literary properties. The studios stocked up on successful titles, setting a
record in February 1942 for number of story buys in a single month (65). War stories
dominated, especially nonfiction accounts of combat like *Guadalcanal Diary* (1942) and
They Were Expendable (1942).[76] Several popular religious novels in 1942–1943—
notably *The Robe, The Song of Bernadette,* and *The Keys of the Kingdom*—also were
bought by Hollywood for hefty sums.[77]

One rather remarkable development which spoke volumes about the wartime fiction
market, the movie industry's reliance on pre-sold properties, and the complex relationship between publishing and moviemaking involved MGM's 1943 hit THE HUMAN
COMEDY. The novelist-screenwriter William Saroyan sold the story to MGM in early
1942, but disagreements over the script led Saroyan to withdraw his story and turn it
into a novel instead of a film. A saccharine comedy-drama about life in small-town,
wartime America, *The Human Comedy* (1943) was an immediate best-seller. That
brought MGM back into the picture, and in March 1943 the film version was released.
Aptly described by Bosley Crowther in the *New York Times* as "sentimental showmanship," the film was even more successful commercially than the novel and brought
Saroyan an Academy Award for his "original" story.[78]

Another significant promotional trend was the boom in low-priced book editions with
direct tie-ins to motion pictures, a strategy that developed along several different lines.
Warners had an arrangement with Grosset & Dunlap to sell low-cost paperbacks based
on original screen stories—a practice that dated back to the 1930s but really took off
during the war with successful "adaptations" like SERGEANT YORK and AIR FORCE.
Pocket Books had a similar arrangement with MGM; its 25-cent edition of MRS.
MINIVER sold 550,000 copies within a year of the film's release. There were other types
of cooperative ventures between publishers and studios, with film adaptations often
turning moderately successful novels into best-sellers. *Kings Row* by Henry Bellamann,
for example, had sold a respectable 30,000 copies before Warners' adaptation came out
in December 1941; in the ensuing year, it sold 500,000.[79]

Another publishing tie-in which boosted the value of the print work was the serialization in newspapers of stories timed to coincide with a film's release. MGM serialized
some thirty-five films in 1942, for instance, usually either in six-chapter versions in daily
newspapers or three-chapter versions in weeklies. Among Metro's releases concurrent-
ly serialized were popular adaptations like RANDOM HARVEST (1942), based on the James
Hilton story, THE HUMAN COMEDY (1943), and THE MOON IS DOWN (1943), an adaptation of John Steinbeck's story which already had appeared as both a play and a novel.[80]

By late 1943, the trend was shifting to popular stage hits. A key trendsetter was
Irving Berlin's *This Is the Army,* a 1942 Broadway hit which Warners in 1943 adapted
into a phenomenally successful movie musical.[81] *Variety* in early 1944 noted the growing controversy and exhibitor dissatisfaction with "war-themed material," especially
combat-related stories, and suggested that the studios were turning to stage hits

The success of William Saroyan's "novelized" screenplay led MGM to reconsider THE
HUMAN COMEDY—*resulting in a 1943 hit starring Mickey Rooney.*

"because Broadway offered more escapist material than the book marts," which many
felt "were following the news headlines too closely for screen-purpose comfort."[82] The
trend to stage adaptations intensified in 1944, a record year for Broadway—and for playwrights cutting motion picture deals.[83] One indication of the feeding frenzy was the
reported asking price of $3 million for John Van Druten's three-character comedy hit
Voice of the Turtle (1943).[84] Warner Bros., which led all companies in play purchases in
1944 (spending $1,650,000 on seven stage hits), eventually bought the rights to Van
Druten's play for $500,000, the same price it paid that year for Clarence Day's *Life with
Father* (1935; dramatized 1939).[85]

This Broadway-to-Hollywood trend eased considerably in 1945 as plays were deemed
overpriced and too many playwrights were demanding percentage deals. Thus, the pen-
dulum swung back to fiction; in early 1945, for instance, the independent star-producer
James Cagney paid a record $250,000 for Adria Locke Langley's novel *A Lion Is in the
Streets* (1945).[86] *Variety* noted the "growing feeling that published works are generally
better source material for the studios than plays," and it later reported that the screen
rights to novels with over $1 million in sales could be bought for as little as $100,000.[87]
Variety also noted that Broadway in 1945 was suffering through its second straight season of musical flops.[88]

While stage musicals were falling on hard times in the later war years, the music and
recording industries were doing record business. Indeed, another of Hollywood's key

wartime marketing strategies involved tie-ins with popular music. Considering the importance of popular music during World War II, with live performances, concerts, recordings, jukebox, and radio plays providing vital amusement for soldiers and civilians alike, music provided Hollywood with a viable presold commodity. Big-name band-leaders like Harry James, Jimmy Dorsey, Tommy Dorsey, Spike Jones, and Guy Lombardo were signed (along with their bands) to studio contracts and worked into pictures.[89] Radio and recording stars like Bing Crosby and the newcomer Frank Sinatra enjoyed unprecedented crossover success. And songwriters enjoyed a boom as well, with sheet-music sales—particularly of songs featured in motion pictures—reaching record heights.[90]

Audience research played an increasingly important role in Hollywood's cultivation of the volatile, high-stakes wartime marketplace. Gallup's Audience Research Institute remained the industry's leading market research firm, and in fact ARI hit its stride during the war. The company began referring to itself as Audience Research "Incorporated" in 1942, and in 1943 Gallup made an important change in ARI's management, replacing David Ogilvy as executive vice president with Albert Sindlinger, who had an extensive background in movie distribution and promotion. ARI's chief clients were still RKO and leading independents like Selznick, Goldwyn, and Disney, but the company also began doing business with other studios and producers as well.[91]

ARI's primary product was still its assessment of the drawing power of Hollywood's top stars, the "Audit of Marquee Values," which it updated every three months. ARI steadily refined its testing of story, casting, and title ideas. By 1942, its surveys were broken down along various lines: male versus female respondents; size of community (over 100,000, between 10,000 and 100,000, under 10,000); frequency of attendance (habitual versus occasional); income level (prosperous, upper-middle, middle, poor); and age (age 12–17, age 18–30, age 31 and older).[92] ARI also refined its "Index of Publicity Penetration" during the war and developed a "jury preview system," which provided far more detailed data on audience response than were generated by traditional studio previews. Clearly ARI's market research was making great strides and becoming increasingly comprehensive. As Shannon James Kelley notes, during the war "the ARI's research program took on a sort of all-inclusive logical closure in regard to 'the average "A" picture' and its audience."[93]

Whatever its claims to scientific validity and predictive reliability, market research in the movie industry was barely out of its infancy and was still far from reliable. Moreover, Hollywood producers and studio executives were not about to put a higher stake in researchers' figures than in their own talent, taste, and intuition. And yet as the economic stakes went up, the marketplace grew more complex, and research methods were steadily refined, market research became an unavoidable if troublesome and costly necessity.

While the studios pursued innovations in marketing and promotion, they continued to rely on established practices as well. Developed along with the vertically integrated industrial system, these practices included a range of promotional tactics, from movie previews ("trailers") shown in theaters to posters and print ads in newspapers and magazines and exploitation stunts in local communities. The vast majority of the studios' efforts and expenditures in their sales campaigns for individual films went toward newspaper ads. In 1945, according to the *Film Daily Year Book*, $52 million of the total industry expenditure of $63 million went to newspaper advertising.[94] The print ad campaign for each film and the national sales campaign were planned in detail in each stu-

Promotion of THE SONG OF BERNADETTE *(1943), which included a specially commissioned Norman Rockwell painting and tie-ins with Franz Werfel's best-seller, reflects the sophistication of wartime movie marketing.*

dio's New York office, and these plans were contained in the "pressbook" which accompanied each studio release. As Mary Beth Haralovich shows in the following section, pressbooks provided a veritable blueprint for a film's national sales campaign, and they also reveal a great deal about the industry's perceptions of its products and its audience.

SELLING MILDRED PIERCE: A CASE STUDY IN MOVIE PROMOTION

Mary Beth Haralovich

Throughout Hollywood's classical era, every studio release was accompanied by a pressbook, an oversized and glossy booklet which outlined the film's national sales campaign and contained basic materials crucial to that campaign. Pressbooks included two types of material: advertising (primarily mats used for newspaper ads) and publicity (stories and exploitation ideas). Advertising was designed to engage the potential moviegoer's interest in the film's story by stressing genre, the conjunctures of star and character, narrative suspense, and the special qualities of a film, such as its adaptation from a popular novel. Publicity presented a film in more detail through prepared reviews, and it also extended beyond the film itself through production stories and stills, merchandising tie-ins, praise for the studio's expertise, suggestions for exploitation stunts, and so on.[95]

Generally speaking, sales campaigns for individual films began in Hollywood and were completed in New York. The sales and promotional campaign for a film was initiated in discussions between advertising personnel and the producer prior to shooting. During production, staff publicists wrote synopses of the plot and created stories about production events and stars, planting these items in newspapers during production. Syndicated columnists like Hedda Hopper and Louella Parsons, as well as feature writers across the country, were fed information about the film and its stars. As shooting drew to a close, studio photographers took production stills and poster-art photographs, which were used by staff artists to create posters and advertising illustrations. Unlike frame enlargements from the film, poster-art stills guaranteed frontal positioning and concentrated on the performers' faces and bodies.[96]

Distribution of films and advertising was conducted out of the New York office, where staff assembled promotional materials and distributed pressbooks and advertising packages to trade papers, magazines, and theaters. Individual exhibitors were given considerable latitude in handling advertising materials and were encouraged to do more on their own to stimulate local interest in the film. Some theaters had staff artists who modified posters and pressbook materials to suit the local environment and the exhibitor's specific ideas. Each issue of the Motion Picture Herald also provided advice for theater owners on advertising layouts and publicity stunts.

Pressbooks invariably opened with a call for exhibitor confidence in the studio's box-office track record, its resources for a national campaign, and its promotional expertise. This appeal was most pronounced with A-class star vehicles and prestige-level films. The pressbook for MILDRED PIERCE (1945) reminds exhibitors about the "full page ads appearing regularly in leading national magazines" for other Warner Bros. films, from CASABLANCA (1942) and THIS IS THE ARMY (1943) to current releases like OBJECTIVE BURMA (1945) and RHAPSODY IN BLUE (1945). The pressbook also lists the magazines in which the ads appear, including Life, Look, Collier's, Time, Fortune, Redbook, Liberty, Cosmopolitan, Parents, Newsweek, Harper's, American Legion, and Foreign Service.[97]

Poster art was crucial to ad campaigns, and in fact newspaper advertising based on posters was a primary use (if not *the* use) of pressbook materials. Pressbooks offered posters in a range of sizes: the familiar one-sheet, larger three- and six-sheets, a gargantuan twenty-four-sheet. Also, variations on the posters were offered in the form of lobby cards, slides, mats in various sizes, and more. Poster ads transmitted the essential attributes of the film, generating viewer expectations and forming what Barbara Klinger has termed "a tentative contract between producer and consumer." Posters identified the genre of the film and placed its stars/characters at a point of narrative suspense. Poster graphics often linked head shots of stars/characters to each other and to a central narrative enigma through glances and tag lines.[98]

A new "maturity" and sexual explicitness introduced in films like THE OUTLAW, as well as the pinup, a prevalent wartime phenomenon, resulted in posters that often displayed much more than head shots, especially during the early-to-mid-1940s. During World War II, the pinup brought a new dimension to poster art, marking a radical change in the presentation of women in movie advertising from the more wholesome, more fully clad, and less overtly sexual depiction in 1930s film posters. This change caused a bit of a stir within the industry's Advertising Advisory Council (AAC), whose task was to approve (and thus regulate) all film advertising. Created in the 1930s as part of the MPPDA's self-regulation effort, the AAC developed and continually refined its own Advertising Code, which underwent considerable revision in the 1940s.

Pressbooks also contained an official billing chart of the cast and top production personnel. This chart tacitly announced the status of these individuals in that the value of each was measured against a common standard: the type size of the title of the film. The names of a film's stars would appear in type size of 50 to 100 percent of the title type size, with top stars invariably appearing "above the title" and in the same type size. Lesser stars and featured players appeared below the title in increasingly smaller type. For prestige-level pictures involving top producers and directors, a type size of 25 percent of the title size was not uncommon. However, type size for other above-the-line talent, while included, could be minuscule; the names of writers and composers often appeared at less than 5 percent of the title size. While these credits were small but legible on posters and in the larger newspaper ads (that appeared on a film's opening day), they were dropped in smaller newspaper ads.

While film advertising was designed for potential ticket buyers and keyed to story, genre, characters, and performers, publicity was designed to "linger" over a film and to treat its personnel and production in a much wider context. While advertising centered on a few well-chosen elements, prepared reviews and stories could elaborate on a film's narrative and commend the cast and other studio personnel for their work on the production. Performance stories could discuss an actor's interpretation of a role or the studio's efforts to build a new star, or they could alert the industry to an Oscar-level performance. The assessment of production values and summary of the story also provided reviewers with basic information, while prompting positive reviews of the film.

Production stories played a complex role in the publicity process. In circulation to the public through newspapers, gossip columns, fan magazines, and so on, these stories illustrated the high level of expertise involved in the production of a film. In circulation to the industry, they gave the studio an opportunity to boast about its excellence and to establish industrial expectations about its products. Rather than maintaining the invisibility of the production process, production stories identified personnel and how they worked, discussing the filmmaking activities and atmosphere in some detail. Thus, these stories assumed an audience interested in and knowledgeable about the production process. As they promoted the film, the stories also served as a means of self-promotion within the industry and of bolstering exhibitor confidence.

Another important form of publicity was the product tie-in, defined by Maria LaPlace as "the display of products in films and of stars in product advertisements." Tie-ins might push specific name-brand products, but they also involved generic statements about fashion and commodities. Moreover, they predominantly were aimed at women. As Maria LaPlace points out, "The main industries involved in tie-ins . . . are all aimed at female consumers: fashion, cosmetics, home furnishings and appliances." In tie-in publicity, a film's actors tended to function simply as models displaying products rather than as people making genuine use of the merchandise. Pressbooks offered premade tie-in stills for display in local shops and also asked exhibitors to develop additional tie-ins with local merchants. While film costumes were not duplicated for the retail market, fashion played an important and complex role in film promotion.[99]

The exploitation section of the pressbook suggested stunts and "ballys" (as in "ballyhoo") to local exhibitors to supplement the studio's advertising and publicity campaign. Designed to grab immediate attention, exploitation often involved amusing and boisterous antics, and unlike the print-oriented ad and publicity campaigns, exploitation could take place inside and outside the theater.

As even this general treatment of movie pressbooks suggests, the studios adopted complex and varied strategies for advertising and publicizing individual films. To indicate the nature and range of these strategies, what follows is a more detailed look at the pressbook and general advertising and promotion campaign of a single film, Warners' 1945 release MILDRED PIERCE.

MILDRED PIERCE was an A-class Warners production starring the newly signed Joan Crawford as the title character and adapted from the recent, controversial best-seller by James M. Cain. The film is an interesting blend of *film noir*-style crime thriller and domestic melodrama, and a brief plot synopsis is necessary to fully appreciate Warners' efforts to market and promote the film. MILDRED PIERCE opens with the murder of a suave, middle-aged man (Zachary Scott) whose dying word is "Mildred." The scene is photographed from the point of view of the killer, who thus is not revealed to the audience; the rest of the film involves the search—mainly through extended flashbacks—to identify the murderer. These flashbacks trace the separation of Mildred from her husband Bruce, her obsessive devotion to her thankless daughter, Veda (Ann Blyth), her partnership in a successful string of restaurants with the lecherous Wally (Jack Carson), and her eventual marriage to Monty Barrigan, the murder victim. Although Mildred initially confesses to the crime, the film ends with two dramatic revelations: that Veda had been carrying on an affair with her stepfather, and that she killed him when he spurned her for Mildred.

Released in September 1945 within weeks of V-J Day, MILDRED PIERCE was accompanied by a lush pressbook with a twelve-page advertising section and a fourteen-page publicity section. The pressbook presents the film as a prestige production in the tradition of other Warners hits and pledges national visibility through an aggressive magazine advertising campaign. "It is in this way the public is being told of the Warner way . . . the American way of motion picture making." Crawford, in her first screen role since leaving MGM in 1943, is accorded the attentive treatment of a star and a valued performer, and the production is lauded as an exemplar of studio craft and expertise.

The advertising for MILDRED PIERCE centers, of course, on the title character, who is presented as a *film noir femme fatale*. Interestingly enough, a primary image used in

Michael Curtiz (lower left, back to camera) directs Zachary Scott and Joan Crawford in MILDRED PIERCE *(1945).*

the ad mats is a drawing which dominates the cover of the pressbook: a figure of a woman who is not immediately recognizable as Joan Crawford. She stands in long shot wearing a low-cut gown, holding a smoking gun in one hand and clutching a drapery with the other, and staring directly at the spectator. The tag line accompanying the image and appearing in most of the advertising mats asserts: "She's the kind of woman men want . . . but shouldn't have!" In the mats which have a clearly recognizable image of Crawford, the star is integrated into the *film noir*-style murder mystery—the primary means of engaging audience interest—with tag lines such as: "She knew there was trouble coming—trouble she made for herself—a love affair—and a loaded gun. . . . She had no right playing around with either!"

Through this focus on *film noir* and the dominance of the title character, Mildred is assigned direct responsibility for aggressive sexuality and for violence. While not precisely faithful to the film, this ad strategy was efficient and effective since it promoted the title of the film and emphasized the lead character (and star) rather than the secondary character of Mildred's daughter, Veda. In both the novel and the film, Veda may have had the more obvious *femme fatale* status and the greater narrative agency (as an adulteress and also as the murderer being sought by the police). But her name was not tied to the title, nor was the actress playing Veda, the relative newcomer Ann Blyth, likely to appeal to potential moviegoers.

Three actors are allocated type size equal to the title: Crawford, Jack Carson, and Zachary Scott. Crawford's name appears first and occasionally above the title; also, her full name shares type size with only the last names of the two male costars. Poster graphics situate the two men in relation to Mildred and *film noir,* as do their respective tag lines. On Zachary Scott/Monty: "He'd rather die than double-cross her . . . so he did both!" On Jack Carson/Wally: "Mildred! . . . she had more to offer a man in a glance than most women give in a lifetime!"

This billing and ad strategy sustained the *film noir* murder mystery and Mildred's *femme fatale* concentration, qualities further reinforced by a small box containing an appeal to the film's entertainment value as suspense: "Please don't tell anyone what she did! We know our patrons will thank us if no one is seated during the last 7 minutes. No One Seated During Last Seven Minutes!" This promise of thrills is reinforced by the ubiquitous reminders that MILDRED PIERCE is adapted from Cain's sensational novel. Many of the mats contain a small drawing of the novel lying open with steam rising from its pages and tag lines like "From the daring book by James M. Cain!" or, "From that sizzling best-seller."

While advertising concentrates on story and stars, it also contains production credits. The MILDRED PIERCE ad mats are peppered with studio name recognition, such as "Warner sensation!" and "Warner hit!" The names of the producer Jerry Wald and the director Michael Curtiz, two of the studio's leading talents, are accorded 25 percent of the title type size—while the screenwriter Ranald MacDougall and the composer Max Steiner are at 3 percent and the novelist Cain at a mere 2 percent. The prepared reviews also praise Wald and Curtiz. The former is described as "Hollywood's most aggressive young movie-maker," and the latter as an "infallible" director and an "Academy Award winner" (for CASABLANCA) who is "liked as well as admired by the people who work for him."

Just as the advertising material focuses on Crawford's title character, the main focus of the publicity material is on Joan Crawford the actress and star. MILDRED PIERCE was termed "the high-water mark in the career of one of screenland's most important ladies"; she "offers an unforgettable, intensely human characterization." And beyond the repeated accolades for her performance, the pressbook stresses that the depth of portrayal was born of human experience as well as professional acumen.[100] In this sense, the pressbook's publicity treatment of Crawford shifts the genre focus from the *film noir* angle to that of the woman's film and motherhood. Stories highlight her experiences—as a woman, mother, and actress—that provide the basis for her "truthful" interpretation of Mildred. The mother, not the *femme fatale,* is privileged here, providing the primary motivations for her character. "Miss Crawford *is* the sacrificing, doubt-ridden, incorruptible Mildred Pierce, squaring off against the world, true to what she conceives to be a duty to her daughter, for whom she unflinchingly undergoes every privation." Crawford, asserts the pressbook, brings "a remarkable knowledge of the inner workings of the mind and heart of a woman for whom life has gone bitterly wrong at every turn."

Only one story in the pressbook, "Actress' Rise to Stardom Was Difficult Journey for Crawford," makes reference to the star's departure from MGM—the result, supposedly, of Crawford's refusal "to accept further roles which she considered trite." And even the history of the star is given a slant which brings it in line with the film. Crawford, like Mildred, "came up the hard way, earning her success." In presenting Crawford's career as an ongoing process of hard work and overcoming obstacles, the star image contributes to her interpretation of Mildred and justifies Warners' expertise in finding a role worthy of Crawford at this point in her career.[101]

The publicity related to merchandising and commercial tie-ins also focuses on Crawford. One story begins with a dual address as luxurious detail about the star's costume invokes the pleasure of consumption as well as the realistic spectacle of the production itself. "Star 'All Dressed To Kill'—Even Herself" treats the opening scene in which Mildred, alone on the Santa Monica pier (actually a studio set) seems to be contemplating suicide. It opens with a description of the "bright green wool dress [the film was shot in black and white], shoes with very high heels and big purse . . . fur cape–style coat with matching fur hat . . . the most expensive items of the wardrobe."

Here and elsewhere, publicity about costumes in MILDRED PIERCE draws on three functions of costuming: the expectation that a Hollywood star will wear glamorous costumes; the role that costumes play in establishing character traits and a plausible story; and the value of costumes as a mark of the stature and prestige of the production. In its treatment of Crawford's costumes, the pressbook highlights the studio's drive for excellence and its achievement of both realism and glamour. But it also acknowledges that in some instances the narrative demands that glamour be subordinated to realism and dramatic clarity: "Joan Crawford usually has a wardrobe to make most women gasp with envy. For her present role, however, she had fourteen aprons and twenty-one house dress changes—a new kind of record for one of the screen's most glamorous personalities." Most of the product tie-ins are of the generic variety—including the quarter-page piece on men's "dresswear," "sportswear," and the like.

The exploitation section of the pressbook concentrates on the adaptation of the Cain novel and "the film's dramatic punch." While the pressbook does not offer newspaper serialization of the novel, which was often done with adaptations, it does promote Tower Books' "special 49¢ movie edition" of *Mildred Pierce* and points out that similar promotion will appear in *Variety*, the *Hollywood Reporter*, and the *New York Times*. Exhibitors are encouraged to tie in to this national campaign through lobby displays of Cain's books, cooperative displays with local libraries and bookstores, and two specific stunts. One stunt is a quiz about movie adaptations involving "the fairer sex." The other is a newspaper "best-seller-to-hit-movie contest" in which contestants identify other recent Warner Bros. adaptations.

The exploitation campaign designed to sell the film's "title and drama" entailed "four attractive teaser ads" for newspapers, lobby displays, and "store windows and counters around town." Like the ad mats, these stress Crawford's *femme noir* status and underscore the mystery angle. One even invites patrons to sign a postcard stating: "I just saw 'Mildred Pierce' and I promise not to tell anyone what Mildred Pierce did." In one radio spot announcement, a woman's voice pleads: "You mustn't tell them what you saw here tonight! . . . Please keep my secret!"

Local promotion for MILDRED PIERCE followed the pressbook's general strategy fairly closely, although both the box-office success and critical accolades for the film were quickly incorporated as well. For example, in Los Angeles, where the film opened at three Warners theaters on Friday, 12 October 1945, each successive day of the preceding week incorporated some facet of the pressbook's *femme noir* and suspense gambits, culminating on opening day with this pitch: "Today!!! Please don't tell anyone what she did! 'Even a woman like me can be hurt once too often!!!' It's all about that talked-about Mildred Pierce, Warner's New Sensation. It's *That* story! The sizzling best-seller by James M. Cain."[102]

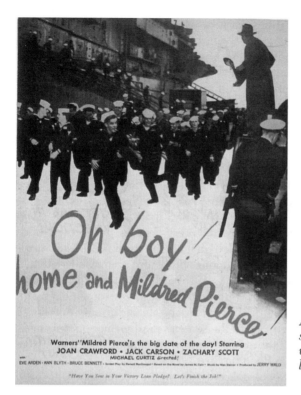

Among the various promotional strategies for MILDRED PIERCE *was this poster tie-in to the millions of returning vets.*

Five days later, Los Angeles advertising was using quotes ("Raves!") from reviews by Louella Parsons, Walter Winchell, and Edwin Shallert of the *Los Angeles Times* that extended beyond the mystery angle to embrace Crawford's performance and to position MILDRED PIERCE as a woman's picture. Two days later, after a full week in release in L.A., the ads began touting the film in terms of its box-office performance. On 26 October, the ads even began an ironic twist on the earlier campaign strategy: "We *MUST* tell you what 'Mildred Pierce' did!!! Broke every existing house record at Warners 3 First-Run Theatres! Earned the critical acclaim of every outstanding reviewer in the nation! Took L.A. by storm with one of the most unusual and engrossing pictures ever produced! Join the throngs!! See for yourself!!!"[103] When the film opened at the Balaban and Katz Roosevelt in Chicago in December, a similar pattern emerged, with the studio-designed promotional campaign augmented by testimony of the film's popular and critical success in New York and Los Angeles.[104]

One aspect of market conditions clearly avoided by the MILDRED PIERCE sales campaign, and by the film itself for that matter, was the war. As discussed in the following chapter, the film managed to convey a range of wartime conditions—working women, absent husbands, housing shortages—without directly invoking the war. In this sense, it was among the more subtle wartime dramas and in fact was more typical of films released toward the end of the war, when Hollywood had grown more adept at incorporating war themes into its feature films. Early on, however, the conversion to war production was decidedly more aggressive and overt, as Hollywood's established stars and genres, indeed its vast filmmaking repertoire, were effectively retooled for the war effort.

7

Wartime Stars, Genres, and Production Trends

Hollywood's On-screen Conversion

On 8 December 1941, a Warner Bros. story analyst filed a report on an unproduced play, "Everybody Comes to Rick's." The story centers on the American expatriate Rick Blaine, whose café in French Morocco is a haven for European war refugees, and whose life is disrupted by the unexpected arrival of Lois Meredith, the wanton American beauty who, years before, had broken up Rick's marriage and family and cost Rick his law practice in prewar Paris. The story analyst considered the property a "box-office natural" and a suitable vehicle "for Bogart, or Cagney, or Raft in out-of-the-usual roles and perhaps Mary Astor."[1]

A few days later, the report reached the desk of the Warners production chief Hal Wallis, who was encouraged to purchase the property by his savvy story department head, Irene Lee. In light of Warners' current hit, THE MALTESE FALCON, Wallis agreed that "Everybody Comes to Rick's" had potential as another near-A, offbeat thriller. But Wallis had bigger plans for the project, seeing it as an ideal A-class vehicle for his own move to unit producer and for Warners' conversion to war production. Weeks later, when Wallis signed a new contract giving him first crack at the studio's contract talent and story properties, he designated "Everybody Comes to Rick's" as the first project for his production unit. He tapped Michael Curtiz to direct and assigned several top writers to overhaul the story, strengthening both the political and romantic angles. He also entered negotiations with David Selznick for the services of his fast-rising contract star Ingrid Bergman, to costar with Warners' own emerging star Humphrey Bogart.[2]

The result, of course, was CASABLANCA, Hollywood's seminal wartime "conversion narrative." The conversion of studio operations and the retooling of established story formulas into war films were crucial factors, but the key factor in this conversion was the narrative itself. The love story was recast in terms of wartime separation and duty by reworking the female lead: the American seductress Lois was transformed into an innocent European refugee, Ilsa, whose commitment to the French Resistance leader Victor Laszlo actually motivated her earlier betrayal of Rick. And the signal conversion, finally, is Rick's. Early on, Bogart's Rick Blaine is very much the hard-boiled Warners hero: cynical and self-reliant, repeatedly muttering, "I stick my neck out for nobody." But in the course of the story, he rediscovers his own self-worth, along with his love of woman and country. Rick's final heroics—sending Ilsa away with Laszlo, killing the Nazi officer, and leaving Casablanca to join the Free French—crystallized the American conversion from neutrality to selfless sacrifice.

In a more general sense, CASABLANCA signaled the wartime conversion of Hollywood's classical narrative paradigm. As Dana Polan suggests in his study of 1940s film narrative, Hollywood's classical paradigm, with its individual protagonist and clearly resolved conflicts, underwent a temporary but profound shift to accommodate the war effort.[3] The two most fundamental qualities of Hollywood narrative, one might argue, were (and remain) the individual goal-oriented protagonist and the formation of the couple. During the war, however, these two qualities were radically adjusted: the individual had to yield to the will and activity of the collective (the combat unit, the community, the nation, the family); and coupling was suspended "for the duration," subordinated to gender-specific war efforts that involved very different spheres of activity (and conceptions of heroic behavior) for men and women.

Actually, Hollywood always had found conflict in its contradictory conception of the idealized male and female—the untrammeled man of action and of few words (and with well-concealed sentiments) who's "gotta do what he's gotta do," and the supportive, sensitive but stoic Madonna whose natural (even biological) destiny is to tame that free-spirited male for the higher cause of civilization. The resolution of the classical film narrative invariably involved the overcoming of that contradiction in the lovers' final embrace. But the war effort created radically different requirements, indefinitely postponing the climactic coupling while celebrating the lovers' dutiful separation and commitment to a larger cause—the lesson learned from Rick in the final moments of CASABLANCA.

By the time CASABLANCA was released in late 1942, Hollywood's wartime transformation had been under way for nearly a year. Within weeks of Pearl Harbor, and with the Senate propaganda hearings only a few months past, Hollywood shifted from outspoken denial of any overt promotion of U.S. involvement in the war to active on-screen support of that involvement. By mid-1942, about one-third of the features in production dealt directly with the war; a much higher proportion treated the war more indirectly as a given set of social, political, and economic circumstances.

Predictably enough, Hollywood's initial response to the war and to FDR's implicit call to arms was to convert established stars and genres to war production. Abbott and Costello stopped doing their service comedies in late 1941, in deference to the gravity of the military recruiting and training effort. That turned out to be a singular exception; the vast majority of stars and genres underwent just the opposite progression, converting to cinematic war production as soon as the United States entered the war. As the war and Hollywood's treatment of it progressed, the fit between various genres and the war conditions became clearer. Spy, detective, and crime thrillers, for instance, were easily reformulated (perhaps too easily) into espionage thrillers or underground resistance dramas in the early war years. The musical and woman's picture were recycled for war production as well and remained enormously effective throughout the war. The backstage musical was recast to depict groups of entertainers putting on military shows "for the boys," while working-girl sagas and melodramas of maternal or marital sacrifice were ideally suited to war conditions.

Hollywood dealt more directly with the war in combat dramas, documentaries, and newsreels. As the war progressed, in fact, the interplay of fiction and nonfiction war films became increasingly significant and complex, with war-related features evincing a documentary realism by 1944–1945 that was altogether unique for Hollywood movies. Meanwhile, *film noir*, a stylistic countertrend, developed; this 1940s period style

There were many reasons for the recasting of Hollywood's romantic idiom,
among them the departure of top male stars like James Stewart and Clark Gable
for military service.

expressed the bleaker side of the American experience during (and after) World War II. Thus, the war era represents a particularly complex and contradictory period in terms of Hollywood's production trends and on-screen accomplishments. Remarkably few canonized film classics were produced during the war, and yet Hollywood's social impact was more pronounced and more profound than ever before. Never in American film history had the relationship between cinema and social conditions been so direct and so politically charged; never had Hollywood films constituted so distinctly a national cinema. While Hollywood stopped short perhaps of functioning as a state-run propaganda agency, clearly the cinema's role as a culture industry was different during the war than at any other time in its history.

Stars and the Star System

As seen in chapter 5, the war's most immediate impact on the film industry—and certainly its most widely publicized impact—was the manpower shortage and the departure of a contingent of Hollywood male stars for military service. The first top star to leave the industry for military service actually was the British actor David Niven, who enlisted in England in October 1939 after the outbreak of war in Europe. The exodus of American stars did not begin until March 1941, when James Stewart joined the Army Air Corps only days after the Academy Award ceremony in which he won the Oscar for best actor (and delivered the shortest acceptance speech on record: "Thanks").[4] Stewart's departure signaled a steady drain of male talent and notably leading men.[5]

There were frequent jokes about male stars being replaced by dogs (Lassie), horses (Flicka), kids (Margaret O'Brien, Baby Jean), and aging character actors (Charles Coburn and Barry Fitzgerald, both of whom won Oscars during the war). The studios also tried to compensate for the loss of male stars by emphasizing other production values—Technicolor, music, presold properties, and so on—and some in Hollywood openly welcomed the opportunity to develop less star-oriented pictures. A new generation of wartime stars emerged, of course, although the male replacements, such as Alan Ladd, Van Johnson, Roy Rogers, Gregory Peck, and Ray Milland, were overshadowed by a coterie of rising female stars, including Betty Grable, Greer Garson, Rita Hayworth, Veronica Lake, Margaret O'Brien, Lauren Bacall, and Jennifer Jones.

Many of the male stars who joined the service maintained high media profiles through popular press and newsreel coverage, particularly those who became decorated officers or qualified as bona-fide war heroes. Clark Gable, for instance, rose from the rank of private to major in the air force, winning an Air Medal for bombing missions over Germany during which he manned both machine guns and newsreel cameras. Douglas Fairbanks Jr. won a Silver Star for his service at Salerno, and two destroyers under Robert Montgomery's command sank in the Pacific. Jimmy Stewart's wartime exploits were perhaps the most celebrated. He began his military career as a private and within nine months had won a commission as a second lieutenant. After serving as a flight instructor in the western United States, he was assigned in 1943 to a Liberator bomber group in England as squadron commander (at the rank of captain) and flew dozens of strategic bombing runs over Germany. In 1944, he rose to the rank of colonel and was awarded the Distinguished Flying Cross.[6]

Besides the drain on male acting talent, the war era also saw the studios' established control of the star system continue to erode. Stars not only took temporary leave for

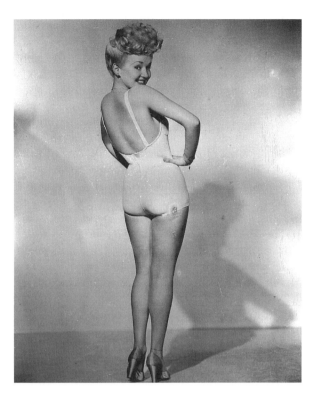

Hollywood's leading female stars served the cause offscreen as well as on—as with Betty Grable's ubiquitous pinup and Greer Garson's christening of a naval warship.

military duty but also went freelance in increasing numbers with no intention of returning to studio employ. Moreover, the studio's established contractual methods were
severely undercut when, in 1943–1944, the courts in California upheld Olivia de
Havilland's suit against Warner Bros. for unreasonable suspension policies, thus establishing an actor's right to refuse roles and to sit out the duration of his or her contract.[7]

Despite the depleted ranks of male stars and eroding studio authority over stars'
careers, the industry remained as star-driven and audiences as starstruck as ever during
the war—arguably more so, considering the stars' unprecedented importance offscreen. Pinups of Betty Grable and Rita Hayworth were taped inside helmets and mess
kits; Donald Duck was featured in more than four hundred official military insignias (the
Disney animators designed well over a thousand such insignias during the war); and
stars actively publicized and promoted the war effort, raising billions in war bonds in
movie theaters across the country and entertaining the troops around the globe.[8]

This last point was especially important in terms of the role, status, and visibility of
movie stars during the war. Carole Lombard's death in a January 1942 plane crash while
on a war-bond tour generated enormous publicity and sympathy, as did the decision of
Myrna Loy to retire for the duration to work for the Red Cross. There was an unprecedented amount of personal contact between stars and the public. Hundreds of thousands of servicemen talked and danced with stars at the Hollywood Canteen and the
Stage Door Canteen while passing through Los Angeles and New York City. And Bob
Hope, whose wartime work for the USO's Foxhole Circuit became legendary, had
appeared before an estimated two million servicemen by late 1944.[9]

Many stars regarded filmmaking as their patriotic duty—as did the government,
which declared Hollywood stars "essential" to the industry (and thus subject to draft
deferment). SAG publicly decried this policy as preferential treatment, and in fact
Mickey Rooney was the only major star whose studio (MGM) applied for such a deferment. The resulting negative publicity was so severe that MGM rescinded the request;
Rooney then proceeded with his induction but failed his draft physical. He remained at
MGM until Roosevelt's "work or fight" edict in early 1944 revoked his deferment, at
which point Rooney joined the army.[10]

The top stars during the war era ranked as follows in terms of their popular and commercial appeal, with the order based on yearly rankings from 1942 to 1945 in the *Motion
Picture Herald*'s annual Exhibitors' Poll.[11]

Table 7.1
TOP-RANKED STARS, 1942–1945

1.	Gary Cooper	11.	Mickey Rooney
2.	Betty Grable	12.	James Cagney
3.	Bob Hope	13.	Clark Gable
4.	Bing Crosby	14.	Walter Pidgeon
5.	Abbott and Costello	15.	Dorothy Lamour
6.	Greer Garson	16.	Wallace Beery
7.	Spencer Tracy	17.	Cary Grant
8.	Humphrey Bogart	18.	Tyrone Power
9.	Judy Garland	19.	Alice Faye
10.	Bette Davis	20.	Van Johnson

SOURCE: *Motion Picture Herald*, 26 December 1942, p. 13; 25 December 1943, p. 13;
30 December 1944, p. 12; 29 December 1945, p. 13.

During the four war years, the stars in the first six positions utterly dominated the box office, and all but Cooper became fixed in the public imagination (and still are widely remembered) as wartime stars. Only four from this elite group—Cooper, Hope, Grable, and Garson—ranked in the top ten all four war years. Crosby and the team of Abbott and Costello placed in the top ten three out of the four years; Crosby climbed to the number-one spot in 1944 and 1945, while the comedy duo started the war at number one but declined slightly each year. A dozen stars remained in the top twenty-five all four years, including all of the top ten in this combined list, plus Rooney and Pidgeon; Pidgeon was the only one of that dozen who failed to crack the top ten at least once during the war.

Several stars fell from the annual Exhibitors' Poll after joining the service: Gable, Autry, Power, and the newcomer Alan Ladd. A few stars who remained in Hollywood during the war also fell from the rankings, notably Cagney and Errol Flynn. A crop of new stars—like Ladd, Van Johnson, and particularly Betty Grable—were virtual unknowns before the war but became top stars by 1944–1945. In fact, nine of the top twenty-five stars in 1944 and eleven in 1945 had not been ranked at all in 1942 or 1943, including Margaret O'Brien, Roy Rogers, Betty Hutton, Ingrid Bergman, Van Johnson, Danny Kaye, Joseph Cotten, and John Wayne.

Productivity was a key factor in the rise of many of these stars. Despite prewar studies by both Gallup and Leo Rosten indicating that top stars should do two to three pictures per year to maintain their currency, Hollywood's elite made fewer films during the war. The top ten stars in the combined list averaged two per year in 1942–1943 but fell to less than one and a half annually in the next two years. The market was changing along with pay scales, tax laws, and war-related obligations, and top stars seemed perfectly willing, in most cases, to cut back. And the market was hot enough that the cuts in productivity barely affected the rankings of several stars. Spencer Tracy maintained his number-five ranking in 1944 and 1945, for instance, while turning out only three pictures; Garson placed in the top ten despite doing only one picture in each of those two years; and remarkably, Bob Hope remained in the top ten both years with only one release in 1944 and none in 1945. Other top stars, including several Oscar nominees and winners—Joan Fontaine, Barbara Stanwyck, and Katharine Hepburn, for example—never even ranked in the top twenty-five, let alone the top ten, owing primarily to low output.

While top stars tended to make fewer films as the war went on, many emerging and second-rank stars gained a competitive edge by working at a much higher rate of output; some actually increased their rate during the war. The ascending male stars, in particular, took advantage of the dearth of leading men and the lighter workloads of their top-ranked colleagues. Ray Milland did eleven pictures during the war, Fred MacMurray did fourteen, and both Van Johnson and John Wayne did fifteen. The war era also saw a reversal of the prewar trend toward male stars atop the rankings: a number of women broke into the top ten. Four of the top ten in the combined listing were women, two of whom (Bette Davis and Judy Garland) were established prewar stars while the other two (Betty Grable and Greer Garson) rose to stardom just as the war broke out.

Greer Garson was a wartime phenomenon of the first order among Hollywood's stars. Arguably the most potent propaganda weapon in Hollywood's arsenal, Garson's stardom coincided almost exactly with the war itself. Born in Ireland in 1908 (and thus well into her thirties when she became a star), Garson was educated in London, where she trained on the stage before joining the MGM-British unit. She was an instant success with Metro, scoring an Oscar nomination in her first role as Robert Donat's dutiful spouse in GOODBYE, MR. CHIPS. The maternal role and Academy nomination set a dual precedent for Garson, although in the future hers would be the title role—invariably with Walter Pidgeon as the dutiful spouse. Pegged by Mayer in 1941 to succeed the poised and well-bred Norma Shearer (who turned down the Miniver role), Garson quickly emerged as Metro's wartime Madonna: a rare beauty of heroic courage, repressed sexuality, and indomitable spirit who nurtured orphans, offspring, and spouse in one lavish melodrama after another. She was nominated as Best Actress every year from 1941 to 1945 for BLOSSOMS IN THE DUST (1941), MRS. MINIVER (1942), MADAME CURIE (1943), MRS. PARKINGTON (1944), and THE VALLEY OF DECISION (1945)—all sizable commercial and critical hits, as was her other major star vehicle during the war, RANDOM HARVEST (1942).

Most of Garson's pictures were period pieces adapted from popular novels and were among MGM's most ambitious wartime productions. She worked with top studio personnel, notably the producer Sidney Franklin, the director Mervyn LeRoy, and the cinematographer Joe Ruttenberg. Her pictures racked up dozens of Academy nominations and quite a few Oscars; MRS. MINIVER was by far the most successful, virtually sweeping the 1942 awards—including Best Actress for Garson. And perhaps the best indication of her popular and commercial success during the war was Garson's legendary

Greer Garson's wartime persona was firmly fixed in the title role of MRS. MINIVER *(1942).*

"monopoly" over Radio City Music Hall. Her films routinely did holdover business there, with MRS. MINIVER and RANDOM HARVEST setting then-record runs of ten and eleven weeks, respectively, in 1942 and 1943. MADAME CURIE enjoyed a long run at Radio City in 1944, and by June 1945, as THE VALLEY OF DECISION began its eighth week there, Garson's playing time at Radio City had reached fully eleven months during the war years alone. The nation's busiest theater, in other words, devoted one-fourth of its screen time during World War II to Greer Garson.[12]

Betty Grable, Hollywood's other leading female star and wartime icon, presented a marked contrast to Garson. Whereas Garson proved ideal for MGM's dignified and somewhat subdued prestige pictures, Grable's brassy blonde with "million dollar legs" and well-honed song-and-dance skills proved ideal for Fox's slick, high-energy musicals. While Garson personified the tastes and sensibilities of Louis B. Mayer and MGM, Grable was the consummate Zanuck-Fox star: unabashedly sexy and attractive, with a screen personality that, like Tyrone Power's in his signature action-romances, utterly dominated one formula picture after another. For Grable the formula was Technicolor musicals with threadbare plots and promising titles that were quite literally constructed around her performance and her figure. While Grable invariably was teamed with an adequate male star like John Payne or Victor Mature, she clearly carried films like SONG OF THE ISLANDS (1942), SPRINGTIME IN THE ROCKIES (1942), CONEY ISLAND (1943), SWEET ROSIE O'GRADY (1943), PIN-UP GIRL (1944), and DIAMOND HORSESHOE (1945). These were money in the bank for Fox, and their success put Grable atop the 1943 Exhibitors' Poll.

Gary Cooper was the leading male star during the war years. Interestingly enough, Cooper's image as an ascetic loner and strong silent type softened during the war, beginning with his initial wartime effort, BALL OF FIRE (1941), a screwball comedy hit costarring Barbara Stanwyck and directed by Howard Hawks. Cooper followed that with a reversion to form and an even bigger hit, THE PRIDE OF THE YANKEES (1942), a biopic of the baseball legend Lou Gehrig (who had died recently at age 37) directed by Sam Wood.

THE PRIDE OF THE YANKEES ended Cooper's association with the producer Sam Goldwyn, although Goldwyn did have a hand in Cooper's next two pictures. Those involved deals with Selznick, Paramount, and Warners, turning on the services of Cooper and Ingrid Bergman (and the directing services of Sam Wood, also under contract to Goldwyn). Goldwyn orchestrated the deal whereby Selznick loaned Bergman to Paramount to costar with Cooper in FOR WHOM THE BELL TOLLS, which led in turn to an arrangement in early 1943 whereby Warners reteamed the pair in SARATOGA TRUNK.[13] Both were directed by Wood, and both were huge hits. FOR WHOM THE BELL TOLLS, a 168-minute Technicolor adaptation of Ernest Hemingway's war romance, emerged as the biggest box-office hit of 1943. SARATOGA TRUNK, another ambitious adaptation of a best-seller (by Edna Ferber), was produced in 1943 but then consigned to Warners' stockpile, where it remained for over two years—reasonably enough, since it was a period piece with two top stars. When Warners finally released SARATOGA TRUNK in early 1946, the Cooper-Bergman vehicle earned over $5 million.

After THE STORY OF DR. WASSELL (1944), a war-related biopic for DeMille and Paramount, Cooper teamed with the screenwriter Nunnally Johnson (who had recently resigned from Fox) to set up an independent unit with UA. Cooper and Johnson collaborated on CASANOVA BROWN (1944), a romantic comedy written and produced by Johnson that reteamed Cooper with Teresa Wright and the director Sam Wood, and ALONG CAME JONES (1945), a Western comedy-drama produced by Cooper and written

Director Sam Wood (left, with script) confers with cinematographer Ray Rennehan and costars Ingrid Bergman and Gary Cooper for a scene in FOR WHOM THE BELL TOLLS *(1943).*

by Johnson that playfully undercut the Cooper persona. While the independent pictures were commercial disappointments, Cooper remained atop the Exhibitors' Poll because of the tremendous "legs" of FOR WHOM THE BELL TOLLS. As of January 1945, the 1943 release had earned over $4 million and still had not gone into widespread general release.[14]

Cooper's laconic individualist was utterly at odds with Hollywood's other top male wartime stars: Hope and Crosby, and Abbott and Costello. Both tandems enjoyed extraordinary wartime success, refining and to some extent varying their prewar routines and musical-comedy personas. Abbott and Costello appeared only as a team in eleven wartime comedies, eight for Universal and three on loan to MGM. After moving away from service comedies once the war broke out, they specialized in genre parodies— including PARDON MY SARONG, a 1942 spoof of the Hope-Crosby Road pictures. They also reworked the "in the navy" angle with ABBOTT AND COSTELLO IN HOLLYWOOD (1945) and IN SOCIETY (1944). The Abbott and Costello comedies relied less on music and musical costars during the war, although a few musical numbers were still worked in. The box-office returns were consistently in the $2 million range, even when the overall market was rising, which helps explain why their ranking fell each year during the war. The team remained invaluable, however, to Universal, which managed to keep their picture costs down to a bare minimum. IN SOCIETY, for example, cost only $660,000, remarkably little for an A-class picture in 1945.[15]

Paramount's Hope and Crosby, whose costarring ventures (with Dorothy Lamour) had propelled them to top stardom, began and ended the war era together with hit Road comedies: ROAD TO MOROCCO in 1942 and ROAD TO UTOPIA, which was produced in 1944 but stockpiled until late 1945. There were no intervening Road pictures, although Hope and Crosby appeared together in several revue-format pictures like STAR SPANGLED RHYTHM (1942) and DUFFY'S TAVERN (1945). Crosby also had a memorable cameo in the climactic battle scene in Hope's 1944 swashbuckling spoof, THE PRINCESS AND THE PIRATE. Hope and Crosby each costarred with Lamour during the war: Crosby in a 1943 musical biopic, DIXIE, and Hope in a 1943 espionage comedy-thriller (increasingly his forte), THEY GOT ME COVERED. Lamour also starred in her familiar tropical excursions, such as BEYOND THE BLUE HORIZON (1942) and RAINBOW ISLAND (1944).

As successful as Hope and Crosby were in tandem, and as firmly as the two are fixed in wartime cultural memory in the Road pictures, they actually had their greatest success during the war in separate and quite different ventures. In fact, Crosby's two biggest wartime hits teamed him with other male costars: Fred Astaire in HOLIDAY INN (1942) and Barry Fitzgerald in GOING MY WAY (1944). The latter was a wartime sensation, netting Paramount $6.5 million, scoring seven Oscars (including Best Actor for Crosby and Best Supporting Actor for Fitzgerald), and propelling Crosby to the number-one spot in the Exhibitors' Poll. He remained on top in 1945, owing largely to THE BELLS OF ST. MARY'S opposite Ingrid Bergman. Hope, meanwhile, devoted himself to the USO, the War Activities Committee, the Hollywood Canteen, and other wartime causes. In fact, Paramount suspended Hope in 1944 for failing to appear in a third picture that year (after THE PRINCESS AND THE PIRATE and ROAD TO UTOPIA).[16] Hope shrugged off the suspension and continued to perform on the Foxhole Circuit overseas, and Paramount eventually relented when Hope was awarded a special Oscar for his war-related humanitarian efforts.

Paramount's suspension of Bob Hope was not for lack of product. The studio had built the industry's largest inventory by 1944—even after unloading that sizable package to UA—and successfully developed new talent as well. In 1942, Paramount scored with Alan Ladd and Veronica Lake in two stylish low-cost thrillers, THIS GUN FOR HIRE and THE GLASS KEY. Military service interrupted Ladd's rise, while war-plant work had a curious impact on Lake's screen persona. She was asked to modify her "peek-a-boo" hairstyle with its wave of hair over one eye; popular with women workers, it interfered with machinery operation. In the later war years, two of Paramount's lesser comedy stars had breakthrough roles in dramatic films: Fred MacMurray in DOUBLE INDEMNITY (opposite Barbara Stanwyck) in 1944, and Ray Milland in an Oscar-winning performance in THE LOST WEEKEND in 1945, both directed and coscripted by Billy Wilder. Meanwhile, the wartime comedies of another Paramount hyphenate, Preston Sturges, helped bring Betty Hutton, Joel McCrea, and Eddie Bracken to star status.

MGM was even more successful in developing new talent during the war. Besides Garson and Pidgeon, several younger Metro players were on the rise, including Lana Turner, Van Johnson, Red Skelton, Robert Walker, and two precocious preadolescents, Margaret O'Brien and Elizabeth Taylor. The wartime ascents of Van Johnson and Margaret O'Brien were particularly impressive. Van Johnson began in 1942 with bit parts and a supporting role in DR. GILLESPIE'S NEW ASSISTANT (replacing Lew Ayres,

Wartime heartthrobs Frank Sinatra and Van Johnson.

who left the series and the studio after declaring himself a conscientious objector to the war).[17] By 1945, Johnson had matured into Metro's consummate boy-next-door type, rising to number two in the Exhibitors' Poll and competing with Frank Sinatra for the hearts and screams of America's bobby-soxers. Margaret O'Brien was five years old in 1942 when she was cast as a wartime waif in the London blitz in JOURNEY FOR MARGARET (1942). After a series of minor roles in major pictures like MADAME CURIE (1943) and JANE EYRE (1944), O'Brien's breakthrough came in MEET ME IN ST. LOUIS (1944), costarring with Judy Garland. In 1945, she joined Johnson, Garson, Tracy, and Garland among the top-ten box-office stars—MGM's strongest showing since the 1930s—and won a special Oscar as Hollywood's top child actor.

In 1942, the MGM stars Spencer Tracy and Katharine Hepburn first teamed up in a hit romantic comedy, WOMAN OF THE YEAR, and then did a somber but effective political drama, KEEPER OF THE FLAME. Each starred in a rather heavy war film in 1944— Hepburn in DRAGON SEED, from Pearl S. Buck's story of Chinese resistance to the invading Japanese, and Tracy as a prisoner of war in THE SEVENTH CROSS. In 1945, they reteamed in a comedy-drama, WITHOUT LOVE, which was something of a disappointment. In fact, Tracy's most effective teaming in the later war years was opposite the fast-rising Van Johnson in A GUY NAMED JOE (1943) and THIRTY SECONDS OVER TOKYO (1944)—two of MGM's biggest hits of the war.

MGM's postadolescent star duo, Judy Garland and Mickey Rooney, teamed success-fully in two more Freed-produced, Berkeley-directed musicals, BABES ON BROADWAY (1941) and GIRL CRAZY (1943), and also enjoyed considerable success working sepa-rately—Rooney in three more Hardy Family installments, and Garland in three other Freed unit musicals, notably MEET ME IN ST. LOUIS. Each also was top-billed in a seri-ous wartime drama: Rooney as Homer Macauley, the telegram delivery boy (and bear-er of bad tidings) in THE HUMAN COMEDY (1943); and Garland opposite Robert Walker in THE CLOCK, a romantic drama directed by Vincente Minnelli (in his first nonmusical) and a surprise hit in 1945.

Another wartime MGM star of note was Wallace Beery, the hard-bitten, semiarticu-late screen veteran who was pushing 60 and, along with a few other aging male actors, enjoyed renewed stardom during the war. Beery had risen to top stardom in the early 1930s opposite Marie Dressler, but her death in 1934 ended that unlikely pairing. In a savvy bit of casting, MGM paired Beery with the equally cantankerous Marjorie Main in THE BUGLE SOUNDS (1941), JACKASS MAIL (1942), and RATIONING (1944). Beery also lumbered through SALUTE TO THE MARINES (1943) and THIS MAN'S NAVY (1945), work-ing his way to number eleven in the 1944 Exhibitors' Poll and winning yet another con-tract from MGM in early 1945.[18]

The Warner Bros. star roster saw heavy changes during the war, although few were due to military service. The studio's only significant loss to the military was Ronald Reagan, who joined up shortly after Pearl Harbor and just as the release of KINGS ROW (1942) put him on the verge of top stardom. Cagney won an Oscar in 1942 for his por-trayal of George M. Cohan in YANKEE DOODLE DANDY, then abruptly left Warners to set up shop at UA. Edward G. Robinson left Warners in 1942 as well, doing his best work of the decade shortly thereafter: in Billy Wilder's DOUBLE INDEMNITY and then in two Fritz Lang psychodramas, THE WOMAN IN THE WINDOW (1944) and SCARLET STREET (1945).

Errol Flynn remained at Warners but faded badly, despite the success of his first two pictures with the director Raoul Walsh, the Custer biopic THEY DIED WITH THEIR BOOTS ON (1941) and as the boxer James J. Corbet in another period biography, GENTLEMAN JIM (1942). Flynn's slide, which began with the subsequent war-related dramas (EDGE OF DARKNESS, NORTHERN PURSUIT, 1943; UNCERTAIN GLORY, 1944), owed less to the material than to his increasingly dissolute lifestyle and difficult behav-ior at the studio, as well as the negative publicity surrounding two separate statutory rape charges in 1942. By 1945, Flynn's star status and matinee-idol appeal had waned, although he did close out the war years with an effective and uncharacteristically grim performance in his one distinguished war picture, OBJECTIVE BURMA (1945).

A more positive wartime note for Warners was the success of Bette Davis in such well-crafted star vehicles as NOW, VOYAGER (1942), OLD ACQUAINTANCE (1943), MR. SKEFFINGTON (1944), and THE CORN IS GREEN (1945)—Warners' prestige equivalents, in effect, to Metro's Greer Garson vehicles. Davis also was effective in Warners' 1943 adaptation of Lillian Hellman's wartime drama WATCH ON THE RHINE, although in a sup-porting role. None of Davis's wartime films was a breakaway hit, but they routinely returned $2–3 million to Warners, which confirmed her value by giving Davis a profit-sharing deal in 1943 and allowing her to do outside pictures—long a sticking point between Davis and Jack Warner.[19]

Warners also made three significant additions to its stable of female stars in 1944, sig-naling a more aggressive pursuit of the women's market. Barbara Stanwyck signed a

Bette Davis, shown here in a costume test for NOW, VOYAGER *(1942), was among a large—and utterly unique—group of "mature" female stars during the war.*

five-year, ten-picture deal (at $100,000 per picture), which took effect in January 1944.[20] In April, Warners signed Rosalind Russell to a three-year, three-picture deal (at $150,000 per picture).[21] That same month, Warners cut a three-picture, three-year deal with Joan Crawford (at $100,000 per picture).[22] Interestingly enough, all three were under consideration by the producer Jerry Wald in May 1944 for the title role in MILDRED PIERCE, and reportedly all three wanted the part.[23] Crawford was particularly eager, having reconsidered her strident refusal to play maternal roles at MGM only a few years before. Crawford won the part and an Oscar in the 1945 picture, thus consolidating her position alongside Davis as Warners' top female star.

The 1944 Warners deals with Stanwyck, Russell, and Crawford signaled not only a significant change in the studio's long-standing male ethos but also an important change in the wartime industry at large. Clearly Warners had plans to increase its output of women's films, and to do so with more mature stars: Russell turned 36 in 1944, as did Bette Davis; Stanwyck was 37, and Crawford 40. By some Hollywood standards, each was well past her prime—as could be said of Garson as well, at age 36. But those standards were changing, both because of the war and because of the increasing importance of women's films and female audiences.

While Warners increased its investment in women's pictures (and female audiences) during the war, it scarcely abandoned its traditional commitment to male action pictures. In fact, the 1942 departure of Cagney and Robinson was countered by the rapid wartime rise of two new resident tough guys, both of whom had been with Warners since the late 1930s. One was John Garfield, reminiscent of the young Cagney and an ideal Warners type in combat dramas such as AIR FORCE, THE FALLEN SPARROW (both 1943), DESTINATION TOKYO (1944), and PRIDE OF THE MARINES (1945). The other was Humphrey Bogart, who emerged during the war not only as Warners' top star but as Hollywood's consummate male hero, a wartime icon as distinctive in his way as Greer Garson or Betty Grable.

CASE STUDY: HUMPHREY BOGART

In December 1941, THE MALTESE FALCON was Warners' surprise hit of the year and Humphrey Bogart's contract option was up for renewal. Bogart had signed a five-year contract back in December 1937 starting at $1,100 per week, with yearly options pushing his salary to $1,850 per week in 1941. Picking up Bogart's final option in that standard term contract would take him to $2,000 per week. Jack Warner had no reservations about renewing the contract, but he was still unsure whether Bogart was top star material. In fact, Warner had just cast Bogart in two second-rate crime thrillers, ALL THROUGH THE NIGHT and THE BIG SHOT (both released in 1942). His star potential was obvious enough, however, and Warners' leading filmmakers considered Bogart a no-nonsense professional with a workhorse mentality. So Warner decided to tear up the 1937 contract, and on 3 January 1942, he signed Bogart to a new seven-year deal starting at $2,750 per week—a reasonable sum but nowhere near what the studio's top stars were making. Flynn at the time was pulling down $6,000 per week, for example, while Cagney was earning $150,000 per film plus 10 percent of the gross over $1.5 million. The Bogart pact was exceptional, however, in that it was a straight seven-year deal with no annual option clauses.[24]

Among Bogart's chief supporters at Warners was Hal Wallis, who as unit producer had two Bogart projects under way. In late December, Wallis secured the rights to a

Saturday Evening Post serial, "Aloha Means Goodbye," and he had the staff writer Richard Macauley rework it with a post–Pearl Harbor angle.[25] Retitled ACROSS THE PACIFIC (1942), the film featured Bogart as an ex-naval officer working undercover who exposes a group of Japanese sympathizers planning to destroy the Panama Canal. Wallis assigned the director John Huston to the film along with two of Bogart's costars from THE MALTESE FALCON, Mary Astor and Sidney Greenstreet. (The picture was completed by the director Vincent Sherman when Huston left for military duty.) Unlike ALL THROUGH THE NIGHT, a fairly clumsy amalgam of gangster and espionage clichés, ACROSS THE PACIFIC was politically subtle and dramatically sharp, winning critical accolades and earning Warners $1.3 million.

While ACROSS THE PACIFIC was an important star turn for Bogart, it was essentially a B-plus project which, like THE MALTESE FALCON, was lifted to A-class status by the talent involved. Bogart's next picture, however, was designed from the outset to be a first-class Warners production. After Wallis bought the rights to "Everybody Comes to Rick's," both Ronald Reagan and George Raft were considered for the role of Rick Blaine. But by April 1942, Wallis had decided on Bogart for the picture, now titled CASABLANCA, and had signed Ingrid Bergman to costar.[26]

With Bogart and Bergman cast, Wallis sent the script into rewrites, and the story underwent extensive changes, as mentioned earlier. As the picture neared production, Wallis had various writers work on different aspects of the script—all of them involving Bogart's hero. Casey Robinson, who specialized in romantic melodrama, worked (uncredited) on the Rick-Ilsa love story. The Epstein twins, Julius and Philip, known for light comedy (and just off a rewrite of YANKEE DOODLE DANDY), did a complete dialogue polish and also worked on the rapport between Rick and Louis Renault, the local prefect of police (played by Claude Rains). Meanwhile, Howard Koch (THE SEA HAWK, SERGEANT YORK, etc.) reworked Bogart's character with an emphasis on both the action and the political intrigue.

CASABLANCA was shot during the summer of 1942, with Michael Curtiz directing, and was completed in November at a final cost of $878,000. Warner and Wallis considered adding a tag scene to clarify the fate of Rick and Louis, but those plans were abandoned when the Allies began Operation Torch, a massive offensive in North Africa in the very region where the film was set. So Warners rushed the picture through postproduction for a Thanksgiving premiere, clarifying the ending simply by redubbing the final exchange between Rick and Louis as they walk away in the fog; Wallis himself reportedly came up with Bogart's immortal closing line, "Louis, this could be the beginning of a beautiful friendship."[27] CASABLANCA officially opened in January 1943, just as Roosevelt and Churchill began a series of summit talks in Casablanca, further exploiting the picture's topical appeal. CASABLANCA became one of Warners' all-time biggest hits, returning $4.1 million, winning an Oscar for best picture, and confirming Bogart's status as an A-class star.

Bogart followed CASABLANCA in 1943 with two straightforward combat films, ACTION IN THE NORTH ATLANTIC and, on loan to Columbia, SAHARA. The former celebrated the U.S. merchant marine convoys, and the latter celebrated the Allies' efforts in North Africa; both reinforced Bogart's wartime persona as the hard-bitten realist who realigns his rugged individualism with the collective war effort and emerges as a natural leader in the process. Both pictures were hits: ACTION IN THE NORTH ATLANTIC returned $2.6 million to Warners, while SAHARA was Columbia's top release of the year, netting $2.3 million. Those pictures, along with CASABLANCA, vaulted Bogart from twenty-fifth to seventh in the 1943 Exhibitors' Poll—the first of seven straight years for Bogart in the top ten.

Wallis developed Bogart's next Warners picture, PASSAGE TO MARSEILLES (1944), as a follow-up to CASABLANCA, reuniting Bogart, Rains, Lorre, Greenstreet, and Curtiz. But the story, depicting a group of disparate losers who escape Devil's Island to join the Free French, was an oddly uneven and disjointed affair which devoted far too little time to Bogart's character. While engaging in retrospect as a consummate example of what might be termed "Warners *noir*," with its convoluted time frame, exotic darkness, and cynical outlook, PASSAGE TO MARSEILLES was Bogart's only wartime disappointment.

Bogart's career then took a rather dramatic turn, owing in large part to Hal Wallis's departure for Paramount and Bogart's collaboration with Howard Hawks on his next two pictures, TO HAVE AND HAVE NOT (1944) and THE BIG SLEEP (1946). Each picture refined the Bogart persona, and each displayed an ideal melding of the Bogart, Hawks, and Warners styles: they are taut, economical thrillers whose action, pace, and penchant for violence are offset by elements of comedy and romance and by a wry self-awareness that typified both Bogart and Hawks at their best. Crucial to this effect was Lauren Bacall, who costarred with Bogart in both pictures.

The first of the Hawks-Bogart pictures was initiated in 1943 when Hawks, after completing AIR FORCE for Warners, created an independent company, H-F Productions (with his agent Charles K. Feldman) and purchased the rights to Hemingway's 1937 novel *To Have and Have Not* from Howard Hughes for $97,000. Hawks then sold the

Bogart and Bacall in one of the additional scenes done to build up Bacall's role and the romantic dimension of THE BIG SLEEP *(1946).*

property to Warners for $108,500 plus 20 percent of the film's gross up to $3 million, and he agreed to produce and direct the picture.[28] H-F also sold Warners the contract of Hawks's 19-year-old discovery, Lauren Bacall.[29] Hawks brought in William Faulkner and Jules Furthman for the adaptation. Furthman had scripted ONLY ANGELS HAVE WINGS for Hawks in 1939 as well as several Von Sternberg-Dietrich films, and at Hawks's behest, he modeled Bacall's character on the surly, sultry Dietrich persona.[30]

Ostensibly an adaptation of Hemingway's best-selling novel, TO HAVE AND HAVE NOT was also indebted to CASABLANCA. Bosley Crowther in the *New York Times* described it as "'Casablanca' moved west into the somewhat less hectic Caribbean," a transformation accomplished "with surprisingly comparable effect."[31] Like CASABLANCA (and unlike the novel), TO HAVE AND HAVE NOT was a romantic intrigue, with a war-related backdrop, whose enigmatic hero finds love and sheds his cynical neutrality to take on the nefarious Nazis. Again the action is set in an exotic foreign locale and centers on a saloon, replete with ceiling fans, sunlight slanting in through the venetian blinds, and an array of colorful characters, including a piano-playing sidekick and an overweight heavy. Despite the similarities, several qualities of TO HAVE AND HAVE NOT, particularly the Bogart-Bacall relationship, set the film off rather dramatically from CASABLANCA. As with many Hawks-directed thrillers and action films, TO HAVE AND HAVE NOT is an offbeat romantic comedy involving a self-reliant, resolutely unattached male and a wisecracking, aggressive woman who violates his space and his all-male group, eventually breaking down his defenses and winning both his affection and his respect. Bacall played the role to perfection, evoking from Bogart an emotional depth that he had not previously displayed on-screen—not even opposite Bergman in CASABLANCA.

While TO HAVE AND HAVE NOT was still in production, Hawks and Bogart decided to follow it with a detective thriller in the mold of THE MALTESE FALCON—only this time with Bogart playing Raymond Chandler's hard-boiled private eye, Philip Marlowe. H-F Productions purchased the screen rights to Chandler's 1939 novel *The Big Sleep,* and Hawks set Faulkner to work on the adaptation with the newcomer Leigh Brackett (while Furthman remained on TO HAVE AND HAVE NOT).[32] By late fall, the Hemingway adaptation was completed and released, and in December 1944 the Hawks unit opened production on THE BIG SLEEP.

Hawks and company initially treated THE BIG SLEEP as a straight detective story and Bogart vehicle, with Bacall relegated to a supporting role. But by the time Hawks finished shooting in the spring of 1945, the full impact of Bacall's popular appeal and of the Bogart-Bacall chemistry in TO HAVE AND HAVE NOT had become evident. The earlier picture was a major hit ($3.65 million in rentals), Bacall had been dubbed "The Look" by the press, and the gossip columns were rife with stories of Bogart's breakup with his wife, Mayo Methot, and his plans to marry Bacall. (They wed in May 1945.) Hawks and Jack Warner were acutely aware of the opportunity missed in THE BIG SLEEP, especially after test audiences responded poorly to preview screenings in early summer. Warner decided to postpone release and to rush out CONFIDENTIAL AGENT (1945), a war-related spy story starring Bacall and Charles Boyer (her only film during the 1940s without Bogart). That gave Bacall additional exposure and gave Hawks time to rework THE BIG SLEEP as a Bogart-Bacall picture.

Actually, the strategy for Hawks's overhaul of THE BIG SLEEP had been outlined by the film critic (and later screenwriter) James Agee in his November 1944 review of TO HAVE AND HAVE NOT in *The Nation:* "The best of the picture has no plot at all, but is a leisurely series of mating duels between Humphrey Bogart at his most proficient and the very entertaining, very adolescent new blonde, Lauren Bacall."[33] That observation turned out to be a blueprint for the later overhaul of THE BIG SLEEP. As Hawks's part-ner Charles Feldman explained in a letter to Jack Warner: "Bacall is more insolent than Bogart [in TO HAVE AND HAVE NOT], and this very insolence endeared her both in the public's and the critic's mind." The retakes, he said, would "give the girl [Bacall] at least three or four additional scenes with Bogart of the insolent and provocative nature that she had in *To Have and Have Not*."[34]

The added scenes effectively recast THE BIG SLEEP as an offbeat romantic intrigue and undoubtedly improved its box office, which netted Warners $3 million after the film's release in early 1946. In fact, the Bogart-Bacall courtship—itself tinged with intrigue, since the girl's allegiance to Marlowe is uncertain until late in the story—may have provided the film with an element of coherence that was otherwise sorely lacking. As Hawks and others have related, the writers had considerable difficulty with Chandler's convoluted plot, as did critics and audiences.[35] The love story made perfect sense, of course, and countered the pervasive darkness and brutality of the film, which was still among the more nihilistic thrillers of the period.

THE BIG SLEEP provided a fitting vehicle to carry Bogart out of the war years, just as THE MALTESE FALCON had fittingly ushered them in. Indeed, there was a remarkable sym-metry to Bogart's career in the early 1940s: his prewar portrayal of the detective Sam Spade and his postwar Philip Marlowe effectively bracketed the war era, while Bogart opened and closed the war period itself with two other oddly symmetrical films, CASABLANCA and TO HAVE AND HAVE NOT. These in turn bracketed several straightfor-ward combat films done in 1943, in the midst of the war. There is a linear trajectory here as well, a clear development of Bogart's screen persona. THE MALTESE FALCON and CASA-BLANCA firmly established Bogart's persona just when Cagney and Robinson left Warners, and they also distinguished Bogart from Warners' other top male star, Errol Flynn. Whereas Flynn was vigorous and athletic, Bogart was contemplative and a bit sedentary. Flynn was hyperkinetic; Bogart was quintessentially "cool." Flynn flashed youthful good looks and exuded sexuality; Bogart was rumpled and pushing middle age. (Bogart was, in fact, ten years older than Flynn.) Flynn was in constant, breathless motion; Bogart was a figure in repose, hunched in a trenchcoat with a cigarette dangling from his lips. Bogart also proved in ACTION IN THE NORTH ATLANTIC and SAHARA to be more adaptable to the war film than Flynn, while he could hold his own in more romantic roles as well.

The intervening war films as well as his rapport with Bacall were crucial to the mat-uration of Bogart's screen persona, motivating a commitment to something beyond him-self while reinforcing the viability of his personal code. Bogart's persona reached full maturity in the Hawks films, which were more than a mere rehash of THE MALTESE FALCON and CASABLANCA, despite the similarities. Thus, the vaguely earnest and aggressive Sam Spade gave way to the postwar Philip Marlowe—older, more subdued, and more world-weary, yet with a sense of humor, a deeper resolve, and the capacity for genuine affection. Bogart, in other words, had become "Bogie."

Genres and Production Trends

Few periods in Hollywood's history were as overtly genre-oriented as World War II; war themes permeated a range of established genres and the war film steadily coalesced into two dominant cycles: the combat film and the home-front drama. These war-related cycles (treated in detail later in this chapter) were distinct, but the fact is that virtually all of Hollywood's major genres were affected by the war and might in some way be included under the general rubric of "war film." This can be said not only of feature films but of Hollywood's secondary products as well—serials, newsreels, live-action shorts, and cartoons. In fact, the cartoon underwent a particularly swift and effective transformation after Pearl Harbor.

Within weeks of the entry of the United States into the war, both Warners and Disney began work on war-related animation projects, which were released in January 1942: "Any Bonds Today?," a two-minute Bugs Bunny cartoon produced by Warners' Leon Schlesinger unit for the Treasury Department; and Disney's "The New Spirit," a Donald Duck cartoon designed, as one Treasury official put it, "to stimulate public interest in the payment of income taxes."[36] The Disney cartoon was the more ambitious and effective of the two, largely because of Disney's investment of resources as it converted its entire operation to war production. It also established Donald Duck as the key figure in Disney's war-related output. Second only to the upbeat, naive Mickey Mouse in the constellation of Disney stars, Donald was deemed more suitable for wartime conversion and thus was featured in a remarkable array of war-related films, from informational cartoons like "The New Spirit" to "good neighbor" films geared to the Latin American market on behalf of the Office of Inter-American Affairs. The latter included not only animated shorts but two featurettes as well, SALUDOS AMIGOS (1943) and THE THREE CABALLEROS (1945).[37]

The most notable of Disney's wartime efforts was a Donald Duck cartoon produced for the War Department, "Der Fuhrer's Face" (1942), which won an Oscar for best short subject and may have been the single most popular propaganda short produced during the war. In it, Donald dreams he works in a Nazi munitions factory where he must constantly salute images of Hitler and other Axis leaders; he awakens to the comforting sight of a small replica of the Statue of Liberty on his windowsill. "Der Fuhrer's Face" and other Disney cartoons did terrific business, and in fact Disney led the Exhibitors' Poll of top moneymaking shorts in 1944.[38]

The other studios' animation units turned their attention to the war more sporadically than Disney, although Hollywood's overall war-related cartoon output was indeed substantial. Paramount's Fleischer unit featured Popeye in such films as "You're a Sap, Mr. Jap" (1942) and "Spinach fer Britain" (1943). In 1942, 20th Century–Fox's Terrytoon unit created "Mighty Mouse," an animated superhero who battles Axis foes in numerous cartoons. MGM's Hanna-Barbera unit won an Oscar in 1943 for their patriotic Tom and Jerry cartoon "Yankee Doodle Mouse"—although by far the more popular wartime cartoons released by MGM involved a cycle based on "Red Hot Riding Hood" (1943) featuring the oversexed Wolf and the alluring showgirl Red. Created by Tex Avery, the Wolf-Red cartoons occasionally deal directly with the war, as in "Swing Shift Cinderella" (1943). But regardless of plot, the lecherous Wolf and voluptuous Red proved remarkably popular with wartime audiences—and especially with military personnel.[39]

Warners' Schlesinger unit was, next to Disney, the most aggressive and successful in its cartoon treatment of the war, the enemy, and the home front. The humor was more scatological, self-reflexive, and irreverent, and thus as propaganda the Warners cartoons were somewhat more complex than their Disney counterparts. The Schlesinger unit, notably the animation directors Friz Freling, Bob Clampett, and Chuck Jones (along with Tex Avery and Frank Tashlin, before their wartime departures to MGM and Fox, respectively), cranked out a remarkable spate of war-related cartoons, from parodies of

Donald Duck's nightmare in Disney's Oscar-winning 1942 cartoon, "Der Fuhrer's Face."

the studio's features, such as "Confusions of a Nutzy Spy" to parodies of their established cartoon stars, such as "The Ducktators," featuring web-footed versions of Hitler, Mussolini, and Hirohito. Bob Clampett created a surrealist pro-Soviet piece, "Russian Rhapsody," wherein a grotesque caricature of Hitler is assaulted by "Gremlins from the Kremlin." Bugs takes on the Germans in "Herr Meets Hare" and the Japanese in "Bugs Bunny Nips the Nips," while Daffy Duck dodges a ubiquitous draft-notice server in "Draftee Daffy."[40]

Bugs also made occasional cameo appearances in the "Private Snafu" cartoons, which Warners and MGM produced for *Army-Navy Screen* magazine. These had modest production values (black-and-white film stock, running times of three to four minutes, etc.), were shown only to military personnel, and were far more raunchy and risqué than theatrical cartoons. Thus, the Private Snafu cartoons gave Hollywood animators the opportunity to experiment with the political, sexual, and topical humor of cartoons, while they gave millions of adult moviegoers a very different cartoon experience. But these experiments were scarcely as significant, finally, as was the retooling of mainstream animated fare, which effectively recast the wartime experience for adults and children alike in the distinctive formal and narrative logic of the Hollywood cartoon.

In terms of features, the musical was the established form most effectively enlisted into the war effort, primarily in a cycle of musical "revues," which were little more than filmed versions of military stage shows. The single biggest hit of the war era, THIS IS

THE ARMY (1943), not only sparked this trend but dominated the entire war era. Produced onstage by the War Department as an all-soldier musical revue with music by Irving Berlin, "This Is the Army" premiered on Broadway on the Fourth of July in 1942 and was a huge hit. Warner Bros. purchased the screen rights later that year and began production in early 1943, while the stage version continued to play to record audiences. The producer Hal Wallis and the director Michael Curtiz (between stints on YANKEE DOODLE DANDY and CASABLANCA) fleshed out the play's paper-thin plot about army recruits staging a big show for the troops, incorporating about a dozen second-rank studio stars (George Murphy, Joan Leslie, Alan Hale, Ronald Reagan, et al.) along with a few cultural icons like the boxer-soldier Joe Louis. On both stage and screen, THIS IS THE ARMY ran uninterrupted throughout the war. Warners' film version returned $8.5 million in rentals, and the stage show enjoyed a thirty-nine-month run from July 1942 to October 1945, generating $19 million for army-navy relief and playing to an estimated 2.5 million servicemen.[41]

The studios turned out revue musicals in record numbers during the war. Most of them were laden with top talent but very thin on plot, and what plot there was invariably involved the war or the military. Widely disparaged or dismissed by critics, the wartime revue musicals also were among the most popular and commercially successful films of the era, and they were relatively inexpensive films by musical standards. The

A scene from Warners' version of THIS IS THE ARMY *(1943), the most successful wartime musical. At far left, in uniform, is boxer Joe Louis.*

most successful revue musicals were Paramount's STAR SPANGLED RHYTHM (1942) with Bob Hope, Bing Crosby, Dorothy Lamour, Veronica Lake, Alan Ladd, Cecil B. DeMille, et al.; Warners' THANK YOUR LUCKY STARS (1943) with Eddie Cantor, Dennis Morgan, Bette Davis, Humphrey Bogart, Errol Flynn, Olivia de Havilland, Ann Sheridan, et al.; UA's STAGE DOOR CANTEEN (1943) with Katharine Hepburn, Paul Muni, Harpo Marx, Benny Goodman, Count Basie, Edgar Bergen, et al.; MGM's THOUSANDS CHEER (1943) with Kathryn Grayson, Gene Kelly, Margaret O'Brien, Mickey Rooney, Judy Garland, June Allyson, Lena Horne, et al.; and Warners' HOLLYWOOD CANTEEN (1944) with Bette Davis, Joan Crawford, the Andrews Sisters, Roy Rogers, Ida Lupino, et al. Some revue-oriented musicals like FOUR JILLS IN A JEEP and HERE COME THE WAVES (both 1944) developed quasi-plausible characters and plot lines, invariably blending comedy and romance, as in the backstage and show musicals of the 1930s. But as with their wartime musical-revue counterparts, the climactic show invariably lapsed into an extended stage-bound revue.

Musicals generally were deemed escapist fare by exhibitors and industry executives, whether they were related to the war or not. Thus, the military revue musicals provided something of an ideal screen formula: they supported the war effort while giving audiences the essential escapist elements of comedy, music, and romance. These elements were evident in traditional musicals as well, particularly the historical period musical—a prewar trend which accelerated during the war. The most successful of these was MGM's MEET ME IN ST. LOUIS (1944), which charted the experiences of a turn-of-the-century midwestern family, culminating in the St. Louis World's Fair.

Fox had been turning out period musicals since before the war and continued to exploit the cycle with films like CONEY ISLAND (1943), DIAMOND HORSESHOE (1945), and STATE FAIR (1945). Bosley Crowther in his *New York Times* review of CONEY ISLAND noted, "Twentieth Century–Fox has a formula for high, wide and fancy musical films which seldom fail." The basic requirements of the formula, wrote Crowther, were a "locale and period of glitter and gaudiness," several standard tunes "of a certain nostalgic quality," and "a pat little love triangle" centering on "a lady singer"—usually Betty Grable.[42] This formula signaled a merger of sorts with the biopic, and in fact a number of wartime period musicals centered on the careers of vaudeville, ragtime, and Tin Pan Alley stars. Warners' YANKEE DOODLE DANDY (1942) typified the trend and was among the biggest hits of the era. Other musical biopics were DIXIE (1943), on the career of Dan Emmett; STORMY WEATHER (1943), an all-black musical based on the career of Bill Robinson; SHINE ON, HARVEST MOON (1944), on Nora Bayes; and INCENDIARY BLONDE (1945), on the nightclub queen Texas Guinan.

While musicals made up a fairly limited proportion of Hollywood's overall output, they generated a sizable share of its income. Twenty-five of the seventy wartime releases earning $3 million or more at the box office were musicals, including three of the top ten (THIS IS THE ARMY, MEET ME IN ST. LOUIS, and YANKEE DOODLE DANDY). Also among the ten biggest wartime hits were Leo McCarey's sentimental quasi-musicals with Bing Crosby, THE BELLS OF ST. MARY'S and GOING MY WAY. As in the prewar era, the studios developed star-genre musical formulas around key personnel—Betty Grable at Fox; Bing Crosby and Betty Hutton at Paramount; Judy Garland, Gene Kelly, and Kathryn Grayson at MGM; and Rita Hayworth at Columbia (notably with Astaire in YOU WERE NEVER LOVELIER in 1942, and with Gene Kelly in COVER GIRL in 1944). MGM also devised a musical formula for the swimmer Esther Williams—notably in BATHING BEAUTY (1944) and THRILL OF A ROMANCE (1945)—reminiscent of Fox's ice-skating musicals with Sonja Henie, whose career was winding down during the war. The genre's wartime currency also was evident at the low end of the spectrum: low-budget musical production surged during the war. While the dominant trend was the ever-popular singing cowboy pictures (with Republic's Roy Rogers succeeding Gene Autry as the top singing B-Western star), the period also saw an increase in musical output by B units at Fox and Paramount.

The Western genre ran directly counter to the musical in output and income during the war. The Western led all genres in sheer numbers, but that output included very few high-end productions or top moneymakers. In fact, the prewar resurgence of the A-Western all but ceased during the war, owing especially to restrictions on sets and location shooting, as well as to the general shift of male action-adventure production to the combat film. The seventy leading moneymakers included only two Westerns: Howard Hughes's much-troubled Jane Russell vehicle THE OUTLAW (produced in 1940–1941 but not released until 1943, with most of its earnings coming after the war), and a 1945 Errol Flynn picture, SAN ANTONIO. Two other A-Westerns of note were THEY DIED WITH THEIR BOOTS ON, Warners' 1942 Custer biopic featuring a romanticized account of the Little Big Horn massacre (giving it considerable resonance in that year of Wake Island, Bataan, and Corregidor), and THE OX-BOW INCIDENT, a dark and somber study of mob violence and social injustice produced by Zanuck and Fox in 1943.

Errol Flynn as George Armstrong Custer in a resonant 1942 "last-stand" drama, THEY DIED WITH THEIR BOOTS ON.

These two films, along with THE OUTLAW, were actually quite important to the Western genre's evolution. THEY DIED WITH THEIR BOOTS ON set the stage for the post-war cavalry film, a fruitful melding of war film and Western; THE OUTLAW was the first A-Western to deal directly and overtly with issues of sexuality and along with THE OX-BOW INCIDENT was a precursor to the "adult" and "psychological" Westerns of the post-war era.

While the A-Western saw limited wartime action, B-Westerns continued to flourish. As with Hollywood's overall output, B-Western production declined during the war—steadily falling from 130 in 1941 to only 80 in 1945. But low-budget Westerns still consistently accounted for one-quarter of all features produced in Hollywood.[43] Out of a total of 572 Westerns produced during the war, only 38 came from the five majors—and over half of those were from RKO, which continued B-picture production longer than the rest of the Big Five. UA released 18 Westerns during the war, most of them Hopalong Cassidy series pictures picked up in the deal with Paramount. Columbia and Universal continued heavy B-Western production, turning out 53 and 35 wartime Westerns, respectively. Virtually all of the remaining 400-odd Westerns released from 1942 to 1945 were from the three minors; Republic's Roy Rogers pictures (SONS OF THE PIONEERS, 1943; KING OF THE COWBOYS, 1943; THE YELLOW ROSE OF TEXAS, 1944; DON'T FENCE ME IN, 1945) and occasional John Wayne Westerns (IN OLD CALIFORNIA, 1942; DAKOTA, 1945) were by far the most successful.

The historical drama and period biopic suffered a wartime decline along with the A-Western, and for many of the same reasons, especially restrictions on location shooting and set construction. Another reason for the biopic's wartime decline was Hollywood's tendency to shy away from any social issues except those related to the war. Thus, biographies of social crusaders, so prevalent in the 1930s, were relatively rare during the war, with a few notable exceptions like MGM's MADAME CURIE in 1943. The musical biography discussed earlier was the most prevalent biopic form during the war, and it illustrated the biopic's wartime penchant for escapist subjects. In fact, the most successful nonmusical biopic of the era was THE PRIDE OF THE YANKEES (1942), a baseball picture that also signaled the tendency of wartime biopics to avoid heavy social subjects.

Yet another sign of this tendency was the commercial failure of Darryl Zanuck's pet wartime project, WILSON (1944), despite tremendous promotional buildup, generally favorable reviews, and half a dozen major Oscar nominations. After returning to Fox from the Signal Corps in July 1943, Zanuck began working on a project he hoped would recapture and revive Woodrow Wilson's League of Nations crusade. Eschewing a star-vehicle approach, Zanuck cast a little-known, Canadian-born, British character actor, Alexander Knox, in the title role.[44] WILSON was a prestige production in every sense of the word, with elaborate sets replicating the House chamber and the Wilson White House, and a final cost of about $4 million.[45]

WILSON was enthusiastically supported by the Office of War Information, but before its initial release Zanuck was informed by the War Department that the picture would not be shown on military bases and camps because of the Soldier Vote Act, which prohibited any media materials "considered to have political content."[46] This restriction was deemed a political setback of little commercial importance, especially after the picture's strong road-show performance. WILSON quickly lost momentum in general release, however, earning a respectable $3.1 million but failing to return a profit or secure a best-picture statuette.[47] Zanuck considered WILSON one of the major disappointments of his career, and its lackluster performance also convinced him to drop plans to adapt

Wendell Willkie's best-selling political memoir, *One World,* purchased in July 1943 (for $100,000) just as Fox began preproduction on WILSON.[48]

An offbeat period biopic that did score for Fox during the war was THE SONG OF BERNADETTE, the surprise hit of 1943 that made an overnight star of Jennifer Jones (on loan from David Selznick). Based on the popular "fictionalized biography" of the peasant girl who had visions of the Virgin Mary at Lourdes, the picture (under the direction of Henry King, who also directed WILSON) displayed simple verities and modest production values and did particularly well with female audiences.

THE SONG OF BERNADETTE signaled a general wartime surge in women's pictures, which ranged from lavish adaptations and period films to contemporary romantic and family melodramas, and which clearly were keyed to the social, industrial, and economic conditions of the time. An important factor was the wartime segregation of male and female audiences; the women's pictures did well at home but were rarely played in military camps. Indeed, the GIs' idea of a "woman's picture" featured pinup stars like Betty Grable, Rita Hayworth, and Dorothy Lamour, who rarely appeared in the kind of wartime melodramas targeted at female moviegoers.

As in the prewar era, women's films during the war focused on female protagonists suffering choices and making sacrifices, and the films tended to fall into five categories: maternal dramas, love stories, working-girl stories, Gothic thrillers, and biopics. Many women's films were quite timely; the war and related social conditions provided ready-made themes and conflicts, particularly for the maternal and romantic dramas. These included wartime home-front dramas like MRS. MINIVER and SINCE YOU WENT AWAY; historical sagas centering on powerful matriarchs, like THE VALLEY OF DECISION, MRS. PARKINGTON, and A TREE GROWS IN BROOKLYN (1945); and a few multigenerational or highly elliptical stories which managed to incorporate both a historical and a war angle, such as RANDOM HARVEST, MR. SKEFFINGTON (1944), and THE WHITE CLIFFS OF DOVER (1944).

Some of the numerous melodramas about separated, soon-to-be separated, or otherwise troubled couples were historical or contemporary stories not directly related to the war—as in two 1942 Bette Davis pictures, IN THIS OUR LIFE and NOW, VOYAGER. In a related vein, MILDRED PIERCE and OLD ACQUAINTANCE (1943) focused on female protagonists whose choices of a career or the company of other women carried wartime resonances as well, although the war was not invoked in either film. Indeed, Hollywood's adaptation of the woman's picture to the war effort was so effective, as Linda Williams notes in her analysis of MILDRED PIERCE, that domestic melodramas could be "about" the female war experience—the working and economic conditions, relationships with husbands and lovers (absent or otherwise), and so on—without even acknowledging the war in the narrative.[49]

The majority of successful romantic melodramas made during the war, however, dealt directly with the war's impact on women and on couples—as in such 1945 hits as I'LL BE SEEING YOU, THE CLOCK, and THE ENCHANTED COTTAGE. The working-girl dramas often involved both war-strained romances and war-related female labor. TENDER COMRADE (1943), for instance, focuses on women war-plant workers sharing an apartment and the pain of loss and separation, and SO PROUDLY WE HAIL (1943) honors military nurses serving and dying with their male military counterparts in the Pacific. Of the various women's subgenres, only the Gothic thrillers consistently avoided the war, although here again hasty marriages and psychologically scarred male protagonists had interesting wartime implications.

Among the more successful home-front dramas was TENDER COMRADE *(1943), starring Ginger Rogers (center).*

As discussed earlier, the wartime woman's picture was dominated by Bette Davis and Greer Garson, both of whom worked almost exclusively in that genre and had a penchant for maternal and romantic melodramas. Joan Fontaine and Ingrid Bergman formed a kind of second rank, specializing in Gothic thrillers such as SUSPICION (1941) and GASLIGHT (1944). Other female stars who specialized in women's pictures included Claudette Colbert, Ginger Rogers, Barbara Stanwyck, and Dorothy McGuire, all of whom could lighten up these otherwise weighty emotional dramas and also worked successfully in wartime comedy.

Screen comedy thrived during the war, sustained largely by a very real need for diversion and by the exhibitors' continual clamoring for escapist product. Hollywood delivered in considerable quantity, although very few major hits were straight (nonmusical) comedies. In fact, Warners' CHRISTMAS IN CONNECTICUT (1945) was the only wartime comedy to earn over $3 million. Still, the mid-range of studio output was dominated by comedy, particularly romantic and screwball comedies, male buddy comedies, and home-front comedies.

The year 1942 marked the wartime peak for screen comedy, and especially for the romantic and screwball strains. The biggest comedy hit of 1942 was ROAD TO MOROCCO, the third Hope-Crosby-Lamour junket. Among the other notable 1942 comedies were Preston Sturges's THE PALM BEACH STORY, with Colbert's delightfully unruly woman opposite Joel McCrea; THE MALE ANIMAL, a campus comedy about socialism and football starring Henry Fonda and Olivia de Havilland, written and directed by Elliott Nugent (from his play); and two George Stevens–directed comedies, THE TALK OF THE TOWN, with Cary Grant, Jean Arthur, and Ronald Colman, and WOMAN OF THE YEAR, the initial Tracy-Hepburn pairing and easily their best comedy until ADAM'S RIB in 1949. Capra's ARSENIC AND OLD LACE with Cary Grant and Priscilla Lane also was "in the can" and ready for release in 1942—and in fact was released to servicemen in early 1943—but was shelved by Warners until 1944.

Interestingly enough, none of these 1942 comedies directly involved the war effort, although all of them treated the anxieties and conflicts related to the changing gender roles and sexual politics that were endemic to the period. One of the few 1942 comedies that did take on a war-related subject was THE MAJOR AND THE MINOR, Billy Wilder's debut as a Paramount writer-director; it costarred Ray Milland as a befuddled and unhappily betrothed military officer on a cross-country train trip who finds himself allied with Ginger Rogers, who is passing as a child because she cannot afford the full fare. While not quite up to Wilder's later standards, the picture was a mild success, suggesting that audiences might take to war-related comedy. Paramount reinforced the point with MY FAVORITE BLONDE, a 1942 war-related spy comedy starring Bob Hope—the first in a series of spy spoofs, including THEY GOT ME COVERED in 1943, playing off Hope's cowardly-hero persona. While Hollywood's output of screen comedies continued during the war, the overall quality (and critical accolades) fell sharply after 1942, in part because the established comedy directors abandoned the genre after 1942 for the duration of the war. Hawks turned exclusively to action films and Wilder to drama, Lubitsch took ill, and both Capra and Stevens joined the service.

One director who stayed with the genre was Preston Sturges, whose meteoric rise continued during the war and peaked with two 1944 home-front farces, HAIL THE CONQUERING HERO and THE MIRACLE OF MORGAN'S CREEK. Those two comedies were in something of a class by themselves during the later war years. Both were all-out comic assaults on motherhood, home, family, hero worship, the military, small-town America, and ultimately the very logic of the home front itself. HAIL THE CONQUERING HERO starred Eddie Bracken as a Marine Corps washout (due to chronic hay fever) who is hustled home and passed off as a war hero by a group of well-meaning marines on a five-day pass. THE MIRACLE OF MORGAN'S CREEK costarred Bracken as a tongue-tied hick and Betty Hutton as a hapless girl he befriends after she finds herself married and pregnant—the result of a drunken frolic with a now-departed soldier whose face and name escape her. Both films sent the PCA and the OWI into paroxysms, while the critics raved and Sturges parlayed his success into an independent venture with Howard Hughes.

Rounding out Hollywood's wartime comedies were the male-buddy escapades of Abbott and Costello, Hope and Crosby, and Laurel and Hardy. Most of these were aggressively escapist farces and genre parodies, treating the wartime male ethos only by radical indirection. Crosby also strolled amiably through GOING MY WAY and THE BELLS OF ST. MARY'S, two contemporary religious fables which blended elements of comedy, sentimental melodrama, and the musical. The huge success of these latter films, along with THE SONG OF BERNADETTE and KEYS OF THE KINGDOM (1944), confirmed that Hollywood was undergoing something of a religious cycle during the war. These rather ponderous religious dramas were complemented, in turn, by such offbeat afterlife comedy-dramas as Lubitsch's HEAVEN CAN WAIT (1943) and MGM's Spencer Tracy-Van Johnson hit, A GUY NAMED JOE.

In Hail the Conquering Hero *(1944), woeful Marine Corps washout Eddie Bracken's chance meeting with a group of soldiers home on leave has comic-chaotic consequences.*

Another noteworthy but limited wartime cycle involved children and animals, spurred largely by the success in 1943 of the MGM Schary unit's Lassie Come Home, costarring Donald Crisp, Elizabeth Taylor, and Roddy McDowall, and Fox's My Friend Flicka, starring McDowall. Both bred offspring in 1945: Son of Lassie and Thunderhead—Son of Flicka. Like their predecessors, these were sentimental family comedy-dramas shot in Technicolor with an emphasis on action scenes and outdoor cinematography. They were near-A's whose solid production values compensated for their second-rank stars and running times of under 90 minutes. MGM actually upgraded the form that same year with National Velvet (1944), which was based on a best-selling children's book, featured a top star (Mickey Rooney), and ran 125 minutes. The result was an A-class hit which earned $4.25 million—and thus outperformed all three of Rooney's wartime Hardy pictures, an MGM family cycle that was clearly fading.

In a darker vein, Universal sustained its signature horror films during the war, primarily through B-grade formula rehash with Lon Chaney Jr., who starred in an incredible nineteen pictures from 1942 to 1945. Most of Universal's reformulations were utterly predictable: the 1932 classic The Mummy, for example, begat The Mummy's Hand (1940), The Mummy's Tomb (1942), The Mummy's Ghost (1944), and The Mummy's Curse (1944). The studio rehashed its Dracula, Frankenstein, and Wolf Man franchises with comparable titles and variations. Universal's one significant wartime innovation with these stock horror figures was the recombination of its horror subgenres in FRANKENSTEIN MEETS THE WOLF MAN (1943), HOUSE OF FRANKENSTEIN (1944), and HOUSE OF DRACULA (1945). Each of these so-called reunion pictures increased the number (and variation) of monsters, mad scientists, and miscreants on-screen, thus providing a remarkable study in the logic and textual limits of Universal's horror formulas. The studio also turned out an occasional A-class horror film, such as the 1943 Technicolor remake of PHANTOM OF THE OPERA starring Claude Rains.

The most innovative and influential horror films during the war era were produced not at Universal but at RKO by the newly formed Val Lewton unit. A former poet, novelist, and screenwriter, and recently a story editor for David Selznick, Lewton joined RKO in 1942 to produce low-budget thrillers. Working with the directors Jacques Tourneur, Robert Wise, and Mark Robson, Lewton produced ten pictures during the war, including CAT PEOPLE (1942), I WALKED WITH A ZOMBIE, THE LEOPARD MAN, THE SEVENTH VICTIM (1943), THE CURSE OF THE CAT PEOPLE (1944), THE BODY SNATCHER, and ISLE OF THE DEAD (1945). Most of them were modest critical and commercial hits, and several now stand as minor horror classics. All ran about seventy minutes, were shot in black and white, and stressed mood and atmosphere rather than star, story value, or special effects. CAT PEOPLE, in fact, managed to be quite frightening without ever showing its "monster." Lewton's earlier productions also brought the horror genre closer to home in that the films were generally set in (or near) the United States.

The fascination with the dark side of America's wartime psyche and the invocation of the female Gothic tradition in Lewton's films evinced another crucial wartime trend— *film noir*. Indeed, although that 1940s period style had its roots in the prewar era and reached full expression after the war, its wartime development was among the more significant and pervasive stylistic trends of the era.

CASE STUDY: *Film Noir*

Throughout the 1940s, an increasing number of Hollywood films displayed an incipient darkness in tone, technique, theme, and narrative form, a style that came to be termed *film noir* by postwar French critics. The term had clear associations with *roman noir*, which French literary critics applied to the recent hard-boiled crime fiction and pulp melodramas by American writers like Dashiell Hammett, Raymond Chandler, James M. Cain, and Cornell Woolrich.[50] And in fact this type of fiction was crucial to Hollywood's development of *film noir* through a remarkable cycle of crime thrillers and detective films in the mid-1940s—notably DOUBLE INDEMNITY, LAURA, MURDER, MY SWEET, PHANTOM LADY, THE WOMAN IN THE WINDOW, THE MASK OF DIMITRIOS, and CHRISTMAS HOLIDAY in 1944; MILDRED PIERCE, CORNERED, DETOUR, SCARLET STREET, and HANGOVER SQUARE in 1945; and THE BIG SLEEP, THE KILLERS, THE POSTMAN ALWAYS RINGS TWICE, and THE BLUE DAHLIA in 1946.

The development of *film noir* into a distinctive period style in the 1940s was evident not only in the dark crime thrillers and hard-boiled detective films of the era but in many other genres and cycles as well. As Robert Sklar aptly points out, *film noir* "describes the psychology and the look not simply of a genre, but of a surprisingly pervasive tone in Hollywood films of the 1940s." Sklar finds evidence of this period style in a range of wartime genres and cycles, from the "psychological thrillers" of Alfred Hitchcock and Fritz Lang to Warners' crime dramas and woman's pictures and the "black comedies" of Preston Sturges.[51]

Despite Sklar's admonition, discussions of *film noir* have focused almost exclusively on the male-oriented action and crime films, with their obvious debt to hard-boiled American fiction and to *serie noire* detective novels. As Deborah Thomas notes, "Most critics and viewers share a sense . . . of the essential male-centeredness of *film noir*." But as Thomas and others argue, this orientation overlooks the role that other genres and cycles played in the development of the *noir* style, particularly the female Gothic variation of the woman's picture.[52] While the emergence of *film noir* can be traced to prewar detective films like THE MALTESE FALCON and CITIZEN KANE, the style was equally pronounced in prewar women's pictures like REBECCA and SUSPICION and continued in a distinctive wartime cycle of female Gothics such as SHADOW OF A DOUBT in 1943; JANE EYRE, GASLIGHT, and EXPERIMENT PERILOUS in 1944; and SPELLBOUND in 1945. And like the crime thriller, the female Gothic found new intensity in the postwar era—as evidenced by such 1946 releases as UNDERCURRENT, THE SPIRAL STAIRCASE, THE LOCKET, DRAGONWYCK, and NOTORIOUS.

As these titles suggest, two key figures in the emergence of the *noir*-style female Gothic were David O. Selznick and Alfred Hitchcock. Selznick personally produced two Hitchcock-directed Gothics, REBECCA and SPELLBOUND. He also loaned Hitchcock and Joan Fontaine to RKO for SUSPICION, and in 1945 he sold RKO the NOTORIOUS package (including the Hecht-Hitchcock script as well as the services of Hitchcock and Ingrid Bergman). Selznick prepared JANE EYRE for Hitchcock but then sold the package (including the script and the services of Fontaine and the director Robert Stevenson) to Fox, which produced the film in 1944. That same year, he loaned Ingrid Bergman and Joseph Cotten to MGM for GASLIGHT. And as mentioned earlier, Val Lewton assisted Selznick in preparing REBECCA and in packaging JANE EYRE, work that clearly influenced his first two RKO productions, CAT PEOPLE and I WALKED WITH A ZOMBIE, two inventive amalgams of the female Gothic and horror and steeped in the *film noir* style.

The roots of *film noir* can be traced to the Gothic romances of the nineteenth century, the more recent popular fiction of Daphne du Maurier (author of the best-selling *Rebecca* [1938]), and the frequently cited detective fiction of Hammett and Chandler. Important cinematic influences included Josef Von Sternberg's exotic Marlene Dietrich vehicles, the horror and gangster pictures of the 1930s, and period styles in European cinema, especially German expressionism in the 1920s and French poetic realism in the 1930s. The European influence was even more direct through the work of filmmakers who migrated from Europe to Hollywood, notably Wilder, Lang, Hitchcock, Otto Preminger, Robert and Curt Siodmak, Edgar Ulmer, Anatole Litvak, and Julien Duvivier.

Film noir was affected by technical and technological developments in the early 1940s as well, especially faster, more sensitive, fine-grain black-and-white film, improved lighting equipment, and coated lenses. A contingent of top cinematographers also played an important role, particularly the monochromatic (black-and-white) specialists who hit their stride in the 1940s, like James Wong Howe, Gregg Toland, John F. Seitz, Lee Garmes, Lucien Ballard, Tony Gaudio, Sol Polito, and John Alton. Moreover, the war-induced confinement to the studio, owing to the myriad restrictions and the demand for production economy and efficiency, led not only to technical invention but to something of a break with the classical film style.

Analyses of *film noir* have tended to treat it in social, psychological, and formal aesthetic terms. Among the more insightful analyses is Paul Schrader's 1972 essay "Notes

Gothic prototypes: Joan Fontaine (with Judith Anderson) in REBECCA *(1940), and (with Orson Welles) in an adaptation of the cycle's literary "foundation,"* JANE EYRE *(1944).*

on *Film Noir,*" which examines the style in both social and aesthetic terms. Schrader notes that "*film noir* attacked and interpreted its sociological conditions, and . . . created a new artistic world which went beyond a simple sociological reflection, a nightmarish world of American mannerism which was by far more a creation than a reflection."[53] Positing THE MALTESE FALCON as the *film noir* prototype, Schrader suggests that "most every dramatic Hollywood film from 1941 to 1953 contains some *noir* elements." He provides an inventory of the "recurring techniques" of *film noir:* most scenes are lit for night; as in German expressionism, oblique and vertical lines are preferred to horizontal; the actors and setting are often given equal lighting emphasis; compositional tension is preferred to physical action; there is an almost Freudian attachment to water (and also to mirrors, windows, and other reflective surfaces); *noir* films have a penchant for voice-over first-person narration which is cynical yet oddly romantic; and often a complex chronological order reinforces a sense of hopelessness and lost time.

David Bordwell argues that *film noir* undercut not only the formal techniques of the period but basic narrative conventions as well—notably in its ambivalent treatment of good and evil and the heroic and the villainous, especially as embodied in the protagonists and antagonists. Bordwell also notes that a fundamental (and often unresolved) antagonism between the principal male and female characters undercuts—through arbitrary, inadequate, or otherwise unsatisfactory "happy endings"—the movies' most basic and cherished narrative operation, the formation of the couple.[54]

While Schrader treats *film noir* in terms of recurring techniques and Bordwell stresses narrative conventions, others have emphasized more subtle or abstract qualities. Sklar, for instance, privileges *noir's* thematic and atmospheric attributes:

> The hallmark of *film noir* is its sense of people trapped—trapped in a web of paranoia and fear, unable to tell guilt from innocence, true identity from false. Its villains are attractive and sympathetic, masking greed, misanthropy, malevolence. Its heroes and heroines are weak, confused, susceptible to false impressions. The environment is murky and close, the settings vaguely oppressive. In the end, evil is exposed, though often just barely, and the survival of good remains troubled and ambiguous. (Robert Sklar, *Movie-Made America: A Cultural History of American Movies* [New York: Random House, 1975], p. 253)

David Cook follows a similar tack, describing *film noir* as a "cinema of moral anxiety" whose films "thrived upon the unvarnished depiction of greed, lust, and cruelty because their basic theme was the depth of human depravity and the utterly unheroic nature of human beings." Cook notes that this style first emerged during the war but reached full maturity only with the paranoia, pessimism, and social angst of the postwar era.[55]

When considering the formal and stylistic qualities of *film noir,* it is scarcely surprising that the detective story has been its privileged domain. In fact, two wartime *noir* classics, DOUBLE INDEMNITY and MILDRED PIERCE, were adaptations that literally imposed a detective framework on what were essentially romantic melodramas. Both were adapted from salacious potboilers by James M. Cain, and in each film the drama is reconstructed as a detective story through a flashback framework and an investigation format. (DOUBLE INDEMNITY was reworked for Paramount by Billy Wilder in collaboration with Raymond Chandler; MILDRED PIERCE was reworked for Warners by various writers and the director Michael Curtiz under the producer Jerry Wald.) The detective structure reinforced the *noir* stylistics and served a number of more practical uses as well. It broadened the potential appeal of the films (especially to male viewers) while retaining the appeal of the novels, provided a more conventional and manageable plot trajectory, and provided a means of mollifying Breen's and the PCA's "compensating moral values" mandate.[56]

Interestingly, critics and historians of 1940s women's pictures have treated the female Gothic in terms quite similar to the detective thriller, although few have related the cycle to the concurrent development of *film noir*. Molly Haskell in *From Reverence to Rape*, for instance, notes the number of wartime women's films wherein "relationships are rooted in fear and suspicion, impotence and inadequacy."[57] Thomas Elsaesser notes that "Hollywood tackled Freudian themes in a particularly 'romantic' or gothic guise, through a cycle of movies inaugurated possibly in Hitchcock's first big American success, *Rebecca*." He finds in these films "an oblique intimation of female frigidity producing strange fantasies of persecution, rape and death—masochistic reveries and nightmares, which cast the husband into the role of sadistic murderer."[58]

Thus, as the two cycles developed during the early 1940s, the female Gothic displayed a remarkable "family resemblance" to the hard-boiled detective film in basic structure, thematic and gender-related concerns, and deployment of *noir* stylistics. Each subgenre's central concerns were gender difference, sexual identity, and the "gender distress" which accompanied the social and cultural disruption of the war and postwar eras. Each had an essentially good although flawed and vulnerable protagonist at odds with a mysterious and menacing sexual other: the *femme noire*, who invariably initiates both the detective's case and an uneasy romance with the hero; the suave, enigmatic husband or lover in the female Gothic, almost always an older man with a past and with something to hide.

In a larger sense, both the hard-boiled detective and the Gothic heroine are at odds with a social milieu that is seen as crass, duplicitous, and amoral. For the Gothic heroine, this conflict is a function of her sexual inexperience and social naïveté—she is an innocent who finds herself in a dark, disturbing world. The detective has "been around" and is in fact a bit seedy and cynical, but there is a commonness and an innocence to his character as well. As Raymond Chandler, in a 1944 essay, said of his hero: "Down these mean streets a man must go who is not himself mean, who is neither tarnished nor afraid. The detective in this kind of story must be such a man. He is the hero; he is everything. He must be a complete man and a common man and yet an unusual man. He must be, to use a rather weathered phrase, a man of honor."[59]

The plot in both subgenres (the detective's case, the Gothic heroine's courtship and marriage) generally is initiated by the sexual other. It gradually becomes evident to the protagonist—and to the viewer, whose knowledge and "identification" are closely allied to the protagonist—that this motivating figure and object of desire is in fact both duplicitous and possibly deadly. This realization is hardly surprising in the detective film, but when the protagonist of the female Gothic finds out that her spouse has something to hide, what began as a romantic drama is transformed into a detective story and, quite often, into a murder mystery. The protagonist in each becomes obsessed with the past, with the discovery of the truth, and also with surviving an embrace that may prove fatal.

As the search develops, the hero's anxieties increase, as does the potential menace of the sexual other. It is notable, however, that even those female Gothics wherein murders do occur—and even those like SHADOW OF A DOUBT and GASLIGHT whose male other is in fact a killer—do not simply lapse into a crime-film mode, nor do they focus on the killer being brought to justice. The stakes in the female Gothic remain primarily domestic rather than social: the problems are identified and worked out in interpersonal and familial terms. But like the detective film, the female Gothic builds to a climactic resolution of its conflicts and enigmas—the truth about the mysterious secret, the real motives of the sexual other, the protagonist's survival (and happiness). In both forms, however, the resolution rarely marks a return to complete stability or moral equilibrium. Sexual tensions and uncertainties linger, as do doubts about the larger social milieu.

Invariably, the solution to the detective's case, when there is one, fails to resolve the deeper issues and conflicts at hand or to bring the appropriate culprits to justice. Ultimately, the hard-boiled hero grimly acknowledges his inability to escape or fully redeem his *noir* netherworld, and thus he simply rediscovers what he already knew and would like to forget. He may prevail over the *femme noire* (as in THE MALTESE FALCON and MURDER, MY SWEET), or she may prove herself to be a genuine love interest after all (as in LAURA and THE BIG SLEEP). But human contact offers the hero little more than a temporary respite from his own malaise and from the mean streets outside his dingy office, and one can be certain that upon meeting the detective hero again in another film, he will be resolutely alone.

Fred MacMurray is no match for Barbara Stanwyck's femme fatale *in* DOUBLE INDEMNITY *(1944).*

In that sense, the *noir* detective film was consummately a matter of style—ultimately of the hero's style, which was perfectly suited to his environment. Once allied with the legitimate forces of social order (the police force, the district attorney's office), the detective hero now works alone as a private eye in a decadent urban milieu. His isolation signals a rejection of that milieu and its values, including those of his former employer. A self-styled existentialist, the detective has refined his personal code of honor and justice, realizing that the cops and the courts are as inept and prone to corruption as the criminal element. A cultural middleman, the detective's streetwise savvy and penchant for violence enable him to operate within the urban jungle, while his moral sensibilities and innate idealism align him with the forces of social order. But that very idealism ultimately dooms him to failure, which he accepts with a shrug, lighting another cigarette and returning to his seedy office to await another case.

This conventionally downbeat resolution was countered in the female Gothic, whose heroine not only tends to survive but to attain a new awareness of herself and her world. This outcome was most prevalent in the wartime Gothics, whose penchant for happy endings suggested that the evil at work in the film is simply a function of the heroine's neuroses and/or the diseased mind of a single criminal. The resolution of the female Gothic involves a redemption of sorts—not only of the heroine but of the world as she has come to know and to see it. And thus the frequent observation that the outcome of these films seems rather perfunctory, as if the *noir* stylistics (and all that they represent) could be overcome by a sunlit tag scene and the heroine's return to emotional equilibrium.

The best of the *noir* Gothics, however, manage to turn this convention back on itself, presenting resolutions so rife with irony as to seem positively Brechtian. Consider SHADOW OF A DOUBT, which is particularly instructive in its variations on the Gothic formula and the detective film. Scripted by Hitchcock and Thornton Wilder, the latter fresh off his stage success with *Our Town,* SHADOW OF A DOUBT was one of the first of the wartime female Gothics to be set not in England but in America; in fact, it was shot almost entirely on location in Santa Rosa, California. The film recasts the marital angle, centering on the dark (and vaguely incestuous) romance between the suave, seductive Uncle Charlie (Joseph Cotten) and his namesake niece (Teresa Wright). On the verge of womanhood and decidedly bored with her middle-class existence, young Charlie welcomes the unexpected arrival of her world-traveler uncle, only to realize that he is a serial killer of wealthy widows and is on the run from the authorities. With that realization, young Charlie steadily descends into darkness and terror, especially once Uncle Charlie realizes she knows the truth and begins engineering her murder as well.

Hitchcock presents young Charlie's descent into the maelstrom in increasingly dark, claustrophobic, and compositionally off-balance visual terms. At one point Uncle Charlie corners her at night in a seedy bar and delivers a veritable testimonial to the world of *film noir*:

> You think you know something, don't you? You think you're the clever little girl who knows something. There's so much you don't know. So much. What do you know, really? You're just an ordinary little girl in an ordinary little town. You wake up every morning of your life and you know perfectly well there's nothing in the world to trouble you. You go through your ordi-

nary little day and at night you sleep your untroubled, ordinary little sleep filled with peaceful stupid dreams. And I brought you nightmares. . . .

How do you know what the world is like? Do you know the world is a foul sty? Do you know if you ripped the fronts off houses you'd find swine? The world's a hell. What does it matter what happens in it?

Young Charlie prevails, but without the help of a well-meaning but ineffectual detective (Macdonald Carey) who, of course, falls in love with her. Carey's soft-boiled detective is a wry parody of his pulp-fiction counterpart, a fact underscored by the obsessive interest of Charlie's father and his best friend (Henry Travers and Hume Cronyn) in dime-store crime magazines. Charlie finally kills her uncle in self-defense, pushing him in front of a train—a fate he had planned for her. In a brief epilogue, young Charlie and the detective sit outside a church in bright sunlight while, inside, her family and neighbors, who suspected nothing about Uncle Charlie, are mourning what they believe was a tragic accident. While the upright detective muses knowingly that "people go crazy now and then, like your Uncle Charlie," young Charlie manages only a wan smile and half-hearted nod of agreement. But the detective cannot understand or explain away the darkness she has seen. She has stared into the abyss, and we get the strong impression that her world, however brightly lit, can never be the same.

That final exchange is the closest anyone comes in SHADOW OF A DOUBT to mentioning the war (although there is a fleeting glimpse of a war-related newspaper headline at one point). Like the hard-boiled detective film, the female Gothic deals with a troubled, wartorn world, but without attributing those troubles to the war itself. Indeed, the conflicts and tensions addressed in these cycles were in many ways deeper and more profound than those of the geopolitical struggle at hand, and they certainly were more endemic to the American experience. Both the female Gothic and the hard-boiled detective film, like the *film noir* style itself, tapped into social conditions and anxieties that not only preceded the war but would gain even greater currency in the postwar era.

The War Film

The dominant wartime production trend, of course, centered on the war itself. Early on, the term "war film" actually was little more than a useful generalization as Hollywood injected war themes into a wide range of genres and formulas. In time, however, the movie industry dealt with the war more directly and effectively, particularly in combat films and documentaries, which provided, in Lewis Jacobs's provocative description, a "vast serialization" of the American and Allied war effort.[60] And remarkably enough, Hollywood's treatment of World War II ended almost as abruptly as the war itself, with combat films and other war-related cycles—military musicals, prisoner-of-war films, home-front dramas, postwar rehabilitation films—disappearing from movie screens soon after V-J Day. Thus, the war film was doubly exceptional: on the one hand, it emerged virtually by social mandate and was refined in direct response to social and historical conditions; on the other, it followed a historical trajectory that coincided almost identically with the events it depicted.

Various studies have charted Hollywood's war-related film production. One conducted by Russell Earl Shain, among the more exhaustive studies, provides these figures on the industry's war-related output from 1940 to 1947:

Table 7.2
WORLD WAR II–RELATED HOLLYWOOD FEATURES, 1940–1947

Year	Total War Films	Total Films	% War Films
1940	12	477	2.5
1941	32	492	6.5
1942	121	488	24.8
1943	115	392	29.3
1944	76	401	19.0
1945	28	350	8.0
1946	13	378	3.4
1947	2	369	0.5

SOURCE: Russell Earl Shain, *An Analysis of Motion Pictures About War Released by the American Film Industry, 1939–1970* (New York: Arno, 1976), p. 31.

Shain notes that during the sustained peak in Hollywood's war-related output from 1942 to 1944, one-fourth of all features (312 of 1,286 releases, or 24 percent) dealt with the war. According to Shain, Hollywood released 340 war-related features during the four war years, or 20 percent of the industry total. Shain's figures cover only films dealing directly with World War II, not films about World War I or the Spanish Civil War, for instance. Studies that examine all war-related films indicate an even heavier overall output. Dorothy B. Jones of the OWI's film reviewing and analysis section, for instance, found that over 28 percent of Hollywood's total output from 1942 to 1944 (376 of 1,313 releases in her sample) were war-related.[61]

Despite the overall decline in the annual output of war-related films from 1942 to 1945, these films remained a viable box-office staple throughout the period. In fact, their stock steadily improved during the war. In 1942, 19 of the 101 films that returned at least $1 million in rentals were war-related. The number and proportion of war-related hits more than doubled in 1943, when they comprised 41 of the 95 releases returning $1 million or more.[62] Moreover, the top two hits in both 1942 and 1943 were war-related: MRS. MINIVER and YANKEE DOODLE DANDY in 1942, THIS IS THE ARMY and FOR WHOM THE BELL TOLLS in 1943. The war-related films' box-office currency peaked in 1944, when they comprised 11 of the 19 releases returning $3 million or more. For the entire wartime period, a remarkable 32 of the 71 $3 million releases were war-related—including 10 musicals, 9 combat films, and 6 home-front comedies or dramas.[63]

Actually, what Hollywood termed "war themes" were likely to show up in any number of genres during the war era. Meanwhile, the term "war film" took on steadily narrower connotations as Hollywood refined specific war-related formulas. The dominant formula was the combat film, although espionage films and home-front dramas involving the training of soldiers and/or the day-to-day experiences of wartime Americans were significant cycles as well. Among the more interesting developments in Hollywood's war-film production, in fact, was the prominence of spy, espionage, and war-related crime thrillers in the early years of the war, especially 1942, and the subsequent surge in home-front dramas and combat films in the later war years. As these figures from Shain's study clearly indicate, by 1944–1945 the combat film was by far the dominant war-related type:

Table 7.3
WORLD WAR II–RELATED FILMS BY TYPE, 1942–1945

Type	1942	1943	1944	1945°
Espionage	59.5%	22.0%	15.6%	17.7%
Combat	24.8	41.5	51.4	60.7
Home-front	16.0	36.7	32.7	18.0

°Note that the figures do not total 100 percent; Shain does not explain this discrepancy.

SOURCE: Shain, *An Analysis of Motion Pictures*, p. 61.

The year 1942, particularly during the first six to eight months after the United States entered the war, was a singularly odd, exceptional period in terms of war-film production. Because Hollywood had been fairly tentative in its treatment of the war until Pearl Harbor, and because top features took nine to twelve months to produce and release, very few A-class war films depicting U.S. involvement were released in 1942. (CASABLANCA, for instance, was optioned within weeks of Pearl Harbor and went into immediate preproduction, but it did not go into general release until January 1943.) Thus, most of the war-related A-class films released in 1942 were initiated in 1941, and they tend to take one of three tacks: they focus on the British war effort (MRS. MINIVER, THIS ABOVE ALL); they depict Americans or "good" Europeans dealing with enemy aggression (Nazis in TO BE OR NOT TO BE, DESPERATE JOURNEY, and THE PIED PIPER; Japanese in SOMEWHERE I'LL FIND YOU and ACROSS THE PACIFIC); or they feature American fliers fighting for other nations (England in EAGLE SQUADRON; Canada in CAPTAINS OF THE CLOUDS).

There were B-grade versions of these trends in 1942 as well, such as MGM's JOURNEY FOR MARGARET, mentioned earlier, and Republic's FLYING TIGERS, in which John Wayne leads a group of fighter pilots assisting the Chinese against Japan. The majority of B-grade war films in 1942, however, had little in common with Hollywood's A-class treatments, nor were they prone to historical accuracy or the depiction of actual combat. Their penchant for exploitation and ability to make their low-budget films rapidly enabled B-class producers to scoop their A-class counterparts in terms of war-related topicality; in fact, on-screen references to Pearl Harbor began turning up in B films within weeks of the Japanese attack.[64] But these were invariably jingoistic celebrations of American heroism and superior know-how, depicted in terms of B-movie formula rather than the conditions at hand.

Hollywood's rapid conversion of various B-grade series to war production in 1942 was actually quite remarkable. Espionage and sabotage films dominated, not only because of genuine public concern but because they were easy reformulations of low-grade crime formulas. B-grade G-men and undercover cops simply turned their sights from gangsters to foreign agents; the trappings of the story—props, sets, costumes, cast, and plot structure—remained much the same. A few A-class features in 1942 dealt with spies and sabotage and did give the formula a certain legitimacy, notably Hitchcock's SABOTEUR. But shrill, jingoistic B-grade thrillers were far more prevalent. Gangster and spy formulas were refitted in pictures like SABOTAGE SQUAD, UNSEEN ENEMY, and

COUNTER-ESPIONAGE, while Sherlock Holmes and Dr. Watson were updated into wartime sleuths in SHERLOCK HOLMES AND THE VOICE OF TERROR and SHERLOCK HOLMES AND THE SECRET WEAPON. B-Western series were recruited in films like Republic's VALLEY OF HUNTED MEN, in which the Three Mesquiteers battle Nazi spies, and Monogram's COWBOY COMMANDOS, in which the Range Busters pursue Nazi saboteurs.[65] Even the Universal horror film was converted to war production in INVISIBLE AGENT; Jon Hall's "invisible man" took on both Nazi and Japanese spies.

Many 1942 B-grade spy and crime thrillers also exploited the American public's anger about Pearl Harbor and anxieties about the Japanese threat—as evidenced by such titles as A PRISONER OF JAPAN, MENACE OF THE RISING SUN, DANGER IN THE PACIFIC, and REMEMBER PEARL HARBOR. These and other 1942 B's demonized the Japanese and embellished the "stab-in-the-back" thesis which was haphazardly applied to all Japanese—including Japanese Americans, in some cases.

The OWI grew increasingly alarmed by these trends; its September 1942 report openly criticizing Hollywood's B-grade war films received extensive coverage in the trade press. The OWI asserted that "the emphasis of the entire industry is still too much on the exciting blood-and-thunder aspects of the war." The report noted that 31 war-related espionage and sabotage pictures had been released in the previous six months, a number that "tended to give the public an exaggerated idea of the menace."[66] In October, the OWI's Bureau of Motion Pictures (BMP) reported that 70 of 220 pictures released in the preceding six months were war-related, but that few of these substantially advanced the war effort. A *Variety* headline in November blared, "OWI Frowns on 'B' Types," and the subhead noted the agency's "Drive to get the studios to lay off cops-and-robbers formula." That story noted that whereas six "saboteur-spy type" war films were released in October 1942, there were none in the OWI's "all-important 'The Issues—What Are We Fighting For' category."[67]

This latter refrain would persist throughout the war years as Hollywood continued to avoid dealing with the conflict in sophisticated social or political terms. As the OWI's Dorothy Jones pointed out in a 1945 assessment of Hollywood's war-related films, no more than fifty or so had "aided significantly, both at home and abroad, in increasing understanding of the conflict." Jones accused the Hollywood community of thinking only in terms of escapist entertainment, asserting that "when faced with the task of making films which would educate the public about the war, most Hollywood movie makers did not know where to begin."[68]

The industry's defense, of course, was that the primary obligation of commercial filmmakers is to make pictures that sell. Walter Wanger, then the Academy president, outlined that rationale in *Public Opinion Quarterly:* "Film with a purpose must pass the same test that the escapist film more easily passes. Theater-goers must want to see the picture." Convinced that the kind of pictures the OWI espoused "can effect no purpose except to empty theaters," Wanger argued that any "truths" about war-related issues "had better be skillfully integrated" into the drama.[69]

By early 1943, when Wanger's article appeared, a growing number of films actually supported his view. While Hollywood would never quite satisfy the OWI, there was a clear improvement in the overall quality of war films as the ambitious first-run features made after Pearl Harbor finally reached the theaters in late 1942. Among the first and most important of these was WAKE ISLAND, a Paramount near-A released in August 1942; starring Brian Donlevy, William Bendix, Macdonald Carey, and Robert Preston, it dramatized the devastating defeat (in December 1941) of a marine contingent on a remote island outpost near Hawaii. As Jeanine Basinger suggests, WAKE ISLAND was a watershed release and in many ways the first true World War II combat film. While incorporating many traits of earlier war films, WAKE ISLAND also "begins to relate the meaning of these 'old' devices directly to World War II." Key factors, according to Basinger, were its focus on an actual U.S. military battle and on the combat unit, "that unique group of mixed individuals, so carefully organized to represent typical Americans."[70] The film also established the conventions of the World War II "last-stand" drama. In WAKE ISLAND and later films such as MANILA CALLING (1942) and BATAAN (1943), a small, isolated unit of American soldiers fights to the death against impossible odds, with the narrative invariably concluding just before the last American is killed.

The popular and critical response to WAKE ISLAND underscored its watershed status. Returning $3.5 million in rentals, it was among the top box-office hits of the year and scored four Oscar nominations, including best picture. Bosley Crowther in the *New York Times* called WAKE ISLAND "a realistic picture about heroes who do not pose as such," and *Newsweek* called it "Hollywood's first intelligent, honest, and completely successful attempt to dramatize the deeds of an American force on a fighting front."[71] Made in cooperation with the Marine Corps and endorsed by the OWI, WAKE ISLAND clearly established the viability of the violent, downbeat, hyperactive combat film, while toning down the jingoistic flag-waving, blatant racism, and gross historical distortions of so many previous B-grade war films. This is not to say that these qualities were eliminated alto-

Macdonald Carey and Brian Donlevy in the seminal World War II combat film WAKE ISLAND *(1942).*

gether. Most of Hollywood's wartime combat dramas were set in the Pacific, and most of them depicted the Japanese enemy as not only uncivilized but essentially inhuman—a view that pervaded the American media and colored the mindset of the public as well. As the war correspondent Ernie Pyle wrote: "In Europe we felt that our enemies, horrible and deadly as they were, were still people. But out here [in the Pacific] I soon gathered that the Japanese were looked upon as something subhuman or repulsive."[72]

In 1943, Hollywood's wave of A-class war-related films hit the nation's theaters with enormous impact. These included big-budget musicals like THIS IS THE ARMY and STAGE DOOR CANTEEN; resistance dramas like WATCH ON THE RHINE and THE MOON IS DOWN; and wartorn romances like CASABLANCA and FOR WHOM THE BELL TOLLS. There was also a marked increase in both the quantity and quality of A-class combat films, including AIR FORCE, ACTION IN THE NORTH ATLANTIC, BATAAN, GUADALCANAL DIARY, THE IMMORTAL SERGEANT, SO PROUDLY WE HAIL, CRY HAVOC, and SAHARA. Moreover, a number of British war films were released in the United States in late 1942 and early 1943—notably IN WHICH WE SERVE, THE IMMORTAL BATTALION (British title THE WAY AHEAD), THE INVADERS (British title 49TH PARALLEL), and ONE OF OUR AIRCRAFT IS MISSING. All were critically well received, and Noel Coward's IN WHICH WE SERVE also was a solid commercial hit.

Critics and the Academy responded enthusiastically to the 1943 surge in A-class war-related films. The National Board of Review's top ten selections for the year included seven war-related pictures, and the Academy's ten nominees for best picture likewise included seven war-related films, with the Oscar going to CASABLANCA. And in the *Film Daily* poll of over 400 critics, every film on the top-ten list was war-related (including RANDOM HARVEST, with a World War I story, and FOR WHOM THE BELL TOLLS, with its Spanish Civil War context).[73]

THE WORLD WAR II COMBAT FILM

The combat film saw significant advances in both quantity and quality of output in 1943. Two key films were AIR FORCE and BATAAN, which solidified the essential conventions of the World War II combat film while establishing its two dominant variations. AIR FORCE, an early 1943 release shot on location (at a Florida air base) and made in cooperation with the Army Air Corps, won critical praise for its semidocumentary style. The story focuses on a group of men isolated within a powerful warship—an authentic B-17 "Flying Fortress"—that was involved in air-sea battles in the Pacific during the early months of the war. The men learn both the value of group cooperation and the finer workings of their bomber, which gradually emerges as the crew's mother, lover, and sacred vessel. The finale of AIR FORCE is relatively upbeat, with the warship taking part in the Battle of the Coral Sea (in May 1942)—one of the first important Allied victories in the Pacific.

BATAAN also involves an early battle campaign in the Pacific theater, but it is a more stylized, studio-bound production, and considerably more brutal and downbeat as well. The story centers on a combat unit of thirteen men in an isolated jungle outpost on Bataan, which is being overrun by invading Japanese troops. The unit is assigned to destroy a bridge and prevent the Japanese from rebuilding it; in carrying out that assignment, the men are killed, one by one, by the relentless, faceless enemy. The consummate last-stand picture, BATAAN ends with the unit leader and lone survivor (Robert Taylor) throwing curses at the swarming Japanese and swinging his machine-gun fire directly into the camera for the film's powerful closing image.

The infantry unit in BATAAN *(1943).*

These two types, centering on the warship and the infantry unit, steadily coalesced into Hollywood's standard, war-issue combat formulas. The group dynamic and celebration of technology of AIR FORCE recur in all manner of warships, from submarines and ships to tanks and aircraft, while the infantry films grimly trace the horrors of combat and the psychopathology of soldiering. For Basinger, AIR FORCE and BATAAN "contain the new genre" of the World War II combat film. "In fact, they *are* the new genre. They are the two most important films . . . because they are the first that are totally in and about World War II combat." She contends, however, that the infantry variation is "the truest and purest combat format," because it is so relentlessly "about" actual fighting. While the bomber can take its crew back to the relative security and domesticity of the barracks, and even the submarine has its social and hospitable attributes, the infantry film offers "no relief from the war."[74]

Basinger considers BATAAN "clearly the seminal film" of the World War II combat genre for three reasons. First, unlike all of the preceding combat films made during the war, BATAAN provides no "denial" of the war through furloughs, returns home, or other noncombat situations but focuses only on soldiering and combat. Second, the nature and composition of the combat unit in BATAAN became a veritable paradigm for subsequent films, along various social and cultural lines—the ethnic, racial, and religious background of unit members; their ideological, economic, and class-related status; their geographical and regional origins; and their military rank, experience, and professionalism. As Basinger notes, BATAAN set the standard not only for the composition of the group in infantry combat films but also for the structure of authority, the likelihood of death, and even the order in which the unit members are killed.[75]

Third and perhaps most important, BATAAN integrated these conventions into a dramatically compelling narrative—and thus into effective propaganda. The group constituted what Lewis Jacobs has termed "a national collective hero," although Basinger aptly notes that the unit's "democratic ethnic mix" necessarily included a leader "who is part of the group, but is forced to separate himself from it because of the demands of leadership."[76] Those demands generally include a military objective (in this case the bridge) related to a specific military campaign, as well as dealing with the inevitable internal conflicts of the group. Meanwhile, the individual group members partake in the myriad rituals of infantry life, the articulation of what they are fighting for, and the necessary horror of fighting and dying. With BATAAN, asserts Basinger, "the foundation of the World War II combat film is in place"; the various "generic requirements" of the form were "firmly established and repeated" in the films that followed, as was readily apparent by late 1943 in films like SAHARA, GUADALCANAL DIARY, CRY HAVOC, and DESTINATION TOKYO.[77]

The infantry and warship variations of the combat film were not altogether distinct from one another, and in fact a few war films effectively combined the two. Among the most notable of these was SAHARA, a late-1943 Columbia release starring Warners loan-out Humphrey Bogart as the leader of a disparate band of Allied soldiers (Dan Duryea, J. Carrol Naish, Rex Ingram, Lloyd Bridges) crossing the Libyan desert aboard a U.S. tank who eventually make a stand at a desert well against an entire Nazi division. One of the more underrated combat films of the war era, SAHARA is noteworthy on several counts—particularly the warship and the military unit involved, the deft blending of the warship and infantry variations, and the heightened realism of the production.

SAHARA opens with the tank commander Sgt. Joe Gunn (Bogart) and his two-man crew crossing the North African desert alone in their tank during the chaotic retreat after the fall of Tobruk. At a bombed-out military hospital, they come across a British medical officer and five infantrymen: two Britons, two Australians, a South African, and a Frenchman. Gunn offers them assistance, but the British dismiss the tank as an "old scow" and a "tin hearse." Gunn takes offense, not only extolling his tank but romanticizing and feminizing it in the process. "She's an M-3 air-cooled job that can cross 200 miles of desert as easily as you'd walk around in that Piccadilly Circus of yours," he says. "When I go into Berlin I'll be riding that tank, the same one that's standin' there with the name Lulubelle on her." With no real choice, the soldiers climb aboard, riding atop the tank while Gunn and his crew (a radioman and a gunner) ride inside.

SAHARA is clearly a star vehicle, with Bogart's Sgt. Joe Gunn another wartime synthesis of rugged individualist and team player. Yet Joe's conversion to the collective war effort has long since been made, and he is presented as the ideal leader; in fact, the ranking British officer readily cedes authority to the American tank commander early in the film. The soldiers eventually are won over by the Lulubelle, of course, as are a black British-Sudanese soldier and his Italian prisoner (a sympathetic figure with relatives in America) who join the ragtag unit in its desert journey. Lulubelle's efficiency is further evinced when the crew shoots down a German fighter plane and captures the pilot, adding a dedicated Nazi to the group. Thus, the group, a diverse amalgam of eleven Allied soldiers and their two Axis prisoners, is complete; it is one of the more remarkable units in any wartime combat film and clearly represents the principal combatants in the Atlantic theater in microcosm.

Humphrey Bogart and director Zoltan Korda discuss a scene in SAHARA *(1943).*

The first half of SAHARA delineates these various characters—and the varied stakes and views of the nations they represent—as they search with increasing desperation for water and fuel. The group discovers water at a modestly fortified well, where they decide to dig in and try to hold off a division of some five hundred parched Nazis en route to El Alemein. Shifting to a last-stand drama, the Allies are killed one by one by the Germans, who themselves die in massive numbers in their repeated assaults on the well. The two prisoners also are killed, each under tellingly symbolic circumstances. The German pilot murders the Italian for defaming Hitler and Nazism, and then while trying to escape he is killed in a desperate hand-to-hand struggle with the black Sudanese—an obvious comment on Aryan superiority. Eventually the Allied force is down to only two men (including Gunn) and low on ammunition. But the Germans, succumbing to thirst and, because of Gunn's successful ploys, unaware of the Allied numbers, suddenly surrender. Thus, SAHARA veers from last-stand drama to an upbeat, updated version of SERGEANT YORK, and its positive outcome is underscored as the two survivors and their Nazi prisoners are met by Allied troops who inform them of the victory at El Alemein.

Despite its star-vehicle status, careening patchwork plot, and upbeat resolution, SAHARA is an altogether effective war film—in large part because of the style and visual treatment of the narrative by a production unit which was nearly as diverse as the mili-

tary unit in the film. Of particular note are the director Zoltan Korda and the cinematographer Rudolph Maté, two Hungarian-born émigrés to Hollywood from wartorn
Europe (Maté via Germany and France, and Korda from England, where he had
worked with his brother, the producer Alexander Korda). The two treated soldiering
and combat in a quasi-documentary style, while bringing a stylized poetic realism to the
depiction of the otherworldly desert milieu. Maté's camera work was nominated for an
Oscar, and the critic James Agee wrote of SAHARA's distinctive style: "It borrows, chiefly
from the English, a sort of light-alloy modification of realism which makes the traditional Hollywood idiom seem as obsolete as a minuet."[78]

As Agee suggests, the realism in SAHARA can be attributed in part to European influence, which came not only from the filmmakers directly involved but from the growing
number of émigrés working in Hollywood and from the British films showing in the
United States at the time. Equally important, however, was the documentary influence
that became increasingly pronounced in Hollywood's combat films of the later war years.

NONFICTION WAR FILMS, DOCUMENTARY REALISM,
AND THE HOLLYWOOD COMBAT FILM

Crucial to the combat film's 1943 surge were the massive advances in news coverage of
the fighting overseas, not only in the print media and on radio but in motion picture
newsreels and documentaries as well. Roughly 80 percent of all newsreels in 1942 were
devoted to the war at home and abroad, and in 1943 that total rose to nearly 90 percent.[79]
As Thomas Doherty notes in chapter 12, the six newsreel companies vastly improved
their coverage in 1942–1943, moving beyond a headline-service role to provide timely
and graphic depictions of military action. This improvement was facilitated by the easing of military restrictions on the filming of actual combat in late 1942 (at FDR's behest)
and by rapid improvements in the technology and logistics of combat reporting.[80]

Documentary film coverage improved as well, as in-depth nonfiction war films—both
shorts and features, many of them created by top Hollywood filmmakers in the military—became standard screen fare in 1943. Several British war documentaries enjoyed
widespread U.S. release and favorable critical response as well. In fact, the Academy
Award for best documentary feature in 1943 went to DESERT VICTORY, a British-
American coproduction on the Allied campaign in North Africa, while the award for best
documentary short went to John Ford's THE BATTLE OF MIDWAY.

Advances in nonfiction war coverage encouraged Hollywood filmmakers not only to
dramatize combat but to do so with a greater degree of verisimilitude and historical
accuracy. In the process, the narrative and dramatic emphases of combat dramas, as
well as the number of Hollywood filmmakers doing documentary work, clearly influenced nonfiction war films. Thus, by 1943 fiction and nonfiction war films were entering a stage of remarkable symbiosis, with combat dramas providing a (belated) fictional
counterpart to the newsreel and documentaries, all of which not only depicted major
military engagements but also defined and dramatized the war experience for millions
of Americans at home.

Regarding the symbiotic interplay of fiction and nonfiction war films, a number of
coincidences and parallels are worthy of note. The breakthrough combat film WAKE
ISLAND was released in 1942 within weeks of Ford's BATTLE OF MIDWAY, which itself was
precedent-setting on several counts. It was the first document of an actual U.S. military
engagement, and it was the first to use 16mm Technicolor photography. Moreover, it

was the first battle record by an established Hollywood director; in fact, Ford's hand-held camera work would set the early standard for first-person combat coverage. In 1943, as other Hollywood filmmakers became involved in documentary production, they introduced dramatic qualities and narrative strategies somewhat similar to their fictional counterparts.[81]

Consider William Wyler's film treatment of bombing runs over Germany from a Flying Fortress in MEMPHIS BELLE (1944), and John Huston's treatment of fierce infantry fighting in the Liri Valley in Italy in THE BATTLE OF SAN PIETRO (1945). Among the more important and critically acclaimed wartime documentaries, both films effectively integrate fiction and nonfiction techniques. They extend and intensify the first-person technique of THE BATTLE OF MIDWAY, and as hourlong documentaries they develop strong narrative and dramatic lines to delve the human as well as the military stakes involved. Moreover, the two are documentary versions of Hollywood's dominant combat trends—the specialized unit operating (and confined within) a high-tech warship; and the isolated, interdependent, war-weary infantry unit trudging from one deadly engagement to another.

As documentarians like Ford, Wyler, and Huston dramatized and humanized their wartime subjects, fictionalized accounts of combat developed a more pronounced documentary realism. In 1944–1945, interestingly enough, the number of fictional and documentary combat films released was almost identical (sixteen and fourteen, respec-

The crew of the Memphis Belle *pose before their warship in William Wyler's 1944 documentary.*

tively), and many critics and historians have argued that these two forms of combat film can (and should) be considered manifestations of the same genre.[82] In fact, James Agee named SAN PIETRO and a dramatic feature, THE STORY OF GI JOE, as the best films of 1945, and for essentially the same reasons: their direct, unsympathetic, anti-romantic portrayal of professional soldiers in combat, and their gauging of military conflict and outcome in human terms.[83]

Released in October 1945, THE STORY OF GI JOE, directed by William Wellman, was the dramatic counterpart of Huston's SAN PIETRO; a grim depiction of an American unit in the Italian campaign, it stars Robert Mitchum as the reluctant unit leader and Burgess Meredith as the war correspondent Ernie Pyle (who had been killed in combat a year earlier). For Agee, THE STORY OF GI JOE was "the first great triumph in the effort to combine 'fiction' and 'documentary' film"—an effort he had been tracing since the release of AIR FORCE in 1943. Besides Wellman's direction, the "great triumphs" of the film also included its "anti-histrionic casting and acting," which Agee considered crucial to this kind of war film. Indeed, Agee's one misgiving about the otherwise effective OBJECTIVE BURMA (1945) was that, for him, it could never quite overcome the onus of being an Errol Flynn picture—a criticism which could be leveled at SAHARA (and Bogart) as well.[84]

Remarkably, both THE STORY OF GI JOE and SAN PIETRO were regarded as antiwar films by some critics, because they were so downbeat in their portrayal of men at war and so sensitive to the psychological and physical trauma involved. THE BATTLE OF SAN PIETRO, in fact, so concerned military officials in Washington that it was withheld from distribution until the end of the war in Europe, and then it was released only in an abridged version under the (also abridged) title, SAN PIETRO.[85] Agee noted the debate that had arisen over the antiwar issue in his October 1945 review of THE STORY OF GI JOE, and his own take was appropriately ambivalent:

> Nobody [in the film] is accused, not even the enemy; no remedy is indicat-
> ed; and though every foot of the film is as full an indictment of war as I ever
> expect to see, it is clearly also demonstrating the fact that in war many men
> go well beyond anything which any sort of peace we have known, or are like-
> ly to know, makes possible for them. It seems to me a tragic and eternal
> work of art. (Reprinted in *Agee on Film* [New York: Grossett and Dunlap,
> 1958], vol. 1, p. 174)

Two other fictional war films released just after the war, THEY WERE EXPENDABLE (December 1945) and A WALK IN THE SUN (January 1946), also displayed the documentary-style realism of THE STORY OF GI JOE, as well as its tone of grim resignation and weary professionalism. Few critics gauged these as antiwar efforts, however. As Roger Manvell points out, the Ford-directed THEY WERE EXPENDABLE clearly accepts "the fatalism bred of combat conditions," while it also "brings out the ancient ethos of war, the aspiration to heroism, a profound acceptance of self-sacrifice for the 'cause' of the nation, the near-worship of the charisma of military authority implicit in such terminol-ogy as *high command* and *supreme command*."[86] At the same time, these films are will-ing to consider both the possible breakdown of the group cohesion as well as the price—in both individual and collective terms—of military victory.

Ultimately, the more realistic and somewhat disillusioned combat films of the later war era marked a significant departure from infantry dramas like WAKE ISLAND, BATAAN,

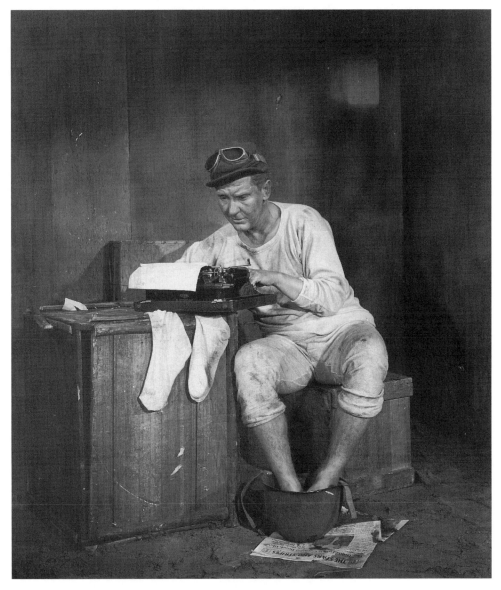

Burgess Meredith as journalist Ernie Pyle in THE STORY OF GI JOE *(1945).*

SAHARA, and GUADALCANAL DIARY. While sharing many qualities with their flag-waving, heroic, and aggressively prowar antecedents, the differences in style and tone of the later combat films clearly set them apart. Again James Agee offers a useful distinction. In his review of BATAAN, Agee termed the film a "war melodrama" much like WAKE ISLAND, and he went on to describe it as "a small triumph of pure artifice," constrained as it was by its star, its obvious studio setting, and its utterly predictable heroic posturing. While Agee found this anything but "realistic," still he recognized the power and appeal of films like WAKE ISLAND and BATAAN: "We may not yet recognize the tradition, but it is essentially, I think, not a drama but a kind of native ritual dance. As such its image of war is not only naive, coarse-grained, primitive; it is also honest, accomplished in terms of its aesthetic, and true."[87] Hollywood continued to produce this type of ritualized war melodrama with films like DESTINATION TOKYO (1943), WINGED VICTORY (1944), GOD IS MY CO-PILOT (1945), and BACK TO BATAAN (1945)—all sizable hits. And while critics praised the documentary-style combat films, audiences clearly preferred the energetic hokum of war melodramas like A GUY NAMED JOE over the grim realism of THE STORY OF GI JOE.

As noted earlier, Hollywood's production of combat films ended rather abruptly after the war, owing mainly to the industry perception that audiences were no longer interested in them.[88] By late 1945, exhibitors and studio executives alike had developed a firm conviction that for a war-weary populace—not to mention the millions of returning veterans—the war film's appeal ended with the war itself. So as the government and the military rapidly dismantled the nation's vast war machine, the movie industry began reconversion as well, mustering out the war-related themes and formulas that had prevailed for the past four years. This was most evident in the combat film, but the home-front drama also underwent a postwar decline as Hollywood shied away from stories of returning vets, postwar rehabilitation, and the domestic "return to normalcy."

The World War II combat film hardly disappeared altogether, of course. After lying dormant for fully three years, the genre would undergo a remarkable, unexpected resurgence in 1949, keyed by three major hits: BATTLEGROUND, TWELVE O'CLOCK HIGH, and SANDS OF IWO JIMA. The genre's currency would continue for decades to come, since the American (and Allied) experience of World War II provided a curious parallel to cold war-era films involving U.S. military conflicts in Korea and Vietnam. Despite its later resurgence, however, the World War II combat film could never be the same—nor, for that matter, could the home-front drama. From 1942 to 1945, Hollywood created a parallel universe for a nation at war, an odd amalgam of information and entertainment, of fact and propaganda, of realism and collective national fantasy. Thus Hollywood's war-related output represents a collective cultural experience altogether unique in American film history.

CASE STUDY: *AIR FORCE* AND *SINCE YOU WENT AWAY*

AIR FORCE and SINCE YOU WENT AWAY provide excellent examples of the combat film and the home-front drama. They reflect other significant wartime trends as well: the relationship between the military and the studios; the increasing authority of top talent and independent producers; the efforts of the OWI as well as the PCA to regulate movie content; and the pronounced wartime distinction between male action films and women's pictures, a function of the marketplace as well as the narrative and thematic qualities of the films themselves. Despite these obvious distinctions, AIR FORCE and SINCE YOU WENT AWAY display a number of significant similarities as well.

Two "fortresses"—the warship Mary Ann in AIR FORCE (*1943*), *and the Hilton family home in* SINCE YOU WENT AWAY (*1944*).

The most basic similarity between the two films is their mutual celebration of distinctive American "fortresses"— one a Boeing B-17 bomber and the other a two-story brick colonial home—while valorizing the occupants and the special wartime rites of each domain. AIR FORCE presented the saga of a B-17 Flying Fortress and its crew, whose training flight of 6 December 1941 across the Pacific becomes an odyssey of the disastrous early months of the war—but then culminates in the Battle of the Coral Sea. SINCE YOU WENT AWAY is an epic of a different sort, dedicated in its opening credits to "the Unconquered Fortress: the American Home." It charts a year in the lives of a woman and her two daughters, beginning in early 1943 with the departure of the husband and father for active duty. The lives of the three are transformed by the war effort and war-related experiences at home, as well as by the fate of the absent patriarch—who is reported missing in action midway through the year (and the film), and whose reported return to safety provides the story's climactic moment.

AIR FORCE was one of many top studio productions initiated immediately after Pearl Harbor. It was made at the behest of Gen. Henry "Hap" Arnold, head of the Army Air Corps and a personal friend of Jack Warner. In early 1942, Arnold began looking to Hollywood for on-screen support, and Warner played a key role in this effort. Warner was commissioned as a lieutenant colonel in the Army Air Corps in April 1942 and assigned as a public relations officer based in Los Angeles. He helped set up the First Motion Picture Unit, a nonfiction production unit housed at the Hal Roach studios that made training films and documentaries for the Air Corps and other military branches. Later in 1942, Warners gave the Air Corps use of its Vitagraph Studios in New York. Jack Warner also took on AIR FORCE as a personal and professional project, with assurances from Hap Arnold of full Army Air Corps support.[89]

While Warner monitored the project, AIR FORCE actually was produced by the executive-turned-unit producer Hal Wallis and the freelance producer-director Howard Hawks, whose new contracts with Warner Bros. in February 1942 specified AIR FORCE as among their initial projects. (Because both contracts also stipulate producer credit, AIR FORCE is introduced as "A Howard Hawks Production" yet Hal B. Wallis receives producer credit.)[90] While Warner and Wallis lined up the production, Hawks signed the screenwriter Dudley Nichols in March 1942 to do an original script based, at Arnold's suggestion, on an actual incident. The *Mary Ann*, a B-17 training plane, was separated from its flying group while heading toward Hickham Field in Hawaii on the morning of the Japanese attack. In the course of the film, the *Mary Ann* sees action in several of the major military engagements during the early stages of the Pacific campaign. Nichols completed the script by early summer, shortly after the Battle of the Coral Sea in May, a spectacular air-sea battle and an early Allied victory which provided an ideal culmination to the story.[91]

AIR FORCE was an ambitious production by Warners' standards but scarcely a star vehicle; it featured the rising star John Garfield and an ensemble of (available) male feature players, notably Harry Carey. The real star of the film was the *Mary Ann*, an authentic Flying Fortress supplied by the Army Air Corps, along with its facilities at a training base in Florida. Filming on location made the picture a wartime rarity, pushing its cost to about $2 million, and allowed Hawks to work without direct studio supervision—and without interference from Wallis and the front office.[92]

The minor problems that Warners ran into with the PCA over language and violence were adjusted (or negotiated away) easily enough. The OWI, however, was then in the midst of its campaign to upgrade the accuracy and curb the blatant racism and xenophobia of war films, and the agency was severely critical of the film. In October 1942, with AIR FORCE in postproduction and nearing release, the OWI complained that virtually all Asians in the film, both enemy soldiers and "friendly" civilians alike, were depicted as treacherous, bloodthirsty savages. (The Japanese were referred to as "stinkin' Nips," "buck-toothed little runts," and so on.) The film also suggested that Japanese sympathizers and saboteurs were in some ways responsible for U.S. defeats in Hawaii and the Philippines. Despite these complaints, however, the filmmakers did little to mollify the OWI—particularly after receiving approval from the Army Air Corps and the PCA.[93]

AIR FORCE was released in early 1943 with considerable fanfare and widespread promotion, including Grossett and Dunlap's publication of John O. Watson's "novelized" version of Nichols's screenplay. The picture returned $2.7 million and was Warners' fourth-biggest hit among nine 1943 releases which earned at least $2 million (seven were war pictures). Critical response was mixed: the film's authenticity and semidocumentary style were often praised, while its war melodrama formulaics were routinely criticized.[94]

Any sense of realism in AIR FORCE results from three factors: the use of an actual B-17 as the principal set for the picture; the story's depiction of actual war-related events; and the incorporation of newsreel footage at various points in the film, notably in the climactic Battle of the Coral Sea. The story and characters, on the other hand, are standard Hollywood war issue. AIR FORCE presents a group of disparate individuals (and two outspoken individualists) who gradually coalesce into a unified, efficient, gung-ho fighting unit. The group hails from all points of the social, ethnic, and geographical map; it includes a Jew, a Pole, an Irishman, a Minnesota farm boy, a Texan, a streetwise New Yorker, and so on—all distinctions that purposefully become meaningless by the end of the film.

Like most combat films, AIR FORCE is a conversion narrative; its conversion theme operates on several levels. In a general sense, the *Mary Ann* herself is converted from a training ship into a fighting machine, and the crew members into functional components of that machine. In terms of human drama, the story focuses on two converts: Winocki (John Garfield) is a surly loner and flight school washout who eventually accepts his role as a team player and gunner; in fact, he is credited with inventing the tail gun for the B-17. Tex Rader (James Brown) is a professional loner, a pursuit pilot forced to ride in the *Mary Ann* when his fighter is shot down. Tex initially denigrates bombers (while the crew, in turn, dismisses his "pea shooter"), but he eventually takes command of the plane after the pilot is killed and the copilot wounded.

The trajectory of AIR FORCE takes the crew from one major Pacific battle to another—from Honolulu to Wake Island to the Philippines. Each stage takes the *Mary Ann* and her crew deeper into the war experience, and each stop is punctuated by a hospital scene which underscores the point. The first involves a nurse at Hickham in Hawaii who is the copilot's sweetheart and the sister of one of the crewmen; she has been wounded during the Japanese attack, indicating the enemy's brutal disregard for helpless women and children. At Wake, the crew visits the wounded base commander, who despite his condition insists on staying with his fliers and the doomed marines trapped on the island. He urges the *Mary Ann*'s crew to proceed to the Philippines, where they encounter heavy combat. The *Mary Ann* is shot down, and Winocki heroically crash-lands the plane after the crew has bailed out and the pilot, Quincannon, has been mortally wounded. The third hospital scene depicts the death of Quincannon, their pilot

The nominal stars of AIR FORCE, *John Garfield (left) and Harry Carey (right).*

and leader, and is perhaps the most dramatic moment in the film. Scripted by William Faulkner during production, the scene features the dying pilot hallucinating a final takeoff in the *Mary Ann,* going through the various verbal procedures as the crew, at his bedside, assume their respective roles as well. This deathbed experience gives an emotional edge to their individual responsibilities as well as to their "family" unity and motivates the crew to return their warship to action.

Inspired by Quincannon's death, the crew literally rebuilds the plane overnight under the supervision of the crusty, paternal crew chief (Carey), assisted by marines awaiting the imminent Japanese attack. They complete the job just as the enemy swarm the airfield; the *Mary Ann* miraculously escapes and joins the Allied air armada over the Coral Sea just as it intercepts the Japanese fleet en route to Australia. The *Mary Ann* asserts her superiority in the ensuing battle, taking the lead in the attack and sinking several enemy vessels—thus marking an early turning point in the war and also the successful conversion of the *Mary Ann* and her crew into a professional fighting machine.

In precise counterpoint to AIR FORCE, David O. Selznick's SINCE YOU WENT AWAY presents an idealized portrait of the fight waged by women, individually and collectively, on the home front. Unlike many women's pictures and home-front dramas which invoked the war more indirectly, SINCE YOU WENT AWAY was quite clearly a war film, tracing the conversion of home and family—the American community in microcosm—to the war effort. Indeed, it was Hollywood's wartime woman's picture *par excellence,* focusing directly on the American female's experience of World War II. And thus, it was quite a bit different from the "American *Mrs. Miniver*" which Selznick set out to produce. Whereas that 1942 MGM film depicts the initial impact of the war on a fully intact British family, SINCE YOU WENT AWAY charts the experiences of a woman and her two daughters in 1943, with her husband overseas and the nation's wartime conversion well under way.

The film was based on a wartime memoir by Margaret Buell Wilder, "Since You Went Away—Letters to a Soldier from His Wife," which had been serialized in *Ladies' Home Journal* and was awaiting publication as a book when Selznick purchased the rights for $30,000 in early 1943. He brought Wilder to Hollywood from her home in Akron, Ohio, where the story was set, and started her to work on the adaptation while he prepared production.[95] Just as AIR FORCE relied for its authenticity and primary setting on the Flying Fortress, so too did Selznick's production rely on its earthbound domestic fortress—a two-story, seven-room brick colonial. Rather than seek out an appropriate location in some Ohio suburb, however, Selznick had a full-scale house constructed (along with a sizable stretch of its city street) as a standing set inside his studio.

In contrast to the nonstar ensemble in Warners' AIR FORCE, Selznick's production featured three top female stars: Claudette Colbert as Ann Hilton, the stalwart matriarch; Jennifer Jones (a sudden star after THE SONG OF BERNADETTE) as the 17-year-old daughter, Jane; and Shirley Temple as the 14-year-old "Brig" (Bridget). Colbert, significantly enough, had just starred in SO PROUDLY WE HAIL, a story of nurses serving in the battle-torn Pacific and a rather odd admixture of women's weepie and wartime action picture. James Agee, in *The Nation,* dismissed SO PROUDLY WE HAIL as "probably the most deadly-accurate picture that will ever be made of what the war looks like through the lenses of a housewives'-magazine romance."[96] This perspective may have accounted for the film's popular success (it earned $3 million and was the twelfth-biggest box-office hit of 1943), as well as for Selznick's decision to cast Colbert in SINCE YOU WENT AWAY.

In the three important male roles, Selznick cast Joseph Cotten as Tony Willett, the longtime friend of the Hiltons who for years has been carrying a torch for Ann (from a discreet distance); Monty Woolley, reprising THE MAN WHO CAME TO DINNER, as the autocratic curmudgeon Colonel Smollett, who rents a room in the Hilton home to help the family make ends meet; and Robert Walker as Corporal Bill Smollett, the colonel's estranged grandson and Jane's love interest. (Walker and Jones were married at the time but would separate during production, with no apparent effect on their portrayal of the innocent young lovers.)

Ever the "creative producer" with a blockbuster mentality, Selznick's creative role and personal stake in SINCE YOU WENT AWAY was exceptional, even for him. The film marked his return to active production after a four-year hiatus; at a cost of $2.78 million, SINCE YOU WENT AWAY was Hollywood's most expensive production since GONE WITH THE WIND. Selznick also had developed a close personal relationship with Jones (whom he would later wed after she had divorced Walker and he had divorced Irene Mayer Selznick), and he recently had added Shirley Temple to his stable of contract stars. He was adamant that the film redefine the screen image of both stars, as Jones looked ahead to more mature romantic roles and Temple entered her teen years.

Selznick's creative involvement began with an overhaul of Wilder's screenplay, which he began to revise immediately after her return to Ohio in August 1943—only weeks before the picture went into production. Selznick's rewriting continued throughout the 127-day shoot, primarily to keep the picture as current as possible with war conditions and to build up Jones's role. He eventually rewrote enough of the script to warrant sole screenplay credit, despite Wilder's appeals to SWG. (The film's writing credits read: "Based on an adaptation of her book by Margaret Buell Wilder," and later, "Screen Play by the Producer.") The director John Cromwell tolerated Selznick's last-minute revisions and also his insistence on seeing a camera rehearsal of every scene before it was filmed. Selznick was unhappy with the camera work and lighting, however; he replaced George Barnes (who had won an Oscar for REBECCA) with Stanley Cortez, and he later replaced Cortez with Lee Garmes, who finished the shoot.

Production closed in February 1944 after five months of principal photography, and Selznick immediately began editing with Hal Kern while Max Steiner composed the score. The completed picture, with its 205 speaking parts and meandering narrative, runs two hours and fifty minutes—long even by wartime standards, though a half-hour shorter than GONE WITH THE WIND. SINCE YOU WENT AWAY was released in June 1944 to uniformly respectful but somewhat tepid reviews. Bosley Crowther, for instance, admired the film but considered it "a rather large dose of choking sentiment."[97] Meanwhile, the public took to it in droves; the picture returned rentals of $4.9 million and was one of the biggest hits of the war.

As a sentimentalized portrait of America's wartime women and the domestic front, SINCE YOU WENT AWAY was enormously effective. Indeed, the film's ardent sentimentality is firmly and effectively established from the very outset. The titles play over a shot of the "home fires" in a hearth, followed by a fade-in on an exterior shot of the Hilton home, framed by a leafless tree in a dark, driving rainstorm. A series of dissolves takes the viewer closer to the home, then closes in on a downstairs window, and finally inside. A long tracking shot surveys a cozy, well-appointed den, moving from an empty leather chair to a bulldog on the floor, then across a desk revealing a calendar (it is January 1943), a telegram (Timothy Hilton, USN, has been ordered overseas), and a memento of Tim and Ann Hilton's honeymoon (they were wed in 1925). The shot continues, sweeping past bronzed baby shoes, a picture of Ann and her daughters, and finally back to the window, as Ann returns home after seeing off her departed soldier-husband. Crucial to the emotional impact of the scene is Steiner's score: the "Since You Went Away Theme" flows subtly, seamlessly into strains of standard American tunes—"You're in the Army Now," "Here Comes the Bride," "Lullaby and Goodnight," and so on—with each transition precisely cued to the visuals. (Steiner's score was the lone Oscar winner among the half-dozen nominations.)

This efficient narrative exposition establishes both the back story and the tone of SINCE YOU WENT AWAY, and Ann's subsequent arrival and voice-over reverie immediately set the dramatic stakes and plot trajectory as well. "This is the moment I've dreaded," says Ann to herself, "coming back to our home—alone." The remainder of the film charts Ann's efforts to confront and eventually to overcome that dread, which intensifies midway through the film when she learns that Tim is missing in action. But in the final moment of the film, a full year after the opening, Ann learns of Tim's imminent safe return—the consummate reward for her sacrifices and efforts in his absence.

While Tim Hilton's departure and return to safety define the film's overarching narrative development, the more immediate dramatic concerns involve the adjustments of the Hilton women—and the household in general—to the war.[98] In that sense, SINCE YOU WENT AWAY represents a consummate wartime conversion narrative. Not only the Hilton females but virtually every other character in the story, as well as the family home and the community at large, are utterly transformed by the war.

Jennifer Jones as Jane Hilton, whose role was built up considerably during the production of SINCE YOU WENT AWAY.

The emphasis is on the home, of course, which is a clear equivalent to the *Mary Ann* in AIR FORCE—a safe (almost womblike) haven which gives definition and meaning and a sense of unity to its occupants. Significantly enough, when Selznick revised Wilder's story and script, he decided to upscale the Hiltons socially, from a modest middle-class to an upper-middle-class family. This change both amplifies and further idealizes their sacrifices—giving up the master bedroom to the crotchety Colonel Smollett; doing without their devoted housekeeper, Fidelia (Hattie McDaniel), although she does find a way to return part-time; planting a victory garden while giving up meat, eggs, and other staples; and so on.

The conversion of Ann, her daughters, and her household to the war effort dominates the first third of the film, providing what Koppes and Black describe as "a virtual compendium of OWI-approved vignettes of American life as changed by the war."[99] This first movement of the story culminates in a dramatic episode which recasts the conversion in a larger social context. Hoping to meet Tim briefly before he ships out, the women embark on a long train ride from Ohio to Washington. Their effort to find Tim proves futile, although it provides an opportunity for the Hiltons (and the viewer) to relate their situation and their sacrifices to those of other Americans—from complaining businessmen and dismembered veterans to relocated workers and other self-reliant wartime women. Aptly enough, the excursion concludes in an intimate and distinctly feminine moment, as a woman lets Brig sleep on her breast and explains to Ann that her own daughter, an army nurse, has been missing since Corregidor.

Shortly after the women return home, Tim Hilton is reported missing, thus initiating the second major movement of the story. As Ann copes with the news, the story shifts focus somewhat to daughter Jane, who takes a job as a nurse's aide (caring for disabled veterans), and who experiences first love with the painfully self-effacing Bill Smollett. The two youngsters mature rapidly in the next few months, and they are considering marriage when Bill is sent overseas—to Salerno in Italy, where he is killed a short time later. Jane's grief gives way to stoic resolve, inspired and reinforced by her mother's example. This section of the story ends with Jane dramatically confronting a longtime family friend and self-centered social matron, Emily Hawkins (Agnes Moorehead). Jane forcefully berates Emily's failure to cooperate with the war effort and her criticism of those who do, clearly articulating the role and responsibilities of the female "recr ats" serving on the home front.

The film's final section returns the focus to Ann, who begins training as a welder and begins to accept the prospect of life without Tim, all the while keeping the vaguely amorous Tony Willett (Cotten) at bay. Her devotion is rewarded on Christmas Eve when she opens a gift which Tim had left and then, alone with her thoughts of her missing husband, she receives word that Tim has been found and is safe. The emotional crescendo and dramatic climax here provide an apt finale to the tearstained, three-hour saga, underscoring both its appeal as a wartime anthem to the home-front warriors and also, in retrospect, its quite remarkable sentimental excess.

The film's unabashed celebration of the attitudes and ideals of wartime America, and its total immersion in the experiences and conditions of the era, may account for the failure of SINCE YOU WENT AWAY to elicit much critical or popular interest over the years, despite its wartime success. As Koppes and Black suggest, "The symbolism and sentimentality of *Since You Went Away* help explain why the picture was a topical smash but suffers badly out of context."[100] They help explain, too, why the combat films of the era, especially those devoted exclusively to warfare, have sustained greater historical and popular interest. Jeanine Basinger states that AIR FORCE "is a great film, still powerful today. In it, one sees the visual strength a genre must have to endure."[101] The enduring appeal of the war film is indeed a function of its distinctive iconography, which has not changed significantly over the past half-century, as well as the timeless rituals of male bonding and the prospect of death in a threatening, alien landscape.

Ultimately, however, the similarities between AIR FORCE and SINCE YOU WENT AWAY are as illuminating as the differences. Both films, most fundamentally, are conversion narratives which trace the adjustments and sacrifices American women and men necessarily had to make for the war effort to succeed. Both redefine family and community, positing a new (albeit temporary) kinship system based on mutual need and commitment to the task at hand. Both depict epic journeys, although of a very different sort: the men in a Flying Fortress, traveling through space and externalizing their war-induced anxieties by fighting and killing; the women in an American domestic fortress, traveling through time and internalizing their anxieties by loving and nurturing—and waiting. Both films end in triumph, although these were only momentary triumphs which could not begin to resolve the larger social and military conflicts the characters still faced. Thus, both AIR FORCE and SINCE YOU WENT AWAY reinforced the basic idea that only when heroism became routine could the war itself finally be won.

8

Regulating the Screen: The Office of War Information and the Production Code Administration

Clayton R. Koppes

Regulating morality and politics on the screen was as critical from 1939 to 1945, during a period of international crisis, as at any time in American film history. While the Production Code Administration (PCA) patrolled moral barricades, major issues arose about the movies' content and their politics. After the PCA tried to eviscerate films against fascism from 1939 through 1941, the U.S. government decided wartime movies were too important to be left to the moviemakers. Through most of the war, the Office of War Information (OWI), the Roosevelt administration's propaganda agency, engaged in the most systematic governmental effort to regulate content that has been seen in any American medium of popular culture.

Together the PCA, policing morality, and the OWI, guarding politics, regulated the American screen more tightly than at any time in its history. The process yielded improvements in film content in certain areas, evasions and outright falsifications in others, high profits, and few great pictures. The unprecedented collaboration between government and the motion picture oligopoly raised questions that go to the heart of issues about control of the media in a democratic society.

The PCA and the Prewar Movie Industry

In the late 1930s, Hollywood and the PCA were still primarily concerned with the sort of pictures that Will Hays liked to describe as "pure entertainment," free of political or social controversy. The PCA under Joseph Breen devoted most of its attention to morality and vulgarity. His forceful administration of the Production Code provided what business prizes most: stability. Critics justifiably deplored the industry's lack of innovation and aversion to serious subjects. Will Hays and the studio heads thought otherwise.

They did not object to the movies' conservative tone and aesthetics, and they were able to make memorable pictures within the Code's strictures. In any case, the industry's profitability since 1934 seemed justification enough. Hays and the Hollywood heads did not want to relive the intense criticism of the early 1930s, which had threatened to bring about tougher censorship (perhaps by the federal government) or antitrust action that would destroy the carefully crafted Hollywood oligopoly.[1]

Although the PCA was a Hollywood fixture by the late 1930s, producers provoked controversies by pushing at the margins of the Code. One of the more recent and celebrated instances, as described in chapter 3, involved David O. Selznick's showdown with Breen over Rhett Butler's final line in GONE WITH THE WIND and Howard Hughes's ongoing feud over the revealing shots of Jane Russell's breasts in THE OUTLAW. Selznick prevailed, of course, and in fact the MPPDA board of directors not only allowed the line but amended the Code to allow *damn* and *hell* to be used in strictly limited cases.[2] Hughes, on the other hand, was ordered to cut some sixty seconds from THE OUTLAW— less than what was first demanded by Breen, who accurately anticipated the more drastic excisions demanded by local censor boards.[3]

The confrontations over *damn* and décolletage afforded comic relief in what was to moral guardians a deadly serious struggle over the theme, tone, and subject matter of motion pictures. In fact, the Catholic Legion of Decency rarely found it necessary to disapprove of PCA-sanctioned pictures. Breen had stumbled, however, when he approved MGM's STRANGE CARGO (1940). The Legion blasted it with a "C" (condemned) rating— the first such divergence between the Legion and the PCA since 1934—on the grounds that it promoted "naturalist religion." The PCA was dumbfounded at this bit of theological arcana. The controversy was an aberration and faded quickly.[4] The Legion's C rating for MGM's TWO-FACED WOMAN in late 1941, shortly after Breen left the PCA for RKO, was an obvious attempt to reassert its authority and to bring Breen's de facto successor, Geoffrey Shurlock, into line.[5] That incident amounted to little, finally, particularly in light of the U.S. entry into the war only a few weeks later.[6]

While battles over marital infidelity, bared breasts, and profanity followed well-worn grooves by the late 1930s, the mounting international crisis that erupted into World War II posed new challenges to the PCA's regulatory apparatus. Hitler's storm troopers, Mussolini's Blackshirts, and the Spanish Civil War offered Hollywood intensely dramatic material. Though most Americans remained resolutely isolationist, many thoughtful observers grew increasingly alarmed about the implications of German, Italian, and Japanese aggression. Hollywood was an intensely political community. Its creative personnel were predominantly liberal to leftist; they were reinforced in the late 1930s by European émigrés who advocated stronger resistance to what they saw as international fascism. Yet little of Hollywood's politics made the transition from the living room or the swimming pool to the screen.

Powerful structural barriers restricted politics on the screen. Hollywood usually eyes "message" pictures coldly, an attitude captured in the bromide attributed to Sam Goldwyn: "If you want to send a message, call Western Union." Like most purveyors of popular culture, the studio moguls tended to view entertainment and social comment as incompatible. Louis B. Mayer's philosophy, said the producer Pandro S. Berman, was that "we were selling beautiful women. . . . And he said if you're selling beautiful women *make* them beautiful. Dress them beautifully. Make them up beautifully. And photograph them beautifully." Many film industry heads were politically and socially conservative. Mayer was a Hoover Republican, and his favorite movies, the Andy Hardy series,

Impromptu wartime conference between PCA chief Joseph Breen (left) and British producer Arthur Rank.

betrayed his nostalgia for a waning Main Street domesticity. Cinema executives' endorsement of the blacklisting of suspected Communists and mere liberals after World War II reflected not merely capitulation to pressure but recognition of their own views.[7]

As seen in previous chapters, foreign trade reinforced Hollywood's caution, since it often meant the difference between break-even and profit. The studio-distributors thus were wary of doing anything that might offend any sizable foreign market. They even went so far as to fire their Jewish employees in Germany when Hitler demanded it. It was no coincidence that studios felt bolder about making antifascist pictures after their films were barred from Germany and Italy in 1940 and the British market thereby assumed greater importance.[8]

The movies' position in American society was paradoxical. Their very popularity gave them power but also encouraged people to attribute great (probably excessive) influence to them. Ongoing anti-Semitic attacks on the Jewish-dominated industry encouraged the moguls, perennially uneasy about their status in their adopted country, to minimize the Jewish presence in the industry and avoid political positions that looked like special pleading for Jewish causes. Will Hays, the master Republican politico and Presbyterian elder, counseled industry self-regulation and avoidance of political controversy on the screen. Politics was not prohibited in the Code, but Hays often invoked the elastic rubric of "industry policy" to pressure studios not to make controversial pictures.[9]

The mounting international crisis in 1937–1938 induced some producers to challenge the institutional barriers to political films. In late 1937, Hitler and Mussolini entered an alliance, which was soon followed by the Fuehrer's *Anschluss* with Austria. The Spanish Republic fell to Franco's Nationalist forces in March 1938, and in September the Munich sellout allowed Hitler to have his way with Czechoslovakia. Some of Hays's lieutenants argued that the screen should be open to more political material, which would be helpful in countering the Justice Department's antitrust suit against the industry in 1938. Filmmakers who attempted projects on the international crisis found, however, that the PCA still threw up roadblocks.[10]

The PCA's institutional bias against political films was reinforced by Breen's anti-Semitism and anticommunism. Although he hid his anti-Semitism in Hollywood, his dislike of Jews poured out in confidential letters to fellow Catholics. "These Jews seem to think of nothing but money making and sexual indulgence," said Breen. "They are, probably, the scum of the scum of the earth." Seemingly unperturbed by the Axis powers' anti-Jewish laws, he dismissed the Hollywood Anti-Nazi League as special pleading. It was "conducted and financed almost entirely by Jews," he said, and used anti-Jewish measures to stir up hostility to Hitler. Breen was sympathetic enough to Mussolini and Hitler in the late 1930s to try to have criticism of their regimes balanced by recognition of their achievements. Like many Catholics, he endorsed Franco and despised the Soviet-aided Spanish Republic. Support for Franco and at least toleration of Hitler and Mussolini was of a piece with the Catholic Church's anticommunism, as was fighting the anti-rightist organizations in Hollywood. Breen believed he was on the front line against red propaganda. In December 1937, he confided to Daniel J. Lord, the Jesuit who had been the Code's chief author, that he was fighting nothing less than a movement to *"capture the screen of the United States for Communistic propaganda purposes."* This hyperbolic statement strained credulity, but it indicated Breen's determination to block or at least dilute criticism of the right.[11]

In 1938, the independent producer Walter Wanger began work on BLOCKADE (1938), which he intended to be sympathetic to the Spanish Republic. Since the screenplay contained no Code violations of any consequence, Breen reluctantly approved it. He insisted, however, that the film avoid identifying either side, a condition that sharply reduced its meaning for the uninitiated. He let stand Henry Fonda's impassioned appeal to the "conscience of the world," since it was cast in vague, general terms. Detached from historical context, the film seems to be a generic war movie. Wanger himself described BLOCKADE as nothing more than a "melodramatic spy story and romance in a modern setting—colorful Spain." The Catholic right nonetheless attacked the film as propaganda, the Legion of Decency warned against it, and Martin Quigley editorialized against it in his *Motion Picture Herald*. Some liberals, on the other hand, charged that Hays worked behind the scenes to sabotage exhibitions. The film had a marginally successful run. Under the PCA, the screen could not speak the name of the conflict that was on everyone's lips.[12]

The persistent, politically minded Wanger tried again with a more daring subject, a film based on the journalist Vincent Sheean's best-selling *Personal History*. The reporter-hero discovers Franco's brutality and Hitler's anti-Semitism and rescues several Jews. Breen was unmoved by this factually based material, dismissing it as "pro-Loyalist propaganda . . . pro-Jewish propaganda, and anti-Nazi propaganda." He warned Wanger that the film would cause him "enormous difficulty" and harm the industry. Wanger shelved the project until 1940, when he retitled it FOREIGN

Laraine Day and Joel McCrea in Hitchcock's espionage thriller FOREIGN
CORRESPONDENT *(1940).*

CORRESPONDENT, hired Alfred Hitchcock for his second Hollywood film, and reduced it
to an espionage story with most of the politics left out.[13]

The PCA was as solicitous of Mussolini as it was of Franco. When MGM bought the
rights to *Idiot's Delight*, Robert E. Sherwood's Pulitzer Prize–winning play of 1936, the
Hays Office expressed opposition to the project. The play offended Mussolini's government because it involved a surprise Italian air attack on Paris and condemned fascism.
Trying to meet the objections of the Italian consul in Los Angeles, Breen demanded
many changes in the screenplay (which Sherwood himself was bowdlerizing for a fee of
$135,000). Metro agreed to most of them. Breen even carried the script to Rome on
his vacation in 1938 and returned with the regime's blessing. The studio finally drew the
line when the consul wanted the title changed to further blur any identification with the
play. IDIOT'S DELIGHT emerged in early 1939 as a showpiece for Clark Gable and
Norma Shearer. Its antifascism was tamed, its location moved to "an Alpine never-never
land," and its language "denatured into esperanto."[14]

The PCA and the War in Europe

Warner Bros. broke through the dual barriers of studio timidity and PCA resistance with
its early-1939 release CONFESSIONS OF A NAZI SPY. PCA staffers labeled it "a portentous
departure," and it was indeed Hollywood's first explicitly antifascist picture.

CONFESSIONS recalled the feisty Warners of the early 1930s. The picture dealt with news as current as the morning's headlines—Nazi spies who were caught and convicted in federal court in New York City. The film reflected the anti-Nazi convictions of its director, Anatole Litvak, and star Paul Lukas, who were German émigrés, and its writer, John Wexley, and other star Edward G. Robinson, who were active in Hollywood's anti-Nazi movement. CONFESSIONS explained how Nazism worked and called for American vigilance against the German menace. Hitler still had some defenders in the PCA who argued that the film was unfair because it ignored "his unchallenged political and social achievements" and detailed his dismemberment of Czechoslovakia, matters they considered "extraneous."[15]

Breen had to concede that the evidence produced at the spy trial substantiated the charges against Germany—Warners' reliance on judicial testimony gave the studio a strong defense. But Breen still wanted to stop the picture. As one PCA staffer put it, why should the industry abandon "the pleasant and profitable course of entertainment to engage in propaganda?" Some industry executives, such as Paramount's Luigi Luraschi, doubted the movie was "smart showmanship." Breen advised Jack Warner to scrap the project, warning that several countries, and possibly even some U.S. censor boards, would ban the film. Warners forged ahead, even though several countries obliged the German government by forbidding its exhibition. While CONFESSIONS now seems melodramatic and the spy threat inflated, many contemporary critics praised it as indeed a portentous breakthrough in moviemaking. Reflecting the desire of many directors and writers to make more serious films, Wexley termed it "the most exciting and exhilarating work I have ever done in Hollywood."[16]

CONFESSIONS OF A NAZI SPY cleared a path for other anti-Nazi films, though the PCA continued to set up roadblocks and detours. When Charles Chaplin decided to put his antifascist political convictions on film in 1938, the Hays Office passed the word that the project was inadvisable. Brooke Wilkinson, head of the British censor board, also indicated that such a film could not play in Britain because of the panel's requirement that a living person could be shown on the screen only if he or she consented. By the time THE GREAT DICTATOR was ready for release in September 1940, Poland and France had been humiliated and the Battle of Britain raged. There was little the PCA could reasonably object to in a screenplay that turned Hitler and Mussolini into buffoons and concluded with a plea for universal brotherhood. Breen hailed it as "superb entertainment" and Chaplin as "our greatest artist." The censor sheepishly insisted, however, that the forbidden word *lousy* be removed; Chaplin agreed, sparing all concerned what would have been an even more embarrassing row than that over Rhett Butler's *damn*. Although anti-Nazi films still faced some opposition, Chaplin's political statement made a handsome profit. THE GREAT DICTATOR suffered, however, because it bore the stamp of its origins in 1938, when satire was still a plausible tool to use against the Axis. By 1940, Hitler was scarcely a laughing matter, and Chaplin later acknowledged that he would not have made such a film if he had known of the horrors of the death camps.[17]

The boldest anti-Nazi release before Pearl Harbor was the British production PASTOR HALL (1940), which portrayed the life of Martin Niemöller, a World War I U-boat captain who became a pacifist minister and was thrown into a Nazi concentration camp. Breen tried to stop American distribution of this "avowedly British propaganda" in June 1940—the very moment Germany overran France—for fear it would expose the industry to charges of "going out of our way to propagandize for the allies." The notion that exhibiting one such picture among the five hundred or so released annually represent-ed an extraordinary propaganda effort suggested how drastically the PCA narrowed the intellectual scope of the screen. None of the major firms would release it. Breen relented only when James Roosevelt, the president's son, arranged to exhibit it through his Globe Productions (and eventually through UA). The American release version boasted the added cachet of a prologue written by Robert Sherwood and read by Eleanor Roosevelt, although the PCA did cut some of the more violent scenes.[18]

Hollywood's products were more timid, owing particularly to Breen's insistence that they continue to employ the Code formula of not offending any nationality by casting its members as uniformly evil; bad Nazis had to be balanced by some good Germans. Metro's THE MORTAL STORM (1940) struck this balance in its essay on anti-Semitism, as did other 1940 releases such as FOUR SONS, ESCAPE, and I MARRIED A NAZI (1940). Fritz Lang, a German émigré, challenged this convention with his MAN HUNT (1941). Dudley Nichols's screenplay, submitted to the PCA in March 1941, depicted all Nazis as "brutal and inhuman" and all British as sympathetic. Breen, backed by Hays, demanded that 20th Century–Fox tone down this "inflammatory propaganda" before issuing a seal.[19]

Hollywood skirted the problem of explicit political statements but got its interven-tionist point across with pictures that glorified the British. In the 1941 releases A YANK IN THE RAF and INTERNATIONAL SQUADRON, Americans aroused by Britain's peril went off to fly with the Royal Air Force. The parallel with American entry into World War I was exploited for all it was worth in SERGEANT YORK, centering on an instinctive pacifist (Gary Cooper as the marksman-hero Alvin York) who wrestles with his conscience, con-cludes that the Allied cause is just, and enlists. By implication, the United States should follow their examples.[20]

Hollywood was moving to an interventionist beat by the summer of 1941, and the White House was delighted. As Lowell Mellett, one of FDR's media aides, put it: "Practically everything being shown on the screen from newsreel to fiction that touches on our national purpose is of the right sort."[21] Roosevelt sent a special message to the 1941 Oscar ceremony in which he praised the industry's contribution to the defense effort. And months later, as seen in chapter 3, isolationist senators led by Gerald Nye openly attacked the industry for its interventionist propaganda—and were routed by the special counsel, Wendell Willkie, who vigorously defended Hollywood for taking an antifascist line.[22] Yet there was less to the screen's interventionism than might have met the eye. Hays and Breen forced the studios to moderate some positions, and their oppo-sition no doubt deterred some producers from making more antifascist films. Though some institutional restraints would have remained, without the Hays Office Hollywood would have taken a stronger, more frequent stand against the Axis and would have been more sympathetic to American intervention.

The Japanese attack on Pearl Harbor made the debate about U.S. involvement in the war moot, and it radically affected both the propaganda function and the regulation of motion pictures as well. The wartime Office of Censorship screened all Hollywood products to determine whether to permit their export. The newly formed Office of the Coordinator of Inter-American Affairs, headed by the youthful Nelson Rockefeller, worked with the MPPDA to improve the portrayal of Latin America. And the most direct and systematic government regulation ever attempted of a popular American medium occurred under the Office of War Information, the propaganda agency.

The OWI in the Early War Years

Roosevelt created the OWI by executive order in June 1942 in an attempt to bring order from the chaos of the half-dozen overlapping propaganda agencies that had operated before the war. Believing the movies were crucial to the propaganda war, he charged the OWI with establishing a liaison with the motion picture industry. FDR insisted that the OWI avoid the "hate the Hun" excesses of the World War I–era Committee on Public Information (the Creel Committee), which had given movie propaganda a bad name. Experienced newsmen were chosen in the hope that they would give the agency credibility. Heading the OWI was the popular radio commentator Elmer Davis, who insisted that his agency's only goal was to "tell the truth."[23] Promoting a war in which rights and wrongs were clearer than in many conflicts, the OWI committed fewer excesses than most propaganda agencies. But controversy, evasion, and falsification were endemic in a context in which, as the *mot* went, "truth is the first casualty."

Whatever his commitment to the truth, Davis also believed, as he confided to his staff, that "the easiest way to propagandize people is to let a propaganda theme go in through an entertainment picture when people do not realize they are being propagandized." Infusing movies with a memorable but subtle propaganda theme fell to the OWI's Bureau of Motion Pictures (BMP). It was run by the former newspaperman Lowell Mellett. His deputy was Nelson Poynter, the 39-year-old liberal publisher of the *St. Petersburg Times.* Operating from a suite in the Taft Building at the corner of Hollywood and Vine, Poynter handled the day-to-day relations with the studios. While these editors' New Deal credentials appealed to the OWI, their lack of experience with film (Poynter seldom even went to the movies) proved to be a serious handicap. Several reviewers, mostly women, analyzed scripts, screened finished pictures, and helped with studio liaison. Dorothy Jones, head of the reviewing unit, devoted her life to movie analysis and political activism; after the war, she wrote a book on the portrayal of Asians in American films and founded Another Mother for Peace. The reviewer Marjorie Thorson parlayed her OWI experience into a job with MGM, where she spent many years as a script doctor.[24]

The BMP insisted that its job was to advise, not to censor. The bureau could not bar production and exhibition of pictures it disapproved. Poynter correctly maintained that the studios could make any films they wanted and distribute them in the United States, so long as they were not treasonable. But the OWI in fact had considerable power. As a government agency in wartime, it had to be taken very seriously; a recalcitrant studio risked accusations of not doing its part. Moreover, the Office of Censorship's control of export licenses gave the government economic leverage that the studios took seriously. Since its recommendations carried weight with the Office of Censorship, the OWI had more than patriotic suasion at its command. As the *Motion Picture Herald* put it: "No one has yet advanced an argument in support of producing a picture known in advance to be doomed to domestic exhibition exclusively."[25]

In the eyes of OWI analysts, Hollywood displayed more zeal about the war than it did political judgment. Bending industry conventions to the OWI's political goals was difficult. The BMP codified its view of the war in the forty-two-page "Manual for the Motion Picture Industry" in July 1942. The first question everyone involved in a production should ask, said the bureau, was, "Will this picture help win the war?" The bureau's war aims were imbued with Vice President Henry Wallace's *Century of the*

Common Man (1943), the bible of liberals and left-liberals at war. The BMP manual described the global conflict as a "people's war" between freedom and fascism. The enemy was not the German, Italian, or Japanese people but the ruling elites and their ideologies. An Allied victory promised a world New Deal, which would combine a regulated capitalism with an extension of social welfare programs; America would abandon isolationism to participate in a system of collective security. Many studios, particularly Warner Bros., whose namesakes admired Roosevelt, distributed the manual widely to their staffs. But other studios, notably Paramount, which was headed by the Georgia conservative Frank Freeman, were wary. To many industry executives, OWI doctrine was too statist and internationalist. Beneath the rhetoric of helping the war effort, the moguls fought with their new regulators over how far they would go in the OWI's liberal crusade.[26]

Conflict began in the summer of 1942 as the Bureau of Motion Pictures screened Hollywood's first war pictures. The OWI reviewers found them appalling. LITTLE TOKYO, U.S.A., a B movie from 20th Century–Fox, encapsulated most of what the OWI disliked. OWI reviewers termed it an "invitation to the Witch Hunt!" The film portrayed all people of Japanese descent in the United States as disloyal and as tools in Tokyo's diabolical plot, decades in the making, to attack Pearl Harbor. BMP reviewers also disliked the glorification of extraconstitutional methods; the detective hero tramples all over the Bill of Rights as he ferrets out traitors in "Little Tokyo" in Los Angeles. But the OWI had little leverage. The army cooperated in making the film, and the Office of

LITTLE TOKYO, U.S.A. *(1942) was precisely the kind of paranoid, jingoistic war film that the OWI railed against in the early war years.*

Censorship gave it an export license. In response to the OWI's objections, Fox made a few changes but did not alter the basic story. After all, it was the picture, rather than OWI's pronouncements, that reflected government policy. LITTLE TOKYO, U.S.A. taught the propaganda agency a lesson. To have maximum influence, the OWI, like the PCA, had to first have a look at screenplays; once a picture was nearly finished, the studios were likely to make only minor changes.[27]

OWI staffers' frustration mounted as they screened other releases in the fall of 1942. Metro's THE MAN ON AMERICA'S CONSCIENCE recklessly strayed into the tinderbox of race relations. The film limned an impossibly noble President Andrew Johnson and in the process traduced his adversary Thaddeus Stevens, the champion of the freed people during Reconstruction. The OWI settled for reshooting some scenes and a change of title to the less provocative TENNESSEE JOHNSON. Sometimes the OWI's concerns were warranted; in other cases, the humorless reviewers lost their perspective. They were convinced that Preston Sturges's THE PALM BEACH STORY, a satire of the idle rich, was a "libel on America at war" and exactly the wrong kind of escape picture for the time.[28]

Alarmed by such pictures, the OWI became increasingly interventionist. When Poynter read the screenplay for SO PROUDLY WE HAIL, Paramount's tribute to the heroic nurses on Bataan, he wrote several pages of suggested dialogue. The finished picture incorporated the thrust of his ideas but not his language, which was more suited to the editorial page than an embattled nurse. Poynter had breached an unspoken but fundamental taboo. Joseph Breen, an industry insider in a way Poynter never could be, might suggest rewriting a line or two, but never whole pages. The conservative Paramount hierarchy was infuriated by the OWI New Dealers' invasion of studio prerogatives.[29]

Compounding Poynter's blunder, Mellett overreached himself. He notified the studios on 9 December 1942 that "it would be advisable" to submit screenplays, and even treatments, to the OWI for early appraisal. Never before had a government agency demanded such control over motion pictures. "CENSORS SHARPEN AXES," bannered *Variety*. Most of the studio heads bitterly criticized the BMP's demand, fretting about the OWI's aspiring screenwriters larding their films with indigestible, liberal dialogue. Recognizing that Mellett's letter was disastrous, the OWI chief, Elmer Davis, quickly backed down and said that submissions were "purely voluntary."[30]

The moguls' outrage at being "censored" would have led the unwary to think Hollywood was a bastion of free speech. In reality, the industry had always lived with censorship. With scarcely a murmur, it had agreed to PCA regulation—a closeted, unaccountable censorship ideologically inspired by a conservative religious minority. The movies accepted censorship by a host of state and local censorship boards, bent to the wishes of pressure groups it deemed important, genuflected to southern racism, and allowed foreign—even hostile—governments to vet screenplays. Yet the industry claimed to be violated when its own government, in wartime, made similar demands. What was at stake was not a First Amendment principle but control of the production process. The PCA was a creature of the industry and had built a stable working relationship with the studios. External censorship boards dealt only with finished pictures, not the production process. Other interventions were episodic. Mellett threatened detailed invasion of studio prerogatives by an outside agency that spoke a language alien to Hollywood and whose minor bureaucrats often bypassed studio executives.

Mellett's and Poynter's blunders proved costly indeed for the OWI. In Congress, the conservative coalition of Republicans and southern Democrats, under the guise of cutting government waste, took aim at the liberal propagandists. Part of this opposition stemmed from Hollywood's complaints. In the spring of 1943, Congress whittled the OWI domestic branch's budget to about 10 percent of its original funding, guaranteeing it would be ineffectual.[31]

Ironically, the virtual demise of the domestic branch enhanced the power of the OWI's Hollywood liaison office. The key to the kingdom of Hollywood lay in the overseas branch. These operations were handled by Ulric Bell, who forcefully presented the case that bad pictures hurt America abroad. The studios thought they were better judges of what American audiences wanted than was the OWI, but they were hardpressed to counter objections based on foreign and military policy. Bell convinced the Office of Censorship to follow OWI recommendations on almost all pictures; by the summer of 1943, his office had become "an advance guard for the Office of Censorship," said the *Motion Picture Herald*. The OWI could now block exhibition, a power that always made the studios more tractable. As the Allied offensive liberated enemy territory, the agency's ability to help the box office interested Hollywood even more. The standard package the liberators handed out included food, DDT louse killer, and OWI-approved movies. As industry executives realized that the OWI wanted "only to be helpful, their attitudes change[d] remarkably," observed Robert Riskin, a top screenwriter who worked for the OWI overseas branch.[32]

The OWI and Hollywood's Portrayal of the Allies

By the autumn of 1943, the once-antagonistic demands of propaganda and popular culture began to dovetail. The result was not unlike the process by which the PCA came to be accepted in Hollywood. As the studios learned that working with the OWI brought predictability and profit without damaging the moguls' control of production, they were only too ready to cooperate. The results were visible in all areas of Hollywood production—the home front, the allies, the enemy, and the hope for a peaceful postwar world.

The OWI's hopes for a suitable treatment of the home front were well realized in David O. Selznick's monumental SINCE YOU WENT AWAY (1944). Bell praised the "corking story," and his successor, William Cunningham, thanked Selznick for his "splendid cooperation with this office." As seen in chapter 7, the film traces the experience of an idealized middle-class Ohio family as they cope with the father departing for war, the mother getting a factory job, and a daughter losing a boyfriend in battle; on a snowy Christmas Eve, the family receives the report of the father's return to safety. Selznick included a host of OWI-approved vignettes to promote the war effort: the family cheerfully enduring travel on a crowded train, a sailor ponying up five months' salary for war bonds, a well-heeled businessman improbably willing to pay 100 percent in income tax, and a stout matron praising the taste of margarine in comparison to butter. SINCE YOU WENT AWAY, concluded *Commonweal's* reviewer, Philip Hartung, was "the definitive home-front movie . . . until a realist comes along to show us what life is really like in America during World War II."[33]

A realist would have found abundant dramatic material in the tensions that suffused the home front. Not surprisingly, neither the PCA-limited studios nor the OWI's propagandists wanted to really tackle those issues. Instead, they crafted a message of reassurance as Americans tried to cope with the bewildering gender, racial, and labor conflicts that Selznick papered over in his idyll of Ohio middle-class domesticity.

Working women raised anxieties that the OWI was eager to dispel. The agency reported "all cheers and hosannas" for RKO's TENDER COMRADE (1943), a Ginger Rogers vehicle that was Hollywood's most systematic treatment of women's wartime role. With a screenplay by the Communist Party member Dalton Trumbo, TENDER COMRADE praised working women, scolded women who hoarded scarce war goods or indulged in the black market, and gave women some of the good speeches that usually went to men about what we were fighting for. Yet for all the film's supposed feminism, the OWI failed to notice that the film remained imprisoned in Hollywood gender conventions. Women are most intent on catching a man; the film implies that, when the war ends, they will leave the assembly line without complaint for their "normal" place in the kitchen and the nursery. Nor did the all-male production staff allow the heroine to grieve over her husband's death in combat. Instead, they converted this private moment into a platform for instructing wives and sweethearts on how to place their loved ones' deaths in geopolitical perspective.[34]

The OWI also hoped to use the movies to improve race relations—one of the most conspicuous wartime problems. Jim Crow still suffused American law and mores, and the United States fought for democracy with a rigidly segregated army and navy. Race riots seared major cities like Detroit. The OWI paid lip service to a campaign led by Walter White, head of the NAACP, and Wendell Willkie, chairman of the 20th Century–Fox board, to improve the depiction of blacks. Some advances were made in improving what had been, with few exceptions, a dismal record. In a few instances, blacks won better roles, although they were often limited, like Lena Horne's role in STORMY WEATHER, to the cinematic ghetto of the song-and-dance revue. In other cases, they were dignified minor roles, such as Leigh Whipper helping to avert a lynching in THE OX-BOW INCIDENT, and LIFEBOAT's Canada Lee being treated at times as an equal by his fellow survivors, though his previous occupation as a pickpocket is also highlighted. MGM's BATAAN sped up the integration of combat units by a decade by adding Kenneth Spencer to a platoon, if in a distinctly secondary position.[35]

On balance, however, Hollywood's vision was little changed by government oversight. TENNESSEE JOHNSON, the first major battle over racial issues, was also the last, since the OWI was not willing to go beyond mild admonitions to the studios about race. Lowell Mellett asked Metro to scrap the nearly completed picture, not because it was unfair to blacks but because it threatened domestic unity. The studio refused, and the OWI was content with some reshooting that softened Thaddeus Stevens's villainy, used Andrew Johnson to spotlight upward mobility and the American dream, and preached progress through the ballot box instead of bullets. The last was surely an ironic message for blacks, who won their freedom in the crucible of war and then saw their right to vote systematically denied by legal chicanery and violence. TENNESSEE JOHNSON included only two black characters and barely hinted of slavery. "Writing out" black characters and racial issues was easier than relearning race relations for wartime Hollywood. Throwbacks to pre–World War II images continued. Selznick transposed Hattie McDaniel from her role as Scarlett's devoted slave in GONE WITH THE WIND to the Hiltons' live-in maid, suggestively named Fidelia, in SINCE YOU WENT AWAY. Ann Hilton can no longer afford Fidelia during the war, but this devoted soul nonetheless returns to cook and clean for the white folks—for free—when she gets off work at the factory. The critic James Agee noted sardonically that, brimming with "malapropisms, comic relief, and mother wit," Fidelia "satisfied all that anyone could possibly desire of a Negro in restive times."[36]

The OWI was willing to fight harder for labor unions, a key component of the Roosevelt coalition. Membership in unions doubled during the war, and their members were a big part of the movie audience. In the original screenplay for his epic AN AMERICAN ROMANCE (1944), MGM's conservative King Vidor glorified his rags-to-riches industrialist hero and implied that unions were violent, subversive organizations. The OWI insisted that labor move from the streets to the conference table. Metro's E. J. Mannix "yelled and screamed," Poynter reported, and charged that the OWI forced him to make a "new deal picture." The agency and the studio eventually agreed to show moderate unions and reasonable management as cooperative rather than antagonistic, in contrast to an early version in which management dispersed strikers with riot police and tear gas. As the union president said, in AN AMERICAN ROMANCE, borrowing from the OWI manual, "Efficient production demands cooperation between labor and management."[37]

Having won a position of power in American politics, moderate labor unions could be accommodated, albeit reluctantly, on the screen. But race and gender raised divisive issues that the national discourse was only beginning to address and often preferred to bury. Both propaganda monitors and popular culture marketers found safe harbor in an illusory national unity.

Just as the home front had to be remodeled into an idealized America, so too were the Allies airbrushed into progressive democracies. This effort required Hollywood to modify some of its cherished stereotypes of foreigners (specifically the British and Chinese) and to tackle a subject it had long avoided—the Russians. The results were misleading and in some cases grossly deceptive—in their own ways as bad, or worse, than Hollywood's old stereotypes. Where Hollywood once tended to exoticize foreigners, the OWI taught how much they resembled Americans.

Great Britain presented the fewest problems. Although Americans generally admired and trusted the British, the OWI feared that hatred of imperialism and the class system might undermine that support. With Churchill determined to hang on to the empire, the OWI decided to ignore the issue. When MGM wanted to re-release KIM, and RKO GUNGA DIN (1939), two Kiplingesque adventures that glorify imperialism, the OWI appealed to the studios to leave them on the shelf, and they agreed. The class issue bedeviled Metro's THE WHITE CLIFFS OF DOVER (1944), peopled by condescending aristocrats who acted as if the war were being fought to preserve Ashworth Manor. Although the studio submitted eighty pages of script changes in response to OWI criticisms in 1943, the film's warm aristocratic haze remained. The studio paid for its indulgence in 1944 when the OWI overseas branch ruled the film could not be shown in the lucrative British market. Ironically, two films that the OWI considered models of how to deal with the class issue—MGM's Oscar-winning MRS. MINIVER and Fox's THIS ABOVE ALL—were both released in 1942 before the OWI began its regulatory efforts. Both films projected a unified Britain, mobilized for war, in which class lines were being dissolved. If the class system proved more durable than these warmhearted films depicted it, they were nonetheless popular propaganda for Americans who believed they were all resolutely middle-class.[38]

"Give us a Mrs. Miniver of China and Russia," Poynter implored studio executives. He was asking the impossible, but Hollywood tried to comply.[39] The Chinese reality scarcely fit either the OWI or Hollywood image. Roosevelt envisioned China as a major power that could serve as one of the "four policemen" of the postwar world. But the country was riven by civil war between Chiang Kai-shek's Nationalists and Mao Tse-tung's Communists, neither of whom resembled FDR's democratic ethos. The OWI wanted China portrayed as "a great nation, cultured and liberal," that had been fighting the Axis since 1933 and was evolving toward democracy. This political mythmaking clashed with Hollywood's mythic China, which veered between the simple, lovable peasantry of THE GOOD EARTH (1937) and the sinister factionalism of SHANGHAI EXPRESS (1932). Hollywood capitalized on China's exotic background for several pictures released in 1942 before the OWI began work. The propaganda agency disliked all of them, such as the John Wayne vehicle FLYING TIGERS, because they showed Americans winning the war single-handedly and the Chinese relegated to inferior positions.[40]

The OWI converted Hollywood to its own myth, with results that were as politically dubious as the studios' prewar fantasies, and certainly more tedious cinematically. The original screenplay for MGM's DRAGON SEED, based on Pearl Buck's novel of the same title, offended the OWI by showing the Chinese as backward illiterates with little political consciousness. The drastically revised screenplay, submitted in 1943, adopted the OWI's vision of politically astute Chinese mobilized for the "people's war." Both the OWI and Hollywood preferred a Westernized China. Since Asians were unthinkable in the leading roles, DRAGON SEED starred (most improbably) Katharine Hepburn, who was Orientalized with slanted eyes.[41]

The OWI took pride in another propaganda victory—KEYS OF THE KINGDOM, starring Gregory Peck as a Roman Catholic missionary in early-twentieth-century China. The OWI objected bitterly to the initial screenplay, by the star writers Nunnally Johnson and Joseph Mankiewicz, which showed a backward China beset by marauding warlords.

Walter Huston (center) and Katharine Hepburn (far right) in DRAGON SEED *(1944).*

The agency rejected the studio's idea of an easy fix—a prologue stating that the film dealt with an earlier China. To the OWI, the screenplay should show the Nationalist forces battling for a new, modern, unified China. T. K. Chang, the influential Chinese consul in Los Angeles, seconded the OWI. Twentieth Century–Fox finally agreed and adopted the OWI's political analysis. As always when Catholicism was portrayed, Catholic priests stood by to oversee church matters. Released in 1944, KEYS OF THE KINGDOM shows Republican Nationalist forces fighting for a new China, and peasants' mud huts are transformed into what elated OWI reviewers described as "neat, little brick places with considerable feeling of civilization about them." The China that Hollywood constructed under OWI regulation offered a reassuring—if grossly inaccurate—tribute to a modern China that was awakening, under Western political and religious tutelage.[42]

Remodeling the image of the Soviet Union was an even more daunting task than Great Britain and China presented. Before the war, Hollywood made few movies about the Soviet Union; the industry had no market there, and Russian subjects did not seem likely to be popular with Western audiences. The PCA was prepared to veto a picture favorable to the Soviets, as Lewis Milestone found in 1934 when Breen warned him against making "Red Square." The most memorable prewar Russian film was NINOTCHKA (1939), in which Melvyn Douglas, an émigré Russian count, induces Greta Garbo, a Communist dominatrix, to defect by plying her with capitalist luxuries and romantic love. In place of such sly satire, Hollywood collaborated with the OWI during the war to humanize the Russians and whitewash Stalinism. As *Variety* said: "War has put Hollywood's traditional conception of the Muscovites through the wringer, and they have come out shaved, washed, sober, good to their families, Rotarians, brother Elks, and 33rd Degree Mason."[43]

The most important—and controversial—wartime film about the Soviet Union was Warners' MISSION TO MOSCOW (1943). The Warners eagerly accepted Roosevelt's request that they make a picture from the memoirs of Joseph E. Davies, who as ambassador to Moscow from 1936 to 1938 displayed a credulous sympathy for the Soviet experiment. Davies worked closely with the studio and twice reported personally to Roosevelt on the film's progress. While the OWI took a backseat in these negotiations, some of its favorite themes emerged, particularly the isolationists' folly and the Soviets' devotion to collective security. In MISSION TO MOSCOW, the Soviet Union became a pleasant land of consumerist plenty, the dreaded secret police bumbling Keystone Kops, Stalin an omniscient world statesman, and the massive purges of the 1930s necessary measures to root out a fifth column. The OWI called the film "a magnificent contribution" and superb entertainment—a judgment in which Jack Warner happily concurred.[44]

To political critics, the film should have been titled, as the bitter joke went, "Submission to Moscow." Breen abhorred the film's politics. But ever the realist, he realized that the PCA had to yield to Washington on wartime political matters. Ruefully noting Davies's and the OWI's sanction of the film, he said: "In the face of all this, it seems to me that we . . . can do little but approve the material." He cautioned Warners, however, that the film would arouse "considerable protest." It did. Outraged editorialists and dogged pickets harried the film; most of the protest was generated by the right wing, but some emanated from tough-minded anti-Stalinist leftists. (In 1947, as the cold war and red-baiting intensified, Jack Warner withdrew MISSION TO MOSCOW from release and delivered Howard Koch, whom he had pressured to write the screenplay, to the wolves of the House Un-American Activities Committee.) Nor was the long, talky

film as entertaining as the OWI and Jack Warner had hoped. "This mishmash is directly and firmly in the tradition of Hollywood politics," said the *New Republic*'s Manny
Farber. "A while ago it was Red-baiting, now it is Red-praising in the same sense—igno-
rantly. To a democratic intelligence it is repulsive and insulting."[45]

Every major studio except Paramount enlisted with a Russian picture, but they tried
to minimize the politics. The OWI and the Soviet embassy read the screenplays. The
best known was Samuel Goldwyn's THE NORTH STAR (1943), written by Lillian Hellman
and directed by William Wyler. THE NORTH STAR tried to humanize average Russians
and to valorize their resistance to the German invaders, but it succeeded mainly in
Americanizing them. Metro offered a musical tribute with SONG OF RUSSIA (1943);
romance leavens politics in United Artists' THREE RUSSIAN GIRLS (1943); love and resistance are joined in RKO's DAYS OF GLORY (1944); and a band of teenagers thwart the
Wehrmacht almost single-handedly in Columbia's BOY FROM STALINGRAD (1943). The
last Russian film, Columbia's COUNTER-ATTACK (1945), boasted a screenplay by John
Howard Lawson, a Communist Party member, who worked in many of the OWI's points.
But by the time of its release in 1945, mounting doubts about Soviet-American friendship led Columbia to downplay ideology for straightforward action.[46]

The propagandists tried to get the studios faithfully to translate national policy about
the Allies to the screen. In this they were, perhaps regrettably, successful. The results
too often were ludicrous: a classless Britain (or worse, a romanticized aristocracy) devoid

*Hollywood's efforts to celebrate—and romanticize—Russia's war with Germany
included* THE NORTH STAR *(1943).*

of imperial ambitions; a progressive, unified China under Chiang Kai-shek instead of a desperately poor society plagued by corruption, brutality, and civil war; and a benign Soviet Union led by an avuncular, farsighted Stalin. Although the movies took on particular colorations because of the OWI's intervention, they reflected a national disposition, which Roosevelt encouraged, to construct artificial allies and avoid hard questions. Experienced political journalists, epitomized by Henry Luce's *Time* and *Life,* constructed the Britains, Chinas, and Soviet Unions they thought would be useful to their political agendas.[47] For all their encomiums to "the truth," neither the White House, the OWI, the news media, nor Hollywood was willing to run the risk that the public would draw the wrong conclusions during wartime from a "warts and all" portrait.

The OWI and Hollywood's Portrayal of the Enemy

The care which the OWI lavished on the portrayal of the Allies was mirrored by its concern for the correct image of the enemies. The propaganda agency warned against the simplistic "hate pictures" which stirred up irrational hatred during World War I and thwarted postwar peace efforts. The enemy, insisted the OWI, was the doctrine of fascism and its ruling cliques, not the German or Japanese people. The Allies would win, but only with a supreme effort against these "cunning, tough, cruel" foes. Movies that showed wisecracking Yanks effortlessly knocking off the enemy deceived the public about how tough this war was. With its penchant for adapting the formulas of Westerns and gangster pictures to the war, Hollywood needed the OWI's correctives. If anything, the propagandists underestimated the brutality of the enemy, particularly Germany, about whose anti-Semitism the OWI remained too cautiously mute.[48]

The portrayal of the Japanese was the single most intractable problem government regulators faced. Pictures such as LITTLE TOKYO, U.S.A. established the themes of diabolical Japanese conspiracy and revealed a deep-seated American racism. The OWI was timid, and largely unsuccessful, in challenging these racist representations. Most movies showed all Japanese as fanatically devoted to the emperor, routinely practicing despicable battlefield tactics, and lacking any redeeming qualities. They were not individuals but, as explained in Frank Capra's "Why We Fight" documentary KNOW YOUR ENEMY—JAPAN (1945), "photographic prints off the same negative." One of the few individualized Japanese characters was the propaganda minister in BEHIND THE RISING SUN (1943), who realized his country's cause was wrong and committed suicide. In such films as BATAAN (1943), GUADALCANAL DIARY (1943), and THE PURPLE HEART (1944), the Japanese were little more than beasts who took naturally to jungle fighting. Faced with the virulent hatred of the Japanese, the OWI seldom fought such portrayals, choosing to block export licenses only in the most flagrant cases.[49]

While the PCA deferred to the OWI on political questions, its preoccupation with profanity and individual guilt remained intact. In Zanuck's THE PURPLE HEART, a young Chinese man murders his traitorous father. The OWI praised the politically conscious character as an exemplar of the new freedom-loving China. But Breen ruled out parricide, even in the cause of democracy, and insisted that the son be tried by the Japanese for murder. The PCA chief also tried to protect the screen from profanity even when it peppered the exact words of none other than General Joseph "Vinegar Joe" Stilwell in a prologue to the Errol Flynn vehicle OBJECTIVE BURMA. Breen initially vetoed Stilwell's comment that U.S. forces took a "hell of a licking," only to reverse himself. But the PCA chief refused to allow the general to say "by God" on the screen because the expression was "intrinsically objectionable." Meanwhile, the PCA allowed repeated references to the Japanese as "dirty yellow rats," "blasted monkeys," and the like to litter the screen.[50]

The Germans received a much more nuanced treatment than the Japanese. As fellow Caucasians, they did not suffer from anti-Asian racism, and they had not launched a surprise attack on American territory. Moreover, the endemic horror of Nazism, culminating in the Holocaust, was inadequately grasped by Americans during the war. In contrast to the evil Japanese mass, Hollywood followed the OWI's lead and created individual German characters and distinguished between good Germans and evil Nazis.

The divergence between German and Japanese representations appears starkly in the 20th Century–Fox release THE MOON IS DOWN (1943). The German officers are sharply differentiated characters. While some officers are Nazi villains, Lt. Tonder is an innocent, handsome, likable farm boy who doubts Hitler's sanity and hates occupation duty in Norway. When he meets his death at the hands of a Norwegian war widow—an opportunity to salute the resistance movements—it is as a fellow human being, not a diabolical enemy.[51]

Dramatizing the resistance movements was a key theme in 1942–1943, since American army contact with the Germans was slow to develop. In THIS LAND IS MINE (1943), a collaboration of the leading talents Jean Renoir and Dudley Nichols, Charles Laughton delivers an impassioned oration against Nazi tyranny. The OWI wanted his speech to stir the townspeople to active uprising, but the agency rested content with the unusually detailed exploration of Nazi ideology. CASABLANCA, probably the most famous film from the war, provided a human story of the war's effects and of various modes of resistance. To the OWI, however, Rick's cynicism persisted too long. They wanted the picture to end not with the immortal line, "This could be the beginning of a beautiful friendship," but with Humphrey Bogart declaiming about the Four Freedoms. Luckily, Hollywood's sense of story overrode the OWI's political agenda. The OWI approved CASABLANCA for export, except to North Africa, where America's tangled relations with Vichy France made the subject too touchy.[52]

However much the OWI wished for serious examinations of Hitlerism, PCA restrictions would have blocked any film that did more than hint at Nazi horror. Paramount and the OWI worked unusually closely to make THE HITLER GANG (1944) a credible explanation of Nazism, only to find the PCA using the Code to block them. The film was not without its problems. Straining for a link between popular ideas of personal perversion and brutal statecraft, Paramount suggested that an impotent Hitler had a perverted attraction to young girls and that many Nazis were homosexual (the latter notion a travesty in view of Nazi persecution of gays). Breen objected that THE HITLER GANG contained "an orgy of bestiality and brutality such as the civilized world has never witnessed." That was, of course, the point Paramount and the OWI were trying to make. Breen insisted that such material be cut, including a blasphemous speech a Nazi had actually given. The OWI was not willing to fight the PCA over sex and blasphemy, just as the PCA deferred, however unhappily, to the OWI on politics. After five months of struggle, Paramount capitulated to the PCA. Even if Paramount and the OWI were wrong about some particulars, their instincts about Nazism's utter depravity were right. This was something which Americans gradually came to comprehend after the war and which millions of Europeans knew from firsthand experience during the war. The PCA, however, was determined to insulate Americans from all but faint intimations of the nature of the enemy.[53]

Both the PCA and the OWI wanted depictions of battlefield violence to be carefully contained. The PCA strictly enforced the Code's warnings against gruesomeness. The OWI encouraged a modicum of battlefield realism in order to prepare the public for casualties, but within rather antiseptic limits. The propagandists primarily wanted to ensure that Hollywood employed a "people's army" with ethnically, religiously, and geographically diverse platoons whose members articulated what they were fighting for. For the most part, battle films, such as WAKE ISLAND (1942), made combat look no more deadly than a football game. Combat pictures often were a variant on a proven genre—the success story. As the OWI wished, dedicated men carry out their civic virtue and are rewarded with the promise of a better life. PRIDE OF THE MARINES (1945) followed the real-life story of a Philadelphia marine who was severely wounded in the Pacific and then restored to health by a loving nurse in a well-equipped service hospital. Virtually the only exception to such formulae was William Wellman's THE STORY OF GI JOE (1945), based on Ernie Pyle's memorable dispatches. Its gritty, documentary-style realism, avoidance of false heroics, and laconic acknowledgment of the randomness of death gave the film an uncharacteristic, uncomfortable verisimilitude. Nevertheless, THE STORY OF GI JOE offered only a glimpse of realism about the war, a perspective that both the OWI and the PCA, for their own reasons, wished to ignore.[54]

Conclusion

Eager to close down war agencies, President Harry Truman abolished the OWI effective 31 August 1945. For three years the propagandists policed film politics while the PCA maintained its accustomed watch over morality and propriety. Hollywood, initially fearful of government demands, learned that propaganda and popular culture were remarkably compatible—and even highly profitable. The studios proved to be surprisingly compliant, once they were reassured that the OWI would not impair their control of production and learned that cooperation paid big dividends with foreign distribution. The OWI's Bureau of Motion Pictures noted happily that from September 1943 to August 1944 the studios changed screenplays in 71 percent of the cases where the agency made suggestions or registered objections.[55]

The OWI added a degree of seriousness and political sophistication to wartime filmmaking. The agency labored within the constraints that the historian Robert A. Rosenstone has noted of feature films: "Dramatic features put individuals in the forefront of the historical process, which means that the solution of their personal problems or their individual redemption substitutes itself for the solution of historical problems."[56] SINCE YOU WENT AWAY, TENDER COMRADE, and PRIDE OF THE MARINES were cases in point. In some instances, the OWI's intervention improved wartime representations: labor unions received better treatment than they otherwise might have, important distinctions were made between the German people and their Nazi overlords, and the ideals for which the Allies fought received more recognition than filmmaking conventions ordinarily allowed. In many cases, however, the OWI supplanted old Hollywood myths with new ones cut to fit wartime fashion. Too often they entailed evasion, distortion, and outright falsification.

The OWI avoided the excesses of the World War I Creel Committee, and the agency was different in kind from the Nazi and Soviet propaganda agencies. The OWI's regulation of Hollywood was not so bad as state control of the cinema in Germany and the

Soviet Union (where, ironically, the studios ground out chiefly nonpolitical escape pictures during the war).[57] And yet in its short life, the American propaganda agency raised in a milder form the danger that government regulation may reinforce the narrow range of opinions expressed by a popular culture oligopoly as it follows a corporate strategy of limiting the scope of permissible content.

Breen's Production Code Administration held to its rigid interpretation of the Code in the face of wartime social upheaval. Moral standards were in flux as a restless nation—and particularly young adults—experienced unprecedented challenges to social conventions. Marriage, birth, and divorce rates soared. Cut loose from their home communities, millions of Americans experienced new sexual freedom. They now enjoyed the experiences the Production Code forbade the movies to display openly or without condemnation. Breen detected "a distinct tendency toward moral laxity" in the material which the studios submitted. But he saw the Code as an expression of unchanging moral precepts. He assured Will Hays that the PCA "uniformly and impartially rejected all such unacceptable material." Lapses from Breen's earlier watchfulness could be cited: the chorus line in the Carmen Miranda spectacle THE GANG'S ALL HERE (1943) that swings giant papier-mâché bananas in and out between their legs; the light treatment of marriage in Preston Sturges's madcap THE MIRACLE OF MORGAN'S CREEK; the adultery and murder that gave DOUBLE INDEMNITY a "sordid flavor." Yet the quiescence of watchdog groups, notably the Legion of Decency, testified to Breen's ability to steer films clear of dangerous territory.[58]

Breen needed all his resolve as the PCA faced new regulatory challenges after the war. With the Legion dug in behind the PCA, every inch of liberated footage in Hollywood would be hard fought. Postwar films like DUEL IN THE SUN prefigured growing opposition to the PCA. From 1939 through 1945, the PCA and the OWI had steered Hollywood through upheavals in morality and politics. Most of the challenges since mid-1934 had focused on particular points of interpretation. By the late 1940s, however, the very notion of the Code came under attack. The Code—and indeed the very structure of the industry—was living on borrowed time. The stability—and the concomitant limitations—that such regulation of content had brought to the industry would face an unprecedented threat in the changing economic, cultural, and moral climate of postwar America.

PART 3

☆

The Postwar Era

THE NAKED CITY (*1948*)

9

The Postwar Motion Picture Industry

After the shooting stops . . . , Hollywood naturally will go back to the business of making films strictly for profit. But it will also do something else. Now that Hollywood has grown up, it knows that it must play a role in creating the world of tomorrow, just as it helped to destroy the kind of world desired by the enemy.

Robert St. John, *Look*, January 1945

The American movie industry faced the postwar era with both relief and euphoria. The war boom had been a mixed blessing for the industry, with record revenues and profits accompanied by material and manpower shortages, severe operational constraints, and ongoing anxiety about the Allied cause. The movie industry had thrived and played an important role in that cause, and in that sense Hollywood had indeed "grown up" during the war along with the nation at large. Now as the United States emerged from World War II as a leading global power, the industry was generally upbeat about its own postwar prospects—particularly in 1946, when Hollywood enjoyed its best year ever.

That postwar optimism faded, however, as Hollywood proved to be singularly ill equipped for "the world of tomorrow." While America's stature as a world power and its economic prosperity continued to grow in the late 1940s, the American movie industry went into an economic tailspin and a sustained fall from social grace. Postwar Hollywood was besieged by labor strife and runaway costs, by rebellious exhibitors and restricted foreign markets, by censorship battles and anti-Communist purges, and, most significantly, by declining domestic revenues and an inglorious end to its decade-long antitrust battles. The Justice Department prevailed in a series of Supreme Court rulings in 1948–1949 that mandated the "dis-integration" of the studio system. Those rulings marked not only the definitive end of the epic Paramount case—arguably the signal event for the American cinema in the 1940s—but also the culmination of Hollywood's postwar woes. It marked, in fact, the climax of the most troubled period in movie industry history.

Postwar America, the Global Economy, and the Cold War

Hollywood's postwar downturn was especially troubling because it contrasted so sharply with the general prosperity of the nation at large. Generally speaking, the United States emerged from World War II in remarkably good shape. The war not only reversed the economic effects of the Depression but also enabled the United States to become a genuine world power. By 1944, America was supplying 40 percent of the world's armaments and feeding citizens and soldiers around the globe. At war's end, estimates put U.S. productivity at nearly half that of the rest of the world combined. And at decade's end, as the British historian Robert Payne noted at the time, "half of the wealth of the world, more than half of the productivity, nearly two-thirds of the world's machines are concentrated in American hands; the rest of the world lies in the shadow of American industry."[1]

U.S. productivity was due in large part to the relatively minor damage inflicted by the war on the nation and its populace. World War II killed an estimated 50 million people and physically devastated much of Europe and the Far East. Major cities and industrial centers were destroyed, and civilian casualties ranged from 60,000 in Britain and 400,000 in France to 6 million in Poland and 7 million in the Soviet Union. The United States was the only principal combatant to suffer few direct civilian casualties and no significant enemy incursions or attacks within its primary borders. U.S. military casualties of some 290,000, while substantial, were relatively light considering both the degree of U.S. involvement in the conflict and also the losses suffered by the other major combatants—Japan with 1.2 million soldiers dead, for example, and the Soviet Union with 7 million (beyond the 7 million civilian casualties).[2]

America's postwar "reconversion" was as rapid and extensive as its conversion to war production in the early 1940s had been, but it scarcely signaled a return to prewar conditions. The high employment and productivity of the war era did ease somewhat, while rising costs and spiraling inflation created financial difficulties for middle- and working-class Americans. But the economy remained strong enough to absorb the millions of returning servicemen, and a boom in housing construction—the largest since the mid-1920s—created affordable homes for the ex-GIs and factory workers, who were marrying in record numbers by the late 1940s.[3] The birth rate soared as well, and by 1948 the term "baby boom" had entered the popular discourse.[4]

The baby boom was simply one aspect of a massive family and housing boom after the war, much of which was fueled by America's vast migration to the suburbs. Keying the migration were low real-estate prices outside urban areas, along with tract housing, improved highway systems, and affordable automobiles. Many cities struggled with the postwar family/baby/housing boom, particularly those which had been war-production centers and had not adequately handled the previous wartime growth. Los Angeles typified this problem. Its population had increased by 300,000 during the war, and during the first postwar year alone the city grew by another 70,000—bringing its total to 2 million. Home construction and transportation simply could not keep up with demand, which drove up costs as well. The cost of living in Los Angeles in 1946 was three times the prewar level, and about twice what it had been only two years earlier.[5]

Rising costs were the result of not only market demand and material shortages but also the rampant labor strife and related wage increases. The war had solidified the role of organized labor in U.S. industry, while the government's general easing of antitrust restrictions (and litigation) during the war enabled the corporate powers in many major industries, from steel and mining to automobile and motion picture production, to further intensify their oligopolistic control. Thus, the government intensified its "trust-busting" efforts after the war, when conditions were ripe for the strikes, wage disputes, and other labor-management discord that would became a way of life for U.S. industry in the late 1940s.[6]

Despite inflation and labor conflicts in the United States, the general postwar economic climate remained upbeat—particularly in comparison to conditions abroad. The Axis nations quite literally had to rebuild their economies and industries, with Germany especially hard hit owing to the heavy bombing in 1944–1945. England also faced massive rebuilding and recovery, and its postwar struggles were of deep concern to the United States, given England's status as a trading partner and its enormous wartime debt. The deepening economic and industrial woes in Britain became front-page news in the United States by 1947 and its economy continued to deteriorate through the next two years, culminating in the devaluation of the pound sterling in 1949.[7]

The postwar global recession coincided with a deepening geopolitical crisis, the cold war, which began soon after World War II and saw the United States radically reshuffle its foreign alliances and redefine its international interests. Anglo-American ties remained strong, although England's economic difficulties caused myriad political prob-

The "March of Time" newsreel "What to Do with Germany" graphically illustrates the impending cold war.

lems. However, the Soviet Union, which had been a crucial ally during the war, was recast immediately afterward as a global menace and as America's principal political foe—along with the other Iron Curtain countries under Soviet control in Eastern Europe. The cold war escalated dramatically in 1949 with the Soviet Union's successful detonation of an A-bomb in August and, some two months later, the fall of China to the Communists.

The cold war seriously limited U.S. economic prospects overseas while fomenting intense anti-Communist fervor and anxiety at home. The cold war also had considerable impact on the American movie industry, in terms of not only overseas trade but also global politics and the nation's international interests. World War II had confirmed the value of Hollywood movies as propaganda, and it had created a direct and intense relationship between the movie industry and the government. But the cold war proved to be a very different kind of war, and thus Hollywood's role as propagandist and its relationship with Washington changed radically as well.

Hollywood and Washington

During the war, the relationship between Hollywood and Washington had been more harmonious than at any time in industry history. There had been a few sore spots, to be sure—the 1943 Senate hearings on the studios' control of and alleged profiteering from military contracts, for instance, or the Justice Department's ongoing (although scaled-back) antitrust campaign. For the most part, however, Hollywood and Washington maintained a state of active and unprecedented cooperation in the war effort. Hollywood lost a valued ally with the death of Roosevelt in early 1945, and in fact his successor Harry Truman, before becoming vice president in 1944, had led the 1943 Senate investigation of the major studios. Not only did the industry garner less support from the White House, but the continued conservative swing in Congress posed an even more direct threat on several fronts, particularly organized labor and purported "un-American activities" in Hollywood.

The most serious postwar threat from Washington involved the government's antitrust campaign against the studios and the large unaffiliated theater circuits—a campaign in which the Justice Department gained increased support from the Supreme Court and the Federal Trade Commission (FTC).[8] The postwar antitrust battles also involved the Federal Communications Commission (FCC), which oversaw the development of the television industry, including the approval of the purchasing and licensing of TV stations. The FCC had the authority to prevent the licensing of stations to any company convicted of antitrust violations, and by the late 1940s, it became clear that the FCC might invoke this authority to forestall the studios' efforts to move into the burgeoning industry through television station acquisition and alliances with the upstart TV networks.

Despite the resumption of these "hostilities" on the home front, Hollywood and Washington maintained an alliance of sorts outside the United States. Immediately after the war, this alliance primarily involved the military, which oversaw Hollywood's return to Europe in 1944–1945 and to the Axis countries in 1945–1946. Then, as the cold war began to heat up, it became evident, ironically enough, that many of the same federal agencies that Hollywood was battling at home would look to the movie industry as an ally overseas. Orchestrating this alliance was the Motion Picture Export

Association (MPEA), an industry trade organization created in 1945 which was, in effect, a postwar merger between the Motion Picture Association of America (MPAA) and the overseas branch of the government's Office of War Information (OWI).[9]

As a branch of the MPAA under Eric Johnston, the MPEA was created to facilitate overseas trade in the complex postwar global marketplace. Initially, the MPEA concentrated on regaining the Axis markets, but as the cold war heated up, it served as the "collective bargaining agent" overseas for Hollywood's eight producer-distributors, concentrating on those markets where, as Johnston put it, "monopolistic pressures have hamstrung the American industry." The MPEA enjoyed Washington's support in this effort, since the government recognized that the movies were valuable to its postwar political and economic strategy in two distinct ways: first, movies were a highly desirable commodity in virtually every market worldwide, regardless of local politics, and thus provided an effective means to gain access to foreign markets; and second, movie content was perceived as a means to sell American ideology and American-made products overseas.[10]

Several government agencies, and three in particular, cooperated with the MPEA. The Commerce Department directly assisted foreign trade, owing to its interest in movies as a means to promote overseas sales of other American goods, from clothing to appliances to automobiles. The Justice Department agreed to relax its trust-busting efforts in the area of the integrated majors' export sales, although the MPEA clearly was a monopolistic enterprise. And the State Department was interested in what the *Wall Street Journal* termed the "propaganda value of the typical American films in portraying the democratic way of life."[11] Indeed, as Thomas Guback points out in his study of the postwar international film industry, the MPEA became known as "the Little State Department" because of the similarity of its "function, scope, and methods" to those of the U.S. Department of State. Besides bargaining for optimal economic advantage on behalf of Hollywood, notes Guback, the MPEA also tried "to win friends and influence local policy."[12]

Thus, the Hollywood-Washington postwar rapport was ruled by two rather remarkable ironies. One was the government's active support of Hollywood's effort to monopolize foreign markets, even though the Justice Department was suing the studios for similar efforts in the United States. The other was the perceived propaganda value of movies themselves: while Hollywood films were deemed a valuable means of promoting Americanism overseas by the State Department and other agencies, Congress continually accused the studios of employing political subversives and of being overly critical of the American way of life.

The Postwar Domestic Marketplace

Hollywood's initial postwar optimism was fueled by a huge box-office surge in late 1945 and into 1946. The surge actually accelerated immediately after the war, thanks to millions of returning servicemen, increased courtship activity, the easing of wartime restrictions, and a generally upbeat populace with both time and wartime savings on their hands. The postwar era was ushered in by three huge late-1945 hits, SPELLBOUND, THE BELLS OF ST. MARY'S, and ROAD TO UTOPIA, and 1946 closed with three even bigger hits, THE JOLSON STORY, DUEL IN THE SUN, and THE BEST YEARS OF OUR LIVES. These hits capped off what was by far Hollywood's biggest year ever in terms of box-office revenues

Recently installed MPAA chief Eric Johnston found his overseas duties vastly expanded after the war as head of the MPEA.

and studio profits. The studios' year-end gross revenues rose from a record $1.45 billion in 1945 to just under $1.7 billion in 1946. And while revenues were up some 10 percent over 1945, profits were astronomical. After record profits of just over $66 million in 1945, the studios' total net in 1946 shot up to $120 million.[13]

Hollywood's staggering profits in 1946 were due in part to its overseas income. But the principal factor was the domestic market, spurred by long-running hits and also by the release of major productions that had been backlogged during the later war years. Top revenues could be earned from pictures that, already "in the can" and awaiting release, had been made when production costs were considerably lower. in fact, three of the top ten hits of 1946, MGM's THE YEARLING, Warners' SARATOGA TRUNK, and Paramount's ROAD TO UTOPIA, had been on the shelf and ready for release for quite some time—over two years in the case of SARATOGA TRUNK.[14]

By late 1946, however, the war boom had peaked and the domestic market began its postwar readjustment. The Hollywood trade papers and the *Wall Street Journal* began to note the decline in early 1947, and by summer both attendance and gate receipts were falling sharply.[15] Many in the industry refused to believe that the boom was over, but in fact the industry had entered a period of serious decline, owing primarily to falling attendance and, despite ticket price hikes, falling box-office receipts.[16] Meanwhile, rising production and operating costs meant eroding profit margins for studios and exhibitors alike. Thus, all sectors of the industry were feeling the squeeze in the late 1940s, as the figures in table 9.1 well indicate:

Table 9.1
POSTWAR ECONOMIC TRENDS IN THE MOVIE INDUSTRY, 1946–1950

Year	Box-Office Gross (in $ billions)	Studio Profits (in $ millions)	Exhibitor Profits (in $ millions)
1946	1.692°	119.9	325
1947	1.594	87.3	253
1948	1.506	48.5	144
1949	1.451	33.6	125
1950	1.376	30.8	111

°Figures on total box-office grosses are based on Department of Commerce statistics and are more conservative and reliable than those reported in the trades. The 1950 Film Daily Year Book reported the postwar grosses as: $1.285 billion in 1945; 1.560 in 1946; 1.565 in 1947; 1.545 in 1948; and 1.350 in 1949.

SOURCE: Christopher H. Sterling and Timothy R. Haight, *The Mass Media: The Aspen Institute Guide to Communications Industry Trends* (New York: Praeger, 1978), p. 187. Studio (producer-distributor) net profits from Joel W. Finler, *The Hollywood Story* (New York: Crown, 1988), pp. 286–87; exhibitor net profits from Sindlinger and Associates, reported in Simon N. Whitney, "Antitrust Policies in the Motion Picture Industry," in Gorham Kindem, ed., *The American Movie Industry* (Carbondale: Southern Illinois University Press, 1982), p. 188.

Figures on theater attendance for this period vary widely, but they all signal a decline. In 1946, *Film Daily* and the MPAA both gauged weekly admissions at 95–100 million, while Gallup's ARI put weekly attendance at only 66 million.[17] By 1949, even the ever-optimistic MPAA acknowledged the slide, reporting a drop from 90 million per week in 1948 to 70 million in 1949—a one-year decline of nearly 30 percent.[18] *Wall Street Journal* figures, meanwhile, indicated a steadier decline, with weekly admissions falling from 80.5 million in 1946 to 78.2 million in 1947, 67 million in 1948, and 62 million in 1949. That 1949 total jibed with the ARI's figures, and in fact most estimates put weekly ticket sales in the 60–65 million range.[19]

Along with declining attendance and revenues, Hollywood saw a decline in the number of top box-office hits as well. In 1946, as the war boom peaked, five films earned over $5 million; THE BEST YEARS OF OUR LIVES and DUEL IN THE SUN both surpassed $10 million. At that point, the succession of big hits simply stopped, and even the mid-range hits tapered off severely. No release earned over $6 million in 1947, although there were a few in the $5–6 million range. In 1948–1949, however, Hollywood's output of big hits—and even modest hits in the $3–5 million range—fell dramatically, as these figures indicate:

Table 9.2
DOMESTIC RENTALS OF TOP HITS, 1946–1949

Earnings	1946	1947	1948	1949
More than $2 million	73	75	65	50
More than $3 million	43	35	22	19
More than $4 million	18	15	7	5
More than $5 million	5	11	0	1

SOURCE: *Variety*, 4 January 1950, pp. 1, 59.

The sharp decline in major hits in the late 1940s brought changes in production and market strategies as rising costs and falling attendance discouraged producers from taking on big-budget pictures designed to clean up at the box office. The postwar era also saw the employment of more defensive market strategies, notably an increase in both B pictures and reissues. in fact, reissues became a veritable programming staple in the late 1940s. While only a half-dozen or so films were re-released in the later war years, the studios reissued twenty in 1946 and forty in 1947. By 1947, remarkably enough, some theaters had gone exclusively to first-run reissues. Exhibitors complained about the increasing number of reissues being offered only on a percentage basis (a sales practice usually reserved for A-class product), but audiences clearly were buying. in fact, a few A-class reissues—MGM's THE GREAT WALTZ (1938) in its 1947 reissue, for instance—were earning more than they had initially.[20] The trend accelerated in the late 1940s: *Variety* reported 105 reissues in 1948 and 136 in 1949.[21] While reissues could scarcely turn around Hollywood's fading postwar fortunes, the booming business for reissues clearly was a major development in the postwar movie industry. Business was so good, in fact, that Paramount's Barney Balaban considered selling "reissue rights" to old pictures, and in 1948 he refused to rent or lease the company's products to television for fear of reducing their theatrical reissue value.[22]

American blacks were an increasingly important market segment in the late 1940s, but they still faced widespread segregation as moviegoers.

The falloff in major box-office hits signaled much more than simply declining attendance. It also indicated changes in the tastes and composition of movie audiences,
changes in the lifestyles and media habits of middle-class Americans, and changes even
in movie theaters themselves. Postwar trends in theater construction are especially
revealing. In the months immediately after the war, with the movie industry's war boom
still going strong, several hundred movie theaters were either under construction or
being planned. Those plans were stymied in March 1946, however, when the Civilian
Production Administration put a freeze on all construction except low-cost housing.
That freeze lasted until June 1948, and by the time it was lifted the movie industry's economic climate had changed drastically.[23] The earlier plans for theater construction were
not revived, and in fact theaters were now closing by the hundreds. From 1945 to 1949,
the number of movie houses operating in the United States fell from more than 20,300
to about 17,350, a decline of 15 percent—the first decline since the early Depression
era, and nearly as severe.[24]

While traditional indoor theaters were closing, however, outdoor theaters underwent
an explosive growth. The drive-in theater phenomenon, begun in the 1930s but stalled
by the war, quickly took off in the late 1940s, and by 1949 drive-ins had compensated
for the decline in operating indoor theaters:

Table 9.3
U.S. MOVIE THEATERS, 1946–1950

Year	Indoor	Drive-in	Total
1946	18,719	300	19,019
1947	18,059	548	18,607
1948	17,575	820	18,395
1949	17,367	1,203	18,570
1950	16,904	2,202	19,106

SOURCE: Christopher H. Sterling and Timothy R. Haight, *The Mass Media: The Aspen Institute Guide to
Communications Industry Trends* (New York: Praeger, 1978), p. 35.

The drive-in explosion was propelled by several crucial postwar factors: suburbanization, affordable automobiles, interstate highways, and, most of all perhaps, the "baby
boom." Designed to accommodate from 250 to more than 1,000 cars, drive-ins clearly
were geared for family traffic. Besides alleviating parking and baby-sitting problems,
drive-ins included playgrounds and elaborate concession stands. in fact, concession
stands still were considered undignified by many indoor exhibitors, and it was the drive-
in that demonstrated the tremendous cost benefits of selling popcorn, soda, candy, and
the like to movie patrons.[25] Thus, the postwar rise of the drive-in coincided with a
marked rise in exhibitors' concession income, which steadily climbed from $34 million
in 1946 to $128 million in 1949.[26]

The drive-in phenomenon gave the movie industry a moderate boost; continuing
through the following decade, the number of outdoor theaters reached 6,000 in 1961.
But the drive-in was yet another sign of the changing times and overall decline of the
motion picture industry—at least as it had evolved since the 1910s. With its clientele of
young marrieds getting out of the house for a few hours with the kids in the family car,
the drive-in heralded the rise of the suburbs and the passing of the downtown area as
the center of social and cultural activity for most Americans. And thus, it signaled the

Drive-in movie theater, ca. 1948.

passing of the downtown deluxe movie house, which had been the lifeblood of the motion picture industry for decades.

There were other signals of the downtown theater's imminent extinction as well. The *Wall Street Journal* reported in 1947 that the once-denigrated "nabes" (neighborhood theaters) were beginning to do better business than the downtown houses—a remarkable development after the tremendous growth of urban markets during the war. Moreover, the *Journal* noted in 1948 that the burgeoning drive-in was a "competitive headache" for neighborhood theaters. Clearly both the nabes and drive-ins were siphoning off the traditional first-run audience. A Gallup study in early 1949 found that the number of "average A customers" had declined from about 16 million in 1946 to 13 million in 1948—a decline of nearly 20 percent in only two years—and that over 60 percent of A-picture customers were now under 30 years old. *Variety* reported in 1949 that the ARI's long-held view that the teenager was the "most faithful" (i.e., habitual) movie-goer was now widely accepted in the industry. And industry studies late that year indicated that the drive-in provided one means of recapturing that "lost" (i.e., over 30) movie audience.[27]

Hollywood's struggle simply to adapt to the changes in the composition and behavior of movie audiences, let alone exploit them, was especially galling because the "lost"—or fast disappearing—audience of young marrieds and suburbanites was remarkably affluent. *Variety* reported that revenues fell 21 percent between 1946 and 1949, while the disposable income of Americans increased 22 percent.[28] Some argued that postwar conditions still compared favorably to prewar levels, but this was scarcely the case. Although Hollywood's 1948 box-office gross of $1.5 billion was up 34 percent over 1941, the increase was due primarily to a 60 percent increase in the average ticket price; meanwhile, attendance was falling despite a population increase of over 10 percent since the prewar era. In 1948, as Hollywood's decline accelerated, personal income in the United States was up 172 percent over 1940, and the gross national product was up 153 percent.[29]

Movie attendance also comprised an ever-smaller portion of Americans' recreational expenditures in the late 1940s. Moviegoers were growing more selective, and they also were opting for other activities as a wider range of amusements and diversions became available—from night baseball to bowling to night classes on the GI Bill. Through the 1930s and into the war years, moviegoing amounted to 20 percent of America's recreation expenditures. That figure climbed to 25 percent during the war but then declined steadily in the late 1940s, falling to 12.3 percent by 1950.[30]

The import of foreign films reflected yet another telling aspect of the changing postwar marketplace. As in the war years, a number of top British films enjoyed considerable success in the United States; most were relatively modest dramas in much the same style as the wartime pictures—David Lean's BRIEF ENCOUNTER (1945; U.S. release 1946), for example, and Carol Reed's ODD MAN OUT (1947). But a number of more ambitious British pictures were released in the United States as well, notably HENRY V (1944; U.S. release 1946), CAESAR AND CLEOPATRA (1946), GREAT EXPECTATIONS (1946), HAMLET (1948), and THE RED SHOES (1948). All of these prestige-level productions were critically well received and did roughly $2 million in the United States, and all were nominated by the Academy for best picture—which HAMLET won in 1948. Moreover, both GREAT EXPECTATIONS and HAMLET were Anglo-American coproductions released via Universal, which underwent a complex merger in 1946 giving such British-made films direct access to the U.S. market. Similarly, Britain's Eagle-Lion in 1947 purchased Producers Releasing Corporation (PRC), a B-grade producer-distributor, to secure access to the U.S. market.[31]

While these Anglo-American deals provided mainstream release for quality English-language imports, the postwar era also saw the rapid rise in the United States of an art cinema movement which catered to foreign-language imports. For the most part, these imports were far more obscure—and far less lucrative—foreign films playing in smaller, more exclusive venues geared to the growing ranks of American cinephiles. Most of the art cinema venues, in fact, were second- and third-run downtown theaters whose owners turned to foreign-language fare rather than close down.

The *1948 Film Daily Year Book* stated that the trend was catching on "because of an alleged product shortage; because some of the low-budget films were disappointing; and because many of the better films were only available as third and fourth runs." The exhibitor operating an art house also did not have to rely on a neighborhood clientele, "since devotees of the foreign film will travel from one end of town to another to see an import."[32] According to successive editions of the *Film Daily Year Book*, 118 foreign films were imported in 1947, 93 in 1948, and 123 in 1949. One major distributor of imports, Vog Films, gauged the number of theaters regularly playing foreign films in 1947 at about 250. *Variety* reported a similar total in late 1949 (226 theaters) and put the total of "strictly artfilm theaters" in the United States at 57. The center of the art-film universe was New York, which had over 30 theaters devoted to foreign films and to the burgeoning market of cinephiles.[33]

The art cinema movement was keyed to the gradual recovery of film production overseas after the war, especially in Western Europe. French and Italian films dominated the movement, and Italian neorealist films such as OPEN CITY (1946), SHOESHINE (1946), and THE BICYCLE THIEF (1949) garnered most of the critical attention and box-office support. By the late 1940s, because European art films were well publicized and actively promoted by major film critics, a few were able to break into major distribution in the United States. Bosley Crowther's rave review of THE BICYCLE THIEF in the *New York Times* in late 1949, for example, and his naming that film and France's DEVIL IN THE FLESH (1946; U.S. release 1949) as the "best foreign language films" of 1949, helped propel both films into the mainstream market.[34]

For the most part, however, foreign films were consigned to play in the marginalized art-house circuit, where both the exposure and economic prospects were limited. Many overseas producers and distributors, in fact, considered that circuit little more than a dumping ground for foreign product—a means, essentially, of preventing foreign films from gaining a foothold in the United States, while the Hollywood studios satisfied market demand with B's and reissues. Even quality British pictures were "not getting proper distribution in America," said Alexander Korda in a blistering tirade in the *New York Times* in late 1946—a situation that would only get worse as the U.S. market declined.[35]

THE BICYCLE THIEF (1949) *was among the critically acclaimed Italian neorealist films released in the United States.*

While these complaints were often justified, the Hollywood studio powers actually grew more sensitive to them as the domestic market declined and foreign sales became more important. Never before, in fact, had the American producer-distributors been so keenly aware of both the importance and difficulty of selling their pictures in foreign markets, and of maintaining favorable relations with their overseas clients.

Postwar Foreign Markets

Hollywood's overseas performance in the late 1940s ran directly parallel to its performance at home—a record high in 1946 followed by a sustained period of economic decline and general disarray. Hollywood's troubles overseas were the result of three postwar developments: first, cold war tensions, which rendered Americans' access to many countries behind the Iron Curtain difficult if not impossible; second, the trend toward tariffs, frozen revenues, and other protectionist policies in nations like Britain, France, and Italy that were determined to build up their own film industries and to prevent Hollywood from completely dominating their markets; and third, Britain's deepening financial crisis.

Even as the U.S. producer-distributors lurched from one foreign crisis to another in the late 1940s, however, overall revenues from overseas held up fairly well. After a record overseas take of about $125 million in 1946, foreign revenues were an estimated $120 million in 1947 and $100 million in both 1948 and 1949.[36] This performance compares favorably to the industry's overseas take of about $110–15 million during the later war years, although rising costs in the late 1940s render such comparisons dubious at best. Moreover, the declining domestic market put increasing pressure on successful sales overseas. By the late 1940s, foreign trade still provided about 35 percent of Hollywood's total revenues, but that income often meant the difference between profit and loss.

This was scarcely the case immediately after the war, when the overseas outlook was remarkably upbeat. The Hollywood studio-distributors saw record overseas revenues in 1946, much of it from pre-1946 films in markets that had been closed during the war.[37] Johnston stated at mid-year that foreign revenues made up fully 45 percent of rental income, and that he hoped to push that total to 50 percent.[38] In October, the *Motion Picture Herald* reported that the "lid" on the foreign markets had been "pried open," and that the MPEA seemed to be fending off protectionism overseas.[39] At year's end, the studios reported that their overseas income of $125 million was virtually identical to their overall net profits—a situation that many in the industry considered ideal, with the domestic market on a break-even basis and overseas income amounting essentially to pure profit.

England remained Hollywood's chief client after the war, and a veritable extension of the U.S. market. Hollywood's total revenues in England were just over $90 million in 1946; roughly $20 million was frozen and remained in England, while $70 million was remitted to the studios. Thus, England accounted for over half of the industry's overseas income—somewhat less than in the war era, when England supplied three-fourths of Hollywood's overseas income, but still a sizable share. So understandably enough, good relations with England remained the single most important item on Hollywood's overseas agenda.

To ensure those positive relations as well as the efficient investment of any funds not remitted, most of the major studios either established production units or studios in

England or entered coproduction deals with British producers. The most significant of these was the 1946 merger of Universal and International Pictures orchestrated by England's J. Arthur Rank. in fact, Rank already had an elaborate coproduction and codistribution deal with Universal; the merger was described by *Variety* as "a major reorganization of the Universal–J. Arthur Rank worldwide film empire."[40] A clear indication of both the unbridled postwar optimism and the need to invest overseas, the merger was designed to coproduce A-class pictures for the global movie market.[41]

The postwar Anglo-American alliance was doomed to failure, however, owing to the declining movie market in the United States and the rapid deterioration of the British economy. With each postwar year the British crisis worsened, with devastating impact on the American movie industry. in fact, in both 1947 and 1948, despite the severe crises at home, the *Film Daily Year Book* gauged the deteriorating British market as the single most acute problem facing the American movie industry.[42] While England did remain Hollywood's major overseas client, by the late 1940s it no longer supplied anywhere near the proportion of foreign revenues (60–75 percent) that it had during the peak war years. Remittances from Britain fell from $70 million in 1946 to $56 million in 1947, $35 million in 1948, and $17 million in 1949.

Indian actor Sabu (center) and British movie mogul J. Arthur Rank (third from right) welcome U.S. exhibitors to the set of BLACK NARCISSUS *in London in 1946, when Anglo-American relations were generally upbeat.*

The so-called Anglo-American impasse stemmed from not only the severe economic situation in Britain but also the long-standing resentment over Hollywood's trade practices by the British government, especially the Board of Trade. Significantly enough, the British film industry in general, and especially the exhibition sector, was far less hostile toward Hollywood than the British government. While some British producers (particularly Rank) often complained that Hollywood films routinely earned at least five times more in England than did British productions, no one really questioned the general superiority of Hollywood product. During the war, the British film industry foundered while the American film industry flourished, and by 1945 the British industry was geared primarily to second-rate product to be double-billed with more popular American films. These "quota quickies" were produced to satisfy government-mandated quotas on the amount of screen time devoted to British product—about 20 percent in 1944 and 1945. These films were barely passable with British audiences, and they simply were not suitable for U.S. release. Both Rank and Korda planned to upgrade production after the war, however, and the various deals with Hollywood promised to improve the general state of the British industry.[43]

Things took a turn for the worse in early 1947, however, when Sir Stafford Cripps, the president of the Board of Trade, started speaking out about the need to "de-Americanize" British exhibition at the same time that the British economy began to show signs of postwar exhaustion.[44] By the summer of 1947, England was mired in an economic crisis which was threatening all of Europe—and much of the globe, for that matter—and the Board of Trade prepared to take active measures against Hollywood and a number of other foreign industries. England's leading producers and distributors warned Cripps that the British film industry could not function without American product, and there was a flurry of activity on both sides of the Atlantic to forestall any serious action by the British government.[45]

Unfazed by these appeals and efforts, the Board of Trade took extreme measures—more extreme, in fact, than anyone expected. On 7 August 1947, an *ad valorem* tax of 75 percent was placed on all future film imports: in effect, foreign distributors were to pay three-fourths of the expected earnings on a picture prior to its release in England. Hollywood's reaction was swift and equally extreme. On 8 August, the MPEA announced an immediate boycott of the British market, to remain in effect until the tax was lifted.[46]

The Board of Trade stood firm despite laments from British exhibitors that they could not "carry on" without American pictures.[47] England's producers were equally disturbed by the tax, since it jeopardized cooperative arrangements with U.S. companies. Several leading British producers did plan to upgrade product in an effort to compensate for (and exploit) the lack of U.S. product.[48] These plans meant little given the state of the British economy, however, and in fact at year's end Rank announced substantial losses for 1947 in his production sector.[49]

The Anglo-American impasse continued into 1948 as conditions in England worsened and as Hollywood faced the prospect of doing without British revenues. The embargo finally ended in early March, when a settlement was announced that was to take effect in May 1948—on the same day as the Supreme Court's momentous *Paramount* decree. The settlement removed the *ad valorem* tax, which was to be replaced by a four-year agreement whereby a maximum of $17 million could be remitted from England by the American companies, plus an amount equal to the combined earnings of all British product released in the United States. The intent here, of course, was to induce the Hollywood studio-distributors to upgrade their efforts to sell British pictures in the United States, the results of which in turn would raise the $17 million remittance ceiling. The excess revenues—those not remitted—would not be taxed by the government but instead could be invested by the studios in various "permitted uses" in England. These included film production, buying story properties, hiring British talent, obtaining real estate (theaters, film labs, or studios, for example, with prior approval from the government), and so on.[50]

The Board of Trade also announced that the government would support the financially troubled British film industry with subsidies and loans, which along with the new accord (and the renewed rapport between British and American producers) promised to improve the quality of British films.[51] Clearly both Hollywood and Britain were counting on that improved quality, and both stood to gain. The benefits to Britain were obvious enough, especially in terms of access to the lucrative U.S. market. Hollywood, meanwhile, could make room for quality British films, whose box-office performance would increase the majors' take at home (in exhibitors' fees) and also in England (in the equivalent add-on to the $17 million).

Unfortunately, however, England's economy continued to slide in 1948, and the British film industry's performance in the U.S. market fell to a postwar low despite the success of HAMLET, THE RED SHOES, and a very few other pictures. Matters worsened with Parliament's passage of the Film Act of 1948, which raised the screen quota on British product from 20 to 40 percent. Again Hollywood countered, this time decreeing (via Eric Johnston) that as of 1 October 1948, no American import could be double-billed in England with a British picture. This announcement dealt a severe blow to British exhibitors, since their patrons generally watched British films only if they played along with Hollywood products.[52]

Britain's film industry and national economy continued to deteriorate, a fact underscored by England's devaluation of the pound sterling in September 1949. One British studio after another closed down as production slowed drastically, especially on what were termed "first features," that is, films which could be dualed with quota quickies in England and released in the United States. Both Rank and Korda were bailed out repeatedly with government subsidies through the National Film Finance Corporation (NFFC), but both were still in desperate straits. Rank lost over $9 million on his production operations in 1949 and was all but inoperative at year's end.[53] Nor did the investment by Hollywood of unremitted funds in England help all that much. The studios found permitted uses for $25 million in 1949, but very little of this money went into actual film production, since more concrete investments (in theaters, film labs, and the like) were less risky. As of June 1949, the studios were sitting on another $40 million and simply waiting for conditions to improve.[54]

Despite the myriad crises in England, Hollywood continued to dominate that market in 1949. Of the 571 features released in Great Britain in 1949, 392 were American-made films—versus 131 British productions and only 22 from France, England's second-largest foreign supplier.[55] And by the same token, England remained Hollywood's major overseas client. No other foreign country played anywhere near the number of American-made films, and while $17 million per annum was far short of what the U.S. studio-distributors had been earning in England in earlier years, it was a good deal more than they earned in any other overseas market.

The limited take from England did force the studios and the MPEA to concentrate more heavily on other markets and to think increasingly in terms of the global market-

Laurence Olivier directed and starred in HAMLET *(1948), which was internationally successful despite the desperate straits of the British movie industry.*

place. There were problems there as well, however, owing primarily to the growing protectionist trend, the deepening cold war, and the painfully slow process of rebuilding the German and Japanese film industries. In the late 1940s, the MPEA handled all distribution of Hollywood films in the dozen or so countries where these problems were most severe, including Austria, Bulgaria, Czechoslovakia, the East Indies, Germany, Hungary, Japan, Korea, the Netherlands, Poland, Rumania, the Soviet Union, and Yugoslavia. There were a few other trouble spots besides Great Britain, like France, Spain, and China, where the MPEA tried to facilitate trade and negotiated agreements but did not serve as the sole bargaining agent for the studios. By 1949, with the former Axis nations on the rebound and now becoming viable U.S. trade partners, the MPEA focused its attention more exclusively on the Soviet Union and other Iron Curtain countries.[56]

As in the prewar era, protectionism inevitably posed a dual problem for Hollywood in that it tended to be most acute in those nations which not only represented the largest overseas markets but also were interested in developing their own indigenous motion picture industries. Consider France in the late 1940s. In 1946, after a year of difficult negotiations (discussed in chapter 5), the MPEA negotiated a Franco-American pact whereby a ceiling of $3,625,000 in remittances was placed on American films. But owing to various difficulties, the studios took out only about $1 million per year in both 1947 and 1948, while roughly $10 million in revenues on U.S. pictures was frozen in France. As in England, the U.S. companies could invest the frozen funds in a number of industry-related areas in France: coproduction with French companies, purchase or construction of theaters, acquisition of distribution rights to French-produced films, and so on.[57]

Meanwhile, France was trying to strengthen its own industry, which had not suffered too severely during the war and in fact had remained in operation under German occupation. This was a daunting task, however, given the difficulties of France's general postwar recovery. In 1946, France produced 91 features at a total cost of $20.3 million (2.4 billion francs)—on a par with B-picture standards in the United States but roughly ten times what France spent on production before the war. Yet the industry showed losses of $7.7 million, while both exhibitors and audiences clamored for more American pictures. In 1948, the Franco-American pact was renewed but limited the total number of Hollywood imports to 121 and set a quota stipulating that French films appear five weeks out of every thirteen.[58] Still, the French industry faced a struggle—mainly because of the deepening economic crisis in Europe in 1948–1949—and it was far from healthy as the decade ended.

Latin America remained an important but generally difficult area for the United States in the late 1940s. Mexico was Hollywood's principal client to the south, returning $3–5 million per year. Mexico's own wartime production boom slowed somewhat in 1946, when its output fell to only 60 pictures. But by 1948–1949, its output was approaching 100 features per annum, and thus it reestablished its position as Hollywood's chief competitor in other Latin markets. Hollywood continued to look longingly at the vast potential in South America, especially Brazil and Argentina, but the slow pace of industrialization and economic development kept those markets from being of any real consequence.[59]

By the end of the decade, the global economic crisis threatened Hollywood's overseas trade in virtually every sector. According to MPAA estimates in late 1949 (in the wake of the devaluation of the British pound), the U.S. film industry would have to increase its foreign revenues by some 50 percent to offset losses due to devalued currency.[60]

Despite that dire forecast, however, the international marketplace was growing at an impressive rate at the time, and Hollywood continued to dominate the global movie business. The number of movie theaters worldwide increased from 79,000 to just over 90,000 between 1947 and 1949, with the Far East and former Axis nations showing tremendous growth. And in every significant overseas region, Hollywood product accounted for anywhere from one-half to three-fourths of the screen time, as these figures indicate:

Table 9.4
WORLD MOTION PICTURE MARKET, 1949

Region	Number of Theaters	% U.S. Product
Europe	53,350	56
South America	5,000	64
Mexico/Central America	1,950	75
Far East	3,500	47
Middle East	2,700	52
South Pacific	2,300	75
Africa	1,300	62
Canada	1,700	75
United States	18,350	95

SOURCE: *Motion Picture Herald*, 4 June 1949, p. 20.

Despite its problems with England, widespread protectionism, and the global recession, 38 percent of Hollywood's revenues in 1949 came from overseas, and its foreign income of roughly $100 million was on a par with the previous year.[61] Thus, Hollywood was clearly holding its own in the turbulent international marketplace of the late 1940s—a vital necessity, considering the deepening crises at home.

Labor Strife, Politics, and the Resurgence of IATSE

Besides the market-related postwar crises, Hollywood faced a number of other industrial and political crises as well. Labor unrest was among the most important and underrated of them. As discussed in chapter 5, the Hollywood labor scene was relatively quiet through most of the war era before flaring up in an early 1945 jurisdictional dispute between the industry's two dominant labor organizations, the International Alliance of Theatrical and Stage Employees (IATSE) and the Conference of Studio Unions (CSU). That conflict led to an eight-month CSU strike, which was resolved in October through the efforts of the MPAA's president, Eric Johnston. Thus, the industry looked to postwar labor conditions with guarded optimism, and in fact, the *Motion Picture Herald* ran a headline in January 1946 boldly asserting: "Labor Amity on Coast Assured for the Future."[62]

At that point, Hollywood's labor arena comprised 43 distinct craft and talent groups, most of which fell under the purview of the American Federation of Labor (AFL). Two-thirds of Hollywood's 30,000 studio employees belonged to craft unions associated with either IATSE or the CSU (both of which were in the AFL). IATSE was the larger and more powerful of the two, with an estimated 12,000 Hollywood members in 13 locals, most of which were involved in the production of films. IATSE had another 50,000 members outside Hollywood; indeed, the IATSE membership of virtually all projectionists in the United States continued to be IATSE's trump card in negotiations with the studios.[63] The CSU, created five years earlier when IATSE was mired in scandal, developed under Herb Sorrell's leadership as a viable challenger to IATSE's dominance over the Hollywood labor scene. By 1946, the Hollywood-based CSU boasted 7,000 members in 12 locals, most of them involved in pre-production crafts (carpenters, set designers, painters, and so on).[64]

Hollywood's other significant labor contingent comprised the talent guilds—the screen actors, directors, and writers guilds, along with the American Federation of Musicians. While all of these organizations attempted to steer clear of the IATSE-CSU dispute, they inevitably were caught in the crossfire and eventually were drawn in, most notably the Screen Actors Guild in league with IATSE and the Screen Writers Guild with the CSU.

Management in postwar Hollywood was represented by three groups, the most powerful of which was, without question, the Association of Motion Picture Producers (AMPP), the major studio-distributors' trade outfit which was presided over by the ubiquitous Eric Johnston (also president of the MPAA and the MPEA). The industry's two dozen or so major independent producers were represented by the Society of Independent Motion Picture Producers (SIMPP), while the minor independents like Monogram and PRC had their own trade outfit and labor negotiator, the Independent Motion Picture Producers Association (IMPPA).

"Movie labor is like nothing else in the labor world," *Fortune* magazine asserted in 1946. Hollywood's labor scene was indeed both volatile and complex, owing to the virtually complete unionization of its workers, the high economic stakes involved (in terms of salaries and wages), and the ongoing struggle between IATSE and the CSU.[65] That struggle had scarcely been resolved with the October 1945 settlement, which in fact had only fanned the flames of jurisdictional conflict. Johnston had won peace among the warring factions by convincing the studios to let the striking CSU workers return to work, while continuing to employ the 1,000 or so set erectors who had replaced the carpenters during the strike. A similar compromise was reached with striking machinists, so there too the studios were employing two workers for every job.

This had led to padded payrolls, gross inefficiency, and endless jurisdictional hassles, with workers arguing over whether a boat was a set or a prop, or whether costumers or makeup artists were responsible for the padding in an actress's undergarments. The conflict went much deeper, of course. As *Fortune* aptly noted in an in-depth piece on Hollywood labor, "Jurisdiction increases fantastically the size of the standing labor force required" for film production. This tendency intensified the rampant "feather-bedding" whereby union contracts required the presence on the set of paid employees who, in effect, did nothing. The studios, meanwhile, seemed resigned to the impasse, leading the *Wall Street Journal* to observe in mid-1946, "By nurturing this rivalry, [the studios] have finally achieved what is described as the 'worst' and 'most complicated' labor situation in the country."[66]

While the CSU's Sorrell pressed for a resolution to the impasse, the studios balked, for two reasons: first, the producers did not want to jeopardize their long-standing (and generally favorable) relations with the IATSE unions; and second, Sorrell was pressing for substantial wage increases.[67] A series of walkouts and continued pressure convinced the IMPPA (Monogram and PRC) to agree to a 25 percent pay hike in June 1946, retroactive to 1 January, but still the majors held out. In July, a two-day "quickie" strike

Show of strength: IATSE pickets outside Columbia Pictures during the decorators strike in 1946.

brought them around, and in what became known as "the treaty of Beverly Hills," the AMPP agreed to a 25 percent wage hike.[68]

The wage hikes put CSU members among the nation's highest-paid salaried workers, but the strike settlement did not resolve the jurisdictional conflicts. In September, the ongoing flap over IATSE set erectors and CSU carpenters led to a full-scale CSU strike against the AMPP.[69] With this interminable squabble over some seventy-five carpenters taking thousands out of work and throwing studio production into turmoil, much of the CSU's credibility and industry support began to erode. A key factor was an effort by the Screen Actors Guild to broker a settlement on behalf of the AFL (with which it also was affiliated). SAG, by now clearly the leading labor organization in Hollywood, abandoned that effort in October and voted to publicly denounce the CSU—an action that was endorsed by twenty-four other Hollywood unions. In November, SAG issued a "Report to the Motion Picture Industry" which stated: "The Guild board reluctantly has been forced to the conclusion that certain of the leaders of the CSU do not want the strike settled." The producers also began to publicly disparage the CSU, arguing that only three hundred jobs were really at issue and that the vast majority of its members did not support the strike. But the CSU stood firm, and in December a pro-CSU rally was held with a sizable turnout at the Hollywood Legion Stadium.[70]

IATSE, meanwhile, proved much more adept at maneuvering through the troubled postwar waters. Much of its success was due to Roy Brewer, IATSE's West Coast head who had arrived in early 1945, sent by the IATSE president, Richard Walsh, at the outset of the first CSU strike. Brewer represented a new breed of IATSE labor leader, without the taint of racketeer associations or big-city labor struggles. He had started in the picture business as a projectionist in Nebraska, and while still in his early twenties (in 1933), he became one of the nation's youngest state-level labor leaders. By the mid-1940s, Brewer was a rising star in the IATSE hierarchy, and he quickly proved himself after his arrival in Hollywood. Indeed, the 1945 strike provided valuable experience for the young labor leader, and in the ensuing labor crises Brewer put that experience to very good use.[71]

Brewer's success and IATSE's postwar resurgence turned on several strategic factors, notably favorable relations with the major studios and the Screen Actors Guild, and Brewer's savvy exploitation of the growing anti-Communist fervor. As in the 1945 strike, IATSE supplied replacements for most of the striking CSU workers during the 1946 walkout. This time, in fact, the studios were counting on it, having conducted secret negotiations with IATSE while the CSU was threatening to strike. Thus, the studios and IATSE effectively joined forces against the CSU, whose militancy disturbed the producers and whose very existence posed a threat to IATSE.[72] And despite the "natural" enmity between labor and management, the alliance between the studios and IATSE was really no surprise given their history of "cooperation" (legal or otherwise) over the previous decade. Brewer also forged an alliance with SAG, based largely on the anti-Communist sentiments he shared with the guild leadership.

in fact, as the labor strife intensified, Brewer took advantage of the anti-Communist climate through two related tactics: flagrant red-baiting of the CSU, with Herb Sorrell as his primary (and admittedly vulnerable) target; and appeals on behalf of IATSE to the studios and the guilds to form an anti-Communist coalition in Hollywood. Brewer found a valuable ally in the Motion Picture Alliance for the Preservation of American Ideals (MPA), the organization of right-wing filmmakers—Sam Wood, Walt Disney, Gary Cooper, et al.—formed in 1944 to counter Hollywood's left-liberal drift. The Alliance not only responded to Brewer's overtures but accepted him into the fold, eventually making him president of the organization.[73]

By 1947, Brewer's red-baiting of Sorrell and his crusade to root out industry subversives began to pay off. The general sentiment in the industry—and elsewhere—was turning against Sorrell and the red-tainted CSU, and political pressures mounted nationwide against left-leaning and strike-oriented organized labor. Congress was now involved, both directly through the pending House Un-American Activities Committee (HUAC) investigation of Hollywood subversives, and indirectly through the Taft-Hartley Act, which became law in August. Essentially a revision of the 1935 Wagner Labor Relations Act, the Taft-Hartley Act required loyalty oaths of union members and outlawed both wildcat and jurisdictional strikes. Meanwhile, the HUAC hearings were scheduled for late October, and the committee's agenda was clearly anti-labor as well as anti-red. The upcoming hearings put enormous pressure on the striking CSU unions, which began returning to work, settling individually with the studios and abandoning the CSU. In late October 1947, days before the HUAC hearings, Sorrell's own painters union voted to cross the picket lines, effectively finishing the CSU.[74]

Thus, by 1948, IATSE had regained control of organized labor in Hollywood, and the industry reverted to a more routine process of labor-management discord over salaries and working conditions. IATSE would continue to win wage concessions from the studios, although as wages increased the total number of union employees in Hollywood fell dramatically. Thomas F. Brady of the *New York Times* in late 1949 noted that IATSE had "established undisputed jurisdiction in its field," but also that Hollywood's overall cost-cutting efforts had been paid for primarily by labor, "not in wage levels, but in the amount of employment." And indeed, union employment in the film production sector had fallen from 22,000 in 1946 to 13,500 in 1949.[75]

HUAC, the Hollywood Ten, and the Birth of the Blacklist

The House Un-American Activities Committee, popularly known as HUAC, became a standing (permanent) committee in 1945, but not until the November 1946 elections did HUAC really become a major political force. In those elections, both the House and Senate attained a Republican majority for the first time since the pre-Depression Hoover era as cold war conservatism swept through the nation and into Congress. The elections brought a new generation of zealous anti-Communist ideologues to Washington—including Richard Nixon and Joseph McCarthy—and it also installed a conservative anti-Communist, J. Parnell Thomas, as chairman of HUAC. It was soon evident that the new Congress would exact its revenge after four terms of FDR and the left-liberal politics of the New Deal, and that the motion picture industry would be in its direct line of fire.

Crucial to HUAC's incursion into Hollywood, and in fact its prime ally, was the Motion Picture Alliance. Since its founding in late 1944, the members of the Motion Picture Alliance had sought to accomplish two goals: first, to demonstrate to the public that the "silent majority" of movie industry employees were conservative, hardworking, freedom-loving Americans; and second, to purge the industry of those who were not. The Alliance already had invited the Dies Committee to look into Hollywood's leftist leanings. That earlier inquiry had come to naught, but the recent conservative swing in Congress encouraged the Alliance to try again. HUAC's Parnell Thomas, a savvy politician and a strident anti-labor, anti-Communist, anti–New Deal Republican, proved most receptive. Thomas was eager to showcase his committee and dramatize the "red menace" in those early months of the cold war, when allegations of Communists working in government and industry were rampant. Seizing the opportunity, Thomas announced that HUAC would be looking into Communist infiltration of the Hollywood movie colony, and into the content of the movies themselves.[76]

MPAA's president, Eric Johnston, hoping to head off a full-blown investigation, went to Washington in April 1947 to testify before HUAC. He acknowledged that there were Communists working in the movie industry but maintained that it was their constitutional right to do so as long as they did not advocate the overthrow of the government. Johnston insisted that "the Communists hate and fear American motion pictures," pointing out the Soviet efforts to prevent Hollywood films from penetrating the Iron Curtain. Johnston also assured the committee that attempts by Communists to attain positions of power in Hollywood or to influence movie content in any way had "suffered an overwhelming defeat." The committee was not persuaded, however, and at one point the archconservative Mississippian John Rankin stated: "Unless the people in control of the industry are willing to clean house of Communists, Congress will have to do it for them."[77]

Hollywood conservative Adolph Menjou testifying in Los Angeles at HUAC's preliminary hearings in May 1947.

HUAC took the initiative in May 1947, when Thomas and two other committee members went to Hollywood and took up residence in the Biltmore for a series of informal interviews. Most of these were with Alliance members who readily identified those in the industry whom they suspected were Communists or "fellow travelers." Convinced that a full investigation was warranted, Thomas revealed (primarily through well-placed news leaks) that subpoenas would be issued and a congressional hearing conducted later in the year.[78] Although Thomas earlier indicated that the investigation would include the CSU strike and the jurisdictional dispute, he ruled that out after the initial sortie to Hollywood. He decided instead to pursue three premises: first, that Communists had attained positions of power in the Screen Writers Guild and in studio writing departments; second, that Communists were successfully introducing subversive propaganda into pictures; and third, that Roosevelt and his administration had pressured Hollywood to produce pro-Soviet pictures during World War II.[79]

From all indications, Hollywood simply did not take HUAC and the pending investigation all that seriously, deeming it little more than a political sideshow—a view that apparently was shared by much of the public and the press. That view changed in September, however, when Congress issued subpoenas to forty-three studio executives, labor leaders, and filmmakers. The summonses were divided about evenly between the so-called friendly and unfriendly witnesses, all of whom were requested to appear in Washington on 20 October to testify about "Communist Infiltration of the Motion Picture Industry." Several summonses went to Alliance members, along with studio executives, like Jack Warner and Louis B. Mayer, who were outspoken anti-Communists; another nineteen went to those suspected of being politically subversive or having direct ties to the Communist Party.[80]

Johnston announced that the industry would be represented by Paul V. McNutt, a liberal attorney and onetime presidential aspirant who had served as national commander of the American Legion, governor of Indiana, head of the War Manpower Commission, and most recently as U.S. ambassador to the Philippines. Reminiscent of the late Wendell Willkie, who had defended Hollywood in the 1941 Senate propaganda hearings, McNutt was highly touted for his legal and courtroom skills, and he was expected to ably defend the industry against the congressional inquisitors. As the battle lines were drawn, however, it quickly became evident that this inquiry would be altogether different from the propaganda hearings. First of all, Congress let it be known that even though many studio executives had been summoned, they and their companies were not under investigation. HUAC, in other words, was convinced that the studios were not knowingly or willingly producing Communist propaganda. There would be questions about such overtly pro-Soviet pictures as Warners' MISSION TO MOSCOW (1943), but the issue was pressure from the Roosevelt administration more than anything else. And second, McNutt was not secured to defend or represent the nineteen unfriendly witnesses; mostly writers and SWG members, they were left to secure counsel on their own.[81]

The only organized industry support for the unfriendly witnesses came from the Committee for the First Amendment. Something of a counter to the Alliance, the Committee was formed shortly before the hearings and was spearheaded by John Huston, Philip Dunne, and William Wyler. Membership included many of the industry's leading liberals: John Garfield, Katharine Hepburn, Billy Wilder, Groucho Marx, Paulette Goddard, Humphrey Bogart, Fredric March, George S. Kaufman, Walter Wanger, and Jerry Wald. After collecting some five hundred industry signatures in support of the First Amendment rights to free speech and peaceable assembly, the Committee planned to send a contingent to Washington at the end of the first week of testimony, just before the unfriendly witnesses were scheduled to testify.[82]

The hearings were held in Washington from Monday, 20 October, to Thursday, 30 October, during which time forty-one witnesses were heard. The first week of testimony was devoted to friendly witnesses; Jack Warner was the first to be called. Warner's testimony set the tone and outlined the studios' general defense strategy. He condemned communism and assured the committee that the vast majority in the Hollywood filmmaking community were deeply patriotic. Warner acknowledged that there were reds in Hollywood, but he testified that any efforts to influence either the industry or the movies had been thwarted. HUAC had flatly stated before the hearings that it expected witnesses to "name names," and Warner readily complied—although most of those he named already were on the roster of unfriendly witnesses. Louis B. Mayer and the Alliance president, Sam Wood, both of whom also appeared on the opening day of the hearings, presented similar testimony.[83]

Through the first week, the hearings followed much the same pattern, which smacked of a carefully rehearsed publicity effort and a setup for HUAC to go after the "unfriendlies" during the following week. Press coverage was mixed, not only in its treatment of the testimony but in its regard for the proceedings in general. The *Washington Post* on the eve of the hearings referred to them as "the biggest show of the fall investigating season" and devoted its front-page coverage to the sideshow aspects as well as the testimony. When the Alliance member Robert Taylor appeared on 22

Members of the Committee for the First Amendment gather in Washington to support
the "unfriendly witnesses" summoned by HUAC.

October, for instance, the *Post*'s page-one headline read "Bobby Soxers and Mothers,"
followed by the subhead "Women Cheer Robert Taylor as He Urges Ban on Reds."[84]
Robert Montgomery, another Alliance member and former president of the Screen
Actors Guild, wryly stated, "For too long a time a vociferous minority has misled the
public to believe that the majority of Hollywood actors and actresses are radicals, crack-
pots or at least New Deal Democrats."[85]

Most of the testimony was deadly serious, of course, and some of it quite vindictive—
Walt Disney testified that Herb Sorrell was "a Commie," for instance, and that reds had
tried to "ruin" him in the strike of 1940–1941. And the industry attorney Paul McNutt
repeatedly maneuvered the testimony into assurances that, despite the Communist
presence in Hollywood, there was no clear evidence of their ideology within the movies
themselves.[86]

While the first week of the hearings produced no major revelations or surprises, the
second week promised a good deal more drama. The unfriendly witnesses received an
obvious boost over the weekend by the much-publicized arrival late Sunday of a twenty-
six-member delegation of the Committee for the First Amendment in Washington (in a
plane furnished by Howard Hughes). In an impromptu 11:00 P.M. press conference at
the Statler Hotel, Committee spokesman John Huston stated that they were there simply to observe, that they intended neither to "attack" HUAC and the friendly witnesses

nor to "defend the hostile witnesses." But the name of the group, along with its full-page ads in various newspapers, left no question as to the Committee's allegiance.[87]

The second week's testimony proved to be even more eventful and dramatic than expected, beginning on Monday morning with the first unfriendly witness, John Howard Lawson. The nineteen had decided not to cooperate with the congressional committee, insisting on their individual rights accorded by the Constitution. The strategy of noncooperation went beyond refusal to answer, however: Lawson demanded to read a prepared statement (as the friendly witnesses had been allowed to do the week before). When Thomas denied the request and demanded answers to the committee's questions ("Are you now or have you ever been . . ."), Lawson launched a verbal tirade against Thomas and the committee. Thomas ordered Lawson removed from the House chamber, and according to the *Post*, he was bodily carried from the packed room "screeching 'Hitler Germany—Hitler tactics!'"[88] Lawson was immediately cited for contempt of Congress, and this pattern of refusal to cooperate, disruptive behavior, and contempt citations was repeated with each of the next ten unfriendly witnesses throughout the week.

Whatever their intent, the general strategy and tactics of the unfriendly witnesses proved to be woefully ill advised. Huston and Philip Dunne, not only a highly respected screenwriter but a student of constitutional law, had encouraged the witnesses to openly disclose their political affiliation outside the House chamber in a press conference, and then once inside to inform HUAC that it had no right to ask them such questions and that they had every right not to answer. Clearly the unfriendly witnesses opted for a more aggressive and hostile strategy. With each raucous confrontation, Huston later recalled, he grew more appalled. "It was a sorry performance," said Huston. "You felt your skin crawl and your stomach turn. I disapproved of what was being done to the [unfriendly witnesses], but I also disapproved of their response."[89]

More reasoned testimony was heard during the second week, notably by Dore Schary (then head of RKO) and the Writers Guild president, Emmett Lavery. But that was lost in the chaos as the hearings degenerated into a sideshow of a very different sort than had occurred in the previous week. On 30 October, after only eleven of the unfriendly witnesses had testified, Parnell Thomas suddenly and unexpectedly suspended the hearings, with assurances that they would resume within a matter of weeks. (The sudden stoppage was never explained, and it would be another three years before HUAC resumed its investigation of Hollywood.) One of the eleven, the German playwright Bertolt Brecht, testified that he was not a Communist and promptly left for France. The remaining unfriendly witnesses, all of whom had been cited for contempt, were dubbed the "Hollywood Ten"—writers Lester Cole, Dalton Trumbo, Albert Maltz, Samuel Ornitz, John Howard Lawson, Alvah Bessie, and Ring Lardner Jr., directors Edward Dmytryk and Herbert Biberman, and producer Adrian Scott.[90]

The Ten returned to Hollywood and, by some accounts, were confident they had faced down the committee and weathered the storm. That was hardly the case. Although HUAC had confirmed virtually none of its charges, still it had been eminently successful. Congress voted overwhelmingly on 24 November to cite the Ten for contempt of Congress. That same day, Eric Johnston convened a two-day, closed-door session in New York's Waldorf-Astoria Hotel with about fifty top industry executives from both the Hollywood studios and the home offices in New York. On 25 November, Johnston, on behalf of the industry, issued what came to be known as the Waldorf Statement.[91]

"Members of the Association of Motion Picture Producers deplore the action of the 10 Hollywood men who have been cited for Contempt of Congress," the statement

*Appearing confident, the "unfriendly" witnesses and their attorneys pose in
Washington on 27 October 1947, as the HUAC hearings entered their second week.
John Howard Lawson (third from left in front row) was cited earlier that day for con-
tempt of Congress.*

began, and it went on to state that none of the Ten would be employed in Hollywood
"until such time as he is acquitted or has purged himself of contempt and declares under
oath that he is not a Communist." And on the "broader issue of alleged subversion and
disloyal elements in Hollywood," the producers asserted that they would not "knowingly
employ" any Communists or subversives. The producers recognized "the danger of
hurting innocent people" and also "the risk of creating an atmosphere of fear," and they
invited "the Hollywood talent guilds to work with us to eliminate any subversives; to protect the innocent; and to safeguard free speech and a free screen."[92]

Thus, the Ten were sacrificed to political expediency, and the Hollywood powers
instituted blacklisting—a practice that technically was illegal in California but that the
studios rationalized via the "morals" clause in workers' contracts. (That rationale ultimately held up in court.) The *Motion Picture Herald* reported in early December that
the talent guilds were "reluctant to rush to the aid of the cited ten but . . . equally reluctant to accept blacklisting as an industry policy."[93] But the guilds and the labor unions
ultimately did accept the blacklist—which was, after all, only a step beyond the loyalty
oaths already mandated by Taft-Hartley.

Gallup's ARI conducted a public opinion study of the HUAC investigation and, interestingly enough, concluded that it would be "easy to overestimate the harm done to

date." The public was evenly split about the way the hearings were handled, and only 10 percent felt that there were "many Communists in Hollywood"—a figure consistent with public opinion about other industries and labor organizations. But that 10 percent included many "citizens over 30 years of age," who happened to be the most strident anti-Communists and also, crucially, the most infrequent moviegoers in the United States. Because this group "offers the greatest opportunity for increasing domestic revenues," said the ARI, their response "warrants serious consideration."[94]

The Ten were tried for contempt in the spring and summer of 1948; all were found guilty, fined, and sentenced to prison terms. They appealed the sentences and also filed a suit against the studios' blacklisting policy in May 1948; SWG filed a similar suit in June. Not surprisingly, considering the cold war mentality of the courts as well as government and industry, all of those legal efforts failed. One clear indication of that mentality was the June 1949 ruling by the U.S. district court of appeals in Washington in the Lawson and Trumbo cases. "No one can doubt in these chaotic times that the destiny of all nations hangs in the balance in the current ideological struggle between communist-thinking and democratic-thinking peoples of the world," said the court. Movies are "a potent medium of propaganda dissemination," and Hollywood "plays a critically prominent role in the molding of public opinion." Thus, reasoned the court, "it is absurd to argue, as these appellants do, that questions . . . [which] require disclosure of whether or not they are or have ever been a Communist, are not pertinent questions."[95]

An "atmosphere of fear" was indeed permeating the landscape, and although the Hollywood producers accepted and even exploited that climate, they scarcely created it. As Robert Sklar has aptly noted, "The behavior of the studios during the period was contemptible, but given their unwillingness to take a stand on principle (along with nearly every American university, newspaper, radio and television station, and the vast majority of intellectuals), what choice did they have?"[96]

The Hollywood labor unions and talent guilds also buckled under to HUAC and to public opinion—even the writers guild, which, as Victor Navasky points out in *Naming Names,* was a "vocal critic of HUAC's practices" but ultimately followed the same pattern as the other guilds, "condemning the Committee's practices but conceding its premises."[97] While Navasky makes a valid point, there is no question but that SWG paid dearly for its leftist bent and its "vocal" challenges of HUAC and the anti-Communist forces. The guild emerged from the HUAC debacle with its reputation tattered, its authority undercut, and its organization in utter disarray. Moreover, its fate stood in sharp contrast to that of the Screen Actors Guild, which not only survived but continued to flourish in the turbulent postwar era. As Gorham Kindem points out in the following section, these two different fates had as much to do with changing economic conditions as the charged political climate.

SAG, HUAC, and Postwar Hollywood

Gorham Kindem

The Screen Actors Guild enjoyed steadily increasing power and influence during the 1940s, owing mainly to the vital importance of top stars in the volatile and uncertain movie industry. In the postwar era, SAG's stature also signaled a shift in the relations of industry power, as the studios' long-standing control of stars—and of the star system in general—began to erode.[98] At the same time, an anti-Communist ideology shared by many stars who were guild leaders reflected the mutual financial interests and a new degree of labor-management cooperation between SAG and the studios.

This cooperation was largely a function of SAG's domination by top stars, of the unique status of stars as workers within the Hollywood system, and also of a basic rift within the guild between the elite stars and the low-salaried rank-and-file players. As the industry's most visible and bankable assets, movie stars also represented a breed of worker very different from their colleagues in the other talent guilds. This difference was evident in not only SAG's privileged status with the producers but also the role which the guild played during the 1940s in the labor disputes and the anti-Communist crusade. SAG generally supported the producers' position concerning strikes, jurisdictional disputes, and even the post–HUAC blacklisting of the late 1940s. These principal issues involved not only national ideology and industry politics but also the mutual economic interests of Hollywood's top stars and its major studios powers.

SAG's postwar rapport with the producers contrasted sharply with the labor-management antagonism which had led to the guild's formation in the 1930s. A relatively conservative union which emerged during a period of fierce labor dispute, SAG was formed in reaction to the studios' attempt in early 1933 to enact both the 50 percent salary cuts and the salary-fixing provisions of the NRA. Responding to public outcry during the Depression about the industry's high-salaried personnel, studio executives sought to extend the salary cuts to movie stars. While previous attempts by stars to organize collectively had been either co-opted or undercut by the studios, SAG succeeded for several reasons: the number of top stars involved; its avowed autonomy from the New York stage actors' unions and relative independence within the AFL; and the Supreme Court's validation of the National Labor Relations Act (the Wagner Act) in April 1937.

This last event served as a catalyst for SAG's official formation and recognition by the studio-producers in May 1937, within days of a SAG vote indicating that 90 percent of its members favored a strike. In that initial agreement, the studios granted SAG a 90 percent closed shop and made a number of important concessions which benefited lower-paid actors by establishing and clarifying minimum standards of employment. In the early 1940s, SAG achieved 100 percent closed-shop status—in other words, only guild members could appear in major studio films—and by then its interaction with the producers was characterized by a spirit more of cooperation than of antagonism.[99]

This cooperation revealed conflicts in the makeup of SAG itself, as well as the guild's paradoxical status as a Hollywood labor union. SAG traditionally had boasted about the altruistic motives for its founding (evinced in the guild motto, "He best serves himself who serves others"), and its major focus had always been to preserve and protect the economic interests of both its lowest- and its highest-paid members. But the background of most stars and feature players was not working-class but middle-class, and the incomes of some stars rivaled those of top studio executives.[100] Meanwhile, the vast majority of SAG's members were relatively little-known players who were low-paid and infrequently employed. Classification of members within SAG gave the more prosperous, more visible, and better-known actors more power, and it eventually led to the departure of screen extras from SAG in 1945.

SAG's fundamentally conservative bent and rapport with the producers first became evident in the guild's involvement with IATSE and the jurisdictional disputes before and after the war. As seen in chapter 2, that earlier dispute involved IATSE and the United Studio Technicians Guild (USTG) in 1939, and it occurred while SAG was still strug-

Screen Actors Guild meeting in 1946. Seated at center (with gavel) is SAG president Ralph Morgan.

gling to establish its own identity and autonomy within the film industry. SAG initially was favorably disposed to the USTG, but the guild became embroiled in its own jurisdictional dispute with the American Federation of Actors (variety actors in nightclubs, cabarets, and vaudeville), which was linked to IATSE. In the heat of the battle between the USTG and IATSE, SAG abandoned the former and forged an agreement with IATSE to protect itself from any incursion by the American Federation of Actors into its domain. While this strategy proved most effective, it brought the guild into an alliance with the IATSE—a labor organization with its own rapport with the producers, albeit one involving collusion, racketeering, and extortion.[101]

SAG again found itself allied with IATSE immediately after the war in IATSE's jurisdictional battle with the Conference of Studio Unions (CSU). But now SAG was operating from a position of strength and seeking to further enhance its power within the industry. The CSU had the support of non-AFL unions, the CIO, and most of Hollywood's independent unions, including the Screen Writers Guild. IATSE had the support of most AFL unions and the producers, who vowed to break the CSU and its leader, Herb Sorrell. Early on, SAG had remained neutral and even tried to broker a settlement, but the guild eventually backed IATSE.

Key to the IATSE-SAG alliance was Roy Brewer's vehement anticommunism, which he shared with several SAG officers—most notably the reformed liberal Ronald Reagan, who became president of the guild in early 1947.[102] IATSE portrayed itself as the bulwark of Americanism throughout its battle with the CSU, and its anti-Communist agenda clearly coincided with SAG's. Indeed, in 1946 the guild had publicly stated that it "has in the past, does now and will in the future rigorously oppose by every power which is within its legal rights any Fascist or Communist influence in the motion picture industry or ranks of labor."[103]

The labor dispute and anti-Communist crusade brought SAG into an alliance of sorts not only with IATSE but with the producers as well. in fact, a special subcommittee of the House Committee on Education and Labor investigating the CSU-IATSE dispute in 1946–1947 took note of this alliance. The hearings were confined to labor grievances and excluded testimony about alleged communism and racketeering. In September 1946, the subcommittee chair, Carroll D. Kearns, a Pennsylvania Republican, made an allegation of conspiracy and collusion between IATSE and the producers, and he suggested that they were aided by unnamed officers and employees of the Screen Actors Guild. Little came of Kearns's hearings, however; they were concluded in September 1947 with a mild condemnation of conspiracy between the producers and IATSE.[104] By then, of course, another House committee, HUAC, had stolen the industry spotlight and the political climate had changed considerably. The CSU was broken, the Taft-Hartley Act had supplanted the Wagner Act, and an anti-Communist—and anti-labor—agenda dominated the proceedings.

SAG avoided HUAC's wrath because of its conservative leadership, its implicit alliance with management, and its avowed anticommunism. This last point is obvious perhaps, but it clearly involved more than simply geopolitical and cold war ideology. The postwar leaders of the guild—Leon Ames, Robert Montgomery, Ronald Reagan, and George Murphy—were staunchly anti-Communist, as were most voting members, by all accounts.[105] But that scarcely explains the motivations behind SAG's opposition to the CSU, SAG's failure to come to the aid of its own members and those in other guilds who were blacklisted, and its general support of producer policies.

To ensure their respective positions of power, IATSE, the producers, and SAG allied in the anti-Communist crusade to rid the industry of "troublemakers." It was convenient for these groups to portray the CSU strike in early 1945 as Communist-inspired, despite the fact that, according to Nancy Lynn Schwartz, the Communist Party opposed the strike and supported the no-strike pledge out of solidarity with the United States as a Soviet ally.[106] in fact, failure initially to support the strike stimulated dissent within the Communist Party. Meanwhile, IATSE publicly adhered to the no-strike pledge, but it also threatened a projectionist shutdown if the producers attempted to conclude negotiations with the CSU. The efforts by SAG, IATSE, and the producers to save the industry from communism clearly were also motivated by a desire to maintain the status quo and protect their common economic self-interests.

SAG's support of the producers and alliance with IATSE also proved to be a crucial factor in the 1947 HUAC investigation and its aftermath. Significantly, all three groups adopted essentially the same position with regard to Communist influence—admitting that radicals, leftists, and even a few CP members had infiltrated their midst and then relying on their own outspoken anti-Communist avowals to convince Parnell Thomas and his committee of their zero-tolerance for these contaminants. This view was hammered home repeatedly in the HUAC testimony by SAG's past and present officers Robert Montgomery, George Murphy, and Ronald Reagan. As Reagan stated in his testimony:

Despite the appearance of cooperation in this October 1946 Los Angeles Times *photo of CSU and SAG officers, the two labor organizations were bitter opponents in the postwar era. Second from left is CSU chief Herb Sorrell; third from left is reformed liberal and future SAG president Ronald Reagan.*

Ninety-nine percent of us are pretty well aware of what is going on, and I think within the bounds of democratic rights . . . we have done a pretty good job in our business of keeping these people's activities curtailed. . . . We have exposed their lies when we came across them, we have opposed their propaganda, and I can certainly testify that in the case of the Screen Actors Guild we have been eminently successful in preventing them from, with their usual tactics, trying to run a majority of the organization with a well-organized minority. (1947 HUAC hearings testimony, p. 217; see also David Prindle, *The Politics of Glamour* [Madison: University of Wisconsin Press, 1988], pp. 53–54)

It should be noted that the SAG officers were included among the friendly witnesses, along with the Alliance members Adolph Menjou, Robert Taylor, and other stars. The one actor among the nineteen unfriendly witnesses, Larry Parks, was not called to testify and continued to work after the 1947 hearings—although he eventually was blacklisted in the course of HUAC's second investigation of Hollywood in the early 1950s.

In November 1947, when HUAC cited the Hollywood Ten for contempt of Congress and the producers issued the Waldorf Statement that they would not employ known Communists, SAG threw its support behind the producers' declaration. SAG did so

despite the pleas of the other guilds, particularly the Screen Writers Guild, which advocated coming to the aid of members who had been cited. In a meeting of the SAG
board on 8 December 1947, Leon Ames argued against supporting the Writers Guild in
its quest to overturn the firings of those cited for contempt of Congress. Ames declared,
"I believe that we must approve their [the producers'] actions in firing the five [mem-
bers of the Writers Guild], from a public relations standpoint, if nothing else," and he
offered two reasons to support the producers' position. The first was that movie stars,
as highly visible members of the Hollywood community, had an obligation to demonstrate their opposition to communism. According to Ames, "enemies of our country . . .
have no right to share in the bounty of our land while conspiring against the American
people." Ames's second reason, which he admitted was "a selfish one," was that, as
highly paid actors, the more prominent members of SAG needed "to protect the economic welfare of the industry."[107]

Ames's second reason for supporting the Waldorf Statement alludes to a fundamental philosophical and economic link between the producers and movie stars—and their
reluctant alliance with IATSE as well. Three of the greatest potential threats to the economic welfare of the industry from both the producers' and stars' viewpoints were (1)
exhibition shutdowns by projectionists, (2) boycotts of films by audiences due to the
unsuitable (read "Communist") content of films, and (3) outside regulation of film content by some agency of the federal government. Producers who were disgruntled with
the leftist leanings of screenwriters and the radical activities of the craft unions found an
acceptable excuse to scapegoat Sorrell and screenwriters like Biberman and Lawson by
supporting IATSE and HUAC. Since many of the most popular and valuable movie
stars seemed unlikely candidates to be cited for contempt of Congress or to be blacklisted, producers saw that cooperation with HUAC would preserve their autonomy and
protect their economic interests. SAG shared those interests and clearly found it prefer-
able to accede to the corruption of IATSE than to succumb to the radicalism of the
CSU, and to support the Waldorf Statement rather than come to the aid of blacklisted
talent—especially if these were less valuable and powerful guild members.

While blacklisted guild members were left to fend for themselves, SAG's lower-paid
rank-and-file members faced severe struggles of a different sort, owing to changes in the
economics and structure of the industry. The general box-office decline and reduced
revenues meant that what the studios had traditionally considered resources and
assets—including contract stars and players—now looked more and more to them like
liabilities. Stars and other personnel under exclusive, long-term contracts suddenly
became expendable. The *Paramount* decree and other antitrust rulings aggravated the
industry's economic problems, further encouraging the studios to reduce overhead and
production costs while stimulating independent production.

For top movie stars, these dramatic structural changes in the postwar film industry
were actually an advantage. Freedom from studio domination and control and renewed
market competition gave many stars greater control over their own careers and a chance
to become actively involved in production. A key factor was the steady shift to a package-unit system as the primary organizational mode of Hollywood production. As Janet
Staiger suggests, the package-unit system "was a short-term film-by-film arrangement,"
and was directly related to the market-induced need "to differentiate the product on the
basis of its innovations, its story, its stars, and its director."[108] With the shift to a package-
unit system, a star's participation and bankability were essential to obtain funding.
Moreover, the increased competition and greater uncertainty in the postwar market-

place proved to be a windfall for the most popular stars as their talent agents bargained for higher and higher salaries and percentages of the profits.

While the top stars were able to turn the changes in the industry to their own economic advantage, their success obscures the fact that the demand for and incomes of less popular actors and actresses fell dramatically during the postwar era. Because of rising costs and declining production in the late 1940s, fewer actors were actively employed in production. The percentage of production costs in the average film budget paid to actors dropped from 25 percent in 1947 to 20 percent in 1948.[109] Many less popular stars moved into television while the most popular stars, who feared overexposure might jeopardize their careers, restricted themselves to film. And the studios, ironically enough, lacking any incentive to develop new stars through their own apparatus and with fewer actors under long-term contract, often looked to competing media for new stars, and especially to the television and recording industries.

As the decade ended, SAG was still the dominant labor force in Hollywood, although it compromised both its own founding principles and the welfare of many of its members to maintain that status. But in the midst of the widespread public outcry against the alleged Communist infiltration of the movie industry, it is not surprising that SAG's leadership and its top stars, as the most visible members of the Hollywood community, felt obliged to demonstrate their opposition to communism. And it clearly was in the actors' economic best interests to cooperate with both the producers and HUAC, even though such cooperation was inconsistent with SAG's altruistic union aims (not to mention IATSE's) and with unionism's presumed struggle between workers and management. The "altruism" of anticommunism shared by SAG and IATSE was based in part on corruption, the quest for individual power, and the middle-class bourgeois values which the leaders of these labor organizations shared with the producers. This is not to suggest that communism posed no real threat to the democratic ideals of the Hollywood unions or to the American political system in general, or that the goals of the Communist Party were purely altruistic. It suggests, rather, that economic preservation and a pragmatic response to the industry's shifting power structure were the primary motives behind SAG's postwar anti-Communist strategy.

Postwar Censorship

While the studios and leading labor forces buckled under to HUAC and the pervasive cold war mentality, the movie industry was being pressured by external conservative forces in other areas as well, particularly in terms of motion picture content. Various conservative institutions, from religious organizations like the Catholic Legion of Decency and the Protestant Motion Picture Council to the state and local censorship boards and even the U.S. Congress, sought to rein in Hollywood's postwar "liberal" inclinations by regulating subject matter. And perhaps inevitably, these efforts became entangled in the other political developments of the period, adding yet another complex dimension to the movie industry's postwar travails.

During the war, the American cinema had matured in many ways, from its heightened social awareness and growing penchant for realism to its treatment of more complex human issues. Many looked to the cinema to take on an even more progressive posture after the war, and as will be seen in more detail in chapter 13, that was in fact what the movie industry did. In the late 1940s, a number of trends and cycles—*noir* thrillers and "adult Westerns," message pictures and social problem films, sex farces and romantic melodramas—displayed a frankness and sophistication quite advanced by Hollywood standards. Meanwhile, European imports continually challenged conventional representations of social conditions and human relationships. While Hollywood's independents tended to be the more progressive filmmakers, even the conservative studios were pushing the boundaries of cinematic expression. The Fox executive Darryl Zanuck, who championed both the social problem film and the semidocumentary crime drama, asserted in 1946 that in the heady postwar climate, Hollywood "can sell almost anything but politics and religion."[110]

The first serious postwar censorship flap involved a film produced before the war and released in 1943, THE OUTLAW. The producer, Howard Hughes, reissued his adult Western in March 1946 to capitalize on the favorable market conditions. In an odd replay of earlier events, Hughes's refusal to cooperate with either the Legion of Decency or the Production Code Administration resulted in a "C" rating from the Legion and removal of the film's Code seal by the PCA. Hughes personally handled the release and promotion of the film, and he deftly manipulated these controversies—along with the local censorship challenges and boycott threats almost everywhere the film played—to fuel audience interest.[111] That led the PCA to challenge Hughes's marketing campaign as well, and ultimately to overhaul its own advertising code. Many deemed Hughes's efforts counterproductive; as *Variety* put it, "The move toward liberalization of censorship . . . has been pretty well shelved by the current ruckus over 'The Outlaw.'"[112] Still, Hughes defied the Legion of Decency and the PCA, and THE OUTLAW was among the biggest box-office hits of the decade.

While the ongoing dispute over THE OUTLAW seemed little more than an extended and somewhat harmless publicity stunt, more serious altercations developed in 1947 over DUEL IN THE SUN, MONSIEUR VERDOUX, and FOREVER AMBER. Selznick's intense Western psychodrama, DUEL IN THE SUN, suffering no doubt from guilt by association with THE OUTLAW, faced a succession of local censorship setbacks, including an outright ban in Memphis. In June 1947, with HUAC gearing up for its assault on Hollywood, Congress announced that it was considering an investigation of the MPAA and the PCA because of the "filthy and obscene" pictures being released by Hollywood, and Rankin introduced a resolution to ban DUEL IN THE SUN from further showings in the D.C. area. (The resolution failed.)[113]

Chaplin's MONSIEUR VERDOUX, a dark comedy marketed as a "sex farce" about the French Bluebeard, was withdrawn from release after a disastrous Broadway opening in April 1947 amid threats of boycott and a torrent of negative publicity directed not only at the film but also at Chaplin's left-wing politics. Matters grew worse when Chaplin received a subpoena from HUAC and then publicly declared that he planned to reopen VERDOUX during the hearings—a strategy that later was abandoned and certainly would not have helped Chaplin's cause. While Chaplin escaped the immediate wrath of HUAC (he was not called to testify), MONSIEUR VERDOUX was an unmitigated popular and commercial disaster upon general release during the same week of the HUAC hearings.[114]

FOREVER AMBER, also released during that fateful week in October 1947, was promptly—and unexpectedly—hit with a C classification by the Legion of Decency. That event was lost in the din generated by the hearings, but as Bosley Crowther wrote in the *New York Times,* "If it hadn't opened against the Washington shindig, [AMBER's C classification] might have . . . bid for the doubtful distinction of being the major 'incident' of the year."[115] Significantly enough, Fox's multimillion-dollar sex farce was

Charlie Chaplin and Martha Raye in Chaplin's ill-fated postwar satire MONSIEUR VERDOUX *(1947)*.

coscripted by Ring Lardner Jr. (of the Hollywood Ten) and Philip Dunne (cofounder of the Committee for the First Amendment). The writers' affiliations may well have been a factor, since the Legion felt compelled to announce that the condemnation was based "solely on the film itself."[116]

Fox's president, Spyros Skouras, reacted angrily, noting that Breen and the PCA had complimented Fox's handling of Kathleen Winsor's sensational best-seller. This response scarcely diminished the criticism: boycotts were threatened by various religious and conservative political groups, including the American Legion. So despite the fact that FOREVER AMBER was the top box-office film in the country in November 1947—owing in part, no doubt, to the controversy itself—Fox acquiesced. The studio withdrew AMBER from release in early December, removed or reshot the offending passages, and had the film back in release within two weeks—with its Legion of Decency classification upgraded from C to B ("objectionable").[117]

While it is difficult to ascertain whether the film's box-office performance was helped by the controversy, the popularity of FOREVER AMBER did suggest that the moral judgments and pressure tactics of the Legion of Decency and the American Legion did not necessarily reflect the opinions of the general public. Still, the efforts of such groups intensified in the postwar era and were directed at film imports as well as Hollywood pictures. Indeed, foreign films were even more offensive to these conservative groups, overall, than the American-made pictures. During the 1947–1948 season, the Legion assigned B classifications to just under 15 percent of Hollywood studios releases; mean-

Cornel Wilde and Linda Darnell in FOREVER AMBER *(1947), the controversial "sex farce" which earned a "condemned" rating from the Catholic Legion of Decency.*

while, over one-third of foreign imports were so classified, and six of the eighty-seven imports classified by the Church were condemned. In 1948–1949, the number of B-rated Hollywood films reached 20 percent, while the number of objectionable imports surpassed 40 percent.[118]

Many filmmakers, studio executives, and critics lamented the pressure by conservative groups, but the groups themselves felt they were fighting a losing battle—particularly as Hollywood increased the on-screen emphasis on both sex and violence in 1948 and 1949 in an effort to stem losses at the box office and appeal to adult viewers. In late November 1949, PCA chief Joe Breen complained to the conservative Catholic publisher Martin Quigley: "We are really having a desperate time of it. During the past month at least, more than half of the material submitted has had to be rejected. We have had nothing like this situation since the early days of 1934."[119]

As Breen certainly realized, however, the industry could scarcely intervene in 1949 as it had in 1934, when Will Hays created the PCA and thus put teeth into the Production Code. Sharpening those teeth by updating the Code or strengthening PCA enforcement was now out of the question, owing less to economic conditions and recalcitrant filmmakers than to the federal government's antitrust campaign. The prospect of theater divestiture threatened the MPAA with the loss of its implicit control over the exhibition end of the business, which it had long maintained through the studios' affiliated chains and selling policies. In other words, theater divestiture would make the Code seal—and the Code itself—essentially meaningless.

The Antitrust Campaign and the Paramount *Decree*

Like so many of the problems dogging the movie industry during the 1940s, the government's antitrust campaign took on a new intensity after the war. The Justice Department had eased its trust-busting efforts during the war, and in fact the only significant antitrust decision against the film industry had involved not the studios but the large unaffiliated theater circuits. In March 1943, the Crescent circuit was found guilty in federal court of restraint of trade in a five-state region in the Southeast. The *Crescent* decision was important to the government's case against the studios as well, however, since it successfully challenged key aspects of vertical integration, particularly the trade policies which enabled the studios and large unaffiliated circuits to control specific regions and markets and to restrain independent exhibitors.[120]

The *Crescent* decision was upheld by the Supreme Court in late 1944, bolstering the Justice Department's view that the major studios as well as the big circuits were vulnerable to antitrust litigation.[121] In the wake of that court decision, and with the war finally coming to an end, the newly appointed attorney general, Tom Clark, decided to reactivate the Paramount case against the major studios. Once again, theater-chain divorcement was the major objective in an overall effort to dismantle the vertically integrated studio system. In October 1945, the Justice Department and the eight studio-distributors returned to New York federal district court, resuming the antitrust battle that had been dormant since 1940.[122]

The government completed its case by late November 1945, and a ruling was handed down by the three-judge panel in June 1946. That ruling was essentially a split decision favoring the studios, and thus it appeared that Hollywood's good fortunes at the box office in 1946 might be matched in the courts. The court found that the eight majors indeed had conspired in what amounted to a nationwide restraint of trade, but it was their sales policies, ruled the court, not the Big Five's theater ownership, that was the primary factor in this restraint. "It would seem unlikely," said the court, "that theater owners having aggregate interests of little more than one-sixth of all the theaters in the United States are exercising such a monopoly of the motion picture business that they should be subjected to the drastic remedy of complete divestiture in order to effect a proper degree of free competition."[123]

"Film Biz Beats Divorcement," blared a page-one banner headline in *Variety*, and indeed this was a tremendous victory for the studios.[124] But the court did rule against the studios on several other major points: it outlawed price fixing, block booking, and all "sweetheart" arrangements between the studios and unaffiliated circuits; it severely curtailed run-zone-clearance policies; it ordered the Big Five either to assume full ownership or to sell off any theaters in which their holdings were between 5 and 95 percent. And in what soon proved to be the most troublesome and controversial outcome of the case, the court demanded that a system of competitive bidding be established to ensure that films were sold on a strict film-by-film, theater-by-theater basis.[125]

Attorney General Clark still was not satisfied. He publicly criticized the court for falling short of theater divorcement, and he vowed to appeal the decision.[126] Nonetheless, in late 1946 a U.S. statutory court upheld the June 1946 decision and issued a new consent decree in line with that ruling.[127] At that point, the Justice Department began a series of formal appeals to the Supreme Court, which agreed to hear the case.[128]

Meanwhile, Justice's pursuit of the large unaffiliated theater circuits also yielded mixed results. After the war, the government's chief targets were the Schine and Griffith circuits in the Northeast and Southwest, respectively. In June 1946, only weeks after the *Paramount* ruling, a federal judge in Buffalo, New York, found Schine guilty of antitrust violations and ordered the circuit to divest seventy-five of its theaters (the total was later reduced).[129] Then in October, a federal judge in Oklahoma found the Griffith circuit not guilty of virtually identical charges. Predictably, appeals were filed in both cases, and they would work their way to the Supreme Court.[130]

While the government battled the studios and unaffiliated circuits on behalf of the nation's independent exhibitors, several independents won significant antitrust victories on their own. In February 1946, the Supreme Court upheld a lower court ruling that the studios and large circuits had conspired to prevent the Jackson Park Theater in Chicago from securing first-run bookings. Then in July, in another federal lawsuit, the Jackson Park was awarded "treble damages" for unreasonable clearance: the competing circuits and studio chains had to pay Jackson Park three times the estimated profits that were lost owing to a mandatory seven-day clearance behind a nearby Balaban & Katz theater—with the latter's gross receipts used as one measure to determine the award.[131] A similar federal court ruling later in the year on behalf of William Goldman Theaters in Philadelphia against the Warner-Stanley chain dealt yet another blow to the industry's entrenched run-zone-clearance system. It also encouraged other exhibitors to sue, and by late 1946 similar cases were filed in Detroit, Baltimore, Memphis, St. Louis, and several other major first-run markets. Both the studios and the unaffiliated circuits appealed the rulings, adding to the tangle of antitrust litigation working its way through the higher courts.[132]

Thus, while 1946 saw an unprecedented number of major court cases involving antitrust suits against the movie industry, the issues were far from resolved. The studios clearly remained at the center of virtually all the antitrust action—even cases involving

Leading independent exhibitor William Goldman, whose lawsuit against the Warner-Stanley chain reached the Supreme Court as part of the Paramount *suit.*

the unaffiliated theater circuits, since the circuits' power was essentially a function of favorable treatment by the studios. The majors were encouraged by the favorable rulings on divorcement to keep battling the Justice Department; their resolve only intensified, no doubt, with the deteriorating economic conditions after 1946. Quite obviously, the loss of the studios' theater revenues, coming in the midst of economic crises both at home and abroad, would mean financial disaster.

The year 1947 was relatively quiet on the antitrust front, although the din of complaints about the court-mandated auction-bidding system grew louder with each passing week. The auction system was hardest on independent exhibitors, precisely those whom it was intended to help. The independents simply could not compete with the larger and better-financed theater circuits, and yet they still had to live with the rising cost of film rentals that inevitably accompanied an auction system. With their interests in both production and exhibition, the majors had a more ambivalent reaction to the new system. While auctioning drove up rental fees and thus benefited production and sales operations, the majors' theater affiliates were livid that their once-guaranteed product flow was now subject to the whims of a more competitive marketplace.[133]

While the antitrust action against the movie industry may have slowed somewhat in 1947, the government's overall trust-busting crusade heated up considerably. A key factor was Truman's campaign strategy, which brought the administration and the Justice

Department into an alignment that would have been unthinkable in the Roosevelt years. As the *Wall Street Journal* noted in August 1947, "The Truman administration has big new plans for hewing a trust-busting program as the capstone of its 1948 presidential campaign."[134] The Federal Trade Commission was on the antitrust warpath as well, and by late 1947 antitrust suits had been filed against many major industries, from cement and sugar to steel and auto tires.[135]

Many of these cases wound up being argued before the Supreme Court in 1948, including various appeals involving the movie industry. By early 1948, the Court had agreed to hear appeals by all of the principals in the recent antitrust cases—the studios, the circuits, and the independent exhibitors as well as the Justice Department. At that point, three distinct types of antitrust cases had emerged: the government's suit against the studios demanding an end to unfair trade practices and theater-chain divorcement (i.e., the Paramount case); the government's suits against the large unaffiliated circuits for conspiring with the studios to monopolize certain regions of the country (the Griffith and Schine cases); and the independent exhibitors' suit against the studios and circuits for withholding product and unreasonable clearance (the Goldman case). These three types of antitrust litigation clearly were interrelated, and thus the Supreme Court decided to consider the Schine, Griffith, and Goldman cases along with the Paramount case, and to rule on all of these cases together.[136]

The Supreme Court handed down its momentous *Paramount* decree on 3 May 1948, with Justice William O. Douglas writing a single opinion on the Paramount, Griffith, and Schine cases and making a separate ruling on the Goldman case. The gist of the Court's unanimous *Paramount* decision can be summarized in four points: first, the mere existence of monopoly power, whether lawfully or unlawfully gained, is basis enough for an antitrust judgment; second, it is not necessary to find specific intent to restrain trade, simply that such restraint results from the defendants' business conduct; third, the Sherman Act can be violated by prevention of competition as much as by destruction of competition; and finally, any theater under any ownership is subject to an antitrust judgment if the theater was acquired or maintained as a result of unreasonable restraint of trade.[137]

The Court ruled against the defendants—the eight majors and the two theater circuits—in all three cases. In the Paramount, Schine, and Griffith cases, the Court sent the suits back to the lower courts for review and for new judgments in line with its findings. In the Paramount case, the Supreme Court asked the New York district court to reconsider theater divorcement, noting that the majors' cooperative control of the first-run market clearly amounted to monopoly practice. The Court upheld the ruling against Schine and reversed the not-guilty ruling in the Griffith case; in both cases, the lower court was instructed to reconsider the extent of the circuit's monopoly and to write a new decree accordingly. And the Court simply refused to review (thus upholding) a lower court judgment in the Goldman case, which awarded the independent exhibitor treble damages of $375,000.[138]

Not surprisingly, given the convoluted history of the decade-old antitrust suit, no one in the industry could quite believe that it was over. And for a while it seemed that perhaps it was not. Among the Big Five, only RKO was willing and ready to comply with the ruling. By November 1948, RKO had worked out a consent decree with the government whereby the studio would divest its theaters by creating a separate exhibition company.[139] Paramount began discussions with the Justice Department in late 1948, but the other majors refused to abide by the *Paramount* decree, hoping to forestall divestiture through interminable legal actions or, failing that, to work out some form of partial

Supreme Court Justice William O. Douglas, author of the
May 1948 Paramount *decision.*

divestiture. Thus, in its year-end review, the 1949 *Film Daily Year Book* stated: "New and most important chapters in the lengthy serial, the so-called New York equity suit, were written in 1948, but not finis."[140]

Not "finis" perhaps, but close to it. Paramount in early 1949 grudgingly signed a consent decree, agreeing to create a separate exhibition company by year's end and to initiate a three-year divestiture process.[141] Once Paramount yielded to divestiture, the handwriting was on the wall, and in fact the Paramount agreement provided a veritable blueprint for the other studios' inevitable divorcement. As the *Motion Picture Herald* stated, the February 1949 consent decree between Paramount and the government represented "a foundation on which the entire future production-distribution-exhibition organization of the industry may be built."[142] Still, Warners, Fox, and Loew's/MGM—now referred to in the industry as the "Big Three"—fought on. Injunctions were filed and arguments heard in New York federal district court, and in July *Variety* ran a headline predicting "No Divorcement Until '55," based on the assumption that "legislation will stall it for years."[143]

Only days later, however, the federal court ordered the Big Three to divest, virtually mandating a divorce procedure like that conducted by RKO and Paramount.[144] Loew's filed yet another appeal to the Supreme Court (which would be refused), but the federal court ruling effectively ended any efforts to sustain the crumbling oligopoly. Aptly enough, the first company to divest was Paramount, and in a corporate reorganization that officially took effect at what was quite literally the end of the decade. At the stroke of midnight, 31 December 1949, Paramount Pictures Incorporated effectively ceased to exist and was replaced by two new entities: Paramount Pictures Corporation, a production-distribution company under Barney Balaban, and United Paramount Theaters, a chain of 1,115 theaters under Leonard Goldenson.[145]

The Paramount divestiture clearly marked not only the end of the decade but the end of an era for the American motion picture industry. Earlier that year, in fact, *Fortune* magazine ran one of its occasional in-depth pieces on the industry under the title "Movies: End of an Era?" The question mark in that title might well have been an exclamation point, as the ensuing cutline well indicated: "With box office down, foreign revenues cut, critics pained, older fans dwindling, reorganization at hand and television looming, the motion-picture industry may be turning a historic corner."[146]

Fortune also noted "a panicky feeling in the air" in 1949 Hollywood, since "the brunt of the recent decline fell . . . on independent producers and on the production end of the integrated companies."[147] Indeed, although the entire American movie industry was pulled into the postwar maelstrom, at the very center of that vortex were the Hollywood studios. And what was at stake was far more than the financial well-being of the major companies, but the very structure of the industry and the nature of the Hollywood studio system itself.

10

The Hollywood Studio System, 1946–1949

In the movie industry's roller-coaster postwar ride from the unprecedented heights of 1946 to the panic of 1949, the Hollywood studio powers underwent enormous changes. Their way of doing business and of making movies changed radically in a few short years as the industry peaked and began its rapid descent. In the process, euphoria steadily gave way to a deepening malaise and a growing nostalgia for Hollywood's halcyon days. By 1949, in fact, trade papers were wistfully invoking the prewar era as "the golden age of Hollywood production."[1] And there was also a bitter desperation about the current state of the industry—made all the worse by the economic conditions in the nation at large. "Hollywood," lamented one major producer in 1949, "is an island of depression in a sea of prosperity."[2]

The studios would endure, of course, and in fact their survival instincts proved to be remarkably acute in the chaotic and uncertain postwar era. In the short term, survival was primarily a matter of controlling costs. *Fortune* magazine deemed Hollywood's "cost-cutting program" of 1948–1949 "the severest the movie colony has known since the great depression."[3] In late 1949, Thomas F. Brady of the *New York Times* wrote, "Hollywood's economy, declining from the 1946 peak of excess profits and lavish waste, reached a nadir early in the year and leveled off." But over the past year, said Brady, the studios "emerged from a state of panic and settled down to the production of films on a reasonable and, by previous standards, a business-like basis."[4]

While controlling costs enabled the studios to survive the postwar downturn, the key to industry fortunes remained the exhibition sector. The theater end of the business was far more profitable than the production end in the postwar era, owing in large part to inflated ticket prices. In January 1948, *Variety* reported that in terms of overall revenues, "the real lifeline has been the company-owned theater chains." *Variety* estimated that of the nearly $100 million in total studio profits for the previous year, roughly 70 percent came from the majors' affiliated chains. The increasingly "steadying influence" these chains had on the majors in a difficult time was "a bright sign for the future if the U.S. Supreme Court permits the Big Five to hold on to them."[5]

The Court did not, of course, and thus a governing irony for the postwar movie industry was that the companies with the most to lose in the antitrust battle—the integrated majors—enjoyed, until divorcement took effect, even greater hegemony than ever, owing to market conditions. This position clearly favored Paramount, with its chain of over 1,200 theaters, while Fox and Warners (with about 500 houses each) held the middle ground. The once-dominant MGM (with only about 125 theaters) steadily lost ground but still remained profitable throughout the late 1940s, thanks to the superiority of both its pictures and its distribution operation. The only integrated company to lose money in the late 1940s was RKO; not only were its holdings limited (about 100 theaters), but it suffered from chronic management troubles. Meanwhile, the three major-minors, without the relative security of theater holdings, struggled simply to stay afloat.

Performance is clearly tied to studio holdings in the postwar studio profits and profit shares outlined in table 10.1:

Table 10.1
STUDIO PROFITS AND PROFIT SHARE, 1946–1949

Company	Profits ($ millions)	Share of Profits
Paramount	110.8	36.0%
20th Century–Fox	68.4	22.0
Warner Bros.	63.7	20.6
Loew's/MGM	38.6	12.5
RKO	14.0	4.5
Columbia	8.7	2.8
Universal	3.5	1.1
United Artists	.2	.06

SOURCE: Joel Finler, *The Hollywood Story* (New York: Crown, 1988), pp. 286–87.

Hollywood began its postwar decline in 1947. That decline accelerated in late 1947, when the effects of falling attendance and the lost British market began to take their toll, and by 1948, as the figures in table 10.2 indicate, every studio was losing ground:

Table 10.2
REVENUES AND PROFITS OF THE BIG EIGHT
STUDIOS, 1947–1948 ($ MILLIONS)

COMPANY	1947		1948	
	GROSS INCOME	NET PROFIT	GROSS INCOME	NET PROFIT
Paramount	186.8°	28.2	170.4	22.6
Warners	164.6	22.1	147.1	11.8
Fox	174.4	14.0	163.4	12.5
Loew's/MGM	161.8	10.5	164.4	4.2
RKO	123.1	5.1	110.0	0.5
Columbia	48.8	3.7	46.9	0.6
Universal	65.0	3.2	58.0	(3.2)
UA	32.0	.5	24.7	(0.5)

°The figures from the two sources do not always correspond; in those instances, Finler's more reliable figures appear. Keep in mind that for the five integrated majors, the gross includes income from both picture rentals and from affiliated theaters.

SOURCE: Joel Finler, *The Hollywood Story* (New York: Crown, 1988), pp. 286–87; *Variety*, 5 January 1949, p. 35.

Besides the general economic downturn, these figures signal several other important postwar developments. First, the integrated majors were making a great deal more in gross revenues and profits than the other companies. Second, a larger portion of the majors' gross income was being retained as profit (i.e., they had wider profit margins). Third, more extensive theater holdings led to proportionately higher revenues and profits. And fourth, to state the obvious, business was declining rapidly. in fact, the falling gross revenues and profits for all the studios would not only continue but accelerate over the coming years with only one exception: Universal's losses bottomed out in 1948 and 1949, and it was the only studio to actually increase revenues and profits in the early 1950s. The Big Five suffered their heaviest losses in 1950—and afterwards, of course, as they began to divest their affiliated theaters.

The figures in table 10.2 also indicate the dwindling profit margins for all of the studios in the late 1940s, and in fact the decline in profits was far more severe than the decline in gross revenues. From 1946 to 1949, the studios' total box-office receipts fell from an all-time high of $1.7 billion to $1.45 billion, a drop of about 14 percent; meanwhile, profits plunged from a record $120 million to $33.6 million, a three-year drop of over 70 percent. Rising production and operating expenses were the main reason for the squeeze, and thus the studios steadily intensified their efforts to cut costs—not only film budgets but also the operating costs of the studio-factories themselves. The belt-tightening was done without significant reductions in overall output. The Big Eight had averaged about thirty-three releases per year in the later war years (1943–1945). This average fell to just under thirty-one releases per annum from 1946 to 1949, with the major-minors accounting for most of the decline. (The Big Five averaged some twenty-nine releases per year from 1943 to 1945, and twenty-eight from 1946 to 1949.)

During the war boom, film costs had inflated considerably, as has been seen, and the majors had helped fuel the inflationary trend by concentrating so heavily on first-run product. They continued this strategy through 1946; the *Wall Street Journal* noted in November that the "big studios" had all but eliminated low-budget production to concentrate exclusively on A-class pictures.[6] In 1946, the average feature film cost about $665,000, roughly double the cost five years earlier.[7] That year, MGM reportedly spent an average of $1.6 million per feature, Paramount $1.5 million, Warners $1.3 million, and Fox $1.25 million. Columbia, Universal, and RKO were close to the industry average, while Republic spent under $500,000 and Monogram only about $200,000 per picture.[8]

The majors' production expenditures paid off in 1946 and early 1947 as top features continued to return record grosses. But as economic conditions worsened, the studios began cutting production and operating costs—an effort that began in earnest in late 1947 after Britain initiated the 75 percent *ad valorem* tax. By 1948, cost-cutting had become a way of life at all of the studios. Reviewing the year 1948 in the *1949 Film Daily Year Book*, the industry analyst J. P. McGowan described "the policy that has been established in most of our studios. Shooting schedules have been reduced 50 percent. Budgets have been cut in half." McGowan reported that the studios had reduced the number of A pictures from 136 in 1947 to 100 in 1948, while increasing B output from 110 to 156. He noted, too, that several companies—including Universal, RKO, and Warners—had actually suspended production in 1948, relying on backlogs while reorganizing and streamlining operations to further cut costs.[9]

Actually, none of the majors achieved quite the reductions that McGowan described, but the cost-cutting was substantial. The *Wall Street Journal* reported in 1949 that budgets and schedules were down roughly 25 percent at the major studios since their post-

*RKO in 1946, by far its most successful year of the decade—although the postwar eco-
nomic crunch would force the studio to suspend operations only two years later.*

war peak. In 1946, for example, Paramount's features had required an average of 55.2
shooting days; in 1949, the average was down to 41.3 days. Paramount's average budget
was down from $1.95 million in 1947 to $1.5 million in 1949. Fox, meanwhile, had cut
its budgets for top features from $2.35 million in 1947 to $1.785 million in 1949.[10] At
year's end, *Variety* announced that Paramount and Fox had set strict budget ceilings (of
$1.5 million and $1.75 million, respectively) on their high-end features. *Variety* also
reported industrywide budget reductions of 25 percent.[11]

Overall, the studios' efforts to control production costs proved to be effective and
were especially impressive in light of the heavy inflation throughout the U.S. economy
in the late 1940s. Hollywood's total production expenditures had doubled during the
war, climbing from around $200 million in 1942 to just over $400 million in 1946, but
over the next three years they rose less than $10 million.[12] The average feature budget
did move past the $1 million mark in 1948, more because of inflation, however, than lax
studio cost controls. in fact, a recent study calculating Hollywood feature production
costs adjusted for inflation found that budgets had increased 100 percent from 1940 to
1946—the biggest periodic leap, by far, in Hollywood's history—but actually declined
about 5 percent from 1946 to 1950.[13]

While the studios focused their cost-cutting campaigns primarily on reducing budgets and shooting schedules for individual films, they pursued other strategies as well. The postwar trend to location shooting was motivated, in part at least, by the fact that production and labor costs were lower outside California, particularly in New York City. The studios also eschewed high-priced presold story properties—or virtually any presold properties, for that matter—relying more heavily on original screenplays. In 1947, the studios spent $4.35 million on screen rights to stage plays; in 1948, they spent only $350,000—the lowest total in two decades, according to the *Motion Picture Herald*.[14] In 1949, *Variety* reported a continued "sharp upswing" in original screenplays; by then, roughly 70 percent of Hollywood films were based on original stories.[15]

The principal means of cutting studio overhead and general operating expenses was simply reducing the labor force; wages had climbed even faster than the rate of inflation after the war. In January 1945, there were 31,000 employees in Hollywood on a combined payroll of $192 million. Within a year, the payroll was $240 million—a 25 percent increase—for roughly the same number of workers. By January 1948, the workforce had declined by some 1,500 while payroll rose to $314 million, having climbed another 30 percent in two years. By then, the studios were cutting both operating costs and the number of employees, and within two years (as of January 1950), the total payroll was reduced to $230 million and the studio workforce to 17,500 employees. Thus, the studios managed to bring wages back to about the 1946 level, but only by eliminating over one-third of their workforce in the span of two years.[16]

Several other factors should be mentioned here in relation to Hollywood's cost-cutting campaign. One was that economies were virtually forced on the studios by lending institutions. With the general inflationary trend in the United States after the war, as well as the decline of the movie industry (which made it an increasingly risky investment), the studios faced higher interest rates and tighter credit terms.[17] These constraints were especially hard on independent producers, but the studios felt the pinch as well. Another factor was the studio management control that accompanied cost-cutting. Simply stated, the tighter economy meant tighter management, which for filmmakers meant that much of the hard-won autonomy and creative control they had enjoyed during the boom years was now lost. Tight money also meant limited opportunities for independent producers, and so many of them, especially producer-directors, returned to the studio fold in order to finance their films—and thus had to submit to tighter management controls.

Another significant factor was the general reassessment, especially by the majors, of both the first-run market and the value of top product in the late 1940s. Given the overall decline of the industry and growing uncertainties about the effects of the suburbanization of the late 1940s on major urban markets, the studios avoided high-cost, high-stakes productions. Indeed, top hits were rare in the late 1940s owing in large part to the fact that the studios simply stopped making the lavish spectacles and pre-sold "event" pictures which were most likely to become major box-office hits. This strategy was confirmed by the late-1940s dearth not only of big moneymakers but even of more modest "sleeper" hits.

Given the uncertain postwar marketplace and the increasing need to cut costs, the studios' management and marketing operations were more important than ever—more so than at any time since the early 1930s, when Hollywood responded to the Depression. And as in that earlier period of sustained (and deepening) crisis, these operations at virtually all of the Hollywood studios underwent extensive and lasting change.

Studio Operations and Market Strategies

THE MAJOR STUDIOS

Paramount Pictures dominated the movie industry throughout the postwar era because of its massive theater holdings, superior resources, and stable and capable management setup. Barney Balaban continued to run the company and to oversee sales and exhibition out of the New York office. Frank Freeman managed the studio, mainly handling contract negotiation and labor relations with the studio's 3,200 employees, while Henry Ginsberg guided filmmaking operations.[18] Paramount had a classic top-down management structure, with virtually all decisions emanating from Balaban. in fact, an inviolable company policy was that Balaban had to approve any expenditure over $100. Balaban gave his top executives ample authority, however, and Ginsberg clearly ruled studio filmmaking operations. As a 1947 *Fortune* profile of the company asserted: "The focus . . . in the whole studio, inevitably, is on Ginsberg. He is the man who makes the decisions in picture making, and although he is in constant consultation with other executives, from Balaban on down, his is the final word."[19]

Paramount's postwar output was essentially a continuation of its wartime efforts—a succession of light comedies and romantic dramas, punctuated by an occasional Road picture with Hope, Crosby, and Lamour (ROAD TO RIO in 1947), an occasional DeMille epic (UNCONQUERED in 1947, SAMSON AND DELILAH in 1949), and an occasional Wilder-Brackett triumph (A FOREIGN AFFAIR in 1948). Hope, Crosby, and Alan Ladd continued to be its dominant stars, with William Holden on the rise and top freelancers like Gary Cooper, Barbara Stanwyck, and Olivia de Havilland coming in for one- and two-picture stints.

Paramount enjoyed tremendous success in the mid to late 1940s, setting an industry record with profits of over $15 million in 1945 and then far surpassing that total in each of the next three years. Its most profitable year was 1946, when net proceeds were nearly $40 million.[20] Significantly enough, even during that period of routine $3 million rentals, the company's record pace owed far more to its "highly profitable and strategically located theater holdings" than to its hit films, as Balaban told *Variety*'s Ira Witt in 1946. "Balaban's disclosure," stated Witt, "indicates that the theater end continues to be the bigger money-getter of the film business."[21] At the time, Paramount had a stake in roughly 1,500 theaters, including about 250 overseas. It held majority ownership in some 1,200 theaters in the United States, most of which were located in major markets. And because of the relative size of these houses, Paramount controlled roughly one-eighth of all the theater seats in the United States (1.45 million out of a total of 11.4 million).[22]

Paramount responded relatively quickly to worsening market conditions in 1947, and by mid-1948 the studio had reduced its overhead by a reported 30 percent.[23] Paramount also reissued films very aggressively throughout the late 1940s, keeping literally dozens in circulation at any given time. This reliance on reissues was more than an effective defensive market strategy; it also enabled Balaban to test his conviction that Paramount's old films would be vital to its anticipated move into television.[24] Indeed, Balaban's hopes for television as the key to Paramount's future helps explain his willingness to divest the all-important theater chain without a serious fight after the *Paramount* decree. By 1949, the company had pretty well abandoned theater-based video projection, and Balaban saw Paramount's future television plans primarily in terms of feature film distribution through Paramount-owned TV stations (see chapter 13). Thus, Balaban, despite his extensive background in exhibition, decided to stay on with Paramount

Pictures after divestiture rather than take over the newly created United Paramount Theaters.

Twentieth Century–Fox, Paramount's chief competitor through the postwar era, also enjoyed stable and capable management, led by Spyros Skouras in New York and Darryl Zanuck at the studio. As in earlier years, Fox's postwar output evinced a fundamental split between Technicolor hokum on the one hand—chiefly Betty Grable musicals and Tyrone Power costume adventures—and relatively ambitious, socially astute drama on the other, much of it supplied by producer-directors like Otto Preminger and Joe Mankiewicz. The latter ranged from *noir* thrillers and realistic crime films to women's pictures and social problem dramas, all trends which Fox developed and dominated in the late 1940s. Perhaps the best example of the studio's split personality can be seen in the two late-1947 films which finished among the top ten box-office hits of 1948: CAPTAIN FROM CASTILE, a color costume drama starring Tyrone Power and directed by the spectacle specialist Henry King, and GENTLEMAN'S AGREEMENT, a drama about anti-Semitism starring Gregory Peck, produced by Zanuck, and directed by Elia Kazan.

Like most of Fox's postwar successes, these were solid but unspectacular hits. Fox relied on a steady supply of profitable A-class films, which it delivered in the late 1940s perhaps as consistently as any studio besides MGM. Moreover, owing to Zanuck's practical approach to the marketplace, Fox relied more heavily on B's than any other major. Actually, Fox hedged its bets in this area by phasing out active B production at the studio in 1946, dismissing the head of the B unit, Bryan Foy (who went to PRC), and subcontracting B-picture production to independent low-budget producers like Sol Wurtzel, Ben Pivar, and Bernard Small. These moves gave Fox considerable flexibility, enabling Zanuck to revert to a high-output strategy, all through outside producers. (The twenty-one B's Fox produced for the 1947–1948 season account for the studio's one-year surge from twenty-seven releases in 1947 to forty-five in 1948). When the strategy did not pay off, Zanuck simply scaled back Fox's outside B commitments, although its thirty-one releases in 1949 still included a few B pictures.[25]

Another measure of Zanuck's pragmatism was his willingness to shoot pictures away from the studio to curb escalating production costs. Fox helped start the trend toward location shooting in 1945 with THE HOUSE ON 92ND STREET, the first film of the era to be shot entirely on location in New York City. That was done more as a production experiment (at the behest of the producer Louis de Rochemont) than as a cost-cutting measure, but by 1947–1948 brutal inflation and labor problems had Fox (and other studios) mounting "runaway" productions for economic reasons as well. in fact, by 1948 Zanuck sometimes had more pictures being shot on location than at the studio.[26]

Like Paramount, Fox was considering its television options as the ascendancy of the new medium and theater divorcement appeared increasingly inevitable in the late 1940s. For Fox, the principal thrust was in video projection for theaters through a cooperative research and development effort with RCA; Fox also actively pursued a plan to purchase ABC-TV in 1948. But as with Paramount, Fox's move into television would be undercut by the FCC in the wake of the 1948 antitrust decree.[27]

MGM, more than any other studio, actively sustained the studio system at all levels during the postwar era, continuing to produce relatively expensive A-class star vehicles and to keep more top talent under contract than any other company after the war. The studio still had nineteen directors and eighty stars under contract in 1949, for example, fifty of whom were top-billed.[28] For its high-end product, Metro continued to rely on costume pictures, historical romances, and especially musicals, many of them in

Seated behind the top executives of Loew's/MGM (Dore Schary, at left; sales chief William Rogers, center; Louis B. Mayer, third from right) at this 1949 sales meeting are the distribution executives who kept the company afloat in the postwar era.

Technicolor. in fact, in 1948–1949 MGM produced twenty-two of Hollywood's seventy-four color releases.[29] And as mentioned earlier, MGM concentrated more on distribution and sales than did its theater-heavy major counterparts.[30]

Thus, MGM did quite well in terms of both gross revenues and rental income in the late 1940s. Combining *Variety*'s annual lists of leading moneymakers from 1946 to 1949, MGM accounted for 65 of the 316 most successful films (versus Fox with 55, Paramount with 49, Warners with 47, and RKO with 40).[31] Cost-efficiency was another matter, however: MGM's steadily narrowing profit margins reached crisis proportions by 1948, when its gross revenues of $164 million, roughly on a par with both Fox's ($163.4 million) and Paramount's ($170.4 million), yielded profits of only $4.2 million, far below Fox's $12.5 million and Paramount's $22.6 million.[32]

At that point, Loew's chief executive, Nick Schenck, and his board of directors demanded that Mayer make wholesale changes in MGM's production and management operations and its general market strategy. The most significant changes involved studio management. In late 1947, Metro announced a realignment of its executive staff and "an abandonment of the executive producer system, which has been in effect for more than 10 years"—that is, since the death of Irving Thalberg in 1936, when Louis B. Mayer initiated his management-by-committee system. Then, in early 1948, Schenck issued his now-famous directive to Mayer: "Find another Thalberg." That resulted in the July 1948 hiring of Dore Schary as the vice president in charge of production (at a salary of $6,000 per week). On his arrival, Schary promised to make "good films about a good world," including five to ten "progressive" films per year—a rather dubious prospect in those days perhaps, but one consistent with Schary's liberal bent.[33]

Schary was successful in reducing production and operating costs at MGM without compromising the overall quality of the company's products. His role, in essence, was to oversee all production except for the musicals, most of which were handled by the producers Arthur Freed (EASTER PARADE, 1948; ON THE TOWN, 1949) and Joe Pasternak (A DATE WITH JUDY, 1948; IN THE GOOD OLD SUMMERTIME, 1949). MGM continued to turn out lavish costume pictures and adaptations like THE THREE MUSKETEERS (1948) and MADAME BOVARY (1949) as well, but Schary's overall effort to reduce both the costs and scale of production was effective. Among MGM's biggest hits in 1949, in fact, was ADAM'S RIB, a lean, high-energy Tracy-Hepburn comedy directed by George Cukor in only thirty-seven days. And Schary did manage to turn out a few "progressive" films, notably an adaptation of William Faulkner's INTRUDER IN THE DUST and his own production of BATTLEGROUND in 1949.[34]

Dore Schary's move to MGM followed a massive shake-up at RKO in May 1948 after Howard Hughes purchased the company from Floyd Odlum. As mentioned earlier, Schary had arrived at RKO in late 1945 to manage a multi-film package put together by David Selznick, and Schary stayed on with the studio after the death of the production chief Charles Koerner in 1946. Under Koerner, RKO had finally achieved stability and financial success, recording profits of over $12 million in 1946 and settling into an ideal balance of modest in-house productions and more ambitious pictures from allied independents like Goldwyn and Disney. Schary shifted from outside producer to production head in January 1947, and among his primary objectives was to upgrade the quality of RKO's high-end productions. The strongest of the in-house A pictures were *noir* thrillers like CORNERED (1945), THE SPIRAL STAIRCASE (1946), and CROSSFIRE (1947). RKO's outside productions in 1946 included some of the best films of the postwar era, including THE BEST YEARS OF OUR LIVES, NOTORIOUS, and IT'S A WONDERFUL LIFE. The studio also scored with two Cary Grant vehicles, THE BACHELOR AND THE BOBBY-SOXER (1947) and MR. BLANDINGS BUILDS HIS DREAM HOUSE (1948), both initiated under Schary's regime.

Schary's efforts to upgrade in-house production increased RKO's revenues in 1947, although its profits fell to $5 million. Still, the studio was clearly in better shape than at any period in its troubled twenty-year history. Hughes's buyout of RKO in May 1948, within days of the *Paramount* decree, effectively ended the climb to profitability. Shortly after his takeover, Hughes fired RKO's president, Peter Rathvon, and closed down the studio, rendering it "practically non-existent during its process of reorganization," according to *Film Daily*'s J. P. McGowan.[35] RKO eventually resumed production, but Hughes's obsessive quest to cut costs, root out subversives, and control production kept the studio in complete turmoil. Hughes ran the company until 1954, but the studio never regained its stability or financial health. The Hughes purchase, as Douglas Gomery aptly states, "signaled the end of RKO as a serious movie concern."[36]

Warner Bros. moved completely to a unit system in the postwar era. Steve Trilling, Jack Warner's longtime aide and casting director, was named executive assistant in charge of production in 1945, but he had far less control over the actual filmmaking process than top producers like Henry Blanke and Jerry Wald or producer-directors like Michael

Curtiz and John Huston. The most significant of these, without question, was Jerry Wald. Allegedly the model for Budd Schulberg's hero Sammy Glick in *What Makes Sammy Run?*, Wald had been Warners' most prolific writer in the late 1930s and developed into an efficient and successful associate producer during the war. Wald hit his stride as a producer in 1945 with two solid hits, OBJECTIVE BURMA and MILDRED PIERCE, and by the late 1940s he was personally producing eight to ten pictures per year—almost half of Warners' output. These tended to be the company's more action- and male-oriented product, although Wald handled Joan Crawford's pictures as well. Meanwhile, Blanke produced most of Warners' prestige pictures, notably its Bette Davis vehicles.[37]

Warners produced very few top hits during the postwar era but did turn out its share of solid box-office performers. Most characteristic perhaps was its string of Bogart vehicles, including THE BIG SLEEP (1946), DARK PASSAGE (1947), THE TREASURE OF THE SIERRA MADRE (1948), and KEY LARGO (1948). A 1947 adaptation of the long-running Broadway hit LIFE WITH FATHER was the only Warners release from 1946 to 1949 to earn over $5 million (it returned $6.25 million), and remarkably enough, in 1949 Warners failed to place a single film even in the top twenty-five. By then, Harry and Jack Warner had closed the studio and were overhauling studio operations and in 1948–1949 began phasing out the contracts with many of its biggest long-term stars, including Bette Davis,

Jerry Wald was Warners' top producer in the postwar era until the company sold his contract to Howard Hughes in 1950.

Humphrey Bogart, Errol Flynn, and Edward G. Robinson. Davis left in 1949 and did not work at the studio again until the early 1960s. More typical was the pattern established by Cagney and Bogart, who played out their contracts but returned for occasional one-picture deals over the next few years.

In early 1950, with divorcement imminent, the Warners began to trim the producer ranks as well. In February 1950, Jack Warner renegotiated Henry Blanke's fifteen-year contract (signed in 1945), cutting his salary and giving him an "advisory capacity" with the studio.[38] In June 1950, Warner sold Jerry Wald's contract for $150,000 to Howard Hughes and RKO—where Wald lasted only a few months before leaving to start his own independent company.[39] The demotion of Blanke and departure of Wald indicated how serious the Warners were about revamping operations and cutting costs. In what was perhaps the consummate irony in the studio's history, Warners' net profits of $10.3 million in 1950 were the highest of any studio. This was the first time Warners had ever finished at the top of the Hollywood heap, but the achievement resulted less from hit pictures than from the elimination of studio personnel to reduce overhead.

THE MAJOR-MINORS AND MINOR STUDIOS

Columbia, Universal, and UA, like the major studios, peaked immediately after the war and in 1947 began a rapid, steady fade. UA and Universal suffered parallel and fairly severe declines, and both companies posted losses in 1948. Columbia, which had not posted a deficit in its history, managed to keep that streak alive through the late 1940s. in fact, it was the only nonintegrated motion picture company, including Republic, Monogram, and Eagle-Lion, to avoid posting losses in the late 1940s. Columbia's management team of Joe and Harry Cohn was crucial to its modest postwar success, as were a few well-timed hits like GILDA and THE JOLSON STORY in 1946, and JOLSON SINGS AGAIN in 1949. Columbia also developed an unlikely star in Broderick Crawford, who scored in ALL THE KING'S MEN (1949) and BORN YESTERDAY (1950).

Columbia always had relied on outside producer-directors for one or two high-class productions per year, but in the late 1940s Harry Cohn began signing multipicture deals with independent companies—including the companies of stars, such as Gene Autry Productions in 1947 and Humphrey Bogart's Santana Productions in 1948.[40] By mid-1949, remarkably enough, Columbia had nine independent pictures in the works and was the most active distributor of independent productions besides UA. Most of these were crime dramas and social problem films rather than the romantic comedies that had been Columbia's trademark in earlier years, although the company did reissue most of its comedy hits from the Depression and prewar era. And as always, Harry Cohn relied on B pictures and series programmers for the company's bread and butter.[41]

Universal had, of course, been relying on in-house independents and outside talent for its A-class pictures throughout the 1940s, and in the immediate postwar era it moved even more emphatically in that direction. In August 1946, J. Cheever Cowdin and Nate Blumberg merged Universal with International Pictures, an independent production company run by Leo Spitz and William Goetz that specialized in prestige productions. The merger was orchestrated by the British producer J. Arthur Rank, who already had an elaborate coproduction and codistribution deal with Universal.[42] Rank clearly planned to play a major role in the reorganized company, albeit from a considerable distance. In terms of studio operations, Goetz and Spitz were to supervise all production at Universal-International, with Cliff Work staying on as "senior studio executive." All B production, including Westerns, was to be phased out as the company concentrated on some twenty-five first-run pictures per year.[43]

At the time of the merger, Universal already had contracts with independent film-makers like Walter Wanger, Fritz Lang, and Mark Hellinger, who leased studio space and distributed what were essentially coproductions through Universal. Now similar deals were cut with Ben Hecht, Garson Kanin, Sam Wood, Douglas Fairbanks Jr., and others. Complex international distribution arrangements also were worked out with Rank and Alexander Korda. In terms of in-house production, Spitz and Goetz eliminated all low-budget series and set a minimum length of seventy minutes for all features. Universal still turned out subpar product as well, but that was scaled back along with the company's overall output. After averaging fifty releases per year during the war (by 1944–1945 roughly twice the majors' output), Universal cut its annual output to thirty-five pictures after the merger.

The results of the Universal-International merger were critically favorable but commercially disastrous. For the first time in a decade, Universal pictures were on ten-best lists and in contention for major Oscars. Not since 1937–1938 had any Universal release been nominated for best picture, best director, best actor, or best actress. Then, from 1946 through 1948, Universal scored ten nominations in these categories. All ten were for outside productions or imports, and seven went to nominees who never set foot on the Universal City lot—including Laurence Olivier, who directed and starred in HAMLET, which won Oscars for best actor and best picture of 1948. But by then it was evident that Universal could ill afford the high cost of prestige. The company had gone into a financial tailspin after the merger, falling from record profits of $4.6 million in 1946 to a net loss of $3.2 million in 1948.

So it was back to basics at Universal City—high-volume, low-cost formula films for the subsequent-run market. And it was back to the old management regime as well. Universal phased out its arrangements with outside producers, along with the management team of Spitz and Goetz (though the two did remain at the studio), while the long-time plant manager Edward Muhl took over production. Universal reversed its market strategy as well, turning from the competitive and uncertain first-run market to the less lucrative but more consistent subsequent-run market. After the *Paramount* decree, escalating rental prices for top features forced smaller exhibitors to settle for second-rate product, and Universal planned to supply it. Key to this effort were several low-budget series initiated late in the decade, notably the Abbott and Costello Meet . . . series begun in 1948, the Ma and Pa Kettle series in 1949, and the Francis the Talking Mule series in 1950. All were targeted for small-town and rural markets, which generally were poorly served by Hollywood except for B-Western production, and all were enormously successful.

The three minor studios, Republic, Monogram, and PRC, also found it tough going in the late 1940s. The British studio Eagle-Lion bought PRC in 1947, securing a distribution setup in the United States and also a source of low-budget product for Britain. While the deal marked yet another effort to exploit the favorable market conditions, the late-1940s industry decline in England and the United States severely undercut this venture.[44] Meanwhile, Monogram and Republic, like the other studios, earned record profits in 1946—$1.1 million for Republic, and $397,000 for Monogram. While minuscule by the majors' standards, these profits were sufficient to encourage both companies to upgrade production. Though financially trying in the short term, upgrading was crucial to their long-term survival. Monogram in 1947 created Allied Artists, a wholly owned subsidiary through which it released productions with budgets ranging up to $1 million, most of them produced by outside independents. Republic in the late 1940s began producing "Premiere" productions, the term it used to designate its high-end releases, which cost $500,000 to $1 million and were done exclusively through arrangements with outside independents.[45]

Independent and Unit Production

Like the major studio powers, Hollywood's major independent producers saw their fortunes swing wildly in the late 1940s. During the immediate postwar period, independents enjoyed tremendous success. Never had industry conditions been better suited to their interests, and never had so many filmmakers sought commercial and creative autonomy. The independent ranks included low-budget specialists like Sol Wurtzel and the team of William Pine and William Thomas as well as mid-range producers like Mark Hellinger and Jack Skirball. But the prestige-level independents garnered the lion's share of the publicity and the revenues in the peak postwar period. in fact, most of the runaway hits released just after the war were independent productions, notably THE BELLS OF ST. MARY'S (McCarey for RKO) and SPELLBOUND (Selznick-Hitchcock for UA) in late 1945, and then in late 1946 THE BEST YEARS OF OUR LIVES (Goldwyn-Wyler for RKO) and DUEL IN THE SUN (Selznick-Vidor for SRO), the two biggest hits of the decade.

The clearest signal of Hollywood's independent-minded shift at the peak of the war boom was the 1946 Universal-International merger, which brought the studio's management, production, and marketing operations in line with the independent movement. But there were scores of other moves to independence in that heady "the sky's the limit" era. In November 1946, as the merger was finalized, the *Wall Street Journal* ran a page-one story on Hollywood's independent outbreak. "Stimulated by the ravenous demand at the box-office and the prospects of a 'freer' market for their pictures," wrote the *Journal*, "these newcomer studios have swollen the industry to grotesque proportions." While Hollywood once could support no more than about thirty independents, now over a hundred independents described themselves as "permanent producing companies," along with the dozens of "single-picture corporations" formed by top talent for tax purposes. The power behind most of these efforts was the "bankable" talent, including stars like Bing Crosby, Edward G. Robinson, Rosalind Russell, and Joan Bennett and producer-directors like Leo McCarey, John Ford, and Howard Hawks.[46]

Because the studio-distributors and large unaffiliated chains continued to control the industry, however, the term "independent filmmaker" still was essentially a misnomer. As Walter Wanger put it, "The independent producer is a man who is dependent on the exhibitors, the studios and the banks."[47] Traditionally, most of the independents enjoyed a privileged arrangement with a studio—as did Wanger with Universal. But now there were signs of real change, especially among the more powerful (and well-financed) independent producers who challenged the established marketing and promotional practices for prestige-level productions.

One clear signal was Howard Hughes's THE OUTLAW, which finally went into widespread release in 1946 after years of wrangling with the PCA, the Legion of Decency, local censors, and the courts. With UA as distributor, Hughes handled the sales and promotion personally, proving remarkably deft at exploiting the picture in a city-by-city campaign that extended into 1948, eventually returning $5 million. Another independent production with an innovative marketing strategy was Rank's HENRY V, which was handled as a road-show special by a three-person team which took the picture from one major market to another, eventually netting some $2 million in the United States.[48]

Selznick's DUEL IN THE SUN, a Western with strong psychosexual themes that also was targeted at more sophisticated "adult" audiences, was the object of perhaps the most significant marketing innovation in the immediate postwar era. While completing the film, Selznick became embroiled in a dispute (and extensive legal difficulties) with the UA owners Charlie Chaplin and Mary Pickford, a conflict that resulted in Selznick leaving his longtime distributor. In late 1946, he created Selznick Releasing Organization (SRO) to handle the nationwide distribution of DUEL IN THE SUN. In fact, Selznick engineered DUEL from the very outset with the postwar marketplace in mind—and in the process he came up with a veritable blueprint for the calculated blockbusters of the 1950s and beyond. As he later confided to Louis B. Mayer: "I set out to make this picture partially as a challenge, partially as an exercise in making a big grossing film."[49] He succeeded, of course, though more because of his creation of SRO and unique promotion and release strategy than the quality of the film. After a heavily promoted and highly successful opening at the Egyptian and Vogue Theaters in Los Angeles over Christmas 1946, Selznick sent the picture into a massive road-show release accompa-

Gregory Peck, Jennifer Jones, and Joseph Cotten in David O. Selznick's "adult" Western DUEL IN THE SUN *(1946).*

nied by aggressive advertising in national magazines and radio as well as the press. DUEL IN THE SUN played some 8,000 road-show dates, nearly twice the number of GONE WITH THE WIND, and in far less time. Within six months, it had already played 2,000 dates and was the talk of the industry.[50]

Variety ran a story on what it termed the "blitz booking" of DUEL, "the policy of opening a picture simultaneously in as many houses as possible in each situation."[51] While *Variety's* view was upbeat, Bosley Crowther of the *New York Times* was less sanguine. He described DUEL IN THE SUN as "spectacularly disappointing" after its simultaneous May 1947 opening in thirty-eight Loew's theaters in the New York City area. Crowther also noted in his review that "a new sales technique in the film business has been cleverly evolving from scientific audience research." If the public's "want to see" scores higher than the reactions of preview audiences to the film itself, wrote Crowther, "you sell your picture in a hurry before the curious have a chance to get wise."[52]

As these developments indicated, movie exhibition and distribution were being radically redefined in 1946–1947. Because of the government's antitrust campaign (and related litigation) and other factors, the postwar era saw the steady dismantling of the studios' long-established sales practices—block booking and blind bidding, the myriad pooling, franchise, and cross-licensing arrangements—as well as the modification of run-zone-clearance constraints. Consequently, movie distribution was becoming an increasingly wide-open affair. The major independents recognized that the movie marketplace was undergoing a massive deregulation, and they devised ways to exploit it. Hughes, Rank, and Selznick all demonstrated that specialized films, particularly those geared for the first-run market, could be handled efficiently and profitably on a market-by-market and a theater-by-theater basis.

While high-end independent films were returning top dollar at the box office, they were also the costliest productions of the period. Selznick spent a reported $5 million on DUEL IN THE SUN, making it the most expensive picture in Hollywood history to date, while costs on both THE BEST YEARS OF OUR LIVES and Capra's initial postwar effort, IT'S A WONDERFUL LIFE, were about $3 million.[53] These costs were far beyond the industry average in 1946 of $665,000, and well beyond what companies like MGM and Paramount were spending even on their top features. Extravagance and waste contributed to these record budgets, although inflation and the difficulty of operating efficiently outside of a studio-factory left their mark as well. And as the market began to decline in 1947 and credit became tighter, the prospects for independent production grew increasingly dismal.

Thus, 1947 was the oddest and most contradictory year ever for independent filmmakers. *Variety* reported in its year-end survey that 1947 saw "the greatest number of new indie production units come into being in the history of Hollywood," with more than one hundred new companies formed.[54] But industry conditions no longer favored independent production—or freelance status, for that matter—and by year's end many of the newly liberated filmmakers were returning to the relative security of studio affiliation. The primary reasons for this reversal were financial, and they extended well beyond the concerns about rising costs and falling attendance.

One key reason was taxes. In July 1946, the Internal Revenue Service closed the legal loophole which rendered the single-picture corporation so attractive as an income-tax dodge. In the words of Commissioner Joseph D. Nunan Jr., "We have ruled that where single pictures are incorporated and the profits for the pictures are divided by liquidation of the corporation, that those profits will be taxed to the individuals concerned as ordinary income at ordinary tax rates instead of as capital gains at a 25 per cent rate." The ruling applied to established independents as well as to the more recent entrepreneurs, and in fact, Goldwyn's "collapsible corporations" were cited by Nunan as prime targets for an IRS audit. The new IRS regulation also was retroactive to 24 July 1943, with back taxes subject to accruing interest of 6 percent—although offending parties would not be subject to criminal penalty.[55]

Expecting Hollywood "corporations" to fight the ruling (they did), the Treasury Department also sponsored new legislation in Congress to legally close the capital gains loophole. By 1947, it was clear not only that the capital gains ruling would hold but that the economic conditions in the industry simply put too high a price on freelance status for most filmmakers. *Variety* reported that "with financial backing getting increasingly difficult to obtain and the film industry beset by uncertainties both domestically and abroad," the "moneymoon" was over for independents, who now had to "backtrack" to the studios.[56] The point was reinforced time and again that year as freelancers and independents sought out permanent financing and distribution deals with major studios. Cagney, for instance, returned to Warners in 1947 after running into trouble financing his UA unit, and he worked out an arrangement whereby he alternated percentage deals and flat salary on each Warners picture. Both Frank Capra and Leo McCarey moved their independent operations—Liberty Films and Rainbow Productions, respectively— from a quasi-independent deal with RKO to a more stable setup with Paramount in 1947, and McCarey announced that it was only a matter of time before all the major studios became "combines" for independent filmmakers.[57]

With the declining market and Britain's *ad valorem* tax, the return to the studio fold gained momentum in late 1947. In November, the *Wall Street Journal* and *Variety* ran stories, under virtually identical headlines, noting the "open door" policy at Warner Bros., 20th Century–Fox, and Columbia, studios that had not previously catered to independents. And interestingly enough, the three studios previously geared to independents—UA, RKO, and Universal—were now the three least attractive prospects for independents seeking a home. Economic conditions had forced Universal, as mentioned earlier, to resume a more modest market strategy and to phase out its in-house independent units. Hughes closed RKO for "reorganization" in mid-1948 and was not actively promoting tie-ups with independents.

Meanwhile, UA, after spearheading Hollywood's independent movement for three decades, was foundering badly in the late 1940s. As Tino Balio aptly summarizes UA's plight: "Nearly all of the majors were beginning to accommodate independents by providing financing, studio space, and attractive distribution terms. UA now had nothing unique to offer producers, and discontent with the company was heightened by the continuous quarrels of the owners. UA failed to attract any producer of distinction during the postwar period."[58]

The 1948 flap between UA and Hawks over RED RIVER was a case in point. After completing his contract with Warners in 1946, Hawks signed with UA. While preparing and producing RED RIVER, a Western starring John Wayne and Montgomery Clift, Hawks grew increasingly concerned about UA's response (or lack thereof) to worsening market conditions and about their handling of the film. On completing RED RIVER, Hawks announced that UA's distribution terms and promotional plans for the film were unacceptable, and he refused to deliver it to UA for release. He later acquiesced, but only on the condition that the film be handled by Gradwell Sears, who had recruited Hawks to UA but had been kicked upstairs to an ineffectual board position during one

Howard Hawks's RED RIVER *(1948) was his only film for UA, and his last of the decade as a "hyphenate" producer-director.*

of UA's frequent management squabbles. RED RIVER went on to earn $4.5 million and was among the top hits of the year; it was also Hawks's only project with UA.[59]

Like many independent producer-directors, Hawks reverted to freelance director status in the late 1940s, choosing to work for hire rather than deal with the risks and hassles of independent production. In 1948, he reteamed with the producer Sam Goldwyn, sacrificing supervisory control for an astounding weekly salary of $25,000 to direct A SONG IS BORN, a remake of his 1941 Goldwyn hit BALL OF FIRE. Then, in 1949, Hawks directed I WAS A MALE WAR BRIDE at Fox for the in-house independent Sol C. Siegel. Once the dust had settled from the *Paramount* decree and the industry had stabilized, Hawks returned to independent producer-director status with his own company.[60]

This pattern was followed by a number of top producer-directors (notably John Huston at MGM and Capra, Wyler, and Stevens at Paramount) in the late 1940s—settling in with a major studio as a highly paid director but without real autonomy or genuine independent status. Several top filmmakers like Leo McCarey and Charlie Chaplin simply remained inactive in the late 1940s. Others like Alfred Hitchcock maintained their independence until financial conditions forced them to retrench. Hitchcock had created Transatlantic Pictures in 1947 after he left Selznick, but after two disappointments (ROPE in 1948 and UNDER CAPRICORN in 1949), he dissolved the com-

pany and signed as an in-house independent at Warners, which had released his
Transatlantic productions.

Still others like John Ford and Orson Welles managed to maintain their independence, but only by radically lowering their sights. Welles began the postwar era at
Columbia, where he teamed with his soon-to-be ex-wife Rita Hayworth for THE LADY
FROM SHANGHAI. Welles wrote, produced, and directed the film in 1946, but it was
shelved for nearly two years by the studio boss Harry Cohn, who found it incompre-
hensible. After extensive reediting, Columbia released the film in 1948 to a disappointing popular and critical response. Welles, meanwhile, produced and directed a highly
inventive adaptation of MACBETH for Republic in 1948 (via his Mercury Productions);
he shot it in twenty-three days for under $200,000. But MACBETH also fared badly, leav-
ing Welles unemployable in Hollywood as a producer-director, although he still was
being offered up to $100,000 per film as an actor. Welles had no interest in devoting
himself to acting—or in becoming a Hollywood star, for that matter—so he set out for
Europe. His next significant opportunity, as it happened, was acting in Carol Reed's
THE THIRD MAN.[61]

Ford also closed out the decade at Republic Pictures in order to maintain his inde-
pendence. In 1946, he completed a long-term contract at Fox with MY DARLING
CLEMENTINE, and over the next few years he turned out a succession of independent
productions through Argosy Pictures with his partner and coproducer Merian C.
Cooper. Ford and Cooper kept Argosy afloat by moving from MGM (THREE
GODFATHERS, 1948) to the struggling RKO (THE FUGITIVE, 1947; FORT APACHE, 1948;
SHE WORE A YELLOW RIBBON, 1949), and finally to Republic in 1949, where their initial
productions (RIO GRANDE and WAGON MASTER, both 1950) launched Republic's risky,
extravagant move to A-class films on million-dollar budgets.[62]

Clearly the postwar picture was growing increasingly bleak for independents, especially producer-directors and small-time independents operating on a picture-by-picture
basis. A *Variety* story in May 1948, under the headline "Bell Tolls for Indie Producers,"
noted that "all but the biggest" independents—that is, Goldwyn, Selznick, Chaplin, and
Disney—were simply unable to secure financing.[63] In fact, even these major independents were struggling in the late 1940s.

As noted earlier, Selznick enjoyed tremendous success in 1946, not only with DUEL
IN THE SUN but also with the highly lucrative sale of NOTORIOUS and several other packages to RKO. But he followed those with two ambitious, costly failures: THE PARADINE
CASE (1948), a final project with Hitchcock, and A PORTRAIT OF JENNY (1948), a bloated
vehicle for Jennifer Jones and Joseph Cotten, his top contract stars, that lost virtually all
of its $4 million production cost. That picture effectively ended Selznick's career as a
major independent in Hollywood. In 1949, he decided to seek production opportunities in England—on THE THIRD MAN, in fact, for which he arranged the financing and
the U.S. distribution.[64]

Sam Goldwyn fared somewhat better in the postwar era, beginning with the tremendous success of THE BEST YEARS OF OUR LIVES in 1946. Besides its $10 million in
rentals, the picture won six Oscars, including best picture and best director (for William
Wyler), along with the Academy's prestigious Thalberg Award to Goldwyn as the industry's top producer. But after BEST YEARS, Goldwyn's key employee and longtime collaborator William Wyler left to join Liberty Films. Then, in 1948, Goldwyn suffered
another huge loss when the cinematographer Gregg Toland, who had shot almost all of
Goldwyn's sound films (thirty-seven in all), died suddenly at age 44. Goldwyn increased

his output to a steady two pictures per annum in the late 1940s, but none was of any real consequence commercially or critically, and by 1950 Goldwyn was easing into semiretirement.[65]

Disney struggled throughout the late 1940s to regain its prewar form, but with little success. The company produced no features in the late 1940s, concentrating instead on package films—compilations of up to ten animated shorts combined into a feature-length release. Disney's initial postwar release, for instance, was MAKE MINE MUSIC (1946), a seventy-minute, ten-cartoon package which included a few excellent pieces like "Casey at the Bat" and "Peter and the Wolf" but was scarcely on a par with its prewar features. By 1949, Disney showed signs of recovery with the release of ICHABOD AND MR. TOAD, comprising two exceptional longer animated works, while it had in production two full-length features, CINDERELLA and TREASURE ISLAND (both 1950)—the latter marking its move into live-action feature films.[66]

In 1949, however, the resurgence of Disney or any other independent appeared to be a long way off. As *Fortune* reported in April: "Independent production, which boomed up to more than a hundred working units in 1946 and 1947, is substantially wiped out. If the independent is producing he has cut costs, like everyone. But more likely he has suspended operations and is waiting for the market to stabilize."[67] In June, the *Wall Street Journal* reported that only about one-third of Hollywood's eighty-five independent companies "have exposed any negative so far in 1949."[68] Perhaps the future belonged to independents and freelance talent, given the thrust of the *Paramount* decree, but the present was discouraging at best, and there was no telling how long it would take for "the market to stabilize."

CASE STUDY: CAPRA, WYLER, STEVENS, AND LIBERTY FILMS

The postwar careers of Frank Capra and his two Liberty Films partners, William Wyler and George Stevens, provide illuminating examples of postwar independence in Hollywood. As seen in chapter 2, Capra had been one of the most successful producer-directors and unit filmmakers in Hollywood's classical era, and he parlayed that success into self-styled independence in 1940–1941. Capra had made films very much on his own terms both financially and creatively before joining the military, and he was determined to resume what he termed his "one man, one film" crusade once the war ended. Thus, in late 1944, Capra and the former Columbia executive Sam Briskin, Capra's unit manager during his studio days, created Liberty Films, and by late 1945 they had lined up Wyler and Stevens as partners.[69]

Wyler signed on while he was preparing THE BEST YEARS OF OUR LIVES for Goldwyn in mid-1945. Wyler had been with Goldwyn for ten years and now enjoyed an excellent profit-participation arrangement—in fact, he was set to receive 20 percent of the net profits on BEST YEARS. But despite Goldwyn's inducements to renew his contract, Wyler was determined to strike out on his own with Capra.[70]

George Stevens, fresh out of the military with no such commitments, readily signed on with Liberty, officially joining the company on 1 January 1946. The last partner to join, Stevens signed a contract that well illustrates the setup at Liberty Films. He signed on as "Producer-Director and Producer," with complete authority over all phases of production, from the inception of a project through post-production. A majority of the four partners had to agree on each project, including budget and casting, but thereafter Stevens had "sole control of the production and direction of the photoplay consistent

Liberty Films partner William Wyler.

with the budget approved for it." Liberty paid Stevens a weekly salary of $3,000, and as an equal partner (and stockholder) with Capra, Wyler, and Briskin, he shared in the company's profits. As with Capra and Wyler, this exclusive contract called for Stevens to deliver three pictures within three years.[71]

The company's title and its Liberty Bell insignia openly announced that Liberty Films was dedicated to independent filmmaking. Capra secured a line of credit with the Bank of America and a favorable financing and distribution deal with RKO, thus ensuring Liberty's freedom from studio control and leading the *Wall Street Journal* to single out the company in 1946 as Hollywood's "leading true independent."[72] Liberty would not maintain that status for long, however, owing largely to its founders' initial postwar productions. At the time of Stevens's signing, the only Liberty project in the works was Capra's IT'S A WONDERFUL LIFE. The film was budgeted at $2.36 million and set to start in April 1946.[73] in fact, Capra recalls starting it on the same day, 8 April, that Wyler started BEST YEARS for Goldwyn.[74] Both films were completed and released in late 1946 and competed head to head not only in the marketplace but at the Academy Awards banquet as well—further solidifying the stature of Capra and Wyler as two of the top filmmakers in Hollywood. BEST YEARS was by far the more successful film, and in fact, IT'S A WONDERFUL LIFE represented a setback for Liberty. Although it earned $3.3 million, the film's $3.2 million cost meant a sizable net loss for Liberty Films.[75]

Capra, meanwhile, planned even more ambitious productions, buying the screen rights to a hit Broadway play, *State of the Union,* and a recent best-seller, *Friendly Persuasion.* But RKO balked at the proposed $2.8 million budget on the former, so Capra was forced to shop the project at other studios, including Paramount and MGM. Thanks largely to Spencer Tracy, MGM took it on as a Tracy-Hepburn vehicle. Capra brought STATE OF THE UNION in under budget at $2.8 million, and when it finally was released in 1948 (after MGM held up its release for another Tracy-Hepburn picture, THE SEA OF GRASS [1947]), the film fared well commercially, returning $3.5 million. But STATE OF THE UNION did not mark a success for Capra or Liberty Films. The critical response to the film was only lukewarm, and because of MGM's sizable promotion and distribution costs, the film failed to turn a profit.[76]

The two Capra films were the only ones made under the Liberty Films trademark, and the only truly independent ventures by the company. Capra later described STATE OF THE UNION as "my last independent production," but in fact Liberty was finished as an independent enterprise even before that film was made. In early 1947, after the weak box-office showing of IT'S A WONDERFUL LIFE and RKO's refusal to back STATE OF THE UNION—and considering the tighter credit terms and the signs of a market decline—Capra began looking for a studio with deeper pockets and better distribution than RKO. In April, he closed a deal with Paramount, which purchased Liberty Films and paid each partner $1 million for his stake in the company. Paramount assumed each filmmaker's three-year, three-film commitment at the same salary ($3,000 per week) but severely limited their creative freedom and authority.[77]

Although the three filmmakers were granted producer-director status at Paramount, there was no question of studio control. As Capra described the situation, he was "an employed contract director taking orders." Thus, Capra's "one man, one film" campaign was over, and he would look back on the Paramount deal as a watershed in movie history. "The more or less continuous downward slide of Hollywood's artistic and economic fortunes that began in 1947 was triggered not by the advent of television, not by the intransigence of foreign governments," wrote Capra in his 1971 biography. "That slide was set in motion by our sale of Liberty Films to Paramount."[78]

Capra found the constraints at Paramount maddening, particularly what was termed "Balaban's law." This decreed that (a) a picture broke even at twice its cost; (b) market projections indicated that $3 million was the top box-office take at the time; and therefore (c) the production costs of top films should not exceed $1.5 million.[79] The numerous projects Capra tried in the late 1940s were nixed by the New York office because of cost, including *Roman Holiday* and *Friendly Persuasion*. After two years of frustration, he finally agreed to take on two lackluster Bing Crosby comedy-dramas in 1950–1951 (one of which, RIDING HIGH in 1950, was a remake of Capra's 1934 hit BROADWAY BILL). In 1951, Capra left Paramount, where he had suffered through what his biographer Joseph McBride aptly describes as "one of the most precipitous collapses in the career of any major American director." And as Capra readily admitted, he himself was largely to blame despite conditions at the studio and in the industry at large. Although only 54 years old, he had lost faith both in the cinema and in himself, and he retired from active feature filmmaking.[80]

Wyler and Stevens, meanwhile, each managed to turn out only one film in the late 1940s after Liberty's move to Paramount—far below what they expected or were contracted to produce, but hardly surprising under the circumstances. Like Capra, both struggled to get projects approved and under way at Paramount, although both eventually adapted to changing industry conditions and did quite well at the studio. After BEST YEARS in 1946, Wyler's next film was THE HEIRESS in 1949, an ambitious adaptation of Henry James's *Washington Square* starring Olivia de Havilland and Montgomery Clift. Critically acclaimed and nominated for a half-dozen Oscars, including best picture, best director, and best actress (which de Havilland won), THE HEIRESS did only moderate business. But Wyler was settling in at Paramount and enjoyed considerable success there over the next few years.[81]

Stevens's stint with Paramount, conversely, was an ongoing struggle with Balaban and the studio brass. His first project, an adaptation of the hit novel and stage play *I Remember Mama*, was turned down by Paramount in 1947 because of its cost. Stevens took the project to Dore Schary at RKO, where it was a critical hit and earned $3.3 million in 1948. I REMEMBER MAMA cost $3.068 million, however, and failed to break even.[82] "Balaban's law" also prohibited both of Stevens's 1948 projects, adaptations of *Madame Butterfly* and *The Young Lions*, and in early 1949 he found himself fighting the Paramount powers over yet another project. On 21 January, Stevens received a memo from Sam Briskin informing him that "Liberty Films, Inc., has disapproved your selection of Theodore Dreiser's *An American Tragedy* as the story for one of your films."[83] (Briskin, still technically a Liberty executive, was in fact working for Paramount, which now owned the company.)

Stevens responded in a memo the following day, challenging the studio's decision and asserting: "I am willing to stake my professional reputation . . . on my judgment of this property." Stevens then received a ten-page scolding from the production chief Henry Ginsberg, who asserted the studio's position in stronger terms. After outlining the troubled history of both the Dreiser novel and a 1931 Paramount adaptation, as well as a recently abandoned Wilder-Brackett adaptation, Ginsberg admonished Stevens: "We refuse to admit that your judgment is better than that of our entire production organization, our sales department, and our New York home office executive's combined. . . . We had expected that you would be most appreciative of the time and effort expended

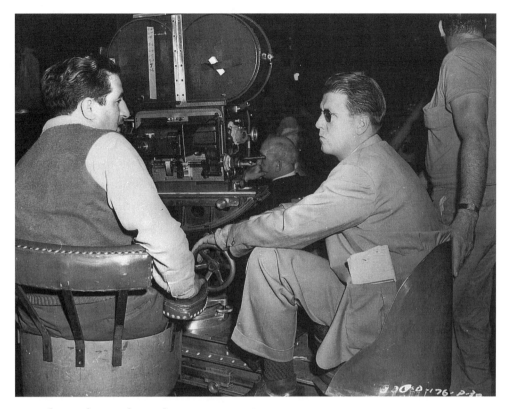

Seated at right, producer-director George Stevens.

not only by me but by everyone including Mr. Balaban in studying the advisability of proceeding with this story." Citing legal, financial, and censorship problems, Ginsberg again refused to approve the story.[84]

Stevens persisted, and the Paramount powers began to yield when he personally secured commitments from Montgomery Clift, a sudden star after RED RIVER and THE HEIRESS, and Elizabeth Taylor (in her first adult role). In September, he submitted a budget of $1,498,000, barely under the Paramount budget ceiling, and a shooting schedule of forty-five days. By then, Balaban and Ginsberg were sold on the project, now titled "A Place in the Sun," and they eventually approved a budget of $1.8 million and a sixty-day schedule.[85] A PLACE IN THE SUN was completed in early 1950 but not released until mid-1951. It was a solid commercial and critical hit, earning $3.5 million and four Academy Awards, including a best-director Oscar for Stevens.

In March 1951, Capra officially left Paramount and dissolved Liberty Films. Stevens stayed on to produce and direct SHANE (1953) before leaving Paramount for genuine freelance status. By then, independent production had returned with a vengeance, and, in fact, Wyler and Stevens were among its leading proponents. The studio system, meanwhile, was a thing of the past—at least where the movie industry was concerned. The major studios in the early 1950s responded to court-ordered dis-integration not only by divesting their theaters but by gradually phasing out feature film production, concentrating instead on movie financing and distribution. Meanwhile, the nascent TV industry steadily adopted Hollywood's factory-oriented system for "telefilm" series pro-duction, which became the industry staple in the late 1950s. Thus, factory-oriented stu-dio production persisted, albeit as a mode of TV production, and the independent film production movement that had been taking hold since the early 1940s, after weathering the stormy postwar era, emerged during the 1950s as the dominant form for making fea-ture films.

11

Postwar Stars, Genres, and Production Trends

Perhaps the single most remarkable aspect of the postwar American cinema was the overall quality and vitality of the movies themselves. Despite the declining market and mounting outside pressures, Hollywood's output in the late 1940s was, by any standards, as strong as in any period in industry history. The war and the war-related flood of new talent brought a spirit of innovation and even a certain progressivism to Hollywood. Among the newcomers were the scores of European émigrés who arrived in Hollywood before the war and had become established filmmakers. Their number also included the influx of new American talent during and just after the war, many of whom had new ideas about the cinema's potential as both a political and an artistic force—the New York dramatists Elia Kazan and Robert Rossen, for instance, who in films like GENTLEMAN'S AGREEMENT (1947) and ALL THE KING'S MEN (1949) injected a new energy and social awareness into the American cinema.

Yet another important group of progressive, American-born postwar *arrivistes*, interestingly enough, were the experienced movie colonists and top filmmakers, like Wyler, Stevens, Ford, Capra, Huston, who had left for military duty and whose postwar films evinced the profound effects of both their documentary work and the war itself. Wyler's THE BEST YEARS OF OUR LIVES (1946) and Huston's THE TREASURE OF THE SIERRA MADRE (1948), for example, provided startling evidence that Hollywood's—and the nation's—wartime experience might bring a new maturity to the American cinema.

This nascent progressivism was countered and contained by the studios, however, which gained increasing control over the industry as economic conditions deteriorated. The studios, although facing imminent extinction, enjoyed their last hurrah in the late 1940s, and their chief strategy in those uncertain times was to sustain the stars, genres, and production practices that had fueled the studio system for the preceding two decades. The system was showing signs of age—quite literally in Hollywood's population of top stars. But there were still some signs of life and vitality in the old system, best evidenced perhaps by the regeneration of the movie musical at MGM and by the studios' efficient reformulation of the crime thriller in a steady flow of trenchant *films noirs*. These were the final flashes of studio brilliance, however, in what proved to be the last gasp of the studio era.

New York stage director Elia Kazan with Spencer Tracy on the set of THE SEA OF
GRASS *(MGM, 1947). Kazan came to Hollywood with the flood of new talent
immediately after the war.*

Stars and the Star System

Since the early 1940s, the Hollywood studio system and the star system had been drift-
ing steadily out of sync, and by 1946 they showed signs of disengaging altogether. Key
factors were the increasing individual authority, diminished output, and shift to freelance status of many top stars and the pronounced turn to independent production. In
1946–1947, stars created their own companies as rapidly as leading producers and directors did, and the stars' bankable status gave them much greater clout both with lending
institutions and with studio-distributors.

Mainly because of the economic downturn and the reassertion of studio authority in
the late 1940s, however, the star system and studio system did remain in sync. While the
industry remained as star-driven as ever, the stars themselves found it increasingly difficult to maintain their independence. Like Hollywood's leading producer-directors, the
top stars declined to risk the financial hazards of freelance status or independence after
1947, returning instead to the security of a studio contract. The studios were eager to
have them back in the fold, of course, since the contract star was the key element in their
production and market strategies. Thus, the studios and stars maintained an uneasy
alliance, waiting for the myriad postwar developments to play themselves out.

Both the immediate postwar surge and the subsequent decline enabled Hollywood's established stars to dominate the industry. In the rush to independence of 1946–1947, only top stars had the leverage to form their own companies. And once the retrenchment mentality set in and stars returned to the studios, these same stars were deemed a safer investment than new talent. Thus, in the late 1940s, there was far less turnover in the rankings of top box-office stars than in the early 1940s, and there were fewer emerging stars as well.

While established stars maintained their currency in the postwar era, gauging star appeal became increasingly difficult. Since the early 1930s, Hollywood's chief means of gauging star value had been the Exhibitors' Poll. In the chaotic postwar marketplace, however, the poll began to lose its credibility and was dismissed by many as a quasi-reliable survey of conservative exhibitor tastes. Consequently, both *Variety* and Audience Research, Inc. (ARI) began measuring star value as well, employing very different methods and coming to very different conclusions about the market value of top stars. Taken together, these different polls illustrate the changing stakes and conditions in the postwar movie industry.

Beginning in January 1947, *Variety* published an index of the top box-office stars of the previous year in its anniversary issue. Designed as a more accurate gauge of a star's audience appeal and market value than the Exhibitors' Poll, *Variety's* rating included the number of pictures in release the previous year, the aggregate rentals of those pictures, and the average rentals per picture; average rentals served as the basis for a star's ranking. Thus, stars with three or four releases in a year would not have an advantage in the rankings over those who appeared in only one or two. While the *Variety* poll was in some ways a more accurate measure of box-office appeal than the Exhibitors' Poll, *Variety* acknowledged that its rankings did not reflect "a star's [box-office] power, per se, since they make no allowance for draw of co-stars or for story, director, production values and the other ingredients which make a film a top-grosser."[1]

ARI, meanwhile, had been gauging star value via social-scientific methods for a number of years, and by 1946 its "Continuing Audit of Marquee Values" was being disseminated widely and had become required reading for studio and production executives, most of whom now were willing to pay for Gallup's services. in fact, *Variety* acknowledged and implicitly criticized ARI's pervasive influence in a May 1946 article under the banner headline "Audience Research Blues." Without mentioning ARI, Variety noted that the "increasing reliance on audience research by the studios has stars looking dreadfully forward to the day when they'll [be] . . . mere percentage figures in a producer's drawer."[2] Actually, that day already had arrived, although producers undoubtedly put less stock in those figures than *Variety* suggested.

ARI, for its part, voiced no doubts about the significance and merits of its research. As its semiannual reports boldly asserted:

> This report shows a screen player's *power to sell tickets at the box office.* . . .
> The Audit does not measure talent, except as talent persuades movie-goers
> to spend money to see a particular personality. The Audit reports the per-
> centage of movie-goers interviewed in a nation-wide cross-section survey
> who say that the name of a particular player on the front of a theater would
> make them want to buy a ticket. ("Continuing Audit of Marquee Values No.
> 27" [emphasis in original] [New York, Princeton, Hollywood: Audience
> Research, Inc., September 1946])[3]

ARI's cross-section was carefully controlled to represent the nation's moviegoers, and its measures indicated interest in a player's name "without regard to title, story, other players, producer, director," or any other factor. ARI did not break down its cross-section in the reports into multiple demographic categories, but it did break out a separate category, the "Upper Price Audit," focused on interviewees who attended first-run theaters. According to ARI, this group, taken as a whole, paid an average of seventy cents per ticket (over twice the norm) and accounted for roughly 60 percent of the total box-office gross.[4]

Interestingly enough, the Exhibitors' Poll, *Variety,* and ARI came up with very different star rankings in the late 1940s—an indication perhaps of the chaotic market conditions as well as the different research methods involved. In 1946, for example, the three services provided these top-ten listings:

Table 11.1
TOP STARS OF 1946

	Exhibitors' Poll	Variety	ARI
1.	Bing Crosby	Bing Crosby	Bing Crosby
2.	Ingrid Bergman	Ingrid Bergman	Ingrid Bergman
3.	Van Johnson	Fred Astaire	Gary Cooper
4.	Gary Cooper	Dorothy Lamour	Alan Ladd
5.	Bob Hope	Gregory Peck	Cary Grant
6.	Humphrey Bogart	Clark Gable	Bob Hope
7.	Greer Garson	Greer Garson	Greer Garson
8.	Margaret O'Brien	Van Johnson	Gregory Peck
9.	Betty Grable	Gene Tierney	Spencer Tracy
10.	Roy Rogers	Joan Caulfield	Clark Gable

SOURCE: Cobbett Steinberg, *Film Facts* (New York: Facts on File, 1980), p. 58; *Variety,* 8 January 1947, p. 8, and 4 January 1950, p. 59; "Continuing Audit of Marquee Values No. 27," September 1946.

The disparity between the three polls is obvious enough—beyond the first two places, at least. Only three of the top ten stars turned up on all three lists, and ten stars appeared on only one of the lists. The 1946 rankings, however, displayed more continuity than usual for the three services. Invariably, only two or three stars turned up on all three lists, and in 1947 and 1949, *Variety's* number-one stars (Jennifer Jones and Jeanne Crain, respectively) were not even included in the top ten in the Exhibitors' Poll ranking.

The increasing fragmentation of both movie audiences and the movie industry itself in the late 1940s made any objective, scientific assessment of star value extremely difficult. in fact, in January 1949, *Variety* had sufficient reservations about its star-ranking efforts—and about star value itself under current market conditions—that it declined to offer any ranking at all. The year's top hits, asserted *Variety,* indicated "more strongly than ever the fact that the draw of star names is no more than a subordinate factor in creating an audience" for a picture. Thus, "tabulation of the top money players during the 12-month period," said *Variety,* was "all but impossible for 1948, for as soon as you get past Bing Crosby, Cary Grant, Lana Turner, Clark Gable, Bob Hope and perhaps a few others [Ingrid Bergman, Jane Wyman, John Wayne], the reasoning becomes spurious."[5]

Variety did return to its star listing the following year, however, and continued the practice throughout the 1950s. Gauging stardom had not become any easier; on the contrary, the industry was even more chaotic and uncertain in the post-divorcement era.

Ingrid Bergman on the set of Notorious *(RKO, 1946), as Alfred Hitchcock gives instruction to his camera operator during a particularly complex shot.*

But as long as movies remained so essentially star-driven, the industry would continue to devise ways of measuring the value and appeal of movie stars.

The vagaries of audience measurement and star evaluation aside, the combined annual rankings of both *Variety* and the Exhibitors' Poll for the period 1946–1949 generate these two lists of top postwar box-office stars:

Table 11.2
TOP STARS, 1946–1949

	Exhibitors' Poll	Variety
1.	Bing Crosby	Bing Crosby
2.	Bob Hope	Cary Grant
3.	Gary Cooper	Clark Gable
4.	Betty Grable	Gregory Peck
5.	Humphrey Bogart	Bob Hope
6.	Ingrid Bergman	Ingrid Bergman
7.	Abbott and Costello	Lana Turner
8.	Clark Gable	Van Johnson
9.	Cary Grant	Larry Parks
10.	Van Johnson	Gene Tierney

SOURCE: Exhibitors' Poll from Cobbett Steinberg, *Film Facts*, p. 58; *Variety* from 8 January 1947, p. 8; 7 January 1948, p. 1; 5 January 1949, p. 3; and 4 January 1950, p. 59.

One striking fact about these lists—beyond their obvious discrepancies—is how few new stars appear. All of the stars listed had established themselves by the late war years, with the lone exception of Larry Parks. After playing leads in second-rate pictures throughout the war, Parks burst to sudden stardom in THE JOLSON STORY in 1946. He kept busy in the late 1940s, but his only subsequent success came in JOLSON SINGS AGAIN in 1949. Parks faded quickly thereafter, a victim of the blacklist when HUAC returned to Hollywood in 1951.

A corollary to the dearth of new stars, of course, was the staying power of established screen figures in the late 1940s—particularly Bing Crosby, Betty Grable, Gary Cooper, Bob Hope, and Humphrey Bogart, who ranked in the top ten on the Exhibitors' Poll in all four postwar years. For the most part, those stars stayed on top by staying very much in character. Crosby and Hope did yet another Road picture for Paramount in 1947, ROAD TO RIO, with predictable box-office results: $4.5 million in rentals. Crosby also starred in his usual light comedy-musical vehicles, notably BLUE SKIES (1946) with Fred Astaire, and he also appeared in a few period musicals like THE EMPEROR WALTZ (1948). Hope, meanwhile, continued to rely on his bumbling, cowardly hero persona and penchant for broad farce in costume jobs like MONSIEUR BEAUCAIRE (1946) and THE PALEFACE (1948). He also turned out a pair of requisite mystery-comedies, MY FAVORITE BRUNETTE (1947) and THE GREAT LOVER (1949), both solid hits. in fact, both Hope and Crosby were popular enough in the late 1940s that virtually all their pictures returned at least $3 million in rentals to Paramount, with whom both had devised profit-sharing deals, and thus they closed out the decade as Hollywood's most dependable, bankable stars.

Like Hope and Crosby, Gary Cooper plodded through a half-dozen utterly pre-dictable postwar roles, including a requisite DeMille epic for Paramount in 1947, UNCONQUERED, which earned over $5 million despite uniformly weak reviews (*Time* called it "a five-million-dollar celebration of Gary Cooper's virility").[6] After disappoint-ing teamings with two top directors—Fritz Lang for the 1946 spy thriller CLOAK AND DAGGER, and Leo McCarey for the upbeat 1948 comedy GOOD SAM—Cooper closed out the decade with portrayals of larger-than-life iconoclasts in THE FOUNTAINHEAD (as a headstrong architect) and TASK FORCE (as a headstrong naval officer). Both were respectable but ponderous dramas and, along with his other postwar films, suggested that Cooper was growing a bit weary and that his stalwart, stoic-heroic persona was wearing a bit thin. in fact, Cooper fell from the Exhibitors' Poll's top ten in 1950 for the first time in a decade. Not until his roles began to exploit his advancing age—as in HIGH NOON (1952)—did Cooper return to top stardom.

Clark Gable suffered much the same fate as Cooper in the late 1940s, appearing in a number of overblown MGM dramas, like ADVENTURE (1945) and COMMAND DECISION (1948), that seemed almost a parody of his prewar persona. Only when he lightened up in THE HUCKSTERS (1947) as an ad-man struggling to "reconvert" after the war did Gable's playful charm and audience appeal seem to return. That picture was a hit, but MGM chose to pursue the weightier dramatic vehicles, which also did well at the box office. And much like Cooper, Gable seemed to strain harder with each role to sustain a persona that was nearing the point of exhaustion.

The postwar efforts of Humphrey Bogart were considerably more interesting and effective than those of Cooper and Gable, for three reasons. First, Bogart, who turned 50 in 1949 and was older than both Cooper and Gable, seemed quite comfortable with the prospect of advancing age. Second, Bogart continually looked for acting challenges and offbeat roles, most notably in THE TREASURE OF THE SIERRA MADRE as a gold prospector who gradually loses his mind. And third, Bogart did three more films with Lauren Bacall—THE BIG SLEEP (1946), DARK PASSAGE (1947), and KEY LARGO (1948)—all of which were hits. And in KEY LARGO, to Bogart's credit, he willingly edged out of the frame to give Edward G. Robinson free rein as the mobster Johnny Rocco in a stun-ning reprise of Robinson's earlier gangster roles.

One male star who managed to mature gracefully while maintaining his romantic appeal was Cary Grant. After playing Cole Porter in the musical biopic NIGHT AND DAY (1946), the inveterate freelancer Grant settled into what was for him a rather lengthy relationship with a single studio, RKO, where he did five films over the next few years. The first of these, NOTORIOUS (1946), was Grant's only dramatic thriller of the period. The remainder were comedies, notably THE BACHELOR AND THE BOBBY-SOXER (1947, with Shirley Temple), THE BISHOP'S WIFE (1947, with Loretta Young), and MR. BLANDINGS BUILDS HIS DREAM HOUSE (1948, with Myrna Loy). He closed out the decade with a comedy hit for Fox, I WAS A MALE WAR BRIDE (1949, with Ann Sheridan).

Gregory Peck, who turned 30 in 1946, was by far the youngest top male star of the postwar period. Peck emerged overnight as a star in KEYS OF THE KINGDOM (1944) (his second screen role) and SPELLBOUND (1945), and he reached top stardom via two 1946 hits, DUEL IN THE SUN and THE YEARLING. But it was not until GENTLEMAN'S AGREEMENT in 1947, playing a journalist who poses as a Jew to expose anti-Semitism, that Peck's screen persona as the decent and reliable (if somewhat dull) hero coalesced. Once established, that persona varied little—there would be no more wild, womanizing renegades as in DUEL IN THE SUN. in fact, his heroic type was becoming altogether pre-

Humphrey Bogart (right) with Tim Holt in THE TREASURE OF THE SIERRA MADRE
*(Warners, 1948). Bogart took on increasingly offbeat and venturesome roles in the
late 1940s.*

dictable until the late-1949 war film TWELVE O'CLOCK HIGH, wherein his portrayal of a
flight commander who agonizes over sending his men to their death brought a new psychological and emotional depth to his screen persona.

Two veteran actors who finally reached top stardom in the late 1940s—and who
would dominate the industry throughout the 1950s—were James Stewart and John
Wayne. Stewart had been on the verge of stardom since winning an Oscar just before
the war, but after returning from the service, he had trouble recovering his prewar form,
despite an excellent performance in IT'S A WONDERFUL LIFE (1946). Roles in two 1948
crime thrillers, CALL NORTHSIDE 777 and ROPE, also failed to ignite audience interest.
Stewart's postwar breakthrough came in 1949 with THE STRATTON STORY, a sentimental
biopic of a baseball pitcher who stages a heroic comeback after losing his leg in an accident. Stewart also left MGM in 1949 and entered a long-term, quasi-independent relationship with Universal that proved remarkably successful.

After Wayne joined the ranks of top stars in 1949–1950, he would dominate for the
next two decades. Signing a producer-star deal with Republic in 1946, Wayne continued to star in formula hokum for the studio such as ANGEL AND THE BADMAN (1947) and
THE FIGHTING KENTUCKIAN (1949).[7] He alternated these with more ambitious projects
elsewhere, including RED RIVER for Howard Hawks in 1948 and SHE WORE A YELLOW
RIBBON for John Ford in 1949. In both films Wayne not only showed his age (he turned

40 in 1947) but evinced a certain vulnerability as well. The lined and cracked features rendered his swagger less imposing, his character more human. RED RIVER also plumbed Wayne's darker nature, revealing an obsessive, brutal side. As David Thomson notes, "Hawks was the first to see the slit-eyed, obdurate side to Wayne's character."[8] These qualities would inform many of his later roles, including the 1949 war film for Republic, SANDS OF IWO JIMA, in which he plays a ruthless, battle-hardened marine top-sergeant. The picture was a huge hit, bringing Wayne an Oscar nomination and solidifying his status as a top box-office star.

Hollywood's leading female stars of the era, Ingrid Bergman and Betty Grable, followed radically different postwar paths. Grable simply extended her wartime success as she posed, sang, and wisecracked her way through a succession of period comedy-musical hits for 20th Century–Fox like MOTHER WORE TIGHTS (1947) and WHEN MY BABY SMILES AT ME (1948). Her one slightly offbeat film of the period was THE BEAUTIFUL BLONDE FROM BASHFUL BEND (1949), a lunatic Western comedy-musical for Fox by writer-director-producer Preston Sturges.

Ingrid Bergman's postwar career, meanwhile, followed a much less stable or predictable course. After completing her contract with Selznick with NOTORIOUS, Bergman struck out on her own. The most significant of her freelance efforts was JOAN OF ARC (1948), a bloated biopic that earned over $4 million. Bergman then turned to Europe, working first in England on a female Gothic with Hitchcock, UNDER CAPRICORN (1949). That was a disappointment, and it was followed by professional disaster. While in Italy for Roberto Rossellini's STROMBOLI (1950), Bergman fell in love with the Italian filmmaker, and in a highly publicized scandal, she left her husband and daughter to wed Rossellini. Chastised by the press, ostracized by conservative political and religious groups, and effectively blacklisted in Hollywood, Bergman would not work again in the United States for nearly a decade.

Olivia de Havilland overtook Bette Davis and Greer Garson as the doyenne of the Hollywood woman's picture in the late 1940s and became arguably the leading dramatic actress of the period. Having won free-agent status from Warners in 1943, de Havilland made the most of her independence after the war in a succession of first-rate melodramas which brought her two Academy Awards and widespread recognition as an actress with beauty, talent, and box-office clout. The best-actress Oscars came with two Paramount melodramas, TO EACH HIS OWN (1946) and THE HEIRESS (1949), while she won her greatest critical acclaim in Fox's THE SNAKE PIT (1948) portraying a recently married woman who descends into madness and battles through a lengthy, horrific recovery.

While de Havilland came into her own after the war, several other veteran female stars went into serious decline. Greer Garson, MGM's wartime matriarch and top box-office star, faded badly despite the studio's best efforts in ADVENTURE (1945), DESIRE ME (1947), and JULIA MISBEHAVES (1948). She enjoyed mild success in the 1949 period drama THAT FORSYTE WOMAN, although by then it was evident that audiences had lost interest in the woman who commanded such devotion only a few years before. The telling blow came in 1950 with the failure of THE MINIVER STORY, a sequel to MRS. MINIVER costarring Walter Pidgeon. The serious decline of Universal's Deanna Durbin actually had begun during the war, when Universal failed to rekindle the appeal of her late-1930s hits. Durbin did several films but nothing of note after the war, despite a Universal salary which in 1948 paid her $366,000, making her the highest-paid female actress in the industry. That same year, while still in her twenties, she suddenly (but not unexpectedly) retired.[9]

Olivia de Havilland in an Oscar-winning performance opposite Montgomery Clift in THE HEIRESS *(Paramount, 1949).*

Warners' top female stars, Bette Davis and Joan Crawford, came out of the war in rare form but also faded badly in the late 1940s. Davis did five pictures with Warners from 1946 to 1949, the first of which, A STOLEN LIFE (1946), was among her best. Then came a series of flops, rendering her $6,000-per-week salary (plus bonuses) a severe drain on Warners' resources.[10] Still, the studio pulled out all the stops for WINTER MEETING (1948) and BEYOND THE FOREST (1949), grand melodramas with Davis's over-the-top performances bordering on self-caricature. When those failed, she left Warners, her career seemingly over—until her next film, ALL ABOUT EVE (1950), which won Davis her third Oscar and gave her career yet another boost. Crawford, meanwhile, followed her Oscar-winning 1945 comeback in MILDRED PIERCE with two excellent *noir* melodramas for Warners, HUMORESQUE (1946) and POSSESSED (1947), and then a more conventional woman's picture for Otto Preminger at Fox, DAISY KENYON (1947). She remained active but did nothing else of note in the late 1940s as her career began winding down.

Other mature women stars, like Katharine Hepburn, Rosalind Russell, and Barbara Stanwyck, held their own in the postwar era. Hepburn, after two disappointing dramatic efforts, UNDERCURRENT (1946) and SONG OF LOVE (1947), reteamed with Spencer Tracy for three solid hits: THE SEA OF GRASS (1947), STATE OF THE UNION (1948), and ADAM'S RIB (1949). The latter two were sharp romantic comedies in the spirit of the initial Tracy-Hepburn hit, WOMAN OF THE YEAR, and they marked a return to form for the screen's "first couple."

While Hepburn turned successfully from drama to comedy in the late 1940s, both Russell and Stanwyck, who had done brilliant comedy early in the decade, concentrated on darker drama in the postwar era. Russell received an Oscar nomination playing the title character in a weighty 1946 biopic, SISTER KENNY; she struggled through an ill-fated 1947 adaptation of MOURNING BECOMES ELECTRA; and she let loose as a headstrong actress who gets away with murder in an effective 1948 *noir* thriller, THE VELVET TOUCH. Stanwyck, who had played the quintessential *femme fatale* in DOUBLE INDEMNITY, portrayed both victimizer and victim in two Oscar-nominated postwar roles: as the homicidal title character in THE STRANGE LOVE OF MARTHA IVERS (1946), and the bedridden hysteric who hears her own murder being plotted in SORRY, WRONG NUMBER (1948).

Although Russell, Stanwyck, and a few other top female stars did well in the late 1940s, their careers clearly had peaked, owing less to diminished skills than to changing industry imperatives and audience tastes. Garson, Davis, Crawford, Russell, Stanwyck, and Hepburn all were in their forties by 1949, and the market for their talents was rapidly drying up. Significantly enough, top male stars like Bogart, Cooper, Grant, Hope, Crosby, Stewart, and Wayne had hit their forties as well, but their careers still were going strong and would continue to flourish. Thus, along with the "graying" of Hollywood's star populace after the war came a gender split of sorts. This bias, in fact, would intensify for decades to come in two distinct ways: the ranks of top stars would be predominantly male, and female stars would tend to be considerably younger than their male counterparts.

While the postwar era was dominated by established stars, a new generation of talent was emerging in the late 1940s. Among the notable female stars were Gene Tierney and Jeanne Crain at Fox, Lana Turner and June Allyson at MGM, Jane Wyman and Ida Lupino at Warners, and the freelancers Dorothy McGuire and Susan Hayward. Of these, only Tierney approached top stardom, although she scarcely enjoyed the success of such emergent wartime stars as Grable and Garson. Tierney and most of the other rising postwar stars were being groomed for melodrama, and few displayed the versatility of Stanwyck, Russell, or Hepburn. Two new arrivals at decade's end, Judy Holliday and Marilyn Monroe, signaled an important change in Hollywood's comic portrayal of female sexuality.

The postwar era saw ascending male stars as well—Alan Ladd and William Holden at Paramount, Glenn Ford at Columbia, Gene Kelly at MGM, and the freelancer Montgomery Clift. The *noir* thriller provided an excellent proving ground for young talent, particularly Robert Mitchum, Kirk Douglas, and Burt Lancaster. Mitchum and Douglas costarred in OUT OF THE PAST (1947), an exceptional postwar thriller, and they did other impressive work as well—Mitchum in THE LOCKET (1946) and CROSSFIRE (1947), for instance, and Douglas in THE STRANGE LOVE OF MARTHA IVERS (his debut) and CHAMPION (1949). Lancaster debuted in THE KILLERS in 1946 and went on to do BRUTE FORCE (1947), SORRY, WRONG NUMBER (1948), and CRISS CROSS (1949). A few established stars also found *film noir* to be their element, notably John Garfield, who did the best work of his career in THE POSTMAN ALWAYS RINGS TWICE (1946, with Lana Turner), BODY AND SOUL (1947), and FORCE OF EVIL (1948).

Another significant postwar development was the emergence of Dean Martin and Jerry Lewis, who made their screen debut in a modest 1949 comedy, MY FRIEND IRMA, and became an overnight sensation—not unlike what Abbott and Costello had done

Both Ethel Waters (left) and Jeanne Crain were nominated for Academy Awards for PINKY *(20th Century–Fox, 1949), an effective merger of the woman's picture and the postwar social problem film.*

early in the decade. And in fact Abbott and Costello themselves enjoyed a return to top stardom in the late 1940s, a comeback that for a number of reasons was even more important than either the emergence of Martin and Lewis or their own burst to stardom in 1940–1941. Indeed, the return of Abbott and Costello was among the more illuminating developments of the period, with implications far beyond simply the careers of the star duo.

CASE STUDY: THE REGENERATION OF ABBOTT AND COSTELLO

Abbott and Costello, a fixture in the Exhibitors' Poll during most of the war, slipped from the top ten to number eleven in 1945. The slide continued for two years amid repeated announcements of their impending split, and the duo was written off as a wartime phenomenon.[11] But remarkably enough, Abbott and Costello returned to the Exhibitors' Poll in 1948 with a number-three ranking, a position they continued to hold in 1949. They remained in the top ten for two more years before executing a successful segue into network television in late 1951.

The resurgence of Abbott and Costello was related to changing audience tastes, of course, but it also evinced other important industry factors in the late 1940s: the changing fortunes of Universal, especially in terms of the International merger; the changing status of A- and B-class product; and the return to efficient star-genre formulation with the late-1940s economic decline and reasserted studio control. The duo's resurgence also indicated the vagaries of star measurement at the time: it was scarcely geared to low-budget production and low-end markets. And on a related note, the success of Abbott and Costello and other low-cost Universal series anticipated the movie industry's convergence with the nascent TV industry.

Abbott and Costello's rapid mid-1940s decline was directly related to the premium on A-class pictures that accompanied the war boom and to Universal's changing production and marketing strategies as well. Mass-produced lowbrow comedy for the subsequent-run market scarcely jibed with Universal's emphasis on top-feature production after its 1946 merger with International Pictures. The studio did try to upgrade the duo's image in 1946 in the costume epic THE TIME OF THEIR LIVES, in which they played a pair of ghosts from the Revolutionary War. And in LITTLE GIANT (1946), a fairly straight comedy, they were introduced separately; Abbott plays a dual role, and one of his characters teams up with Costello in the course of the story.

Both of those fared poorly, so Universal reverted to low-cost genre parodies much like the Abbott and Costello films of the war years. These included THE WISTFUL WIDOW OF WAGON GAP (1947) and THE NOOSE HANGS HIGH (1948), which were more cost-efficient and somewhat more successful at the box office, and thus more profitable than the ambitious 1946 vehicles. But the duo's glory days seemed to be over, best evidenced perhaps by the 1947 release of BUCK PRIVATES COME HOME, a lackluster effort to capitalize on the initial Abbott and Costello hit—to the extent of including footage from the original BUCK PRIVATES in the form of flashbacks.

In early 1948, with the genre parodies doing reasonable business, producer Robert Arthur and writer John Grant, who had collaborated on Abbott and Costello's initial hits, developed the idea for a horror-comedy. Initially titled "The Brain of Frankenstein," the project was designed to rework an earlier series of genre recombinations at Universal— the horror "reunion" pictures of the war years, such as FRANKENSTEIN MEETS THE WOLF MAN (1943), HOUSE OF FRANKENSTEIN (1944), and HOUSE OF DRACULA (1945). Those films had not fared well, and now after Hiroshima and the birth of the atomic age, Universal's horror cycle seemed not only exhausted but antiquated. Moreover, the currency of horror stars Bela Lugosi and Lon Chaney Jr. was even lower than Abbott and Costello's. Thus, while the effort to recombine its horror and Abbott and Costello formulas may have seemed like a desperate and ill-fated exercise, Universal actually had little to lose—especially in light of the modest cost of the venture. In 1947, with the average cost per feature over $1 million and top features costing two to three times that, "The Brain of Frankenstein" was budgeted at only $750,000. Abbott and Costello shared a flat-fee salary of $105,000 on the film, while Chaney and Lugosi each earned $2,000 per week.[12]

In Grant's story, Abbott and Costello were to play their usual bumbling selves, while Lugosi and Chaney did straightforward horrific versions of their signature roles as Dracula and the Wolf Man. The story centered on two hapless freight agents in Florida who handle the encased forms of Dracula, Frankenstein's monster, and various other props for a horror theme park. The vampire (Lugosi) and the monster turn out to be authentic, however—part of a diabolical plot by a mad scientist determined to carry on the work of Frankenstein in America. Meanwhile, the monsters are being pursued by the Wolf Man (Chaney), who has vowed to rid the world of them forever. The film's title refers to a plot by the scientist to transplant Costello's brain into the Frankenstein monster, which not only ties together the comedy and horror formulas but also provides a climactic "birth scene" in the tradition of the original Frankenstein films.

In February 1948, Universal began shooting "The Brain of Frankenstein," which was completed by March with characteristic Universal efficiency, coming in on schedule and only $10,000 over budget. The title was changed to ABBOTT AND COSTELLO MEET FRANKENSTEIN during postproduction, and the film was released in June 1948. The Abbott and Costello (and Lugosi and Chaney) vehicle proved to be an appealing mix of genre conventions—*Variety* deemed it "a happy combination both for chills and laughs."[13] A happy combination of income and efficiency for Universal, the film also translated into considerable profit. ABBOTT AND COSTELLO MEET FRANKENSTEIN earned $2.2 million in 1948, generating a profit of over $1 million—a significant take under the market conditions of the late 1940s, as indicated by the film's performance relative to other releases with comparable earnings. *Variety's* year-end tabulation placed ABBOTT AND COSTELLO MEET FRANKENSTEIN at number fifty-one in rental returns for the year, just behind Warners' THE TREASURE OF THE SIERRA MADRE ($2.3 million) and THE PARADINE CASE ($2.2 million). Significantly, the Warners picture cost $2.74 million to produce, and the Selznick production cost $3.2 million.[14] Thus, both pictures were far from breaking even after their domestic release.

The success of ABBOTT AND COSTELLO MEET FRANKENSTEIN vaulted the duo back into the Exhibitors' Poll's top ten, and Universal immediately initiated a follow-up, ABBOTT AND COSTELLO MEET THE KILLER, BORIS KARLOFF (1949). That gave Universal another low-cost, high-yield hit and enabled the comedy team to maintain their number-three ranking (behind Hope and Crosby) in 1949. But Abbott and Costello were not similarly rated by *Variety* or ARI. in fact, in 1949, with their comeback by now a widely acknowledged industry phenomenon, the duo was not even ranked in *Variety's* top twenty-five. Nor were they included in ARI's 1950 listing of the top twenty-five *male* stars.[15]

These omissions ultimately say less about Abbott and Costello's star value and audience appeal than about the different assumptions and methods involved in the three polls. *Variety's* method of ranking stars according to average box-office performance

Publicity shot for ABBOTT AND COSTELLO MEET FRANKENSTEIN *(Universal, 1948), featuring the comedy duo along with Lon Chaney Jr. (as the Wolf Man) and Bela Lugosi (as Dracula).*

per annum clearly favored stars who appeared predominantly in only a few big first-run-market pictures each year. This emphasis on top hits discriminated against any stars who appealed to small-town and rural audiences—from Abbott and Costello to B-Western stars like Roy Rogers and Gene Autry, who also failed to show up in *Variety's* top twenty-five. Moviegoers polled by ARI's interview-based method, on the other hand, may have been reluctant to voice their interest in the likes of Abbott and Costello when asked which stars would draw them into the theater.

Star rankings aside, Universal's revised Abbott and Costello formula was set by 1949, and over the next few years the duo would "meet" the Invisible Man, Dr. Jekyll and Mr. Hyde, and the Mummy. Moreover, the success of the Abbott and Costello films led Universal to develop other low-cost comedy series as well. In 1949, the studio created a spin-off of its 1947 A-class comedy hit THE EGG AND I, starring Claudette Colbert and Fred MacMurray. Two supporting players from that film who played a farm couple, the veteran character actors Marjorie Main and Percy Kilbride, starred in MA AND PA KETTLE, a 1949 hit which returned $2.5 million—nearly ten times its production cost, initiating a series that ran in nine annual installments through 1957. In 1949, the long-time Universal producer-director Arthur Lubin, who had directed many of Abbott and Costello's early hits, went to work on another low-budget buddy comedy, FRANCIS THE TALKING MULE, a 1950 hit which generated yet another comedy series.

Thus, the comeback of Abbott and Costello marked a reversion by Universal as well—a return to the factory-based production geared to the mass market that once had been its forte. That strategy would provide a pattern for the emerging television industry as well, particularly in terms of telefilm series production. in fact, several of these same Universal series eventually were reworked for TV. In 1951, Abbott and Costello took their slapstick comedy and vaudeville shtick to television's *Colgate Comedy Hour*, among the first Hollywood-based telefilm series. The Ma and Pa Kettle and Francis films would spark TV's "rural sitcoms" of the late 1950s and 1960s: the Kettles were reworked into *The Real McCoys*, and Arthur Lubin himself created *Mr. Ed*, a TV version of the Francis series.

Genres and Production Trends

During the immediate postwar period, the most significant genre-related development was the rapid phasing-out of the war film, and particularly the combat drama. In a matter of months, the genre that had so completely dominated movie screens for the previous five years virtually disappeared from view. The combat film went out in impressive fashion, however, with two major independent productions just after the war: John Ford's THEY WERE EXPENDABLE (December 1945) and Lewis Milestone's A WALK IN THE SUN (January 1946). Ford's account of a PT-boat during the early months of the war in the Pacific actually did well at the box office, returning $3.2 million. Milestone's searing account of a combat outfit's experiences during one day in the Italian campaign of 1943, although critically acclaimed, fared poorly at the box office. That hastened the combat film's demise, and by the summer of 1946, not a single war film was in release or in production. ARI had announced early in 1946 that the audience "want to see" factor on war films was virtually nil—something that the nation's exhibitors had been proclaiming for two years—and the production community now seemed to concur.[16]

After 1946, war film production stalled completely for several years. It began a tentative return in 1948–1949 in a variety of war-related pictures: an aerial combat film FIGHTER SQUADRON (1948); two dramas about the trials and tribulations of military leadership, COMMAND DECISION (1948) and TASK FORCE (1949); a Hawks-directed screwball comedy, I WAS A MALE WAR BRIDE (1949); a geopolitical postwar romance with Humphrey Bogart, TOKYO JOE (1949); and a drama about racial prejudice in the military, THE HOME OF THE BRAVE (1949). All of these were in release in 1949, and several were solid hits. While none of them was of any singular importance as a war film, together they overcame the stigma that had been attached to the genre since the war.

Then, in late 1949, the combat film staged an impressive comeback via three first-rate dramas: BATTLEGROUND, the story of an infantry unit during the Battle of the Bulge, personally produced for MGM by Dore Schary; TWELVE O'CLOCK HIGH, a Zanuck-produced study of a bomber unit commander (Gregory Peck) who begins to crack under the mounting pressures; and SANDS OF IWO JIMA, a John Wayne vehicle from Republic that veered between grim realism in its harrowing battle scenes and more traditional war melodrama. Like the superior films from the late war era, particularly THE STORY OF GI JOE and THEY WERE EXPENDABLE, these focused primarily on the psychology and camaraderie of men at war and on the brutal responsibilities of leadership in combat. All three were major hits: BATTLEGROUND and SANDS OF IWO JIMA both surpassed $5 million in domestic earnings, virtually ensuring the return of the combat film. They were

Robert Montgomery and John Wayne in THEY WERE EXPENDABLE *(MGM, 1945),
among the last of the World War II films before the genre went on a three-year hiatus.*

critically acclaimed as well; in fact, Bosley Crowther in the *New York Times* called
BATTLEGROUND "the best of the World War II pictures that have yet been made in
Hollywood," and he endorsed the current view that it was as important a postwar epic
as THE BIG PARADE (1925) had been in the aftermath of World War I.[17]

While the combat film was on hiatus from 1946 to 1949, Hollywood maintained its
action-adventure output in various other venues like the Western and the *noir* thriller.
An important related development was the postwar trend toward serious drama with a
strong male focus. in fact, there emerged in 1946 a distinctive form of prestige-level
"male melodrama," invariably centering on the efforts of a vaguely despondent male
beset by postwar angst to "find himself." This search often took place in a dark and
alienating milieu and clearly was related to the postwar *film noir* and social problem
trends. At the same time, certain themes and concerns of the war film were displaced
onto these melodramas.

A clear indication of this postwar trend was the Academy's list of nominees for best
picture of 1946: THE BEST YEARS OF OUR LIVES, IT'S A WONDERFUL LIFE, THE RAZOR'S
EDGE, HENRY V, and THE YEARLING. All except Olivier's adaptation of Shakespeare's
Henry V (actually produced in 1944 as a British call-to-arms) were male melodramas,
and even Olivier's film dealt with war-induced male anxiety. THE YEARLING was a com-
ing-of-age story focusing on a boy's relationship with his father—played by Gregory
Peck, who was nominated for an Oscar as best actor. THE RAZOR'S EDGE, Zanuck's care-

fully designed comeback vehicle for Fox star Tyrone Power on his return from the service, was an adaptation of Somerset Maugham's novel about a World War I veteran's search for "the meaning of life." Both THE YEARLING and THE RAZOR'S EDGE were enormously popular, returning just over $5 million and finishing among the top five box-office hits of 1946.

By far the most successful film of the lot was THE BEST YEARS OF OUR LIVES, Goldwyn and Wyler's postwar readjustment drama focusing on three returning servicemen (Fredric March, Dana Andrews, and Harold Russell). The biggest commercial hit of the decade, it returned over $10 million on its initial release.[18] BEST YEARS also provides an interesting complement to IT'S A WONDERFUL LIFE, Frank Capra's postwar paean to a "home-front veteran" (Jimmy Stewart) whose travails are presented as no less severe. Both are male melodramas focused squarely on the postwar American experience, incorporating romantic and comic dimensions and a generally upbeat outcome, although both have darker moments as well.

BEST YEARS, with its three-hour running time and multiple principals and plot lines, was the more accomplished of the two, bringing a new maturity to the screen. Scripted by Robert Sherwood and photographed by Wyler's longtime collaborator Gregg Toland, who like Wyler had done documentary work during the war, BEST YEARS was at once a Hollywood movie and a clear attempt to create a more realistic portrayal of the postwar American experience. Employing a visual style which relied on elaborate compositions, location shooting, and Wyler and Toland's usual deep-focus, long-take approach to filming individual scenes, BEST YEARS evinced a technical realism that jibed well with its social and thematic aspects. The film addresses timely and acute postwar issues—anxieties brought on by physical and emotional trauma, troubled marriages, the prospect of unemployment, problems with alcohol—with uncommon subtlety and dramatic power. And despite well-drawn female roles and excellent performances, especially by Myrna Loy and Teresa Wright, these issues are treated from a distinctly male viewpoint.

James Agee devoted two of his review columns in *The Nation* to BEST YEARS under the title "What Hollywood Can Do." He was especially impressed with the film's delicate interplay of narrative intimacy and documentary technique, writing that Wyler "has come back from the war with a style of great purity, directness and warmth."[19] Terry Ramsay, reviewing the film in the *Motion Picture Herald,* also noted its "decided documentary quality," although he qualified the point by referring to "a glossy sort of realism."[20] Bosley Crowther in the *Times* simply saw it as a first-rate Hollywood product and "enthusiastically" endorsed the film "not only as superlative entertainment but as food for quiet and humanizing thought."[21] The heaviest praise came from the Academy: THE BEST YEARS OF OUR LIVES won eight Oscars, including best picture of 1946, along with the Thalberg Award for producer Sam Goldwyn.

Despite the huge commercial and critical success of BEST YEARS, only one other postwar male melodrama centered on the trauma of readjustment, TILL THE END OF TIME (1946). Produced by Dore Schary and directed by Edward Dmytryk for RKO (which also released BEST YEARS), TILL THE END OF TIME starred Guy Madison, Robert Mitchum, and Bill Williams as three ex-marines struggling to adjust after coming home. (in fact, the Williams character lost his legs in the war and suffers from much the same trauma as Harold Russell in BEST YEARS, who lost his hands.) TILL THE END OF TIME added another dimension through Madison's romance with an emotionally devastated war widow (Dorothy McGuire), thus taking its romantic subplot well beyond the stand-by-your-man mentality of BEST YEARS.

Postwar reunion: a returning veteran (Fredric March) is welcomed by his daughter (Teresa Wright) in William Wyler's acclaimed postwar drama THE BEST YEARS OF OUR LIVES *(RKO, 1946).*

While the male melodramas addressed the emotional and psychological aspects of the postwar male experience, the deluge of Westerns provided a more traditionally male and mythic Hollywood treatment. The output of both A- and B-Westerns accelerated in the late 1940s, owing no doubt to the cutback of combat films. All told, Westerns comprised more than one-fourth (27 percent) of all films released from 1946 through 1949. In 1948, a peak year to that point in the genre's history, fully 30 percent of all Hollywood features were Westerns.[22]

The Big Eight's output of Westerns, which had fallen to only twenty-eight features in 1945, steadily climbed after the war, peaking in 1950 at sixty-one. Most of the A-class Westerns came from Fox, MGM, Warners, and Paramount, which collectively produced twenty Westerns from 1946 through 1949 (up slightly from the war era). RKO produced twenty-five Westerns in the late 1940s, mostly B's. Universal's changing market strategy cut its postwar Western output to only fourteen, including only one in 1948. Columbia cranked out an astounding seventy-two Westerns from 1946 through 1949, nearly half of the total (152) released by the Big Eight. The minor independents like Republic and Monogram, meanwhile, produced 246 Westerns from 1946 through 1949. Although Republic was edging into the A-Western arena (the first was Ford's RIO GRANDE in 1950), virtually all of these were B-Westerns. And like Columbia's, they were split between "singing cowboys" and straight "actioners."[23]

While the B-Western maintained its naive charm and largely adolescent appeal, the A-Western continued to incorporate adult themes, most notably in Selznick's DUEL IN THE SUN (1946) and Howard Hawks's RED RIVER (1948). The chief antagonists in Selznick's sexual psychodrama are Gregory Peck and Jennifer Jones, both cast against type as libidinous, violent renegades. in fact, the most basic of Western conventions, the climactic shootout, occurs in the desert (hence the title) between these two, who then crawl into a dying embrace. RED RIVER, conversely, is a remarkable study in male heroism and a veiled remake of MUTINY ON THE BOUNTY (1935)—John Wayne's aging, obsessive rancher feuds with his adopted son (Montgomery Clift) during an epic cattle drive.

Two other significant and vastly underrated Westerns of the period were PURSUED (1947) and YELLOW SKY (1948). PURSUED, an independent production directed by Raoul Walsh and released through Warners, is a bizarre tale of familial abuse, vengeance, and murder. The story centers on star-crossed lovers and adoptive siblings (Robert Mitchum and Teresa Wright) who reconstruct their fated lives while waiting in the ruins of Mitchum's childhood home for a crazed relative (Dean Jagger) who has sworn to kill him. Aptly described by Edward Buscombe as "Walsh's exquisitely 'noir' masterpiece," the film is a remarkable amalgam of postwar themes, styles, and genres.[24] So is William Wellman's YELLOW SKY, a hybrid of Shakespeare's *The Tempest* and John Huston's THE TREASURE OF THE SIERRA MADRE. The story is about an outlaw band (Gregory Peck, Richard Widmark, et al.) on the run. They stumble into a ghost town where a crazed prospector and his spitfire daughter (James Barton and Anne Baxter) have struck gold. Here, too, Freudian themes and a complex interplay of lust, greed, and violence push the traditional Western into areas anticipated by films like THE OUTLAW and DUEL IN THE SUN.

Another significant trend in the late 1940s was a spate of military Westerns, the most notable of which were John Ford's so-called cavalry trilogy—FORT APACHE (1948), SHE WORE A YELLOW RIBBON (1949), and RIO GRANDE (1950). Besides refining the Wayne persona (he starred in all three), the cavalry films were also veiled combat dramas focusing on the Indian wars of the late nineteenth century. Like their World War II counterparts, they dealt with military command and leadership, the psychopathology of combat, and the myriad rituals of soldiering. On a very different note, the currency of the postwar Western was further reinforced by a cycle of genre parodies released in the late 1940s, the most successful of which was the 1948 Bob Hope vehicle THE PALEFACE.

Despite the postwar bias toward male stars and genres, the period saw its usual array of women's pictures and romantic dramas. Indeed, the marked increase in love stories in the late 1940s was scarcely surprising given the social conditions at the time.[25] Most of these were light romances—modest contemporary films celebrating the courtship and coupling rites of postwar America. There were weightier romances as well: prestige-level adaptations and period films like FOREVER AMBER (1947), GREEN DOLPHIN STREET (1947), THE THREE MUSKETEERS (1948), and THE HEIRESS (1949). The last, an eminently successful adaptation of Henry James's *Washington Square* costarring Olivia de Havilland and Montgomery Clift, was among the many late-1940s spinster melodramas, a subgenre whose stock was rising for two fairly obvious reasons: the pressure on women to marry and the aging of stars like de Havilland, Davis, Crawford, Stanwyck, and Rosalind Russell, all of whom took a turn at this type of melodrama.

A related postwar strain was the domestic comedy-drama, which enjoyed a remarkable postwar popularity in films like EASY TO WED (1946), LIFE WITH FATHER (1947), THE EGG AND I (1947), SITTING PRETTY (1948), I REMEMBER MAMA (1948), MOTHER IS

FORT APACHE *(RKO, 1948), the first of John Ford's "cavalry trilogy," recombined the Western and war film in a distinctive postwar cycle.*

A FRESHMAN (1949), MA AND PA KETTLE (1949)—and on and on in a seemingly endless procession of films celebrating the American hearth and home. Many were based on best-sellers (or, as with LIFE WITH FATHER, on long-running stage plays), although few were high-cost prestige productions. They were, for the most part, modest celebrations of the postwar marriage-family-baby boom, which later critics have treated in terms of an emergent postwar "cult of domesticity" that encouraged women to return to the home after doing their part in the workforce during the war.[26] This message, so crucial not only to restabilizing the social and familial structure but also to promoting postwar consumer culture, was reinforced on radio's domestic comedies and soap operas. Like Hollywood's domestic comedy-dramas, radio dramas were selling sanitized versions of American family life—and the myriad goods and services that came with it. This effort was even more pronounced on early television, and in fact several Hollywood films made their way to TV as situation comedy series, notably *Mama,* a long-running (1949–1957) CBS series based on I REMEMBER MAMA.[27]

"Working-girl" dramas and comedies represented another significant strain of postwar women's pictures, most of which follow one of three tacks: they disparage the "pink-collar ghetto" positions that awaited most women who remained in the workforce, invariably portraying them as desperately trying to get out via a husband; they portray women caught between a professional vocation and true love; or they dramatize the price paid by women who sacrificed love and home for a career. Among the most prominent of this last type were DAISY KENYON (1947), with Joan Crawford trying to choose between her career and two men; THE FARMER'S DAUGHTER (1947), with Loretta Young playing a maid-turned-politician; and ADAM'S RIB (1949), a Tracy-Hepburn film in a class by itself among postwar portrayals of working women—and working couples, for that matter. ADAM'S RIB centers on a married couple who are opposing attorneys in a highly publicized lawsuit (involving marital infidelity) and whose courtroom battles create comic havoc in their domestic lives.

While most of these films portray the postwar American female in a positive light, a significant countercurrent developed in a number of heavier, darker dramas. Particularly important was the late-1945 Fox release LEAVE HER TO HEAVEN, starring Gene Tierney, Cornel Wilde, and Jeanne Crain. A Technicolor prestige drama based on a current best-seller, the film stars Tierney as a new bride who resorts to murder to maintain control over her husband and her marriage. Zanuck later described the film as "an uncompromising character story of a vicious woman who . . . deliberately kills her own unborn child, drowns the crippled brother of her husband and endeavors to send her own adopted sister to the electric chair. And yet despite all of this, there are certain things about her that you rather like."[28] LEAVE HER TO HEAVEN was a huge hit, earning $5.5 million, securing Tierney's stardom, and wielding tremendous influence on the postwar woman's picture.[29]

The success of LEAVE HER TO HEAVEN surprised even Zanuck, particularly after the critical beating it took upon release. Bosley Crowther in the *New York Times* dismissed it as "a moody, morbid film," and called Tierney's performance "about as analytical as a piece of pin-up poster art."[30] James Agee in *Time* magazine said that "the story's central idea might be plausible enough in a dramatically lighted black and white picture," but in the "rich glare of Technicolor" it was simply too much.[31] Although the Academy differed with these views—Tierney was nominated for best actress, and Leon Shamroy won an Oscar for his color cinematography—the filmmaking community seemed to concur. The subsequent spate of romantic dramas focusing on sympathetic, murderous heroines generally featured Hollywood's top female talent—Barbara Stanwyck in THE STRANGE LOVE OF MARTHA IVERS, for instance, and Merle Oberon in TEMPTATION (both 1946)—and were done in the "dramatically lighted" style of *film noir*.

Meanwhile, Hollywood's postwar musicals provided a much more upbeat, colorful, and romantic view. The genre veered away from its wartime emphasis on revues and show musicals, although the wartime male bias was still evident in some areas. Several Bing Crosby vehicles, particularly his costume musicals like THE EMPEROR WALTZ (1948) and A CONNECTICUT YANKEE IN KING ARTHUR'S COURT (1949), featured an individual male protagonist, as did the madcap musicals of the emerging musical star Danny Kaye, such as THE KID FROM BROOKLYN (1946) and THE INSPECTOR GENERAL (1949). The musical biopic also tended to focus on great men: Columbia's THE JOLSON STORY (1946) and JOLSON SINGS AGAIN (1949); Warners' Cole Porter biopic NIGHT AND DAY (1946); MGM on Jerome Kern in TILL THE CLOUDS ROLL BY (1946) and on Rogers and Hart in WORDS AND MUSIC (1948).

Complementing these male-dominant musicals were those featuring Hollywood's two biggest female musical stars of the era, Betty Grable and Esther Williams. These musicals were clearly designed for the individual stars, despite their predictable romantic subplots, and in fact each star refined a characteristic subgenre unto herself: Grable's Technicolor period musicals from Fox, like MOTHER WORE TIGHTS (1947) and WHEN MY BABY SMILES AT ME (1948), which generally had a vaguely biographical dimension;

and Williams's enormously popular water ballets, such as ON AN ISLAND WITH YOU (1948) and NEPTUNE'S DAUGHTER (1949). Produced by MGM, these aqua-musicals were altogether unique among the studio's postwar musical output, which was dominated by the distinctive dance musicals produced by Arthur Freed.

CASE STUDY: THE MGM FREED UNIT MUSICAL

The musical had been a key genre in MGM's repertoire since the arrival of sound, and not even the rampant cost-cutting and retrenchment of the late 1940s diminished its currency. in fact, even after Dore Schary arrived in the late 1940s and attempted to build up more economical genres like the crime thriller and romantic comedy, Metro actually increased its musical output, though by then the genre represented a tremendous strain on studio resources. As Nick Schenck, Louis B. Mayer, and Schary well realized, the musical was MGM's signature genre and chief revenue-generator, and studio operations were geared to the output of musicals. They realized too that as other studios cut musical production after the war, MGM's musicals would further differentiate its high-end output and its house style.[32]

MGM produced eight to ten musicals per year during Schary's tenure at the studio (1948–1956). Most of them were Technicolor pictures, and in fact MGM's postwar shift to color was directly related to its musical production. In the early 1940s, MGM had been somewhat tentative about doing Technicolor pictures, releasing only twenty from 1940 to 1945 (versus thirty-eight from Fox, the industry leader). The success of MEET ME IN ST. LOUIS in 1944–1945 convinced Mayer and company of the market value of color—and of color musicals, whose output steadily increased over the next few years. By decade's end, MGM was the industry leader in color releases, with twelve in 1948 and ten in 1949 (versus six from Fox in each of those years). Of MGM's twenty-two color releases in 1948–1949, fifteen were musicals.[33]

MGM utterly dominated the musical genre after the war and into the 1950s. In the decade following World War II, musicals comprised more than 25 percent of MGM's total output (81 of 316 total releases), while MGM musicals comprised more than half the total made in Hollywood.[34] Musicals ruled the box office—particularly MGM musicals. The *Wall Street Journal* reported in 1949 that musicals traditionally comprised roughly 10 percent of Hollywood's A-class output while accounting for about one-third of its top box-office hits. *Variety*'s summary of top hits in 1949 indicated that the trend was continuing: five MGM musicals along with Columbia's JOLSON SINGS AGAIN finished among the year's top fifteen box-office performers.[35]

Musical production at MGM was dominated by three producers, Arthur Freed, Joe Pasternak, and Jack Cummings. Pasternak and Freed were the most prolific, each turning out about a dozen musicals from 1946 through 1949, while Cummings produced about half that many. Cummings did produce a few sizable hits, notably Esther Williams vehicles like FIESTA (1947) and NEPTUNE'S DAUGHTER. Pasternak and Freed each had a remarkable run of hits during the period, and in fact they were Hollywood's two top moneymaking producers in 1948.[36] But while Pasternak and Freed were roughly equal in terms of productivity and box-office performance, Freed garnered most of the critical acclaim—and deservedly so. Freed's productions defined the trajectory of Hollywood's musical golden age, from MEET ME IN ST. LOUIS in 1944 to GIGI in 1958. While Freed's greatest success came in the early 1950s with AN AMERICAN IN PARIS (1951), SINGIN' IN THE RAIN (1952), and THE BAND WAGON (1953), he clearly hit

*Arthur Freed, the chief
architect of MGM's
"musical golden age."*

his stride in 1948–1949, producing such musical masterworks as WORDS AND MUSIC, THE PIRATE, EASTER PARADE, THE BARKLEYS OF BROADWAY, TAKE ME OUT TO THE BALL GAME, and ON THE TOWN.

Two factors in Freed's success were the production unit he assembled in 1947–1948 and the unit's emphasis on dance. While Freed, Pasternak, and Cummings all drew from the same pool of MGM personnel, only Freed assembled a consistently coherent group of above-the-line talent. Besides directors, stars, writers, and composers, the most vital members of his production units were four choreographers—Gene Kelly, Stanley Donen, Charles Walters, and Robert Alton—whom Freed developed into directors. The role of the director-choreographer was by no means common in Hollywood or even at MGM—except in the Freed unit, where it was the dominant and defining feature.

Among the other top artists who worked closely with Freed at MGM, director Vincente Minnelli had the most intense alliance with the producer. All of Minnelli's MGM musicals were done in collaboration with Freed. All told, Kelly, Donen, and Minnelli worked in various combinations on half of Freed's two dozen musicals from 1943 to 1958. Freed also developed strong alliances with his performers, writers, and composers. Gene Kelly starred and danced in nine Freed musicals, and Fred Astaire in six. Alan Jay Lerner and the team of Betty Comden and Adolph Green wrote virtually all of the top Freed unit hits, often the lyrics as well as the "book" (i.e., the dialogue and other nonmusical portions of the script).

The dance musical was scarcely new to postwar Hollywood; it dated back to such earlier cycles as RKO's Fred Astaire–Ginger Rogers films of the 1930s. in fact, THE

BARKLEYS OF BROADWAY marked the couple's celebrated reunion after a ten-year separation. The Freed unit's dance musicals were distinctive, however, for several reasons. Foremost perhaps was the integration of music and dance directly into the narrative as a means of both personal and romantic expression. In earlier musicals, the song-and-dance numbers tended to be realistically motivated through a backstage musical format, or else they were treated as distinct breaks wherein the characters momentarily escape from the circumstances and conflicts of the story. The Freed unit musicals overcame the break between the musical's story and its "show"—and thus the tension between the star as dramatic character and as musical performer. And in the process, the narrative universe itself, the virtual world of the film, was steadily infected by music and energy and transformed into a distinctly utopian realm.

Music and narrative had been integrated in earlier musicals, notably in the musical operettas of Ernst Lubitsch, like THE LOVE PARADE (1929), and in MGM's 1930s hit operettas with Jeanette MacDonald and Nelson Eddy, like NAUGHTY MARIETTA (1935) and ROSE MARIE (1936). Donen later remarked that the objective of the Freed unit was to develop a musical form with "its own reality," as in those operettas. But as Donen noted, the Freed unit musicals also had a distinctive "energy, which has mainly to do with (a) America and (b) dancing."[37] Nowhere was that more evident perhaps than in the 1949 codirectorial debut of Gene Kelly and Stanley Donen in ON THE TOWN. A consummate integrated musical romance, the film went beyond the melding of song, dance, and narrative through its location shooting in New York City, thus melding reality and artifice.

ON THE TOWN was produced at a cost of just over $2 million and on a production schedule of thirty weeks, with ten weeks devoted to rehearsal and twenty to actual shooting. Based on Leonard Bernstein's score and a script by Comden and Green (adapted from their 1944 stage hit), the film centered on three sailors (Gene Kelly, Frank Sinatra, and Jules Munshin) who spend a twenty-four-hour liberty in New York City. The tone is established in an elaborate opening number as the men disembark from the Brooklyn Navy Yard and dance their way across Manhattan. This dynamic routine not only showcases New York but also, by intercutting from one locale to another in an otherwise seamless musical number, integrates the city's familiar landmarks into a high-energy celebration of the modern urban metropolis. The men team up with three women (Ann Miller, Vera-Ellen, and Betty Garrett), each a thorough New Yorker with a comic-topical dilemma: one is an overworked cabbie, another is belly dancing to finance ballet lessons, and the third suffers loudly from war-induced sexual neglect. The men successfully liberate the three women, enabling them to express themselves musically and to overcome their woes. In the process, the couples gradually transform the most familiar of cities into an arena of musical play and expression.

Released during the 1949 holiday season, ON THE TOWN was a strong critical hit and earned $2.9 million. It underscored the currency and vitality of the MGM dance musical while securing the ascent of Donen and Kelly to director status. (Their next collaboration as codirectors would be SINGIN' IN THE RAIN.) The location shooting in New York brought a new dimension to the postwar musical and marked a curious complement to the dramatic films shot there in the late 1940s. Most of the dramas were done in black-and-white, however, and often employed a documentary realist style which corresponded closely to their downbeat view of postwar urban life. in fact, the upbeat Technicolor musicals with their idealized couples and utopian milieu provide a fascinating contrast to the *noir* thrillers and urban crime films, whose protagonists are utterly alone in a world gone terribly wrong.

Film Noir, *Documentary Realism,* and the *Social Problem Drama*

In 1946, after five years of enforced optimism and prosocial posturing, American movie screens suddenly darkened. "Whoever went to the movies with any regularity in 1946 was caught in the midst of Hollywood's profound postwar affection for morbid drama," wrote *Life* magazine's David Marsham. "From January through December deep shadows, clutching hands, exploding revolvers, sadistic villains and heroines tormented with deeply rooted diseases of the mind flashed across the screen in a panting display of psychoneuroses, unsublimated sex and murder most foul."[38]

What Marsham described, of course, was *film noir,* which underwent a tremendous surge in 1946 that actually intensified in the coming years. And beyond its now-familiar terrain of hard-boiled detective thrillers and female Gothics, *film noir* also had a significant impact on two other postwar cycles: the semidocumentary crime film and the social problem drama (or message picture). Both cycles—as outgrowths, in a sense, of the war film—reflected Hollywood's increasing preoccupation with realism. in fact, these *film noir,* realist, and social problem trends actively, perhaps inevitably, cross-fertilized in the postwar era. A 1946 *New York Times* review of the detective *noir* THE DARK CORNER, for instance, noted the "atmospheric realism" in what was essentially a "sizzling piece of melodrama."[39] And James Agee, discussing a spate of 1946 *noir* thrillers in *The Nation,* praised THE KILLERS for its "journalistic feeling" and its "jazzed-up realism." In terms of social immediacy, Agee saw THE KILLERS as symptomatic of the crime thriller generally: "For many years so much has been forbidden or otherwise made impossible in Hollywood that crime has offered one of the few chances for getting any sort of vitality on the screen."[40]

Despite its social-realist dimension, *film noir* was at base a highly stylized treatment of contemporary social and human conditions. As noted earlier, *film noir's* distinctive way of telling stories and distinctive way of seeing included: low-key lighting and expressive camera work; a penchant for night scenes, rain-slick streets, and dark claustrophobic interiors; convoluted narrative construction, often employing romantic voice-over narration, flashbacks, nonlinear plot development, and an unsatisfactory or ambiguous outcome; an emphasis on character psychology and obsessive sexuality; an overall mood of anxiety, alienation, and despair; and a general distrust of legitimate social authority and institutions that, together with the preceding elements, often created a powerful (albeit implicit) social critique.

Immediately after the war, these elements were most clearly evident in the hard-boiled detective film, which reached a peak of sorts in 1946 with films like THE BIG SLEEP, THE KILLERS, THE BLUE DAHLIA, THE LADY IN THE LAKE, THE DARK MIRROR, THE DARK CORNER, and BLACK ANGEL. The year's "morbid dramas" also included a number of dark romances featuring star-crossed lovers, like THE POSTMAN ALWAYS RINGS TWICE (John Garfield and Lana Turner) and GILDA (Glenn Ford and Rita Hayworth), with money and murder as well as adultery on their minds. As in their predecessor DOUBLE INDEMNITY (1944), the dominant viewpoint in these films is that of a cynical male who falls victim to a duplicitous *femme fatale.* The female viewpoint, meanwhile, was privileged in films like THE STRANGE LOVE OF MARTHA IVERS and TEMPTATION, which center on a murderous heroine (Barbara Stanwyck and Merle Oberon, respectively), thus effectively melding the woman's picture with the *noir* thriller.

Hollywood's two pioneering *noir* stylists, Alfred Hitchcock and Orson Welles, continued to shape its development in 1946—Hitchcock with NOTORIOUS and Welles with THE STRANGER, each of which effectively blends the Gothic romance with the war-related espionage thriller in a classic *noir* film. Another film worth mentioning here is Welles's THE LADY FROM SHANGHAI (costarring Orson Welles, who also wrote and directed), a Rita Hayworth vehicle initiated in late 1946 as a follow-up to GILDA. Veering wildly from black comedy to sexual psychodrama to murderous intrigue, the film presents Hayworth as coolly homicidal and sexually manipulative—the consummate *femme noire*. Upon its completion in early 1947, however, Columbia's Harry Cohn was not happy with the film or the depiction of his top star, and he withheld THE LADY FROM SHANGHAI until 1948.

In 1947, Hollywood's *film noir* output accelerated and took on a new complexity as the period style began to cross-fertilize with other emerging postwar strains. Sometimes *noir* only slightly shaded an established formula or recombined a bit with another genre. CROSSFIRE, for example, is very much a hard-boiled crime thriller except for two elements which interject elements of both the message picture and the police procedural: the killer (Robert Ryan) is an ex-GI motivated by rabid anti-Semitism, and he is eventually brought to justice by a police detective (Robert Young) operating very much by the book. Other genres were also effectively reworked in 1947 as *noir* intrigues with a social angle: the boxing film in BODY AND SOUL, tracing the rise of a fighter (John Garfield) by any means necessary, including his cooperation with the mob; and the prison drama BRUTE FORCE, in which inmates (led by Burt Lancaster) revolt against a sadistic head guard and a corrupt criminal justice system. The gangster genre collided with *film noir* in KISS OF DEATH (1947), a downbeat film about a mobster (Victor Mature) who is captured and turns state's evidence; after testifying, he and his family are stalked by a former cohort (Richard Widmark in his stunning film debut as a cackling, psychopathic killer).

KISS OF DEATH also evinced an emerging realist trend, both in its depiction of police procedures and its use of location shooting and sound. The film was directed by Henry Hathaway, whose two previous films, THE HOUSE ON 92ND STREET (1945) and 13 RUE MADELEINE (1946), were produced for Fox by the March of Time veteran Louis de Rochemont. Those films established the currency and basic conventions of the semi-documentary investigative drama—including objective voice-over narration, location shooting, use of nonactors, and little or no musical scoring. Those films had been war-related espionage thrillers involving U.S. federal agents, but KISS OF DEATH was a straight crime film. Other crime thrillers pushed even more aggressively into the realm of documentary realism, notably BOOMERANG and T-MEN in 1947, and CALL NORTHSIDE 777 and THE NAKED CITY in 1948. Shot on location and based on actual criminal cases, all of these films followed an investigation through its various procedures to an inevitably favorable outcome.

At first glance, the semidocumentary crime dramas seem antithetical to *film noir,* and in fact these films do indicate important changes in the Hollywood crime film. "The semi-documentaries are a good example of the shift away from the radicalism of *film noir,*" notes Michael Walker, in that they "celebrate the efficacy of the American crime-fighting institutions" and tend to "marginalize or discredit" the low-life types and losers who are more sympathetically portrayed in *noir* thrillers. Although shot on location, they favor daylight scenes and well-lit interiors, and the dominant setting of a police

Film noir, *social problem drama, and police procedural effectively coalesced in*
CROSSFIRE (RKO, 1947).

headquarters conveys a sense of order. The voice-over in most semidocumentaries, like
the authoritative "voice of God" of the documentary and newsreel, is "completely foreign to the highly subjective, frequently painful" narration in *noir* films. And the linear,
cause-and-effect development of the semidocumentary narrative is fundamentally at
odds with the convoluted structure of most *noir* thrillers.[41] In terms of character and
theme, as Frank Krutnik argues, the semidocumentary crime thrillers "signaled a shift
away from the 'tough' thriller's obsession with psychological breakdown and sexual
malaise, or at least they recast these elements within a perspective which stressed the
normative processes of law and social order."[42] Generally eschewing a romantic subplot
or central female character, these films focus closely on "the case," which invariably is
solved by film's end.

As both Walker and Krutnik recognize, however, few semidocumentary thrillers maintained this clear distinction from *film noir.* in fact, the two seemingly antithetical forms—
the realistic, reactionary, reassuring, authoritative, upbeat semidocumentary versus the
expressionistic, subversive, disturbing, confusing, and downbeat *film noir*—clearly began
to intermingle as soon as the semidocumentary veered from war-related spy films to
crime thrillers after the war. BOOMERANG, for example, was a de Rochemont production
for Fox filmed entirely on location in a small town in the Northeast and was based on an
actual case. It traces the dogged efforts of a disillusioned state's attorney (Dana Andrews)
to prove that a maladjusted war veteran (Arthur Kennedy) did not murder a local priest.

Directed by Elia Kazan (his second feature), BOOMERANG was far darker and more complex than the previous de Rochemont productions and was scarcely a testimonial to institutional authorities and the machinery of social justice. Nor did it commend the process of postwar rehabilitation. Andrews's attorney does manage to overcome his own malaise and clear the wrongly accused vet, but only by exposing local prejudices and the ineptitude of the criminal justice system. Moreover, the failure to apprehend the actual murderer offsets the film's upbeat outcome.

Kazan directed another breakthrough film for Fox in 1947, GENTLEMAN'S AGREEMENT, an investigative drama with an explicit social problem theme centering on socially sanctioned anti-Semitism. Shot largely on location in New York City, GENTLEMAN'S AGREEMENT features a journalist (Gregory Peck) who poses as a Jew to experience firsthand the deep-seated prejudices of mainstream American society. A prestige project scripted by Moss Hart (from Laura Z. Hobson's best-seller) and costarring John Garfield and Dorothy McGuire, the Zanuck production was a tremendous hit. Considered daring and progressive in its day, GENTLEMAN'S AGREEMENT impressed critics, scored Oscars for best picture and best director, and was among the year's top box-office performers. Coming on the heels of THE LOST WEEKEND in 1945 and THE BEST YEARS OF OUR LIVES in 1946 (both of which also won best-picture Oscars), GENTLEMAN'S AGREEMENT affirmed the currency of the realistic, male-oriented social problem film. Along with CROSSFIRE, GENTLEMAN'S AGREEMENT indi-

Gregory Peck in GENTLEMAN'S AGREEMENT *(20th Century–Fox, 1947).*

cated that Hollywood movies might effectively present more liberal-humanist, if not openly leftist, political views.

The burgeoning social realism and left-liberalism in postwar Hollywood was due to several factors, particularly the influx of new talent and the impact of the war and of war-related films. The war and immediate postwar era saw the emergence of a new crop of writers and directors in Hollywood, many of whom brought with them a progressive political agenda and a strong interest in film realism. Among these were Kazan, Robert Rossen, Jules Dassin, Abraham Polonsky, Nicholas Ray, Joseph Losey, Fred Zinnemann, and Anthony Mann. Many were trained in the New York theater during the 1930s, often working with politically and aesthetically radical companies, such as the Group Theatre, the Actors Studio (cofounded by Kazan), and the Theatre Union. Equally important was the war itself and its on-screen treatment in Hollywood features and documentaries. In a sense, the war had presented Hollywood with a massive "social problem" which utterly consumed the industry from 1942 through 1945 and demanded a more overtly social, political, and realistic approach to filmmaking than ever before. Filmmakers continued to refine this approach after the war, despite the phasing-out of the war film itself, and audiences (and critics) clearly responded.

By late 1947, however, serious counterforces were militating against Hollywood's nascent social realist movement. In fact, GENTLEMAN'S AGREEMENT was released only weeks after the HUAC hearings, the Waldorf Statement, and RKO's consequent firing of Adrian Scott and Edward Dmytryk (the producer and director of CROSSFIRE). As these and other developments indicated, the conservative forces both inside and outside the movie industry meant to stifle any trace of left-leaning liberalism in movies. The Motion Picture Alliance railed against the "sizable doses of Communist propaganda" in scores of recent movies, including PRIDE OF THE MARINES, THE STRANGE LOVE OF MARTHA IVERS, and THE BEST YEARS OF OUR LIVES. The right-wing novelist and screenwriter Ayn Rand, on behalf of the Alliance, drafted a "Screen Guide for Americans" with such headings as "Don't Smear the Free Enterprise System," "Don't Deify the 'Common Man,'" "Don't Glorify Failure," and "Don't Smear Industrialists." Even Eric Johnston, head of Hollywood's Motion Picture Association of America (MPAA), climbed onto the conservative bandwagon. "We'll have no more *Grapes of Wrath*, we'll have no more *Tobacco Road*s," vowed Johnston in 1947. "We'll have no more films that show the seamy side of American life."[43]

In the aftermath of HUAC and the blacklist, many questioned whether Hollywood would dare to venture beyond the safe and predictable forms of light entertainment, while others saw the emerging realistic aesthetic as a reason for optimism. James Agee voiced both of those views in a January 1948 piece in *The Nation* as he pondered the success of GENTLEMAN'S AGREEMENT and CROSSFIRE in light of recent events: "It is hard to believe that absolutely first-rate works of art can ever again be made in Hollywood, but it would be idiotic to assume that flatly. If they are to be made there, they will most probably develop along the directions worked out during the past year or two; they will be journalistic, semi-documentary, and 'social-minded,' or will start that way and transcend those levels."[44]

Other indications were less encouraging, however. John Huston told the *New Yorker*'s Lillian Ross about battling Warners simply to include the word *labor* in THE TREASURE OF THE SIERRA MADRE, which he had recently completed; he was having similar problems on his current Warners project, KEY LARGO, over a line of dialogue that quoted FDR on the United Nations and the reasons for fighting World War II. Ross also reported that she had been told by William Wyler "that he is convinced that he could not make [THE BEST YEARS OF OUR LIVES] today and that Hollywood will provide no more films like *The Grapes of Wrath* and *Crossfire*."[45]

Hollywood's more progressive efforts were indeed stifled in the late 1940s; the careers of both Huston and Wyler are cases in point. The difficulties faced at Paramount by Wyler and his Liberty Films partners already have been described—imagine Capra making a film that did not deify the common man or smear industrialists. Huston was similarly constrained at Warners, once deemed the bastion of film realism and a haven for left-leaning filmmakers. After writing and directing THE TREASURE OF THE SIERRA MADRE and KEY LARGO, both released in 1948 to excellent critical and popular response, Huston left Warners in disgust. "The complexion of the place was changing," Huston later said of the studio. "Its great innovative period was in decline, if not over."[46] JOHNNY BELINDA, a dark social problem drama about a young deaf-mute woman (Jane Wyman) who is a victim of rape and of small-town gossip and prejudice, is another example of Warners' conservative turn in 1948. Jack Warner so disliked the film that, before its release, he refused to renew the contract of the director, Jean Negulesco. JOHNNY BELINDA went on to become a huge critical and commercial hit, earning $4.25 million and nine Oscar nominations—including best director. At that point, Warner relented, but Negulesco had no interest in returning to the studio.[47]

RKO underwent a reversal similar to Warners' after the Howard Hughes takeover in May 1948. Hughes's archconservative political views were utterly at odds with those of RKO's liberal production chief, Dore Schary, and their differences affected the studio's filmmaking. A strong proponent of the social problem film and the socially astute crime thriller, Schary had a number of projects in the works at RKO that Hughes intensely disliked. When Schary left for MGM a few months after the takeover, Hughes quashed the "liberal" trends at RKO and temporarily shelved several of Schary's pet projects, notably Joseph Losey's antiwar fable THE BOY WITH GREEN HAIR (1948) and Nicholas Ray's *noir* thriller THEY LIVE BY NIGHT (1949).

Schary found the political climate less tense but quite conservative at MGM under Nick Schenck and Louis Mayer. By 1948, MGM's only ventures into *film noir* or message pictures were through a Loew's distribution deal with Enterprise Pictures, whose releases that year included the masterful *film noir* FORCE OF EVIL and a semidocumentary drama about European war orphans, THE SEARCH. While Schary subdued his progressive bent at MGM, he did initiate a few low-cost crime thrillers with strong social elements that were released in 1949, notably INTRUDER IN THE DUST, an adaptation of a Faulkner novel with an anti-lynching theme, and BORDER INCIDENT, a semidocumentary about illegal Mexican migrant workers.

Twentieth Century–Fox was the only studio to sustain a steady output of *films noirs*, semidocumentary thrillers, and social problem dramas in the late 1940s, owing largely to the interests and efforts of Darryl Zanuck. Zanuck had been a proponent of drama "torn from the day's headlines" since his early career as a writer and production executive at Warner Bros., and he continued to pursue that strategy at Fox. Indeed, his predilection for message pictures resulted in the two "seamy" prewar pictures, THE GRAPES OF WRATH and TOBACCO ROAD, that Eric Johnston had so fervently disclaimed in 1947. And at the time of that disclaimer, Zanuck had his usual run of seamy projects in the works, including GENTLEMAN'S AGREEMENT, THE SNAKE PIT, and CALL NORTHSIDE 777.

THE SNAKE PIT was perhaps the darkest of the lot. Based on a true story (and best-selling book) about a woman's descent into mental illness, the film also presents a powerful critique of the treatment of the mentally ill. Directed by Anatole Litvak in a semi-documentary style, THE SNAKE PIT was released in late 1948 to a strong critical and commercial response, earning over $4 million. CALL NORTHSIDE 777, a semidocumentary crime thriller shot in Chicago, recounts the crusade of a cynical reporter (James Stewart) to prove the innocence of a death row inmate awaiting execution. Clearly influenced by BOOMERANG, CALL NORTHSIDE 777 incorporates *noir* elements and is less than flattering in its portrayal of the authorities and the criminal justice system. Fox also turned out more straightforward *noir* films in 1948, such as ROAD HOUSE (directed by Jean Negulesco after leaving Warners) and CRY OF THE CITY. The studio countered these darker crime films in 1948 with an upbeat semidocumentary cold war spy thriller, THE IRON CURTAIN, an exposé of Soviet espionage in Canada.

By decade's end, Fox was by far the most aggressive studio in the production of message films and socially sensitive thrillers, and it was the only company willing to risk an occasional prestige-level social problem film. As *Fortune* magazine observed in early 1949: "Innovations in the shape of crusading themes, realism, the psychological view, and documentary style have been adopted notably by Darryl Zanuck of Twentieth Century-Fox." But *Fortune* also noted that Zanuck "could risk a 'Snake Pit' because he had twenty-five or more other pictures a year and Betty Grable."[48] Zanuck's principal risk at the time was PINKY, another ambitious social drama in the mold of GENTLEMAN'S AGREEMENT. Personally produced by Zanuck and directed by Elia Kazan, PINKY centers on the struggles of a light-skinned black woman (Jeanne Crain) who has been living in the North and passing as white; upon returning to her small-town southern home, she decides to forgo her white existence—including her betrothal to a prosperous doctor—and to accept her racial and social identity. Once again, Zanuck and Kazan struck just the right balance of realism and melodrama, of social commentary and personal anguish. And while PINKY was not quite the critical success of GENTLEMAN'S AGREEMENT or THE SNAKE PIT, its $4 million in rentals was on a par commercially with those two previous hits.[49]

While PINKY dominated the box office in 1949, most of the critical accolades went to ALL THE KING'S MEN, a political drama which took top honors from the New York Film Critics, won the Golden Globe (voted best picture by Hollywood's foreign press), and also won the Academy Award for best picture. Adapted from Robert Penn Warren's 1946 best-seller, ALL THE KING'S MEN was written, produced, and directed by Robert Rossen in a quasi-independent deal with Columbia. Loosely based on the career of the infamous Louisiana governor Huey Long, the film traces the rise and seemingly inevitable corruption of small-town politician Willie Stark (Broderick Crawford), who becomes a ruthless yet effective demagogue and eventually is assassinated. In both film technique and narrative construction, ALL THE KING'S MEN is a stylistic *tour de force*. Rossen shot the film entirely on location (in an unnamed state) using only available light; he cast third-rate character actor Crawford as Willie and used nonactors in minor roles. (Crawford won an Oscar for his performance, as did newcomer Mercedes McCambridge in a supporting role.) Rossen employed various *noir* techniques as well, notably a complex flashback structure and the brooding voice-over narration by Stark's introspective and deeply disillusioned political aide (John Ireland). Beyond the downbeat nature of the climactic assassination, the deeper moral and political questions raised are left unresolved.[50]

Judging from the success of PINKY and ALL THE KING'S MEN, Hollywood had not yet written off the social problem drama, and in fact 1949 saw the release of three other successful "race" pictures—THE HOME OF THE BRAVE, LOST BOUNDARIES, and INTRUDER IN THE DUST. It should be noted, however, that all three were relatively low-risk ventures; none was a high-cost star vehicle based on a celebrated presold property, and each packaged its social message in familiar narrative terms.[51] INTRUDER IN THE DUST is a *noir* intrigue set in the South about an old woman and a young boy, both white, who solve a murder and thereby prevent the lynching of a black man. LOST BOUNDARIES, an independent de Rochemont production, is a semidocumentary based on a true story and shot on location in small-town New England; the white community discovers that the local doctor and his wife are actually of black descent. THE HOME OF THE BRAVE, produced by the independent Stanley Kramer, traces the efforts of an army psychiatrist to discover the cause of a black soldier's psychologically induced paralysis, which turns out to be the result of racist treatment.

All three films did well critically and commercially; Bosley Crowther of the *Times* was a particularly vocal advocate of the "race drama" trend. In May, he termed THE HOME OF THE BRAVE "a drama of force and consequence" and "a most propitious 'first' in the cycle of Negro prejudice pictures which Hollywood now has in the works." In July, he wrote that the "statement of the anguish and ironies of racial taboo [in LOST BOUNDARIES] is clear, eloquent and moving." In September, he noted that in PINKY, Zanuck and Fox "shift the scope of observation into that more noted arena of racism, the

The late-1940s cycle of "race pictures" included HOME OF THE BRAVE *(UA, 1949), which also marked the war film's resurgence. James Edwards (left) and Lloyd Bridges (center) costarred.*

Deep South . . . [in] a picture that is vivid, revealing and emotionally intense." Crowther was most enthusiastic about MGM's INTRUDER IN THE DUST, which he described in November as "probably this year's pre-eminent picture and one of the great cinema dramas of our time." He acknowledged, however, that the "deeper meanings might be utterly missed" by those simply looking for a crime thriller.[52] *Variety* also was enthusiastic and optimistic about the recent spate of message films dealing with "anti-Negro prejudice." These films, asserted *Variety* in late 1949, "proved that there is no subject that is taboo in Hollywood."[53]

That was scarcely the case, however. In 1950, Hollywood went into a full-scale retreat from message pictures and prestige-level social problem dramas. The retreat was due to a range of factors, many of them well outside industry control—HUAC's ongoing investigation of Communists in the U.S. government and the 1949 Alger Hiss trial; the Soviet A-bomb tests and the fall of China to the Communists later that same year. Inside the industry, however, the blacklist of the Hollywood Ten was augmented in 1948–1949 by a steadily expanding "graylist" which included many of Hollywood's more progressive filmmakers. By 1950, there were rumors of HUAC's imminent return, which in fact occurred in early 1951, resulting in the complete collapse of Hollywood liberalism, the blacklisting of hundreds of "subversives," and the end of the American cinema's erstwhile social realist movement.

While progressive message pictures and high-stakes social problem films disappeared from American screens, Hollywood continued to turn out *noir* films in the early 1950s, including such classics as SUNSET BOULEVARD and THE ASPHALT JUNGLE in 1950. The resurgent war film also displayed a distinct *noir* influence, most prominently in Fox's late-1949 release TWELVE O'CLOCK HIGH. But besides that Zanuck-produced hit reexamining the "problem" of war—albeit as a more personal and psychological than social problem—Fox backed completely away from the prestige-level social problem drama, opting instead for low-cost, low-risk thrillers like PANIC IN THE STREETS, NO WAY OUT, NIGHT AND THE CITY, and WHERE THE SIDEWALK ENDS (all 1950). A few of these treated significant social issues but did so without incurring the wrath of conservative critics and social watchdogs. As Brian Neve notes in *Film and Politics in America:* "Even when political controversy made explicit social content a liability, *films noirs* generally evaded scrutiny."[54] But by 1950, the disillusioned heroes, subcurrents of anxiety, and implicit social critiques of earlier message pictures and crime thrillers were noticeably absent. The moral ambiguity and existential angst so essential to these forms had been excised. *Film noir,* for the time being at least, was undergoing a belated postwar rehabilitation.

CASE STUDY: MARK HELLINGER'S *THE KILLERS,* *BRUTE FORCE,* AND *THE NAKED CITY*

As seen in chapter 4, Mark Hellinger played a key role in the prewar overhaul of the Warner Bros. crime film on pictures like THE ROARING TWENTIES, THEY DRIVE BY NIGHT, and HIGH SIERRA. During the war, Hellinger rose to producer status, and in 1945 he signed with Universal as an in-house independent. Hellinger produced three films for Universal after the war: THE KILLERS in 1946, BRUTE FORCE in 1947, and THE NAKED CITY in 1948. All three were hits, and all three were indicative of the dominant postwar trends in the crime film: THE KILLERS is a hard-boiled detective *noir;* BRUTE FORCE is a prison drama with social problem overtones and a dynamic blend of realism and *film noir;* and THE NAKED CITY is a semidocumentary police procedural which depicts urban life and day-to-day police work in much more immediate terms than other postwar semidocumentary thrillers.

The formation of Mark Hellinger Productions and Hellinger's deal with Universal were announced in a page-one *Daily Variety* story in August 1945. As *Variety* noted, Hellinger's contract as an in-house independent was modeled on Walter Wanger's— although the actual details were somewhat different. Universal paid Hellinger a salary on a flat-fee, per-film basis: $25,000 for script development and another $25,000 to produce each picture. Universal also would "loan" Hellinger up to one-half the production costs and arrange financing, if necessary, for the balance. Once his film was released, the loan would be repaid and Hellinger would take 25 percent of the profits.[55]

With his initial Universal project, THE KILLERS, Hellinger confirmed his efficiency and creative acumen as a producer, and his savvy sense of the crime thriller as well. The film was based on Ernest Hemingway's short story "The Killers," which describes an enigmatic figure named Swede who calmly waits in his dark rooming house for two hired assassins, whom he knows are coming, to find and kill him. Hellinger's plan, as he explained to Hemingway's attorney, was "to use the story practically in toto as an open-

Mark Hellinger (right) signs newcomer Burt Lancaster to star in THE KILLERS *(Universal, 1946).*

ing sequence and then carry on from there with the same two killers and in the same established mood."[56]

After securing the rights to the story, Hellinger hired Tony Veiller to do the adaptation (with eventual uncredited assistance from John Huston).[57] In the script, an insurance investigator learns through a complex, randomly ordered mélange of flashbacks—and flashbacks within flashbacks—that Swede was a washed-up prizefighter and small-time hood who was murdered for betraying his accomplices in a heist, a fatal decision motivated by Swede's love of a double-crossing *femme fatale.* Thus, much like the recent reconstructions of James M. Cain's *Double Indemnity* and *Mildred Pierce,* the adaptation of "The Killers" took on obvious *noir* dimensions—the flashback structure and convoluted time frame, an obsession with the past and with fate, the enigmatic central character betrayed by a heartless black widow—none of which was in the Hemingway story, though it all seemed to emerge quite naturally from the motivating situation.[58]

To direct THE KILLERS, Hellinger hired *noir* stylist Robert Siodmak (PHANTOM LADY, THE SPIRAL STAIRCASE, etc.). He cast Burt Lancaster (in his screen debut) as Swede, Edmund O'Brien as the detective, and Ava Gardner as the deadly love interest. The picture was a straight studio shoot with no location work and few exteriors; it was scheduled for nine weeks and budgeted at $875,000.[59] Hellinger closely supervised production, which closed in late June, two days behind schedule but almost $50,000 under budget. Hellinger oversaw editing in July and had the picture ready for release by August.[60] Completed within weeks of the International merger, THE KILLERS was heavily promoted by Universal as an exemplary product of the "new" U-I.

THE KILLERS was a hit, returning domestic rentals of $2.5 million and worldwide earnings of $3 million. Net profits to Universal were nearly $1 million—with $250,000 going to Mark Hellinger Productions.[61] The film was critically well received and scored Academy Award nominations for Veiller's script, Siodmak's direction, and Miklos Rozsa's score. Hellinger won critical praise as well. The "good strident journalistic feeling for tension, noise, sentiment, and jazzed-up realism," wrote James Agee in *The Nation,* "is probably chiefly to the credit of the producer, Mark Hellinger."[62]

Hellinger's next project, BRUTE FORCE, was another well-crafted, moderately priced thriller starring Burt Lancaster. The dark, violent prison drama centers on six convicts (Lancaster, Howard Duff, Jeff Corey, et al.) who rebel against a sadistic head guard (Hume Cronyn) in an inhumane, incompetently run prison. While the film is as stylized in some ways as THE KILLERS, especially in its use of chiaroscuro lighting and expressive camera work, BRUTE FORCE also employed realist techniques and included some location shooting. Crucial to this blend was the collaboration between director Jules Dassin and cinematographer William Daniels. Dassin, a relative newcomer with stage experience in New York (including the Group Theatre), had come into cinema by way of radio writing and had directed only a few B-grade features. Daniels, on the other hand, was an accomplished cinematographer—although his celebrated work as Garbo's cameraman at MGM scarcely seemed to prepare him for something like BRUTE FORCE. But Daniels was a consummate professional, who readily adapted to the demands of the shoot, and he worked well with the inexperienced but talented Dassin.

Despite its aggressively downbeat story, BRUTE FORCE did well commercially, with domestic earnings of $2.2 million in 1947. But it drew mixed reviews, owing largely to the uncommonly violent and depressing story of brutalized inmates and a deadly prison riot in which the rebellious convicts are killed in an apocalyptic finale—although not

Howard Duff and Yvonne De Carlo in BRUTE FORCE *(Universal, 1947).*

before the sadistic Cronyn is thrown from a guard tower. A number of critics noted that the film's condemnation of prison conditions gave it a social problem dimension; many drew comparisons to Nazi concentration camps. Bosley Crowther in the *New York Times,* for instance, posited a direct parallel, "with the prisoners the pitiable victims and the authorities the villains." Crucial to his view was the portrayal of Cronyn's sadistic guard: with the inclinations of a Nazi stormtrooper, he is an obvious fascist who listens to Wagner while torturing prisoners.[63]

For his next picture, tentatively titled "Homicide," Hellinger wanted to chronicle the day-to-day police work of a New York City homicide squad. Reteaming Jules Dassin and William Daniels, the film would be shot on location in a semidocumentary style, and it would be the first such film to follow a murder investigation exclusively from a police detective's viewpoint. The film also would present an authentic portrait of Hellinger's beloved New York City, where his own writing career began. In September 1946, just after the release of THE KILLERS and while BRUTE FORCE was in postproduction, Hellinger sold Universal on the project and sent writer Malvin Wald to New York on what was essentially a month-long research junket, mainly to observe the Manhattan Police Department. "At this point I am making no effort to figure out a story line," Wald wrote to Hellinger in October. "Every case gives me more and more story material and characters. I think when I get back to Hollywood it will be more a job of editing what I have

learned than creating something new. The important thing is that I come back . . . knowing more about New York homicide detectives than any writer in Hollywood."[64]

By April 1947, Wald and Al Maltz, whom Hellinger hired to coscript the film, had
completed a shooting script for "Homicide." The story, based on actual case files, centers on the brutal murder of a young woman and the subsequent manhunt for her killer,
who eventually is apprehended after a chase across the Williamsburg Bridge. While the
murder investigation provided the spine of the story, the writers recognized the opportunities inherent in the semidocumentary format to rework the crime thriller. Maltz
even included a page of "Production notes for Mark Hellinger" in his final screenplay
draft, including this suggestion: "This film will depend for its effect on a sense of
absolute authenticity, upon its honest portrayal of people and life, upon the absence of
forced effects, forced scenes, forced melodramatics."[65]

In May 1947, Universal officially approved the film—now titled "The Naked City"—
and a $1.2 million budget. Hellinger then dispatched a second unit to New York for an
intensive twenty-four-day shoot.[66] The second unit shot in New York for two weeks
without the cast, simply filming the various locations where the story was to take place.
Bad weather plagued the shoot, as did myriad technical and logistical problems. For a
period of four straight days, for example, rain, unruly crowds, and equipment problems
kept the second unit from doing a single camera setup. These difficulties underscored
the value of working in a studio, but Hellinger was satisfied with the trade-off—capturing the authenticity and atmosphere of Manhattan on film.[67]

In June, Hellinger and Dassin took the cast and first unit to New York for eight weeks
of principal photography, with just over half the script to be filmed on location. The
shoot went well, but shortly after returning to the studio in August, Hellinger suffered
a mild heart attack and was forced to monitor the remainder of the production from his
hospital room. Dassin closed production in mid-September, staying on to supervise cutting with Hellinger, who by then was out of the hospital. Frank Skinner and Miklos
Rozsa scored the film later in the fall, and Hellinger himself recorded the voice-over
narration for the picture, including its now-famous epitaph, "There are eight million stories in the naked city. This has been one of them." By mid-December, THE NAKED
CITY was ready to preview, but Hellinger never saw the finished product. On 22
December 1947, at age 44, Hellinger died of a massive coronary.

THE NAKED CITY was released in early March 1948 and gave Hellinger Productions
another hit, returning $2.4 million and finishing among the top fifty box-office releases
of the year.[68] The semidocumentary form by then was quite familiar; in fact, de
Rochement's CALL NORTHSIDE 777 and Anthony Mann's T-MEN (on U.S. Treasury
agents) both were released a few weeks earlier. But THE NAKED CITY is in a class by
itself among semidocumentary crime films. It is relentlessly authentic in its treatment
of police procedures and makes no effort to idealize or romanticize the central character (Barry Fitzgerald as a police lieutenant), the other detectives, or the criminals. The
investigation itself is routine to the point of banality, although the final chase does provide a solid dramatic payoff. Equally important, the film presents a remarkable portrait
of postwar New York in all its brutal grandeur, much of it captured by the hidden cameras used in many scenes to augment the documentary quality.

Critical response to THE NAKED CITY was rather uneven, owing largely to the film's
unrelenting documentary quality. Agee in *Time* praised Daniels's "lovely eye for space,
size, and light" as well as the "visually majestic finish" (the final chase), but he found little else to recommend the film.[69] Crowther in the *Times* called it "virtually a Hellinger

Preparing to shoot the final chase scene in THE NAKED CITY *(Universal, 1948) on the Williamsburg Bridge.*

column on film," but he found the investigation, except for the "roaring 'Hitchcock' end," altogether tedious: "The drama is largely superficial, being no more than a conventional 'slice of life'—a routine and unrevealing episode in the everyday business of the cops."[70] Interestingly enough, other critics would praise THE NAKED CITY for precisely that quality. George Sadoul, for instance, later noted that "the banal plot of this crime thriller is merely an excuse for a semidocumentary portrait of the life of ordinary people in a major city"; he considered that portrait the film's principal achievement.[71] The Academy also responded favorably to the film's documentary quality, awarding Oscars to Daniels for his cinematography and to Paul Weatherwax for film editing. (Wald also was nominated for his screen story.)

THE NAKED CITY marked a sharp departure from most postwar crime thrillers, even semidocumentary films like BOOMERANG and CALL NORTHSIDE 777. The film's aggressive quest for authenticity, its focus solely on the police, and its unsentimentalized view of the workaday cop set it apart from the more socially astute—and at least implicitly progressive—realistic crime dramas of the period. These qualities set the tone for the more conservative police procedurals to come, and also for television "cop shows" such as *Dragnet* and, of course, *The Naked City*, the ABC-TV series which ran from 1958 to 1963 and was shot largely on location in New York. Despite its influence, however, THE NAKED CITY remained an exceptional film during the late 1940s—a crime film with virtually no trace of *noir* stylistics, and a semidocumentary drama with no social problem dimension.

Postscript: Paramount, DeMille, and SAMSON AND DELILAH

While forces both outside and inside the movie industry subdued Hollywood's progressive impulse after the late-1949 burst of race dramas and social problem films, perhaps the most significant development in the conservative swing at decade's end was the release of SAMSON AND DELILAH. Produced and directed by Cecil B. DeMille for Paramount and released in December 1949—only days before the studio's epochal theater divorcement took effect—SAMSON AND DELILAH was utterly at odds with the dominant genres, stylistic trends, and market strategies of the period. It was not only a throwback to an earlier era but an augur of things to come.

The first studio-produced, calculated blockbuster effort in years, SAMSON AND DELILAH was a lavish historical spectacle starring Victor Mature, Hedy Lamarr, and "a cast of thousands." Paramount raised its budget ceiling to $3.5 million for the production, and DeMille reportedly brought it in some $600,000 under budget in early 1949. Paramount devoted nearly a full year to postproduction and promotion, and the studio's investment paid off. SAMSON AND DELILAH became the first picture in nearly three years to earn over $5 million en route to total domestic earnings of $11.5 million, surpassing THE BEST YEARS OF OUR LIVES as the biggest box-office hit of the decade.[72]

The tremendous success of SAMSON AND DELILAH both in the United States and overseas rekindled Hollywood's hit-driven mentality while reasserting the currency of the big-budget historical spectacle, and it heralded a radical redirection of the movie industry in the 1950s. Indeed, although it recalled DeMille's earlier biblical epics like THE TEN COMMANDMENTS (1923) and THE SIGN OF THE CROSS (1932), SAMSON AND DELILAH was actually quite radical by postwar standards. The film was a lavish spectac-

George Sanders and Hedy Lamarr in Cecil B. DeMille's Technicolor costume epic
Samson and Delilah *(Paramount, 1949)*.

ular with global appeal designed to exploit Paramount's strengths as a producer-distributor rather than its once-vast theater chain. And "bringing together the Old Testament and Technicolor for the first time," as Bosley Crowther put it, the film also anticipated the marriage of large-scale epics with other technological innovations like CinemaScope and Cinerama.[73]

The success of SAMSON AND DELILAH spawned two similar hits in 1951, QUO VADIS? and DAVID AND BATHSHEBA, and much bigger hits were yet to come—THE ROBE in 1953, THE TEN COMMANDMENTS in 1956, and BEN-HUR in 1959. Each was a monumental international success which redefined the revenue potential of top movie hits, and each reinforced the blockbuster mentality of the New Hollywood. Thus, SAMSON AND DELILAH, clearly a watershed film, was more a film of the 1950s than the 1940s. in fact, it underscored the distinctive nature of the period that preceded it—the tense and heady postwar years, the vibrant twilight of Hollywood's classical era.

PART 4

☆

Ancillary Developments

12

Documenting the 1940s

Thomas Doherty

In 1940, the documentary presentation of real life, whether in newsreel, short subject, or feature-length form, was a subordinate entry in the staple program of classical Hollywood cinema, an attendant-in-waiting to the unchallenged supremacy of fanciful motion picture fiction in categories A or B. By the middle of the decade, however, news on-screen and the documentary contended with the entertainment feature film for impact and import. The war years witnessed the mature prime of the newsreel, theretofore little more than a moving image headline service, and the dynamic reemergence of the documentary, an option that had lain dormant in the American cinema since the silent era. Yet their elevation in status from the inconsequential to the indispensable was short-lived. Without the spectacle of a world at war and its intimate link to the world at home, attention to the newsreel and documentary waned. By 1950, both forms were diminished and disparaged—and one was facing extinction from a newly born rival, television.

Nonfiction Film Before World War II

On the eve of the Second World War, "the creative treatment of actuality" on screen came in four main versions—the newsreel, the screen magazine, the travelogue, and the exploration film.[1] All were ancillary entries in the theatrical package known as "the staple program," the moving image lineup that strung together A picture, B movie, short subject, cartoon, singalong, public service announcements, and charity appeals. Ushers announced movie showtimes from the moment the A picture started because the wraparound material was simply not the main attraction.

Despite their second-class status in the staple program, the newsreel and the documentary could claim an illustrious genealogy. In the silent era, when audiences still thrilled to the miracle of the moving image, the presentation of exotic and unvarnished reality was sufficient to induce spellbound attention and provided viable competition to comedy shorts and feature-length melodrama. On occasion, the commercial documentary might even challenge the feature film in popularity and prestige. Robert Flaherty's NANOOK OF THE NORTH (1922) not only gave the 1920s one of its most identifiable screen characters but pioneered a major cycle of ethnographic entertainments. The exploration and adventure films of Ernest B. Schoedsack and Meriam C. Cooper (GRASS, 1925; CHANG, 1927) and the moving-image photo albums of the husband-wife team of Martin and Osa Johnson (SIMBA, 1928) were emblematic of the silent documentaries that, while anthropomorphizing the animals and Americanizing the natives, offered sensational glimpses of creatures and civilizations never before recorded by motion picture cameras.[2]

Yet not since the silent era had feature-length documentaries competed on anything like equal footing with studio-style entertainment. In 1940, there was no contest. Determinedly illusionist, classical Hollywood cinema was by reputation and self-image a dream factory, a story machine whose assembly-line fictions were designed to transport moviegoers to an alternative sphere. "I've been to Paris, France, and I've been to Paris, Paramount," the director Ernst Lubitsch was reported to have said. "I think I prefer Paris, Paramount."[3]

Travelogue excursions aside, Lubitsch's soundstage Paris was not merely the preferred but the only version of Paris appearing regularly on screen.[4] Though audiences in metropolitan areas enjoyed a wider selection of options, a devoted moviegoer in a hinterland "nabe" (neighborhood theater) might never have seen a full-fledged documentary on the order of Robert Flaherty's MAN OF ARAN (1934), Pare Lorentz's THE PLOW THAT BROKE THE PLAINS (1936) and THE RIVER (1937), or Joris Ivens's SPANISH EARTH (1937) and THE POWER AND THE LAND (1940). In the late 1930s, the federal government, mainly through the U.S. Film Service, and the New Deal's Tennessee Valley Authority ventured tentatively into the production of a few informational films on farming, electricity, and nutrition, shown mainly to captive audiences in church basements and relief agencies. The filmmaker Margaret Cussler, working on educational films for the nutrition division of the Office of Defense Health and Welfare Services, described such officially sponsored projects, without irony, as "the kind of movie usually billed a 'selected short,' only in a smaller size." Prior to the war, the "documentary" label was deemed a "damning designation" by exhibitors, and Hollywood moguls avoided it. "Commercial picture circles were scarcely aware of the existence of such films," recalled Arthur L. Mayer, owner and operator of New York's Rialto Theater.[5]

The two universally accepted documentary formats were the newsreel and the screen magazine. Over two-thirds of the nation's approximately 16,500 theaters included one of five commercial newsreels as a component of the staple program: Paramount News (1927–1957), 20th Century–Fox's Movietone News (1927–1963), RKO-Pathé News (1931–1956), MGM's News of the Day (1927–1967), and Universal Newsreel (1929–1967). (In 1942 Warner Bros. briefly considered producing its own flagship newsreel, but the shortage of raw film stock during wartime, the unavailability of equipment, and the already cluttered market foreclosed the project. Warners ultimately bought the rights to Pathé News from RKO in 1947.) Issued twice weekly, and running approximately eight minutes in length, the newsreels provided a haphazard overview of current but not breaking news, a "pictorial parade" of headlines, human interest stories, sports highlights, and celebrity outings. Like the film stock, the news was in black-and-white: a sixth commercial newsreel, the All-American Newsreel, catered to African Americans. Founded in 1942, the All-American Newsreel was seen in weekly issues in 365 of the estimated 450 "Negro houses" that made up the segregated "race circuit."[6]

Two screen magazines, "The March of Time" (1935–1951, distributed by RKO until 1942 and by 20th Century–Fox thereafter) and "This Is America" (1942–1951, distributed by RKO), provided longer, more in-depth coverage of individual stories. Where the newsreels functioned mainly as a headline service, the screen magazines were comparable to the feature article of a newsweekly. Unhurried and expansive, their segments supplemented newsreel news by offering more background information, historical footage, staged scenes, and editorial opinion. In the mid-1930s, the "March of Time" lineup usually included three separate reports, but after May 1938 the monthly issue was devoted exclusively to one topic—a practice actually begun in January 1938 with its controversial "Inside Nazi Germany—1938." Issued monthly and running about twenty minutes, the screen magazines were defined by expert editing, compact exposition, and a tendency toward bombast. (A good index of the format is the "News on the March" sequence at the top of CITIZEN KANE, where Orson Welles parodied the "March of Time" style with corrosive accuracy.)[7]

Certainly prolonged exposure to the newsreel/screen magazine style invited a satiric response. With a calm authority whose tonalities bespoke a "crisis-crashing firmness," stern masculine voices modulated from sonorous baritone to buoyant tenor as segments switched from the seriousness of hard news to the frivolity of fads and fashion.[8] Disembodied, the voice seemed to preside over a "found" series of clips and intertitles, an anonymous Virgil to a motion picture world born of spontaneous generation—for

After September 1939, "The March of Time" devoted more and more of its coverage to the war in Europe—as in this sequence from "On Foreign Newsfronts," focusing on the Battle of Britain.

though the veteran radio voices were familiar enough, they spoke the company line with an omniscient detachment that effaced the individual personality from the editorial commentary.

A jumble of unrelated stories, a typical newsreel issue jump-cut a swath through national news, foreign pageantry, bathing beauties, baby shots, animal antics, and the off-beat candid shot, publicity stunt, or celebrity sighting. The contents of a Fox Movietone issue from the second week of January 1940 (vol. 22, no. 35) illustrate the scope and priorities of the sound newsreel before American entry into the Second World War: a battle between a German plane and a British warship; fighting on the Karelian front; a cutter breaking ice in the Hudson River; Sonja Henie performing in a Chicago ice show; Frank Murphy being named to the Supreme Court; Robert Jackson being named attorney general; Mrs. Roosevelt speaking out for an infantile paralysis drive; ice boating; horse racing on ice; and ski jumping. Though the leadoff items showcasing the most exciting footage are positioned at the top of the newsreel, and sports already finds its level at the close of the issue, the arrangement of the individual segments abides by no discernible hierarchy of importance or logical order: the momentous war news is followed by pallid scenes of a boat breaking ice in the Hudson River, while the skating star Sonja Henie precedes the announcements of Supreme Court and executive branch nominations.

The lineup was called the "smorgasbord," a potluck course of weighty news, light-hearted human interest stories, and a side dish of cheesecake. Infinitely adaptable, it was often prepared to suit ethnic and regional tastes. A metropolis like New York City warranted a special clip for local distribution (frequently featuring Mayor Fiorello La Guardia), but newsreel editors also obliged more obscure locales with stories of "sectional interest only," highlighting hometown teams in the sports clips and tailoring coverage to market demands. As a Fox Movietone editor explained, somewhat wearily: "Exhibitors in the Michigan area want that hardy annual from Holland, Michigan, which shows the goodly descendents of those highly sanitary Dutch burghers turning out en masse to clean their city streets. This is picturesque only the first time you see it, but Michiganders expect it every year. So we make a special of it for that territory."[9]

Newsreel journalism benefited from and encouraged innovations in motion picture camera technology, from higher-speed film stock to multiple lens turrets, from battery-driven motors to telephoto lenses. Obviously, the equipment requirements of studio system photography—a Hollywood style dependent on huge, stationary 35mm cameras requiring tripods, mounts, and precision lighting—needed to be modified for field situations, which required mobility and quick setups. In 1925, Bell & Howell developed the first of its famed 35mm Eyemo models specifically for newsreel coverage. For the next forty years, updates and improvements on the basic Eyemo model made it the camera of choice for field photography. After 1938, the 35mm Mitchell BNC studio camera and the Mitchell NC sound model also saw steady newsreel service, especially the Mitchell NC, which was lighter in weight, possessed a four-lens turret, and kept quiet enough for the filming of most spot news. Since both Mitchells required tripods, they were employed most frequently for the coverage of stationary events announced in advance, such as congressional hearings and awards ceremonies. By the late 1930s, the hand-held Bell & Howell Filmo model, the Eyemo's 16mm cousin, was the workhorse of the newsreel cameraman in the field, favored for its durability, portability, and ease of operation under duress.

Within the mass media matrix that included radio news reports, the photojournalism of *Life* and *Look,* and the coverage of daily newspapers, the weeklies *Time* and

Newsweek, and monthly magazines, the newsreel played a unique and, to the modern spectator, elusive role. Properly speaking, its purpose was neither to transmit information nor to provide perspective. The appeal of the newsreel was in the image, not the news. The classical Hollywood audience attended to the newsreels for the motion picture imprint of news already heard and digested. Radio brought the information first and fastest—the newsreel, days, weeks, or sometimes months afterwards—provided a visual analog, imprinting mental images of dramatic moments that audiences were already well acquainted with through radio reports and newspaper articles—black smoke billowing from sunken battleships in the aftermath of the Japanese attack on Pearl Harbor, President Roosevelt before a joint session of Congress demanding a declaration of war, the bodies of American GIs in the surf at Omaha Beach, and on and on. Such screen moments became pictorial shorthand for a whole series of historical touchstones—but only *after the fact*. The *simultaneous* arrival of image and information (today's network news "bulletin") is a legacy of television technology.[10]

In the main, the newsreel left muckraking and partisanship to the press. It was a force for cultural cohesion, not disruption, a medium with more allegiance to the codes of Hollywood cinema than to the principles of crusading journalism. Even before World War II and the implementation of military censorship, the newsreel abided complacently by the strictures of semiofficial oversight from civilian and military authorities. In 1937, at the insistence of the Senate's La Follette Committee, the newsreels withheld for months coverage of the brutal strikebreaking at Republic Steel. The next year, at the request of Joseph P. Kennedy, then U.S. ambassador to Great Britain, the Hays Office persuaded Paramount Newsreel to delete from its overseas issue clips criticizing Prime Minister Neville Chamberlain's handling of the Munich Crisis. The most famous instance of restraint reveals the archaic manners of what could not then be called a predatory media pack: throughout FDR's twelve years in office, the commercial newsreels, as well as still photographers, refrained from showing the disabled and, by 1944, visibly infirm president to disadvantage. Editorial opinion approvingly cited such deference to the commander in chief because "a reasonable and patriotic citizenry would be wanting him always to look his best."[11]

The newsreels' dual status as staple program offerings and hard news bearers created a curious journalistic ethos, a kind of gentleman's agreement to spare the viewing public any gritty unpleasantness in order not to disturb unduly a mood conducive to a good night out at the movies. To be sure, as flagship operations of the studios, the newsreels were required to abide by the Production Code, whose regulations on permissible images, proper language, and correct opinions mandated discretion in the exposure of blunt reality. Up against the (comparatively and in context) unrestrained coverage of the tabloid metropolitan press, the Code prohibitions against profanity, vulgarity, and "repellent subjects" (also known as the stuff of hard news) severely compromised both the integrity and competitiveness of screen journalism. Yet the Code never subjected newsreel content to the systematic scrutiny given the Hollywood feature film, always the prime target of Hays Office interest. The location of the newsreel operations (in New York, not Los Angeles, a coast away from the hawk eyes of the PCA administrator Joseph I. Breen) and the necessarily fast pace of production of the twice-weekly issues (in extreme cases, a news event shot at 9:00 P.M. in the evening could be edited and shipped to New York exhibitors by 3:00 A.M. the next morning) militated against a meticulous review process.[12] Distance, time, and the nature of the business granted the newsreels some informal dispensation in complying with the Code standards, especially in regard to the Code's "Special Regulations on Crime in Motion Pictures," which, against all common journalistic sense, decreed that "details of crime must never be shown." Thus, the body of John Dillinger, laid out on a slab, was shown in the newsreels a week after the gangster's death on 22 July 1934, a gruesome tableau that would never have been allowed in the realm of fiction.[13]

A self-censorship originating from *within* the newsreel ranks—an internal compass that told editors what boundaries not to stray beyond in the depiction of carnage and combat—could be as confining as any restrictions imposed from without. Moreover, motion picture exhibitors routinely cut newsreel sequences they felt would disturb or antagonize moviegoers, especially female patrons, whose sensibilities were deemed too delicate to withstand the harsher news and more explicit images. Although the Motion Picture Theater Owners of America (MPTOA) cautioned its membership against reckless in-house censorship, "in order that we may do our part in keeping the public fully informed," wary exhibitors deleted not only newsreel footage of violent military action from abroad but even coverage of peacetime defense preparations in America. "We have definitely ascertained," a Dallas theater manager reported in 1940, "that most of our patrons, especially women, want complete escape from the [European] war when they attend a movie." Newsworthy but unsettling images were left to offscreen imaginations and elliptical intimations by commentators. No matter how horrendous the happening or chaotic the occurrence, the visible world of the newsreel screen appeared ordered, contained, and sanitized—"edited compilations of forced optimism, story, travel, and comedy."[14]

The war changed everything. From 1941 to 1945, the status and significance of news on-screen grew exponentially, and the latitude accorded it expanded beyond the bounds of Hays Office propriety. Suddenly the faraway images acquired a direct urgency; the remoteness of foreign locales and obscure events was bridged by the blood ties between the moviegoers and the mobilized, the intense knowledge that news on-screen had an immediate consequence for home-front life and frontline death. The Second World War, an event preserved in celluloid more completely than any other happening in human history, presented a reality that, for once, surpassed the imaginations of Hollywood screenwriters.

Images of War

The war brought about a sustained commitment to comprehensive newsreel reportage and elaborate documentary production. The exigencies of "the present emergency"—the need to inform, educate, and inspire—propelled the recalibration of news on-screen and the revitalization of a dormant documentary tradition. For the first time in American history, documentaries were backed by the full resources of the studios and the cooperation, sometimes coordination, of the U.S. government. Washington and Hollywood, military photographic units and studio employees, initiated an intensive and extensive venture into motion picture production. From 1941 to 1945, the nonfiction film was a theatrical attraction in its own right, attended to as avidly as the putative top of the bill—sometimes more. The war years remain the dynamic center of filmic record-keeping, "the Great Struggle" (as the director Frank Capra labeled Hollywood's war work) being also the great high renaissance of the American documentary.

Coordination between newsreel services, the military, and the government brought images of war to moviegoers with remarkable speed and efficiency. Here a navy cameraman on an aircraft carrier deck continues filming during heavy fighting.

The transforming influence of the war on newsreel reporting expressed itself most clearly in two areas of protracted contention: delays in getting war footage to home-front screens and deletions of vivid combat material. The progressive speedup in timely coverage of headline-worthy happenings was the first noticeable shift. Newsreel images of the first year of war had arrived on-screen so tardily as to seem an afterthought. The Japanese attack on Pearl Harbor, which by pure coincidence was recorded in part by the 20th Century–Fox cameraman Al Brick, who was on assignment in Hawaii to obtain location footage for TO THE SHORES OF TRIPOLI (1942), was withheld from release until 27 February 1942. Moreover, when it did reach the home-front screen, the Pearl Harbor footage was heavily censored by nervous navy officers. For the next year, the deletion of spectacular combat action was as bothersome as the delays in arrival.[15]

Subject to official censorship and dependent on the armed forces for access to remote battlefields, the commercial newsreels could do naught but comply with a system of cooperative, military-supervised coverage known in the jargon of the day as "rota-coverage" ("pool reporting" in current broadcast vernacular). But the rota-coverage accounted for relatively few of the combat images that came to the commercial newsreel screen. The Army Signal Corps and the navy photographic units superseded (scooped?) the newsreels by strictly regulating independent access to overseas locales and battle sites. The military then provided official footage, shot by its own combat photographers and censored by security officers, to the commercial newsreels. During the war, the five newsreels shared this identical stock of raw material supplied by the armed forces. Hence, the differences between their war reporting became largely a matter of logo, commentator, and editing. This explains why so many compilation flashbacks to World War II resurrect the exact same archival footage.

Throughout the first year of war, interminable delays and perplexing deletions were the main sources of antagonism between newsreel editors and news makers. Playing the patriotic card, newsreel editors argued that timely combat footage was essential for home-front education and morale. In 1942, surveying the "tepid, serene recital of an entire world at war" on exhibition at a newsreel theater in New York, *Variety* sardonically recorded a fair sampling of early wartime newsreel fare: "American doughboys are on parade in Iceland (Paramount). An RAF squadron tees off for a raid on the French coast (Fox). Congressman [Martin] Dies recalls how his [House Un-American Activities] committee once came in possession of a map that showed that the Japs had heinous designs on the United States (Universal). A cavalry troop somewhere in the northwest demonstrates how this arm of the service has been mobilized for reconnaissance (RKO-Pathé)." Nary a shot was shown fired in anger.[16]

Not until the autumn of 1943 did the military and the newsreels reach a mutually advantageous accommodation. The shift in policy was precipitated by the very public protests of Francis S. Harmon, vice chairman of the War Activities Committee of the Motion Picture Industry (WAC), who argued that to apprehend the war fully the home front needed to see shots of frontline combat—and American casualties—on the newsreel screen, and "not merely pictures of Yanks riding jeeps and dispensing cigarettes to natives." Before a meeting of East Coast exhibitors, Harmon openly appealed to Donald M. Nelson, chairman of the War Production Board, and Palmer Hoyt, head of the domestic branch of the Office of War Information, to persuade the military to release realistic, even harrowing, scenes of combat to the newsreels. In September 1943, the dispute was finally resolved by executive action. After a conference with the OWI chief Elmer Davis and representatives of the War and Navy Departments, FDR himself ordered a more newsreel-friendly policy. The army then lifted its ban on featuring weapons such as the bazooka and the flamethrower in action and (the most sensitive issue) on showing Americans dead in battle. Moreover, as a measure of good-faith compliance, the army thereafter indicated "the number of feet deleted and the type and locale of the deleted subject" in the footage it supplied the newsreels.[17]

After FDR's directive, the evasive omissions and "Pollyanna slants" that characterized newsreel coverage of the first year and a half of war gave way to a more comprehensive and unvarnished depiction of combat action. Given the expressive and explicit photojournalism in wire-service photos and *Life,* the newsreels warranted the extra measure of latitude and respect. Besides, the newsreels had become *the* medium for apprising the home front of frontline action and government policy. In 1944, RKO-Pathé's Walton C. Ament, chairman of the newsreel division of the War Activities Committee, claimed that "every week, 100 million people in the United States see at least one of the twice weekly releases of the various companies, viewing historical happenings of the year," with an estimated 88 percent of the clips dealing with some facet of the war effort.[18]

Working in tandem with the newsreel was the renascent documentary, whose abrupt promotion in status was underscored by the establishment in 1941 of a best-documen-

The proximity of this 16mm camera to a gun installation clearly indicates the immediacy—and the danger—of newsreel coverage. According to a press release, this September 1943 photo was taken shortly after a Japanese bomb killed the entire crew manning the gun at right.

tary category by the Academy of Motion Picture Arts and Sciences. Wartime necessity and the symbiosis between Hollywood and Washington spawned three distinct documentary forms: the nuts-and-bolts training film, the orientation picture, and the combat report. Some were perfunctory and unimaginative, but others offered a fertile field of expression for technical experimentation and artistic talent. All were part of an unprecedented and unparalleled deployment of government and studio resources in the service of documentary production.

The daunting task of military education, of schooling 12 million armed forces recruits in the skills of modern warfare, fell mainly to what was christened the nuts-and-bolts film. First through the Hollywood-based Research Council of the Academy of Motion Picture Arts and Science, later on a strict contract basis, the studios fulfilled government contracts for production of arcane training and information films with titles such as "The 60mm and 81mm Mortar Sights and Sight Setting" and "The Anti-Aircraft Searchlight Battery—Emplacement." With ranks swollen by draftees from the motion picture industry, the military's own production units—located at Fort Monmouth, New Jersey; Wright Field, Ohio; Culver City, California; and the Signal Corps Photographic Center housed in the old Paramount Studios in Astoria, New York—also churned out literally hundreds of training films on the nuts and bolts of war. Typically running from ten to twenty minutes, and often instructing GIs in subjects of utmost secrecy (radar, bomb sights, coding), the films were restricted to use by the military.

Of course, the military exploited its Hollywood moviemakers for more than dry assembly-disassembly, connect-the-dots lessons. Mechanical training was necessarily supplemented with behavioral instruction. The military's famous "Fighting Man" films (1942–1945), a stark series of lessons on the mental attitudes and physical skills needed to survive in combat, evoked a full gamut of spectator emotions—fear, courage, loyalty, sadism, loneliness—as it taught how "to kill or be killed." BAPTISM OF FIRE (1943) uses interior monologue to render the psychological turmoil of a soldier anticipating combat, shedding first blood, and steadying himself to go on fighting.[19]

The second documentary category allowed for more creative filmmaking opportunities: the orientation film—or, more accurately, wartime propaganda (a word uttered with some trepidation in Hollywood and Washington because of its Axis associations). Orientation films taught not technical skills but worldviews—history, values, morality, politics. The War Department's fulsome embrace of the inspirational or morale-building role of motion pictures can be attributed to the vision of one man, Army Chief of Staff George C. Marshall, who insisted upon motivated men in a democratic armed services. "In this war a very special effort was made to care for the minds of men as well as their bodies," Marshall wrote in one of his biennial war reports. "From the very beginning, the Army recognized that [the] strain [of war] must be counteracted by healthy informational and recreational activities." On 14 February 1942, the responsibility for the execution of that mandate fell to a newly commissioned major and former Hollywood maestro, Frank Capra.[20]

On 6 June 1942, Capra took command of the 834th Signal Service Photographic Detachment, a unit activated "especially for the purpose of producing orientation films" and initially comprising "eight officers and thirty-five enlisted men drawn from the various technical fields of the motion picture company on the west coast." Under Capra's supervision, the 834th Photo Signal Detachment (as it became known) produced a legendary series of orientation films for the Army Pictorial Service. The 834th might be thought of as the first fully operating and professionally staffed documentary studio in American history. Capra's seven-part "Why We Fight" series (1942–1945) remains the enduring landmark, the most influential and widely seen of all wartime documentaries and perhaps the most influential documentary series ever. For the first time in U.S. history, the full inventory of motion picture magic was marshaled for overt instructional and propaganda purposes.[21]

Capra's unit fashioned a wholly new canvas for the documentarian's art. The wartime innovation was the compilation film, a fluid reworking of archival footage orchestrated by the documentarian as historical survey and political argument. The newsreel boys and the early documentary adventurers had always highlighted the spot coverage of on-location fieldwork, capturing images in inaccessible locales and transporting them back to American bijous for inspection. The members of Capra's 834th Photo Signal Detachment molded their documentaries from archival footage (called "library material" in the jargon of the day). Their workplace was not in the field, shooting on location and framing the fabulous "money shot" at risk of life and limb, but at the editing table scanning a moviola. From material unearthed and made to order, they arranged a rich mosaic of motion picture images and created a new movie from old movies. Capra and his crew (which included the director Anatole Litvak and the writers John Gunther,

William L. Shirer, and Eric Knight) pillaged old newsreels, documentaries, and Hollywood movies; shot special scenes for exposition and transition; designed maps and illustrations; and then bound the strains together into a seamless cinematic web. No one had done anything quite like it before.[22]

The art of weaving together archival footage to create a new tapestry of cinema was the product of historical synchronicity and the cooperation of the enemy. The Nazis had not merely recorded their pageants on film but orchestrated them *for* film. "Why We Fight" could review the past through the medium of motion pictures because, for the first time, the past was accessible through cinema: the rise of fascism coincided with the development of the sound motion picture in the 1930s. Recasting the motion picture work of Joseph Goebbels's *Reichsfilmkammer* and of the Japanese High Command, "Why We Fight" usurped images from their original context. The written prologue to KNOW YOUR ENEMY: JAPAN (1945) explained the counteroffensive: "This film has been compiled from authentic newsreel, official United Nations, and captured enemy film. Free use has been made of certain Japanese motion pictures with historical backgrounds. When necessary, for purposes of clarity, a few re-enactments have been made under War Department supervision."

No "captured enemy film" was incorporated more regularly into American orientation than Leni Riefenstahl's TRIUMPH OF THE WILL (1935), the official party record of the 1934 Nazi Party Congress at Nuremberg. Part of the reason for the incessant recurrence of TRIUMPH OF THE WILL in wartime orientation films was sheer necessity: it was one of the few lengthy documents of the militaristic Nazi ethos available in the early years of the war. With the exception of the freelance cameraman Julien Bryan, whose restricted photography appeared in the "March of Time" segment "Inside Nazi Germany—1938," almost no independent footage of Nazi Germany was available in stateside library stock. But availability alone does not explain the dominance of Riefenstahl's footage. Capra himself wrote of the sheer visual attraction of the images, the "blood-chilling spectacle" that was "the classic, powerhouse propaganda film of our times." Resolving to "mount a counter-attack," Capra marshaled the enemy's own images against him (or her). In "Why We Fight," the images were no less impressive, but the context of grim analysis and moral outrage framed and contained them. Riefenstahl's dynamic forces became Capra's deluded automatons. By 1945, her images had become iconic, visual shorthand for the Nazi menace.[23]

At the order of General Marshall, every American in uniform was required to see the Capra series as part of his or her military training. Three entries were released commercially to home-front theaters (PRELUDE TO WAR, 1943; THE BATTLE OF RUSSIA, 1943; and WAR COMES TO AMERICA, 1945) and the complete series played widely in a "16mm circuit" comprising church basements, lodges, and factory assembly halls. For an entire generation of Americans, "Why We Fight" was the proclamation that ordered the past, explained the present, and envisioned the future.[24]

Though "Why We Fight" was the most influential and well remembered of the orientation films, literally hundreds of other morale-building and informative shorts— made on the cuff by the studios, by individual branches of the armed forces, under the aegis of one of the myriad new government agencies, and by state legislatures and private companies "doing their wartime bit"—unspooled on the commercial screen. From 1941 to 1945, WAC arranged for the regular screening of nearly 160 "Victory" films to the nation's home-front theaters, carefully monitoring exhibitors to make sure the films were screened during every program. Occasionally, a "Victory" film received favorable publicity as a theatrical attraction in its own right, particularly when matinee idols eased the transition from fictional entertainment to documentary education. Stars in uniform made especially attractive narrators when they spoke from experience. Two of the most popular, Lt. James Stewart in WINNING YOUR WINGS (1942) and Lt. Clark Gable in WINGS UP (1943), assumed the guise of friendly narrators to recruit for the Army Air Corps or review the rigors of officer candidate school. In a much lighter vein, the biweekly "Army-Navy Screen Magazine" resembled a khaki-colored version of the newsreel/screen magazine smorgasbord, serving its all-GI audience with everything from cautionary VD vignettes to starlet shenanigans by request.[25]

Combat Reports

The third documentary category born of war was the combat report. Where Capra's orientation was instructional in purpose and archival in creative spirit, the combat reports were rushed dispatches from the battle front. Providing a warrior's-eye view of frontline action, it embraced a gritty aesthetic and exuded a mean, sometimes bloodthirsty attitude. The fluid montage and storyboarded construction of the orientation films bespoke controlled perspective and level calm. The cinematic grammar of the combat report, conversely, signified camera work under fire: obstructed, jerky, out of focus, off-kilter, up close, and jagged. In accentuating the danger of photography shot under duress, it harkened back to the silent-era adventures of cameramen who forayed into "darkest Africa" to "bring 'em back alive" (and on film). But here the dangerous game was human, and the subject matter and imminent theme death by violence.

The screen credits of the combat reports—or rather the unacknowledged filmmakers, since the military documentaries were not credited to individuals but instead to the unit and responsible branch of the armed services—reflect another significant feature of the documentary. For the first time, many of Hollywood's most seasoned and talented directors turned collectively away from feature entertainment to documentary production. A pantheon of top-notch directors and prestige producers entered the fray to deploy what the motion picture trade press and studio boosters called the "celluloid weapon." Not coincidentally, the most popular of the combat reports then, and best known now, were supervised and directed by famed and accomplished filmmakers: John Ford's THE BATTLE OF MIDWAY (1942), Darryl Zanuck's AT THE FRONT IN NORTH AFRICA (1943), John Huston's REPORT FROM THE ALEUTIANS (1943) and THE BATTLE OF SAN PIETRO (1945), and William Wyler's THE MEMPHIS BELLE (1944). However, no auteurist touch adorned the series of blunt combat reports that captured the peculiar ruthlessness of the war in the Pacific theater—the eerie terrain, hidden enemy, and impulse to utter extermination on display in THE BATTLE FOR THE MARIANAS (1944), FURY IN THE PACIFIC (1945), ATTACK! THE BATTLE FOR NEW BRITAIN (1944), WITH THE MARINES AT TARAWA (1944), and TO THE SHORES OF IWO JIMA (1945).

The combat reports functioned as a military-minded screen magazine and expanded on stories first covered by the five newsreels. Newsreel accounts of any major military action were followed up by a documentary recapitulation from the armed services involved. After a couple of months, a two- to four-reel government issue reviewed the campaign and retraced its movements, reassuringly structuring and cinematically framing the completed action. For example, the campaign in Italy, climaxing with the entry

WE ARE THE MARINES (*1943*) *was among the dozens of feature-length documentaries providing a "warrior's-eye" view of battlefield action. It was produced by "The March of Time" in cooperation with the Marine Corps and was released by 20th Century-Fox.*

of the U.S. Army into Rome on 4 June 1944, was expeditiously underscored with the WAC-coordinated release of the Army Signal Corps' THE LIBERATION OF ROME (1944). Film taken of the battle of Okinawa on 22 March 1945 arrived in Washington on 29 March and hit newsreel screens the next week, on 3 April. (The footage was then shipped *back* to Okinawa for viewing by Admiral Chester W. Nimitz and his aides by 13 April.) The combat report expansion arrived on 26 July: THE FLEET THAT CAME TO STAY.

Perhaps the most extraordinary combat footage and the most astonishing testimony to the cinematic ordering of the chaos of combat was the filming of the battle of Iwo Jima. A total of fifty thousand feet of footage was shot by some sixty combat cameramen from the U.S. Navy, the Marine Corps, and the Coast Guard under the supervision of Lt. Cdr. John W. McLain, a former Hollywood screenwriter, and Lt. Cdr. William Park, a former Paramount News executive who supervised the newsreel coverage. Several weeks prior to the operation, McLain was given access to the Iwo Jima invasion plan, the better to storyboard his own beachhead tactics. Even under fire, his cameramen were expected to abide by proper film grammar. McLain reported that "photographers were instructed to shoot American action right to left, and enemy action left to right, thus enabling the public to get a good perspective of the action from the screen and also to help the film cutters do a better job." The spectacular and brutal Iwo Jima footage left the island on 21 February 1945 in McClain's personal custody and reached newsreel screens (in black-and-white) on 8 March 1945. All five newsreels devoted their entire issue to the battle. Editors at Warner Bros. had compiled the footage into To THE SHORES OF IWO JIMA, a searing Technicolor record of the bloodiest days in the history of the Marine Corps.[26]

Throughout the war years, therefore, combat-laden newsreels and documentary shorts accompanied the full-length feature presentation on the theatrical staple program—and frequently outstripped it in spectacular imagery and dramatic impact. It stood to reason. Ignoring the consternation of civilian editors, the armed services would often hold back their best footage from the newsreels and use it to punch up the action in their own films. "Run *To the Shores of Iwo Jima* as soon as you can," a wartime exhibitor urged in the pages of *Motion Picture Herald*. "It is one of the best twenty-minute shorts that has been released yet."[27]

Distilled to essentials, the military ethos and cinematic style of the combat report yoked Hollywood convention to documentary innovation. Familiar codes of cinematic orientation were interwoven with radically new screen moments and filmic techniques. The easily identifiable voices of Hollywood actors narrated the action, dissolves and set pieces signaled transition or provided exposition, and staged scenarios prefaced unstaged action. But amid the Hollywood convention was a new screen aesthetic that not only permitted technical flaws in photography but showcased them as verification of fidelity to reality. Prior to the war, a professional-quality 35mm studio focus and resolution was a sine qua non of classical Hollywood projection. Suspending the studio "tradition of quality" and the rigid regulations of the American Association of Cinematography, the jagged edges of photography under the gun—not the classically framed vision of soundstage Hollywood—provided the drama, danger, and awe of the combat report.

As in classical Hollywood cinema, however, the combat report granted the spectator a privileged perspective on the action. Wherever possible, home-front moviegoers were given the best seat in the house. Whether aiming from behind the crosshairs of fifty-caliber machine guns, through the slits of tanks, or over the top of landing barges, hugging the sand of besieged beachheads or looking down at enemy cities through bombsights, the camera lens was a surrogate for the warrior's field of vision. Typically, the danger of photography shot in the line of fire is accentuated by the visible presence on-screen of the photographer himself. Personal risk was implicit in the acquisition of any combat scene and explicit in the credits and advertising. "Nine of my cameramen buddies were killed or wounded filming this picture," an illustrated marine said in the ad sheets for FURY IN THE PACIFIC. Sometimes the on-screen appearance of the photographer confirmed his participation in the thick of the action, as when Darryl Zanuck is spied clenching his cigar during an aerial attack in AT THE FRONT IN NORTH AFRICA. More often, the presence of the filmmaker-photographer is felt or heard rather than seen, as when John Ford's camera is knocked out of frame from the concussion of an exploding bomb in THE BATTLE OF MIDWAY or when John Huston provides eyewitness narration to REPORT FROM THE ALEUTIANS and THE BATTLE OF SAN PIETRO.

Besides self-aggrandizement, the presence of the photographer lent testimonial verification to the authenticity of the on-screen action. A pivotal refutation to the duplicity of Axis propaganda, the verity of the combat report—its certified, unstaged, spontaneous reality—was a sacred covenant between screen and spectator. In at least two films, the British Ministry of Information's DESERT VICTORY (1943) and Frank Capra's TUNISIAN VICTORY (1944), combat footage was staged—more to assist narrative coherence than to send out false information, said defenders when the Hollywood trade press pointed out the fabrications. John Ford's December 7th (1943), the official navy record of the Japanese attack on Pearl Harbor, also reenacted scenes, but here the purpose was avowedly a historical review; only to a later generation, unfamiliar with the extant footage, has Ford's material, created on a backlot at 20th Century–Fox, been mistaken for authentic footage. Rumors of staged combat footage were widespread enough among the viewing public to prompt the army to issue an official statement of denial in 1943, a striking corroboration of the sharp eyes and cinematic sophistication of the wartime audience.[28]

Another perceptible difference between the newsreels and the combat reports was that some of the most memorable examples of the latter—At the Front in North Africa, The Battle of Midway, The Memphis Belle, and To The Shores of Iwo Jima—were shot on color stock, generally in 16mm Kodachrome, which was then "bumped up" to 35mm Technicolor for release prints. Color stock, once associated mainly with cartoons, musicals, and costume dramas, was relied on increasingly as the war went on. Its use was more common in the Pacific than the European theater, owing to the navy's need for vibrant hues to discern meteorological and geographic details amid vast expanses of ocean and sky. The aerial perspective of the army air force likewise made color stock a medium well suited for battle damage assessment and intelligence gathering. Yet to some eyes, by evoking the frivolity of Hollywood's escapist fare, the full spectrum of primary colors seemed incongruous with the stark horror of war. A Technicolor war disclosed for the first time a paradox of documentary aesthetics: though reality is in color, black-and-white looks more "realistic."

The realist aesthetic of the combat report was enhanced by a series of new and sophisticated cameras that made possible the recording of realities heretofore unexposed to the lens. The exigencies of war greatly accelerated the development of all manner of esoteric camera technology: underwater and aerial cameras, magazine-loaded, lightweight 16mm cameras, and high-speed specialty cameras that could microscopically photograph ballistics, the stress on machines and vessels, and surgical procedures. Often military designers worked side by side with Hollywood technicians and directors to advance the effectiveness of "the celluloid weapon." For example, Harry Cunningham, one of the motion picture industry's most respected camera designers, devised a special combat camera equipped with a gunstock and four lenses built into a revolving turret—35mm, 75mm, six-inch, and ten-inch. Late of the Battle of Midway, Lt. Cdr. John Ford found these lenses to have the most useful range for combat photography. A combat camera crew might thus be issued four of Cunningham's cameras, with each member assigned to shoot the combat action with a particular lens. To facilitate construction of Cunningham's camera, RKO Studio opened up its machine shop to the U.S. Navy.[29]

Finally, the combat report served as a kind of chapter ending to a completed campaign, closing out the action and punctuating the victorious finale. As the war moved toward its climax, the combat reports unspooled like episodes of a serial. The Pacific theater combat reports trace an east-to-west (to Far East) trajectory congenial to the American eye for frontier progress, sweeping in line across the mid-Pacific (With the Marines at Tarawa, Attack! The Battle for New Britain, and The Battle for the Marianas) through the Philippines, Peleliu, and Saipan (Brought to Action, 1945; and Fury in the Pacific), and on to the main island of Japan (Target Tokyo, 1945; To the Shores of Iwo Jima; and The Fleet That Came to Stay).

Before the combat report was mustered out of the staple program, two *fin de guerre* recapitulations memorialized the form. THE TRUE GLORY (1945), a documentary overview of the Allied campaign in Europe from D day to VE day, was a kind of combat report compilation film, meting out new footage and reviewing the best of the old. Jointly produced by British and American units overseen by Carol Reed and Garson Kanin, respectively, THE TRUE GLORY took a from-the-bottom-up perspective on the largest amphibious assault in history. Though introduced by and featuring privileged remarks from General Eisenhower, a chorus of disparate voices dominates the sound-track, speaking the interior monologue of men and women of all ranks and nations. In the combat report's most sustained and eloquent use of the film soundtrack, the voices do not so much narrate the action as confide personal impressions to counterpoint the Big Picture. Reversing the conceit of John Ford's DECEMBER 7TH, which uses one voice to speak the posthumous lines of a band of multi-ethnic Pearl Harbor casualties ("How does it happen that all of you talk and sound alike?" "We *are* all alike. We are all Americans"), THE TRUE GLORY records a rich and idiosyncratic polyphony of accents to sing the message of Allied diversity: southern drawls and Scottish burrs, New York slang

THE TRUE GLORY, *one of the most ambitious feature-length combat reports, traced the Allied campaign in Europe from D day to VE day. Coproduced by the British Ministry of Information and the OWI, and codirected by Carol Reed and Garson Kanin, the film was released in October 1945 by Columbia Pictures. Here, troops of the U.S. First Army advance through the ruins of Cologne, Germany.*

and the queen's English. Not a one is prone to the bluster or sentimentality that characterized some of the omniscient narrators of the early combat reports. In contrast, THE ATOM STRIKES (1945) seems to recognize the need for silent reflection when contemplating the final death blows of the Pacific theater. Despite the visible devastation apparent in aerial shots of the two most famous targets of the Second World War, the official military account of the bombing of Hiroshima and Nagasaki managed to include not a single shot of a burnt body or scarred victim.

Ironically, neither the violence of combat battle nor the horrors of landscapes after battle would have the indelible impact of the most appalling documentary images of the war. Army Signal Corps footage of Nazi concentration camps, soon supplemented by British and Soviet footage, began appearing in the newsreels in late April 1945. General Eisenhower insisted that the footage be shown in every American community—in theaters, factories, high schools, and civic arenas. Through circulation in the newsreels (each of which devoted whole issues to the camps) and in documentaries such as the WAC release THAT JUSTICE BE DONE (1945), the Soviet Union's NAZI ATROCITIES (released stateside by Artkino in 1945), and the War Department's DEATH MILLS (1946), Americans learned a set of place names that, no less than Pearl Harbor, would live in infamy: Bergen-Belsen, Buchenwald, Dachau, Treblinka, Auschwitz. . . .

Postwar News

After the most spectacular news story of the century, after a series of progressively explicit and unimaginably horrifying images in the final months of the war, the content of the newsreels and documentaries seemed almost to diminish visibly in energy after 1945. In the immediate postwar period, the cultural work of restoration and readjustment modulated the tone, urgency, and force of documentary cinema. To scan the newsreels of the period is to witness a prolonged denouement to the fury of war: strangers embracing in Times Square, joyful family reunions in small-town America, streams upon streams of parading battalions disembarking from troopships and smothered by ticker tape, and soon housing shortages and classrooms crowded with ex-servicemen on the GI Bill.

Only the Berlin Airlift of 1948–1949 "provided newsreel photographers in Europe with the first real postwar 'news subject' [of a] magnitude equal that of any wartime event," averred the veteran Paramount newsreel photographer John Dured. Back in Europe after a three-year absence, Dured likened his feelings to those of a Hollywood cameraman returning to a studio to find "the stages in ruin and his best actors gone and replaced by new faces devoid of personality and color." Who save an American newsreel photographer could look back on continent-wide slaughter with such wistful nostalgia? Lamented Dured: "Gone was the incredulous Goering, the pompous Mussolini, the sinister Hitler, . . . gone were they all from the European scene and my camera viewfinder."[30]

The fate of the documentary was no less bleak. Despite high hopes for its potential as a commercial attraction, the documentary in postwar America received few veteran's benefits for its wartime service. Toward the close of the war, critics and industry insiders hailed the progress of the American documentary, approvingly cited the popularity of the combat reports, and predicted great things for the form that had at last "come of age" and attracted talent, resources, and audience. Yet as a theatrical draw or artistic form, it was relegated to antebellum status, little heeded beyond a small coterie of buffs and intellectuals. If not quite the staple program oddity it was before 1941, the documentary—short-form or feature-length—was certainly nothing like the welcomed entry it had been during wartime. The occasional exception underscored its anomalous status. MGM's THE SECRET LAND (1947), a serene seventy-one-minute documentary record of Robert E. Byrd's expedition to the South Pole in 1946, was described as "one of the few documentary films ever compiled and edited by a major company." Though it continued the war-born process of shooting in 16mm Kodachrome and bumping up the footage to 35mm Technicolor for theatrical release, and of using celebrities for voice-over commentary (Robert Montgomery, Robert Taylor, and Van Heflin), THE SECRET LAND never enjoyed the popularity of THE MEMPHIS BELLE or TO THE SHORES OF IWO JIMA. To be counted a tolerable attraction by American moviegoers, the viability of the documentary depended on its intrinsically spectacular allure or the uncontested immediacy and importance of its subject matter.[31]

Throughout the postwar era, the late war remained the preeminent measure of documentary spectacle. The compilation film was an important continuity; appropriately, many of the postwar documentaries were compilations of World War II film. As the Allies uncovered enemy footage and the War Department cleared previously censored material for commercial release, the moving image record of the Second World War became an expanding archival treasure chest. RKO's DESIGN FOR DEATH (1947) supplemented extant American material with Japanese newsreels and historical films lately released by the Alien Property Custodian of the U.S. Customs Service. An independent outfit, American Film Producers, scavenged the newsreel vaults for THE LOVE LIFE OF ADOLF HITLER (1948), mainly for glimpses of Eva Braun in a bathing suit.

A goodly portion of the material that saw postwar release was far more explicit than the footage shown during 1941–1945. Freed from security restrictions and morale considerations, the War Department archives and newsreel outtakes revealed a world at war even more brutal than the one the wartime screen had so recently projected. Always inveterate record-keepers, the Nazis had preserved on film a thorough inventory of their wartime horrors: gruesome experiments, routine depredations, and mass executions. As Allied investigators into war crimes gathered evidence against the surviving Axis leaders, the motion picture record became an eloquent witness for the prosecution. At the outset of the first round of Nuremberg trials in November 1945, the original newsreel footage of Bergen-Belsen, Buchenwald, and Dachau was screened for the tribunal in a decision made not "out of logic but by felt necessity," recalled the historian Telford Taylor, then an army colonel on the American prosecution staff. To bolster their case, the Americans also offered in evidence a documentary record of the Nazi ascent to power called THE NAZI PLAN (1945).[32]

For their part in the Nuremberg prosecutions, the Soviet Union entered into evidence THE ATROCITIES BY THE GERMAN FASCIST INVADERS IN THE USSR (1946). The Soviet film was an exceptionally chilling record of the mass murder of Russian POWs and the implementation of "the final solution" in Poland. In time, its images would help shift the filmic memory of the Holocaust away from the Nazi concentration camps on the western front (liberated by Anglo-American armies) and toward the camps on the eastern front (liberated by the Soviet Union), where the technology of genocide operated at full power. The Soviet footage bequeathed two unforgettable screen moments to the documentary record of World War II: the residue of mass death piled up in mountains of shoes, eyeglasses, and women's hair, and a row of children at Auschwitz unrolling their shirtsleeves to expose the serial numbers tattooed on their arms. The War Department incorporated the Soviet images of Auschwitz into its troop education film DEATH MILLS, as did the Allied command in an overview of the trials entitled NÜRNBERG UND SEINE LEHRE (1947).

World War II aside, the most popular compilation film of the late 1940s was probably THE ROOSEVELT STORY (1947), an eighty-minute documentary supervised by Elliot Roosevelt, the late president's son. THE ROOSEVELT STORY—which a mere decade before might have been the title of a studio-produced epic—heralded what was to become an influential subgenre of the compilation film: the documentary biopic. Having lived a good portion of their lives in front of the moving camera, great men of the twentieth century left behind an imposing celluloid legacy. Certainly the media-savvy FDR had played before the cameras with nearly as much frequency and facility as on the radio. A hagiography-via-cinema of the beloved leader, THE ROOSEVELT STORY showed just how comprehensive a motion picture recapitulation of a twentieth-century figure could be, how thoroughly a full-length feature captured the arc of a man's life. Buttressed with still photographs and lent expository drama by Canada Lee as "the Voice of the Depression" and Ed Begley as "the Voice of the Opposition," THE ROOSEVELT STORY reviewed a photo album that began with Franklin and Eleanor Roosevelt's wedding (filmed for the newsreels in 1905), continued through economic crisis, wartime burdens, and the rigors of four presidential election campaigns (including his last great public speech lambasting Republicans for criticizing "my little dog Fala"), and concluded with the funeral procession and grieving multitudes in the streets of Washington, D.C. For many in the contemporaneous audience, the review of FDR's motion picture life was a measure of their own histories, his very public scrapbook calling up personal memories of a parallel journey through history.

But even THE ROOSEVELT STORY failed to break into *Variety's* annual list of the eighty top-grossing films of 1947. Lacking theatrical appeal, studio interest, and generous subsidies from the OWI or War Department, the postwar documentary depended for survival on foundation support, corporate sponsorship, or government contracts. One of the most reliable and generous patrons of documentary production was the United States Information Agency (USIA). Forbidden to distribute materials domestically, the USIA financed half-hour portraits of Americana at $50,000 an episode for the edification of foreign audiences. As the peacetime descendant of the overseas branch of the Office of War Information, the agency incorporated its war-taught lessons about the power of film as a weapon in American foreign policy. (Congress had also learned a lesson from Joseph Goebbels: it forbade the executive branch agency from distributing any of its propaganda domestically.) Likewise, a few special-interest groups with political motives used the documentary as a leaflet for their causes. Similar in spirit to the USIA films, if premature as foreign policy, was Meyer Levin's THE ILLEGALS (1948). The independently produced documentary, financed by the Jewish Distribution Agency, depicted the plight of displaced persons making their way from Poland to Palestine. It played mainly in temples and town halls as a fund-raiser for Zionist causes.

Along with official Washington and special-interest groups, corporate boardrooms registered the value of documentary orientation films as advertisements for themselves. Few companies were naive enough to assume that a paean to the company line would have theatrical appeal, but a modest investment in motion picture production yielded a palpable product in film form, tangible evidence of prestige and ongoing goodwill for corporate giants. Doing what the USIA could not, the Ford Motor Company in 1948 underwrote a series of regional self-portraits called "America At Home," whose entries included MEN OF GLOUCESTER, PUEBLO BOY, and SOUTHERN HIGHLANDERS. Taking not a single screen credit for its $200,000 investment, Standard Oil of New Jersey bankrolled Robert Flaherty's LOUISIANA STORY (1948), an on-location record of the pristine relationship between oil rigs and the backcountry bayou, a film as aesthetically gorgeous as it is ecologically suspect.[33]

Surveying the paltry entries on the postwar screen and revising the rosy predictions of 1945, one friend of the documentary could only reiterate the standard prewar diagnosis: "The documentary film has not yet come into its own in America." Even for captive audiences—students, soldiers, job trainees—documentaries had to be short, since anything longer than two reels (about twenty minutes) failed to engender "sustained interest."[34] In 1948, *Motion Picture Herald* editor Terry Ramsaye, himself a former newsreel and documentary editor, summed up the disappointments of the besieged aficionados of the form. "The place of the non-fiction picture in the entertainment world is yet to be made."[35]

With an estimated sixty thousand 16mm sound projectors flickering around the nation in 1948, a burgeoning nontheatrical market seemed a promising outlet for documentary films that, as 35mm attractions, had no box-office potential. Hence, Flaherty's LOUISIANA STORY was released in 16mm a year after its standard theatrical run in 35mm. Cinema 16, a pioneering film society founded in the fall of 1947, provided one of the first regular venues devoted exclusively to alternatives to mainstream Hollywood fare and in the process set an early pattern for what by the 1960s would be a thriving network of university film societies and art houses. In 1948, the critic James Agee evoked the distribution and exhibition limitations (and some of the romance of atmospheric screenings) in the alternative 16mm circuit: "Some of [the films] do get shown around, more or less, in union halls, parish houses, schools; some others, I imagine, by societies of amateur moviemakers, or in the homes of friends, or, in a sort of extension of shop talk, among the people who made them in the first place." To Agee's dismay, however, the insulation from the commercial marketplace fostered more dullness and elitism than innovation and populism. He was speaking about more than the standard venues for 16mm cinema when he detected "a churchly smell to the whole business."[36]

For the 35mm commercial documentary, meanwhile, escalating production costs exacerbated the theatrical doldrums. Costs for the production of a typical documentary short subject had risen an estimated 40–60 percent from the war years, yet exhibitors balked at paying higher rentals or risking advertising budgets to publicize nonfeatured attractions. Moreover, the kind of subject that possessed theatrical appeal before the war—mainly travelogues and nature films—looked quaint to a war-tempered generation on intimate terms with exotic locales and heart-pounding adventure. Acknowledging in 1948 that filmgoers "have lived through a lot of reality in the last ten years," RKO-Pathé's Phil Reisman Jr. unaccountably proposed a movement *away* from short subjects to feature-length documentaries. "If you can't sell documentary shorts for what they cost," reasoned Reisman, "make 60-minute fact films and sell them for the bottom half of that double bill. Many a *March of Time* or *This Is America* could be expanded to six reels of more solid entertainment than a lot of present features." Reisman's critical judgment may have been sound, but his commercial sense was flawed. The screen magazines, at a price tag in excess of $50,000 per issue and long unprofitable as theatrical attractions, were in no better shape than the venerable travelogues.[37]

Ironically, as the documentary film languished and the screen magazines expired, documentary style thrived. The impact of the wartime documentary tradition found an unexpectedly friendly reception in, of all places, the Hollywood entertainment feature. After 1945, a studied incorporation of newsreel and documentary technique challenged the illusionist aesthetic of classical Hollywood cinema. When a generation of directors, cameramen, and sound technicians returned from the battlefield to the Hollywood soundstage, they were animated by a desire to move beyond the confines of closed-in studio sets. Because the war had accelerated the development of everything from light-weight 16mm cameras to underwater photography, technical advances abetted the urge, particularly the faster film speeds and higher-quality film stocks that made location shooting practicable and cost-effective. The climate-controlled environment of the soundstage, deemed essential for professional quality lighting, sound, and set design, was a frustrating constraint for men who had weathered artillery bombardment and automatic weapons fire. The cinematographer James Wong Howe spoke for a genera-tion of photographers anxious to liberate themselves from the reins of studio conven-tion. "We confine and restrain movement because of the problems created by ponderous equipment," argued Howe in 1948. "When you pan or tilt a camera on a tri-pod as we do today with 35mm, it is quite different from panning or tilting by hand." For the stadium fight scenes in Robert Rossen's boxing melodrama BODY AND SOUL (1947), Howe unleashed four ex-combat cameramen to prowl the stands with hand-held cameras for cutaway coverage. He then donned roller skates and had a grip maneuver him around the boxing ring—giving moviegoers a better-than-ringside seat on the action. "Our stuff will have the same quality as the combat footage," Wong told Rossen. "If a few shots are out of focus, so much the better. We'll have a real fight on the screen for the first time."[38]

The motion picture industry called it "newsdrama cinematography," an amalgam of the best elements of "studio and newsreel technique." Deemed most appropriate for gritty urban melodramas and social problem films, it was characterized by a full range of war-taught skills: location shooting, hand-held mobile photography, and reliance on high-resolution black-and-white grain, available lighting, and actual "sets." Exemplars include THE HOUSE ON 92ND STREET (1945), 13 RUE MADELEINE (1946), BOOMERANG (1947), THE NAKED CITY (1948), and CITY ACROSS THE RIVER (1949). "The result has been an authentic newsreel atmosphere, surprisingly different from a studio made film, and one that is especially vital and dramatic for factual stories," reported Henry Hathaway, director of 13 RUE MADELEINE. In 1949, when the Academy of Motion Picture Arts and Sciences awarded the Oscar for best cinematography to William Daniels for THE NAKED CITY, the gesture was seen as "a most welcome nod of approval for the documentary style of photography that has characterized some of Hollywood's most outstanding photoplays during the last two years." Even the MGM musical—the epitome of studio-bound, choreographed artificiality—moved on location to the streets of New York to shoot portions of ON THE TOWN (1949).[39]

If the postwar commercial cinema is a credible signpost, then a perceptual shift in the quality of moving image spectatorship, difficult to gauge but impossible to discount, occurred in the wake of the war and as a result of the war-born documentary technique. For a generation of wartime cinephiles educated, oriented, and uplifted by news on-screen and documentary cinema, the movies were no longer a dream screen and Hollywood no longer purely a factory for entertainment. In form (the newsreel style) and in content (the social problem film), Hollywood might have a relationship to reality that, if at heart no less illusionist, was at least less fantastical and glamorous.

TV Newsreels

The durable appeal of documentary aesthetics did not rebound to the advantage of the forms that developed them. When television began to broadcast live images, when the simultaneous arrival of news and moving image became a living-room reality, the diagnosis for the theatrical newsreel was terminal. Though prewar trade press reports had warned of looming competition from television since its public demonstration at the 1939 New York World's Fair, the diversion of resources from research and development unrelated to the business of war caused many motion picture executives to mistake a postponement for a cancellation. The stunning financial success and cultural esteem the Hollywood system had earned during the wartime interregnum imbued them with a heady sense of invulnerability. Already though, in 1945, television news reports and sports events were being broadcast to a few pioneering tele-families. In BREWSTER'S MILLIONS (1945), a group of returning war veterans convene in an upscale office and watch a televised horse race. The celluloid (television) image is newsreel footage, not broadcast transmission, but the nonchalance of the scene must have been tantalizing. Inadvertently, Hollywood had held out the promise that the returning veteran would preside over the newsreel in private space. A few years later, with the motion picture industry's lifeblood threatened by the new medium, references to television in feature films would be conspicuously absent or defensively condescending.[40]

During television's infancy, motion picture industry executives watched in denial and disbelief as their once-devoted public pursued the new and younger suitor. Obviously, the coverage of live events was the unchallenged purview of the new medium, and the two most popular spectator sports in the nation—baseball and politics—were forthwith annexed by television. Yet for a time it seemed that the theatrical newsreel and television news could coexist profitably, as if there were enough news (and enough money) to go around. Far from supplanting newsreel photography, television's appetite for 16mm coverage in the field was initially voracious. Early broadcasting technology (suffocating klieg lights and unwieldy cameras tethered to huge electrical cables) put television in something of the position of the Hollywood studios during the conversion to sound. As a news-gathering (as opposed to news-disseminating) medium, television was bolted to the floors of broadcast booths and restricted to controlled environments. For television, the spot coverage of seasoned newsreel film crews was a way to expand its field of vision and supplement its programming.[41]

Three groups competed for a piece of the action in the lucrative television news market: the networks themselves (through their own news divisions), the three wire services (Associated Press, United Press, and International News Service), and the five commercial newsreels. Of the three, the newsreels possessed the tradition and training for the swift acquisition of 16mm motion picture news. Yet they were at a disadvantage against their two rivals because, in providing news footage to television, they undercut themselves in theaters. Moreover, the major studios at this point were reluctant to traffic with the enemy, and, naturally, movie exhibitors protested any newsreel distribution deals with television.

Early television news adopted not only the strategies but the actual facilities used to cover the war. Here, Walter Cronkite narrates an early TV news story filmed at the Army Pictorial Center, Long Island, New York.

The wire services felt no compunction about breaking into the wholesale supply of moving image news. In January 1947, Associated Press, United Press, and International News Service all entered the field of newsreel production for television broadcasting. The wire services shot their footage in 16mm, struck individual prints for each broadcaster, and airmailed the reels to subscriber stations, a process that allowed for television broadcast of a filmed report in "all parts of the country within 36 hours" after the camera rolled. Possessing a mere twenty-six licensed television stations that served some forty million Americans, mainly on the East Coast, the embryonic medium was soon outrunning the theatrical newsreel in breadth of coverage and speed of arrival. That summer, NBC televised pictures of a flood in Oregon, flying the footage to New York for telecast within twenty-four hours. "It is expected that sufficient flow of footage will ensue to provide a daily presentation of news subjects by each station," remarked a prophetic editor for *American Cinematographer* in 1948, describing what became the nightly news.[42]

Attempts to beat back "tele-news" by accentuating the theatrical superiority of newsreel photography evoked the pathos of a condemned medium groping for a last-minute commutation. In 1947, Warner Pathé News opted to film the Tournament of Roses Parade and the Rose Bowl in color under the delusion that "what's being lost in timeliness is being compensated for in the color spectacle which only the newsreels will have." Alas, the next week the newsreel's hopes "fizzled out in a blur of orange and green tints" as a botched two-color Cinecolor process projected a spectacle that was multichromic but indiscernible. Vivid color registration required time—and time was what the news-reels could not afford.[43]

A revamped kind of screen journalism that could provide a judicious summary of news highlights seemed an answer. "News-plus-background" issues devoting their full running time to one selected topic (rather than the staccato smorgasbord approach) had become commonplace in the final months of the war, with entire issues devoted to the liberation of Paris, the fighting on Iwo Jima, and the Nazi concentration camps. Promising a new niche and a possible reprieve, the war-born strategy was resurrected in the postwar era. Thus, all the commercial newsreels devoted their end-week issue (26 January 1949) to coverage of Truman's inauguration. "They couldn't compete with video in fullness of coverage, of course, but it is open to question whether or not theater audi-ences didn't do just as well as TV watchers in having the highlights edited and packed tightly into eight or nine minutes," *Variety* commented. Editors at all five commercial newsreels conceded that "the reel must change its style to a more three dimensional treatment of news to meet the tele challenge."[44]

Ultimately, faced with competition from the wire services and a dawning sense of the inevitable, the commercial newsreels cut deals with the television networks for their ser-vices. The studios could not resist the lure of ready cash in a declining market for their theatrical features, especially since—a guilty secret for years—the newsreels had typi-cally operated in the red since the onset of the sound era, functioning "more as a service to exhibitors than as a money making venture." Twentieth Century–Fox moved first. In a deal bankrolled by Camel cigarettes, Movietone News agreed to supply NBC with daily editions of a newsreel beginning 16 February 1948, a date that marks "the first time any outfit has attempted to turn out a daily newsreel." This experiment, however, lasted less than a year. Television news preferred a media-friendly format: a video mon-tage of film clips, live reporting, and live commentary by a talking-head anchor. Over the next years, the network news divisions would maintain a variety of different finan-cial arrangements with the commercial newsreels. With broadcast television soon gar-nering the resources to field its own newsreel cameramen, it turned to the older newsreels only for supplementary material or on those increasingly rare occasions when their own divisions were scooped. And as news on the small screen thrived, news on the big screen wilted.[45]

The lingering illness and progressive dissolution of the newsreel was little noticed and largely unmourned. Recycling a vintage metaphor, *Variety* remarked caustically that the "flashing of the newsreel on the screen in most theaters today [1948] usually marks a breather for the majority of customers to hike out to the lobby for a smoke." "We appeal to a small audience that is shrinking," a spokesman for New York's Embassy Newsreel Theater conceded when his house switched over to a feature film program in 1949. With moving image news elsewhere more readily and promptly available (if not more clearly visible), the theatrical newsreel was a moot medium.[46]

As if on a long death watch, the motion picture trade press tracked the degenerative decline of newsreel and screen magazine exhibition over the next decade and a half. The two screen magazines succumbed early. Citing "rising costs and a desire to switch its creative talent to TV," "The March of Time" ceased production in July 1951. "This Is America" followed the next month. Of the newsreels, RKO-Pathé was first to go, on 23

August 1956, followed by Paramount on 15 February 1957 and Fox Movietone in 1963. MGM and Universal held out longest, with MGM ending 30 November 1967 and Universal flickering out on 31 December 1967. Longtime money losers—by the mid-1950s the newsreels were losing $1 million per annum for the studios—they kept going mainly on deals with television and to carry the studio flag. In an elegiac obituary that named the killer and mourned the victims, *Motion Picture Herald* wrote: "The television era in approximately fifteen years put an end to one of the oldest established features of the theater screen, the twice a week newsreel." In truth, as a stateside theatrical entity, the newsreel had been dead on its feet since the mid-1950s, consigned to exhibition in foreign lands and remote U.S. military bases.[47]

Appropriately perhaps, the last time the newsreel appears prominently and persuasively in a prestige A picture is at the end of SUNSET BOULEVARD (1950). A new Hollywood slant on the old Hollywood, Billy Wilder's black comedy harkens back to a lost era of silent filmmaking even as the classical studio system contemplated its own decline in the age of television. In a final scene of dementia and delusion, Paramount News cameras whir and record the last big screen close-up of the washed-up screen star Norma Desmond (Gloria Swanson). By then, the newsreels too were facing the same fate as the silent cinema.

13

Television and Hollywood in the 1940s

CHRISTOPHER ANDERSON

Television enchanted Hollywood in 1940, but in that regard Hollywood was no different from the rest of the country. Heralded by stories of scientific breakthroughs and by occasional demonstrations of the technology, television's arrival as a popular medium had been anticipated for more than a decade by 1940. As early as 1928, the chairman of RCA, David Sarnoff, had predicted that within five years television would become "as much a part of our life" as radio. Executives in the movie industry may have questioned Sarnoff's time frame, but few ignored his prediction, since press reports throughout the 1930s assumed that television loomed just over the technological horizon. The motion picture trade press certainly fueled speculation, as when the *Hollywood Reporter* announced in November 1934 that commercial TV sets would hit the market by January of the following year. "Television Is Ready," the headline brashly—and prematurely—reported. Los Angeles was also the site of one of the country's most active experimental television stations, Don Lee's W6XAO, which conducted numerous demonstrations over the course of the decade. By the time *Business Week* assured executives that 1939, at last, would be the breakthrough "Television Year," the climate of prophecy had nurtured an intense public fascination with television—in Hollywood as in the rest of the country.[1]

American television made its long-awaited public debut in April 1939, when NBC launched regular service with its coverage of the opening ceremonies of the New York World's Fair. Subsequent broadcasts by NBC and CBS were conducted only on an experimental basis, beamed to a few thousand receivers in the New York area, and yet public awareness of television continued to grow during 1939, fueled by clever publicity campaigns that featured exhibitions of the technology at trade shows and in department stores.[2] Valuable publicity came also from televised events, which had few viewers but captured public attention through accounts in newspapers and magazines.

The motion picture industry participated in one of these televised events when NBC broadcast the Atlanta premiere of GONE WITH THE WIND in December 1939. Perhaps more than any single event, that premiere marked the pinnacle of the movie industry's influence in American culture. With the attention of the national press focused on

422

Atlanta, NBC seized the opportunity for self-promotion, stationing four video cameras near the theater marquee and using them to transmit the first televised movie premiere to its small audience in New York.[3] It was a technical feat that served both the movie industry and the nascent TV business, and the experimental broadcast gained stature by paying homage to the country's preeminent form of popular culture.

This early broadcast offered Hollywood a tantalizing glimpse of the future. Though staged mainly for publicity, it appeared at the time to presage an almost certain bond between the movie and television industries. From the earliest days of commercial radio, the studios had explored the field of broadcasting; many had made unsuccessful bids to form their own radio networks. Now as the new decade dawned, it seemed logical, if not inevitable, that Hollywood would play a key role in shaping American television. Even the Federal Communications Commission (FCC), the government agency responsible for regulating the country's airwaves, hoped that Hollywood studios would apply their particular acumen to the challenge of forming a viable television industry. In August 1940, the FCC chairman, James L. Fly, paid a diplomatic visit to Hollywood, touring the production facilities at Warner Bros., Paramount, and RKO. Before leaving, he invited the major studios to seek licenses for television stations and to stake their claim as television producers.[4]

Studio executives, however, were not satisfied merely to experiment in a medium controlled by the existing radio networks; they wanted to *command* the television industry just as they dominated the movie industry, by controlling the channels of distribution. Consequently, Hollywood approached broadcasting with two goals. First, studios or their parent companies invested directly in stations, networks, and electronics manufacturers as part of their general strategies for corporate diversification. Second, the studios sought to influence the development of television technology, which they anticipated would become a revolutionary new mode of distribution and exhibition for motion pictures.

The networks had developed a particular model of broadcasting based on transmitting commercially sponsored programs to home receivers. The studios, on the other hand, envisioned alternative uses for the technology, uses that would conform more closely to the economic exchange of the theatrical box office. These included theater television, in which programs would be transmitted to theaters and shown on movie screens, and subscription television, in which home viewers would pay directly for the opportunity to view exclusive, commercial-free programming. By recognizing these ambitions, the historian Michele Hilmes argues, "a new picture emerges of Hollywood as an active experimenter with the new technology, presenting a serious challenge to the established broadcasting interests."[5]

Entering the 1940s, the Hollywood studios were eager to explore television, and the federal government endorsed their ambitions. Yet the radio networks, which quickly adapted radio's economic practices and program forms, exerted a far greater influence over television's development as a national medium. Given Hollywood's expressed interests, why didn't the movie industry play a larger role in the development of television during the 1940s? Why did the television industry come to be controlled by the radio networks instead of the studios? And why have so many subsequent stories testified to the hostility of studio executives, who were often said to have despised television during its early years?

This chapter explores the history of television in Hollywood during the 1940s in order to understand how the conditions and events of that decade combined to thwart the ambitions of the major studios. Because American television was suspended during the war and did not really develop as a popular medium until the networks introduced regular prime-time programming in 1948, television during much of this decade existed in an inchoate form, more a projection of social and commercial fantasies than a public institution. Television gradually achieved definition during this period of anticipation and experimentation, publicity and policy making, demonstration and debate. Under these circumstances, Hollywood tried to ensure that television would never be strictly defined as a domestic medium aimed at individual homes, nor as the logical domain of the radio networks, but that it would be equally viable as an extension of the studio system, perhaps even as a public medium based in movie theaters.

Launching Television, 1939–1942

From the time of NBC's inaugural telecast in 1939 until World War II forced the suspension of consumer electronics manufacturing in 1942, Americans witnessed a flurry of activity surrounding television, including a series of debates over proposed technical standards, the beginning of commercial broadcasts, and the first demonstrations of theater television. The period was dominated by RCA, which pushed hard to see its technology adopted as the technical standard for the entire industry. For RCA, according to the historian J. Fred MacDonald,

> the launching of television in 1939 was a double-edged business enterprise intended to sell TV sets to the public and impose RCA technical standards on the industry. If RCA/NBC could develop, produce, and market receivers as well as programs, the corporation could establish itself as the technological, manufacturing, commercial, and programming giant of television. With such an advantage it could monopolize the emerging industry from the outset. (J. Fred MacDonald, *One Nation Under Television: The Rise and Decline of Network TV* [New York: Pantheon, 1990], p. 14)

The motion picture industry, however, did not concede control of television to RCA. For years the Hollywood community had monitored technological developments in the field described initially by the trade journals as "visual broadcasting."[6] Because the major studios had extensive experience in radio, they eagerly awaited the moment when it would be feasible to diversify into television. The Motion Picture Producers and Distributors of America (MPPDA), the industry trade organization, prepared several studies of television for the studios during the 1920s and 1930s.[7]

Individual studios and independent producers sought their own advantage in television during the 1930s. Warner Bros. carefully monitored television patents filed by Theodor Nakken, Ludwig Silberstein, and others. Rumors in the trade press even claimed that Warner Bros. attempted to lure the television research pioneer Vladimir Zworykin away from RCA during this period.[8] Contracts negotiated by studios and independent producers began to contain clauses governing television rights. Indeed, television played a central role in Walt Disney's decision in 1936 not to renew his distribution contract with United Artists. When United Artists refused to grant Disney the television rights to his feature films, he abandoned the company and signed with RKO—a decision that paid huge dividends for the producer in years to come.[9] Hollywood's fascination with television in the years leading up to its commercial introduction can be seen in a remark by the producer David O. Selznick after he had attended a demonstration of the technology in the laboratory of the inventor Philo T. Farnsworth in 1937. "I do not believe that television can be stopped," he reported to his board of directors. "Some day, it will undoubtedly have a future so stupendous that we cannot even foresee its possibilities."[10]

The first major studio to move beyond enthusiastic endorsements and actually invest in television was Paramount, which had forged an initial alliance with the broadcasting industry by purchasing a substantial interest in the CBS radio network during the late 1920s. Although Paramount liquidated its CBS investment by 1932, the studio continued to seek opportunities in broadcasting once it had begun to recover from the effects of the Depression.[11] In July 1938, Paramount paid $164,000 for a 25 percent interest in DuMont Laboratories, a television manufacturing firm founded by the inventor Allen B. DuMont. According to Paul Raibourn, the studio executive in charge of television, Paramount made the investment to ensure that the movie industry would not be squeezed out of TV by the radio networks and to direct DuMont research toward theater television.[12] For the second time in less than a decade, Paramount asserted its leadership in broadcasting, setting a precedent that was recognized immediately in the movie industry.

The MPPDA's 1939 study of television, the latest in a series of reports by the industry's trade organization, expressed the belief that television could be shaped to the major studios' advantage, particularly if the studios committed themselves to developing theater television. Courtland Smith, the report's author, advised the studios to follow Paramount's lead and seek greater influence in the medium—by participating in experimental broadcasts and by lobbying the FCC as it considered technical standards. The timing would never be better for the movie industry to control distribution by establishing their own networks. "Television needs us, and very badly," he reported. "Most television people hope to relegate film to a minor position and bring the direct pick-up [live broadcast] into all programs. In fact, if networks were now possible they might adopt the policy of excluding film. . . . There being no networks, film will start unopposed and as an essential factor."[13]

Though Smith encouraged the studios to participate in the market that would develop around home TV receivers, he argued that Hollywood's success in television would rest ultimately on its ability to foster the growth of theater TV, since video projection technology promised benefits for both the studios and theater owners. In part, this meant fighting a rhetorical battle against established radio interests in an effort to influence the FCC, which already seemed predisposed to view television as primarily a domestic medium like radio. "We never should let the idea become generally accepted that television means pictures in the home *instead* of pictures in the theater," Smith argued. "It would seem to be wise to combat the idea at once. It seems obvious now that television, as it affects the motion picture industry, is not only a matter of film production for the home but also of a new type of show for the motion picture theaters. It may well be at the box office of the motion picture theater that television will make its first profit."[14]

The historian Michele Hilmes has noted that the movie industry, by conceiving of theater television as a viable alternative to home receivers, proposed not only to develop a mode of reception for television that differed from radio but also to create an alternative to the economics of commercial broadcasting, one that substituted the direct revenue from theater attendance for the indirect revenue of advertising.[15] Instead of waiting for advertisers to shift to television only after the medium had attracted a critical mass of viewers, the movie industry could hasten the adoption of television by using box-office admissions as the medium's economic foundation. Theater TV, speculated one industry reporter, offered an obvious solution to the cost of TV production: "Many television programs will probably be so expensive to produce that they will not be sent over the air free to anyone who has a receiver in his home but to theaters by special wires or on a separate wavelength which cannot be received on home sets."[16]

Private demonstrations of television projection systems had been conducted in research laboratories since 1930, but the technology was not presented to the public until 1939, when the British companies Baird Television and Scophony Ltd. equipped several London theaters, making it possible for movie patrons to view live broadcasts of prizefights and horse races. The first public demonstrations in the United States took place at the New York World's Fair, where Baird and RCA introduced their systems. RCA quickly became the leader in theater TV research, developing an electronic system that used a cathode-ray tube similar to that in home TV sets in order to project a video image directly onto a theater screen. RCA staged private demonstrations for FCC commissioners in February 1940 and for stockholders in April.[17]

The first full-scale public screening took place at the New Yorker Theater in New York City during January 1941. This initial telecast, presented to representatives of the FCC, advertising agencies, and the movie industry, consisted of a one-act play and performances of ballet, opera, and vaudeville. In May, RCA arranged a second demonstration specifically for movie industry distributors and exhibitors, who would be the target audience for the company's imminent marketing campaign. Executives from the studios' New York offices joined a standing-room-only crowd of 1,500 people to view a live program transmitted from the NBC studios. The program featured a variety of live events, including a news report by NBC's Lowell Thomas, a roundtable discussion concerning the potential for covering sporting events via theater TV, a prizefight taking place in Madison Square Garden, and a dramatic sketch staged in the NBC studios. Able to project an image of 15 x 20 feet at a cost of $30,000 per unit, the RCA system offered adequate sound and visual quality but did not measure up to the standards of a Hollywood feature. The critic Terry Ramsaye, who attended the event as a reporter for the *Motion Picture Herald,* was generally unimpressed by the technical quality. "If theatre television proves to be an art," he reported shortly afterwards, "it was the first art to be born in the doghouse."[18]

According to Ralph Beal, the head of television research at RCA, the electronics manufacturer assumed that American television ultimately would consist of two separate services, one directed at home receivers and the other at movie theaters. As a manufacturer of radio and TV receivers, and as the parent company of NBC, RCA believed that television should be targeted primarily at audiences in the home. Television, according to its chairman David Sarnoff, was destined to be a "vital element" in a culture increasingly centered on the family home.[19] On the other hand, RCA was also the leader in developing the technology for theater television, for which it made equally definitive claims. "Theater television has great promise," stated one RCA brochure. "It heralds the linking of playhouses in the nation into television networks that can transform every village theater into a Madison Square Garden or a Metropolitan Opera House."[20]

These types of statements began to define a potential relationship between home and theater television: theater TV would serve as a forum for public events and perfor-

Besides its theater-projection television systems, RCA also experimented with video projection in its home receivers. Here a kinescope image projected onto a translucent screen provides a "big-screen" (13 x 18 inches) TV image.

mances, while home television would incorporate the programming strategies of radio, relying on advertiser-sponsored series. RCA concentrated on the market for home receivers but also envisioned theater TV as the "public" form of television, the ideal technology for screens located in hotels, cafés, small newsreel theaters, and regular movie theaters. The movie industry also encouraged the notion that theater television would provide moviegoers with privileged access to public events. For instance, a 1940 Paramount short subject, "Ted Husing's Television Revue," introduced theater patrons to the notion of theater TV and extolled the virtue of witnessing live events, suggesting that theater TV would connect the movie theater to the public sphere. "No longer will you have to stay at home from the movies just to hear what's going on in the world," the narrator explained. "Come to the movies to see and hear."[21] Paramount's president, Barney Balaban, used a similar rationale in explaining his company's investment in theater TV. "Instead of being competition, television may be an asset to the theater business," Balaban said. "On nights when a big fight is being held, or perhaps the President is making an important address, imagine how much more business could be obtained by televising the event. Instead of a patron sitting at home and hearing an audible broadcast, he will be able to come to our theaters and not only hear the broadcast but see the entire show on the television screen."[22]

As these comments indicate, RCA and the movie industry shared complementary visions of a dual television system able to serve both home and theater with separate types of programming. Since RCA needed to market its video projection technology to theaters, many of which were controlled by the studios, it initially had a strong incentive to ally itself with the movie industry in calling for the development of theater TV. But once the studios began venturing further into television, conflicts arose between RCA and Hollywood, primarily because RCA opposed any form of competition that threatened its dominance over the television industry or its hopes for seeing its own technology adopted as the industrywide standard.

Paramount's investment in DuMont created tensions between the movie and broadcasting industries because Paramount immediately emerged as a rival to RCA, just as it had during its brief partnership with CBS in the early 1930s. The tone of this renewed rivalry was set during the FCC's 1940 hearings over television's technical standards when DuMont, along with other electronics manufacturers, challenged RCA's proposed standards. DuMont asked the FCC to support competition and not to freeze technological development by accepting RCA's proposals. The FCC, according to MacDonald, "wavered between reluctant support for the bullying enterprise of Sarnoff and RCA, the desire to keep the new industry open to competition, and the desire to protect consumers from buying TV sets that would become obsolete quickly."[23]

In February 1940, the FCC announced that commercial broadcasting would begin in September, although the commission had not yet established technical standards. Following the announcement, RCA launched an energetic marketing campaign in order to flood the market with its own receivers and perhaps establish the *de facto* industry standard. To prevent consumers from purchasing sets that might soon be obsolete, the FCC reacted by postponing the introduction of commercial broadcasts and calling for new hearings in April 1940.[24]

At these hearings, RCA went on the offensive against its competitors, explicitly accusing Paramount of inhibiting the development of television through its investment in DuMont. In a brief filed with the FCC, RCA claimed, "The motion picture interests which are financing DuMont Laboratories have a much greater financial stake in the movie industry than they have in television. Their recent interest in television is primarily for the purpose of 'protecting' their larger interest in the movie and theater industry and not to develop the new art of television. Therefore, they desire the adoption of systems and methods that would make television inferior rather than superior to motion pictures."[25] By leveling such charges against Paramount, RCA introduced two ideas that would come to influence the government's response to the movie industry's increased presence in television. First, RCA implied that the movie industry would exploit television solely for commercial gain, whereas the experienced radio networks recognized the responsibility of broadcasters to serve the "public interest," as policy mandated. Second, it suggested that the movie studios were masking their true motives, which were not to promote television but to slow its growth in order to protect their theaters.[26]

On the contrary, Paramount had moved aggressively into television following its 1938 investment in DuMont. In July 1939, the studio formed a television subsidiary, Television Productions, Inc. And in spite of RCA's aspersions, the FCC granted Paramount and its related companies four experimental television permits, while giving RCA only three. Paramount capitalized on this opportunity by announcing that it had purchased a vehicle for use as a mobile television unit capable of feeding live remote telecasts to DuMont and its experimental stations. Paramount also began using television as a lure for its movie theaters, installing DuMont TV sets in the lobbies of its Chicago-based Balaban & Katz theaters, with the sets tuned to the theater circuit's own experimental TV station, W9XBK.[27]

RCA's accusations about Paramount had little immediate influence on the FCC; in fact, it was shortly after the hearings that FCC Chairman Fly visited Hollywood with an invitation for the studios to participate more actively in developing television. But over the next few years—as the studios faced new charges of antitrust violations—the FCC began to have its own doubts about allowing the Hollywood studios to play a major role in the television industry.

The War Years, 1942–1945

The FCC approved technical standards for television in April 1941 and authorized commercial broadcasts beginning in July 1941. With manufacturers prepared to market TV receivers, American television appeared to be on the verge of fulfilling the predictions of the previous decade. But World War II intervened, and television's development came to a halt by mid-1942 as manufacturers ceased producing consumer electronics and turned instead to making equipment for the military. Ten commercial stations were broadcasting in mid-1942, and six remained on the air throughout the war. As advertisers drifted away, these stations reduced their schedules to a token four hours per week, transmitting to the roughly ten thousand TV sets in the United States mainly concentrated in New York, Chicago, and Los Angeles.

Commercial television was suspended for the duration of the war, but the federal government was eager to pave the way for a quick launch once the war ended. "During the postwar period," FCC Chairman Fly predicted, "television will be one of the first industries arising to serve as a cushion against unemployment and depression."[28] During 1944–1945, the FCC conducted hearings to establish spectrum allocation for television, and many historians believe that these hearings were the single most important event in determining the eventual structure of American television. The critical issue at these hearings was whether television broadcasting should remain in the VHF band of the electromagnetic spectrum (as advocated by RCA), thus restricting its channel capacity, or whether it should be moved to the UHF band, which had a much greater capacity. These hearings were a turning point because they offered the last opportunity to shift U.S. broadcasting to the UHF band without severely disrupting manufacturers and consumers.[29]

In May 1945, however, the FCC approved a system of thirteen-channel VHF broadcasting and encouraged the use of UHF solely for experimental broadcasts. By restricting the number of available channels, the FCC created an artificial scarcity that guaranteed fierce competition in the television industry. As J. Fred MacDonald has written, "To make channels so scarce effectively guaranteed that U.S. television would be broadcast TV, dominated by those few corporations able to afford stations in the largest cities, provide attractive programs, attract national advertisers, and quickly build a chain of affiliates eager to appeal to the mass audience."[30] In other words, the high demand for a limited number of channels meant that radio's mode of commercial network broadcasting was likely to dominate television as well; there would be no opportunity to explore alternative forms of television. As a result of the FCC's decision, small networks and independent stations—like those envisioned by the studios—were placed at a competitive disadvantage in relation to NBC and CBS, which were prepared to sign affiliates as soon as commercial broadcasting resumed after the war.

During the war, the major studios still assumed that they would be competitive in the television industry. As the movie industry prospered, the major studios jockeyed for position in television because they recognized that commercial television would be launched almost immediately after the war ended. At the same time, however, the studios were aware that conditions in the movie industry—a new round of antitrust litigation, an uncertain international market, and a rise in independent production—would necessitate changes in the studio system. Eager to stake out the future of distribution and exhibition through television, each of the studios made substantial investments in station ownership and theater TV. The studios were not alone in pursuing these investments: a 1945 survey reported that 50 percent of exhibitors intended to operate TV stations, while nearly 60 percent planned to install theater TV systems.[31]

In late 1943 the studios began applying for station licenses and developing plans for production. MGM in December 1943 assigned Nat Wolf to form a television department, and Wolf subsequently hired the radio writers George Wells and Norman Corwin, assigning them to write screenplays until they could be used in actual television production. MGM's parent company, Loew's, subsequently applied for permits to construct stations in New York, Los Angeles, and Washington, D.C.[32] RKO hired Ralph Austrian from NBC, giving him responsibility for exploring all phases of television. In June 1944, Austrian helped form RKO Television Corporation, a subsidiary that would produce TV news and entertainment. RKO became the first major studio to produce for television with the telecast of "Talk Fast, Mister," a one-hour drama filmed at RKO-Pathé studios in New York and broadcast by DuMont's New York station in December 1944. Later RKO created a series of ten-minute short subjects for TV by recycling stock footage to create a quiz show titled *Do You Know?* and a nostalgia series titled *Ten Years Ago Today.*[33] Warner Bros. in 1944 filed an application for a Hollywood television station to be operated by its radio station, KFWB, and purchased seventeen acres on Mulholland Drive to be used for constructing the station. Twentieth Century-Fox, through its theater circuits, filed applications in Los Angeles, New York, Boston, Seattle, Kansas City, and St. Louis. Even the independent producer Walt Disney anticipated the future growth of television by applying for a permit to construct a station at the Disney studio.[34]

Paramount continued to set the pace for the integration of television into the movie industry. Its subsidiary Television Productions, Inc., launched a Los Angeles experimental station, W6XYZ, in February 1943. The Balaban & Katz station in Chicago, WBKB, became a commercial station in October 1943. Many of the studio's theater circuits prepared station applications across the country, in New England, Michigan, Texas, Pennsylvania, and Florida. Paramount also kept pace with RCA by joining with British Scophony and General Precision Equipment (the single largest shareholder of 20th Century-Fox) in 1943 to form the Scophony Corporation of America, a U.S. subsidiary of Britain's leader in theater TV research.[35]

Of course, technological innovation alone could not ensure the success of theater TV; studios also had to devise a system for producing and distributing the necessary programming. The studios stressed the need to create networks of theaters in order to cover the expense of production. "All that theatre television needs to become a reality," claimed RKO's Ralph B. Austrian, "is a means of interconnecting a chain of theatres. . . . It is not beyond the bounds of possibilities to visualize a nationwide chain of theatres

Allen DuMont, with his wife at a Paramount dinner. A key figure in Paramount's television plans, DuMont's research-and-development operations, projection-TV patents, and TV station holdings gave the movie studio a range of options as it looked to the future.

reaching out for home television personalities as fast as they are developed, and paying them enough to make it worth their while to perform for theatres only, rather than for the home audience." *Variety* reported that some in the movie industry even wanted to create streamlined theaters devoted exclusively to television, relying on programming transmitted from a central network source. In 1944, Paramount asked the FCC to approve two microwave relay networks that would connect the studio's stations and theaters in just such a network. Indeed, frequency allocation would prove to be a crucial factor in determining the eventual success or failure of theater TV. In 1945, the Society of Motion Picture Engineers (SMPE) testified before the FCC that theater TV would not be able to exist without the allocation of special frequencies reserved exclusively for the studios to transmit programming to theaters. In response, the FCC agreed to set aside several frequencies for experimental applications of theater TV but chose not to allocate channels for its commercial development.[36]

As this decision suggests, during the war years the federal government became increasingly skeptical of the movie industry's role in television and seldom encouraged further expansion by the studios. Although the FCC welcomed the studios in 1940, the atmosphere in Washington had changed dramatically by 1945, when FCC Chairman Paul A. Porter addressed a meeting of industry leaders in Hollywood and warned them that the movie industry should not expect a significant role in television after the war; his agency would see to it that television would not become a "Hollywood bauble."[37]

This surprising shift occurred because Washington had become increasingly concerned about the threat of monopolies forming in the television industry. The FCC's 1938 hearings on network monopoly in radio broadcasting had led to its 1941 *Report on*

Chain Broadcasting. The FCC concluded that NBC and CBS had restricted competition in radio by exercising inordinate control over affiliated stations and that NBC should be forced to divest one of its two radio networks in order to foster competition. In October 1943, after the courts had upheld the FCC's findings, NBC sold its Blue network to Edward H. Noble, who later changed the name to the American Broadcasting Company.

The major studios increasingly fell under a cloud of suspicion as they once again faced antitrust allegations in charges filed by the Justice Department in August 1944. While these antitrust proceedings moved through the courts, Washington scrutinized the movie industry more carefully. In December 1945, for instance, the Justice Department filed suit against American Scophony, charging that Paramount and its associates had monopolistic control over theater TV patents and had delayed the technology's development for fear that theater TV would undermine the movie business.[38] These charges, which obviously echoed RCA's previous allegations about Paramount, signaled a dramatic change in the relationship between Washington and Hollywood. The FCC's commitment to VHF virtually guaranteed that a precious few networks would exert enormous influence over television. It was becoming apparent that these networks were likely to be formed by the radio networks and not by the studios.

Thwarted Ambitions of the Major Studios, 1946–1950

In spite of the intense expectations that surrounded television by the end of World War II, commercial television was slow to develop after the war. The FCC had received 116 license applications from 50 cities by the end of 1945, but two years later there were still only 16 stations on the air and fewer than 200,000 TV sets in the country. Of course, television was solely a metropolitan phenomenon, with stations and viewers concentrated mainly along the East Coast and in Chicago and Los Angeles. The electronics industry needed time to retool for consumer markets, but lingering uncertainty over technical standards also made manufacturers and consumers wary about moving forward. Those interested in television awaited a definitive ruling about which of the competing color standards—a mechanical system developed by CBS or an electronic system advocated by RCA—would receive the FCC's approval. In March 1947, the FCC rejected the CBS color system, which was incompatible with existing technology, and this decision launched the expansion of American television because it established that, for the foreseeable future, television would be broadcast in black-and-white.[39]

Following the war, the major studios continued to lay the groundwork for the eventual role of television in the studio system. Faced with a pending antitrust ruling that threatened to disrupt the movie industry, the studios had an unusually strong incentive for exploring opportunities for diversification. Warner Bros. and Paramount were the most aggressive studios attempting to diversify into television.

To compete with Paramount, Warner Bros. in 1947 joined 20th Century-Fox and RCA in a project to develop and market RCA's technology for theater TV. This collaborative research led to a public screening of the Joe Louis-Jersey Joe Walcott heavyweight prizefight at the Fox-Philadelphia Theater in June 1948 and to demonstrations on the studio's Burbank lot in late 1948 and early 1949.[40] In April 1948, Warner Bros. also filed an application for a Chicago TV station and prepared applications in five other cities. Two months later, Warner Bros. asked the FCC to allow the studio to purchase two radio stations and Los Angeles TV station KLAC from Dorothy Thackery, former publisher of the *New York Post*.[41] For Warner Bros., these investments represented the first steps in organizing a broadcast network that would support an expansion into television.

It is no coincidence that Warner Bros. stepped up its TV-related activities in 1948, a year in which studio executives faced the worst destabilization of the studio system since the Depression. After the industry's peak year of 1946, nationwide box-office attendance had declined steadily, while foreign revenue also diminished as a result of protectionist legislation enacted by European countries.[42] The *Paramount* decision threatened to curtail another source of revenue by eliminating the steady profits delivered by studio-controlled theaters once the studios divested themselves of their theater circuits. Under these conditions, Warner Bros. virtually ceased studio operations from November 1948 to February 1949. When the trade press interpreted the shutdown as a distress signal, Jack Warner denied the rumors; the studio's temporary inactivity was not a shutdown per se, he claimed, but an opportunity for "appraisal, analysis, and planning for the future."[43]

As a result of this reflection, Warner Bros. executives devised a new production strategy that promised to salvage aspects of the studio system by integrating film and television production. Harry Warner declared in January 1949 that Warner Bros. would introduce television production at its Burbank studios as soon as the FCC approved the purchase of the Thackery stations. Planning to use owned-and-operated stations as the cornerstone for expansion into further station ownership or the development of a network, the company would produce programming both for broadcast television and for theater TV. Jack Warner would continue to supervise the production of theatrical features, while Harry would assume responsibility for the television division.[44] This decision marked the origins at Warner Bros. of the policy that ultimately would lead the studio system into the television age. Increasingly, theatrical features would be produced individually by independent units, while the studio's traditional mode of production would be dedicated to serving the television market. The studio would balance the shift toward unique, expensive films with a standardized product that served the same function as had its more routine features during much of the studio era.

Paramount continued to pursue an even wider range of interests in television. Its experimental Los Angeles station began commercial broadcasts in 1947 as KTLA, the first commercial station west of the Mississippi. In 1948, Television Productions, Inc., formed the Paramount Television Network to distribute filmed programs produced at KTLA. This was not a true broadcast network but an alternative source of programming using film distribution instead of live broadcasts to supply local stations. Through American Scophony, Paramount also began to explore the potential for subscription TV, an early precursor of pay cable that used wired transmissions to bypass broadcasters altogether. This technology was being developed in the late 1940s but was not tested in actual markets until the 1950s. In general, however, Paramount's interest in American Scophony diminished following the antitrust suit filed by the Justice Department in 1945. Paramount and General Precision eventually signed a consent decree in January 1949, agreeing to divest all stock interest in Scophony, but Paramount already had begun to develop its own version of theater television even before leaving Scophony.[45]

Unlike the electronic systems developed by RCA and Scophony, which projected a video image directly onto a movie screen, Paramount's theater TV employed an "intermediate film system": in the theater, a video image was filmed from a TV monitor, the footage developed immediately, and the film projected through a normal projector; the entire process took about one minute. Paramount's intermediate film system made its public debut in April 1948 by presenting live coverage of a boxing match to three thousand people in New York's Paramount Theater. The studio assumed that its TV stations, WBKB in Chicago and KTLA in Los Angeles, would function as centers for networks of TV-equipped theaters. By February 1949, the equipment had been installed in theaters in both cities; in June, Paramount launched theater TV telecasts at the Balaban & Katz flagship Chicago Theater. Subsequent telecasts at the Chicago Theater and at other Balaban & Katz theaters in the Chicago area continued to use theater TV for covering special live events, especially sports (boxing matches, Big Ten football, the 1949 World Series) and occasional news events (such as speeches by Dwight Eisenhower and Douglas MacArthur).[46]

All plans for expanding into station ownership and theater television were dashed, however, when the FCC stepped in following the *Paramount* ruling to investigate whether the major studios legitimately had the right to own television stations. Senator Edwin C. Johnson, chairman of the Senate Interstate Commerce Committee, which monitored the broadcasting industries, decried the fact that "interests who have accepted consent decrees stand defiantly at the counter demanding the right to get into television." The Communications Act of 1934 had authorized the FCC to refuse station licenses to any individual or organization convicted of monopolistic practices, and the commission was now prepared to decide whether this provision should be applied to the movie studios whose collusion had precipitated the *Paramount* decision. FCC Chairman Wayne Coy even asked the Justice Department to determine whether the studios' activities in television constituted further violations of antitrust laws.[47]

The FCC never actually delivered a ruling on this question because the station application process was abruptly suspended in September 1948 when the commission declared a freeze on the licensing of TV stations, postponing decisions on all pending applications until solutions had been found for various technical problems that still plagued television, including lingering questions about spectrum allocation, signal interference, and color standards. The station application freeze began as a six-month moratorium to allow the FCC to reevaluate television policy, but the issues involved were too complicated to untangle in such a short period; the freeze ultimately lasted four years, until the commission delivered its *Sixth Report and Order* in May 1952.

Still, American television was hardly frozen during this four-year period. As stations approved before the freeze went on the air, advertisers and the public were drawn to the new medium. The number of stations rose from 50 in 1948 to 108 in 1952, and the number of sets in U.S. homes increased from 1.2 million to 15 million. Historians have argued that because of this growth the freeze actually gave NBC and CBS an insurmountable advantage in the television industry, enabling them to solidify their positions in local markets during a period of limited competition.[48] With the tacit support of the FCC, the radio networks extended their power into the TV industry by establishing owned-and-operated stations in major cities and by signing affiliate contracts with the vast majority of these early stations—which were owned primarily by radio broadcasters who were accustomed to the network structure. Allen B. DuMont, who had launched his own ill-fated network, complained that "the freeze reserved to two networks the almost exclusive right to broadcast in all but 12 of the 63 markets which had television service. It meant that [DuMont and ABC] did not have . . . an opportunity to get programs into the markets so necessary . . . to attract advertisers."[49]

The government's role in excluding the major studios from owning television stations during this period was critical in determining the eventual structure of the television industry. As Douglas Gomery has noted, the *Paramount* decision not only broke up the studio system but "guaranteed that the majors would not secure a significant place in the ownership of U.S. television networks and stations. The radio industry was able to secure a hold which continues to the present day."[50] Hollywood's major studios watched helplessly during the freeze as their plans for television disintegrated. Hoping to force a decision by the FCC, a frustrated 20th Century–Fox petitioned the Justice Department in March 1949 for a ruling on whether the studios should be eligible for broadcast licenses. Meanwhile, Warner Bros. dismissed its Chicago station application in May 1949, after a studio survey concluded that the first year of operation in Chicago—if that year ever came—would cost nearly $800,000. Ultimately, the Thackery TV interests grew tired of waiting for the FCC to approve Warner Bros.' purchase of their Los Angeles stations and pulled out of the deal.[51] With all licensing decisions delayed indefinitely by the freeze, the other studios dismissed their remaining applications as well.

Even as the *Paramount* decision was used by the government to thwart the studios' plans to establish their own stations and networks, the FCC's reluctance to support alternative technologies by allocating frequencies for their use also made theater TV financially untenable. As Michele Hilmes explains, "Through a tendency to protect established interests against innovative competition . . . and [in] what is surely one of the worst examples of regulatory foot-dragging in history, the FCC managed to delay, avert, and handicap testing and operation of these systems to the point that the companies involved could no longer support their efforts."[52]

Although Warner Bros. had planned an initial network of twenty-five theaters equipped with video projection, it would install television systems in only thirteen of its theaters in the coming years.[53] Paramount was also unable to make a profit on theater television and withdrew the systems from its Chicago theaters in 1951. Theater television expanded briefly in the early 1950s, though it never achieved any sort of widespread acceptance. In 1950, ten theaters in the United States were equipped for video projection, and the number peaked in 1952 with seventy-five theaters in thirty-seven cities.[54]

As many in the industry had predicted, theater television failed in part because the FCC would not assign broadcast frequencies exclusively for theater use. Because the studios were unable to acquire stations, they also found it impossible to form a network capable of linking theaters across the country; consequently, the cost of theater TV broadcasts fell on individual theaters and could not be subsidized by a network structure. By the early 1950s, television had become overwhelmingly oriented toward the family home. Not even a single theater added video projection in 1953, and the system slowly disappeared, replaced in theaters by new exhibition technologies like CinemaScope and 3-D.

In spite of their clear designs on the television business, most of the major studios found themselves in the late 1940s with no substantial connections to the new medium and no incentive to forge ahead (the exception being Paramount, which still owned Los Angeles TV station KTLA and an interest in DuMont). Because the major studios had been thwarted from gaining control of distribution, the integration of television in Hollywood occurred through television production, which originated as the domain of independent producers with razor-thin profit margins and little stake in the studio system.

Television Production in Hollywood, 1946–1950

The major studios clearly saw promise in television during the 1940s, but they were not blinded by ambition; they proceeded cautiously by the end of the decade because they were reluctant to take any action that would leave them subservient to the existing radio networks. Yet even though the major studios withdrew from television, Hollywood's engagement with the medium continued apace, fueled by independent producers who rushed forward to supply the new medium's demand for programming.

As small-scale entrepreneurs, Hollywood's first television producers experienced few of the reservations that deterred the movie industry's major powers. They had grown accustomed to squeezing themselves into the cracks and crevices of the studio system— operating on tiny budgets, surviving on minimal profits, designing products that earned money in the neglected areas of a market defined by larger companies. Independent producers and small studios, like Monogram and Republic, typically filled the exhibitors' need for such products as B features, short subjects, serials, and travelogues, the less prestigious and profitable entertainment that completed a theater's daily program, but that the major companies produced with less frequency after the early 1940s. Adaptability was the key to survival in a market that discriminated against any small producer. By necessity, then, independent producers worked with a much broader definition of filmed entertainment, considering many formats that strayed from the major studios' dominant feature-length narratives. Unburdened by commitment to any particular system of distribution or exhibition, to a certain conception of the producer's autonomy and authority, or to any particular definition of the cinematic text, these producers were less devoted to a single medium than to exploiting the potential of any market and any product that promised a return on their investment.

The television industry during the late 1940s and early 1950s was not an ideal alternative to the studio system, since the networks were beginning to monopolize the nation's TV stations as effectively as the studios had controlled theaters. By comparison, however, the market for TV programming was relatively open. Though the majority of network programs were produced for live broadcast by such New York-based advertising agencies as J. Walter Thompson and Young and Rubicam, Hollywood producers discovered a welcome market; the successful ones, like William "Hopalong Cassidy" Boyd or Hal Roach, were able to license filmed programming to networks and local stations or to national, regional, and local sponsors who would then purchase broadcast time. Early television offered meager financial rewards, but it opened new channels of distribution outside the influence of the major studios, providing refuge to producers whose movies traditionally had languished in tiny neighborhood or rural theaters.

An entrepreneur like Jerry Fairbanks epitomized the spirit of the early telefilm pioneers. A producer of short subjects at Paramount for many years, Fairbanks chased the lure of television riches in 1946 when he opened his own telefilm production company in a small studio at the heart of Sunset Boulevard's Poverty Row studios. Inspired by the general corporate culture at Paramount, the studio most committed to television, and by the ingenuity of the studio's short-subject division, Fairbanks envisioned TV production as his opportunity to surpass the studio system. Although there were only a dozen TV stations broadcasting at the time, Fairbanks believed the most optimistic forecasts that more than a thousand stations would bombard the nation's airwaves by 1953. While many of these thousand stations would be network affiliates broadcasting live programs from New York, Fairbanks and others speculated that they would have an insatiable appetite for filmed programming because they would quickly exhaust the network's ability to supply new programs. Although TV production did not promise to be immediately profitable, Fairbanks imagined this imminent demand and saw no ceiling on the potential value of filmed TV programs, which could be circulated indefinitely among the country's new TV stations.

Fairbanks was a tinkerer and a cut-rate visionary; he relished the challenge of adapting studio system production techniques to the demanding economies of television during an era when a half-hour television program, like his 1948 series *Public Prosecutor*, could not count on more than a $20,000 budget. During the late 1940s, in the trade journals and popular press, Fairbanks touted his "Multicam" production system, which adapted live TV's three-camera shooting technique for film production. While there were precedents for multi-camera shooting in the film industry, Fairbanks used 16mm Mitchell cameras mounted on tripod dollies to approximate video's capacity for quick, continuous shooting while creating a product—a motion picture print—that was durable, reproducible, and transportable; moreover, its visual quality surpassed that of live TV's kinescopes, which were filmed off the screen of TV monitors airing the live production.

Because of his limited budget, Fairbanks could not afford to duplicate video's practice of running all three cameras simultaneously. To economize on film stock, much of

Among the more successful Hollywood-based producers of early filmed television programming was Jerry Fairbanks Productions, created in 1946 and housed in a renovated B-film studio.

the editing was completed "in-camera," with only one designated camera running at any given moment. This technique necessitated rigorous preproduction planning in which lighting, camera angles, editing decisions, and the movement of cameras and performers had to be orchestrated precisely before the cameras rolled. Cables and banks of 300-watt reflector lights were suspended from the ceiling so that they would not impede the movement of actors or cameras. Newly developed zoom lenses were fitted onto the cameras to facilitate rapid shifts in focus or changes in composition. Fairbanks registered a number of patents related to this process, including the tripod dollies, an electronic method for marking synchronization among all three cameras and the sound recorder, and a device for following focus on the Mitchell camera's parallax viewer. At a time when other filmed half-hour episodes had production schedules of two or three days, Fairbanks could shoot an episode in a matter of hours. Production costs were kept so low that the single most expensive item in the budget was the film stock and processing, which accounted for only 3 percent of a feature film budget but was 25 to 30 percent of the budget for any Fairbanks program.[55]

In 1948, NBC contracted Fairbanks to produce the first filmed series for network TV, *Public Prosecutor,* starring John Howard. The program looks primitive by the standards of contemporary feature film production. Narrated by Howard, who addresses the camera throughout much of the story, the bare-bones mystery plots are condensed to fit into fifteen-minute segments modeled after the format of radio episodes. The verbal exposition is so insistent that the images begin to seem redundant; the episodes truly resemble radio with pictures. Sets are often undecorated. Actors appear distracted, if not anguished, as they try to hit their marks consistently in the first take. In spite of the opportunities for shot selection offered by the Multicam system, the camera work consists mainly of single-take medium shots or simple over-the-shoulder dialogue sequences. In promoting his Multicam system, Fairbanks claimed that his minimum length per take was five minutes, with the average take lasting between seven and eight minutes. Although this may be true of other Fairbanks programs, an episode of *Public Prosecutor* contains frequent, seemingly unnecessary editing within any given sequence. The network-financed budget for the series was $8,800 per episode. Still, the network could not find sponsors—even after reducing the asking price to $5,000 per episode. With each episode's production costs exceeding $10,000, Fairbanks discontinued production before completing a season's worth of episodes.[56] Fairbanks's company survived the setback, going on to produce series such as *Silver Theater* (1950) and *Front Page Detective* (1951–1953), but it certainly was not an impressive debut for filmed programming on the networks.

Many other independent producers joined Fairbanks in this first speculative period of telefilm production, which extended from 1946 through the 1951-1952 TV season. "Everybody who could buy or borrow a little drugstore movie camera announced himself as a TV-film producer," Fairbanks claimed in describing these early days.[57] News accounts during this period estimated that over eight hundred producers sought telefilm riches in the years prior to 1952. As a result, over two thousand unsold pilots languished on storage shelves or rotted in trash bins, having failed to attract a sponsor for network broadcast or syndication. Neglected studios, empty warehouses, supermarkets, and family garages were transformed into temporary soundstages; 16mm cameras disappeared from stores; personal savings accounts were drained—all in the frantic gold rush years of the early telefilm industry.

The most visible producers to emerge in telefilm production during the late 1940s were the B-movie cowboys, who quickly became icons of the early video age: William "Hopalong Cassidy" Boyd, Gene Autry, and Roy Rogers. Boyd provided the telefilm industry's first unabashed success story, fueling every independent producer's wildest fantasies about deliverance from the studio system. During the 1940s, he had shrewdly invested $350,000 to acquire the television rights to the series of Hopalong Cassidy feature films in which he had starred since 1935; in addition, he acquired the rights to use the Hopalong Cassidy character in other media, including television, and in character merchandising. After marketing the features to local stations during the late 1940s, Boyd produced a *Hopalong Cassidy* TV series for NBC beginning in 1949.

By tapping into the growing postwar youth market and by taking advantage of television's emergent position at the center of an expanding popular culture marketplace, Boyd founded a Hopalong Cassidy industry that within only a few years included a radio series, a comic strip, comic books, a popular fan club, and a dazzling array of licensed merchandise—with an estimated total value of $200 million.[58] Spurred by Boyd's canny reincarnation, Autry and Rogers also revived moribund careers and earned fantastic wealth, beginning in the late 1940s, by producing television Westerns on the same dusty backlots that once had provided the settings for their B Westerns.

From the pack of fly-by-night producers that surrounded these cowboy heroes in the early telefilm business, five significant production companies emerged: Fairbanks, the Hal Roach Studios, Bing Crosby Enterprises, Ziv Television Programs, Inc., and Louis Snader Productions. The varied backgrounds of these producers give some sense of the many career routes that delivered early entrepreneurs to the telefilm industry.[59]

The Hal Roach Studios arrived in television as an established Poverty Row movie studio. After years at the margins of the movie industry, the Roach studio was familiar with the many low-budget alternatives to standard narrative features. The studio itself was virtually dormant in 1949 when Hal Roach Jr., after years of kicking around the industry, joined the company and convinced his father to rent space to telefilm producers and to form their own TV production unit. Roach produced situation comedies such as *The Stu Erwin Show* (1950–1955) and *My Little Margie* (1952–1955), and crime dramas like *Racket Squad* (1950–1953). As the studio increased its output, Hal Jr. became one of the early influential figures in the telefilm business, helping to found both the Television Film Producers' Association and the Academy of Television Arts and Sciences.

Bing Crosby was a performer and shrewd businessman, who always had moved easily between movies, radio, recordings, and live performances. Under the guidance of Basil Grillo and Crosby's brother Everett, Bing Crosby Enterprises during the 1940s had diversified into a number of unrelated businesses, producing orange juice, ice cream, sport shirts, and a wide variety of endorsed merchandise. An early proponent of the shift from live radio broadcast to transcribed performances, Crosby also was a chief investor in Ampex's development of videotape. As a result of these investments, Crosby was probably the most reputable and highly capitalized of the early telefilm producers. Crosby's company during its early years focused primarily on anthology series like *Fireside Theater* (1950–1958) and *Rebound* (1952).

Frederick Ziv, a syndicator of radio transcriptions to local stations, viewed telefilm production as an obvious extension of his existing business—an alternative to live broadcasting that provided local radio stations with some autonomy from the networks. Ziv Television Programs, Inc., packaged fifteen-minute sports and news programs for TV

William Boyd secured the rights to the films featuring his on-screen persona Hopalong Cassidy and successfully entered the TV market through reissued B-Western movies and, beginning in 1949, a television series for NBC.

beginning in 1948. In 1949, his company began production on *The Cisco Kid* (1950–1956), its first dramatic TV series. By shooting the series in color when all other producers were using black-and-white film, Ziv ensured the residual value of the series for decades. Ziv's subsequent work consisted primarily of action series with male heroes, such as *Boston Blackie* (1951–1953) and *Dangerous Assignment* (1951–1952).

Louis Snader, an ex-musician and real estate tycoon, was probably the least likely member of this group, and his success was the shortest-lived. Louis Snader Productions produced the television version of *Dick Tracy* in 1950, but Snader hoped to make his real mark through his introduction in 1949 of "Telescriptions," three-minute filmed musical performances featuring stars like Peggy Lee, Mel Torme, and the Jordanaires. Producing twelve per day at a cost of $2,500 each, Snader imagined that his short films could be programmed flexibly into the daily schedule of local stations. Snader antici-pated that Telescriptions would be hosted by TV jockeys who would become as influen-tial as radio's newly celebrated disk jockeys.[60] Snader's peculiar contribution to the early telefilm—imagining TV mimicking radio's new recorded-music format and unwittingly anticipating the form of music videos—gives some idea of the flexibility of these pro-ducers, of their willingness to explore the options made possible by TV.

Only two of Hollywood's major studios attempted to move into television production during the late 1940s, and these were two of the least profitable studios in the studio sys-tem: Universal-International and Columbia. At first glance, it seems ironic that Universal and Columbia were the first studio system pioneers in TV production since they traditionally had demonstrated the least interest in broadcasting. But in fact Universal and Columbia were best equipped to adapt to the programming demands and economic relations of television. While the five largest studios jockeyed for position—buying radio stations, investing in television research, applying for TV station licenses—Universal and Columbia never had the investment capital to diversify into broadcasting. Along with United Artists, Universal and Columbia did not own the revenue-generating theater chains that provided the major studios with the financial security to consider diversification. Universal and Columbia saw their relationship to the TV industry as an extension of their subordinate status in the studio system: they were prepared to supply product to a market beyond their control.

Universal first began television production in 1947 as one measure in a desperate attempt to put the brakes on runaway financial losses that had piled up following the box-office failure of a number of prestige independent productions financed and dis-tributed by the studio starting in 1946.[61] Universal turned to the production of TV com-mercials as a side venture of its New York-based subsidiary United World Films, the world's largest distributor of 8mm and 16mm film. The company immediately estab-lished itself by producing for clients such as Lever's Lux Soap, General Electric, and Gulf Oil. By 1949, the company had moved its TV operations to Los Angeles in hopes of expanding into the production of documentaries and other types of programming. Since the TV division's net profits for the first year were less than $40,000, the studio probably did not intend for TV production to boost its profits so much as to buy time by paying for facilities and labor at a time when lack of funds even forced the studio tem-porarily to shut its doors.[62] Universal staked its eventual movie comeback on a series of low-budget, proto-situation comedies featuring Ma and Pa Kettle and Francis the Talking Mule, but it never sold a television series and consequently remained in TV solely as a producer of commercials.

Although Columbia initially entered television under much the same circumstances as Universal, its rapid diversification beyond commercials made it more successful. In the spring of 1949, Columbia's president, Harry Cohn, hired his nephew Ralph, the son of the studio cofounder Jack Cohn, to conduct a preliminary study of Columbia's immediate and long-range prospects in the field of television. For the previous two years, Ralph Cohn had acquired a firsthand knowledge of television while running a two-man organization, Pioneer Television, which produced TV commercials in New York. Cohn presented a fifty-page analysis in which he advised that Columbia immediately assemble an organization to produce TV commercials and, ultimately, filmed programs for both network and local broadcast.[63]

In June 1949, Columbia formed a television production subsidiary through Screen Gems, the former animation company that had produced the studio's short subjects since the Cohns purchased it from Charles Mintz in 1934. During its first two years, Screen Gems produced only commercials, delivering more than two hundred for such clients as American Tobacco, Hamilton Watch, and BVD.[64] Soon thereafter, Screen Gems began producing television series, and within a few years its success with series like *Father Knows Best* (1954–1960) would elevate it into the ranks of Hollywood's major powers.

Created under severe economic constraints, Hollywood's earliest filmed television programs scarcely affected the movie industry's major studios. During the first stage of television production in Hollywood, roughly 1946 until 1951, telefilm production took place on the distant fringes of the studio system. The province of Hollywood outsiders and castoffs, telefilm's underfinanced, uncoordinated early ventures merited little attention from industry leaders. Gradually, however, the market for telefilm production solidified as sponsors and the networks looked to Hollywood for programming and as more established independent producers turned to television in hopes of reaping profits through syndication and merchandising. As early as 1951, these producers began to leave their mark on the medium. During the fall of that year, Desi Arnaz and Lucille Ball premiered *I Love Lucy* (1951–1957), the first filmed situation comedy to have a national impact. Jack Webb followed later that season with *Dragnet* (1952–1959), the first successful crime series shot on film. Within a year, *I Love Lucy* and *Dragnet,* two filmed series produced in Hollywood, stood atop the network ratings as the most popular series on TV.

Conclusion

Jack Warner's legendary antagonism toward television was not evident until the end of the 1940s. Considering his studio's long-term commitment to television, it was a significant departure from Warner Bros. tradition when he announced in early 1950 that "the only screens which will carry Warner Bros. products will be the screens of motion picture theaters the world over."[65] Warner's hostility to television has sometimes seemed like the natural result of competition between the movie industry and an upstart rival; in fact, it might never have existed were it not for FCC actions that prevented the studio from forming its own network or seeing its investment in theater TV pan out. Judging by the plans that Warner Bros. unveiled in 1949, the studio executives conceived of television as a central component of the postwar studio system, a new source of income in an unpredictable economic environment.

For much of the 1940s, it was possible for Hollywood's major studios to imagine that they would play a significant role in shaping American television, that television under their influence might not simply duplicate the model of broadcasting established during the radio era. They envisioned two complementary forms of television which would feature different types of programming, one designed for home audiences and the other for theaters. By the dawn of national television service in the late 1940s, however, it was already clear from the FCC's actions that American television would follow the radio model: television would be an advertiser-supported medium dominated by the established broadcast networks, with programming transmitted almost solely to home receivers.

The FCC's growing distrust of the studios may have seemed gratuitous, perhaps even willfully biased in favor of the radio networks, but the antitrust charges of the 1940s cast grave doubts on the worthiness of the studios to hold broadcast licenses. Michele Hilmes has shown that the FCC's suspicion echoed more general public criticism of the movie industry following the *Paramount* decision. An article in the February 1949 *Consumer Reports,* for instance, forecast dire problems for the future of television should the studios, with their acknowledged record of monopolistic practices, find a foothold in the medium. Given power in both the movie and television industries, these oppressors of independent theater owners might be tempted to commit any number of abuses; most important, as RCA warned in 1940, they could slow the development of

By the late 1940s, RCA's efforts were focused squarely on the production and sale of home receivers—here being mass-produced in RCA's factory in Camden, New Jersey.

television to protect the movie business or erode broadcasting's public service standards in their quest for profits.[66]

According to Hilmes, the *Paramount* decision helped to foster the contrasting images that justified the FCC's discrimination between the movie and broadcast industries: Hollywood appeared to be a potential public menace, while the radio networks—which had themselves engaged in a host of monopolistic practices—posed as beneficent public servants. Supported by public sentiment, the FCC's inquiries into Hollywood antitrust violations and general reluctance to support technological or economic alternatives to the broadcast networks blocked virtually every plan for television that originated in Hollywood.

During the 1940s, even Paramount, the studio that diversified most aggressively into television, could not succeed beyond its interest in DuMont and its ownership of local stations in Los Angeles and Chicago. Blocked from owning individual stations, building networks, or developing theater TV, Hollywood's leaders recognized at the end of the decade that they had lost the opportunity to compete with the broadcast networks, which became firmly entrenched during the freeze. Producing for television without controlling distribution was an unthinkable compromise for the studios. Doubtless the studio system would have to adapt in order to survive the postwar era, but the studios were not yet prepared to create a product that they would neither distribute nor exhibit; distribution was still the key to a studio's power and self-determination. Therefore, while the major studios other than Paramount retreated from television at the end of the 1940s, independent film producers began to integrate television into the movie industry. The history of television in the studio era is a chronicle of thwarted ambitions. The full-scale integration of television in Hollywood would not occur until the 1950s, when the major studios themselves would begin to produce for television.

14

Experimental and Avant-Garde Cinema in the 1940s

Lauren Rabinovitz

After World War II, non-Hollywood films became a more visible part of U.S. urban movie culture, and a greater number of people experienced new types of cinema. A perceived difference emerged between Hollywood fare and independent or foreign cinemas, an opposition that theater exhibitors and critics alike promoted in the practice of differentiating customer groups for their movies. Within this divergence, independent cinema (any movies made independently from or outside of Hollywood production studios) developed a widespread film culture similar to that of the prewar European cine club movement.[1] While such a model for film culture held sway in the United States in the 1930s among leftist cultural-political clubs like the Workers Film and Photo League (WFPL) and the John Reed Clubs, it reemerged after the war as the model for a system of alternative cinema as art rather than of cinema conceived as a political weapon.

The European Exodus and Other War-Related Developments

Various wartime developments had resulted in significant shifts in U.S. art institutions. During World War II, the international art capital or marketplace changed from Nazi-occupied Paris to New York City. A similar transcontinental displacement occurred in independent filmmaking activities. European painters immigrated to America to escape the Nazis, and they subsequently influenced a generation of American painters and sculptors; among the European artists who immigrated to the United States were a number of filmmakers who acted as mentors to a new generation of young filmmakers. For example, Luis Buñuel immigrated from Spain and spent the war years in Manhattan at the Museum of Modern Art (MOMA) Circulating Film Library, where he reedited, dubbed, and directed documentaries for Latin American distribution. The American expatriate Man Ray left Nazi-occupied Paris and lived in Los Angeles for the duration of the war. His good friend and Dada collaborator, the artist-filmmaker Marcel

Duchamp, moved to New York City and became active among surrealist artists and film-makers there.

Although some European filmmakers spent the war years in exile in the United States, other filmmakers immigrated permanently to New York and Los Angeles and actively contributed to transforming a new American experimental cinema. The German animator Oskar Fischinger, who specialized in what Goebbels decreed was "forbidden" abstract art, left Berlin and went to work for Paramount Pictures in Hollywood in 1936. Fischinger had great difficulty working within a studio system of production that depended upon regimentation and division of labor, first with Paramount and then with Disney Studios, to whom he brought the idea of a feature-length animated movie set to classical music (FANTASIA). When he met the curator of the Solomon Guggenheim Foundation during a trip to New York City in 1938, he found someone who would help him receive a series of grants during the war years when he could not obtain employment because of his German citizenship. Back in Los Angeles, he continued to work on his animated abstract films, and he gathered around him a group of young musicians and film artists that at times included John Cage, Edgard Varèse, the Whitney brothers, Maya Deren, and Kenneth Anger. Both Cage's and Varèse's compositional experiments drew upon Fischinger's experiments with synthetic sounds.

Another important European abstract painter-animator, Hans Richter, immigrated from Germany to the United States. In 1940, he came to New York City, where he began the Film Institute of the City College of New York in 1943. He befriended and encouraged Maya Deren and later, in the 1950s, the filmmakers Jonas Mekas and Shirley Clarke. His live-motion, feature-length film DREAMS THAT MONEY CAN BUY (1944–1947) was a collection of surreal vignettes suggested by various friends of his who were well-known European artists in exile in New York City—Marcel Duchamp, Man Ray, Alexander Calder, Fernand Leger, and Max Ernst.

The animated films Richter made in the 1920s (RHYTHM 21, 1921; RHYTHM 23, 1923; and RHYTHM 25, 1925) and Fischinger's films (especially MOTION PAINTING 1, 1947) were prominently featured in the landmark "Art in Cinema" series held at the San Francisco Museum of Art in the late 1940s. Richter's films inspired Jordan Belson, a recent graduate of the California School of Fine Arts, to make his first films.[2] TRANSMUTATION (1947) and IMPROVISATION #1 (1948), both now lost, were abstract paintings set in motion. Fischinger's work was an important model for a kind of abstract animation that attempted to coordinate visual and sound sensations. During the 1940s, a few filmmakers were working independently on animation as a natural extension of experiments in abstract painting and time, or in modern music and composition, or in both. Harry Smith batiked abstractions directly on celluloid in a series of hand-painted films, NOS. 1–3 (1939–1947). The artist Dwinell Grant, an assistant curator at the Solomon Guggenheim Foundation during the time when Fischinger was a fellowship recipient, exhibits Fischinger's influences in his nonobjective, stop-motion COMPOSITIONS, 1–4 (1940–1945). The filmmaker and composer John Whitney and his brother, the painter James Whitney, worked together to develop a unified relationship between film and music in their animated paper cut-out films that explore sound and image synchronization (FILM EXERCISES, NOS. 1–5, 1943–1944). Norman McLaren used techniques first introduced by Fischinger in visualizing synthetically produced sound pitches in a series of direct-drawings-on-film that he made while working at the New York City Museum of Non-Objective Art (1939–1941) before he began his lifelong association with the National Film Board of Canada in 1941. Mary Ellen Bute's "seeing-sound" films, color abstractions rhythmically set to classical music (TARENTELLA, 1940; POLKA GRAPH, 1947; COLOR RHAPSODIE, 1948), have often been compared to Fischinger's films but are more sensuous and tactile in form and color, are less rigidly patterned, and more frequently use the music for counterpoint effects.[3] The painter-animator Douglass Crockwell's GLEN FALLS SEQUENCE (1946) explores the pictorial qualities of a series of abstract painterly images. His film THE LONG BODIES (1946–1947) uses a sliced-wax animation technique similar to one invented by Fischinger.

In addition to the influx of several leaders of the arts in Europe, greater availability and commercial marketing of affordable film technology and materials revolutionized the possibilities for independent filmmaking. Sixteen-millimeter film stock and equipment offered an economical alternative to the 35mm gauge stock and equipment employed in Hollywood studios. Film stock and printing cost less for 16mm than for 35mm, and the equipment was lighter in weight, portable, and more easily manipulated by one or two individuals. Although not widely circulated before the 1940s, 16mm stock and equipment had existed since 1923. Only when the government adopted 16mm during World War II for military use in training films and war documentaries and as the medium for exhibition on military bases around the world were the advantages of 16mm widely publicized. More important, the surplus of used equipment after the war and Eastman Kodak's need to find new markets to replace dwindling military consumption resulted in more economical and more readily available materials and processing.

The advantages of the 16mm format had been revealed to a new generation of filmmakers who were watching government films during World War II or reading about how the government made its films. Others became familiar with 16mm while making films in the armed services or working for the government. Alexander Hammid, Willard van Dyke, and Peter Glushanok were among the independent filmmakers who worked in film services for the Office of War Information. The experimental filmmaker Marie Menken learned how to work in 16mm while she was employed during the war at Time News Services.

Postwar Film Culture

After the war, more students were able to learn the techniques of 16mm filmmaking because military veterans' benefits packages and a booming postwar economy provided new sources of funding support for new educational programs. Not only did the GI Bill subsidize college-bound veterans, but the resulting increase in college enrollments and tuition revenues allowed schools to expand curricula and to introduce such new subjects as filmmaking and film appreciation. In 1947, the California School of Fine Arts became the first art school in the United States to teach 16mm filmmaking as a regular part of its curriculum. The integration of filmmaking into arts curricula helped to legitimate independent cinema's status as an artistic medium among the vanguard arts. Such institutional integration occurred in a number of key places and through a number of significantly decisive moves, such as the George Eastman House's 1947 opening of a film archive to preserve cinema's history as an art form. Even New York City film societies took field trips to Rochester to view cinematic art at Eastman House.

Measuring the growth of a postwar film culture in numbers is just as impressive as the measure of institutional "firsts." By 1949, there were more than 200 film societies in the United States, with an estimated audience of approximately 100,000, whereas at the beginning of the decade only a handful of film societies had operated, with a small membership.[4] Museum art schools and colleges that had begun to teach filmmaking also began to sponsor film societies that screened classic European movies and independent cinema. As an analog to their filmmaking courses, they offered film appreciation courses. One could see experimental cinema almost anywhere because the MOMA Circulating Film Library distributed movies nationwide to colleges, universities, museums, film appreciation clubs, and study groups.

At both East and West Coast art centers, new film societies especially became important models for a national culture of experimental cinema. In 1947, two students at the San Francisco Museum of Art launched a series of screenings on independent cinema. Their program was so successful that the "Art in Cinema" series ran at the museum until the early 1950s as a film society with approximately six hundred members.[5] Because they also published their screening lists and program notes as an art catalog, they offered a widely circulated prototype of experimental cinema canon formation and aesthetics.

On the East Coast, Cinema 16 became the preeminent showcase for independent film, as well as the largest film society in the United States—by 1949 it boasted a membership of 2,500.[6] In addition, Cinema 16 began distributing independent films in 1948. From their first screenings, Cinema 16's directors, Amos and Marcia Vogel, emphasized a discourse of film appreciation in the selection, arrangement, and presentation of film programs. The film critic Scott MacDonald characterizes this programming policy: "One form of the film collides with another so as to create a maximum intellectual engagement on the part of the audience, not simply in the individual discrete films, but with film itself and the implications of its more conventional uses."[7] Programs regularly included scientific films, government-sponsored documentaries, independently made documentaries, experimental films, animation, foreign features, and classics. The Vogels supplemented the films with written program notes and even with appearances by the filmmakers themselves. Among those who authored program notes were the film critics Arthur Knight, Parker Tyler, and Siegfried Kracauer.[8] The program notes discussed cinematic aesthetics within a context of modern psychological and literary thought. They implicitly defined artistic cinema through the use of symbols and spatio-temporal experimentation.

At the same time that film societies experienced significant growth, postwar expansion of art-house cinemas and a small system for commercial distribution of independent cinema facilitated significant theatrical alternatives to Hollywood movies. When the major Hollywood studios reduced the number of films released annually and booked them for longer runs at first-run theaters, they were slowly squeezing smaller second- and third-run theaters out of the distribution circuit. As the film historian Janet Staiger describes the economic situation: "The growth of art houses may have been due less to any new audience demand per se than to an opening of exhibition options arising from changes in the U.S. film industry's structure and conduct."[9] Smaller theaters then, needing an alternative product, increasingly turned to foreign films, documentaries, and reissued classics. While not a direct economic or institutional model for the emergent cine club culture of independent cinema, foreign films differentiated through art-house marketing and exhibition practices provided a highly visible discourse for the future of aesthetics and sexuality, issues that would be explored in experimental cinema.

It is interesting that Americans would patronize movies other than Hollywood fare at precisely the moment when Hollywood was experiencing a postwar drop in theater

Among the most obvious signs of an emergent postwar "film culture" was the art-cinema movement—with theaters, like this one in Wilmington, California, adopting a first-run policy for European imports.

attendance. By articulating its difference from Hollywood cinema primarily in terms of social consciousness, explicit sexuality, and artistry, art-house cinema promoted a new type of movie to patrons who, for various reasons, sought alternatives to standard Hollywood fare. Literary journals and art magazines provided an important base for thinking about and defining foreign, experimental, and independent films in these ways. Such periodicals as *Saturday Review, New Directions, Kenyon Review,* and *Theater Arts* featured stories on independent cinema, and magazines such as the *New Republic* and *The Nation* regularly reviewed non-Hollywood films in the latter half of the 1940s. By the very act of including cinema in discussions of the arts, these popular magazines promoted cinema's status as a contemporary radical art form.

Critical discourse about experimental cinema emphasized the preoccupation of new short films with interior psychology or the experience of interiority. The criteria for understanding the new cinema was not so much the intelligibility of its narratives but more importantly the ways that it disrupted time and space logics for self-expressive purposes. The discussions foregrounded the new stylistic strategies, which countered narrative causality with dream logic and challenged the dominant conventions of established film style—the linear story film, Hollywood styles and genres, standards of professionalism, and mainstream production values.[10]

MESHES OF THE AFTERNOON *and the Poetic Psychodrama*

The best-known experimental films of the decade, influenced by surrealism's dynamic presence in New York City during World War II, were poetic psychodramas that could be readily understood within the charged contexts of art cinema as sexually explicit, scandalous, and radically artistic. They emphasized a dreamlike quality, tackled questions of sexual identity, featured taboo or shocking images, and used editing to liberate spatio-temporal logic from the conventions of Hollywood realism. In 1943, Maya Deren and Alexander Hammid made MESHES OF THE AFTERNOON, the first American example of this type of filmmaking. The film is about a woman's dream of her quest for self-identity as expressed through a series of surrealist encounters between her multiple selves inside an ordinary house. Deren made two more films about women's self-identities, AT LAND (1944) and RITUAL IN TRANSFIGURED TIME (1946), as well as two films that were short exercises in editing dance or dancelike movements across different geographic spaces (A STUDY IN CHOREOGRAPHY FOR CAMERA, 1945; MEDITATION ON VIOLENCE, 1947). Curtis Harrington's FRAGMENT OF SEEING (1946) and PICNIC (1948) continued in the same vein, exploring the logic of spatio-temporal discontinuities in dream narratives about an isolated protagonist whose quest is for self-identity.

Made in the same year as MESHES OF THE AFTERNOON, Willard Maas and Marie Menken's GEOGRAPHY OF THE BODY is a series of extreme close-ups of the naked body edited together with the spoken description of a fantastic travel narrative to remote regions. This film and Maas's IMAGE IN THE SNOW (1948) emphatically narrativize images through poetic, sexually expressive commentary.

Menken's VISUAL VARIATIONS ON NOGUCHI (1945) is a poetic essay of sensuous abstract forms and rhythms, a stylistic hybrid between the abstract animations and the cinematically psychological realism of the introspective dramas. Menken made the film while house-sitting at the studio of the sculptor Isamu Noguchi when he was away on a trip; she freely swung her camera in smooth, rhythmic motions around the artist's rounded, polished organic forms.

THE POTTED PSALM (1946), Sidney Peterson and James Broughton's first film, is a more freewheeling dream that combines distorted images, obvious optic effects, disjointed narrative progressions, and wild camera movements to pose a pseudo-narrative about a set of adventures that take a schizophrenic man from the graveyard to the city and back to the graveyard. It was an important model for their individual efforts over the next several years: THE CAGE (1947), HORROR DREAM (1948), MR. FRENHOFER AND THE MINOTAUR (1948), THE PETRIFIED DOG (1948), and THE LEAD SHOES (1949). Peterson's films, often made for little money with his students at the California School of Fine Arts, consistently depend on distorted imagery made with an anamorphic lens that undermines the illusion of realism heralded by Deren. They operate at an intersection between their attention to formal abstraction and their referentiality to dream modes filled with sexual icons, Freudian scenarios, and schizoid adventures that result in picaresque pseudo-narratives about the unconscious. They are psychodramas that masquerade as witty sexual fantasies marked by a sense of anarchic humor.

James Broughton's MOTHER'S DAY (1948) is a more lyrical examination of sexual identity as a perverse nostalgic exploration of the Oedipal complex. It is a meditative attempt "to fathom the awesome sexuality of Mother," as Lucy Fischer says.[11] Stylistically similar to the individually made films of his friend Sidney Peterson, Broughton's MOTHER'S DAY is a surrealistically played-out montage of Freudian fragments about memory, Mom, and the remembrance of childhood as a denial of sexuality.

A few of the psychodramas of the 1940s represented homosexual desire and employed explicit images about what was a taboo subject, a situation that made the films not only controversial but in violation of censorship laws in some states. The best known and most enduring of these films is Kenneth Anger's dream narrative FIREWORKS (1947). Gregory Markopoulis's PSYCHE-LYDIS-CHARMIDES (1948), made while he was a student at the University of Southern California, is a reverie of homoeroticism that combines such sexually charged images and Freudian fragments as a battering ram that becomes a phallic symbol and close-ups of the male body.

For succeeding generations of college students and film critics, however, MESHES OF THE AFTERNOON has remained the most famous as well as the most important work of U.S. experimental cinema. The origins of MESHES OF THE AFTERNOON lie in the relationship and collaboration between the newlyweds Maya Deren, a poet and secretary to the New York–based Katherine Dunham Dance Company, and Alexander Hammid, an émigré filmmaker from Czechoslovakia. Deren met Hammid in Los Angeles when she accompanied Dunham's dance company to Los Angeles, where it was to work in a Hollywood feature film. Deren and Hammid married, and with his lighting, photographic, and editing expertise and her desire to extend her previous experience as a poet to film, the two made an eighteen-minute, black-and-white, silent film for $260 in their rented California bungalow.[12] Although the film owes some stylistic and conceptual debts to Hammid's AIMLESS WALK (1930), MESHES expresses more intense emotions and an overall mood unlike anything that Hammid had previously done.[13]

By plotting the film according to the coordinates of a woman's inscription in a heterosexual relationship, an obsessively fetishistic southern California domestic scene, and a visual style indebted to Hollywood *film noir*, MESHES OF THE AFTERNOON culturally and psychosexually moves well beyond Hammid's previous intellectual allegiances and experience to American cultural conditions and constructions of woman's identity in the early 1940s. Maureen Turim associates the film's images of domestic disorder—a telephone off the hook, a record player turntable spinning relentlessly, a knife stuck in a loaf of bread—and the detailed attentiveness to the architectural space of domesticity with the biographical elements of the home movie, a genre obsessively about "writing" the familial and psychological identity of the filmmaker.[14] It is both the domestic woman-centered subject matter and the manner of its presentation that have allowed critics to understand the film's author as Deren rather than Hammid.

MESHES OF THE AFTERNOON begins by introducing a woman—played by Deren—who is seen only as an extended arm, legs running up stairs, and a shadow projected onto the sidewalk. The initial sequence of events comprises only close-ups: an arm reaches for a paper flower, the hand lifts the flower, sandaled feet alternate with a profile in shadow moving up a flight of stairs to the door of a house. The hand takes a key from a purse and drops the key; the key falls in slow motion to the ground, bounces, and heads offscreen. A hand enters following the same trajectory of movement as the key. Across several similarly composed shots alternating the hand, the key, and the feet, one continuous trajectory of movement implies a spatio-temporal metamorphosis from object to body part to object to body.

The body parts substitute for an unseen but implied "whole" woman. But the arm, legs, shadow, and flower as objects of equal size and depth are positioned within the die-

Maya Deren in MESHES OF THE AFTERNOON, *one of several 1943 experimental films that helped initiate the American avant-garde movement.*

gesis as autonomous agents rather than as extensions of any unified subject that controls the movement. The relation of subject to object is reversed: the woman becomes passive while the objects act aggressively. Deren herself wrote program notes explaining that the film presents a malevolent vitality in inanimate objects.[15] The result is a fragmented subject and a narrative organized around an initial act of dislocation that underlies the simple linear progression of a woman doing an everyday activity in an ordinary environment.

From the outset, MESHES OF THE AFTERNOON plays with a meaning it refuses to assign, giving way to self-reflexivity on the nature of cinema itself as well as to the imagistic body of woman as the material through which signification is played out and questioned. While it may borrow cinema vocabulary from Hollywood cinema and especially from *film noir,* the overall organization and purpose of spatio-temporal fragmentations, extremely oblique camera angles, high-contrast lighting and deep shadows, and character point-of-view shots are *anti-Hollywood.* The film refuses to conform to simple cause-and-effect story relationships and rejects the idea of psychological motivation expressed through character development and fullness, even the idea of character identity expressed through bodily unity: MESHES is about a woman contending with her own fragmentation and disequilibrium. As Julian Wolfreys has noted, "The shadow is itself [simultaneously both] a signifier of the female and not the woman (nor her image) at all" and instead functions as a trace of the nature of filmic projection itself.[16] In this regard, then, he argues that the film's beginning refuses to make meaning in any conventional way. Instead, it locates the fulfillment of meaning in the self-reflexive trope of a "signature of a signature"—or rather, in the image of a projection on a wall (the shadow) that is contained within an image that is really a projection on a screen (thus, a *mise en abyme*). In this case, it is not the body of *any* woman that bears this burden of both meaning constructions and denials but the bodily index of one of the filmmakers. The image is thus also a referent to authorial trace, which functions in its capacity both to construct and deconstruct the authorial role in cinema.

Such double-edged play on meanings, offered from a more modern context of feminist and post-structuralist criticism, suggests the rich capacity of this film for different reception contexts. Since the 1940s, MESHES OF THE AFTERNOON has been linked to several agendas for independent cinema. In the 1970s, it entered into several discussions as a model of formalist aesthetics.[17] Since the 1980s, it has figured in discussions of woman's discursive strategies, the poetics of home movies, psychoanalytic and especially Lacanian interpretive strategies for understanding the formation of gender, and, finally, Derridean deconstructionist techniques for understanding the film as an expressive act of linguistic resistance.[18] One critic has even suggested that the film's "innovative spatio-temporal ordering transformed its audience's concept of film."[19] The perennially central position of MESHES in shifting discourses about experimental cinema suggests not merely a chameleonlike adaptability to changing critical fashion but the density of Deren and Hammid's production.

In the 1940s, however, MESHES OF THE AFTERNOON was more modestly hailed in discussions of surrealist influence on U.S. experimental cinema. A dance reviewer in 1946 compared MESHES to important surrealist psychodramas: "*Seashell and the Clergyman* might have sprung from the heart of an identical twin of Maya Deren. Jean Cocteau's *Blood of a Poet,* too, is not far from *Meshes of the Afternoon.*"[20] Writing for the *Kenyon Review,* the film critic Parker Tyler compared Deren's film to "the visions of Cocteau and Dali."[21] Although Deren herself consistently refused any linkage with surrealist goals or aesthetics, the surrealist films of the 1920s provided the critics with the primary cinematic comparisons for dream imagery, logic disturbances, and concern for the subconscious that they saw in her film.

From the film's opening, MESHES suggests a strong sense of subject fragmentation, psychological disturbance, and spatial dislocation. Once the woman enters the house, she stops to rest in an easy chair and falls asleep. A close-up of her eye followed by a point-of-view iris or telescopic shot makes her eye an objectively rendered gateway to the internal world of her dream imagination, where she chases a hooded figure with a mirrored face into the house and encounters ordinary domestic objects such as a phonograph and a telephone. The sequence of events occurs three times, each constructed around a search through the space whereby the staircase provides a pathway to dramatic spatial and temporal disruptions of the environment. The searches end with the three "dream" Mayas facing off around the dining room table in order to determine which one will kill the fourth Maya asleep in the chair. At the moment when the woman's self-destruction in this world seems imminent—a dream Maya lowers a knife toward the sleeping Maya—the dream is abruptly replaced by the sleeping woman's point of view of a man's face bending over her. They go upstairs to the bedroom, where his viewpoint and actions control the flow of images. He returns her to normalcy, that is to say, to representation within a narrative where her body is portrayed as a sexual object of desire in relation to the male gaze. But following this possibility held out for the spectator of a conventional ending and of closure is a rapid montage organized around many of the same iconic images that figure earlier in the film: a paper flower, a knife, an eye, a broken mirror. The narrative then returns the spectator to the outside of the home and to another entry into the domestic realm. The man who awoke the sleeping woman approaches the house, enters, and sees the woman with her throat slit, mirror fragments strewn around her, and seaweed dripping down her clothing. His final point-of-view close-up images are of her dead eyes and bloody mouth.

The ending is ambiguous and raises many questions. How does one interpret the woman's "death"? Is it, as Mary Ann Doane observes about women characters who appropriate the camera's subjective "gaze" in the Hollywood genre of women's pictures in the 1940s, that her desire is so excessive the only closure possible is her death?[22] Or is the ending the result of a revolt against conventional cinematic structures of containment? Or is it dramatically signifying her end as a construction of Woman within his dream world? Or her dream world? As Maureen Turim similarly questions, "Is it the dream of the man or the woman, is it an act performed by the woman that shatters the man/mirror of her self? Or is she drowned already as she sits dreaming on the easy chair in her living room?"[23] What is important is that the ending is the outcome of a combined series of spatio-temporal fragmentations and shifts in signification that progressively develop around a theme of latent domestic violence and the politically resistant potential of a nonunitary identity.

In this regard, MESHES appropriates the psychological realism that was in vogue in classical Hollywood cinema but expresses it through spatio-temporal *dis*continuities rather than through the verisimilitudinous continuity that was typical of Hollywood films. For example, the woman is unable to master the environment not because of her psychological motivation and character traits as expressed within the contours of a plot set in a stable diegesis but because abruptly changing camera angles and jump cuts present the space itself as constantly changing around her as she tries to traverse it. Turim writes: "The house space is magical. Its architecture includes an infinite staircase, a second story window that one can leap into from the outside, a picture window that becomes a tele-scopic tunnel into the space of dreams."[24] It is a domestic world of dream logic where objects turn into other objects, where the speed of motion does not correspond to phys-ical laws, and where geography is neither constant nor consistent. Time and space are so fractured that such everyday occurrences as walking up the stairs, entering a bedroom, or answering the telephone become traumatizing experiences. The film critic Parker Tyler describes the process: "Physical laws are transcended and implemented by filmic devices. Slow motion, weird angles, magical mutation and transitions. Time is not literal, but a means of poetic expression. *Meshes* is an afternoon reverie of erotic suspense."[25] It is worth noting that Tyler enjoins both the narrational motivating terms associated with female desire in two Hollywood genres, the erotic element of the woman's film and the suspense of *film noir,* to describe a dream narrative largely preoccupied with the woman's physical placement and inability to find containment in a traditionally female world of domesticity that has suddenly become *noir*-esque.

More important, however, the anti-Hollywood position taken by Meshes is most pointed in its on-screen inscription of multiple Mayas, who literalize the film's perfor-mance of modernist fragmentation and pluralization of subjectivity. Julian Wolfreys argues that the three Mayas framed together around the dining room table intercut with their active gazing and reaction shots of each other is a performance that denies "the [notion of] unitary consciousness which it has been the project of both filmic and liter-ary realism to promote." The multiple Mayas, who also stand in for the artist-author, denote a fragmented subject who must contend with her own objectification and the resistance to any unitary subjectivity. Their multiple corporeality ultimately questions the capacity of the female body as a material signifier for subjectivity. This scene is the culmination of the film's terms of subjectivity: a refusal of and resistance to Hollywood's classical treatment of a woman who occupies physical space insofar as she is physically fragmented within a system of shots organized by a male gaze so as to objectify female subjectivity into an eroticized and fetishized Woman. In Meshes, the figuration of the multiple Mayas—constructed across the narrative, its cinematic logic, and even its iconography—"is not the classical objectification of women, but belongs instead to what is potentially a feminist poetics—and politics—of refusal."[26]

GEOGRAPHY OF THE BODY *and* FIREWORKS

In the same year that Deren and Hammid made MESHES OF THE AFTERNOON in their Los Angeles bungalow, Marie Menken and Willard Maas in their New York City apart-ment made a different type of poetic drama that also examined the representation of subjectivity. In a differently structured example of domestic collaborative filmmaking, Menken, her husband, Maas, and their poet-friend George Barker filmed each other. A friend had left his 16mm camera with them when he entered the army, and they exper-imented with it by taping a set of cheap magnifying glasses to the camera lens. They shot extreme close-up views of the details of each other's bodies. Barker wrote a poem and then recited it for the film's soundtrack, an account of a fantastic journey. It is the juxtaposition of the sounds and images that unifies meanings as a reverie of Eros. According to Lucy Fischer's characterization, "By fragmenting images of body parts and sequentializing them in time, the sense arises of the body as a navigable landscape and of its comprehension as a psycho-physical journey."[27] Contrary to MESHES, GEOGRAPHY

OF THE BODY strives to make comprehensible that which Deren set adrift, dislocated, and dissembled by relocating subjectivity in the spaces of the body itself.

GEOGRAPHY OF THE BODY does, however, share with MESHES the oneiric or dream-like purpose of expressing a poetics of psychological interiority. Like MESHES, it gives a privileged position to the eye viewed in close-up, a potent index of the bridge between psychological interiority and objective exteriority. The framing device of a close-up of an eye opens and closes the film, suggesting that the content of the film is a dream, a reverie, a psychological landscape of sexual subjectivity.

GEOGRAPHY OF THE BODY, like MESHES, relies on editing together disparate images, but for the purpose of constructing a unified bodily presence. If MESHES relies on editing strategies for reversing subject-object relations and making active the spaces in which the bodies move, GEOGRAPHY OF THE BODY reverses this process in order to "cement fragmented body parts" into one composite body and to allow sound-image relationships to recover the gaps between the parts.[28] For example, an image of an ear is accompanied by a sound reference to the entrance of an Indian temple, and an image of the navel occurs during a poetic phrase inquiring about the opening passage to the mysterious cavern. In this way, the narrative of the film is the body itself, which becomes a spatial frontier imbued with the abstract visual properties of magnification and a sound adventure narrative of wondrous exploration. One is reminded more of strategies of pornography associated with cinematic or visual exploration of the surfaces of bodies and sexual organs viewed close up than of the erotic associated with woman's desire in the woman's film or in its imbrication in MESHES OF THE AFTERNOON. The erotic here is located in anatomical space and given a powerful sexual aura through visual magnification and its narrative capacity to signify more than its materiality, that is, to signify psychic mysteries through the linguistic, rhythmic journey of the soundtrack. GEOGRAPHY OF THE BODY exemplifies the importance of oneirism and formal expressivism as the means for making cinema a potentially liberating force. Like MESHES and Deren's subsequent films that further explored woman's psychological identities in the shifting registers of dream worlds (AT LAND and RITUAL IN TRANSFIGURED TIME), GEOGRAPHY OF THE BODY taps the deep undercurrents of sexuality and gendered identities commonly argued as most explicitly realized in the dream states that draw upon the reservoir of the human subconscious. By giving expression to deep psychological realities, the filmmakers hoped to make conscious psychological truths of human nature through the very structures of cinema itself and to achieve a higher degree of psychological realism than that offered by Hollywood cinema's conventional telling of psychological truth in story formats that served as fables or moral tales about psychological states of awareness.

FIREWORKS (1947) furthers this set of assumptions in its efforts to overcome the sexual repression of homoerotic desire in a dream expression that sets the interior subject free through the dream itself. Like MESHES, the film's exploration of subjectivity is played out through the body of the filmmaker as the film's protagonist. But FIREWORKS is more closely wedded to the surrealist conceptions of dream logic than either MESHES or GEOGRAPHY. More than any other American film, it is the heir to Jean Cocteau's classic oneiric fantasy of the artist's homoerotic self-identity as an artist, LE SANG D'UN POETE (BLOOD OF A POET, 1930). The basic assumption of FIREWORKS is that the dream world is Other to the waking world; sexual repression is overcome, and the interior subject can be set free.

FIREWORKS, a film made by Kenneth Anger when he was only 17 years old, synthesizes the corporeal dream landscape of GEOGRAPHY OF THE BODY and the labyrinthine dream *noir* narrative of MESHES OF THE AFTERNOON for a study of the homosexual man as a sexual subject. Unlike Deren, whose exposure to Hollywood production practices was minimal and who spent almost the entirety of her artistic career in New York City as a cinema advocate in anti-Hollywood terms, Anger grew up surrounded by both the business and allure of Hollywood filmmaking. He was born and raised in Los Angeles, where he seems to have relished the fascinations of the mythical Tinseltown. At an early age, he had a small movie role as the changeling in Max Reinhardt's 1934 A MIDSUMMER NIGHT'S DREAM, and he later boasted about taking tap-dancing classes with the child star Shirley Temple. Using 16mm home movie equipment, he began making his own movies when he was only 11 years old.

Even from the beginning of what has been a long and sustained career as an experimental filmmaker, Anger drew upon the iconic imagery of American popular culture in wholly unique and unexpected ways in order to explore deep sexual undertones and to offer some subversive reworkings of Hollywood's best clichés. In this regard, FIREWORKS is indeed different from contemporary experimental films because, while it explores sexual identity through "new ways of seeing," it defines itself more aggressively as anti-Hollywood in homoerotic readings of Hollywood's staging of masculine heterosexuality through images of cowboys, pilots, and sailors. As Anger has said, "This flick is

Kenneth Anger's 1947 film FIREWORKS *opens with dream-state images of a sailor holding a bloodied, half-naked, young male—portrayed by the artist himself, in an elaborate coming-out/coming-of-age psychodrama.*

all I have to say about being seventeen, the United States navy, American Christmas, and the Fourth of July."[29] It is about what was then considered a taboo subject: the elaborate "coming out" of a high school adolescent who, as Vito Russo said, "dared to film one of his own wet dreams."[30]

FIREWORKS begins with a uniformed sailor posing and holding a half-naked, bloody figure (Anger) in his arms. It is followed by Anger awakening in bed. Richard Dyer suggests that the opening image is "a visual rhyme with the Christian *pieta*" and a deliberate inscription of Christian iconography, which has provided endless detailed images of beautiful, suffering men and of masochism (of punishment as pleasure), utilized here for a conflation of homosexual desire and masochism, of homosexuality and Christian persecution of gays. Dyer says: "This photograph, often used to evoke the film and the filmic world of its director, Kenneth Anger, is in itself an image of masochistic homosexual desire. In the film it is looked at by the young man and thus represents his memory or fantasy. Thus an image of gay desire is also an image of what the gay person is. The face of the young man, in its soft, troubled expression, is an icon of beautiful melancholy."[31]

This all-important iconic image recurs later as a self-referential photograph or still from the film that appears in the diegetic space. Like MESHES, the opening offers retrospective play on its signifying capacity. Is it the dream he has just dreamed or a foreshadowing of the events in which the film culminates? Is the image an interior point of view in Anger's dream world? Is the oneiric state in which the filmmaker's body signifies the protagonist an expression of the filmmaker's true self, and the film an autobiographical revelation about the author's sexuality? Or is it an objective image of a material entity? Is the material image of the photograph or the movie being projected on the screen substantially different from the dreamer's dream image? In this regard, FIREWORKS opens with an elaborate display much like the representation in MESHES of the process of textual construction, although the psychoanalytical overtones are more overt here.

When the dreamer awakens and finds himself alone in bed, he arises with a mock erection, dresses, and zips up his fly. As he dresses, a plaster cast of a broken hand figures prominently in the foreground. He leaves the room through a door with an exaggerated "Gents" sign. Once through the door, he enters a spatio-temporal realm comparable to that of MESHES, where the continuity of the subjective positions undergoes continuously changing spatial and temporal relationships to the spectator. In other words, the identity of the figure remains constant, but he is subject to constant movements into and out of the spatial field, rearrangements across geographies, and rigorously formalized poses within the frame.

Within this transforming diegesis, the protagonist in FIREWORKS meets a sailor in a bar. Through a cut, he and the sailor are transported back to the bedroom. The encounter with the sailor continues across the geographic spaces of a side street at night and the bedroom. Eventually, a group of sailors approaches Anger and attacks him. In the ritualistic beating that ensues, the sailor tears open his chest to reveal a ticking meter in the place of his heart. Roman candles are set off, a Christmas tree is carried aloft, and the dreamer awakens from the dream. The bedroom is the same except that he is in bed with another man whose face has been scratched out, and the broken plaster cast by his bedside is now restored as whole.

Like MESHES, FIREWORKS relies upon a stylistic vocabulary associated with Hollywood *film noir* to convey this sense of psychological disturbance—extremely oblique camera angles, figures isolated in deep shadows, prominent foreground objects, point-of-view shots, nighttime exterior settings. But FIREWORKS fairly vibrates with the romantic sadism that is present but invariably only latent in the American *film noir.* As P. Adams Sitney notes, "There is a comic or satiric element in the hyperbolic symbolism of this film. . . . [Its roots] lie in French Romantic decadence of the late nineteenth century."[32] Anger makes this hyperbole not only the manifest content of his film but a celebration of the inversion of the Hollywood myth.

MESHES OF THE AFTERNOON and FIREWORKS, the two most significant dream dramas of the 1940s, stylize violence in different ways for radically different effective outcomes about sexual identity. The violence in MESHES may confuse and refuse the logic of feminine identity, but the refusal also carries a potential for destruction. The narrative and narrational violence effected on the bodily subject in FIREWORKS culminates in a sexual aggression that is mocked with phallic imagery and the liberation of waking. The objects linked to sexual violence—Roman candles, the Christmas tree, the metered heart, and the broken (castrated) plaster hand—are the shifters that traverse the spaces of the dream and waking worlds within the film, positing the two worlds as oppositional. The sexual violence of which the figure of Anger is the target is also the filmmaker's satirical target for the rationality and sexual repressions of the exterior waking world. Yet, the alternative that he imagines, one that counters Hollywood's mythologized heterosexuality, is an expression of the very icons of the sad young man through which Hollywood castigated homosexuality. The radical otherness that Anger proposes through sexual liberation can be expressed only through a dialectical relationship to Hollywood's dominant representational and ideological practices.

Conclusion

The rise of an independent cinema after World War II, a cinema specifically defined as anti-Hollywood, had important political and cultural consequences. As the film critic J. Hoberman has observed, "A film practice that opposes the dominant culture, resists commodity status, invents its own means of production, and sets out to challenge habitual modes of perception is political—no matter what it seems to be about and sometimes because it's not 'about' anything."[33] Hoberman's characterization, made more than thirty years after the fact, that the postwar experimental cinema was an important political alternative to Hollywood cinema is echoed by the participants themselves in the late 1940s. The legendary story of the diarist Anaïs Nin about Deren's 1946 public screening at the Provincetown Playhouse in New York City's Greenwich Village resonates with the same sense of cultural import: "The crowd was dense, and some policeman thought he should investigate. He asked: 'Is this a demonstration?' Someone answered: 'It is not a demonstration, it is a revolution in film-making.'"[34] Independent cinema in the 1940s that became understood as anti-Hollywood, sexually and aesthetically daring as well as intellectually elite, allied cinema more broadly as a medium to other avant-garde media understood as radical artistic activity.

Once the booming postwar economy of New York City and the West Coast art worlds opened up the means through which an alternative cinema in the United States could flourish, cinema was increasingly identified as an object divided on the basis of the intellectual discourse associated with different groups of media objects. By the end of the decade, "highbrow," "lowbrow," and "middlebrow" had become the popular designations of hierarchical categories of aesthetic taste. Such categories signaled the ways in

which popular and conventional cinema had become differentiated from more experimental or avant-garde films, and intellectual dispositions or aesthetic interests at the
movies could be identified with certain moviegoing audiences. More important, these
sets of interests shared among filmmakers, critics, and audiences were organized
through an apparatus understood as a challenge to the hegemony of the Hollywood studio system. The implications then of independent cinema practices in the United States
immediately after World War II are far-reaching, because they did nothing less than signify that resistance to Hollywood's practices of meaning construction could also reform
cinema's place in culture.

Appendix 1

Total Number of Theaters in the United States, 1940–1950

Year	Indoor Theaters	Drive-ins	Total
1940	19,032		19,032
1941	19,645	95	19,740
1942	20,281	99	20,380
1943	20,196	97	20,293
1944	20,277	96	20,273
1945	20,355	102	20,457
1946	18,719	300	19,019
1947	18,059	548	18,607
1948	17,575	820	18,395
1949	17,367	1,203	18,570
1950	16,904	2,202	19,106

SOURCE: *Film Daily Year Book.*

Appendix 2

AVERAGE WEEKLY ATTENDANCE IN THE UNITED STATES, 1940–1950 (MILLIONS OF ADMISSIONS)

1940	80	1946	90
1941	85	1947	90
1942	85	1948	90
1943	85	1949	70
1944	85	1950	60
1945	85		

SOURCE: U.S. Bureau of the Census, *Historical Statistics of the United States, 1960*, pp. 242–44.

Appendix 3

NUMBER OF FEATURE FILMS RELEASED IN THE UNITED STATES, 1940–1949

TOTAL NUMBER OF FEATURE FILMS RELEASED

YEAR	MAJOR STUDIOS		INDEPENDENTS		TOTAL
	U.S.-Produced	Imports	U.S.-Produced	Imports	
1940	348	15	129	181	673
1941	368	11	124	95	598
1942	346	12	142	33	533
1943	279	10	118	20	427
1944	262	8	139	33	442
1945	228	6	122	21	377
1946	239	13	139	76	467
1947	234	15	135	103	487
1948	225	23	141	70	459
1949	224	10	132	113	479

NUMBER OF FEATURE FILMS RELEASED BY THE BIG EIGHT STUDIOS

STUDIO	1940	1941	1942	1943	1944	1945	1946	1947	1948	1949
Columbia	51	61	59	47	51	38	51	49	39	52
MGM	48	47	49	33	30	31	25	29	24	30
Paramount	48	45	44	30	32	23	22	29	25	21
RKO	53	44	39	44	31	33	40	36	31	25
20th-Century Fox	44	50	51	33	26	27	32	27	45	31
UA	20	26	26	28	20	17	20	26	26	21
Universal	49	58	56	53	53	46	42	33	35	29
Warner Bros.	45	48	34	21	19	19	20	20	23	25
TOTAL	358	379	358	289	262	234	252	249	248	234

SOURCE: *Film Daily Year Book.*

Appendix 4

MAJOR STUDIO REVENUES AND PROFITS, 1940–1949 ($ MILLIONS)

YEAR	PARAMOUNT		20TH CENTURY–FOX		LOEW'S/MGM	
	Revenues	Profits	Revenues	Profits	Revenues	Profits
1940	96.0	6.3	47.8	(0.5)	121.9	8.7
1941	101.3	9.2	49.6°	4.9	113.9	11.0
1942	123.3	13.1	67.3°	10.6	119.5	11.8
1943	140.9	14.5	154.3	10.9	138.8	13.4
1944	153.2	14.7	172.6	12.5	145.1	14.5
1945	158.2	15.4	178.2	12.7	154.2	12.9
1946	193.5	39.2	190.3	22.6	165.4	18.0
1947	186.8	28.2	174.4	14.0	161.8	10.5
1948	170.4	22.6	163.4	12.5	164.4	4.2
1949	78.8†	3.3	169.5	12.4	160.2	6.0

YEAR	WARNER BROS.		RKO	
	Revenues	Profits	Revenues	Profits
1940	100.3	2.7	54.2	(1.0)
1941	98.1	5.4	53.3	0.5
1942	114.9	8.6	61.4	0.7
1943	127.3	8.2	78.8	7.0
1944	136.1	7.0	84.9	5.2
1945	141.5	9.9	96.1	6.0
1946	158.6	19.4	120.1	12.2
1947	164.6	22.1	123.1	5.1
1948	147.1	11.8	110.0	0.5
1949	135.0	10.5	N.A.#	1.7

464

YEAR	UNIVERSAL		COLUMBIA		UNITED ARTISTS	
	Revenues	Profits	Revenues	Profits	Revenues	Profits
1940	27.6	2.2	22.2	0.5	22.5	0.2
1941	30.2	2.3	21.6	0.6	23.9	0.1
1942	39.1	3.0	27.2	1.6	22.8	0.1
1943	46.5	3.8	32.4	1.8	28.3	0.1
1944	51.6	3.4	37.1	2.0	24.1	(0.3)
1945	51.0	3.9	36.0	1.9	34.4	0.6
1946	53.9	4.6	46.5	3.5	37.0	0.4
1947	65.0	3.2	48.8	3.7	32.1	0.5
1948	58.0	(3.2)	46.9	0.6	24.7	(0.5)
1949	56.7	(1.1)	53.3	1.0	23.0	(0.2)

TOTAL STUDIO PROFITS ($ MILLIONS)

1940	19.1	1945	63.3
1941	34.0	1946	119.9
1942	49.5	1947	87.3
1943	60.6	1948	48.5
1944	59.0	1949	33.6

° Fox totals in 1941 and 1942 do not include theater chain income.

† Paramount's revenue total for 1949 is estimated.

RKO divested its theaters in 1949.

SOURCE: Joel Finler, *The Hollywood Story* (New York: Crown, 1988), pp. 286–87. Finler's figures, the most accurate and well supported of any available, are culled from the annual financial reports of the various film companies, the *Film Daily Year Book, Moody's Manual of Investments, Motion Picture Almanac,* and the *U.S. Department of Commerce Survey of Current Business.*

Appendix 5

TOP BOX-OFFICE PICTURES, 1940–1949

1940

BOOM TOWN ($4.6 million)
THE GREAT DICTATOR (3.5)
REBECCA (3.0)
NORTHWEST MOUNTED POLICE
THE FIGHTING 69TH
STRIKE UP THE BAND

ALL THIS, AND HEAVEN TOO
TIN PAN ALLEY
I LOVE YOU AGAIN
THE GRAPES OF WRATH
ANDY HARDY MEETS THE
    DEBUTANTE

1941

SERGEANT YORK ($6.1 million)
THE GREAT DICTATOR (4.0)
HONKY TONK (2.65)
A YANK IN THE RAF (2.5)
THE PHILADELPHIA STORY (2.5)
DIVE BOMBER (2.2)

CAUGHT IN THE DRAFT (2.2)
CHARLEY'S AUNT (2.2)
MEN OF BOYS TOWN (2.2)
ANDY HARDY'S PRIVATE
    SECRETARY (2.2)

1942

MRS. MINIVER ($5.4 million)
YANKEE DOODLE DANDY (4.7)
RANDOM HARVEST (4.6)
REAP THE WILD WIND (4.0)
HOLIDAY INN (3.8)

ROAD TO MOROCCO (3.8)
THE PRIDE OF THE YANKEES (3.67)
WAKE ISLAND (3.5)
SOMEWHERE I'LL FIND YOU (3.0)

1943

THIS IS THE ARMY ($8.5 million)
FOR WHOM THE BELL TOLLS (7.1)
THE OUTLAW (5.0)
THE SONG OF BERNADETTE (4.7)
STAGE DOOR CANTEEN (4.34)
CASABLANCA (4.15)

STAR SPANGLED RHYTHM (3.9)
MADAME CURIE (3.5)
CONEY ISLAND (3.3)
DIXIE (3.1)
GIRL CRAZY (3.0)
SO PROUDLY WE HAIL (3.0)

1944

GOING MY WAY ($6.5 million)
MEET ME IN ST. LOUIS (5.1)
THIRTY SECONDS OVER TOKYO
    (4.47)
A GUY NAMED JOE (4.125)
THE WHITE CLIFFS OF DOVER
    (4.04)
HOLLYWOOD CANTEEN (3.83)
BATHING BEAUTY (3.5)
FRENCHMAN'S CREEK (3.5)

THOUSANDS CHEER (3.5)
TWO GIRLS AND A SAILOR (3.5)
UP IN ARMS (3.34)
DESTINATION TOKYO (3.2)
WILSON (3.1)
GASLIGHT (3.0)
THE HITLER GANG (3.0)
MRS. PARKINGTON (3.0)
THE PICTURE OF DORIAN GRAY (3.0)
THE SEVENTH CROSS (3.0)

1945*

THE BELLS OF ST. MARY'S ($8.0
    million)
LEAVE HER TO HEAVEN (5.5)
SPELLBOUND (4.97)
SINCE YOU WENT AWAY (4.92)
ANCHORS AWEIGH (4.8)
THE VALLEY OF DECISION (4.56)
ROAD TO UTOPIA (4.5)
WEEKEND AT THE WALDORF (4.36)

THRILL OF A ROMANCE (4.34)
THE LOST WEEKEND (4.3)
NATIONAL VELVET (4.24)
ADVENTURE (4.23)
STATE FAIR (4.02)
THE DOLLY SISTERS (3.95)
TO HAVE AND HAVE NOT (3.65)
SAN ANTONIO (3.55)
MILDRED PIERCE (3.5)

1946†

THE BEST YEARS OF OUR LIVES
    ($11.3 million)
DUEL IN THE SUN (11.3)
THE JOLSON STORY (7.6)
THE YEARLING (5.56)
SARATOGA TRUNK (5.15)
THE RAZOR'S EDGE (5.0)
NIGHT AND DAY (4.9)
NOTORIOUS (4.8)

TILL THE CLOUDS ROLL BY (4.76)
ROAD TO UTOPIA (4.5)
TWO YEARS BEFORE THE MAST (4.4)
THE GREEN YEARS (4.22)
THE HARVEY GIRLS (4.13)
MARGIE (4.1)
EASY TO WED (4.0)
THE KID FROM BROOKLYN (4.0)
SMOKY (4.0)

1947#

WELCOME STRANGER ($6.1 million)
BLUE SKIES (5.7)
THE BACHELOR AND THE BOBBY-
    SOXER (5.5)
THE EGG AND I (5.5)
UNCONQUERED (5.25)

LIFE WITH FATHER (5.05)
FOREVER AMBER (5.0)
ROAD TO RIO (4.5)
GREEN DOLPHIN STREET (4.4)
MOTHER WORE TIGHTS (4.1)

1948**

RED RIVER ($4.5 million)
THE PALEFACE (4.5)
THE THREE MUSKETEERS (4.3)
JOHNNY BELINDA (4.26)
EASTER PARADE (4.2)
JOAN OF ARC (4.1)
THE SNAKE PIT (4.1)

THE EMPEROR WALTZ (4.0)
GENTLEMAN'S AGREEMENT (3.9)
A DATE WITH JUDY (3.7)
HOMECOMING (3.7)
CAPTAIN FROM CASTILE (3.6)
SITTING PRETTY (3.6)
STATE OF THE UNION (3.5)

1949††

SAMSON AND DELILAH ($11.3 million)
BATTLEGROUND (5.05)
JOLSON SINGS AGAIN (5.0)
SANDS OF IWO JIMA (5.0)
I WAS A MALE WAR BRIDE (4.1)
THE STRATTON STORY (4.025)

PINKY (3.8)
MR. BELVEDERE GOES TO COLLEGE (3.7)
LITTLE WOMEN (3.6)
NEPTUNE'S DAUGHTER (3.5)
WORDS AND MUSIC (3.5)

° Another 14 films earned between $3 and 3.5 million in 1945.
† Another 25 films earned between $3 and 4 million in 1946.
# Another 25 films earned between $3 and 4 million in 1947.
°° Another 10 films earned between $3 and 3.5 million in 1948.
†† Another 11 films earned between $3 and 3.5 million in 1949.

SOURCE: For 1940, *Variety,* 18 December 1940, p. 1; these are rank-ordered, but no dollar figures are given. For 1941, *Variety,* 31 December 1941, p. 1. Note that both are year-end summaries and thus do not reflect the total earnings for films released late in the year.

For 1940–1949, "All-Time Film Rental Champs," *Variety,* 24 February 1992, pp. 125–68. This listing is exceptional in that it organizes the films by decade; it includes films earning at least $3 million. Because very few films from 1940–1941 earned that amount, the *Variety* year-end summaries from 1940 and 1941 are included. Three Disney features (FANTASIA and PINOCCHIO in 1940 and DUMBO in 1941) are included in *Variety's* 1992 report, but these actually were box-office disappointments on initial release and earned nowhere near $3 million. Many of these films were reissued, and thus the totals may include multiple releases.

Appendix 6

Exhibitors' Poll of Top Ten Box-Office Stars, 1940–1949

1940

Mickey Rooney
Spencer Tracy
Clark Gable
Gene Autry
Tyrone Power
James Cagney
Bing Crosby
Wallace Beery
Bette Davis
Judy Garland

1941

Mickey Rooney
Clark Gable
Abbott and Costello
Bob Hope
Spencer Tracy
Gene Autry
Gary Cooper
Bette Davis
James Cagney
Judy Garland

1942

Abbott and Costello
Clark Gable
Gary Cooper
Mickey Rooney
Bob Hope
James Cagney
Gene Autry
Betty Grable
Greer Garson
Spencer Tracy

1943

Betty Grable
Bob Hope
Abbott and Costello
Bing Crosby
Gary Cooper
Greer Garson
Humphrey Bogart
James Cagney
Mickey Rooney
Clark Gable

1944

Bing Crosby
Gary Cooper
Bob Hope
Betty Grable
Spencer Tracy

Greer Garson
Humphrey Bogart
Abbott and Costello
Cary Grant
Bette Davis

1945

Bing Crosby
Van Johnson
Greer Garson
Betty Grable
Spencer Tracy

Humphrey Bogart/Gary Cooper
Bob Hope
Judy Garland
Margaret O'Brien
Roy Rogers

1946

Bing Crosby
Ingrid Bergman
Van Johnson
Gary Cooper
Bob Hope

Humphrey Bogart
Greer Garson
Margaret O'Brien
Betty Grable
Roy Rogers

1947

Bing Crosby
Betty Grable
Ingrid Bergman
Gary Cooper
Humphrey Bogart

Bob Hope
Clark Gable
Gregory Peck
Claudette Colbert
Alan Ladd

1948

Bing Crosby
Betty Grable
Abbott and Costello
Gary Cooper
Bob Hope

Humphrey Bogart
Clark Gable
Cary Grant
Spencer Tracy
Ingrid Bergman

1949

Bob Hope
Bing Crosby
Abbott and Costello
John Wayne
Gary Cooper

Cary Grant
Betty Grable
Esther Williams
Humphrey Bogart
Clark Gable

SOURCE: *Motion Picture Herald* (Quigley Publications).

Appendix 7
MAJOR ACADEMY AWARDS, 1940–1949

1940

Picture: REBECCA (Selznick/UA)
Director: John Ford, THE GRAPES OF WRATH
Actor: James Stewart, THE PHILADELPHIA STORY
Actress: Ginger Rogers, KITTY FOYLE
Supporting Actor: Walter Brennan, THE WESTERNER
Supporting Actress: Jane Darwell, THE GRAPES OF WRATH
Writing:
  (Original story) ARISE, MY LOVE—Benjamin Glazer and John S. Toldy
  (Original screenplay) THE GREAT MCGINTY—Preston Sturges
  (Screenplay) THE PHILADELPHIA STORY—Donald Ogden Stewart
Cinematography:
  (Black-and-white) REBECCA—George Barnes
  (Color) THE THIEF OF BAGHDAD—George Perinal
Art Direction:
  (Black-and-white) PRIDE AND PREJUDICE—Paul Groesse and Cedric Gibbons
  (Color) THE THIEF OF BAGHDAD—Vincent Korda
Editing: NORTHWEST MOUNTED POLICE—Anne Bauchens
Sound Recording: STRIKE UP THE BAND—Douglas Shearer
Music:
  (Song) "When You Wish upon a Star" (PINOCCHIO)—music by Leigh Harline; lyrics by Ned Washington
  (Score) TIN PAN ALLEY—Alfred Newman
  (Original Score) PINOCCHIO—Leigh Harline and Paul J. Smith

1941

Picture: HOW GREEN WAS MY VALLEY (20th Century–Fox)
Director: John Ford, HOW GREEN WAS MY VALLEY
Actor: Gary Cooper, SERGEANT YORK

Actress: Joan Fontaine, SUSPICION
Supporting Actor: Donald Crisp, HOW GREEN WAS MY VALLEY
Supporting Actress: Mary Astor, THE GREAT LIE
Writing:
  (Original story) HERE COMES MR. JORDAN—Harry Segall
  (Original screenplay) CITIZEN KANE—Herman J. Mankiewicz and Orson Welles
  (Screenplay) HERE COMES MR. JORDAN—Sidney Buchman
Cinematography:
  (Black-and-white) HOW GREEN WAS MY VALLEY—Arthur Miller
  (Color) BLOOD AND SAND—Ernest Palmer and Ray Rennehan
Art Direction:
  (Black-and-white) HOW GREEN WAS MY VALLEY—Richard Day, Nathan Juran
  (Color) BLOSSOMS IN THE DUST—Cedric Gibbons and Urie McCleary
Editing: SERGEANT YORK—William Holmes
Sound Recording: THAT HAMILTON WOMAN—Jack Whitney
Music:
  (Song) "The Last Time I Saw Paris" (LADY BE GOOD)—music by Jerome Kern;
lyrics by Oscar Hammerstein II
  (Scoring of a dramatic picture) ALL THAT MONEY CAN BUY—Bernard Herrmann
  (Scoring of a musical) DUMBO—Frank Churchill and Oliver Wallace
Documentary: CHURCHILL'S ISLAND (UA)
Irving G. Thalberg Award: Walt Disney

1942

Picture: MRS. MINIVER (MGM)
Director: William Wyler, MRS. MINIVER
Actor: James Cagney, YANKEE DOODLE DANDY
Actress: Greer Garson, MRS. MINIVER
Supporting Actor: Van Heflin, JOHNNY EAGER
Supporting Actress: Teresa Wright, MRS. MINIVER
Writing:
  (Original story) THE INVADERS—Emeric Pressberger
  (Original screenplay) WOMAN OF THE YEAR—Michael Kanin and Ring Lardner Jr.
  (Screenplay) MRS. MINIVER—George Froeschel, James Hilton, Claudine West, and
Arthur Wimperis
Cinematography:
  (Black-and-white) MRS. MINIVER—Joseph Ruttenberg
  (Color) THE BLACK SWAN—Leon Shamroy
Art Direction:
  (Black-and-white) THIS ABOVE ALL—Richard Day and Joseph Wright
  (Color) MY GAL SAL—Richard Day and Joseph Wright
Editing: PRIDE OF THE YANKEES—Daniel Mandell
Sound Recording: YANKEE DOODLE DANDY—Nathan Levinson
Music:
  (Song) "White Christmas" (HOLIDAY INN)—music and lyrics by Irving Berlin

(Scoring of a drama or comedy) NOW, VOYAGER—Max Steiner
(Scoring of a musical) YANKEE DOODLE DANDY—Ray Heindorf and Heinz
Roemheld
Documentary:
(Short) THE BATTLE OF MIDWAY (20th Century–Fox)
(Feature) PRELUDE TO WAR (U.S. Army Special Services)
Irving G. Thalberg Award: Sidney Franklin

1943

Picture: CASABLANCA (Warner Bros.)
Director: Michael Curtiz, CASABLANCA
Actor: Paul Lucas, WATCH ON THE RHINE
Actress: Jennifer Jones, THE SONG OF BERNADETTE
Supporting Actor: Charles Coburn, THE MORE THE MERRIER
Supporting Actress: Katina Paxinou, FOR WHOM THE BELL TOLLS
Writing:
(Original story) THE HUMAN COMEDY—William Saroyan
(Original screenplay) PRINCESS O'ROURKE—Norman Krasna
(Screenplay) CASABLANCA—Julius J. Epstein, Philip G. Epstein, and Howard Koch
Cinematography:
(Black-and-white) THE SONG OF BERNADETTE—Arthur Miller
(Color) PHANTOM OF THE OPERA—Hal Mohr and W. Howard Greene
Art Direction:
(Black-and-white) THE SONG OF BERNADETTE—James Basevi and William Darling
(Color) PHANTOM OF THE OPERA—Alexander Golitzen and John B. Goodman
Editing: AIR FORCE—George Amy
Sound Recording: THIS LAND IS MINE—Stephen Dunn
Music:
(Song) "You'll Never Know" (HELLO, FRISCO, HELLO)—music by Harry Warren;
lyrics by Mack Gordon
(Scoring of a drama or comedy) THE SONG OF BERNADETTE—Alfred Newman
(Scoring of a musical) THIS IS THE ARMY—Ray Heindorf
Documentary:
(Short) DECEMBER 7TH (U.S. Navy)
(Feature) DESERT VICTORY (British Ministry of Information)
Irving G. Thalberg Award: Hal B. Wallis

1944

Picture: GOING MY WAY (Paramount)
Director: Leo McCarey, GOING MY WAY
Actor: Bing Crosby, GOING MY WAY
Actress: Ingrid Bergman, GASLIGHT
Supporting Actor: Barry Fitzgerald, GOING MY WAY

Supporting Actress: Ethel Barrymore, NONE BUT THE LONELY HEART
Writing:
  (Original story) GOING MY WAY—Leo McCarey
  (Original screenplay) WILSON—Lamar Trotti
  (Screenplay) GOING MY WAY—Frank Butler and Frank Cabett
Cinematography:
  (Black-and-white) LAURA—Joseph La Shelle
  (Color) WILSON—Leon Shamroy
Art Direction:
  (Black-and-white) GASLIGHT—Cedric Gibbons and William Farrari
  (Color) WILSON—Wiard Ihnen
Editing: WILSON—Barbara McLean
Sound Recording: WILSON—E. H. Hansen
Music:
  (Song) "Swinging on a Star" (GOING MY WAY)—music by James Van Heusen; lyrics by Johnny Burke
  (Scoring of a drama or comedy) SINCE YOU WENT AWAY—Max Steiner
  (Scoring of a musical) COVER GIRL—Carmen Dragon and Morris Stoloff
Documentary:
  (Short) WITH THE MARINES AT TARAWA (U.S. Marine Corps)
  (Feature) THE FIGHTING LADY (U.S. Navy, 20th Century–Fox)
Irving G. Thalberg Award: Darryl F. Zanuck

1945

Picture: THE LOST WEEKEND (Paramount)
Director: Billy Wilder, THE LOST WEEKEND
Actor: Ray Milland, THE LOST WEEKEND
Actress: Joan Crawford, MILDRED PIERCE
Supporting Actor: James Dunn, A TREE GROWS IN BROOKLYN
Supporting Actress: Anne Revere, NATIONAL VELVET
Writing:
  (Original story) THE HOUSE ON 92ND STREET—Charles G. Booth
  (Original screenplay) MARIE-LOUISE—Richard Schweizer
  (Screenplay) THE LOST WEEKEND—Charles Brackett and Billy Wilder
Cinematography:
  (Black-and-white) THE PICTURE OF DORIAN GRAY—Harry Stradling
  (Color) LEAVE HER TO HEAVEN—Leon Shamroy
Art Direction:
  (Black-and-white) BLOOD ON THE SUN—Wiarn Ihnen
  (Color) FRENCHMAN'S CREEK—Hans Drier, Ernest Fegte
Editing: NATIONAL VELVET—Robert J. Kern
Sound Recording: THE BELLS OF ST. MARY'S—Stephen Dunn
Music:
  (Song) "It Might as Well Be Spring" (STATE FAIR)—music by Richard Rodgers; lyrics by Oscar Hammerstein II

(Scoring of a drama or comedy) SPELLBOUND—Miklos Rozsa

(Scoring of a musical) ANCHORS AWEIGH—George Stoll

Documentary:

(Short) HITLER LIVES? (Warner Bros.)

(Feature) THE TRUE GLORY (the governments of Great Britain and the United States)

1946

Picture: THE BEST YEARS OF OUR LIVES

Director: William Wyler, THE BEST YEARS OF OUR LIVES

Actor: Fredric March, THE BEST YEARS OF OUR LIVES

Actress: Olivia de Havilland, TO EACH HIS OWN

Supporting Actor: Harold Russell, THE BEST YEARS OF OUR LIVES

Supporting Actress: Anne Baxter, THE RAZOR'S EDGE

Writing:

(Original story) VACATION FROM MARRIAGE—Clemence Dane

(Original screenplay) THE SEVENTH VEIL—Muriel Box and Sydney Box

(Screenplay) THE BEST YEARS OF OUR LIVES—Robert E. Sherwood

Cinematography:

(Black-and-white) ANNA AND THE KING OF SIAM—Arthur Miller

(Color) THE YEARLING—Charles Rosher, Leonard Smith, and Arthur Arling

Art Direction:

(Black-and-white) ANNA AND THE KING OF SIAM—Lyle Wheeler and William Darling

(Color) THE YEARLING—Cedric Gibbons and Paul Groesse

Editing: THE BEST YEARS OF OUR LIVES—Daniel Mandell

Sound Recording: THE JOLSON STORY—John Livadary

Music:

(Song) "On the Atchison Topeka and the Santa Fe" (THE HARVEY GIRLS)—music by Harry Warren; lyrics by Johnny Mercer

(Scoring of a drama or comedy) THE BEST YEARS OF OUR LIVES—Hugo Freidhofer

(Scoring of a musical) THE JOLSON STORY—Morris Stoloff

Documentary:

(Short) SEEDS OF DESTINY (U.S. War Department)

(Feature) None nominated

Irving G. Thalberg Award: Samuel Goldwyn

1947

Picture: GENTLEMAN'S AGREEMENT (20th Century–Fox)

Director: Elia Kazan, GENTLEMAN'S AGREEMENT

Actor: Ronald Colman, A DOUBLE LIFE

Actress: Loretta Young, THE FARMER'S DAUGHTER

Supporting Actor: Edmund Gwenn, MIRACLE ON 34TH STREET
Supporting Actress: Celeste Holm, GENTLEMAN'S AGREEMENT
Writing:
  (Original story) MIRACLE ON 34TH STREET—Valentine Davies
  (Original screenplay) THE BACHELOR AND THE BOBBY-SOXER—Sidney Sheldon
  (Screenplay) MIRACLE ON 34TH STREET—George Seaton
Cinematography:
  (Black-and-white) GREAT EXPECTATIONS—Guy Green
  (Color) BLACK NARCISSUS—Jack Cardiff
Art Direction:
  (Black-and-white) GREAT EXPECTATIONS—John Bryan
  (Color) BLACK NARCISSUS—Alfred Junge
Editing: BODY AND SOUL—Francis Lyon and Robert Parrish
Sound Recording: THE BISHOP'S WIFE—Gordon Sawyer
Music:
  (Song) "Zip-a-dee-doo-dah" (SONG OF THE SOUTH)—music by Allie Wrubel; lyrics
by Ray Gilbert
  (Scoring of a drama or comedy) A DOUBLE LIFE—Miklos Rozsa
  (Scoring of a musical) MOTHER WORE TIGHTS—Alfred Newman
Documentary:
  (Short) FIRST STEPS (UN Division of Films and Visual Information)
  (Feature) DESIGN FOR DEATH (RKO)

1948

Picture: HAMLET (Universal-International)
Director: John Huston, THE TREASURE OF THE SIERRA MADRE
Actor: Laurence Olivier, HAMLET
Actress: Jane Wyman, JOHNNY BELINDA
Supporting Actor: Walter Huston, THE TREASURE OF THE SIERRA MADRE
Supporting Actress: Claire Trevor, KEY LARGO
Writing:
  (Motion picture story) THE SEARCH—Richard Schweizer and David Wechsler
  (Screenplay) THE TREASURE OF THE SIERRA MADRE—John Huston
Cinematography:
  (Black-and-white) THE NAKED CITY—William Daniels
  (Color) JOAN OF ARC—Joseph Valentine, William V. Skall, and Winton Hoch
Art Direction:
  (Black-and-white) HAMLET—Roger K. Furse
  (Color) THE RED SHOES—Hein Heckroth
Editing: THE NAKED CITY—Paul Weatherwax
Sound Recording: THE SNAKE PIT—Thomas T. Moulton
Music:
  (Song) "Buttons and Bows" (THE PALEFACE)—music and lyrics by Jay Livingston
and Ray Evans
  (Scoring of a drama or comedy) THE RED SHOES—Brian Easdale

(Scoring of a musical) EASTER PARADE—Johnny Green and Roger Edens
Documentary:
  (Short) TOWARD INDEPENDENCE (U.S. Army)
  (Feature) THE SECRET LAND (U.S. Navy, MGM)
Irving G. Thalberg Award: Jerry Wald

1949

Picture: ALL THE KING'S MEN (Columbia)
Director: Joseph L. Mankiewicz, A LETTER TO THREE WIVES
Actor: Broderick Crawford, ALL THE KING'S MEN
Actress: Olivia de Havilland, THE HEIRESS
Supporting Actor: Dean Jagger, TWELVE O'CLOCK HIGH
Supporting Actress: Mercedes McCambridge, ALL THE KING'S MEN
Writing:
  (Motion picture story) THE STRATTON STORY—Douglas Morrow
  (Screenplay) A LETTER TO THREE WIVES—Joseph L. Mankiewicz
  (Story and screenplay) BATTLEGROUND—Robert Pirosh
Cinematography:
  (Black-and-white) BATTLEGROUND—Paul C. Vogel
  (Color) SHE WORE A YELLOW RIBBON—Winton Hoch
Art Direction:
  (Black-and-white) THE HEIRESS—John Meehan and Harry Horner
  (Color) LITTLE WOMEN—Cedric Gibbons and Paul Groesse
Editing: CHAMPION—Harry Gerstad
Sound Recording: TWELVE O'CLOCK HIGH—Thomas T. Moulton
Music:
  (Song) "Baby, It's Cold Outside" (NEPTUNE'S DAUGHTER)—music and lyrics by
Frank Loesser
  (Scoring of a drama or comedy) THE HEIRESS—Aaron Copland
  (Scoring of a musical) ON THE TOWN—Roger Edens and Lennie Hayton
Documentary:
  (Short) A CHANCE TO LIVE (March of Time, 20th Century–Fox)
  (Feature) DAYBREAK AT UDI (British Information Services)

SOURCE: Paul Michael, *The Academy Awards: A Pictorial History,* 5th ed. (New York: Crown, 1982).

Appendix 8

NATIONAL BOARD OF REVIEW, 1940–1949

Note: The National Board's ten-best-films category changed during the decade, moving from the ten best American films in 1940–1941 to the ten best English-language films in 1942–1944, and then to a general ten-best-films category from 1945 to 1949 that included documentaries and foreign-language features.

1940

Best American Films:
THE GRAPES OF WRATH
THE GREAT DICTATOR
OF MICE AND MEN
OUR TOWN
FANTASIA
THE LONG VOYAGE HOME
FOREIGN CORRESPONDENT
THE BISCUIT EATER
GONE WITH THE WIND
REBECCA
Best Foreign Film: THE BAKER'S WIFE
Best Documentary: THE FIGHT FOR LIFE

1941

Best American Films:
CITIZEN KANE
HOW GREEN WAS MY VALLEY
THE LITTLE FOXES
THE STARS LOOK DOWN
DUMBO
HIGH SIERRA
HERE COMES MR. JORDAN
TOM, DICK AND HARRY
ROAD TO ZANZIBAR
THE LADY EVE

Best Foreign Film: PEPE LE MOKO
Best Documentaries: TARGET FOR TONIGHT, THE FORGOTTEN VILLAGE,
   KU KAN, and THE LAND

1942

Best English-Language Films:
IN WHICH WE SERVE
ONE OF OUR AIRCRAFT IS MISSING
MRS. MINIVER
JOURNEY FOR MARGARET
WAKE ISLAND
THE MALE ANIMAL
THE MAJOR AND THE MINOR
SULLIVAN'S TRAVELS
THE MOON AND SIXPENCE
THE PIED PIPER
Best Foreign Film: none cited
Best Documentary: MOSCOW STRIKES BACK

1943

Best English-Language Films:
THE OX-BOW INCIDENT
WATCH ON THE RHINE
AIR FORCE
HOLY MATRIMONY
THE HARD WAY
CASABLANCA
LASSIE COME HOME
BATAAN
THE MOON IS DOWN
NEXT OF KIN
Best Foreign Films: none cited
Best Documentaries: DESERT VICTORY, THE BATTLE OF RUSSIA,
   PRELUDE TO WAR, SALUDOS AMIGOS, and THE SILENT VILLAGE

1944

Best English-Language Films:
NONE BUT THE LONELY HEART
GOING MY WAY
THE MIRACLE OF MORGAN'S CREEK
HAIL THE CONQUERING HERO
THE SONG OF BERNADETTE
WILSON
MEET ME IN ST. LOUIS
THIRTY SECONDS OVER TOKYO

THUNDER ROCK
LIFEBOAT
Best Foreign Film: none cited
Best Documentaries: THE MEMPHIS BELLE, ATTACK! THE BATTLE FOR
    NEW BRITAIN, WITH THE MARINES AT TARAWA, BATTLE FOR THE
    MARIANAS, and TUNISAN VICTORY

1945

Best Film: THE TRUE GLORY
Ten Best Films (including documentaries and English-language features):
THE TRUE GLORY
THE LOST WEEKEND
THE SOUTHERNER
THE STORY OF GI JOE
THE LAST CHANCE
COLONEL BLIMP
A TREE GROWS IN BROOKLYN
THE FIGHTING LADY
THE WAY AHEAD
THE CLOCK

1946

Best Picture: HENRY V
Ten Best Films (including foreign):
HENRY V
OPEN CITY (also voted best foreign-language film)
THE BEST YEARS OF OUR LIVES
BRIEF ENCOUNTER
A WALK IN THE SUN
IT HAPPENED AT THE INN
MY DARLING CLEMENTINE
DIARY OF A CHAMBERMAID
THE KILLERS
ANNA AND THE KING OF SIAM

1947

Best Picture: MONSIEUR VERDOUX
Ten Best Films (including foreign):
MONSIEUR VERDOUX
GREAT EXPECTATIONS
SHOESHINE
CROSSFIRE
BOOMERANG
ODD MAN OUT
GENTLEMAN'S AGREEMENT

TO LIVE IN PEACE
IT'S A WONDERFUL LIFE
THE OVERLANDERS

1948

Best Picture: PAISAN
Ten Best Films (including foreign):
PAISAN
DAY OF WRATH
THE SEARCH
THE TREASURE OF THE SIERRA MADRE
LOUISIANA STORY
HAMLET
THE SNAKE PIT
JOHNNY BELINDA
JOAN OF ARC
THE RED SHOES

1949

Best Picture: THE BICYCLE THIEF
Ten Best Films (including foreign):
THE BICYCLE THIEF
THE QUIET ONE
INTRUDER IN THE DUST
THE HEIRESS
DEVIL IN THE FLESH
QUARTET
GERMANY YEAR ZERO
THE HOME OF THE BRAVE
A LETTER TO THREE WIVES
THE FALLEN IDOL

SOURCE: Cobbett Steinberg, *Film Facts* (New York: Facts on File, 1980).

Notes

CHAPTER 1 (Introduction)

1. W. H. Auden, *The Age of Anxiety* (London: Faber & Faber, 1948).

CHAPTER 2 (The Motion Picture Industry in 1940–1941)

1. *Motion Picture Herald,* 2 December 1939, p. 8.
2. *Motion Picture Herald,* 13 January 1940, p. 9. See also Ronald Haver, *David O. Selznick's Hollywood* (New York: Knopf, 1980), pp. 299–309. According to Haver (p. 309), by May 1940, as GONE WITH THE WIND completed its initial roadshow release, the film had grossed an astounding $20 million.
3. Roy Chartier, "The Year in Pictures," *Variety,* 3 January 1940, p. 5.
4. Here and elsewhere, unless otherwise noted, figures on motion picture industry finances are taken from Joel W. Finler, *The Hollywood Story* (New York: Crown, 1988). Of particular value here is Finler's summary of studio revenues and profits from 1920 on (pp. 286–287). My reliance on Finler's figures is the result of a growing conviction throughout the extensive research for this book that his data, culled primarily from movie industry trade journals (*Variety, Motion Picture Herald*), the annual *Film Daily Year Book,* the annual *Motion Picture Almanac,* and the U.S. Department of Commerce Survey of Current Business, are the most reliable and comprehensive currently available. According to Finler, total studio profits in 1936 were $30.9 million; in 1937, $37.7 million; in 1938, $22.3 million; in 1939, $19.4 million; and in 1940, $19.1 million.
5. *Motion Picture Herald,* 2 December 1939, p. 9; *Variety,* 10 January 1940, p. 3. See also *Motion Picture Herald,* 16 March 1940, p. 9.
6. *Variety,* 17 January 1940, p. 3.
7. *Variety,* 3 January 1940, p. 8.
8. On congressional anti-block-booking efforts, see Garth Jowett, *Film, The Democratic Art: A Social History of American Film* (Boston: Little, Brown, 1976), pp. 276–279.
9. For in-depth histories and analyses of the vertically integrated studio system, see Tino Balio, ed., *The American Film Industry,* rev. ed. (Madison: University of Wisconsin Press, 1985); Tino Balio, *Grand Design: Hollywood as a Modern Business Enterprise, 1930–1939* (New York: Scribner's, 1993); Douglas Gomery, *The Hollywood Studio System* (New York: St. Martin's Press, 1986); and Thomas Schatz, *The Genius of the System: Hollywood Filmmaking in the Studio Era* (New York: Pantheon, 1988).
10. *Motion Picture Herald,* 26 August 1939, p. 25.
11. *Variety,* 6 September 1939, p. 6; *Wall Street Journal,* 3 October 1939, p. 1. See also "U.S. Takes Film Industry Apart Statistically: 'Worth 2 Billions,'" *Motion Picture Herald,* 30 March 1940, p. 70.
12. See Mae D. Huettig, "Economic Control of the Motion Picture Industry," in Balio, *The American Film Industry,* pp. 299–300; Leo Rosten, *Hollywood: The Movie Colony, the Movie Makers* (New York: Harcourt Brace, 1941), pp. 62–65; Gomery, *The Hollywood Studio System,* p. 3. See also Chapter 4, "Feeding the Maw of Exhibition," in Balio, *Grand Design: Hollywood as a Modern Business Enterprise, 1930–1939.*

13. John C. Flinn, "Motion Picture Industry a $2,000,000,000 Biz," *Variety*, 8 January 1941, p. 25.
14. *1941 Film Daily Year Book*, p. 45.
15. Jowett, *Film, the Democratic Art*, p. 276; Gomery, *The Hollywood Studio System*, p. 17.
16. *1941 Film Daily Year Book*, pp. 43, 45.
17. *Motion Picture Herald*, 27 April 1940, p. 9.
18. Quoted in Balio, *The American Film Industry*, p. 285. Note that Huettig's study was conducted in 1939 and published in 1944.
19. *1941 Film Daily Year Book*, pp. 35–47.
20. Figures from the financial section of the *1942 Film Daily Year Book*, pp. 897ff. See also Gomery, *The Hollywood Studio System*.
21. Gomery, *The Hollywood Studio System*, p. 2.
22. "Exhibition in 1939," *1940 Film Daily Year Book*, p. 45.
23. Tino Balio, *United Artists: The Company Built by the Stars* (Madison: University of Wisconsin Press, 1976), p. 257.
24. Figures are from Gomery, *The Hollywood Studio System*; *Variety*, and various editions of the *Film Daily Year Book*. Note that the figures on studio-affiliated theaters vary considerably, owing to the number of houses in which the studios held only partial interest—as little as 5 percent in some cases. The 1940 estimates in annual industry surveys by *Variety* (8 January 1941, p. 254) and the *1941 Film Daily Year Book* (p. 43), for instance, put Paramount's chain at 1,400 and 1,210 theaters, respectively.
25. Quoted in Balio, *The American Film Industry*, p. 304.
26. Jowett, *Film, the Democratic Art*, p. 276.
27. See Gomery, *The Hollywood Studio System*, p. 13.
28. Jowett, *Film, the Democratic Art*, p. 276.
29. For an overview of the creation and development of Allied States, see *Variety*, 14 January 1939, p. 17.
30. Balio, *United Artists*, p. 99.
31. *Motion Picture Herald*, 2 November 1940, p. 13.
32. "'Trust Trial' Nears," *Motion Picture Herald*, 10 February 1940, p. 8.
33. Quoted in *Motion Picture Herald*, 7 January 1939, p. 7.
34. *Motion Picture Herald*, 11 February 1939, p. 15.
35. *Variety*, 15 February 1939, p. 3; *Motion Picture Herald*, 18 February 1939, p. 12.
36. *Variety*, 15 February 1939, p. 3.
37. *Motion Picture Herald*, 25 February 1939, p. 24.
38. *Variety*, 1 March 1939, p. 24; *Motion Picture Herald*, 1 April 1939, p. 12.
39. *Variety*, 31 May 1939, p. 2.
40. *Variety*, 14 June 1939, p. 1.
41. *1940 Film Daily Year Book*, p. 49; *Variety*, 3 January 1940, p. 5.
42. *Motion Picture Herald*, 27 January 1940, p. 8; 16 March 1940, p. 8.
43. *Motion Picture Herald*, 27 April 1940, p. 14.
44. *Variety*, 12 June 1940, p. 5.
45. *Variety*, 23 October 1940, p. 5; "'Divorcement in Abeyance' as U.S. Approves Negotiations for Decree," *Motion Picture Herald*, 15 June 1940, p. 13; "U.S. Considers 'Final' Draft of Decree While Majors Still Differ," *Motion Picture Herald*, 10 August 1940, n.p.; "U.S. and 'Big Five' At Truce," *Motion Picture Herald*, 31 August 1940, p. 17.
46. "Allied Joins Fight on Decree," *Motion Picture Herald*, 26 October 1940, p. 8; "Exhibitor Groups Protest on Blocks-of-Five Clause," *Motion Picture Herald*, 2 November 1940, p. 55.
47. *Motion Picture Herald*, 26 April 1941, p. 9.
48. *New York Times*, 6 October 1940, p. x3.
49. *Motion Picture Herald*, 19 July 1941, p. 47. A total of 95 cases were filed, and 46 resolved.
50. *Motion Picture Herald*, 13 December 1941, p. 18.
51. *1942 Film Daily Year Book*, p. 681.
52. *Ibid.*, p. 683.
53. Quoted in *ibid.*, p. 633.
54. Frank Nugent, "War's Double-Entry," *New York Times*, 17 September 1939, p. x3.
55. *Wall Street Journal*, 2 January 1941, p. 48.

56. *Motion Picture Herald,* 11 March 1939, p. 6. According to the *Herald,* prior to 1938 Japan imported about 400 U.S. pictures per year (21 January 39, p. 9), and Italy imported about 200 (13 January 1940, p. 8).

57. *Motion Picture Herald,* 4 February 1939, p. 38.

58. *Variety,* 19 July 1939, p. 11.

59. There were reportedly about 30,000 "theaters" in the Soviet Union, although very few of these were permanent facilities wired for sound. The 6,200 theaters in the Far East and Middle East included 1,750 in Japan, 1,370 in Australia, 1,025 in India, 720 in New Zealand, and 275 in China. There were 880 theaters in Africa and the Near East, including 300 in South Africa. And in Latin America, an increasingly important market for Hollywood, there were 5,240 theaters, including 1,450 in Brazil, 1,020 in Argentina, 825 in Mexico, and 375 in Cuba. Figures from *Motion Picture Herald,* 11 February 1939, p. 28; see also various issues of the *Film Daily Year Book.*

60. *Variety,* 6 September 1939, p. 6.

61. *Wall Street Journal,* 3 October 1939, p. 1.

62. *1941 Film Daily Year Book,* p. 57.

63. *Wall Street Journal,* 2 January 1941, p. 48.

64. *Variety,* 4 January 1939, p. 5.

65. Quoted in *Variety,* 6 September 1939, p. 7.

66. *Motion Picture Herald,* 16 September 1939, p. 9; *Motion Picture Herald,* 17 August 1940, p. 8. While attendance was approaching normal, the number of prints shipped to England fell sharply, from over 700 in the first six months of 1939 to barely 300 during the same period in 1940.

67. *Motion Picture Herald,* 7 June 1941, p. 18; *Wall Street Journal,* 7 July 1941, p. 1.

68. *Variety,* 16 April 1941, p. 5.

69. *Wall Street Journal,* 2 January 1941, p. 48.

70. *Motion Picture Herald,* 1 November 1941, p. 8; *1941 Film Daily Year Book,* p. 71.

71. *Motion Picture Herald,* 7 January 1939, p. 14.

72. *Variety,* 15 February 1939, p. 11.

73. *Motion Picture Herald,* 3 February 1940, p. 22.

74. *Motion Picture Herald,* 29 April 1939, p. 13.

75. *Variety,* 16 April 1941, p. 5; *Motion Picture Herald,* 10 May 1941, p. 8.

76. *Motion Picture Herald,* 24 May 1941, p. 44.

77. *Motion Picture Herald,* 25 October 1941, p. 27.

78. *1942 Film Daily Year Book,* p. 89.

79. Quoted in *Variety,* 31 December 1941, p. 3.

80. *1941 Film Daily Year Book,* pp. 43, 45. As will be seen in chapter 3, the industry figures on weekly ticket sales and weekly attendance were hotly contested in 1940–1941. On potential audience, see *Motion Picture Herald,* 15 February 41, p. 44. According to these figures, some 23 percent of the American public was too young, old, ill, poor, disinterested, or otherwise unable to attend.

81. Finler, *The Hollywood Story,* p. 288.

82. *Motion Picture Herald,* 22 June 1940, p. 8. By Poor's estimate, an increase of only 7 percent in U.S. box-office receipts would offset a 50 percent decline in foreign business.

83. Figures on total admissions income are reported in Christopher H. Sterling and Timothy R. Haight, *The Mass Media: The Aspen Institute Guide to Communications Industry Trends* (New York: Praeger, 1978), p. 187.

84. *Wall Street Journal,* 2 January 1941, p. 48.

85. *Variety,* 28 May 1941, p. 15. The subhead queried: "Defense Boom Just a Mirage?" Crowther in *New York Times,* 1 June 1941, p. x4.

86. *Motion Picture Herald,* 25 October 1941, p. 13.

87. *Variety,* 9 July 1941, p. 5.

88. *Wall Street Journal,* 10 September 1941, p. 1.

89. *Motion Picture Herald,* 25 October 1941, p. 13; *Variety,* 26 November 1941, p. 7.

90. *Motion Picture Herald,* 1 November 1941, p. 13.

91. *Motion Picture Herald,* 17 August 1940, p. 25.

92. *Motion Picture Herald,* 17 May 1941, p. 16.

93. *Motion Picture Herald,* 4 October 1941, p. 43; *Variety,* 15 February 1941, p. 44.

94. *Motion Picture Herald,* 31 August 1940, p. 39.

95. *Motion Picture Herald,* 3 May 1941, p. 9.

96. Douglas Gomery, *Shared Pleasures: A History of Movie Presentation in the United States* (Madison: University of Wisconsin Press, 1992), p. 152.

97. *Motion Picture Herald*, 15 July 1939, p. 9. See also Gomery, *Shared Pleasures*, ch. 9, "Ethnic Theatres and Art Cinemas." According to Gomery, the number of foreign-language theaters peaked in the early 1930s at about 500 houses (p. 176).

98. *Motion Picture Herald*, 15 July 1939, p. 41. These figures, cited in an in-depth article on African-American theaters and moviegoing, were supplied by the motion picture division of the Department of Commerce.

99. *Variety*, 3 January 1940, p. 36.

100. *Ibid.*, p. 18.

101. Gomery, *Shared Pleasures*, p. 161.

102. Sterling and Haight, *The Mass Media*, pp. 184, 187.

103. Technically, the guild agreements and other union contracts were signed with the Association of Motion Picture Producers (AMPP), not to be confused with the Motion Picture Producers and Directors of America (MPPDA), the studios' trade association.

104. David Prindle, *The Politics of Glamour* (Madison: University of Wisconsin Press, 1988), pp. 31–32. See also Balio, *Grand Design*, pp. 153–155.

105. For a detailed treatment of Capra's role in securing the SDG agreement, see Joseph McBride, *Frank Capra: The Catastrophe of Success* (New York: Simon & Schuster, 1992), pp. 375–408.

106. *Variety*, 18 June 1941, p. 5.

107. Rosten, *Hollywood*, p. 318.

108. *Variety*, 4 January 1939, p. 51.

109. David Prindle, *The Politics of Glamour*, p. 7.

110. *Variety*, 18 February 1939, p. 27; 14 June 1939, p. 3.

111. *Motion Picture Herald*, 29 July 1939, p. 29; *Variety*, 23 August 1939, p. 1.

112. Prindle, *The Politics of Glamour*, pp. 31–33; *Motion Picture Herald*, 26 August 1939, p. 18.

113. Prindle, *The Politics of Glamour*, pp. 33–36; *Variety*, 16 September 1939, p. 3; *Motion Picture Herald*, 4 November 1939, p. 8.

114. *Motion Picture Herald*, 13 January 1940, p. 8.

115. *Motion Picture Herald*, 8 June 1940, p. 8; 15 March 1941, p. 33; 19 April 1941, p. 9. Joe Schenck was officially the president of the Association of Motion Picture Producers (AMPP).

116. *Motion Picture Herald*, 15 November 1941, p. 12.

117. Prindle, *The Politics of Glamour*, pp. 37–40.

118. *Ibid.*, p. 36.

119. *New York Times*, 12 February 1939, p. E12.

120. *Motion Picture Herald*, 24 February 1940, p. 28.

121. *Variety*, 21 August 1940, p. 3.

122. *Motion Picture Herald*, 24 August 1940, p. 48; *New York Times*, 25 August 1941, p. 3x; *Motion Picture Herald*, 2 August 1941, p. 9.

123. *Variety*, 6 August 1941, p. 3.

124. *1942 Film Daily Year Book*, p. 95.

125. Leonard J. Leff and Jerold L. Simmons, *The Dame in the Kimono* (New York: Grove Weidenfeld, 1990), pp. 33–54, 284. See also *Motion Picture Herald*, 28 June 1941, p. 61.

126. Selznick to J. H. Whitney, 6 September 1939, REBECCA censorship file, David O. Selznick Collection, Harry Ransom Humanities Research Center, University of Texas at Austin (hereafter Selznick Collection, UT).

127. *Motion Picture Herald*, 10 May 1941, p. 23; Leff and Simmons, *The Dame in the Kimono*, pp. 116–118.

128. *New York Times*, 26 February 1939, p. 4x.

129. *Motion Picture Herald*, 1 April 1939, p. 22.

130. "Hays Office Clarifies Prod. Code; Realism Up to Individual Producer, But There's Been No Relaxing by PCA," *Variety*, 22 February 1939, p. 4. The Hays Office was responding to controversies involving a number of other films besides BLOCKADE, notably a recent Warners romantic comedy, YES, MY DARLING DAUGHTER (1939).

131. Clayton R. Koppes and Gregory D. Black, *Hollywood Goes to War: How Politics, Profits, and Propaganda Shaped World War II Movies* (New York: Free Press, 1987), pp. 33–34. See also *Motion Picture Herald*, 18 January 1941, p. 9; 15 February 1941, p. 9; and *New York Times*, 19 January 1941, p. x5.

132. *Motion Picture Herald,* 3 May 1941, p. 8; see also Leff and Simmons, *The Dame in the Kimono,* 109–117.
133. *Variety,* 3 December 1941, p. 3. The *Variety* review of 22 October 1941 is quoted in the same article.
134. *Variety,* 3 December 1941, p. 3.
135. *Ibid.; Motion Picture Herald,* 6 December 1941, p. 13.
136. *Motion Picture Herald,* 12 December 1941, p. 8.
137. *Motion Picture Herald,* 9 August 1941, p. 26; 16 August 1941, p. 8; August 1941, p. 8.
138. *Variety,* 10 September 1941, p. 1.
139. *Motion Picture Herald,* 13 September 1941, n.p.
140. *Motion Picture Herald,* 4 October 1941, pp. 12–18.
141. *Motion Picture Herald,* 15 November 1941, p. 8; 29 November 1941, p. 9.

CHAPTER 3 (The Hollywood Studio System in 1940–1941)

1. "Industry Statistics," *1941 Film Daily Year Book,* p. 35.
2. Robert Sklar, *Movie-Made America: A Cultural History of American Movies* (New York: Random House, 1975), pp. 164–165.
3. Tino Balio, *Grand Design: Hollywood as a Modern Business Enterprise, 1930–1939* (New York: Scribner's, 1993), pp. 25–26.
4. Janet Staiger, "The Producer-Unit System: Management by Specialization After 1931," in David Bordwell, Janet Staiger, and Kristen Thompson, *The Classical Hollywood Cinema: Film Style and Mode of Production to 1960* (New York: Columbia University Press, 1985), p. 320.
5. *New York Times,* 21 February 1940, p. 5x.
6. *Variety,* 1 April 1940, p. 3.
7. Warners' assets in 1930 were $230 million; by 1934 its total assets stood at $168 million, where they remained for the rest of the decade. Loew's/MGM, meanwhile, showed assets of $128 million in 1930, and its total climbed slowly during the decade, reaching $157 million by 1939. Douglas Gomery, *The Hollywood Studio System* (New York: St. Martin's Press, 1986), pp. 52, 102.
8. *1941 Film Daily Year Book,* p. 3.
9. John Douglas Eames, *The MGM Story* (New York: Crown, 1975), p. 166.
10. Figures from Warner Bros. legal file, United Artists Collection, Wisconsin Center for Film and Theatre Research, State Historical Society, University of Wisconsin—Madison (hereafter Warner Legal Collection, UW—M).
11. ARSENIC AND OLD LACE file, Warner Legal Collection, UW—M. The deal gave Capra 10 percent and the playwrights 15 percent of all gross receipts above $1.25 million.
12. The prototype for Daffy Duck was introduced in "Porky's Duck Hunt" in 1937, and the model for Bugs first appeared in "Porky's Hare Hunt" a year later. It was in Tex Avery's 1940 cartoon "A Wild Hare" that the name Bugs Bunny was first used. See Joe Adamson, *Bugs Bunny: Fifty Years and Only One Grey Hare* (New York: Henry Holt, 1990).
13. Gomery, *The Hollywood Studio System,* pp. 86–88.
14. Joel W. Finler, *The Hollywood Story* (New York: Crown, 1988), 94–95.
15. Richard B. Jewell, *The RKO Story* (New York: Arlington House, 1982), p. 140. See also Jewell, "RKO Film Grosses, 1929–1951: The C. J. Tevlin Ledger," *Historical Journal of Film, Radio, and Television,* vol. 14, no. 1 (1994), pp. 37–49.
16. Finler, *The Hollywood Story,* p. 169.
17. *Variety,* 24 April 1940, p. 1. The two films mentioned in the article were THAT'S RIGHT, YOU'RE WRONG (1939) and TOO MANY GIRLS (1940).
18. Jewell, "RKO Film Grosses," p. 45.
19. Universal released 49 films in 1940, and 58 in 1941; Columbia released 51 films in 1940, and 61 in 1941. See Finler, *The Hollywood Story,* p. 280.
20. Figures from Clive Hirschhorn, *The Universal Story* (New York: Crown, 1983), pp. 115–121. In 1940, 28 features ran 65 minutes or less; in 1941, 30 of 57 releases ran 65 minutes or less. The average on all features was 69.2 minutes in 1940 and 68.7 minutes in 1941.
21. Todd McCarthy and Charles Flynn, eds., *Kings of the B's* (New York: Dutton, 1975), p. 19.
22. For general histories of Republic and Monogram, see *ibid.,* and also Gomery, *The Hollywood Studio System,* pp. 180–187.

23. McCarthy and Flynn, *Kings of the B's,* p. 20.
24. Gomery, *The Hollywood Studio System,* p. 183.
25. According to the *1942 Film Daily Year Book* (p. 902), Consolidated in 1940–1941 had total assets of $6.7 million.
26. McCarthy and Flynn, *Kings of the B's,* p. 25.
27. *Motion Picture Herald,* 16 November 1940, p. 33; 28 June 1941, p. 18.
28. *Motion Picture Herald,* 11 October 1941, p. 13.
29. *Motion Picture Herald,* 12 April 1941, p. 13.
30. *Variety,* 3 January 1940, p. 7; *Motion Picture Herald,* 16 November 1940, p. 33; *Motion Picture Herald,* 22 July 1939, p. 9. The number of presold literary and stage properties increased about 40 percent in 1939 over the previous year (from 230 to 319).
31. *Motion Picture Herald,* 29 March 1941, n.p.
32. *Motion Picture Herald,* 1 March 1941, p. 8.
33. *Motion Picture Herald,* 23 August 1941, p. 64.
34. "Outstanding Campaigns of 1940," *1941 Film Daily Year Book,* p. 763.
35. *Motion Picture Herald,* 23 December 1939, n.p.
36. *Motion Picture Herald,* 30 December 1939, p. 8.
37. *Motion Picture Herald,* 2 July 1940, p. 9; *Motion Picture Herald,* 7 December 1940, p. 9.
38. *Motion Picture Herald,* 26 April 1941, p. 29.
39. *Motion Picture Herald,* 13 January 1940, n.p.
40. *Motion Picture Herald,* 27 April 1940, p. 9.
41. For rental terms, see *Motion Picture Herald,* 28 September 1940, p. 10; for figures on its long run, see *Motion Picture Herald,* 29 March 1941, p. 8.
42. *Motion Picture Herald,* 10 August 1941, p. 50.
43. "Film Showmanship," *Variety,* 3 January 1940, p. 10; *Variety,* 15 February 1939, p. 5. "Outstanding Campaigns of 1939," *1940 Film Daily Year Book,* p. 801.
44. "Film Showmanship," *Variety,* 3 January 1940, p. 10.
45. *1941 Film Daily Year Book,* p. 716.
46. *1942 Film Daily Year Book,* p. 91.
47. For an excellent analysis of the studios' in-house research efforts, see Leo Handel, *Hollywood Looks at Its Audience: A Report of Film Audience Research* (1950; reprint, New York: Arno, 1976).
48. Shannon Kelley, "Gallup Goes to Hollywood: Motion Picture Audience Research in the 1940s" (M.A. thesis, University of Texas—Austin, 1989), pp. 6–9.
49. *Ibid.,* p. 9; *Motion Picture Herald,* 26 July 1941, pp. 33–34. On Handel's MPRB, see Handel, *Hollywood Looks at Its Audience.* See also Ernest Borneman, "The Public Opinion Myth," *Harper's,* July 1947. Borneman noted that "Dr. Gallup shares the ownership of AR [Audience Research] with Raymond Rubicam of . . . Young & Rubicam" (p. 34).
50. Handel, *Hollywood Looks at Its Audience,* p. 94.
51. *Motion Picture Herald,* 21 September 1940, p. 8.
52. *Motion Picture Herald,* 26 July 1941, p. 33.
53. Handel, *Hollywood Looks at Its Audience,* p. 100.
54. Handel's general survey of production-oriented research is covered in chs. 3–5 of his study (pp. 21–92). The various methods he describes of gauging audience response included the use of polygraph recorders (lie detectors) and such voting mechanisms as the Lazarsfeld-Stanton Program Analyzer, the Cirlin Reactograph, and the Hopkins Electric Televoting Machine (*Hollywood Looks at Its Audience,* pp. 45–52).
55. *Motion Picture Herald,* 10 August 1940, p. 21.
56. "B's Become Near-A's," *Variety,* 3 January 1940, p. 19.
57. *Motion Picture Herald,* 27 January 1940, p. 29.
58. *Variety,* 31 December 1941, p. 1.
59. *Variety,* 10 July 1940, p. 5.
60. *1941 Film Daily Year Book,* p. 45.
61. *Motion Picture Herald,* 6 June 1940, p. 13; *Motion Picture Herald,* 25 February 1939, pp. 12–14; *Motion Picture Herald,* 20 March 1948, p. 26.
62. Roy Chartier, "The Year in Pictures," *Variety,* 4 January 1939, p. 48.
63. "Increasing Profits with Continuous Audience Research," *Princeton Audience Research Institute, 1941—Gallup Looks at the Movies: ARI Reports 1940–1950* (Princeton, N.J.: Audience Research

Institute) (hereafter ARI Reports); Bosley Crowther, "Doubles, or Maybe Nothing," *New York Times,* 11 July 1940, n.p.; "Goldwyn-Gallup Survey Reports 57% Against Duals, 43% in Favor," *Motion Picture Herald,* 10 August 1940, p. 21; "Gallup's Pan on Pix Adv.," *Variety,* 14 August 1940, pp. 5, 19.

64. Thomas M. Pryor, "Random Notes on the Film Scene," *New York Times,* 23 February 1941, n.p.; Pryor, "The Screen Grab-Bag," *New York Times,* 18 August 1940, p. 4.

65. See also Handel, *Hollywood Looks at Its Audience,* p. 131.

66. Broidy interview in McCarthy and Flynn, *Kings of the B's,* p. 275.

67. Edward R. Beach, "Double Features in Motion Picture Exhibition," *Harvard Business Review* 10 (July 1932), p. 512; Howard T. Lewis, *The Motion Picture Industry* (New York: D. Van Nostrand Co., 1933), pp. 325–333; "New Experiment in Duals," *Variety,* 5 February 1941, p. 7.

68. Richard deCordova, "Regulating Childhood: The Children's Matinee Movement," 1990 Society for Cinema Studies conference, Washington, D.C., 26 May 1990.

69. See, for example, "H'wood to Continue Low-Budgeters Despite Shortage of Raw Material," *Variety,* 6 January 1943, p. 37.

70. In 1933, Karl Hoblitzelle in Dallas agreed to operate the Paramount-Publix Theaters in Texas. The chain operated from 1920 to 1973.

71. Hoblitzelle Interstate Theatre Circuit, "Interstate Short Subject Manual," box 2, Hoblitzelle Theatre Arts Collection, Harry Ransom Humanities Research Center, University of Texas—Austin.

72. See Beach, "Double Features," pp. 505–515; Lewis, *The Motion Picture Industry,* pp. 325–333.

73. See also Broidy interview in McCarthy and Flynn, *Kings of the B's,* p. 270.

74. "25% of Theatres Use Dual Features Only, MPAA Says," *Motion Picture Herald,* 26 June 1948, p. 28.

CHAPTER 4 (Prewar Stars, Genres, and Production Trends)

1. Tino Balio, *Grand Design: Hollywood as a Modern Business Enterprise, 1930–1939* (New York: Scribner's, 1993), p. 73.

2. Wanger to UA's Lynn Farrol, 9 February 1939, John Ford Manuscripts Collection, Indiana University (hereafter Ford Collection, IU).

3. Nichols to Ford, 26 February 1939, Ford Collection, IU.

4. Frank Nugent, "Speaking of Directors," *New York Times,* 19 February 1939, p. x5.

5. *New York Times,* 2 April 1939, quoted in Leo Rosten, *Hollywood: The Movie Colony, the Movie Makers* (New York: Harcourt Brace, 1941), p. 302.

6. *Variety,* 8 March 1939, p. 5. See also *Variety,* 3 January 1940, p. 1.

7. "Directors' Best Break," *Variety,* 11 December 1940, p. 3.

8. *Motion Picture Herald,* 6 September 41, p. 13.

9. David Bordwell, "The Bounds of Difference," in David Bordwell, Janet Staiger, and Kristen Thompson, *The Classical Hollywood Cinema: Film Style and Mode of Production to 1960* (New York: Columbia University Press, 1985), pp. 77–78.

10. *Ibid.*

11. *Motion Picture Herald,* 11 May 1940, p. 42.

12. Throughout the section on the Zanuck-Ford collaborations at Fox, I am relying on information culled from the Twentieth Century–Fox Script Collection in the UCLA Film and Theater Arts Library (hereafter Fox Script Collection, UCLA), particularly the script and story files on individual titles, as well as the general script inventory.

13. Story conference memo, 22 May 1940, HOW GREEN WAS MY VALLEY file, Fox Script Collection, UCLA.

14. Fox script inventory, Fox Script Collection, UCLA.

15. Zanuck to Ford, 10 July 1941, Ford Collection, IU.

16. Originally stated in a 1970 interview by Mel Gussow for his biography of Zanuck; quoted in Rudy Behlmer, ed., *Memo from Darryl F. Zanuck* (New York: Grove, 1993), p. xix.

17. In a letter of 25 June 1946 in which he informs Ford that he is about to recut MY DARLING CLEMENTINE (1946) after a poor preview, Zanuck reminds Ford that he, Zanuck, edited both GRAPES and HOW GREEN, and that "you [Ford] did not see either picture until they were playing in the theatres"; Ford Collection, IU. See also Dunne and Johnson comments in Behlmer, *Memo*

from Zanuck, p. xviii. (Dunne: "Writers at Twentieth never wrote 'for' directors, as most critics and movie historians assume; they wrote for Darryl Zanuck." Johnson said of Zanuck in a 1969 *American Film Institute* interview: "He was far and away the most valuable man I've ever been associated with in the business. One of the very few who really made contributions and was a collaborator.")

18. *Variety,* 21 September 1938, p. 1.
19. Frank Capra, *The Name Above the Title* (New York: Macmillan, 1971), p. 219. See also Joseph McBride, *Frank Capra: The Catastrophe of Success* (New York: Simon & Schuster, 1992), pp. 365–374.
20. Capra file, Selznick Collection, UT. This offer was first made in 1937, as indicated in a letter of 12 August 1937 from David Selznick to John Hay Whitney and John Wharton of SIP.
21. Copy of the contract of 21 February 1940 between Frank Capra Productions, Inc., and Warner Bros. Pictures, Inc., Capra file, Selznick Collection, UT. See also McBride, *Frank Capra,* pp. 429–430.
22. *Variety,* 31 December 1941, p. 1.
23. Contract of 1 August 1941, ARSENIC AND OLD LACE legal file, Warner Legal Collection, UW—M.
24. On the details of the purchase of the REBECCA motion picture rights, see the extensive correspondence between Selznick and Kay Brown, his East Coast story department head. The details of the purchase are contained in an "Agreement" of 29 September 1938; REBECCA story file, Selznick Collection, UT. See also Ronald Haver, *David O. Selznick's Hollywood* (New York: Knopf, 1980), pp. 312–313; Thomas Schatz, *The Genius of the System: Hollywood Filmmaking in the Studio Era* (New York: Pantheon, 1988), pp. 271–277.
25. The agreement between Selznick and Wanger for Hitchcock's services was reached on 26 September 1939, stipulating that the director would report to Wanger upon completion of principal photography on REBECCA. Production closed on 20 November, and Hitchcock reported to Wanger one week later; REBECCA file, Wanger legal file, Selznick Collection, UT. See also Matthew Bernstein, *Walter Wanger: Hollywood Independent* (Berkeley: University of California Press, 1995), pp. 157–158; and Schatz, *The Genius of the System,* pp. 287–289.
26. Hitchcock file, Selznick Collection, UT. The RKO deal is contained in an agreement dated 15 August 1940; Hitchcock's compensation for the first two years with Selznick is outlined in a memo from Frances Ingles to Selznick, 22 September 1941.
27. Agreement of 21 December 1940 between Selznick and RKO, Fontaine file, Selznick Collection, UT.
28. SABOTEUR deal outlined in Selznick to Ernest L. Scanlon, 20 December 41, Hitchcock file, Selznick Collection, UT.
29. David Thomson, *The Autobiographical Dictionary of Film* (New York: Morrow, 1976), p. 605.
30. Barbara Leaming, *Orson Welles* (New York: Penguin, 1985), p. 170.
31. Quoted in *Motion Picture Herald,* 15 March 1941, p. 27.
32. Actually, Welles had first experiminted with film as an offshoot of his theater interests, creating a dramatic short, *The Hearts of Age,* in 1934, and also producing an extended (40-minute) film drama which was to accompany his 1938 stage production of William Gillette's *Too Much Johnson.* See Leaming, *Orson Welles,* pp. 155–157.
33. *Ibid.,* p. 169.
34. On the writing of KANE, see Robert L. Carringer, *The Making of* Citizen Kane (Berkeley: University of California Press, 1985), pp. 21–30. See also Pauline Kael's account in *The* Citizen Kane *Book* (Boston: Little, Brown, 1971).
35. See Kael, "Raising Kane," *The* Citizen Kane *Book,* pp. 86–87.
36. George Turner, "Xanadu in Review: *Citizen Kane* Turns 50," *American Cinematographer,* August 1991, p. 35.
37. Carringer, *The Making of* Citizen Kane, p. 69; Gregg Toland, "Realism for *Citizen Kane,*" in *American Cinematographer,* August 1991, p. 42.
38. Bordwell, "Deep-Focus Cinematography," p. 347.
39. Toland, "Realism for *Citizen Kane,*" p. 37. See also Charles Henry Harpole, *Gradients of Depth in the Cinema Image* (New York: Arno, 1978).
40. Quoted in Turner, "Xanadu in Review," p. 34.
41. Carringer, *The Making of* Citizen Kane, p. 81.

42. Toland, "Realism for *Citizen Kane*," pp. 38–40.
43. Carringer, *The Making of* Citizen Kane, pp. 69–70.
44. Leaming (*Orson Welles*, pp. 205–206) suggests that Hedda Hopper, Parsons's principal competitor in Hollywood, first informed Hearst of the content of CITIZEN KANE. The source was Parsons, according to most other accounts, however, including a detailed story in the *Motion Picture Herald*, "Hearst Dislikes 'Kane'" (18 January 1941, p. 9).
45. Quoted in Harlan Lebow, *Citizen Kane* (New York: Doubleday, 1990), p. 212.
46. *Motion Picture Herald*, 15 March 1941, p. 27.
47. Leaming, *Orson Welles*, p. 232.
48. *Ibid.*, p. 217; Turner, "Xanadu in Review," p. 34.
49. *Variety*, 8 January 1941, p. 29.
50. *Motion Picture Herald*, 26 July 1941, p. 33; *Motion Picture Herald*, 16 August 1941, p. 11.
51. The separate circuit and independent listings seem to have been primarily a matter of industry politics; there were only minor differences in the two.
52. *Variety*, 3 January 1940, p. 1.
53. *New York Times Film Reviews* (hereafter *NYTFR*), 18 March 1940.
54. The deal essentially had Warners loaning Bette Davis to Goldwyn for THE LITTLE FOXES in exchange for Cooper for YORK, with Cooper going to Paramount for FOR WHOM THE BELL TOLLS, along with Selznick's Ingrid Bergman, after Bergman completed Warners' CASABLANCA and SARATOGA TRUNK (in which she costarred with Cooper). See legal files for SERGEANT YORK, CASABLANCA, and SARATOGA TRUNK, Warner Legal Collection, UW—M. See also Bergman file, Selznick Collection, UT; and *Variety*, 7 December 1940, p. 12.
55. *Motion Picture Herald*, 18 May 1940, p. 8.
56. *Variety*, 8 January 1941, p. 1.
57. Janet Staiger, "Individualism Versus Collectivism," *Screen* 24, nos. 4–5 (July-October 1983), p. 70.
58. "Hollywood Places Greater Value on Stars in Blocks-of-5 Selling," *Motion Picture Herald*, 1 March 1941, p. 12.
59. *Motion Picture Herald*, 16 August 1941, p. 11.
60. See Hugh Fordin, *The World of Entertainment* (Garden City, N.Y.: Doubleday, 1975).
61. Most of the material on the Hardy Family pictures was culled from the George B. Seitz Collection, Louis B. Mayer Library, American Film Institute, Los Angeles (hereafter Seitz Collection, AFI). Additional material on the Hardy pictures is available in the MGM Script Collection, Cinema-Television Library, University of Southern California.
62. See Aljean Hermetz, *The Making of* The Wizard of Oz (New York: Limelight, 1977).
63. Information on BABES IN ARMS and subsequent Freed-produced musicals was found in the Arthur Freed Collection, Department of Special Collections, Doheny Library, USC (hereafter Freed Collection, USC).
64. BABES IN ARMS production file, Freed Collection, USC.
65. Hermetz, *The Making of* The Wizard of Oz, p. 288.
66. Balio, *Grand Design*, pp. 17–80.
67. *Variety*, 3 January 1940, p. 5. See also *Variety*, 2 July 1941, p. 3.
68. *Variety*, 1 March 1939, p. 5.
69. *New York Times*, 12 March 1939, p. x5.
70. For an excellent, informative study of Hollywood's A- and B-Western production, see Edward Buscombe, *The BFI Companion to the Western* (London: BFI Publishing, 1988).
71. According to Buscombe, Hollywood's B-Western output totaled 114 in 1939, 130 in 1940, and 121 in 1941. While the majority of these came from the minor studios, most of the Big Eight cranked them out as well. In 1941, for example, Republic released 33 B-Westerns, Monogram released 19, and PRC 13; meanwhile Paramount released 10, Fox 6, RKO 7, Columbia 16, and Universal 9. *The BFI Companion to the Western*, pp. 426–427.
72. *Variety*, 23 August 1939, p. 3.
73. See, for example, Bosley Crowther, "Boxoffice Blues," *New York Times*, 1 June 1941, p. x4.
74. *Variety*, 4 January 1939, p. 5.
75. In October 1938, Robinson signed a new three-year, six-picture contract at $85,000 per picture, giving him approval of both story and role; Robinson pact of 3 October 1938, BROTHER ORCHID file, Warner Legal Collection, UW—M. In July 1939, Cagney signed a new three-year, eleven-

picture deal for $150,000 per picture plus 10 percent of the gross revenues above $1.5 million, as well as story and role approval—a remarkable contract by current industry standards. Cagney pact of 7 July 1939, THE BRIDE CAME COD file, Warner Legal Collection, UW—M.

76. Garfield first attracted attention in a minor role in a 1938 woman's picture for Warners, FOUR DAUGHTERS. The long-term pact was signed 13 February 1939; DUST BE MY DESTINY file, Warner Legal Collection, UW—M.

77. Raft contract, 15 June 1939, BACKGROUND TO DANGER file, Warner Legal Collection, UW—M.

78. Bogart contract, 31 December 1937, THEY MADE ME A CRIMINAL file, Warner Legal Collection, UW—M.

79. Walsh contract, 16 May 1939, Walsh legal file, Warner Bros. Archives, Department of Special Collections, Doheny Library, University of Southern California (hereafter Warner Archive, USC).

80. See Hellinger deal (option taken at $1,750 per week) of 1 July 1940, Hellinger legal file, Warner Archive, USC. The Walsh deal was more complicated. In its original contract of 13 May 1939, Warners inserted a clause indicating that 30 days after the preview of THE ROARING TWENTIES it could exercise the first of five yearly options (at $1,750 per week)—which the studio did in August 1939. See Jack Warner to Hal Wallis, 21 August 1939 (outlining the option pickup), Walsh legal file, Warner Archive, USC.

81. See HIGH SIERRA file, Warner Legal Collection, UW—M.

82. Letter of 21 March 40, quoted in Rudy Behlmer, ed., *Inside Warner Bros. (1935–1951)* (New York: Viking, 1985), p. 126.

83. John Huston, *An Open Book* (New York: Knopf, 1980), p. 79.

84. Thomson, *A Biographical Dictionary of Film*, p. 595.

85. *NYTFR*, 25 January 41.

86. See Hellinger to Wallis, 17 February 1941, and also Warners' "release" of Hellinger, 10 March 1941, Hellinger legal file, Warner Archive, USC.

87. See Wald reassignment as "associate producer" on 29 March 1941. See also Wald's new contract (as "Supervisor") of 19 July 1941. Wald legal file, Warner Archive, USC.

88. See the contract of 26 May 1941, IN THIS OUR LIFE file, Warner Legal Collection, UW—M.

89. For a detailed treatment of the making of THE MALTESE FALCON, see Rudy Behlmer, *America's Favorite Movies* (New York: Ungar, 1982).

90. Quoted in Behlmer, *Inside Warner Bros.*, p. 151.

91. See billing memoranda of 10 June 41 and 8 September 41, THE MALTESE FALCON production file, Warner Archive, USC.

92. *New York Times*, 4 October 1941, n.p.

93. See ch. 2, "Hollywood Turns Interventionist" (pp. 17–47), in Koppes and Black, *Hollywood Goes to War.*

94. National Board quoted in the *1940 Film Daily Year Book*, p. 81.

95. Koppes and Black, *Hollywood Goes to War*, p. 30.

96. *Motion Picture Herald*, 7 September 1940, p. 47.

97. Russell Earl Shain, *An Analysis of Motion Pictures About the War Released by the American Film Industry, 1939–1970* (New York: Arno, 1976), pp. 31, 61.

98. Koppes and Black, *Hollywood Goes to War*, p. 32.

99. *New York Times*, 8 September 1940, p. x3.

100. *New York Times*, 22 September 1940, p. x3.

101. *NYTFR*, 21 June 40.

102. *NYTFR*, 3 August 40. In his review, Crowther suggests that THE MAN I MARRIED was in fact the first Hollywood film to use the term "Jew."

103. Shain, *An Analysis of Motion Pictures*, pp. 31, 61.

104. Roger Manvell, *Films and the Second World War* (New York: Delta, 1974), pp. 15–17, 86–92.

105. *Motion Picture Herald*, 2 November 1940, p. 9.

106. *Motion Picture Herald*, 30 August 1941, p. 15.

107. Information on the Abbott and Costello films was culled from production files on IN THE NAVY and other Universal films co-starring the comedy team in the Universal Collection, Department of Special Collections, Doheny Library, University of Southern California (hereafter Universal Collection, USC).

108. Navy Lt. Cdr. A. J. Bolton to Universal production supervisor A. J. Murphy, 14 March 1941, IN THE NAVY production file, Universal Collection, USC.

109. Joe Breen to Universal's Maurice Pivar, 20 March 1941; transcription of 31 March 1941 phone conversation between Arthur Lubin and Navy Lt. Cdr. Herman Spitzel; IN THE NAVY production file, Universal Collection, USC.

110. Alex Gottlieb to Arthur Lubin et al., 17 May 1941 (with script revisions attached); Herman Spitzel to Lubin, 21 May 1941; IN THE NAVY production file, Universal Collection, USC.

111. Information on EAGLE SQUADRON culled primarily from the Walter Wanger Collection, Wisconsin Center for Film and Theatre Research, State Historical Society, University of Wisconsin—Madison (hereafter Wanger Collection, UW—M), as well as the Walter Wanger file, Selznick Collection, UT.

112. Summary of Wanger-UA productions, 28 April 1945, Wanger Collection, UW—M.

113. Watt and Schoedsack to Wanger, 20 August 1941, EAGLE SQUADRON file, Wanger Collection, UW—M.

114. Watt to Wanger, 19 September 1941, EAGLE SQUADRON file, Wanger Collection, UW—M.

115. See correspondence between Wanger and Raine, 30 September 1941 and 1 October 1941, EAGLE SQUADRON file. On FOREIGN CORRESPONDENT costs, see undated summary of "negative cost," FOREIGN CORRESPONDENT production file. Details are specified in Wanger's Universal contract of 15 November 41, EAGLE SQUADRON file. All in Wanger Collection, UW—M.

116. Wanger contract with Universal Pictures, 15 November 1941, EAGLE SQUADRON file, Wanger Collection, UW—M.

117. See income summaries of 31 October 1942 and 29 May 1943, EAGLE SQUADRON file, Wanger Collection, UW—M.

CHAPTER 5 (The Motion Picture Industry During World War II)

1. Robert St. John, "Preface" to *Look* magazine, *Movie Lot to Beachhead: The Motion Picture Goes to War* (Garden City, N.Y.: Doubleday, 1945), p. i.

2. R. A. C. Parker, *Struggle for Survival: The History of the Second World War* (New York: Oxford University Press, 1989), p. 131.

3. John Keegan, *The Second World War* (New York: Viking, 1989), p. 219; Richard R. Lingeman, *Don't You Know There's a War On? The American Home Front, 1941–1945* (New York: Putnam's, 1970), pp. 67, 114, 141. For more on unemployment in the United States, see Richard S. Kirkendall, *The United States, 1929–1945: Years of Crisis and Change* (New York: McGraw-Hill, 1974), pp. 121, 214.

4. Michael Renov, *Hollywood's Wartime Women* (Ann Arbor, Mich.: UMI Research Press, 1988), p. 40; Lingeman, *Don't You Know There's a War On?*, p. 155. See also William H. Chafe, *The American Woman: Her Changing Social, Economic and Political Roles, 1920–1970* (New York: Oxford University Press, 1975).

5. Lingeman, *Don't You Know There's a War On?*, p. 135; Parker, *Struggle for Survival*, p. 143.

6. *Ibid.*, p. 135.

7. *Ibid.*, p. 133.

8. Nelson Lichtenstein, *Labor's War at Home* (New York: Cambridge University Press, 1982), p. 111.

9. Lingeman, *Don't You Know There's a War On?*, p. 70.

10. *Ibid.*, p. 351.

11. On the marriage rate, see Susan Hartmann, *The Home Front and Beyond: American Women in the 1940s* (Boston: Twayne, 1982), p. 164. According to Hartmann (pp. 169–170), the birthrate during the Depression had hovered between 18 and 19 births per 1,000 population, the lowest in the nation's history. The rate rose above 20 per 1,000 in 1941, peaked at 22.7 in 1943, then declined during the last two years of the war, when the number of men overseas reached a sustained peak.

12. Lingeman, *Don't You Know There's a War On?*, p. 94.

13. Lichtenstein, *Labor's War at Home*, pp. 133–134.

14. *Ibid.*, pp. 123–124; see also Leila J. Rupp, *Mobilizing Women for War: German and American Propaganda, 1939–1945* (Princeton, N.J.: Princeton University Press, 1978), pp. 150–153.

15. Lichtenstein, *Labor's War at Home*, p. 125.

16. Lingeman, *Don't You Know There's a War On?*, p. 388.

17. Parker, *Struggle for Survival*, p. 143.

18. *Ibid.*, 124–125.
19. *Motion Picture Herald,* 13 January 1945, p. 13.
20. *Motion Picture Herald,* 27 December 1941, p. 17. See also Garth Jowett, *Film, the Democratic Art: A Social History of American Film* (Boston: Little, Brown, 1976), p. 311.
21. On training films, see *Motion Picture Herald,* 1 August 1942, p. 8; on reissues, see *Variety,* 26 September 1945, p. 9; *Motion Picture Herald,* 16 June 1945, p. 13.
22. *Wall Street Journal,* 26 January 1942, p. 1.
23. Clayton R. Koppes and Gregory D. Black, *Hollywood Goes to War: How Politics, Profits, and Propaganda Shaped World War II Movies* (New York: Free Press, 1987), p. 58–60; *Motion Picture Herald,* 20 June 1942, p. 9.
24. Jowett, *Film, the Democratic Art,* p. 357.
25. *Motion Picture Herald,* 3 January 1942, p. 16; *1946 Film Daily Year Book,* p. 145.
26. *Motion Picture Herald,* 19 September 1942, p. 9.
27. Koppes and Black, *Hollywood Goes to War,* p. 69.
28. *Ibid.,* p. 323.
29. Lingeman, *Don't You Know There's a War On?,* p. 181.
30. *Wall Street Journal,* 29 October 1942, p. 1; *Motion Picture Herald,* 17 October 1942, p. 13.
31. *Motion Picture Herald,* 2 January 1943, p. 8.
32. *Motion Picture Herald,* 7 October 1944, p. 9.
33. *1943 Film Daily Year Book,* pp. 37, 150.
34. *Motion Picture Herald,* 27 March 1943, p. 9; *Motion Picture Herald,* 5 June 1943, p. 28.
35. *Variety,* 5 January 1944, p. 12.
36. *Variety,* 6 May 1942, p. 6.
37. *Motion Picture Herald,* 29 May 1943, p. 22; *Variety,* 15 April 1942, p. 7; *Motion Picture Herald,* 29 May 1943, p. 22.
38. *Motion Picture Herald,* 31 October 1942, p. 28; *Variety,* 11 November 1942, p. 22.
39. *Variety,* 18 October 1944, p. 6.
40. Lingeman, *Don't You Know There's a War On?,* p. 184.
41. *Motion Picture Herald,* 21 February 1942, p. 8. See also "Beachhead Bijou," in *Look* magazine, *From Movie Lot to Beachhead,* pp. 104–105.
42. *Motion Picture Herald,* 13 January 1945, p. 9.
43. *1943 Film Daily Year Book,* p. 77; *Motion Picture Herald,* 22 January 1944, p. 9; *Motion Picture Herald,* 27 October 1945, p. 8. These figures contradict a common assumption of the period, expressed in *Look's From Movie Lot to Beachhead:* "War movies do not appeal to fighting men, nor do Westerns. Men who have seen real shooting do not care for the synthetic variety," (p. 105).
44. *Motion Picture Herald,* 22 January 1944, p. 38.
45. *Look* magazine, *From Movie Lot to Beachhead,* p. 104.
46. *Motion Picture Herald,* 16 May 1942, p. 9.
47. *Variety,* 7 April 1943, p. 3.
48. *Motion Picture Herald,* 29 July 1944, p. 9.
49. *Motion Picture Herald,* 13 January 1945, p. 9.
50. *Motion Picture Herald,* 6 October 1945, p. 8; *1946 Film Daily Year Book,* pp. 147–148.
51. *Look* magazine, *From Movie Lot to Beachhead,* pp. 82–83; Jowett, *Film, the Democratic Art,* pp. 314–315.
52. *Variety,* 12 April 1944, p. 10; *Motion Picture Herald,* 6 October 1945, p. 61; *1946 Film Daily Year Book,* p. 148.
53. *Motion Picture Herald,* 30 October 1943, p. 9.
54. Otto Friedrich, *City of Nets* (New York: Harper & Row, 1987), p. 108.
55. *Motion Picture Herald,* 2 October 1943, p. 8.
56. *Motion Picture Herald,* 14 March 1942, p. 8.
57. *Motion Picture Herald,* 11 May 1942, p. 65; *Motion Picture Herald,* 8 August 1942, p. 13.
58. *Variety,* 8 April 1942, p. 5.
59. *Motion Picture Herald,* 29 August 1942, p. 31.
60. *Variety,* 6 January 1943, p. 47.
61. *Look* magazine, *From Movie Lot to Beachhead,* p. 204.
62. *1946 Film Daily Year Book,* pp. 145–146; *Look* magazine, *From Movie Lot to Beachhead,* p. 205.

63. *Variety,* 15 April 1942, p. 7.

64. *Variety,* 8 April 1942, p. 9.

65. *Variety,* 18 November 1942, p. 5.

66. *Motion Picture Herald,* 15 July 1943, p. 13.

67. *Motion Picture Herald,* 27 June 1942, p. 29; *Motion Picture Herald,* 11 July 1942, p. 8; *Motion Picture Herald,* 18 July 1942, p. 9; *Motion Picture Herald,* 15 August 1942, p. 9.

68. *Variety,* 5 September 1945, p. 7. Note that, according to the *1944 Film Daily Year Book* (p. 49), the average run of a Hollywood feature still was only four and a half days.

69. *Motion Picture Herald,* 30 October 1943, p. 12.

70. *Variety,* 3 January 1945, p. 1.

71. *Motion Picture Herald,* 16 June 1945, p. 13; *Variety,* 26 September 1945, p. 9. Among the pictures scheduled for reissue in 1945–1946 were NAUGHTY MARIETTA (1935), WATERLOO BRIDGE (1940), NORTHWEST MOUNTED POLICE (1940), CALL OF THE WILD (1935), IMITATION OF LIFE (1934), AIR FORCE (1943), and THIS GUN FOR HIRE (1942). Republic also announced plans to reissue seven Gene Autry films first released between 1935 and 1940.

72. *Variety,* 3 May 1944, p. 3; *Variety,* 14 June 1944, p. 3.

73. *Variety,* 1 August 1945, p. 5.

74. *1941 Film Daily Year Book,* p. 41; *Variety,* 6 December 1944, p. 5; *1946 Film Daily Year Book,* p. 51. The number of houses playing double bills increased from a reported 10,350 in 1941 (60 percent of the theaters in operation) to 12,280 (64 percent) in 1945.

75. *1942 Film Daily Year Book,* p. 49; *1946 Film Daily Year Book,* p. 49.

76. *1943 Film Daily Year Book,* p. 48; *1944 Film Daily Year Book,* p. 47; *1946 Film Daily Year Book,* p. 49.

77. *Motion Picture Herald,* 8 April 1944, p. 34.

78. Joel W. Finler, *The Hollywood Story* (New York: Crown, 1988), p. 15; Jowett, *Film, the Democratic Art,* p. 475.

79. *Variety,* 6 January 1943, pp. 1, 58.

80. *Variety,* 5 January 1944, p. 9.

81. *Variety,* 8 March 1944, p. 7.

82. *Variety,* 29 November 1944, p. 1 (on Broadway stage); *Variety,* 13 December 1944, p. 1 (on the music industry).

83. *Motion Picture Herald,* 29 September 1945, p. 9.

84. *Motion Picture Herald,* 3 February 1945, p. 53.

85. *Motion Picture Herald,* 10 June 1944, p. 9.

86. *Variety,* 4 November 1942, p. 7; *Motion Picture Herald,* 7 November 1942, p. 8.

87. *Motion Picture Herald,* 28 November 1942, p. 29.

88. *Motion Picture Herald,* 27 May 1944, p. 8; *1946 Film Daily Year Book,* pp. 649–670.

89. *Variety,* 11 October 1944, p. 3.

90. Marcia Landy, *British Genres: Cinema and Society, 1930–1960* (Princeton, N.J.: Princeton University Press, 1991), pp. 25–31.

91. *Variety,* 11 October 1944, p. 3; *Motion Picture Herald,* 27 January 1945, p. 8.

92. *Motion Picture Herald,* 19 June 1943, p. 29; *Motion Picture Herald,* 27 February 1944, p. 26; *Variety,* 17 May 1944, p. 3; *Motion Picture Herald,* 4 August 1945, p. 22.

93. *1946 Film Daily Year Book,* pp. 649–651.

94. *Variety,* 9 August 1944, p. 3. There were 4,579 theaters in South America (including 1,680 in Argentina, the largest market) and 2,368 theaters in Central America (including 1,410 in Mexico); *1946 Film Daily Year Book,* p. 49.

95. On output, see *Motion Picture Herald,* 6 January 1943, p. 27; *Variety,* 19 April 1944, p. 18; *Motion Picture Herald,* 5 August 1944, p. 24. On strikes and labor discord, see *Motion Picture Herald,* 19 August 1944, p. 54; *Variety,* 16 August 1944, p. 13; *Motion Picture Herald,* 3 March 1945, p. 9.

96. Charles Ramirez Berg, *Cinema of Solitude* (Austin: University of Texas Press, 1992), pp. 14–15.

97. *Variety,* 26 July 1944, p. 19.

98. *Motion Picture Herald,* 29 August 1944, p. 8; *Motion Picture Herald,* 20 May 1944, p. 9; *Motion Picture Herald,* 27 January 1945, p. 9.

99. *Motion Picture Herald,* 29 April 1944, p. 8; *Motion Picture Herald,* 20 May 1944, p. 8; *Variety,* 30 August 1944, p. 15; *Motion Picture Herald,* 5 August 1944, p. 24.

100. *Motion Picture Herald*, 10 March 1945, p. 8.
101. *Motion Picture Herald*, 16 September 1944, p. 14.
102. *Motion Picture Herald*, 11 February 1939, p. 28.
103. *1944 Film Daily Year Book*, p. 67; *Motion Picture Herald*, 16 January 1947, p. 17.
104. *Motion Picture Herald*, 7 August 1943, p. 17.
105. *Variety*, 24 January 1945, p. 1. The view was voiced by Ulrich Bell.
106. *Variety*, 24 January 1945, p. 3; *Variety*, 21 March 1945, p. 1; *Motion Picture Herald*, 28 July 1945, p. 28; *Variety*, 1 August 1945, p. 3; *Motion Picture Herald*, 11 August 1945, p. 9; *Variety*, 22 August 1945, p. 13.
107. *Motion Picture Herald*, 28 July 1945, p. 28.
108. *1946 Film Daily Year Book*, p. 53.
109. *Motion Picture Herald*, 7 April 1945, p. 8; *Motion Picture Herald*, 28 April 1945, p. 8.
110. *Motion Picture Herald*, 29 September 1945, p. 9; *Motion Picture Herald*, 6 October 1945, p. 9.
111. *Variety*, 19 December 1945, p. 1.
112. *Motion Picture Herald*, 7 February 1942, p. 8; *Motion Picture Herald*, 4 April 1942, p. 17.
113. *1942 Film Daily Year Book*, p. 79.
114. *Motion Picture Herald*, 23 May 1942, pp. 13–14.
115. Quoted in *Variety*, 19 August 1942, p. 5.
116. *Motion Picture Herald*, 22 August 1942, p. 12.
117. Quoted in *Motion Picture Herald*, 2 January 1943, p. 9.
118. *Motion Picture Herald*, 20 February 1943, p. 9.
119. *Motion Picture Herald*, 12 June 1943, p. 17.
120. *Motion Picture Herald*, 15 May 1943, p. 17; *Motion Picture Herald*, 30 September 1944, p. 8.
121. *Variety*, 20 January 1943, p. 7.
122. *Motion Picture Herald*, 1 January 1944, p. 8. Decisions on these cases ran about 50–50 between distributor and exhibitor.
123. *Motion Picture Herald*, 9 September 1944, p. 13.
124. *Motion Picture Herald*, 30 September 1944, p. 8.
125. *Motion Picture Herald*, 1 January 1944, p. 27.
126. *Motion Picture Herald*, 19 February 1944, p. 15.
127. *Variety*, 13 December 1944, p. 3.
128. See, for example, *Motion Picture Herald*, 24 October 1942, p. 23; and *Motion Picture Herald*, 15 April 1944, p. 13.
129. *Motion Picture Herald*, 31 March 1945, p. 20.
130. *Motion Picture Herald*, 2 June 1945, p. 9.
131. *Motion Picture Herald*, 13 October 1945, pp. 15, 18.
132. *Motion Picture Herald*, 24 November 1945, p. 16; *Variety*, 21 November 1945, p. 11.
133. *Variety*, 19 December 1945, p. 1; see also *Motion Picture Herald*, 22 December 1945, p. 23.
134. David Prindle, *The Politics of Glamour* (Madison: University of Wisconsin Press, 1988), p. 39.
135. For figures on IATSE and CSU membership, see *Variety*, 3 January 1945, p. 41; *Variety*, 14 March 1945; and Friedrich, *City of Nets*, p. 247. Reported figures tend to vary widely (the very point, of course, of the jurisdictional conflicts); some saw CSU by 1945 as reaching a stage of near-parity with the IATSE.
136. *Variety*, 3 January 1945, p. 41.
137. *Variety*, 9 February 1944, p. 8; *Motion Picture Herald*, 26 February 1944, p. 9.
138. *Variety*, 26 April 1944, p. 1.
139. *Variety*, 5 July 1944, p. 3; *Motion Picture Herald*, 8 July 1944, p. 29.
140. *Variety*, 20 December 1944, p. 4. The tally was 1,451 votes for SPU to SAG's 456.
141. *Motion Picture Herald*, 6 January 1945, p. 46; Prindle, *The Politics of Glamour*, p. 38.
142. *Motion Picture Herald*, 14 October 1944, p. 39.
143. *Variety*, 3 January 1945, p. 41.
144. *Variety*, 14 March 1945, p. 1; *Motion Picture Herald*, 17 March 1945, p. 16; *1946 Film Daily Year Book*, p. 81.
145. *Variety*, 6 June 1945, p. 8.
146. *Motion Picture Herald*, 2 June 1945, p. 25; *Motion Picture Herald*, 27 October 1945, p. 13.
147. Friedrich, *City of Nets*, p. 248; *Variety*, 11 July 1945, p. 12; Prindle, *The Politics of Glamour*, p. 39.

148. *Motion Picture Herald,* 18 August 1945, p. 19.

149. *Motion Picture Herald,* 20 October 1945, p. 35.

150. Friedrich, *City of Nets,* p. 249; *Motion Picture Herald,* 27 October 1945, p. 13.

151. *Motion Picture Herald,* 27 October 1945, p. 13; *Variety,* 31 October 1945, p. 2; *Motion Picture Herald,* 10 November 1945, p. 40.

152. *Variety,* 9 January 1946, p. 79.

CHAPTER 6 (The Hollywood Studio System, 1942–1945)

1. Richard Lingeman, *Don't You Know There's a War On? The American Home Front, 1941–1945* (New York: Putnam's, 1990), p. 181. For an excellent survey of Hollywood's initial response to Pearl Harbor, see ch. 1, "Prologue to War," in Editors of *Look* magazine, *From Movie Lot to Beachhead: The Motion Picture Goes to War and Prepares for the Future* (Garden City, N.Y.: Doubleday, 1945), pp. 4–25.

2. Lingeman, *Don't You Know There's a War On?,* p. 178; Leonard Mosley, *Zanuck: The Rise and Fall of Hollywood's Last Tycoon* (Boston: Little, Brown, 1984), p. 179.

3. Joel W. Finler, *The Hollywood Story* (New York: Crown, 1988), p. 280. The Big Five released 1,268 pictures in the five prewar years, and only 788 from 1942 to 1946. The Little Three during these two periods released 615 and 607, respectively.

4. *Ibid.,* pp. 31, 286–287. For a detailed accounting of studio revenues and profits, see appendix 4.

5. According to the U.S. government (in statistics compiled in its antitrust suits), the majors' theater holdings on the eve of World War II were: Paramount, 1,273; Warner Bros., 557; 20th Century–Fox, 538; RKO, 132; Loew's/MGM, 122.

6. *Motion Picture Herald,* 9 May 1942, p. 17.

7. *Variety,* 12 August 1942, p. 5.

8. For figures on the 1942–1943 season, see *Variety,* 2 September 1942, p. 3. According to *Variety* (3 November 1943, p. 5), for the 1943–1944 season Fox scheduled only 27 pictures on a total budget of $36 million; Paramount and MGM each planned to spend $40 million on about 30 pictures; and Warners budgeted 24 pictures at $30 million.

9. *1946 Film Daily Year Book,* summary, p. 43.

10. *Variety,* 28 October 1942, p. 5.

11. According to a study cited in *Motion Picture Herald* (11 November 1944, p. 41), the studios at that time were equipped to produce over 700 features per year; the output for the previous year was less than 400.

12. For figures on stockpiling, see *Variety,* 22 April 1942, p. 7; *Variety,* 25 February 1942, p. 5; *Motion Picture Herald,* 22 August 1942, p. 33; *Motion Picture Herald,* 20 June 1942, p. 14; *Variety,* 22 July 1942, p. 5; *Variety,* 28 October 1942, p. 5; *Variety,* 30 December 1942, p. 5; *Motion Picture Herald,* 27 February 1942, p. 13; *Variety,* 27 October 1943, p. 5; *Motion Picture Herald,* 12 February 1944, p. 13; *Motion Picture Herald,* 26 August 1944, p. 23. Note that the figures vary widely owing to two factors: the way companies defined a "completed" film (some still in the later stages of post-production were included among stockpiled films); and the relatively high concentration of releases during the holidays (Thanksgiving to New Year's).

13. *Variety,* 7 March 1945, p. 9; *Motion Picture Herald,* 26 May 1945, p. 13.

14. *Variety,* 21 November 1945, p. 3.

15. *Variety,* 29 April 1942, p. 22; Tino Balio, *United Artists: The Company Built by the Stars* (Madison: University of Wisconsin Press, 1976), pp. 192–193.

16. *Motion Picture Herald,* 29 January 1944, p. 33.

17. Balio, *United Artists,* p. 188.

18. *Ibid.,* p. 189.

19. Todd McCarthy and Charles Flynn, eds., *Kings of the B's* (New York: Dutton, 1975), p. 32. Monogram's wartime net income was in the $100,000–200,000 range.

20. *Variety,* 5 January 1944, p. 55.

21. *Variety,* 12 April 1944, p. 7.

22. *Variety,* 9 January 1946, p. 36.

23. McCarthy and Flynn, *Kings of the B's,* p. 24; *Variety,* 12 April 1944, p. 7; *Variety,* 9 January 1946, p. 36. The definition appeared in the latter piece, which recapped 1945 trends and ran under the headline "'Exploitation Pictures' Paid Off Big For Majors, Also Indie Producers."

24. See Wheeler Dixon, ed., *Producers Releasing Corporation: A Comprehensive Filmography and History* (Jefferson, N.C.: McFarland, 1986).

25. See obituary in *Motion Picture Herald,* 21 March 1942, p. 9. Kent's death has been erroneously (and frequently) reported elsewhere as occurring in 1941.

26. Douglas Gomery, *The Hollywood Studio System* (New York: St. Martin's Press, 1986), p. 89.

27. *1943 Film Daily Year Book,* p. 53; see also Gomery, *The Hollywood Studio System,* pp. 131–132.

28. *Motion Picture Herald,* 9 July 1942, p. 23; *Variety,* 4 March 1942, p. 5.

29. *Variety,* 4 March 1942, p. 5.

30. Jack Warner to Foy, 6 September 1941 (releasing Foy from contract of 6 June 1938), Foy legal file, Warner Archive, USC.

31. Agreement between Warner Bros. and Wallis of 12 January 1942 (releasing Wallis from contract of 27 June 1935); new Wallis contract of 2 February 1942; both in Wallis legal file, Warner Archive, USC. Hellinger contract of 26 February 1942, Warner Archive, USC. Hawks contract of 12 February 1942, Warner Legal Collection, UW—M.

32. *Variety,* 1 April 1942, p. 6.

33. *The Screen Writer,* July 1945, p. 40. Fox reportedly had 42 under contract, Columbia 39, Warners 34, and Paramount 33.

34. *Variety,* 18 February 1942, p. 3.

35. There was considerable disagreement between Welles and Chaplin about the extent of Welles's contributions to both the script and the finished product. See, for example, Chaplin's *My Autobiography* (New York: Simon & Schuster, 1964), pp. 418–419, and Barbara Leaming, *Orson Welles* (New York: Penguin, 1985), pp. 219–221.

36. *Variety,* 16 February 1944, p. 7.

37. Balio, *United Artists,* pp. 172–174, 186–187; John Douglas Eames, *The MGM Story* (New York: Crown, 1975), p. 203.

38. *Motion Picture Herald,* 13 March 1943, p. 8. Note that FANTASIA saw only limited release on a roadshow basis in 1940 but was not put into general release by RKO until 1942. See also Doherty, *Projections of War: Hollywood, American Culture, and World War II* (New York: Columbia University Press, 1993), p. 68.

39. Ernest Borneman, "Rebellion in Hollywood: A Study in Motion Picture Finance," *Harper's,* October 1946, pp. 337, 338–339. When he wrote the article, Borneman was director of foreign distribution for the National Film Board of Canada.

40. Balio, *United Artists,* p. 190.

41. On Cagney, see Kevin Hagopian, "Declarations of Independence: A History of Cagney Productions," *Velvet Light Trap* 22 (1986), pp. 16–32. On Goldwyn, see A. Scott Berg, *Goldwyn: A Biography* (New York: Knopf, 1989), pp. 381, 545.

42. Borneman, "Rebellion in Hollywood," p. 339.

43. *Variety,* 5 January 1944, p. 13; *Motion Picture Herald,* 29 January 1944, p. 33.

44. *Motion Picture Herald,* 11 November 1944, p. 29; *Variety,* 1 November 1944, p. 3.

45. Wanger's contract of 10 April 1942 for ARABIAN NIGHTS became the model for future Universal deals. Wanger Collection, UW—M.

46. Wanger signed the five-picture deal with Universal on 6 April 1945, with each picture set up on roughly the same terms as the earlier contracts. The Diana contracts were signed 13 March 1945; Wanger Collection, UW—M. For a detailed treatment of both the formation of Diana Productions and the making of SCARLET STREET, see Matthew Bernstein, "Fritz Lang, Incorporated," *Velvet Light Trap* 22 (1986), pp. 33–52. See also Bernstein, *Walter Wanger: Hollywood Independent* (Berkeley: University of California Press, 1994), pp. 197–216.

47. *Variety,* 9 January 1945, p. 77.

48. Lewton to Selznick, 10 December 1942, Lewton correspondence file, Selznick Collection, UT.

49. *Variety,* 14 July 1943, p. 5.

50. *Variety,* 28 April 1943, p. 5; *Variety,* 14 July 1943, p. 5.

51. Contract of 12 January 1942 (to take effect on 2 February 1942), Wallis legal file, Warner Archive, USC. Regarding Warners' central-producer setup, note that Wallis's contract stated that "for several years past" he had been "the executive having general charge and supervision of substantially all the Class-A motion picture photoplays produced by the Company."

52. Contract of 12 February 1942, THE BIG SLEEP file, Warner Legal Collection, UW—M.

53. On Hellinger's departure in 1941, see Hellinger to Jack Warner, 17 February 1941. See also new contract of 26 February 1942. Both in Hellinger legal file, Warner Archive, USC.

54. See agreement of 10 June 1943 between Davis and Warners in A STOLEN LIFE legal file, Warner Legal Collection, UW—M. A STOLEN LIFE (1946) was the one picture produced under the auspices of B.D. Inc.

55. *Variety,* 17 May 1944, p. 3; *Variety,* 25 May 1944, p. 3; *Variety,* 21 June 1944, n.p.

56. *Variety,* 16 August 1944, p. 1.

57. Schary legal file, Selznick Collection, UT.

58. See the synopses of the "Rapf Group" and the "Rapf-Schary unit" producers meetings, 3 April 1941–17 November 1941; Schary Papers, UW—M.

59. *NYTFR,* 4 April 1942.

60. Recapitulations of 2 June 1942 and 4 March 1943, MGM Unit 43 (the Rapf-Schary unit), Schary Papers, UW—M.

61. See minutes of MGM executive committee meetings, 20 January 1943 and 9 February 1943, Schary Papers, UW—M.

62. Schary legal file, Selznick Collection, UT.

63. Schary to Selznick, 8 December 1943, Selznick Collection, UT. See also *Variety,* 5 April 1944, p. 2.

64. Selznick to Schary, 1 March 1944 (on title suggestion); Selznick to Schary and Dan O'Shea, 20 July 1944 (on title test); both in Selznick Collection, UT.

65. *Variety,* 19 July 1944, p. 34.

66. Vanguard Films income statement of 21 June 1946, I'LL BE SEEING YOU production file, Schary Papers, UW—M. Production information on the film also is included in both the Schary Papers at UW—M and the Selznick Collection, UT. Rogers had a profit-sharing arrangement as well; her share came to $162,000.

67. *Variety,* 25 April 1945, p. 3.

68. See agreements of 31 May 1947, 11 September 1947, 13 November 1945, et al. between Vanguard (Selznick) and RKO, Selznick Collection, UT.

69. *Variety,* 9 September 1942, p. 15; *Motion Picture Herald,* 10 April 1943, p. 15. *Advertising Age* cited in the *Variety* story.

70. *Variety,* 14 April 1943, p. 7.

71. *Motion Picture Herald,* 25 September 1943, p. 9.

72. *Motion Picture Herald,* 14 April 1944, p. 19.

73. *Variety,* 5 January 1944, p. 54. The theory of compensating production values was made graphically clear in the headline to this story: "$7,500,500 in Literary Buys by Pix As Offset to Loss of Male Stars."

74. *Variety,* 3 January 1945, p. 30.

75. See YANKEE DOODLE DANDY file, Warner Legal Collection, UWM.

76. Lingeman, *Don't You Know There's a War On?,* pp. 285–286; *Motion Picture Herald,* 4 July 1942, p. 50.

77. *Variety,* 3 June 1942, p. 1; *Variety,* 5 January 1944, p. 14.

78. *NYTFR,* 3 March 43. In his review of the film, Bosley Crowther provides a detailed account of the story's rather odd journey from page to screen.

79. *Motion Picture Herald,* 3 April 1943, p. 14.

80. *Ibid.; Variety,* 4 January 1944, p. 14.

81. *Variety,* 5 January 1944, p. 54.

82. *Ibid.,* p. 14.

83. *Motion Picture Herald,* 13 January 1945, p. 27.

84. *Motion Picture Herald,* 1 April 1944, p. 9.

85. *Variety,* 3 January 1945, p. 30.

86. *Motion Picture Herald,* 17 March 1945, p. 9.

87. *Variety,* 13 June 1945, p. 3; *Variety,* 4 July 1945, p. 3.

88. *Variety,* 14 November 1945, p. 1.

89. *Variety,* 5 January 1944, p. 54.

90. *Motion Picture Herald,* 8 May 1943, p. 9.

91. Shannon James Kelley, "Gallup Goes Hollywood: Motion Picture Audience Research in the 1940s" (M.A. thesis, University of Texas—Austin, 1989), pp. 2, 12.

92. This information is culled from various ARI reports in the Selznick Collection, UT. See also *Variety*, 5 August 1942, p. 3; *Variety*, 1 September 1943, p. 1.

93. Kelley, "Gallup Goes Hollywood," p. 101.

94. *1946 Film Daily Year Book*, p. 43.

95. On movie promotion and particularly the role of pressbooks, see Maria LaPlace, "Producing and Consuming the Woman's Film: Discursive Struggle in *Now, Voyager*," in *Home Is Where the Heart Is: Studies in Melodrama and the Woman's Film*, Christina Gledhill, ed. (London: BFI, 1987), pp. 138–166; Barbara Klinger, "Much Ado About Excess: Genre, Mise-en-Scène, and the Woman in *Written on the Wind*," *Wide Angle* 11 (1989), p. 4; Mary Beth Haralovich, "The Proletarian Woman's Film of the 1930s: Contending with Censorship and Entertainment," *Screen* 31, no. 2 (Summer 1990), pp. 172–187. On early motion picture promotion, see Janet Staiger, "Announcing Wares, Winning Patrons, Voicing Ideals: Thinking About the History and Theory of Film Advertising," *Cinema Journal* 29, no. 3 (Spring 1990), pp. 3–31. On commercial tie-ins, see Jane Gaines, "The *Queen Christina* Tie-ups: Convergence of Show Window and Screen," *Quarterly Review of Film and Video* 11, no. 1 (1989), pp. 35–60.

96. Mary Beth Haralovich, "Mandates of Good Taste," *Wide Angle* 6, no. 2 (1984), pp. 50–57. For more information on studio still photographers and their work on poster art and publicity, see Haralovich, "Film Advertising, the Film Industry, and the Pin-up: The Industry's Accommodations to Social Forces in the 1940s," *Current Research in Film*, vol. 1, ed. Bruce Austin (New York: Ablex, 1985), 127–164.

97. All references to the MILDRED PIERCE pressbook materials are from the MILDRED PIERCE pressbook, Warner Archive, USC.

98. Mary Beth Haralovich, "Advertising Heterosexuality," *Screen* 23, no. 2 (July–August 1982), pp. 50–60; see also Klinger, "Much Ado About Excess," pp. 20–21.

99. LaPlace, "Producing and Consuming the Woman's Film," p. 141. In his study of Edith Head, Robert Gustafson finds that clothing is not often explicitly modeled after costumes; "The Power of the Screen: The Influence of Edith Head's Film Designs on the Retail Fashion Market," *Velvet Light Trap* 12 (1982), pp. 8–15. For more on fashion and film, see Jane Gaines and Charlotte Herzog, eds., *Fabrications: Costume and the Female Body* (New York: Routledge, 1990), esp. Maureen Turim, "Designing Women: The Emergence of the New Sweetheart Line," pp. 212–228.

100. In his biography of Crawford, Bob Thomas discusses her hard work on MILDRED PIERCE and argues that the studio early on realized the potential of the Crawford performance. Thomas reports that a publicity campaign for an Academy Award for Crawford was launched when "Wald sensed that something extraordinary was happening" during production. *Joan Crawford* (New York: Simon & Schuster, 1978), pp. 145–149.

101. This explanation of the actress is akin to what Robert Allen and Douglas Gomery found in their study of how Crawford's star image developed over the decades. She was a "self-made star" with the "strength of character to overcome all material obstacles" and a "regenerating star [with the] unique power to transform herself to meet demands"; *Film History: Theory and Practice* (New York: Knopf, 1978), pp. 178–181. Richard Dyer argues that "stars are examples of the way people live their relation to production in a capitalist society. . . . [T]hey articulate a dominant experience of work itself under capitalism." *Heavenly Bodies: Film Stars and Society* (New York: St. Martin's Press, 1986), pp. 6–8.

102. *Los Angeles Times*, 8 October 1945, p. 9; 11 October 1945, sect. 2, p. 8; 12 October 1945, sect. 2, p. 9.

103. *Los Angeles Times*, 17 October 1945, sect. 1, p. 11; 26 October 1945, sect. 2, p. 3.

104. *Chicago Tribune*, 9 December 1945, p. 3; 30 December 1945, sect. 1, pp. 1, 6; 16 December 1945, p. 6 (graphic); 25 December 1945, p. 25.

CHAPTER 7 (Wartime Stars, Genres, and Production Trends)

1. Report of 8 December 1941, CASABLANCA production file, Warner Archive, USC. For an excellent analysis of the story and script development of the film, see ch. 9 in Rudy Behlmer, *America's Favorite Movies* (New York: Ungar, 1982), which is devoted to the film. Wallis recalls first reading the play on 12 December. For Wallis's account, see Hal Wallis and Charles Higham, *Starmaker: The Autobiography of Hal Wallis* (New York: Macmillan, 1980), pp. 83–93.

2. Irene Lee's role in both pursuing and securing the project is detailed by Aljean Harmetz in *Round up the Usual Subjects: The Making of* Casablanca (New York: Hyperion, 1992), pp. 17–18. Harmetz also states flatly that "Hal Wallis was the creative force behind *Casablanca*," noting "how thoroughly he shaped the movie, from the quality of the lighting to the exact details of the costumes" (p. 29).

3. Dana Polan, *Power and Paranoia* (New York: Columbia University Press, 1986).

4. The Editors of *Look* magazine, *Movie Lot to Beachhead: The Motion Picture Goes to War and Prepares for the Future* (Garden City, N.Y.: Doubleday, 1945), pp. 70, 77.

5. The 1,500 figure is from SAG; *Variety*, 6 January 1943, p. 58. *Look* put the total of male stars at 49; *Movie Lot to Beachhead*, p. 58. See also *Motion Picture Herald*, 29 August 1942, p. 8; *Variety*, 7 October 1942, p. 1.

6. On Gable, see *Motion Picture Herald*, 16 October 1942, p. 8; on Stewart, et al., see *Motion Picture Herald*, 17 June 1944, p. 9; *Look* magazine, *Movie Lot to Beachhead*, pp. 60–71.

7. *Motion Picture Herald*, 13 November 1943, p. 8; *Motion Picture Herald*, 1 April 1944, p. 9; *Variety*, 13 December 1944, p. 3; *Variety*, 7 February 1945, p. 3. De Havilland's case went to the appellate state supreme court in late 1944 and early 1945. Prior to that judgment, the studios simply added the time an actor was on suspension to the "end" of the contract period, thus making it impossible to wait out one's contract.

8. John Taylor, *Storming the Magic Kingdom* (New York: Knopf, 1987), p. vii; *Motion Picture Herald*, 13 November 1943, p. 9; *Motion Picture Herald*, 15 January 1944, p. 8.

9. See "Foxhole Circuit," in *Look* magazine, *Movie Lot to Beachhead*, pp. 82–85.

10. *Motion Picture Herald*, 6 March 1943, p. 8; *Variety*, 10 March 1943, p. 21; *Motion Picture Herald*, 11 March 1944, p. 8.

11. The top 25 stars for each of these years were as follows:

	1942	**1943**
1.	Abbott and Costello	Betty Grable
2.	Clark Gable	Bob Hope
3.	Gary Cooper	Abbott and Costello
4.	Mickey Rooney	Bing Crosby
5.	Bob Hope	Gary Cooper
6.	James Cagney	Greer Garson
7.	Gene Autry	Humphrey Bogart
8.	Betty Grable	James Cagney
9.	Greer Garson	Mickey Rooney
10.	Spencer Tracy	Clark Gable
11.	Dorothy Lamour	Judy Garland
12.	Bing Crosby	Alice Faye
13.	Tyrone Power	Bette Davis
14.	Walter Pidgeon	Tyrone Power
15.	Bette Davis	Alan Ladd
16.	Ann Sheridan	Cary Grant
17.	Errol Flynn	Errol Flynn
18.	Wallace Beery	Wallace Beery
19.	Judy Garland	Spencer Tracy
20.	Red Skelton	Dorothy Lamour
21.	John Payne	Jean Arthur
22.	Rita Hayworth	Walter Pidgeon
23.	Lana Turner	Claudette Colbert
24.	Cary Grant	Red Skelton
25.	Humphrey Bogart	Lana Turner

	1944	**1945**
1.	Bing Crosby	Bing Crosby
2.	Gary Cooper	Van Johnson
3.	Bob Hope	Greer Garson
4.	Betty Grable	Betty Grable
5.	Spencer Tracy	Spencer Tracy

6.	Greer Garson	Bogart/Cooper
7.	Humphrey Bogart	Bob Hope
8.	Abbott and Costello	Judy Garland
9.	Cary Grant	Margaret O'Brien
10.	Bette Davis	Roy Rogers
11.	Wallace Beery	Abbott and Costello
12.	Dorothy Lamour	Betty Hutton
13.	Walter Pidgeon	Ingrid Bergman
14.	Judy Garland	Bette Davis
15.	Faye/Skelton	Alan Ladd
16.	Ginger Rogers	Dane Clark
17.	Mickey Rooney	Joseph Cotten
18.	Claudette Colbert	Claudette Colbert
19.	Irene Dunne	Walter Pidgeon
20.	O'Brien/Cagney	Fred MacMurray
21.	Barry Fitzgerald	Danny Kaye
22.	Roy Rogers	Gregory Peck
23.	Betty Hutton	Ginger Rogers
24.	MacMurray/Bergman	John Wayne
25.	Deanna Durbin	Mickey Rooney

12. *Motion Picture Herald,* 29 January 1944, p. 9; *Motion Picture Herald,* 23 June 1945, p. 8.

13. For the FOR WHOM THE BELL TOLLS deals, see the Ingrid Bergman contract of 6 August 1942 and the deal memo of 10 October 1942, Bergman legal file, Selznick Collection, UT. For the SARATOGA TRUNK deals, see the 8 April 1942 deal between Warners and Goldwyn for Sam Wood, and the contracts of 22 February 1943 (for Bergman) and 23 February 1943 (for Cooper), SARATOGA TRUNK legal file, Warner Legal Collection, UW—M.

14. *Variety,* 3 January 1945, p. 1.

15. IN SOCIETY file, Universal Collection, USC.

16. *Motion Picture Herald,* 3 April 1943, p. 29; *Motion Picture Herald,* 11 December 1943, p. 9; *Motion Picture Herald,* 18 November 1944, p. 8.

17. *Variety,* 8 April 1942, p. 7.

18. *Motion Picture Herald,* 27 January 1945, p. 8.

19. Contracts of 7 June 1943 and 10 June 1943, Davis legal file; Warner Archive, USC.

20. Stanwyck contract of 16 December 1943, CHRISTMAS IN CONNECTICUT file, Warner Legal Collection, UW—M.

21. Russell contract of 3 April 1944, ROUGHLY SPEAKING file, Warner Legal Collection, UW—M.

22. Crawford contract of 10 April 1944, MILDRED PIERCE file, Warner Legal Collection, UW—M.

23. Wald casting memo of 15 May 1944, MILDRED PIERCE file, Warner Legal Collection, USC.

24. Bogart contract of 3 January 1942 in PASSAGE TO MARSEILLES file; Cagney contract of 7 July 1939 in THE BRIDE CAME COD file; 1 July 1941 modification of Flynn contract of 17 August 1938 in EDGE OF DARKNESS file; all in Warner Legal Collection, UW—M.

25. Contract of 31 December 1941, Warners story file, Warner Legal Collection, UW—M.

26. Bergman contract of 24 April 1942, CASABLANCA file, Warner Legal Collection, UW—M.

27. Wallis and Higham, *Starmaker,* p. 91.

28. Contracts of 20 October 1943 and 8 November 1943, TO HAVE AND HAVE NOT file, Warner Legal Collection, UW—M.

29. Hawks signed "Betty Bacal" to a personal contract in May 1943 for $100 per week; Warners picked up her contract (as "Lauren Bacall") in early 1944, while TO HAVE AND HAVE NOT was still in development. In 1945, during production of THE BIG SLEEP, Warners renegotiated her contract—now as "Betty Bogart"—and increased her salary to $1,000 per week. See Betty Bacal contract of 3 May 1943 and Lauren Bacall contract of 3 May 1944 in TO HAVE AND HAVE NOT file; Betty Bogart contract of 26 July 1945, THE BIG SLEEP file; Warner Legal Collection, UW—M.

30. See "The Hawksian Woman," in Joseph McBride, *Hawks on Hawks* (Berkeley: University of California Press, 1982), pp. 98–102.

31. *NYTFR,* 12 October 1944.

32. See drafts of 11 September 1944 and 26 September 1944, THE BIG SLEEP script file, Warner Legal Collection, UW—M.

33. Reprinted in James Agee, *Agee on Film,* vol. 1 (New York: Grossett and Dunlap, 1958), p. 121.

34. Charles K. Feldman to Jack Warner, 16 November 1945, quoted in Rudy Behlmer, ed., *Inside Warner Bros. 1935–1951* (New York: Viking, 1985), pp. 248–249.

35. See, for example, Hawks's description of the adaptation in an interview with Joseph McBride in *Hawks on Hawks,* pp. 103–105. Hawks relates the oft-told anecdote about the writers contacting Chandler about the murder of a particular character (Owen Taylor, Bacall's chauffeur), and Chandler himself admitted that he did not know the identity of the killer.

36. Quoted in Eric Smoodin, *Animating Culture: Hollywood Cartoons from the Sound Era* (New Brunswick, N.J.: Rutgers University Press, 1993), p. 169.

37. See Christopher Finch, *The Art of Walt Disney* (New York: Abrams, 1973), pp. 92, 108.

38. *Motion Picture Herald,* 13 January 1945, p. 28.

39. For a detailed historical treatment of Hollywood animation, see Leonard Maltin, *Of Mice and Magic: A History of American Animated Cartoons* (New York: McGraw-Hill, 1980). See also Mitchell Alan Abney, "The Economical and Institutional Value of Cartoons: A Case History of the Warner Bros. Cartoon Division" (M.A. thesis, University of Texas—Austin, 1996).

40. Maltin, *Of Mice and Magic,* pp. 250–251.

41. *Motion Picture Herald,* 27 October 1945, p. 8.

42. *NYTFR,* 17 June 1943.

43. See Ed Buscombe, *The BFI Companion to the Western* (London: BFI Publishing, 1988), pp. 426–427. There were 110 Westerns out of a total of 488 films made in 1942, 103 of 397 in 1943, 95 of 401 in 1944, and 80 of 350 in 1945.

44. Zanuck first pursued Joseph Cotten for the role of Wilson, but Selznick refused to loan his contract player for the role. See Selznick to Zanuck, 9 August 1943; Zanuck to Selznick, 13 August 1943; both in Selznick Collection, UT.

45. Clayton R. Koppes and Gregory D. Black, *Hollywood Goes to War: How Politics, Profits, and Propaganda Shaped World War II Movies* (New York: Free Press, 1987), pp. 322–324; *Motion Picture Herald,* 16 September 1944, p. 9.

46. On the OWI response, see Koppes and Black, *Hollywood Goes to War,* p. 321; on the army camp prohibition, see *Motion Picture Herald,* 12 August 1944, p. 9.

47. *Motion Picture Herald,* 23 September 1944, p. 46; *Motion Picture Herald,* 30 September 1944, p. 56. Zanuck later claimed the picture lost $2 million; see *Variety,* 20 March 1946, p. 3.

48. *Motion Picture Herald,* 29 May 1943, p. 8; *Motion Picture Herald,* 24 July 1943, p. 8.

49. Linda Williams, "Feminist Film Theory: *Mildred Pierce* and the Second World War," in E. Deidre Pribram, ed., *Female Spectators* (New York: Verso, 1988), pp. 12–29.

50. David A. Cook, *A History of Narrative Film* (New York: Norton, 1981), p. 467; David Bordwell, in David Bordwell, Janet Staiger, and Kristen Thompson, *The Classical Hollywood Cinema: Film Style and Mode of Production to 1960* (New York: Columbia University Press, 1985), p. 76.

51. Robert Sklar, *Movie-Made America: A Cultural History of American Movies* (New York: Random House, 1975), p. 253.

52. Deborah Thomas, "How Hollywood Deals with the Deviant Male," in Ian Cameron, ed., *The Movie Book of Film Noir* (London: Verso, 1992), p. 59. On the issue of *film noir* as a male form, see also Andrea Walsh, *Women's Film and Female Experience* (New York: Praeger, 1984); and Frank Krutnik, *In a Lonely Street: Film Noir, Genre, Masculinity* (New York: Routledge, 1991).

53. Paul Schrader, "Note on *Film Noir,*" *Film Comment,* Spring 1972, p. 16. Note that the critic-turned-filmmaker Schrader developed many *noir* techniques in his own work, most notably perhaps in his script for TAXI DRIVER (1976) and in AMERICAN GIGOLO, which he wrote and directed in 1979.

54. Bordwell, "The Bounds of Difference," pp. 75–76.

55. Cook, *A History of Narrative Film,* pp. 467–468.

56. Breen openly opposed both projects and was particularly critical of Warners' efforts to adapt MILDRED PIERCE. In a letter of 2 February 1944 to J. L. Warner, Breen wrote of the initial studio treatment: "The story contains so many sordid and repellent elements that we feel that the finished picture would not only be highly questionable from the standpoint of the Code, but would, likewise, meet with a great deal of difficulty in its release. . . . In the face of all this, we respectfully suggest that you dismiss this story from any further consideration." MILDRED PIERCE PCA file, Warner Archive, USC.

57. Molly Haskell, *From Reverence to Rape: The Treatment of Women in the Movies* (New York: Holt, Rinehart, & Winston, 1974), pp. 195–196.

58. Thomas Elsaesser, "Tales of Sound and Fury: Observations on the Family Melodrama," *Monogram* 4 (1973), p. 11. For a particularly detailed and illuminating study of the female Gothic cycle during the 1940s, see Diane Waldman, "Horror and Domesticity: The Modern Gothic Romance of the 1940s" (Ph.D. diss., University of Wisconsin, 1981).

59. Raymond Chandler, "The Simple Art of Murder," *Atlantic Monthly*, October 1944, p. 59.

60. Lewis Jacobs, "World War II and the American Film," *Cinema Journal*, Winter 1967–1968, p. 21.

61. Dorothy B. Jones, "The Hollywood War Film: 1942–1944," *Hollywood Quarterly* 1, no. 5 (October 1945), pp. 2–3. Jones's study is cited in Jowett and Jacobs as well. The variance between Shain's and Jones's total release figures for the period is not surprising given inconsistencies between the official and actual release dates.

62. *Variety*, 6 January 1943, p. 58; *Variety*, 4 January 1944, p. 54.

63. Figures are taken from an accounting of Hollywood's leading all-time box-office hits, organized by decade, in *Variety*, 24 February 1996, pp. 168–169.

64. The first reference, according to various sources, was in a Rapf-Schary B picture, A YANK ON BURMA ROAD, which was reviewed in the *New York Times* on 29 January 1942. See also Richard Lingeman, *Don't You Know There's a War On? The American Home Front, 1941–1945* (New York: Putnam's, 1970), p. 176; and Jeanine Basinger, *The World War II Combat Film: Anatomy of a Genre* (New York: Columbia University Press, 1986), pp. 26, 281.

65. Buscombe, *The BFI Companion to the Western*, pp. 243–244; Koppes and Black, *Hollywood Goes to War*, p. 61.

66. *Motion Picture Herald*, 19 September 1942, p. 9.

67. *Variety*, 25 November 1942, p. 7.

68. Dorothy Jones, "Hollywood War Films, 1942–1944," *Hollywood Quarterly* 1 (October 1945), pp. 12–13.

69. Walter Wanger, "The OWI and Motion Pictures," *Public Opinion Quarterly*, Spring 1943, pp. 103–104.

70. Basinger, *The World War II Combat Film*, pp. 30, 37.

71. *NYTFR*, 2 September 1942; *Newsweek*, 13 August 1942, p. 260.

72. Quoted in Koppes and Black, *Hollywood Goes to War*, p. 248.

73. *1944 Film Daily Year Book*, p. 105. The films were RANDOM HARVEST, FOR WHOM THE BELL TOLLS, YANKEE DOODLE DANDY, THIS IS THE ARMY, CASABLANCA, THE HUMAN COMEDY, WATCH ON THE RHINE, IN WHICH WE SERVE, SO PROUDLY WE HAIL, and STAGE DOOR CANTEEN.

74. Basinger, *The World War II Combat Film*, pp. 42, 21–22.

75. *Ibid.*, pp. 37–55.

76. Jacobs, "World War II and the American Film," p. 19; Basinger, *The World War II Combat Film*, p. 37.

77. Basinger, *The World War II Combat Film*, pp. 62–63.

78. James Agee, review in *The Nation*, 8 October 1943, reprinted in *Agee on Film*, vol. 1, p. 53.

79. *1943 Film Daily Year Book*, p. 152; *1944 Film Daily Year Book*, p. 144. The figure for 1943 in the latter is 87.7 percent.

80. *Motion Picture Herald*, 11 September 1943, p. 8.

81. Roger Manvell, *Films and the Second World War* (New York: Delta, 1974), p. 176; *Variety*, 10 June 1942, p. 3; *Motion Picture Herald*, 5 September 1942, p. 8.

82. The figures on fiction and nonfiction war-film output are from Basinger, *The World War II Combat Film*, pp. 281–283. Basinger is among the critics and historians who treat these two forms as variations of the same narrative paradigm.

83. James Agee, "The Best of 1945," *The Nation*, 19 January 1946, reprinted in *Agee on Film*, vol. 1, p. 186.

84. James Agee, review in *The Nation*, 15 September 1945, reprinted in *Agee on Film*, vol. 1, p. 173.

85. Richard Meran Barsam, *Nonfiction Film* (New York: Dutton, 1973), p. 196; *Agee on Film*, vol. 1, p. 186.

86. Manvell, *Films and the Second World War*, p. 190.

87. James Agee, review in *The Nation*, 13 July 1943, reprinted in *Agee on Film*, vol. 1, p. 45.

88. See, for example, *Variety*, 8 August 1945, p. 1; *Motion Picture Herald*, 18 August 1945, p. 19; *Motion Picture Herald*, 8 September 1945, p. 18; *Variety*, 31 October 1945, p. 1; *Motion Picture Herald*, 29 December 1945, p. 9.

89. Behlmer, *Inside Warner Bros.*, p. 165; Wallis and Higham, *Starmaker*, p. 78; *Motion Picture Herald*, 10 October 1942; *Motion Picture Herald*, 6 October 1945; see also Max Wilk, ed., *The Wit and Wisdom of Hollywood* (New York: Atheneum, 1971), pp. 261–262.

90. Contract of 12 January 1942, Wallis legal file, Warner Archive, USC; Howard Hawks contract of 12 February 1942, THE BIG SLEEP file, Warner Legal Collection, UW—M.

91. Dudley Nichols agreement of 25 March 1942 and contract of 9 July 1942, AIR FORCE file, Warner Legal Collection, UW—M. For background on the production, see Wallis and Higham, *Starmaker*, pp. 79–82; and Joseph McBride, *Hawks on Hawks*, pp. 90–93.

92. The location shoot facilitated Hawks's usual practice—which caused continual problems with Wallis—of revising the shooting script during production. In fact, Wallis, as nominal executive producer, ordered Hawks and company back to the studio in August 1942, before they had finished shooting the film. Hawks flatly refused. See Wallis's account in *Starmaker*, pp. 80–81; see also Behlmer, *Inside Warner Bros.*, p. 237. On the production of AIR FORCE, see Koppes and Black, *Hollywood Goes to War*, pp. 78–79.

93. Koppes and Black, *Hollywood Goes to War*, p. 79.

94. Watson agreement in AIR FORCE legal file, Warner Legal Collection, UW—M; box-office figures in *Variety*, 5 January 1944, p. 54.

95. See Ronald Haver, *David O. Selznick's Hollywood* (New York: Knopf, 1980), pp. 333–343, for detailed treatment of the production of SINCE YOU WENT AWAY; see also Rudy Behlmer, *Memo from David O. Selznick* (New York: Viking, 1972), pp. 337–347.

96. James Agee, review in *The Nation*, 25 September 1942, reprinted in *Agee on Film*, vol. 1, p. 51.

97. *NYTFR*, 21 July 1944 .

98. Walsh, *Women's Film and Female Experience*, p. 99.

99. Koppes and Black, *Hollywood Goes to War*, p. 156.

100. *Ibid.*, p. 156.

101. Basinger, *The World War II Combat Film*, p. 44.

CHAPTER 8 (Regulating the Screen)

1. On the controversies over films in the late 1920s and early 1930s and the formation of the PCA, see Richard Maltby, "Censorship, Self-Regulation and the Hays Office," in Tino Balio, *Grand Design: Hollywood as a Modern Business Enterprise, 1930–1939* (New York: Scribner's, 1993); Leonard J. Leff and Jerold L. Simmons, *The Dame in the Kimono* (New York: Grove Weidenfeld, 1990); Lea Jacobs, *The Wages of Sin* (Madison: University of Wisconsin Press, 1991); Gregory D. Black, *Hollywood Censored* (New York: Cambridge University Press, 1994); Steven Vaughn, "Morality and Entertainment: The Origins of the Motion Picture Production Code," *Journal of American History* 77 (1990), 39–65; Kevin Brownlow, *Behind the Mask of Innocence* (New York: Knopf, 1990), ch. 1; and Clayton R. Koppes, "Film Censorship: Beyond the Heroic Interpretation," *American Quarterly* 44 (December 1992), 643–649.

2. Leff and Simmons, *The Dame in the Kimono*, ch. 5.

3. Breen to Hays, 28 March 1941, THE OUTLAW case file, PCA Files, Motion Picture Association of America Files, Margaret Herrick Library, Academy of Motion Picture Arts and Sciences Center for Motion Picture Study, Beverly Hills, Calif. (hereafter PCA Files); Leff and Simmons, *The Dame in the Kimono*, pp. 111–118.

4. Francis S. Harmon to Breen, 15 March 1940 (telegram); Breen to Harmon, 4 April 1940; Breen to Hays, 15 April 1940; all in STRANGE CARGO file, PCA Files.

5. Breen to Louis B. Mayer, 13 and 17 June 1941; PCA staff memorandum to files, n.d., ca. December 1941; *Memphis Commercial Appeal*, 2 December 1941; TWO-FACED WOMAN file, PCA Files; Geoffrey Shurlock oral history, Louis B. Mayer Library, American Film Institute, Los Angeles, Calif., p. 250.

6. Shurlock oral history, p. 257; Leff and Simmons, *The Dame in the Kimono*, pp. 118–121.

7. Pandro S. Berman oral history (interviewed by Barbara Hall), Margaret Herrick Library, Academy of Motion Picture Arts and Sciences Center for Motion Picture Study, Beverly Hills, Calif., p. 104. On the studio executives, see generally Leo Rosten, *Hollywood: The Movie Colony, The Movie Makers* (New York: Harcourt, Brace, 1941), pp. 30–39, 133–162, and Thomas Schatz, *The Genius of the System: Hollywood Filmmaking in the Studio Era* (New York: Pantheon, 1988).

8. Ruth Vasey, "Foreign Parts: Hollywood's Global Distribution and the Representation of Ethnicity," *American Quarterly* 44 (December 1992), p. 618.

9. Breen to Mayer, 31 January 1936, IT CAN'T HAPPEN HERE file, PCA Files; *New York Times,* 15 June 1935; Neal Gabler, *An Empire of Their Own: How the Jews Invented Hollywood* (New York: Doubleday, 1989), pp. 338–347.

10. Richard Maltby, "'It Can't Happen Here': The Politics of Censorship in Hollywood, 1936–1939," unpublished paper read at American Studies Association annual meeting, Costa Mesa, Calif., 6 November 1992. Although some Hays Office staffers in New York and Washington pressed for greater freedom for political pictures, Breen continued to resist. Any weakening on his part must take account of not only the antitrust threat but the swiftly moving international scene—which had created great tension by the summer of 1939—and the outbreak of the war against Poland on 1 September 1939.

11. Breen to Wilfrid Parsons, 10 October 1932, quoted in Vaughn, "Morality and Entertainment," p. 63; Breen to Daniel J. Lord, 5 December 1937, Daniel J. Lord Papers, Jesuit Missouri Province Archives, St. Louis, Mo. (emphasis in original). On the issue of fascism and American film in the late 1930s, see Clayton R. Koppes and Gregory D. Black, *Hollywood Goes to War: How Politics, Profits, and Propaganda Shaped World War II Movies* (New York: Free Press, 1987), ch. 2; Maltby, "Censorship, Self-Regulation, and the Hays Office"; and Larry Ceplair and Steven Englund, *The Inquisition in Hollywood* (Berkeley: University of California Press, 1979). On American Catholics' diverse views toward Mussolini, see John P. Diggins, *Mussolini and Fascism* (Princeton, N.J.: Princeton University Press, 1972), pp. 185–197, 329–333.

12. Breen to Wanger, 4 January 1938, BLOCKADE FILE, PCA Files; Larry Ceplair, "The Politics of Compromise in Hollywood: A Case Study," *Cineaste* 7, no. 4 (1978), pp. 2–7.

13. Breen to Wanger, 18 June 1938, PERSONAL HISTORY file, PCA Files.

14. R. Caracciolo to Breen, 8 June 1937 and 20 June 1938; Breen to Mayer, 26 August 1938; all in IDIOT'S DELIGHT file, PCA Files. John Mason Brown, *The Worlds of Robert E. Sherwood* (New York: Harper & Row, 1962), p. 338.

15. K.L. to Breen, n.d.; Breen to Hays, 30 December 1938, CONFESSIONS OF A NAZI SPY file, PCA Files; Eric J. Sandeen, "Confessions of a Nazi Spy," *American Studies* (1979), 69–81.

16. Breen to Warner, 30 December 1938, CONFESSIONS OF A NAZI SPY file, PCA Files.

17. Breen to Al Reeves, 6 September 1940, THE GREAT DICTATOR file, PCA Files; Charles Chaplin, *My Autobiography* (New York: Simon & Schuster, 1964), p. 392.

18. Breen to Francis Harmon, 8 June 1940; Breen to James Roosevelt, 7 July 1940; both in PASTOR HALL file, PCA Files.

19. Breen to Hays, 4 March 1941, MAN HUNT file, PCA Files.

20. See SERGEANT YORK production file, Warner Archive, USC.

21. Mellett to FDR, 17 March 1941, White House—1941 folder, Lowell Mellett Papers, Franklin D. Roosevelt Library, Hyde Park, N.Y. (hereafter Mellett Papers).

22. U.S. Senate Committee on Interstate Commerce, *Propaganda in Motion Pictures: Subcommittee Hearing on S.R. 152,* 77th Cong., 1st sess., 9–26 September 1941; Gerald Nye, "War Propaganda," *Vital Speeches of the Day,* 15 September 1941, 720–723; Koppes and Black, *Hollywood Goes to War,* pp. 40–47.

23. The fullest account of OWI relations with Hollywood is found in Koppes and Black, *Hollywood Goes to War.* See also Richard R. Lingeman, *Don't You Know There's a War On? The American Home Front, 1941–1945* (New York: Putnam's, 1970); Sydney Weinberg, "What to Tell America: The Writers' Quarrel in the Office of War Information," *Journal of American History* 55 (June 1968), 76–88; Allan M. Winkler, *The Politics of Propaganda: The Office of War Information, 1942–1945* (New Haven, Conn.: Yale University Press, 1978); and Bernard F. Dick, *The Star-Spangled Screen: The American World War II Film* (Lexington: University of Kentucky Press, 1985).

24. Davis to Byron Price, 27 January 1943, box 3, records of the OWI, record group 208, Federal Records Center, Suitland, Md. (hereafter OWI Files); Koppes and Black, *Hollywood Goes to War,* pp. 56–60; Dorothy Jones, *The Portrayal of China and India on the American Screen* (Cambridge, Mass.: MIT Press, 1955).

25. Nelson Poynter, interviewed by Clayton R. Koppes, St. Petersburg, Fla., 8 January 1974; *Motion Picture Herald,* 10 July, 24 July, and 14 August 1943.

26. "Government Information Manual for the Motion Picture Industry," summer 1942, box 15, OWI Files.

27. Feature review, LITTLE TOKYO, U.S.A., 9 July 1942, box 3518, OWI Files; script review, "Air Force," 27 October 1942, box 3515, OWI Files; Larry Suid, ed., *"Air Force"* (Madison: University of Wisconsin Press, 1983).

28. Mellett to Mayer, 25 November 1942; feature review, TENNESSEE JOHNSON, 1 December 1942; both in box 3510, OWI Files; Dorothy B. Jones to Poynter, 6 November 1942; feature review, THE PALM BEACH STORY, 4 November 1942; both in box 6, Mellett Papers.

29. Poynter to Mark Sandrich, 28 October 1942; "The Chaplain Speech—*So Proudly We Hail*," 25 November 1942; "Re Janet's Speech," 25 November 1942; all in box 3511, OWI Files; Poynter interview, 1974.

30. Mellett to various studios, 9 December 1942; excerpts from Davis press conference, 23 December 1942, both in box 1443, OWI Files; *Variety*, 23 December 1942; William Goetz to Gardner Cowles, 22 December 1942, box 12a, OWI Files.

31. Koppes and Black, *Hollywood Goes to War*, pp, 134–137.

32. *Motion Picture Herald*, 10 July 1943; Riskin to Bell, 22 October 1943, box 3510; Riskin to Edward Barrett, 12 August 1944; both in box 19, OWI files; *Wall Street Journal* quoted in Ian Jarvie, *Hollywood's Overseas Campaign: The North Atlantic Movie Trade, 1920–1950* (New York: Cambridge University Press, 1992), p. 384.

33. Bell to Selznick, 28 September 1943; Cunningham to Selznick, 21 July 1943; feature review, SINCE YOU WENT AWAY, 20 July 1944; all in box 3525, OWI files; *Commonweal* 40 (1944), pp. 374–375.

34. Bell to Riskin, 10 December 1942, OWI Files.

35. On blacks and World War II films, see Koppes and Black, "Blacks, Loyalty, and Motion-Picture Propaganda in World War II," *Journal of American History* 73 (September 1986), 383–406.

36. James Agee, *Agee on Film* (New York: Grossett & Dunlap, 1958), p. 108.

37. Poynter to Mellett, 12 November 1942; script review, "America," 5 November 1942; both in box 3525, OWI Files.

38. Mellett to Goldwyn, 20 August 1942; Goldwyn to Mellett, 22 August 1942; both in box 1433b, OWI Files; script review, "The White Cliffs of Dover," 1 March 1943, box 1556, OWI Files; feature review, THE WHITE CLIFFS OF DOVER, 10 March 1944; Ferdinand Kuhn Jr. to Bell, 24 March 1944; both in box 3529, OWI Files.

39. OWI logs, 13 June 1942, box 1556, OWI Files.

40. "Government Information Manual for the Motion Picture Industry," summer 1942, box 15, OWI Files.

41. Script reviews, "Dragon Seed," 10 and 15 September 1942; feature review, DRAGON SEED, 3 July 1944; both in box 3525, OWI Files.

42. Script review, "Keys of the Kingdom," 19 January 1944; Cunningham to Sailor, 13 April 1944; both in box 3518, OWI Files.

43. *Variety*, 28 October 1942.

44. Feature review, MISSION TO MOSCOW, 29 April 1943, box 3523, OWI Files; David E. Culbert, ed., *Mission to Moscow* (Madison: University of Wisconsin Press, 1980).

45. Breen to Warner, 1 July 1943, MISSION TO MOSCOW production file, Warner Archive, USC; Stephen J. Whitfield, *The Culture of the Cold War* (Baltimore: Johns Hopkins University Press, 1991), p. 129; *New Republic*, 10 May 1943, p. 636.

46. See Koppes and Black, *Hollywood Goes to War*, ch. 7.

47. See in particular the special Soviet issue of *Life*, 29 March 1943, in which Davies was featured as the principal commentator on Soviet affairs. On the American media's approach to the Soviet Union during the war generally, see Clayton R. Koppes and Gregory D. Black, "The Soviet Palimpsest: The Portrayal of Russia in American Media in World War II," unpublished paper read at Second Annual US-USSR Symposium on History of World War II, Franklin D. Roosevelt Library, Hyde Park, N.Y., 19–23 October 1987; and Clayton R. Koppes, "Conference Calls: Representations of American-Soviet Relations in American Media from Quebec to Yalta," unpublished paper read at CIS/US/GB symposium on History of World War II, Yalta, Crimea, Ukraine, 23–28 April 1992.

48. "Government Information Manual for the Motion Picture Industry," summer 1942, box 15, OWI Files.

49. Feature review, BEHIND THE RISING SUN, 8 June 1943; Cunningham to Little, 11 September 1944; both in box 3522, OWI Files.

50. Breen to Jason Joy, 14 October 1943, THE PURPLE HEART file, PCA Files; Breen to Warner, 21 December 1944; Susan Seidman to Hays, OBJECTIVE BURMA file, PCA Files.

51. Warren Pierce to Joy, 2 December 1942; Bell to Riskin, 23 February 1943; both in box 3521, OWI Files.

52. Riskin to Bell, 8 January 1943, box 3510, OWI Files.

53. Breen to file, 8 September 1943; Breen to Luraschi, 9 August 1943; Breen to Hays, 6 July 1944; all in HITLER'S GANG file, PCA Files.

54. "The Manual for the Motion Picture Industry," 27 April 1943; feature review, PRIDE OF THE MARINES, 11 July 1945; both in box 15, OWI Files.

55. "Report on Activities, 1942–1945," 18 September 1945, box 65, OWI Files.

56. Robert A. Rosenstone, "Like Writing History with Lightning: Historical Films/Historical Truths," *Contention: Debates in Society, Culture, and Science* 2 (Spring 1993), p. 195.

57. On Soviet films, see Peter Kenez, *Cinema and Soviet Society, 1917–1953* (New York: Cambridge University Press, 1992), ch. 9; on German movies, see David Welch, *Propaganda and the German Cinema, 1933–1945* (Oxford: Clarendon Press, 1983).

58. Joseph Breen, PCA annual report, 23 February 1945, PCA Files.

CHAPTER 9 (The Postwar Motion Picture Industry)

1. John Keegan, *The Second World War* (New York: Viking, 1989), p. 219. Payne is quoted in David Halberstam, *The Fifties* (New York: Fawcett Columbine, 1993), p. 116.

2. Keegan, *The Second World War,* pp. 590–591.

3. *Wall Street Journal,* 5 July 1946, p. 2; *Wall Street Journal,* 11 January 1949, p. 2.

4. See, for instance, *Wall Street Journal,* 23 December 1948, p. 1.

5. *Wall Street Journal,* 20 June 1946, p. 1; *Wall Street Journal,* 3 January 1947, p. 1.

6. On trust-busting, see *Wall Street Journal,* 28 August 1947, p. 1.

7. *Wall Street Journal,* 17 February 1947, p. 1; *Wall Street Journal,* 6 March 1947, p. 1; *Wall Street Journal,* 19 September 1949, p. 1.

8. *Wall Street Journal,* 28 August 1947, p. 1; *Wall Street Journal,* 3 June 1948, p. 1.

9. In late 1945, shortly after Johnston succeeded Hays as president of the MPPDA, its title was changed to the Motion Picture Association of America (MPAA).

10. Johnston quoted in *Motion Picture Herald,* 13 April 1946, p. 14.

11. *Wall Street Journal,* 11 July 1946, p. 1; the story appeared under the page-one subhead "Foreign Sales Pushed 'Good Propaganda,' Potent Trade Stimulus." See also *Variety,* 21 August 1946, p. 3.

12. Thomas Guback, *The International Film Industry* (Bloomington: Indiana University Press, 1969), p. 92.

13. On the sustained wartime rate of increase, see *Variety,* 13 February 1946, p. 7; *Motion Picture Herald,* 20 April 1946, p. 23; *Motion Picture Herald,* 2 November 1946, p. 14. On box-office grosses, see Christopher H. Sterling and Timothy R. Haight, *The Mass Media: The Aspen Institute Guide to Communications Industry Trends* (New York: Praeger, 1978), p. 187; Joel Finler, *The Hollywood Story* (New York: Crown, 1988), pp. 30–31.

14. Sterling and Haight, *The Mass Media,* p. 184; *Variety,* 21 August 1947, p. 31. Note that both SARATOGA TRUNK and ROAD TO UTOPIA were released in late 1945.

15. *Wall Street Journal,* 2 January 1947, p. 16; Wall Street Journal 20 May 1947, p. 1.

16. The *Motion Picture Herald* was especially ardent in its postwar optimism. One typical example: on 8 November 1947, the *Herald* reported on the analysis by "experts and statisticians" based on Treasury Department data which refuted the "prophets of pessimism." According to their analysis, "the prosperous days of the war years have not gone, and there is no reason to suppose they will fade in the foreseeable future" (p. 12).

17. Reported in *Motion Picture Herald,* 23 February 1946, p. 8.

18. *1950 Film Daily Year Book,* p. 71; based on MPAA estimates.

19. *Wall Street Journal,* 16 September 1949, p. 1; *Wall Street Journal,* 29 November 1949, p. 1.

20. *Variety,* 2 October 1946, p. 5; *Variety,* 29 January 1947, p. 5; *Motion Picture Herald,* 26 April 1947, p. 12; *Wall Street Journal,* 14 October 1947, p. 1.

21. *Variety*, 16 November 1949, p. 7.
22. *Variety*, 12 July 1948, p. 9.
23. *Variety*, 6 March 1946, p. 3; *Variety*, 13 March 1946, p. 25; *Motion Picture Herald*, 26 June 1948, p. 36.
24. According to Sterling and Haight, the number of "four-wall theaters" wired for sound in the United States actually increased during the early Depression, which hit while many theaters had not yet converted to sound. Most of the closings involved silent houses. The overall decline was from 23,344 house theaters in 1929 to 15,273 in 1935 (*The Mass Media*, p. 35).
25. *Variety*, 27 March 1946, p. 9; *Motion Picture Herald*, 28 September 1946, p. 8; *Variety*, 5 January 1949, p. 30.
26. Figures for the other postwar years were $63 million in 1947, $105 million in 1948, and $160 million in 1950. Simon N. Whitney, "Antitrust Policies of the Motion Picture Industry," in Gorham Kindem, ed., *The American Movie Industry: The Business of Motion Pictures* (Carbondale: University of Illinois Press, 1982), p. 188.
27. On "nabes" versus downtown theaters, see *Wall Street Journal*, 20 May 1947, p. 1. On nabes versus drive-ins, see *Wall Street Journal*, 9 July 1948, p. 1. On the Gallup study, see *Variety*, 23 February 1949, p. 5. On teenage audiences, see *Variety*, 10 August 1949, p. 5; on the "lost audience," see *Variety*, 26 October 1949, p. 3.
28. *Variety*, 16 November 1949, p. 10.
29. *Fortune*, 4 April 1949, p. 140.
30. Sterling and Haight, *The Mass Media*, p. 187. See also *Motion Picture Herald*, 15 January 1949, p. 12.
31. On Eagle-Lion/PRC, see *Motion Picture Herald*, 23 August 1947, p. 28.
32. *1948 Film Daily Year Book*, p. 185.
33. See, for instance, "Foreign Films Pour Into U.S. Market; 190 on Way," *Motion Picture Herald*, 27 December 1947, p. 17; *Variety*, 27 July 1949, p. 13.
34. *New York Times*, 18 December 1949, p. x5; *New York Times*, 25 December 1949, p. x5. See also Douglas Gomery, *Shared Pleasures: A History of Movie Presentation in the United States* (Madison: University of Wisconsin Press, 1992), pp. 183–193.
35. Korda quoted in *Motion Picture Herald*, 16 December 1946, p. 14.
36. See *Motion Picture Herald*, 3 January 1948, p. 23; *Motion Picture Herald*, 11 December 1948, p. 20; *1950 Film Daily Year Book*, p. 71; *Variety*, 4 January 1950, p. 175. Some sources report Hollywood's postwar foreign revenues as somewhat higher. The figures reported here are supported by other studies (Guback in *The International Film Industry*, for instance), but they remain even less reliable than figures on domestic earnings.
37. *Variety*, 7 January 1948, p. 31.
38. *Motion Picture Herald*, 29 September 1946, p. 23.
39. *Motion Picture Herald*, 19 October 1946, p. 19.
40. *Variety*, 31 July 1946, p. 3.
41. *Motion Picture Herald*, 3 August 1946, p. 69; *Variety*, 16 October 1946, p. 3.
42. *1948 Film Daily Year Book*, p. 46; *1949 Film Daily Year Book*, p. 47.
43. On the British quota, see *Motion Picture Herald*, 1 June 1946, p. 9; *1947 Film Daily Year Book*, p. 41; *Motion Picture Herald*, 1 February 1947, p. 48.
44. Cripps quoted in *Motion Picture Herald*, 25 January 1947, p. 48; on the economic slump, see *Motion Picture Herald*, 18 January 1947, p. 30; see also *Variety*, 5 March 1947, p. 3.
45. *Motion Picture Herald*, 21 June 1947, p. 19; *Motion Picture Herald*, 5 July 1947, p. 21; *Motion Picture Herald*, 23 August 1947, p. 28; *Motion Picture Herald*, 21 June 1947, p. 19.
46. *Motion Picture Herald*, 9 August 1947, p. 13; *Variety*, 13 August 1947, pp. 1, 3, 5; *Motion Picture Herald*, 16 August 1947, p. 12; *1948 Film Daily Year Book*, p. 45.
47. *Motion Picture Herald*, 16 August 1947, p. 12, 16.
48. *Motion Picture Herald*, 15 November 1947, p. 24. Rank announced plans to spend $37 million on 44 pictures in 1948, while Korda reportedly planned to spend $20 million on 13 films.
49. *Motion Picture Herald*, 20 December 1947, p. 22.
50. *Motion Picture Herald*, 13 March 1948, p. 13; *Variety*, 17 March 1948, p. 1; *Motion Picture Herald*, 29 March 1948, p. 13.
51. *Variety*, 14 April 1948, p. 9.
52. *1949 Film Daily Year Book*, p. 47; Balio, *United Artists*, p. 233.

53. On devaluation, see *Wall Street Journal*, 19 September 1949, p. 1. On government subsidies and the failing industry, see *Variety*, 2 February 1949, p. 7; *Motion Picture Herald*, 5 February 1949, p. 28; *Wall Street Journal*, 9 March 1949, p. 1. On Rank, see *Variety*, 28 September 1949, p. 7; *Variety*, 9 November 1949, pp. 3, 14.

54. *Variety*, 25 February 1948, p. 24; *Variety*, 5 January 1949, p. 201. On the studios sidestepping production and sitting on $40 million in frozen revenues, see *Variety*, 22 June 1949, p. 7. See also *1950 Film Daily Year Book*, p. 51.

55. Guback, *The International Film Industry*, p. 44.

56. *Motion Picture Herald*, 13 April 1946, p. 14; *1948 Film Daily Year Book*, p. 99; *1949 Film Daily Year Book*, pp. 766, 926; *Motion Picture Herald*, 19 March 1949, p. 28. On the rebuilding of the German industry, see *Wall Street Journal*, 5 August 1947, p. 6; *Motion Picture Herald*, 5 February 1949, p. 34.

57. *Motion Picture Herald*, 3 August 1946, p. 9; *1949 Film Daily Year Book*, p. 801; Guback, *The International Film Industry*, p. 19.

58. *Motion Picture Herald*, 22 February 1947, p. 52; *1950 Film Daily Year Book*, pp. 91, 767–768.

59. *Variety*, 5 January 1949, p. 21; *1950 Film Daily Year Book*, p. 71.

60. *1950 Film Daily Year Book*, p. 51.

61. *1950 Film Daily Year Book*, p. 71; *Variety*, 4 January 1950, p. 175.

62. *Motion Picture Herald*, 12 January 1946, p. 66.

63. For a detailed survey of organized labor in Hollywood after the war, see "More Trouble in Paradise," Fortune, November 1946, pp. 154ff.

64. *Ibid.*, p. 156; *Wall Street Journal*, 2 May 1946, p. 1.

65. "More Trouble in Paradise," p. 154.

66. *Ibid.*, p. 157; *Wall Street Journal*, 2 May 1946, p. 1.

67. *Motion Picture Herald*, 2 February 1946, p. 14; *Variety*, 13 February 1946, p. 1. See also *Wall Street Journal*, 2 May 1946, p. 1; and "More Trouble in Paradise," p. 154.

68. "More Trouble in Paradise," p. 159; *Variety*, 3 July 1946, p. 3; *Variety*, 10 July 1946, p. 21; *Motion Picture Herald*, 19 October 1946, p. 40; *1947 Film Daily Year Book*, pp. 41, 93.

69. *Wall Street Journal*, 2 October 1946, p. 1; *Motion Picture Herald*, 19 October 1946, p. 40; *1947 Film Daily Year Book*, pp. 41, 93.

70. Report quoted in David Prindle, *The Politics of Glamour* (Madison: University of Wisconsin Press, 1988), p. 47. See also Otto Friedrich, *City of Nets* (New York: Harper & Row, 1987), p. 280; *1947 Film Daily Year Book*, pp. 93, 846.

71. On Brewer's rise, see Friedrich, *City of Nets*, pp. 277–280; Prindle, *The Politics of Glamour*, pp. 41–51; Tino Balio, *The American Film Industry*, rev. ed. (Madison: University of Wisconsin Press, 1985), p. 278.

72. Balio, *The American Film Industry*, pp. 278–279; Friedrich, *City of Nets*, 277–279.

73. Prindle, *The Politics of Glamour*, p. 51.

74. On Taft-Hartley, see *Wall Street Journal*, 9 August 1947, p. 2; on the painters union, see *New York Times*, 28 October 1947, n.p. See also Friedrich, *City of Nets*, p. 283.

75. *New York Times*, 25 December 1949, p. x5.

76. Garth Jowett, *Film, the Democratic Art: A Social History of American Film* (Boston: Little, Brown, 1976), pp. 393–394; Prindle, *The Politics of Glamour*, pp. 51–53; A. Scott Berg, *Goldwyn: A Biography* (New York: Knopf, 1989), p. 433.

77. *Motion Picture Herald*, 5 April 1947, p. 21.

78. Berg, *Goldwyn*, p. 433; Prindle, *The Politics of Glamour*, pp. 52–54; *Motion Picture Herald*, 3 May 1947, p. 34.

79. Balio, *The American Film Industry*, p. 408.

80. Ceplair, "The Unfriendly Hollywood Nineteen," in Gary Crowdus, ed., *A Political Companion to American Film* (Chicago: Lakeview Press, 1994), p. 437; Prindle, *The Politics of Glamour*, p. 52. The 19 "unfriendly" witnesses were Alvah Bessie, Herbert Biberman, Bertolt Brecht, Lester Cole, Richard Collins, Edward Dmytryk, Gordon Kahn, Howard Koch, Ring Lardner Jr., John Howard Lawson, Albert Maltz, Lewis Milestone, Samuel Ornitz, Larry Parks, Irving Pichel, Robert Rossen, Waldo Salt, Adrian Scott, and Dalton Trumbo.

81. *Variety*, 17 September 1947, p. 1; *Motion Picture Herald*, 27 September 1947, p. 14.

82. Friedrich, *City of Nets*, p. 304; Berg, *Goldwyn*, p. 535.

83. *New York Times*, 21 October 1947, p. 1; *Motion Picture Herald*, 25 October 1947, p. 13.

84. *Washington Post,* 23 October 1947, p. 1.
85. Quoted in the *Motion Picture Herald,* 25 October 1947, p. 13.
86. *Washington Post,* 25 October 1947, p. 1; *Motion Picture Herald,* 25 October 1947, p. 13; *Motion Picture Herald,* 1 November 1947, p. 13.
87. *Washington Post,* 27 October 1947, p. 1; *New York Times,* 27 October 1947, p. 1. The group comprised sixteen stars, six writers, three producers, and one composer.
88. *Washington Post,* 28 October 1941, p. 1; *New York Times,* 28 October 1947, p. 1.
89. John Huston, *An Open Book* (New York: Knopf, 1980), p. 133.
90. *Washington Post,* 30 October 1947, p. 1; *New York Times,* 31 October 1947, p. 1.
91. *Variety,* 26 November 1947, p. 1; *Motion Picture Herald,* 29 November 1947, p. 13; *Motion Picture Herald,* 6 December 1947, p. 20. The House vote was 346–317 on Maltz, and 240–215 on Trumbo. At that point, a simple voice vote was taken. Among those who considered the unfriendly witnesses' strategy to have been successful is Larry Ceplair, who has written extensively on HUAC and the Hollywood blacklist. Ceplair suggests that the hearings were suddenly suspended because of negative publicity against HUAC in response to the unfriendly witnesses' testimony. See also Ceplair and Steven Englund, *The Inquisition in Hollywood: Politics in the Film Community, 1930–1960* (Garden City, N.Y.: Anchor Press, 1980); and Ceplair, "The Unfriendly Hollywood Nineteen," in Crowdus, *A Political Companion to American Film.*
92. The full text of the Waldorf Statement is in the HUAC file, Schary Papers, UW—M.
93. *Motion Picture Herald,* 6 December 1947, p. 20.
94. ARI, "Congressional Investigation of Communism in Hollywood—What the Public Thinks," 17 December 1947, Schary Papers, UW—M.
95. *Motion Picture Herald,* 6 March 1948, p. 20; *Motion Picture Herald,* 17 April 1948, p. 14; *Motion Picture Herald,* 29 May 1948, p. 28; *Motion Picture Herald,* 19 June 1949, p. 22.
96. Robert Sklar, *Movie-Made America: A Cultural History of American Movies* (New York: Random House, 1975), p. 267.
97. Victor S. Navasky, *Naming Names* (New York: Viking, 1980), p. 177.
98. See Janet Staiger, "The Package-Unit System: Unit Management After 1955," in David Bordwell, Janet Staiger, and Kristen Thompson, *The Classic Hollywood Cinema* (New York: Columbia University Press, 1985), pp. 330–337.
99. Murray Ross, *Stars and Strikes* (New York: Columbia University Press, 1941), pp. 89–174.
100. *Ibid.,* pp. 173–174. Ross also cites Leo Rosten's study of the background of motion picture players published in *Screen Actor,* December 1940, p. 16. See also Rosten, *Hollywood: The Movie Colony, the Movie Makers* (New York: Harcourt, Brace, 1941).
101. Ross, *Stars and Strikes,* p. 202; *New York Times,* 24 May 1941, p. 1.
102. Prindle, *The Politics of Glamour,* p. 49.
103. SAG press release, 17 June 1946.
104. Nancy Lynn Schwartz, *The Hollywood Writers' Wars* (New York: Knopf, 1982), pp. 252–253. Schwartz quotes a 2 March 1948 letter from SAG President Ronald Reagan to Congressman Ralph W. Gwinn in which he calls Kearns's allegation "astounding, unsupported" (p. 3).
105. SAG press release, 15 January 1948.
106. Schwartz, *The Hollywood Writers' Wars,* p. 243.
107. Talk given to the board by Leon Ames, 8 December 1947.
108. Janet Staiger, "The Package-Unit System: Unit Management After 1955," pp. 330–332.
109. See the production statistics from the 1948 and 1949 editions of the *Film Daily Year Book.* See also Douglas Ayer et al., "Self-Censorship in the Movie Industry: A Historical Perspective on Law and Social Change," in Kindem, *The American Movie Industry,* pp. 215–253.
110. *Variety,* 20 March 1946, p. 3.
111. On the C rating, see *Variety,* 3 April 1946, p. 1; *Motion Picture Herald,* 20 April 1946, p. 52. On local problems, see *Variety,* 3 April 1946, p. 46. On Hughes's battles with both the MPAA and the PCA, see *Motion Picture Herald,* 27 April 1946, p. 15; *Motion Picture Herald,* 14 September 1946, p. 26.
112. *Variety,* 22 May 1946, p. 5.
113. *Variety,* 23 April 1947, p. 3; *Motion Picture Herald,* 28 June 1947, p. 13.
114. *Variety,* 14 May 1947, p. 3; *Variety,* 30 July 1947, p. 13; *Motion Picture Herald,* 11 November 1947, p. 15; Balio, *United Artists,* pp. 210–214.
115. *New York Times,* 26 October 1947, p. x1.

116. *Motion Picture Herald,* 25 October 1947, p. 20.

117. *Motion Picture Herald,* 15 November 1947, p. 15; *Variety,* 3 December 1947, p. 6; *Variety,* 10 December 1947, p. 7; *Motion Picture Herald,* 13 December 1947, p. 26.

118. According to the *Motion Picture Herald,* the Legion of Decency assigned 52 B ratings and one C rating to 367 Hollywood studio releases during the 1947–1948 season; during that same period, it assigned 30 B ratings and 6 C ratings to 84 foreign films (27 November 1948, p. 22). For the figures on 1948–1949, see *Motion Picture Herald,* 3 September 1949, p. 38.

119. Quoted in Leonard J. Leff and Jerold L. Simmons, *The Dame in the Kimono* (New York: Grove Weidenfeld, 1990), p. 146.

120. *Motion Picture Herald,* 1 January 1944, p. 27.

121. *Variety,* 13 December 1944, p. 3.

122. *Motion Picture Herald,* 6 October 1945, p. 19; *Motion Picture Herald,* 13 October 1945, p. 12; *Variety,* 21 November 1945, p. 11; *Motion Picture Herald,* 24 November 1945, p. 16.

123. *Variety,* 12 June 1946, p. 1; see also Whitney, "Antitrust Policies of the Motion Picture Industry," p. 172.

124. *Variety,* 12 June 1946, p. 1.

125. *Variety,* 12 June 1946, p. 1; court ruling quoted in *Motion Picture Herald,* 15 June 1946, p. 12.

126. *Motion Picture Herald,* 19 October 1946, p. 13; *Motion Picture Herald,* 30 November 1946, p. 98.

127. *1948 Film Daily Year Book,* p. 41; *Variety,* 8 January 1947, p. 4; *Motion Picture Herald,* 4 January 1947, p. 10a.

128. *Motion Picture Herald,* 22 February 1947, p. 19; *Motion Picture Herald,* 17 May 1947, p. 21; *1948 Film Daily Year Book,* p. 45.

129. *Variety,* 26 June 1946, p. 3; *Variety,* 10 July 1946, p. 9.

130. *Motion Picture Herald,* 12 October 1946, p. 9; *Motion Picture Herald,* 19 October 1946, p. 14.

131. Whitney, "Antitrust Policies of the Motion Picture Industry," p. 174; *Variety,* 27 February 1946, p. 5; *Motion Picture Herald,* 13 July 1946, p. 15; *Variety,* 19 October 1946, p. 8; *1947 Film Daily Year Book,* p. 41.

132. Whitney, "Antitrust Policies of the Motion Picture Industry," p. 174; *1947 Film Daily Year Book,* p. 41.

133. *Motion Picture Herald,* 27 July 1946, p. 16; *Motion Picture Herald,* 14 September 1946, p. 13; *Variety,* 23 October 1946, p. 3; *Motion Picture Herald,* 25 January 1947, p. 13; *Variety,* 4 June 1947, p. 5; *Variety,* 3 December 1947, p. 7.

134. *Wall Street Journal,* 28 August 1947, p. 1.

135. *Wall Street Journal,* 9 January 1948, p. 1.

136. See Jowett, *Film, the Democratic Art,* p. 345; *Variety,* 21 August 1946, p. 3; *Variety,* 5 January 1949, p. 35.

137. Whitney, "Antitrust Policies of the Motion Picture Industry," p. 170; *Wall Street Journal,* 4 May 1948, p. 1; *New York Times,* 4 May 1948, p. 1; *Motion Picture Herald,* 8 May 1948, p. 12; Sklar, *Movie-Made America,* p. 273.

138. *Motion Picture Herald,* 8 May 1948, 12.

139. *Wall Street Journal,* 2 November 1948, p. 2; *Motion Picture Herald,* 6 November 1949, p. 13.

140. *1949 Film Daily Year Book,* p. 47.

141. *Wall Street Journal,* 10 February 1949, p. 14; *Motion Picture Herald,* 12 February 1949, p. 14.

142. *Motion Picture Herald,* 12 February 1949, p. 14.

143. *Variety,* 27 July 1949, p. 3.

144. *Motion Picture Herald,* 30 July 1949, p. 13; *Variety,* 3 August 1949, p. 3; *1950 Film Daily Year Book,* p. 51.

145. *1950 Film Daily Year Book,* p. 51; see also Gomery, *The Hollywood Studio System,* pp. 49–50.

146. *Fortune,* April 1949, pp. 99, 102.

147. *Ibid.,* p. 102.

CHAPTER 10 (The Hollywood Studio System, 1946–1949)

1. *Motion Picture Herald,* 5 February 1949, p. 15.

2. *Fortune,* April 1949, p. 148.

3. "Movies: End of an Era?," *Fortune,* April 1949, pp. 102, 140.

4. *New York Times,* 25 December 1949, p. x5.

5. *Variety,* 7 January 1948, p. 31.
6. *Wall Street Journal,* 20 November 1946, p. 1.
7. *1947 Film Daily Year Book,* p. 49. The average cost of a feature in 1942 was $375,000.
8. *Variety,* 8 January 1947, p. 39.
9. *1949 Film Daily Year Book,* p. 941.
10. *Wall Street Journal,* 23 August 1949, p. 1.
11. *Variety,* 4 January 1950, p. 23.
12. Figures from Joel Finler, *The Hollywood Story* (New York: Crown, 1988), p. 31, and various editions of the *Film Daily Year Book.*
13. Finler, *The Hollywood Story,* p. 30. Finler's figures are actually quite interesting in that they indicate that the biggest periodic leap in picture costs, by far, was during World War II. In 1986 dollars, a picture in 1940 cost $4.4 million; in 1946, $9 million; in 1950, $8.5 million; in 1960, $9 million; in 1976, $8 million; in 1980, $10.5 million; and in 1986, $12 million.
14. *Motion Picture Herald,* 5 February 1949, p. 15.
15. *Variety,* 7 September 1949, p. 1.
16. Figures from the 1945, 1946, 1948, and 1949 editions of the *Film Daily Year Book.*
17. *Wall Street Journal,* 31 January 1948, p. 1; *Wall Street Journal,* 6 June 1949, p. 11.
18. See "Paramount: Oscar for Profits," *Fortune,* June 1947, pp. 89+. See also Douglas Gomery, *The Hollywood Studio System* (New York: St. Martin's Press, 1986), p. 35; Finler, *The Hollywood Story,* p. 140.
19. *Fortune,* June 1947, p. 218.
20. Accounts vary; note that whereas Finler puts Paramount's 1946 net earnings at $39.2 million, *Fortune* (June 1947, p. 90) and the trade press reported its 1946 profits as $44 million.
21. *Variety,* 21 August 1946, p. 16.
22. *Fortune,* June 1947, p. 92. According to *Fortune,* Paramount wholly owned 7 of the nation's biggest theaters; owned over 95 percent of 14 chains totaling 455 theaters; and owned over 50 percent of another 755 theaters. It owned between 25 and 50 percent of some 275 theaters and owned less than 25 percent of only 25 theaters.
23. *Variety,* 23 June 1948, p. 5.
24. According to *Variety,* 31 August 1946, p. 13, Paramount releases accounted for 31 of the 71 reissues in circulation at the time. For Balaban on reissues and television, see *Variety,* 12 May 1948, p. 9; and Gomery, *The Hollywood Studio System,* p. 49.
25. *Variety,* 24 April 1946, p. 5; *Motion Picture Herald,* 11 May 1946, p. 8; *Motion Picture Herald,* 27 September 1947, p. 23.
26. *Motion Picture Herald,* 27 September 1947, p. 23; *Variety,* 5 November 1947, p. 9; *1949 Film Daily Year Book,* p. 941.
27. *Variety,* 30 June 1948, p. 1; *Motion Picture Herald,* 27 November 1948, p. 9. See also Christopher Anderson, *Hollywood TV* (Austin: University of Texas Press, 1994), p. 37.
28. John Douglas Eames, *The MGM Story* (New York: Crown, 1975), p. 222.
29. Finler, *The Hollywood Story,* p. 281.
30. *Variety,* 8 January 1947, p. 8. *Variety* estimated in 1946 that MGM's sales policies brought in approximately $1 million on each of its top releases beyond what the other majors earned.
31. *Variety,* 8 January 1947, p. 8; *Variety,* 7 January 1948, p. 1; *Variety,* 5 January 1949, p. 3; *Variety,* 4 January 1950, p. 59. The definition of a "commercial hit" changed slightly owing to declining box office: for 1946, it comprised the 60 pictures returning $2.25 million or more; in 1947, the 75 returning $2 million or more; in 1948, the 93 returning $1.5 million or more; and in 1949, the 92 returning $1.5 million or more. Of the other studio-distributors, Universal had 26 hits, Columbia 17, UA 12, Republic and Eagle-Lion 2 each, and Monogram one.
32. Finler, *The Hollywood Story,* pp. 286–287. Again, accounts vary. Note that Eames in *The MGM Story* (p. 216) puts MGM's gross income in 1948 at $185 million.
33. *Motion Picture Herald,* 17 July 1948, p. 8; *Variety,* 11 August 1948, p. 5.
34. On ADAM'S RIB, see Eames, *The MGM Story,* p. 230.
35. *1949 Film Daily Year Book,* p. 941.
36. Gomery, *The Hollywood Studio System,* p. 132.
37. Jerry Wald and Henry Blanke legal files, Warner Archive, USC; see also *Variety,* 5 January 1949, p. 35.
38. Jack L. Warner to studio attorney Mendel Silberberg, 22 February 1950; Blanke legal file, Warner Archive, USC.

39. Wald legal file, Warner Archive, USC.

40. On the Autry deal, see *Variety*, 8 January 1947, p. 39; on Santana, see Finler, *The Hollywood Story*, p. 81.

41. *Wall Street Journal*, 6 June 1949, p. 1.

42. *Variety*, 31 July 1946, p. 3.

43. *Motion Picture Herald*, 3 August 1946, p. 69; *Variety*, 16 October 1946, p. 3.

44. *Motion Picture Herald*, 23 August 1947, p. 28.

45. Todd McCarthy and Charles Flynn, eds., *Kings of the B's* (New York: Dutton, 1975), pp. 24–25.

46. *Wall Street Journal*, 5 November 1946, p. 1.

47. Quoted in *Wall Street Journal*, 5 November 1946, p. 1.

48. *Motion Picture Herald*, 30 March 1946, p. 56 on HENRY V's special handling. See also Tino Balio, *United Artists: The Company Built by the Stars* (Madison: University of Wisconsin Press, 1976), p. 220, and *Variety*, 8 January 1947, p. 33.

49. Selznick to Mayer, 16 September 1953, Selznick Collection, UT.

50. *Variety*, 8 January 1947, p. 33; *Motion Picture Herald*, 11 January 1947, p. 20; *Motion Picture Herald*, 28 June 1947, p. 18; *Motion Picture Herald*, 30 August 1947, p. 23; *Variety*, 11 June 1947, p. 5.

51. *Variety*, 11 June 1947, p. 5.

52. *NYTFR*, 8 May 1947.

53. While costs on DUEL IN THE SUN, according to readily available archival material, were indeed in the $5 million range, A. Scott Berg in *Goldwyn* (New York: Knopf, 1989) puts the production cost of BEST YEARS at $2.1 million, with another $400,000 spent on advertising (pp. 217–218).

54. *Variety*, 7 January 1948, p. 43.

55. *Motion Picture Herald*, 3 August 1946, p. 73.

56. *Variety*, 12 February 1947, p. 3; *Variety*, 16 April 1947, p. 3.

57. On Cagney, see Kevin Hagopian, "Declarations of Independence: A History of Cagney Productions," *Velvet Light Trap* 22 (1986). See also *Variety*, 1 June 1949, p. 3. On Rainbow-Paramount, see *Variety*, 7 January 1948, p. 43. On Paramount-Liberty, see *Variety*, 12 February 1947, p. 3; and *Variety*, 30 April 1947, p. 3. McCarey quoted in *Variety*, 7 January 1948, p. 23.

58. Balio, *United Artists*, 219.

59. *Variety*, 17 July 1946, p. 5; Balio, *United Artists*, pp. 217–218; Joseph McBride, *Hawks on Hawks* (Berkeley: University of California Press, 1982), pp. 121–122.

60. Berg, *Goldwyn*, p. 441.

61. Barbara Leaming, *Orson Welles* (New York: Penguin, 1985), pp. 331–345; Joseph McBride, *Orson Welles* (New York: Viking, 1972), pp. 92, 112.

62. McCarthy and Flynn, *Kings of the B's*, p. 30.

63. *Variety*, 19 May 1948, p. 25.

64. Ronald Haver, *David O. Selznick's Hollywood* (New York: Knopf, 1980), pp. 374–386. Selznick did mount a major comeback project in 1956, a remake of A FAREWELL TO ARMS costarring Jennifer Jones and Rock Hudson; it too was a major box-office disappointment.

65. Note that Berg devotes an entire chapter in *Goldwyn* to THE BEST YEARS OF OUR LIVES (pp. 393–429), and that he covers the remainder of the decade in a single chapter (pp. 430–459).

66. On Disney after the war, see Christopher Finch, *The Art of Walt Disney* (New York: Abrams, 1973), pp. 271–300. The two featurettes in ICHABOD AND MR. TOAD were adaptations of Kenneth Grahame's *The Wind in the Willows* (1908) and Washington Irving's "The Legend of Sleepy Hollow" (1819). Also note that TREASURE ISLAND was shot in Great Britain and 90 percent of the financing came from blocked funds. *Wall Street Journal*, 6 June 1949, p. 11.

67. *Fortune*, April 1949, pp. 142, 144.

68. *Wall Street Journal*, 6 June 1949, p. 11.

69. Capra and Briskin formed Liberty Films in late 1944, announced that formation in January 1945, and officially incorporated the company in April, with Capra as president and major stockholder. Joseph McBride, *Frank Capra: The Catastrophe of Success* (New York: Simon & Schuster, 1992), p. 506.

70. Berg, *Goldwyn*, p. 423.

71. Stevens contract with Liberty (signed by Capra) of 1 January 1946, George Stevens Collection, Academy of Motion Picture Arts and Sciences, Los Angeles (hereafter Stevens Collection). See also Frank Capra, *The Name Above the Title* (New York: Macmillan, 1971), pp. 372–373; Capra's

account of the deal with RKO and the partners basically corresponds with the legal documents in the Stevens Collection.

72. *Wall Street Journal,* 5 November 1946, p. 1. On the formation of Liberty Films, see Capra, *The Name Above the Title,* ch. 19, "Give Me Liberty"; and "The Story of Liberty Films," Stevens Collection.

73. Liberty memo of 30 June 1946, Stevens Collection.

74. Capra, *The Name Above the Title,* p. 382.

75. *Variety,* 8 January 1946, p. 39. According to McBride, the production cost on IT'S A WONDERFUL LIFE was $3.18 million, and the total cost, including distribution charges to RKO, was $3.78 million.

76. Capra, *The Name Above the Title,* pp. 386–398. See also McBride, *Frank Capra,* pp. 532, 546–547.

77. *Variety,* 12 February 1947, p. 3; *Variety,* 30 April 1947, p. 3. See also Stevens to Liberty Films, memo of 22 January 1949, Stevens Collection, which describes Paramount's buyout, with the final stock purchase executed in May 1947.

78. Capra, *The Name Above the Title,* pp. 400, 402.

79. *Variety,* 4 January 1950, p. 23; *Wall Street Journal,* 23 August 1949, p. 1; Capra, *The Name Above the Title,* p. 401.

80. McBride, *Frank Capra,* p. 548; *Variety,* 21 March 1951, n.p.; Capra, *The Name Above the Title,* pp. 403–406.

81. The films which Wyler produced and directed for Paramount were THE HEIRESS (1949), DETECTIVE STORY (1951), CARRIE (1952), ROMAN HOLIDAY (1953), and THE DESPERATE HOURS (1955).

82. Richard B. Jewell with Vernon Harbin, *The RKO Story* (New York: Arlington House, 1982), p. 227; see also the I REMEMBER MAMA story and production files, Stevens Collection.

83. Briskin to Stevens, 21 January 1949; Stevens to Liberty Films, 22 January 1949; both in A PLACE IN THE SUN file, Stevens Collection.

84. Ginsberg to Stevens, 3 February 1949, A PLACE IN THE SUN file, Stevens Collection.

85. Stevens's projected budget and schedule are included in a memo of 7 September 1949 to Ginsberg; the approved budget and schedule are included in a memo of 30 September 1949 from Ginsberg to Stevens; both in Stevens Collection.

CHAPTER 11 (Postwar Stars, Genres, and Production Trends)

1. *Variety,* 8 January 1947, p. 8.

2. *Variety,* 8 May 1946, p. 5.

3. This and other reports can be found in various financial files in the Selznick Collection, UT.

4. ARI, "Continuing Audit of Marquee Values No. 42" (Autumn–Winter 1950).

5. *Variety,* 5 January 1949, p. 3.

6. Quoted in Leslie Halliwell, *Halliwell's Film Guide,* 3d ed. (New York: Scribner's, 1982), p. 1050.

7. On Wayne's producer pact at Republic, see *Variety,* 27 March 1946, p. 5.

8. David Thomson, *The Autobiographical Dictionary of Film* (New York: Morrow, 1976), p. 602.

9. *Motion Picture Herald,* 9 April 1949, p. 9; see also Ephraim Katz, *The Film Encyclopedia* (New York: Putnam's, 1971), p. 367.

10. Davis contract of 4 February 1946, JUNE BRIDE legal file, Warner Legal Collection, UW—M. Regarding her 1947 salary, see Clive Hirschhorn, *The Warner Bros. Story* (New York: Crown, 1979), p. 264.

11. On the threatened split, see *Variety,* 16 May 1945, p. 1.

12. Abbott and Costello's salary for this and other postwar pictures was split 60–40, with the larger portion going to Costello—the result of continued feuding between the two over each comedian's relative value to the "team."

13. *Variety,* review of 26 June 1948, in *Variety Film Reviews 1943–1948,* vol. 7 (New York: Garland, 1983).

14. On the cost of THE PARADINE CASE, see Rudy Behlmer, ed., *Memo from Darryl F. Zanuck* (New York: Grove, 1993), p. 378; Ronald Haver, *David O. Selznick's Hollywood* (New York: Knopf, 1980), p. 378; on the cost of SIERRA MADRE, see undated summary of costs and income on Henry Blanke's productions, Henry Blanke legal file, Warner Archive, USC. The cost of the Abbott and

Costello picture is from the ABBOTT AND COSTELLO MEET FRANKENSTEIN production file, Universal Collection, USC.

15. Cobbett Steinberg, *Film Facts* (New York: Facts on File, 1980), p. 58; *Variety,* 4 January 1950, p. 59; ARI, "Continuing Audit of Marquee Values No. 42" (Autumn–Winter 1950).

16. *Motion Picture Herald,* 13 March 1946, p. 13; ARI on the war film in *Variety,* 30 January 1946, p. 5; on the box-office failure and fate of the war film, see *Variety,* 7 August 1946, p. 4.

17. *NYTFR,* 12 November 1949.

18. Actually, THE BEST YEARS OF OUR LIVES finished its initial run in a virtual dead heat with the December 1949 release SAMSON AND DELILAH, which, of course, generated most of its revenue in 1950.

19. James Agee, reviews in *The Nation,* 14 and 28 December 1946, reprinted in James Agee, *Agee on Film,* vol. 1 (New York: Grossett & Dunlap, 1958), p. 232.

20. *Motion Picture Herald,* 23 November 1946, p. 20.

21. *NYTFR,,* 22 November 1946.

22. Statistics from Ed Buscombe, *The BFI Companion to the Western* (London: BFI Publishing, 1988), pp. 426–428. According to Buscombe's data, Hollywood's proportionate output of Westerns would reach an all-time high of 34 percent in 1950. See also *Variety,* 16 June 1947, p. 9; *Motion Picture Herald,* 8 November 1947, p. 17.

23. Buscombe, *The BFI Companion to the Western,* p. 426.

24. *Ibid,* p. 290.

25. In a *Women's Home Companion* poll conducted in mid-1946, for example, "romantic drama" was cited as the top preference of women moviegoers, with a 54 percent preference; musicals (48 percent), musical comedy (42 percent), and light romance (39 percent) were the next choices. Reported in *Motion Picture Herald,* 8 June 1946, p. 28.

26. See, for example, Molly Haskell, *From Reverence to Rape: The Treatment of Women in the Movies* (New York: Holt, Rinehart, & Winston, 1974); Marjorie Rosen, *Popcorn Venus* (New York: Avon, 1974); and Andrea S. Walsh, *Women's Film and the Female Experience, 1940–1950* (New York: Praeger, 1984).

27. Richard B. Jewell with Vernon Harbin, *The RKO Story* (New York: Arlington House, 1982), p. 227; Tim Brooks and Earl Marsh, *The Complete Directory of Prime Time Network TV Shows* (New York: Ballantine, 1979), p. 372.

28. Zanuck to writer Jules Furthman, 2 April 1947, reprinted in Behlmer, *Memo from Darryl F. Zanuck,,* p. 127.

29. *Variety,* 8 January 1947, p. 8.

30. *NYTFR,* 26 December 1945.

31. James Agee, review in *Time,* 7 January 1946, reprinted in Agee, *Agee on Film,* p. 360.

32. Schary was not pleased with this situation, as indicated by a bit of selective recollection in a 1973 interview in which he discussed MGM's musical "golden age" in relation to his role at the studio. Acknowledging that "we had a kind of musical stock company at MGM," Schary stated: "If we had ten good ideas for musicals [in any given year], . . . we made ten. If we had one, we made one. My feeling was, let's not count how many melodramas, or how many dramas or comedies, or musicals." Quoted in Donald Knox, *The Magic Factory: How MGM Made* An American in Paris (New York: Praeger, 1973), pp. 38–39.

33. Joel Finler, *The Hollywood Story* (New York: Crown, 1988), p. 281.

34. John Douglas Eames, *The MGM Story* (New York: Crown, 1975), pp. 206–277. See also Christopher H. Sterling and Timothy R. Haight, *The Mass Media: The Aspen Institute Guide to Communications Industry Trends* (New York: Praeger, 1978), p. 294.

35. *Wall Street Journal,* 4 November 1949, p. 1; *Variety,* 4 January 1950, pp. 1, 59. The five MGM musicals (some of which were released in late 1948) were WORDS AND MUSIC, IN THE GOOD OLD SUMMERTIME, THE BARKLEYS OF BROADWAY, NEPTUNE'S DAUGHTER, and TAKE ME OUT TO THE BALL GAME. Not included were several late-1949 releases, such as the MGM musical hit ON THE TOWN.

36. *Variety,* 5 January 1949, p. 47. Pasternak produced five films which earned a total of $13.85 million, and Freed produced four films which earned $10.5 million.

37. "Interview with Stanley Donen," *Movie,* Spring 1977, pp. 27, 28.

38. *Life,* 25 August 1947, n.p..

39. *NYTFR,* 9 May 1946.

40. James Agee, review in *The Nation,* 14 September 1946, reprinted in Agee, *Agee on Film,* pp. 216–217.

41. Michael Walker, introduction to Ian Cameron, ed., *The Movie Book of Film Noir* (London: Verso, 1992), pp. 37–38.

42. Frank Krutnik, *In a Lonely Street* (New York: Routledge, 1992), pp. xiii–xiv.

43. Johnston quoted in Brian Neve, *Film and Politics in America* (New York: Routledge, 1992), p. 90; see also Neve on the Alliance, p. 90. Rand's "Screen Guide for Americans" quoted in Lillian Ross, "Come in, Lassie!," *New Yorker,* 21 February 1948, p. 42.

44. James Agee, review in *The Nation,* 10 January 1948, reprinted in *Agee on Film,* pp. 289–290.

45. *New Yorker,* 21 February 1948, p. 46.

46. John Huston, *An Open Book* (New York: Knopf, 1980), p. 150.

47. See Negulesco's two-year contract of 31 August 1945, JOHNNY BELINDA file, Warner Legal Collection, UW—M. See also William R. Meyer, *Warner Brothers Directors* (New Rochelle, N.Y.: Arlington House, 1978), pp. 259–260.

48. *Fortune,* April 1949, pp. 138, 141.

49. Accounts of the film's rental earnings vary slightly. The 4 January 1950 issue of *Variety* puts them at $4.2 million (p. 1); *Variety*'s 24 February 1992 listing of all-time rental champs (pp. 168–169) puts its earnings at $3.8 million.

50. For an excellent treatment of the production and an analysis of ALL THE KING'S MEN, see Neve, *Film and Politics in America,* pp. 142–144.

51. William Faulkner, author of *Intruder in the Dust,* did win the Nobel Prize for Literature in 1949, but at the time none of his novels were in print. Note too that in Arthur Laurents's original stage version of *Home of the Brave,* the central character is a Jew, not a black.

52. *NYTFR,* THE HOME OF THE BRAVE, 13 May 1949; LOST BOUNDARIES, 1 July 1949; PINKY, 30 September 1949; and INTRUDER IN THE DUST, 23 November 1949.

53. *Variety,* 28 December 1949, p. 1.

54. Neve, *Film and Politics in America,* p. 147.

55. Daily *Variety,* 6 August 1945, p. 1. See agreement of 15 May 1946 between Mark Hellinger Productions and Universal Pictures; the contract is also outlined in Martin Gang (Hellinger's attorney) to Universal, 9 May 1946, Universal Collection, USC.

56. Hellinger to attorney Maurice Speiser, 28 August 1945, Universal Collection, USC.

57. *Ibid.*; details of story deal in Universal agreement of 24 November 1945 with Hellinger. Hellinger paid Hemingway $36,750 for the film rights to his story. Universal Collection, USC.

58. On script development, see Hellinger to Veiller, 14 February 1946, and Veiller to Hellinger, 12 March 1946; on screenplay approval, see Universal agreement of 8 March 1946; all in Universal Collection, USC.

59. Budget compiled 25 April 1946; in final accounting (27 December 1947), the picture had grossed $2,903,000 worldwide. Universal Collection, USC.

60. Daily production reports for THE KILLERS, 29 April 1946 to 28 June 1946, Universal Collection, USC.

61. Final accounting of 27 December 1947, Universal Collection, USC. For domestic rentals, see *Variety,* 8 January 1947, p. 8.

62. James Agee, review in *The Nation,* 14 September 1946, reprinted in *Agee on Film,* p. 217.

63. *NYTFR,* 17 July 1947. See also Georges Sadoul, *Dictionary of Films* (Berkeley: University of California Press, 1975), p. 45.

64. Universal story approval, Universal agreement of 17 October 1946 with Hellinger, who also was paid $5,000 for the "original story." Wald to Hellinger, 16 October 1946, and several other undated letters updating Hellinger on the progress of the research, Universal Collection, USC.

65. Maltz notes appended to final script of 7 May 1947 (with same date), Universal Collection, USC.

66. Final script/project approval, Universal agreement of 5 May 1947 with Hellinger; budget and schedule 6 June 1947; both in Universal Collection, USC.

67. All discussion of the production of THE NAKED CITY, unless otherwise noted, is culled from the daily production reports (31 May 1947 to 12 September 1947), THE NAKED CITY production file, Universal Collection, USC.

68. *Variety,* 5 January 1949, p. 46.

69. James Agee, review in *Time,* 24 April 1948, reprinted in *Agee on Film,* p. 301.

70. *NYTFR,* 5 March 1948.

71. Sadoul, *Dictionary of Films,* p. 234.
72. On the budget and production costs, see *Variety,* 5 January 1949, p. 21; on marketing and promotion, see *Variety,* 28 December 1949, p. 3. According to both contemporaneous and more recent accounts in *Variety,* SAMSON AND DELILAH returned $11.5 million, and BEST YEARS $11.3 million. Both films have been surpassed by Disney features like BAMBI and CINDERELLA, owing to the enormous success of the Disney films as theatrical reissues over the years. See "All-time Film Rental Champs," *Variety,* 24 February 1992, pp. 160–164.
73. *NYTFR,* 22 December 1949.

CHAPTER 12 (Documenting the 1940s)

1. Rather than replay a tedious meditation on the metaphysics of screen reality and screen illusion, I've decided to rely on the commonsense appreciation of the points of difference—and convergence—between documentary cinema and the entertainment film. The British documentarian John Grierson's classic definition is as serviceable as any: "the creative treatment of actuality." John Grierson, *Grierson on Documentary* (New York: Harcourt, Brace, and Company, 1947), p. 5.
2. Of the early documentary adventure films, a contemporaneous historian of the motion picture industry, Benjamin H. Hampton, observed: "None of these pictures told a story in accordance with accepted patterns of the studios, yet each attracted large audiences." He estimated that the Johnsons' SIMBA earned over $2 million in America and abroad. *History of the American Film Industry from Its Beginnings to 1931* (1931; New York: Dover, 1970), p. 422.
3. Quoted in Peter Bogdanovich, *Pieces of Time* (New York: Dell), p. 223.
4. Although there were a number of ethnic or foreign-language cinemas in the big cities (twenty-five in New York City alone), the non-Hollywood market was peripheral to the American experience of motion pictures. In the 1930s, "a handful of such hybrid operations were able to make a go of it," observes the cultural historian Douglas Gomery, but with World War II, "the marginal theater that had turned to foreign films in the 1930s now could make far more money showing anything from Hollywood." Gomery, *Shared Pleasures: A History of Movie Presentation in the United States* (Madison: University of Wisconsin Press, 1992), pp. 179, 180, 171–196.
5. Margaret Cussler, *Not by a Long Shot: Adventures of a Documentary Film Producer* (New York: Exposition Press, 1952), p. 9. Though no fewer than twenty-seven government agencies were engaged in film production during the 1930s under FDR, the only documentaries that got any appreciable distribution outside of federal outposts such as military bases and Civilian Conservation Corps campgrounds were THE PLOW THAT BROKE THE PLAINS, with more than 3,000 theater playdates, and THE RIVER, with more than 5,000 playdates. Angry that the Roosevelt administration was producing motion pictures without specific authorization, and amid Republican charges of federally financed "New Deal propaganda," Congress terminated the U.S. Film Service on 30 June 1940. "Fight in Congress over 'Fight for Life' Hits U.S. Documentary Films," *Motion Picture Herald,* 30 March 1940, p. 13.
6. The standard and essential account of the commercial Hollywood newsreel is Raymond Fielding, *The American Newsreel 1911–1967* (Norman: University of Oklahoma Press, 1972). With the exception of Paramount, each of the newsreels has a labyrinthine corporate history. As Fielding notes, "Four of the five major names associated with the history of the American newsreel had introduced their series" by 1918: Pathé, Hearst (MGM), Universal, and Fox. A necessary bibliographical companion is K. R. M. Short, *World War II Through the American Newsreels 1942–1945: An Introduction and Guide to the Microfiches* (New York: Oxford Microfilm Publications, 1985). For a useful overview, see David H. Mould, "Historical Trends in the Criticism of the Newsreel and Television News," *Journal of Popular Film and Television,* Fall 1984, pp. 118–126.
7. On the screen magazine, see Raymond Fielding, *The March of Time, 1935–1951* (New York: Oxford University Press, 1978), and Richard T. Elson, "Time Marches on the Screen," and Richard Meran Barsam, "'This Is America': Documentaries for Theaters, 1942–1951," in Barsam, ed., *Nonfiction Film Theory and Criticism* (New York: Dutton, 1976), pp. 95–114; 115–135.
8. Bosley Crowther, "'Time' Marches Off," *New York Times,* 15 July 1951, sect. 2, p. 1. The *Times* film critic was writing on the occasion of the screen magazine's decision to cease production.

9. Dan Doherty, "Editing the Newsreel," *Journal of the Society of Motion Picture Engineers,* November 1946, p. 358. The coinage "smorgasbord" comes from the documentary filmmaker Newton Meltzer.

10. Again, the date of the event would predate the date of its newsreel appearance. Although by 1940 the five commercial newsreels were the fourth-largest user of air express (after machinery, printed matter, and clothing), the circulation life of each newsreel issue was about four weeks.

11. Newton E. Meltzer, "Are the Newsreels News?," *Hollywood Quarterly* 2 April 1947, p. 271; Ferdinand Kuhn Jr., "Kennedy Helped Censor Newsreel, Commons Learns," *New York Times,* 24 November 1938, pp. 1, 22; "White House Pictures," *Motion Picture Herald,* 11 November 1944, p. 8.

12. Two eyewitness accounts of the frenzied pace of newsreel production in the 1930s are Janet Mabie, "Reeling up the Newsreels," *Christian Science,* 19 June 1935, pp. 3, 12; and Robert W. Desmond, "News About the Newsreel," *Christian Science,* 28 September 1938, pp. 5, 15.

13. The newsreel coverage of the death of Dillinger is anomalous and instructive. Though only a month before, on 13 June 1934, the MPPDA had put in effect stringent new enforcement mechanisms for the Production Code, the new standards and practices had not yet become a shared set of commonly acknowledged cultural and cinematic boundaries. That the portrait of Dillinger in death was a departure from normative newsreel content, and that exhibitors might have reason to be wary of such unpleasant scenes, is indicated by *Variety*'s angle on the newsreel program at New York's Embassy Theater the week after Dillinger was gunned down: "Death of Dillinger has established another precedent for the newsreels and assignments for the cameramen. After this the boys will have to add the morgue to their coverage. A genuine semi-close-up of the dead gunman's face is graphic to say the least." The reviewer concluded with a telling warning about the lingering impact of the image on movie-house patrons: "It will stay with an audience of any imagination for a long time. *And the immediate memory might even distract them from the rest of the program* [italics added]" "Newsreels," *Variety,* 31 July 1934, p. 17.

14. "Newsreel War Scenes Get Theatre Attention," *Motion Picture Herald,* 29 June 1940, p. 42; Tom Waller, "Checking the Newsreels," *Variety,* 2 January 1934, p. 5.

15. "Filming Pearl Harbor(s)," *Motion Picture Herald,* 2 February 1942, p. 9.

16. "House Reviews: Embassy, N.Y.," *Variety,* 11 March 1942, p. 49.

17. "More Criticism on 'Pollyanna' War Newsreels," *Variety,* 11 March 1942, pp. 4, 27; "Harmon Is Army's No. 1 'Poison Guy' in Scrap Releasing Censored Reels," *Variety,* 8 September 1943, p. 4.

18. *1944 Film Daily Year Book,* p. 147.

19. The editors of *Look* magazine offer a colorful account of Hollywood's military work in *Movie Lot to Beachhead: The Motion Picture Goes to War and Prepares for the Future* (Garden City, N.Y.: Doubleday, 1945).

20. *The War Reports of General of the Army George C. Marshall, et al.* (New York: J. B. Lippincott, 1947), p. 281.

21. The Office of Military History's official history of the Army Signal Corps in the Second World War provides lucid clarification of the myriad acronyms, nomenclatures, units, and branches of the various military groups engaged in wartime motion picture production. Capra actually produced the early entries in the "Why We Fight" series for the Special Services Branch, a special status that caused a good deal of resentment within the regular Army Signal Corps ranks. Eventually, a directive on 1 September 1943 put him under the authority of the Army Pictorial Service. See all three volumes of Office of the Chief of Military History's *The Signal Corps: The Emergency, the Test, the Outcome* (Washington, D.C.: Government Printing Office, 1957), esp. vol. 2, pp. 387–426. Capra tells his version in *The Name Above the Title* (New York: Macmillan, 1971), pp. 359–408. For a succinct overview, see Richard Dyer MacCann, "World War II: Armed Forces Documentary," in Barsam, *Nonfiction Film Theory and Criticism,* pp. 136–157.

22. Since little in film history is absolutely sui generis, Sergei Eisenstein's OCTOBER (1928) and the documentarians at KINO in the Soviet Union can claim a kind of priority over Frank Capra and the War Department.

23. Fielding, *The March of Time,* pp. 187–201; Capra, *The Name Above the Title,* pp. 362–364. On the lack of independent newsreel coverage of the Nazis, see "Rambling Reporter," *Hollywood Reporter,* 30 November 1938, p. 2.

24. Here and throughout, the dates given for orientation films and combat reports mark the commercial release dates according to the War Activities Committee. The actual production dates and dates when military service people may have seen the films might well have been much earlier. For example, PRELUDE TO WAR was completed in 1942 and released commercially by WAC on 27 May 1943. Likewise, John Huston's REPORT FROM THE ALEUTIANS was made in summer of 1942, actually before Darryl F. Zanuck's AT THE FRONT IN NORTH AFRICA, although Zanuck's film was released by WAC before Huston's film.

25. The 1945 volume of *Movies at War,* WAC's annual report, on file in the MPAA New York office, lists 161 combat reports and "Victory" films released to home-front theaters during 1941–1945. This figure does not include studio-made shorts and charity appeals produced at the encouragement of the government and distributed to member theaters through normal chains of distribution, nor does it include imported and independently produced documentaries. On the screening of the "Victory" films, see "Industry Police System Proposed to Ensure 100% Showing Gov't Shorts," *Variety,* 25 March 1942, p. 4; and "94% Using 'Em," *Variety,* 15 April 1942, p. 5.

26. "Newsreels Bring Bloody Iwo Home," *Motion Picture Herald,* 10 March 1945, p. 36.

27. *Motion Picture Herald,* 14 July 1945, p. 36.

28. "Review of *Desert Victory,*" *Variety,* 31 March 1943, p. 8; and "Army Forbids Faking of Any Battle Shots," *Hollywood Reporter,* 21 April 1943, p. 2; each noted the staged shots in DESERT VICTORY. See also "War Shots Faking Officially Denied," *Hollywood Reporter,* 1 April 1943, p. 8.

29. William Stull, "Combat Camera," *Flying,* April 1943, p. 98.

30. John Dured, "Newsreeler's Dilemma," *American Cinematographer,* June 1949, p. 201.

31. "Metro's Documentary on Byrd's Expedition," *Variety,* 11 November 1947, p. 5.

32. Telford Taylor, *The Anatomy of the Nuremberg Trials: A Personal Memoir* (Boston: Little, Brown, 1992), p. 200. Taylor recalls that the reaction of the conspirators to THE NAZI PLAN surprised the prosecution. "Far from viewing the film as another nail in their coffins, they enjoyed it hugely."

33. Charles Loring, "Americans at Home: Documentary Series in Color," *American Cinematography,* March 1948, pp. 94–95. The review of LOUISIANA STORY in *Variety* (22 September 1948) deemed it "invaluable public relations for Standard Oil of New Jersey" and observed: "The firm has no rights and no identification in the film, but stands to get across the idea that oil companies are beneficently public spirited, their employees honest, industrious, and amiable, and their operations productive and innocuous."

34. Loring, "Americans at Home," p. 94.

35. Terry Ramsaye, "Semi-Documentary," *Motion Picture Herald,* 7 February 1948, p. 7.

36. James Agee, "Films," *The Nation,* 3 July 1948, pp. 24–25.

37. "Feature-Length Documentaries, Tel Offered as Solutions to Shorts Snarl," *Variety,* 21 January 1948, p. 4.

38. Ezra Goodman, "Postwar Motion Pictures," *American Cinematographer,* May 1945, pp. 160, 176. Goodman averred: "The majority of photographers in the armed forces are former Hollywood moviemakers, and it seems unlikely that they will discard their new found techniques when they return to cinema city." Robert Parrish, *Growing up in Hollywood* (Boston: Little, Brown, 1976), p. 173.

39. Herb A. Lightman, "13 Rue Madeleine—Documentary Style in the Photoplay," *American Cinematographer,* March 1947, p. 88; Lightman, "Documentary Style," *American Cinematographer,* May 1949, p. 161. In *The American Film Musical* (Bloomington: Indiana University Press, 1987), Rick Altman offers a useful caution about hyping the originality of the location work in ON THE TOWN, noting that King Vidor's HALLELUJAH (1929), for example, also showcased on-location musical numbers. But it was only after the war, and because of the war, that on-location shooting and documentary style became a standard procedure for classical Hollywood cinema.

40. Regarding Hollywood's grudging acknowledgment of the existence of television in feature films, *Variety* cited the video sequences in Universal-International's SOMETHING IN THE WIND (1947), Paramount's RED, HOT, AND BLUE (1949) and 20th Century–Fox's MY BLUE HEAVEN (1950) as markers of the studios' realization "that the new medium has taken too big a hold on the public to be ignored." "H'Wood to Go Steady with TV," *Variety,* 28 September 1949, pp. 1, 30.

41. "World Series Big Boom for Midwest Tele," *Variety,* 6 October 1948, pp. 27, 36; and Fred Hift, "Newsreel and Video Will Slug It out in Political Ring," *Motion Picture Herald,* 5 June 1948, pp. 22–23.

42. "News Services Launching 16mm Television Newsreel," *American Cinematographer,* February 1948, p. 53. See also "Hollywood Bulletin Board," *American Cinematographer,* July 1948, pp. 224, 247.

43. "Newsreels in Color as Offset to Television?" *Variety,* 31 December 1947, p. 3; and "Warner Color News NSG," *Variety,* 14 January 1948, p. 10.

44. "Newsreels' Nifty Inaugural Job," *Variety,* 26 January 1949, p. 11; "Video's Quicker Coverage Alters Newsreels' Format," *Variety,* 26 April 1949, p. 6.

45. "Metro, INS Linked to Telenews Deal," *Variety,* 12 December 1947, p. 24; "Cig Coin Cupids Pix-Tele Match," *Variety,* 28 January 1948, p. 1; "Camel Cancels Fox 'Newsreel' for 'Hot' News," *Variety,* 1 January 1949, p. 31.

46. "Cig Coin Cupids Pix-Tele Match," *Variety,* 28 January 1948, p. 61; "Embassy to Drop Newsreels," *New York Times,* 6 November 1949, sect. 2, p. 5.

47. "Richard de Rochemont Seen Exiting Time Org. as March of Time Folds," *Variety,* 11 July 1951, p. 4. "In effect," observed the *Variety* obituary, "the *March of Time* was a prestige series which, almost from the start, did not return earnings to the parent company"; "Economics Crushing Newsreels; Looks Like Two Go, Three Stay; 'Pooling' Idea Never Developed," *Variety,* 25 July 1956, pp. 3, 16; "Last Two Newsreels Call It a Day," *Motion Picture Herald,* 29 November 1967, pp. 1, 4.

CHAPTER 13 (Television and Hollywood in the 1940s)

1. J. Fred MacDonald, *One Nation Under Television: The Rise and Decline of Network TV* (New York: Pantheon, 1990), p. 8; "Television Is Ready," *Hollywood Reporter,* 28 November 1934, p. 1; Joseph H. Udelson, *The Great Television Race: A History of the American Television Industry, 1925–1941* (Tuscaloosa: University of Alabama Press, 1982); "1939—Television Year," *Business Week,* 1 December 1938, pp. 17–31. See also Garth Jowett, "Dangling the Dream? The Presentation of Television to the American Public, 1928–1952," *Historical Journal of Film, Radio and Television* 14, no. 2 (1994), pp. 121–145. According to Jowett, the climate of prophecy surrounding television also sowed considerable skepticism among a public that had witnessed many premature predictions and lackluster demonstrations during the 1930s.

2. MacDonald, *One Nation Under Television,* pp. 19–20.

3. Ronald Haver, *David O. Selznick's Hollywood* (New York: Bonanza Books, 1980), p. 304; "Television for 'GWTW' Premiere," *Hollywood Reporter,* 12 December 1939, p. 1.

4. "Fly Sees Hollywood as Source of Television Program Supply," *Motion Picture Herald,* 31 August 1940, p. 59; "Fly Impressed by Tour of Movie Lots," *Broadcasting,* 1 September 1940, p. 40.

5. Michele Hilmes, *Hollywood and Broadcasting: From Radio to Cable* (Champaign: University of Illinois Press, 1990), p. 8.

6. "Warner Seeking MBS Interest but Rejection of Offer Is Seen," *Broadcasting,* 1 May 1936, p. 8.

7. "Film Industry Advised to Grab Television," *Broadcasting,* 15 June 1937, p. 7, quoted in David Alan Larson, "Integration and Attempted Integration Between the Motion Picture and Television Industries" (Ph.D. diss., Ohio University, 1979), p. 31. For more on the movie industry's consideration of television during the 1930s, see Eric Smoodin, "Motion Pictures and Television, 1930–1945: A Pre-History of Relations Between the Two Media," *Journal of the University Film and Video Association* 34, no. 3 (Summer 1982), pp. 3–8. For a more detailed discussion of Hollywood's role in radio, see Richard B. Jewell, "Hollywood and Radio: Competition and Partnership in the 1930s," *Historical Journal of Film, Radio, and Television* 4, no. 2 (1984), pp. 125–141, and Hilmes, *Hollywood and Broadcasting,* pp. 53–74.

8. Warner Bros. Pictures, general television file, 1930–1936, Warner Bros. Pictures Collection, Department of Special Collections, Doheny Library, University of Southern California; Lawrence Bergreen, *Look Now, Pay Later: The Rise of Network Broadcasting* (New York: New American Library, 1980), p. 121.

9. Tino Balio, *United Artists: The Company Built by the Stars* (Madison: University of Wisconsin Press, 1976), pp. 136–138.

10. Selznick to John Hay Whitney, 17 November 1937; Selznick to John Wharton, 24 November 1937; both in Selznick Collection, UT.

11. For more on the CBS-Paramount merger, see Jonathan Buchsbaum, "Zukor Buys Protection: The Paramount Stock Purchase of 1929," *Cine-Tracts* 2 (Summer–Fall 1979), pp. 49–62; Douglas

Gomery, *The Hollywood Studio System* (New York: St. Martin's Press, 1986), pp. 124–132; Hilmes, *Hollywood and Broadcasting*, pp. 36–46.

12. "Paul Raibourn of Par Stresses Why Film Co. Bought into DuMont," *Variety*, 1 May 1940, p. 4. For a more complete account of Paramount's investment in DuMont, see Timothy R. White, "Hollywood's Attempt at Appropriating Television: The Case of Paramount Pictures," in Tino Balio, ed., *Hollywood in the Age of Television* (Boston: Unwin Hyman, 1990), pp. 145–163; and Timothy R. White, "Hollywood on (Re)Trial: The American Broadcasting–United Paramount Merger Hearing," *Cinema Journal* 31, no. 3 (Spring 1992), pp. 19–36.

13. "Television vs. Theatre," *Variety*, 3 May 1939, p. 1, 30.

14. *Ibid.*

15. Hilmes, *Hollywood and Broadcasting*, p. 117.

16. "Television Comes to That Corner Again," *Motion Picture Herald*, 11 January 1941, p. 27.

17. "Prize Fight's Telecasting Irks Exhibs," *Variety*, 1 March 1939, p. 1; "Non-commercial BBC Embarrassed by Runaway Theatre Television," *Variety*, 8 March 1939, p. 1; "Baird Vision to Enter U.S. During N.Y. Fair," *Variety*, 1 March 1939, p. 2; "RCA Shows Wide-Screen Television for Theaters to Its Stockholders," *Motion Picture Herald*, 11 May 1940, p. 5.

18. "Television Brought to Theatre by RCA Large Screen Showing," *Motion Picture Herald*, 1 February 1941, pp. 30–31; "Theatre Television," *Motion Picture Herald*, 10 May 1941, p. 9; Terry Ramsaye, "Wired Television Makes Debut," *Motion Picture Herald*, 17 May 1941, p. 15. Movie industry executives in attendance included Paramount's Barney Balaban, Columbia's Jack Cohn, Loew's Nicholas Schenck, 20th Century–Fox's Spyros Skouras, and Warner Bros.'s Albert Warner.

19. "Paramount First Film Studio to Turn to Production," *Motion Picture Herald*, 14 September 1940, p. 19; "Television a Home Element, Says Sarnoff," *Motion Picture Herald*, 1 July 1939, p. 33.

20. Quoted in William Boddy, *Fifties Television: The Industry and Its Critics* (Champaign: University of Illinois Press, 1990), p. 23.

21. Douglas Gomery, "Failed Opportunities: The Integration of the U.S. Motion Picture and Television Industries," *Quarterly Review of Film Studies* 9, no. 3 (Summer 1984), p. 221; "Paramount Produces a Film to Show Advantages of Television," *Motion Picture Herald*, 16 March 1940, p. 29.

22. "Balaban Stresses Television Value," *Motion Picture Herald*, 1 February 1941, p. 32.

23. MacDonald, *One Nation Under Television*, p. 18.

24. "Commercial Television Is Delayed," *Motion Picture Herald*, 30 March 1940, p. 31.

25. "Paramount in Television, First Active Film Tieup," *Motion Picture Herald*, 20 April 1940, p. 14; "Motion Picture Industry Accused by RCA of Trying to Hamstring Television," *Motion Picture Herald*, 11 May 1940, p. 41.

26. See White, "Hollywood's Attempt at Appropriating Television," pp. 146–147; Hilmes, *Hollywood and Broadcasting*, p. 134.

27. "Paramount's Television Victory," *Variety*, 24 April 1940, p. 3; "FCC Gives Paramount Group Four Telecast Permits," *Motion Picture Herald*, 29 June 1940, p. 24; "Paramount First Film Studio to Turn to Television Production," *Motion Picture Herald*, 14 September 1940, p. 19; "B & K Will Telecast to Chicago Theatres Within Three Months," *Motion Picture Herald*, 18 January 1941, p. 29. DuMont introduced stations in New York and Washington, D.C.; the studio's Balaban & Katz theater circuit began broadcasting from a station in Chicago; and Television Productions, Inc., was given a permit for a station in Los Angeles. RCA, meanwhile, received permits for stations in New York, Chicago, and Washington, D.C.

28. MacDonald, *One Nation Under Television*, p. 34.

29. Boddy, *Fifties Television*, p. 44.

30. MacDonald, *One Nation Under Television*, p. 38.

31. Al Steen, "Television Developments," *1946 Film Daily Year Book*, p. 75.

32. "Majors Bolster Stake in Postwar Television," *Motion Picture Herald*, 5 June 1943, p. 31; "Hollywood Eyes Television as Postwar Customer," *Motion Picture Herald*, 25 December 1943, p. 25; Al Steen, "Television in 1943," *1944 Film Daily Year Book*, p. 685; "Television for Leo," *Motion Picture Herald*, 2 December 1944, p. 9.

33. "Hollywood Eyes Television as Postwar Customer," *Motion Picture Herald*, 25 December 1943, p. 25; "Television Group to See First Film Made for Medium," *Motion Picture Herald*, 9 December 1944, p. 15; Al Steen, "Television Developments of 1944," *1945 Film Daily Year Book*, p. 722; "RKO Unwraps Pix Package for Tele," *Variety*, 20 March 1946, 3.

34. "Warners Buys Station Site," *Motion Picture Herald*, 23 September 1944, p. 32; "Hollywood Digs In," *Business Week*, 24 March 1945, pp. 94–95; Ralph Wilk, "Television in Hollywood," *1946 Film Daily Year Book*, p. 742.

35. "Trade Plans for Postwar Boom in Television," *Motion Picture Herald*, 27 February 1943, p. 23; "Majors Bolster Stake in Postwar Television," *Motion Picture Herald*, 5 June 1943, p. 31.

36. Larson, "Integration and Attempted Integration," pp. 57–58; "Tele Theaters in All Keys," *Variety*, 12 January 1944, p. 5; Gomery, "Failed Opportunities," p. 224; "Theatre Television's Slice of the Spectrum Must Wait," *Motion Picture Herald*, 20 January 1945, p. 35; "Theatre Television Battles Again for Spectrum Space," *Motion Picture Herald*, 10 March 1945, p. 27.

37. "Closed Circuit," *Broadcasting*, 9 April 1945, p. 4, quoted in Larson, "Integration and Attempted Integration," p. 65.

38. "U.S. Suit Charges Film Cartel Bars Theatre Television," *Motion Picture Herald*, 22 December 1945, p. 23; "Release Video Patents Is Answer of Justice Dept. to Par," *Variety*, 26 December 1945, 3.

39. MacDonald, *One Nation Under Television*, p. 42; Boddy, *Fifties Television*, pp. 47–48.

40. "Link Warners to NBC Television," *Variety*, 30 January 1946, p. 1; "Warner-RCA Deal Unlocks Theatre Television Gate," *Motion Picture Herald*, 19 July 1947, p. 17; "RCA, 20th-Fox in Television Pact," *Motion Picture Herald*, 13 September 1947, p. 44; "Infant Theater Television Stuck with Diaper Pins," *Motion Picture Herald*, 3 July 1948, 13.

41. "Warners Buys Station Site," *Motion Picture Herald*, 23 September 1944, p. 32; "Hollywood Digs In," *Business Week*, 24 March 1945, pp. 94–95; Larson, "Integration and Attempted Integration," pp. 59, 73–74; Gomery, "Failed Opportunities," pp. 221, 225; Thomas F. Brady, "Warners to Make Television Films," *New York Times*, 4 January 1949, p. 21; "Suit Against Warner Holds up Radio Deal," *New York Times*, 18 February 1949, p. 37.

42. For a more detailed account of these conditions, see Douglas Gomery, "The Coming of Television and the 'Lost' Motion Picture Audience," *Journal of Film and Video* 38 (Summer 1985), pp. 5–11; and Thomas H. Guback, "Hollywood's International Market," in Tino Balio, ed., *The American Film Industry*, rev. ed. (Madison: University of Wisconsin Press, 1985), pp. 470–475.

43. Thomas F. Brady, "Hollywood Studio in Contract Field," *New York Times*, 22 November 1948, p. 29.

44. Thomas F. Brady, "New Hollywood Enterprise," *New York Times*, 9 January 1949, sect. 2, p. 5.

45. White, "Hollywood's Attempt at Appropriating Television," p. 148; Gomery, "Failed Opportunities," pp. 225–226.

46. Gomery, "Failed Opportunities," pp. 221–223.

47. "Par Under Fire for Its TV Plans," *Variety*, 27 April 1949, p. 6; "Quiz Justice Dept. on Legality of Pix' Entry into Video," *Variety*, 1 December 1948, p. 3.

48. Boddy, *Fifties Television*, pp. 50–52; MacDonald, *One Nation Under Television*, pp. 60–61.

49. MacDonald, *One Nation Under Television*, pp. 60–61.

50. Gomery, "Failed Opportunities," p. 227.

51. "Film Cos. Stymied Till FCC Rules Whether They're Anti-trust Violators," *Variety*, 16 March 1949, p. 26; "Suit Against Warners Holds up Radio Deal," p. 37.

52. Hilmes, *Hollywood and Broadcasting*, p. 130.

53. "Warners Wants out on Chi TV, but Assures FCC on Coast Aspirations," *Variety*, 11 May 1949, p. 26; "FCC Okays WINS, KLAC-TV Sales, Approves Other Transfers," *Variety*, 30 December 1953, p. 33.

54. Gomery, "Failed Opportunities," p. 223.

55. Jerry Fairbanks, "New Low-Cost TV Film Technique," *Television*, November 1949, pp. 23, 28; Jerry Fairbanks, "Multiple-Camera Techniques for Making Films," *American Cinematographer*, July 1950, pp. 238, 244.

56. Mary Gannon, "Hollywood and Television Try New Financial Patterns," *Television*, November 1948, p. 32.

57. "Film for '52," *Newsweek*, 11 August 1952, p. 54.

58. See J. Fred MacDonald, *Who Shot the Sheriff? The Rise and Fall of the TV Western* (New York: Praeger, 1987), pp. 20–24.

59. Much of this information is taken from "The Men Who Make and Sell TV Film," *Television*, July 1953, pp. 19–21. See also Barbara Moore, "The Cisco Kid and Friends: The Syndication of Television Series from 1948 to 1952," *Journal of Popular Film and Television* 8 (Spring 1980), pp. 26–33.

60. "Hollywood Can Grind out Film Fare for TV," *Business Week,* 24 November 1951, pp. 122–126.
61. Gomery, *The Hollywood Studio System,* pp. 148, 157.
62. "The Feature Is the Commercial," *Broadcasting,* 13 January 1958, p. 46.
63. "Screen Gems Has New Iron in Fire," *Broadcasting,* 13 April 1958, p. 76.
64. Albert R. Kroeger, "Steady as She Goes—Upward," *Television,* December 1965, p. 52; "Screen Gems Has New Iron," *Broadcasting,* 13 April 1958, p. 76.
65. "No Warners Films on Video, Jack L. Tells Sales Chiefs," *Los Angeles Daily News,* 14 July 1950, p. 27.
66. Hilmes, *Hollywood and Broadcasting,* p. 136.

CHAPTER 14 (Experimental and Avant-Garde Cinema in the 1940s)

1. The cine club movement of the 1920s that began in France and spread to several European cities was a loose network of film-screening and discussion groups comprising students, poets, and painters who often lived together on the fringes of universities that hosted lively intellectual atmospheres. Cine club participants watched European and Soviet avant-garde films, made their own experimental movies, and often wrote about the aesthetics of artisanal filmmaking in small journals and newsletters. For example, the documentary filmmaker Alexander Hammid was first exposed to experimental cinema at a Prague cine club, where he shortly thereafter began to write about cinema for local art journals and then turned to filmmaking itself. Thomas E. Valasek, "Alexander Hammid: A Survey of His Filmmaking Career," *Film Culture* 67–69 (1979), pp. 250–322.
2. P. Adams Sitney, *Visionary Cinema: The American Avant-Garde, 1943–1978,* 2d ed. (New York: Oxford University Press, 1979), p. 263.
3. See, for example, Lewis Jacobs, "Experimental Cinema in America," *Hollywood Quarterly* 3, no. 2 (Winter 1947–1948), p. 124.
4. M. Pryor, "Film Society Movement Catches On," *New York Times,* 18 September 1949, quoted in Stephen J. Dobi, "Cinema 16: America's Largest Film Society" (Ph.D. diss., New York University, 1984), p. 116.
5. Frank Stauffacher, ed., *Art in Cinema* (San Francisco: San Francisco Art in Cinema Society, San Francisco Art Museum, 1947).
6. Dobi, "Cinema 16," p. 117.
7. Scott MacDonald, "Amos Vogel and Cinema 16," *Wide Angle* 9, no. 3 (1987), p. 43.
8. *Ibid.,* p. 42.
9. Janet Staiger, *Interpreting Films: Studies in the Historical Reception of American Cinema* (Princeton, N.J.: Princeton University Press, 1992), p. 183.
10. James Agee was among the mainstream critics to regularly promote experimental and avant-garde cinema, particularly in his writing for *The Nation.* See, for instance, his 5 and 12 July 1947 reviews of Jean Vigo's ZERO DE CONDUITE (ZERO FOR CONDUCT) and L'ATALANTE, and his 3 July 1948 piece on Cinema 16, reprinted in *Agee on Film* (New York: Grossett & Dunlap, 1969), pp. 263–266, 307–309.
11. Lucy Fischer, "Program 1: 1943–1948," in John G. Hanhardt, ed., *A History of the American Avant-Garde Cinema* (New York: American Federation of the Arts, 1976), p. 80.
12. The musical soundtrack that now accompanies most extant prints of the film was made in the middle 1950s by Deren's third husband, the composer Teiji Ito.
13. For a more detailed discussion of Hammid's past films and his role in MESHES OF THE AFTERNOON, see Thomas E. Valasek, "Alexander Hammid: A Survey of His Filmmaking Career," pp. 250–322.
14. Maureen Turim, "Childhood Memories and Household Events in the Feminist Avant-garde," *Journal of Film and Video* 38 (Summer-Fall 1986), p. 87.
15. Maya Deren, "Program Notes on Three Early Films," n.d., Maya Deren Papers, reprinted in *Film Culture* 39 (Winter 1965), p. 1, and in VeVe A. Clark, Millicent Hodson, and Catrina Neiman, eds., *The Legend of Maya Deren,* vol. 1, pt. 2 (New York: Anthology Film Archives, Film Culture, 1988), p. 78.
16. Julian Wolfreys, "*Meshes of the Afternoon:* Hollywood, the Avant-garde, and Problems of Interpretation," *CineAction!* (Winter 1987–1988), p. 39.
17. See especially Lucy Fischer, "Program 1: 1943–1948," pp. 69–73; Sitney, *Visionary Cinema,* pp. 3–24.

18. See especially Lauren Rabinovitz, *Points of Resistance: Women, Power, and Politics in the Avant-Garde Cinema, 1943–1971* (Champaign: University of Illinois Press, 1991), pp. 55–65; Turim, "Childhood Memories and Household Events in the Feminist Avant-garde," pp. 86–93; Wolfreys, *"Meshes of the Afternoon,"* pp. 38–41.

19. Turim, "Childhood Memories and Household Events in the Feminist Avant-garde," p. 87.

20. Richard Lippold, "Dance and Film—A Review in the Form of a Reflection," *Dance Observer* 13, no. 5 (May 1946), p. 59, reprinted in Clark, Hodson, and Neiman, *The Legend of Maya Deren,* vol. 1, pt. 2, p. 393.

21. Parker Tyler, "Experimental Film: A New Growth," *Kenyon Review* 11, no. 1 (1949), p. 143.

22. Mary Ann Doane, *The Desire to Desire: The Woman's Film of the 1940s* (Bloomington: Indiana University Press, 1987), pp. 34–35. For an extended discussion of the way that MESHES OF THE AFTERNOON responds to and capitalizes on the woman's picture, see my discussion of the film in Rabinowitz, *Points of Resistance,* pp. 61–65.

23. Turim, "Childhood Memories and Household Events in the Feminist Avant-Garde," p. 88.

24. *Ibid.*

25. Parker Tyler, "Maya Deren as Filmmaker," *Filmwise* 2 (1962), p. 3.

26. Wolfreys, *"Meshes of the Afternoon,"* p. 39.

27. Fischer, "Program 1: 1943–1948," p. 75.

28. *Ibid.*

29. Quoted in Sitney, *Visionary Cinema,* p. 101.

30. Vito Russo, *The Celluloid Closet: Homosexuality in the Movies* (New York: Harper & Row, 1981), p. 98.

31. Richard Dyer, *The Matter of Images: Essays on Representations* (New York: Routledge, 1993), p. 44.

32. Sitney, *Visionary Cinema,* p. 100.

33. J. Hoberman, "Three Myths of Avant-garde Film," *Film Comment* 17, no. 3 (May–June 1981), pp. 34–35.

34. Anaïs Nin, *The Diary of Anaïs Nin, 1944–1947,* vol. 4, ed. Gunther Stuhlmann (New York: Harcourt Brace Jovanovich, 1971), p. 137.

Bibliography

PRINCIPAL ARCHIVAL SOURCES

John Ford Manuscripts Collection, Lilly Library, Indiana University, Bloomington (Ford Collection, IU).

Arthur Freed Collection, Department of Special Collections, Doheny Library, University of Southern California (Freed Collection, USC).

Mark Hellinger Collection, Department of Special Collections, Doheny Library, University of Southern California (Hellinger Collection, USC).

Alfred Hitchcock Collection, Margaret Herrick Library, Academic of Motion Picture Arts and Sciences, Beverly Hills, California (Hitchcock Collection, Academy).

Daniel J. Lord Papers, Jesuit Missouri Province Archives, St. Louis, Missouri (Lord Papers).

Lowell Mellett Papers, Franklin D. Roosevelt Library, Hyde Park, New York (Mellett Papers).

MGM Script Collection, Doheny Library, University of Southern California (MGM Script Collection, USC).

Oral History Collection, Louis B. Mayer Library, American Film Institute, Los Angeles (Oral History, AFI).

Records of the Office of War Information, record group 208, Federal Records Center, Suitland, Maryland (OWI Files).

Production Code Administration File, Margaret Herrick Library, Academy of Motion Picture Arts and Sciences, Beverly Hills, California (PCA Files).

Dore Schary Papers, Wisconsin Center for Film and Theatre Research, State Historical Society, University of Wisconsin—Madison (Schary Papers, UW—M).

David O. Selznick Collection, Hoblitzelle Theatre Arts Library, Harry Ransom Humanities Research Center, University of Texas at Austin (Selznick Collection, UT).

George Stevens Collection, Academy of Motion Picture Arts and Sciences, Los Angeles (Stevens Collection).

Twentieth Century–Fox Script Collection, Theatre Arts Library, University of California—Los Angeles (Fox Collection, UCLA).

United Artists Collection, Wisconsin Center for Film and Theatre Research, State Historical Society, University of Wisconsin—Madison (UA Collection, UW—M).

Universal Collection, Department of Special Collections, Doheny Library, University of Southern California (Universal Collection, USC).

Walter Wanger Collection, Wisconsin Center for Film and Theatre Research, State Historical Society, University of Wisconsin—Madison (Wanger Collection, UW—M).

Warner Bros. Archive, Department of Special Collections, Doheny Library, University of Southern California (Warner Archive, USC).

Warner Bros. Legal File, United Artists Collection, Wisconsin Center for Film and Theatre Research, State Historical Society, University of Wisconsin—Madison (Warner Legal Collection, UW—M).

PRINCIPAL NEWSPAPERS AND TRADE JOURNALS

Motion Picture Herald
New York Times
Variety
Wall Street Journal
Washington Post

BOOKS

Adamson, Joe. *Bugs Bunny: Fifty Years and Only One Grey Hare.* New York: Henry Holt, 1990.
————. *Tex Avery: King of Cartoons.* New York: Da Capo, 1985.
Agee, James. *Agee on Film.* Vol. 1. New York: Grossett & Dunlap, 1958.
Allen, Robert C., and Douglas Gomery. *Film History: Theory and Practice.* New York: Knopf, 1985.
Altman, Rick. *The American Film Musical.* Bloomington: Indiana University Press, 1987.
Anderson, Christopher. *Hollywood TV.* Austin: University of Texas Press, 1994.
Balio, Tino, ed. *United Artists: The Company Built by the Stars.* Madison: University of Wisconsin Press, 1976.
————. *The American Film Industry.* Rev. ed. Madison: University of Wisconsin Press, 1985.
————, ed. *Hollywood in the Age of Television.* Boston: Unwin Hyman, 1990.
————. *Grand Design: Hollywood as a Modern Business Enterprise, 1930–1939.* New York: Scribner's, 1993.
Barnouw, Erik. *Documentary: A History of the Non-Fiction Film.* New York: Oxford University Press, 1974.
Barsam, Richard Meran. *Nonfiction Film: A Critical History.* New York: Dutton, 1973.
————, ed. *Nonfiction Film Theory and Criticism.* New York: Dutton, 1976.
Basinger, Jeanine. *The World War II Combat Film: Anatomy of a Genre.* New York: Columbia University Press, 1986.
Behlmer, Rudy, ed. *Memo from David O. Selznick.* New York: Viking, 1972.
————. *America's Favorite Movies: Behind the Scenes.* New York: Frederick Ungar, 1982.
————, ed. *Inside Warner Bros. 1935–1951.* New York: Viking, 1985.
————, ed. *Memo from Darryl F. Zanuck.* New York: Grove Press, 1993.
Berg, A. Scott. *Goldwyn: A Biography.* New York: Knopf, 1989.
Berg, Charles Ramirez. *Cinema of Solitude: A Critical Study of Mexican Cinema, 1967–1983.* Austin: University of Texas Press, 1992.
Bergreen, Lawrence. *Look Now, Pay Later: The Rise of Network Broadcasting.* New York: New American Library, 1980.
Bernstein, Matthew. *Walter Wanger: Hollywood Independent.* Berkeley: University of California Press, 1995.
Black, Gregory D. *Hollywood Censored: Morality Codes, Catholics, and the Movies.* New York: Cambridge University Press, 1994.
Boddy, William. *Fifties Television: The Industry and Its Critics.* Champaign: University of Illinois Press, 1990.
Bordwell, David, Janet Staiger, and Kristen Thompson. *The Classical Hollywood Cinema: Film Style and Mode of Production to 1960.* New York: Columbia University Press, 1985.
Brown, John Mason. *The Worlds of Robert E. Sherwood.* New York: Harper & Row, 1962.
Brownlow, Kevin. *Behind the Mask of Innocence.* New York: Knopf, 1990.
Buscombe, Edward. *The BFI Companion to the Western.* London: BFI Publishing, 1988.
Cameron, Ian, ed. *The Movie Book of Film Noir.* London: Verso, 1992.
Capra, Frank. *The Name Above the Title: An Autobiography.* New York: Macmillan, 1971.
Ceplair, Larry, and Steven Englund. *The Inquisition in Hollywood: Politics in the Film Community, 1930–1960.* Garden City, N.Y.: Anchor Press, 1980.
Chafe, William H. *The American Woman: Her Changing Social, Economic and Political Roles, 1920–1970.* New York: Oxford University Press, 1975.
Chaplin, Charles. *My Autobiography.* New York: Simon & Schuster, 1964.
Cogley, John. *Report on Blacklisting.* New York: Fund for the Republic, 1956.

Conant, Michael. *Antitrust in the Motion Picture Industry: Economic and Social Analysis.* Berkeley: University of California Press, 1960.

Cook, David A. *A History of Narrative Film.* 2d ed. New York: Norton, 1981.

Cripps, Thomas. *Slow Fade to Black: The Negro in American Film, 1900–1942.* New York: Oxford University Press, 1977.

Crowdus, Gary, ed. *A Political Companion to Film.* Chicago: Lakeview Press, 1994.

Cussler, Margaret. *Not by a Long Shot: Adventures of a Documentary Film Producer.* New York: Exposition Press, 1952.

Dick, Bernard F. *The Star-Spangled Screen: The American World War II Film.* Lexington: University of Kentucky Press, 1985.

Diggins, John P. *Mussolini and Fascism.* Princeton, N.J.: Princeton University Press, 1972.

Dixon, Wheeler, ed. *Producers Releasing Corporation: A Comprehensive Filmography and History.* Jefferson, N.C.: McFarland, 1986.

Doane, Mary Ann. *The Desire to Desire: The Woman's Film of the 1940s.* Bloomington: Indiana University Press, 1987.

Doherty, Thomas. *Projections of War: Hollywood, American Culture and World War II.* New York: Columbia University Press, 1993.

Dyer, Richard. *The Matter of Images: Essays on Representations.* New York: Routledge, 1993.

———. *Heavenly Bodies: Film Stars and Society.* New York: St. Martin's Press, 1986.

Eames, John Douglas. *The MGM Story.* New York: Crown, 1975.

Fielding, Raymond. *The American Newsreel 1911–1967.* Norman: University of Oklahoma Press, 1972.

———. *The March of Time, 1935–1951.* New York: Oxford University Press, 1978.

Finch, Christopher. *The Art of Walt Disney.* New York: Abrams, 1973.

Finler, Joel W. *The Hollywood Story.* New York: Crown, 1988.

Fordin, Hugh. *The World of Entertainment.* Garden City, N.Y.: Doubleday, 1975.

Friedrich, Otto. *City of Nets: A Portrait of Hollywood in the 1940s.* New York: Harper & Row, 1987.

Gabler, Neal. *An Empire of Their Own: How the Jews Invented Hollywood.* New York: Doubleday, 1989.

Gaines, Jane, and Charlotte Herzog, eds. *Fabrications: Costume and the Female Body.* New York: Routledge, 1990.

Goldman, Eric F. *The Crucial Decade.* New York: Knopf, 1956.

Gomery, Douglas. *The Hollywood Studio System.* New York: St. Martin's Press, 1986.

———. *Shared Pleasures: A History of Movie Presentation in the United States.* Madison: University of Wisconsin Press, 1992.

Guback, Thomas. *The International Film Industry.* Bloomington: Indiana University Press, 1969.

Halberstam, David. *The Fifties.* New York: Fawcett Columbine, 1993.

Hambley, John, and Patrick Downing. *The Art of Hollywood: Fifty Years of Art Direction.* London: Thames Television, 1979.

Hampton, Benjamin H. *History of the American Film Industry from Its Beginnings to 1931.* 1931. Reprint. New York: Dover, 1970.

Handel, Leo A. *Hollywood Looks at Its Audience: A Report of Film Audience Research.* Urbana: University of Illinois Press, 1950.

Hanhardt, John G. *A History of the American Avant-garde Cinema.* New York: American Federation of the Arts, 1976.

Harmetz, Aljean. *The Making of* The Wizard of Oz. New York: Limelight, 1977.

———. *Round up the Usual Suspects: The Making of* Casablanca: *Bogart, Bergman, and World War II.* New York: Hyperion, 1992.

Hartmann, Susan. *The Home Front and Beyond: American Women in the 1940s.* Boston: Twayne, 1982.

Haskell, Molly. *From Reverence to Rape: The Treatment of Women in the Movies.* New York: Holt, Rinehart, & Winston, 1974.

Haver, Ronald. *David O. Selznick's Hollywood.* New York: Knopf, 1980.

Hilmes, Michele. *Hollywood and Broadcasting: From Radio to Cable.* Urbana: University of Illinois Press, 1990.

Hirschhorn, Clive. *The Warner Bros. Story.* New York: Crown, 1979.

———. *The Universal Story.* New York: Crown, 1983.

Huettig, Mae D. *Economic Control of the Motion Picture Industry.* Philadelphia: University of Pennsylvania Press, 1944.

Huston, John. *An Open Book.* New York: Knopf, 1980.

Jacobs, Lea. *The Wages of Sin: Censorship and the Fallen Woman Film, 1928–1942.* Madison: University of Wisconsin Press, 1991.

Jacobs, Lewis. *The Rise of the American Film: A Critical History.* New York: Teachers College Press, 1968.

———, ed. *The Documentary Tradition: From Nanook to Woodstock.* New York: Hopkins and Blake, 1971.

Jarvie, Ian. *Hollywood's Overseas Campaign: The North Atlantic Movie Trade, 1920–1950.* New York: Cambridge University Press, 1992.

Jewell, Richard B., with Vernon Harbin. *The RKO Story.* New York: Crown, 1982.

Jowett, Garth. *Film, the Democratic Art: A Social History of American Film.* Boston: Little, Brown, 1976.

Kael, Pauline. *The* Citizen Kane *Book.* Boston: Little, Brown, 1971.

Katz, Ephraim. *The Film Encyclopedia.* New York: Putnam's, 1971.

Keegan, John. *The Second World War.* New York: Viking, 1989.

Kenez, Peter. *Cinema and Soviet Society, 1917–1953.* New York: Cambridge University Press, 1992.

Kindem, Gorham, ed. *The American Movie Industry: The Business of Motion Pictures.* Carbondale: University of Illinois Press, 1982.

Kirkendall, Richard S. *The United States, 1929–1945: Years of Crisis and Change.* New York: McGraw-Hill, 1974.

Knox, Donald. *The Magic Factory: How MGM Made* An American in Paris. New York: Praeger, 1973.

Koppes, Clayton R., and Gregory D. Black. *Hollywood Goes to War: How Politics, Profits, and Propaganda Shaped World War II Movies.* New York: Free Press, 1987.

Krutnik, Frank. *In a Lonely Street: Film Noir, Genre, Masculinity.* New York: Routledge, 1992.

Landy, Marcia. *British Genres: Cinema and Society, 1930–1960.* Princeton, N.J.: Princeton University Press, 1991.

Leaming, Barbara. *Orson Welles.* New York: Penguin, 1985.

Lebow, Harlan. *Citizen Kane.* New York: Doubleday, 1990.

Leff, Leonard J., and Jerold L. Simmons. *The Dame in the Kimono: Hollywood, Censorship, and the Production Code from the 1920s to the 1960s.* New York: Grove Weidenfeld, 1990.

Lewis, Howard T. *The Motion Picture Industry.* New York: Van Nostrand, 1933.

Lichtenstein, Nelson. *Labor's War at Home: The CIO in World War II.* New York: Cambridge University Press, 1982.

Lingeman, Richard R. *Don't You Know There's a War On? The American Home Front, 1941–1945.* New York: Putnam's, 1970.

Look magazine, the Editors of. *Movie Lot to Beachhead: The Motion Picture Goes to War and Prepares for the Future.* Garden City, N.Y.: Doubleday, 1945.

MacDonald, J. Fred. *One Nation Under Television: The Rise and Decline of Network TV.* New York: Pantheon, 1990.

Maltby, Richard. *Harmless Entertainment: Hollywood and the Ideology of Consensus.* Metuchen, N.J.: Scarecrow Press, 1982.

Maltin, Leonard. *Of Mice and Magic: A History of American Animated Cartoons.* New York: McGraw-Hill, 1980.

Manvell, Roger. *Films and the Second World War.* New York: Delta, 1974.

May, Lary, ed. *Recasting America: Culture and Politics in the Age of the Cold War.* Chicago: University of Chicago Press, 1990.

McBride, Joseph. *Orson Welles.* New York: Viking, 1972.

———. *Hawks on Hawks.* Berkeley: University of California Press, 1982.

———. *Frank Capra: The Catastrophe of Success.* New York: Simon & Schuster, 1992.

McCann, Richard Dyer. *The People's Films: A Political History of U.S. Government Motion Pictures.* New York: Hastings House, 1973.

McCarthy, Todd, and Charles Flynn, eds. *Kings of the Bs.* New York: Dutton, 1975.

Meyer, William R. *Warner Brothers Directors.* New Rochelle, N.Y.: Arlington House, 1978.

Michael, Paul. *The Academy Awards: A Pictorial History.* 5th ed. New York: Crown, 1982.

Mosley, Leonard. *Zanuck: The Rise and Fall of Hollywood's Last Tycoon.* Boston: Little, Brown, 1984.

Navasky, Victor S. *Naming Names.* New York: Viking, 1980.

Neve, Brian. *Film and Politics in America: A Social Tradition.* New York: Routledge, 1992.

Nin, Anaïs. *The Diary of Anaïs Nin, 1944–1947.* Vol. 4. Edited by Gunther Stuhlmann. New York: Harcourt Brace Jovanovich, 1971.

Office of the Chief of Military History. *The Signal Corps: The Emergency, the Test, the Outcome.* Washington, D.C.: Government Printing Office, 1957.

Parker, R. A. C. *Struggle for Survival: The History of the Second World War.* New York: Oxford University Press, 1989.

Parrish, Robert. *Growing up in Hollywood.* Boston: Little, Brown, 1976.

Polan, Dana. *Power and Paranoia: History, Narrative, and the American Cinema, 1940–1950.* New York: Columbia University Press, 1986.

Powdermaker, Hortense. *Hollywood: The Dream Factory.* New York: Grossett & Dunlap, 1950.

Pribram, E. Deirdre, ed. *Female Spectators: Looking at Film and Television.* London and New York: Verso, 1988.

Prindle, David F. *The Politics of Glamour: Ideology and Democracy in the Screen Actors Guild.* Madison: University of Wisconsin Press, 1988.

Rabinovitz, Lauren. *Points of Resistance: Women, Power and Politics in the Avant-garde Cinema, 1943–1971.* Champaign: University of Illinois Press, 1991.

Renov, Michael. *Hollywood's Wartime Women.* Ann Arbor: UMI Research Press, 1988.

Roddick, Nick. *A New Deal in Entertainment: Warner Brothers in the 1930s.* London: British Film Institute, 1983.

Rosen, Marjorie. *Popcorn Venus: Women, Movies, and the American Dream.* New York: Avon, 1974.

Ross, Murray. *Stars and Strikes.* New York: Columbia University Press, 1941.

Rosten, Leo. *Hollywood: The Movie Colony, the Movie Makers.* New York: Harcourt, Brace, 1941.

Rupp, Leila J. *Mobilizing Women for War: German and American Propaganda, 1939–1945.* Princeton, N.J.: Princeton University Press, 1978.

Russo, Vito. *The Celluloid Closet: Homosexuality in the Movies.* New York: Harper & Row, 1981.

Schatz, Thomas. *Hollywood Genres: Formulas, Filmmaking, and the Studio System.* New York: Random House, 1981.

———. *The Genius of the System: Hollywood Filmmaking in the Studio Era.* New York: Pantheon, 1988.

Schwartz, Nancy Lynn. *The Hollywood Writers' Wars.* New York: Knopf, 1982.

Shain, Russell Earl. *An Analysis of Motion Pictures About the War Released by the American Film Industry, 1939–1970.* New York: Arno, 1976.

Shipman, David. *The Great Movie Stars: The International Years.* New York: St. Martin's Press, 1972.

Short, K. R. M. *World War II Through the American Newsreels 1942–1945: An Introduction and Guide to the Microfiches.* New York: Oxford Microfilm Publications, 1985.

Sitney, P. Adams. *Visionary Cinema: The American Avant-garde, 1943–1978.* 2d ed. New York: Oxford University Press, 1979.

Sklar, Robert. *Movie-Made America: A Cultural History of American Movies.* New York: Random House, 1975.

Smoodin, Eric. *Animating Culture: Hollywood Cartoons from the Sound Era.* New Brunswick, N.J.: Rutgers University Press, 1993.

Staiger, Janet. *Interpreting Films: Studies in the Historical Reception of the American Cinema.* Princeton, N.J.: Princeton University Press, 1992.

Stauffacher, Frank, ed. *Art in Cinema.* San Francisco: San Francisco Art Museum, 1947.

Steinberg, Cobbett. *Film Facts.* New York: Facts on File, 1980.

Sterling, Christopher H., and Timothy R. Haight. *The Mass Media: The Aspen Institute Guide to Communications Industry Trends.* New York: Praeger, 1978.

Taylor, John. *Storming the Magic Kingdom: Wall Street, the Raiders, and the Battle for Disney.* New York: Knopf, 1987.

Taylor, Telford. *The Anatomy of the Nurenberg Trials: A Personal Memoir.* Boston: Little, Brown, 1992.

Thomson, David. *The Autobiographical Dictionary of Film.* New York: Morrow, 1976.

Udelson, Joseph H. *The Great Television Race: A History of the American Television Industry, 1925–1941.* Tuscaloosa: University of Alabama Press, 1982.

Wallis, Hal, and Charles Higham. *Starmaker: The Autobiography of Hal Wallis.* New York: Macmillan, 1980.

Walsh, Andrea. *Women's Film and the Female Experience, 1940–1950.* New York: Praeger, 1984.

The War Reports of General of the Army George C. Marshall. et al. New York: J. B. Lippincott, 1947.

Whitfield, Stephen J. *The Culture of the Cold War.* Baltimore: Johns Hopkins University Press, 1991.

Wilk, Max, ed. *The Wit and Wisdom of Hollywood.* New York: Atheneum, 1971.

Winkler, Allan M. *The Politics of Propaganda: The Office of War Information, 1942–1945.* New Haven: Yale University Press, 1978.

ARTICLES, THESES, AND PARTS OF BOOKS

Abney, Mitchell Alan. "The Economical and Institutional Value of Cartoons: A Case History of the Warner Bros. Cartoon Division." M.A. thesis, University of Texas at Austin, 1996.

Beach, Edward R. "Double Features in Motion Picture Exhibition." *Harvard Business Review* 10 (July 1932).

Bernstein, Matthew. "Fritz Lang, Incorporated." *Velvet Light Trap* 22 (1986).

Borneman, Ernest. "Rebellion in Hollywood: A Study in Motion Picture Finance." *Harper's* (October 1946).

Ceplair, Larry. "The Unfriendly Hollywood Nineteen." In Gary Crowdus, ed., *A Political Companion to American Film.* Chicago: Lakeview Press, 1994.

———. "The Politics of Compromise in Hollywood: A Case Study." *Cineaste* 7 (1978).

Desmond, Robert W. "News About the Newsreel." *Christian Science* (28 September 1938).

Doherty, Dan. "Editing the Newsreel." *Journal of the Society of Motion Picture Engineers* (November 1946).

Donen, Stanley. "Interview with Stanley Donen." *Movie* (Spring 1977).

Dured, John. "Newsreeler's Dilemma." *American Cinematographer* (June 1949).

Fortune. "More Trouble in Paradise" (November 1946).

Fortune. "Paramount: Oscar for Profits" (June 1947).

Fortune. "Movies: End of an Era?" (April 1949).

Gaines, Jane. "The Queen Christina Tie-ups: Convergence of Shop Window and Screen." *Quarterly Review of Film and Video* 11, no. 1 (1989).

Gomery, Douglas. "The Coming of Television and the 'Lost' Motion Picture Audience." *Journal of Film and Video* 38 (Summer 1985).

Goodman, Ezra. "Postwar Motion Pictures." *American Cinematographer* (May 1945).

Gustafson, Robert. "The Power of the Screen: The Influence of Edith Head's Designs on the Retail Fashion Market." *Velvet Light Trap* 19 (1982).

Hagopian, Kevin. "Declarations of Independence: A History of Cagney Productions." *Velvet Light Trap* 22 (1986).

Haralovich, Mary Beth. "Advertising Heterosexuality." *Screen* 23, no. 2 (July–August 1982).

———. "Film Advertising, the Film Industry, and the Pin-Up: The Industry's Accommodations to Social Forces in the 1940s." In *Current Research in Film,* vol. 1, edited by Bruce Austin. New York: Ablex, 1985.

———. "The Proletarian Woman's Film of the 1930s: Contending with Censorship and Entertainment." *Screen* 31, no. 2 (Summer 1990).

Hoberman, J. "Three Myths of Avant-garde Film." *Film Comment* 17, no. 3 (May–June 1981).

Jacobs, Lewis. "Experimental Cinema in America." *Hollywood Quarterly* 3, no. 2 (Winter 1947–1948).

Jewell, Richard B. "Hollywood and Radio: Competition and Partnership in the 1930s." *Historical Journal of Film, Radio, and Television,* 4, no. 2 (1984).

———. "RKO Film Grosses, 1929–1951: The C. J. Tevlin Ledger." *Historical Journal of Film, Radio, and Television* 14, no. 1 (1994).

Jones, Dorothy. "Hollywood War Films, 1942–1944." *Hollywood Quarterly* 1 (1945).

Jowett, Garth. "Dangling a Dream? The Presentation of Television to the American Public, 1928–1952." *Historical Journal of Film, Radio, and Television* 14, no. 2 (1994).

Kelley, Shannon James. "Gallup Goes Hollywood: Motion Picture Audience Research in the 1940s." M.A. thesis, University of Texas at Austin, 1989.

Klinger, Barbara. "Much Ado About Excess: Genre, Mise-en-Scène, and the Woman in *Written on the Wind.*" *Wide Angle* 11, no. 4 (1989).

Koppes, Clayton R. "Film Censorship: Beyond the Heroic Interpretation." *American Quarterly* 44 (December 1992).

Koppes, Clayton R., and Gregory D. Black. "Blacks, Loyalty, and Motion-Picture Propaganda in World War II." *Journal of American History* 73 (September 1986).

LaPlace, Maria. "Producing and Consuming the Woman's Film: Discursive Struggle in *Now, Voyager.*" In *Home Is Where the Heart Is: Studies in Melodrama and the Woman's Film,* edited by Christine Gledhill. London: British Film Institute, 1987.

Lightman, Herb A. "13 Rue Madeleine—Documentary Style in the Photoplay." *American Cinematographer* (March 1947).

———. "Documentary Style." *American Cinematographer* (May 1949).

Lippold, Richard. "Dance and Film—A Review in the Form of a Reflection." *Dance Observer* 13, no. 5 (May 1946).

Loring, Charles. "Americans at Home: Documentary Series in Color." *American Cinematography* (March 1948).

Mabie, Janet. "Reeling up the Newsreels." *Christian Science* (19 June 1935).

Meltzer, Newton E. "Are the Newsreels News?" *Hollywood Quarterly* 2 (April 1947).

Moore, Barbara. "The Cisco Kid and Friends: The Syndication of Television Series from 1948 to 1952." *Journal of Popular Film and Television* 8 (Spring 1980).

Mould, David H. "Historical Trends in the Criticism of the Newsreel and Television News." *Journal of Popular Film and Television* (Fall 1984).

Ross, Lillian. "Come in, Lassie!" *New Yorker* (21 February 1948).

Sandeen, Eric J. "*Confessions of a Nazi Spy,*" *American Studies* (1979).

Smoodin, Eric. "Motion Pictures and Television, 1930–1945: A Pre-History of Relations Between the Two Media." *Journal of the University Film and Video Association* 34, no. 3 (Summer 1982).

Staiger, Janet. "Individualism versus Collectivism." *Screen* 24, nos. 4–5 (July–October 1983).

———. "Announcing Wares, Winning Patrons, Voicing Ideals: Thinking About the History and Theory of Film Advertising." *Cinema Journal* 29, no. 3 (Spring 1990).

Stull, William. "Combat Camera." *Flying* (April 1943).

Thomas, Deborah. "How Hollywood Deals with the Deviant Male." In *The Movie Book of Film Noir,* edited by Ian Cameron. London: Verso, 1992.

Toland, Gregg. "Realism for *Citizen Kane.*" *American Cinematographer* (August 1991).

Turim, Maureen. "Childhood Memories and Household Events in the Feminist Avant-garde." *Journal of Film and Video* 38 (Summer–Fall 1986).

Turner, George. "Xanadu in Review: *Citizen Kane* Turns 50." *American Cinematographer* (August 1991).

Tyler, Parker. "Maya Deren as Filmmaker." *Filmwise* 2 (1962).

Vasey, Ruth. "Foreign Parts: Hollywood's Global Distribution and the Representation of Ethnicity." *American Quarterly* 44 (December 1992).

Vaughn, Steven. "Morality and Entertainment: The Origins of the Motion Picture Production Code." *Journal of American History* 77 (1990).

Waldman, Diane. "From Midnight Shows to Marriage Vows: Women, Exploitation, and Exhibition." *Wide Angle* 6, no. 2 (1984).

Wanger, Walter. "The OWI and Motion Pictures." *Public Opinion Quarterly* (Spring 1943).

Whitney, Simon N. "Antitrust Policies of the Motion Picture Industry." In *The American Movie Industry: The Business of Motion Pictures,* edited by Gorham Kindem. Carbondale: University of Illinois Press, 1982.

Williams, Linda. "Feminist Film Theory: *Mildred Pierce* and the Second World War." In *Female Spectators: Looking at Film and Television,* edited by E. Deirdre Pribram. London and New York: Verso, 1988.

Wolfreys, Julian. "*Meshes of the Afternoon:* Hollywood, the Avant-garde, and Problems of Interpretation." *CineAction!* (Winter 1987–1988).

General Index

Italic numerals signify illustrations.

Index of Films

Italic numerals signify illustrations.